Fundamentals of Philately

by
L.N. Williams

Revised Edition
1990

Published by the
American Philatelic Society
State College, Pennsylvania

An American Philatelic Society Handbook

Published by the American Philatelic Society
P.O. Box 8000, State College, Pennsylvania 16803

Revised Edition

Previous Publication

Sections 1 through 5 first appeared as a series in Volumes 67 through 76 of *The American Philatelist*. Copyright 1954, 1955, 1956, 1957, 1958, 1959, 1960, 1961, 1962, 1963 by the American Philatelic Society Inc. and L.N. and M. Williams. Sections revised and published separately: Section 1 of the First Edition (1958), Section 2 (February 1960), Section 3 (June 1963), Section 4 (1966), Section 5 (1969), Copyright 1958, 1960, 1964, 1966, 1969 by the American Philatelic Society and L.N. and M. Williams. The first edition of this book was published in 1971.

Library of Congress Cataloging-in-Publication Data

Williams, L.N. (Leon Norman), 1914 —
  Fundamentals of Philately / by L.N. Williams. — Rev. ed.
  880 p., 23.3 cm.
  Includes bibliographical references and index.
  ISBN 0-933580-13-4
  1. Postage-stamps — Collectors and collecting. I. Title.
HE6213.W5473 1990
769.56 — dc20

Printed in the United States of America by
CONSOLIDATED BUSINESS FORMS
Lock Haven, Pennsylvania

DEDICATION

To the memory of my elder brother

MAURICE WILLIAMS
(August 19, 1905 — June 15, 1976)

with whom I enjoyed a philatelic writing partnership
for more than forty years.

Contents

Preface

The dictionary states that "fundamental" means "that which serves as a groundwork" and in *Fundamentals of Philately,* within the limits imposed on any work that is not to be endless, an attempt is made to survey the subjects. It does not pretend to be exhaustive. The work is intended primarily to be of assistance to adult "beginners" seeking guidance, but there is reason to hope that collectors and students with advanced knowledge will find some help in the pages that contain matters of record and some fundamental considerations. Sometimes, problems that seem intractable on a single line of inquiry yield to inquiry based on comparative study.

Philately and philatelic study are not bounded by reference exclusively to methods of producing the object studied as being primarily (to re-use some of the relevant words of Rowland Hill) "a bit of paper just large enough to bear the stamp, and covered at the back with a glutinous wash, which . . . might, by applying a little moisture" be attached to the letter. Nevertheless, knowledge of those methods is essential for the elucidation of problems arising from observation of characteristics presented by the studied objects.

Throughout the text four principles have been activated: (1) to make the text readily understandable and reasonably comprehensive — the world of stamps bristles with technicalities and exceptions to general rules; (2) to pay special regard to the pictorial representation of instances referred to in the text — to re-use the words of W. Dudley Atlee in *The Philatelist* for December 1869 (Volume III, Page 138), "nothing is so satisfactory as ocular demonstration"; (3) to provide adequate references to specific stamps — anyone who wishes to follow a point more closely may search for an item rather than a class; (4) to pay particular attention to the elucidation of technical terms — appended to each relevant chapter is an alphabetical list of terms, definitions and examples germane to the subjects referred to in the chapter.

The study of stamps and their methods of production and the diagnosis of the cause of certain effects observable on the finished product are not limited to issues newly emanating from the presses. Problems arising from study of contemporary issues are, sometimes, solvable by reference to the house producing them. The student is more likely to encounter problems of more difficult means of diagnosis in issues made long ago. The endeavor, therefore, has been to attempt to light the way to solving such problems. To that end I have — usefully, I hope — sought to represent in actual and word pictures processes that are not necessarily still current. It is to be clearly understood that a description in the present tense does not necessarily

ix

mean to imply that the process as described is in current use. My intention has been to give immediacy to the description as though the reader was present during the production of the stamp or issue or process being described. It has not been thought necessary to strive to picture varieties in current issues rather than issues immediately or long past. The fundamentals are no better pictured by modern stamps than those others and no benefit is to be gained by striving after the ultimate part of Shakespeare's fifth age of man.

This book owed its inception to the late David Lidman, erstwhile editor of *The American Philatelist,* who requested for the journal a survey of the basic knowledge requisite to serve as a groundwork of philately. There is, as has been averred, no end to philately, and one could have paraphrased, perhaps with justification, the psalmist in the New English idiom by saying to him I "see that all things come to an end, but thy commandment has no limit" — and a limit had, perforce, to be set. The fundamentals of philatelic knowledge are in no sense bounded by an understanding of some of its history and the processes of stamp production; however, such understanding is one of the qualifications of anyone who wishes justifiably to lay claim to being called "a philatelist."

Serialization of *Fundamentals of Philately* in *The American Philatelist* began in April 1954 and continued issue by issue until June 1963, punctuated by publication of five sections until 1968 and followed by the unabridged edition, first printing, in 1971. Throughout, the sub-editing and layout of the work was carried out by David Lidman. For many years I regarded his initial request as being light-hearted. However, I am not sure. By the time of that request, my late brother, Maurice, and I had corresponded frequently with David Lidman and he knew, must have known, that the request was really directed to me alone so far as concerned the production of stamps, for Maurice's learning and studies lay in other philatelic directions and David Lidman certainly knew about my abhorrence of perpetrating unconscious fiction in the guise of fact, for that subject had featured more than once in our letters. His enthusiasm for the work was scarcely less than that of myself, who wrote every single word of that marathon — although, of course, consonant with the fraternal writing policy that Maurice and I had adopted from the outset in 1934 or even earlier, the publication appeared under the joint names "L.N. and M. Williams." Even so, merely the fact that Maurice died in 1976, more than four years before the present, substantially revised, edition was embarked upon, suffices to explain its appearance under my name alone, while I shall always acknowledge the pleasure that more than forty years of philatelic writing partnership gave me.

As before, I have constantly borne in mind that the usual approach of the collector and student is to look at the stamp or other item and work backward. Accordingly, in surveying the processes extending substantially beyond a century and a half I have, as a general rule, written in the historic present and related them as though the practices were current. That, of course, is scarcely ever the case.

Fundamentals of Philately originally was more than fifteen years in the writing, and the revision has occupied more than eight years. It has been my constant endeavor to record fact. Nevertheless, it is, perhaps, too much to hope that nowhere unwittingly have I condescended to fiction. For such errors of omission or commission as exist, I can do no more, or less, than cover myself with confusion.

I am grateful to many philatelists throughout the world who readily lent material for illustration (their names are listed); to the late David Lidman; to Ray Van Handel, the artist, who improved almost beyond recognition the rough sketches that I provided to illustrate various points; to stamp printers, manufacturers, the librarian of the London College of Printing, postal authorities, and many others who met my often quite unreasonable demands with unfailing courtesy and cooperation.

As to the technicalities of the present edition, I record and acknowledge my thanks to Bill Welch, editor of *The American Philatelist*; former assistant editor Jane M. Andrews, who, although resigning her post, continued her years-long work on *Fundamentals*; and design manager Barbara Boal. The indexing — based on the superb index to the first edition prepared with his usual thoroughness by James Negus — has been carried out by Gini Horn, librarian of the American Philatelic Research Library.

I acknowledge the following philatelists, collectors and others past and present who have assisted in one way or another in my endeavors to make the present volume of service generally:

Amateur Collector Ltd., N.J.D. Ames, Royal C. Anderson, Earl P.L. Apfelbaum.

Dr. David Berest, George W. Brett, Trustees of the British Museum (and also the British Library), David H. Burr, Ed. and Sophie Buser.

George W. Caldwell, Sylvester Colby Inc., Edward S. Conger, F.J. Coomer, R.W. Crabtree & Sons Ltd., S. Cross-Rudkin, Crown Agents Stamp Company Ltd.

Thomas De La Rue & Company Ltd.

G.B. Erskine.

C.W. Fawdry, John A. Fox, Henry H. Frenkle.

W.E. Gerrish, Gimbel's Stamp Department, Grover & Company Ltd.

K.S. Haldane, H.R. Harmer Inc., Harmer, Rooke & Company, Harris Seybold Potter Company, Harrison & Sons Ltd., Emanuel Hatzakos, Harrison D.S. Haverbeck, C.W. Hennan, Karl Heumann, Hunter- Penrose Ltd., I.L. Hurt.

H.F. Johnson, F.S.J. Jordan.

Herman Kerst, E.G. Kinsey, Brainerd Kremer.

Con A. Larsen, J.E. Lea.

Colin McCaig, Mrs. Ethel McCoy, Machines Chambon, Joseph Mandos, George Mann & Company Ltd., Mercury Stamp Company, Brigadier F.M. Montresor, Mosden Stamp Company, Erwin Mueller.

National Philatelic Museum, Jim Negus, Nicholas Sanabria Company Inc., Harry Nissen.

Odhams Books Ltd., Dr. Harry Osborne, Pierson Ostrow.

George Pearson, Carl Pelander, Philatelic Foundation, W. Pickering & Sons Ltd., Her Majesty's Postmaster General, J.R.W. Purves.

Stephen G. Rich, Peter C. Rickenback, Stuart A. Robertson, Robson Lowe, Royal Mint.

Dr. Gregory S. Salisbury, Scott Publications, James W. Shaver, Robert A. Siegel, G.H. Simpson, J.N. Sissons, Stanley Gibbons Ltd., J. & H. Stolow, C.T. Sturton.

John Taylor, Allen M. Thatcher, E.V. Toeg.

United States Postal Service.

Brigadier G.A. Viner.

Dr. Gordon Ward, Waterlow & Sons Ltd., Raymond H. Weill Company, Denise Williams, M.K. Williams, H.E. Wingfield & Company

R.H. Yorke.

If I have omitted to name anyone whose name should have appeared, I give assurance that the omission was inadvertent and I tender my apologies.

L.N. Williams
London
January 10, 1990

About L.N. Williams

Born on March 25, 1914, Leon Norman Williams — known as Norman — has collected, studied, spoken of, and written about stamps and their production for more than fifty years.

His philatelic writing career in separate publications began in September 1938 with a booklet he co-authored with his late brother, Maurice (d. 1976), entitled *The Propaganda Forgeries: A History and Description of the Austrian, Bavarian and German Stamps Counterfeited by Order of the British Government During the Great War 1914-1918.* The following year saw publication of *Philately: An Outline of Its Elements.* Together, the Williams brothers wrote more than thirty separate books about stamps.

Mr. Williams has contributed to philatelic periodicals and the daily press throughout the world since 1934. There is scarcely an aspect of philatelic interest and study that he has not covered during his fifty years of writing. For more than fourteen years, he has been engaged in compiling and writing *Encyclopaedia of Rare and Famous Stamps* for publication by David Feldman S.A. of Geneva, Switzerland.

In 1946, he made the first of many television appearances, this time on a British Broadcasting Corporation program devoted to stamps, "For the Children." He often has spoken on radio about philatelic subjects, has lectured on philately in continuing education courses, has acted as judge at exhibitions and, apart from all that, has presented many displays and given many talks to philatelic societies.

In addition to being a Fellow of the Royal Philatelic Society, London — the oldest extant philatelic society — Mr. Williams is a life member of the American Philatelic Society, an honorary life member of Britain's National Philatelic Society, and founder member and vice president of the Cinderella Stamp Club. He also has been the editor of *The Cinderella Philatelist*, the club's quarterly journal, since its inauguration in 1961. In 1980 he was elevated to the Philatelic Writers Hall of Fame of Writers Unit 30 of the American Philatelic Society, and he is a founder member and vice chairman of Britain's Philatelic Writers Society.

A barrister, Mr. Williams has appeared as an expert philatelic witness for several litigants on both sides of the Atlantic. He is a reporter to the Incorporated Council of Law Reporting for England and Wales, a regular contributor to the law reports published in *The Times* and, since 1970, the editor of a specialized series of law reports in England, *Road Traffic Reports.*

He has been married to his wife, Denise, since 1943 (when, as a lieutenant in the Royal Regiment of Artillery, he came home on leave from service overseas). They have two sons, Marcus (b. 1950) and Robin (b. 1960), both of whom are married. Marcus and Wendy have three sons, Daniel (b. 1979), Benjamin (b. 1982), and Joseph (b. 1985), and are interested in stamps and philatelic material related to the national sport, cricket. Robin is involved with computers and Ann is a talented florist, and they have produced the first girl in the immediate family, Avital (b. 1990).

About the
American Philatelic Society

Founded in 1886, the American Philatelic Society is the oldest and largest national organization of stamp collectors. From its headquarters in the American Philatelic Building at 100 Oakwood Avenue, State College, Pennsylvania, a staff of more than forty employees provides a full range of services to 57,000 members in some 100 countries.

Among the benefits and services enjoyed by APS members are:

- A monthly 100-page journal, *The American Philatelist*.
- A Sales Division that circulates by mail some 70,000 books of philatelic material valued in excess of $9 million. More than 12,000 members participate as buyers or sellers.
- A low-cost, high-coverage stamp insurance program.
- Member-discounts on APS publications such as *Fundamentals of Philately*.
- Member-discount fees for the American Philatelic Expertizing Service, which gives expert opinions, respected worldwide, on the genuineness of stamps, covers, and related items.
- Access to special-interest collecting information through fellow members and the more than 180 specialty groups allied with the APS as affiliates.
- Access to the American Philatelic Research Library, the largest facility of its kind in the English-speaking world. Also located in the American Philatelic Building, it contains more than 75,000 books, periodicals, auction catalogues, and other materials, which are available by mail or by photocopy.

Both the APS and the APRL are authorized tax-exempt, non-profit institutions under Section 501(c)3 of the U.S. Internal Revenue Code. Gifts, donations, and bequests are tax-deductible.

Information about membership may be obtained by writing to the American Philatelic Society, P.O. Box 8000, State College, Pennsylvania 16803.

1. Philatelic Trends

TODAY the range of interests associated with stamp collecting is vast: it is the product of well over a century's development. During that time there have been innumerable variations and off-shoots from the simple ideas that activated the earliest collectors, but there have been, also, some general trends, and these can be traced as a shadowy pattern overlaying the philatelic world — a pattern with no sharp outlines, and with overlapping spheres of interests, but one which can be traced, tentatively, to give an appearance of form to the almost formless growth of one of the most popular of the indoor hobbies and pursuits of the present day.

It is my purpose here only to outline some of the interests that from time to time have engaged the attention of the ever-growing numbers of people who are termed and term themselves philatelists, and at a later stage to deal with these interests and others in greater detail.

The general trends are reflected by the literature that has poured in an ever-increasing stream from the philatelic presses since the early 1860s; but, as is in the nature of things, it is dangerous to form any fixed ideas from a mere perusal of the literature, since literature nearly always lags behind the inception of a trend, yet might be the means of giving it a stimulus by flood-lighting the path and encouraging followers.

The simple idea which lay behind the activities of the earliest collectors was to form a representative collection of as many different stamps as were in existence and could be obtained. Stamp collecting in that form had its inception somewhere in the Old World about the middle or late 1850s.

Aim of the Earliest Collectors

These early collectors accepted as axiomatic that the printed design comprised the stamp. It is noteworthy that the same idea was in the mind of Rowland Hill when, in 1837, he projected the use of adhesive stamps in his pamphlet *Post Office Reform: Its Importance and Practicability*. He wrote that use might be made of "a bit of paper just large enough to bear the stamp, and covered at the back with a glutinous wash, which the bringer might, by applying a little moisture, attach to the back of the letter. . . . "

Two comments may be made on that extract. The first is that Hill's idea was all of a piece with the idea enunciated some two centuries earlier by Henry Bishop, postmaster-general from 1660 to 1663 under King Charles II. Bishop wrote, "a stamp is invented that is putt upon every letter. . . . " The "stamp" was a handstamped circular impression in ink.

The second comment is that the use of the word "bringer" gives a glimpse of an outstanding paradox. The paradox is that Hill's stamp — the foundation of stamp collecting and the literature of philately — was introduced to enable people unable to write to post letters. An explanation and a longer extract from Hill's pamphlet will justify the paradox.

Hill based his hopes on what became the Mulready covers and envelopes. They were central to his plan for penny postage. The letter-writer would use them, enclose his letter in them, write the address on them and then bring them to the post. Just one moment though! Letter-writers might send servants to post the letters. Most servants in those days were illiterate. What then? Hill was prepared:

The only objection which occurs to me to the universal adoption of this plan [of covers and envelopes bearing the stamp] is the following: Persons unaccustomed to write letters, would, perhaps, be at a loss how to proceed. They might send or take their letters to the Post Office without having had recourse to the stamp. It is true that on presentation of the letter the Receiver instead of accepting the money as postage, might take it as the price of a cover, or band in which the bringer might immediately inclose the letter, and then redirect it. But the bringer would sometimes be unable to write. Perhaps this difficulty might be obviated by using a bit of paper just large enough to bear the stamp, and covered at the back with a glutinous wash, which the bringer might, by applying a little moisture, attach to the back of the letter, so as to avoid the necessity for re-directing it.

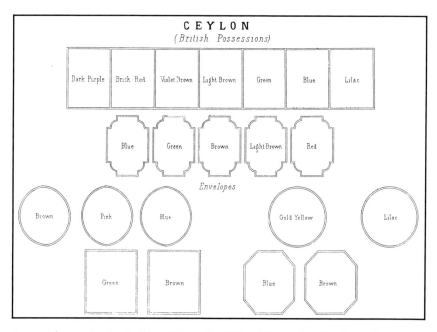

A page from a Justin Lallier album, English edition, showing how the spaces were allocated to stamps and why so many early stamps still extant are cut to shape. (Photo courtesy V.T. Short)

2

A typical example of a non-rectangular stamp trimmed to shape by the correspondent.

To early collectors it was immaterial whether or not all the design or only part of it was available on the example collected: so long as it existed and was demonstrably and patently different from any other example in the collection, it was desirable — and that is all there was to it. Signs of those times, and indicative of them, were the people with used foreign postage stamps to sell — and there were very few traders until the early 1860s, and comparatively few different issues — those people used to spike the stamps on nails affixed to boards in order to display their wares.

The stamp consisted of only the printed design; and the stamp was the be-all and end-all of collecting.

However, this crudeness lasted for, perhaps surprisingly, few years, and by 1862 and 1863, one finds writers such as Mount Brown in his catalogue stating, "The value of stamps in present use depends upon their 'condition,' whether used or unused," and Dr. C.W. Viner in *The Stamp Collector's Magazine*, Vol. 1, Page 113 (August 1863), writing, "A black penny English in good condition is worth the current value."

Good condition then meant that the whole of the printed design was available. That the design might be difficult to perceive because of a heavy obliteration was immaterial. That the presence or absence of perforations or margins was equally immaterial is evidenced by some of the albums that were published in those days: a "Justin Lallier" album completely filled with early classics has wrung the hearts of many a more modern collector because the stamps have had their margins trimmed to fit the space bearing representations merely of the printing and at times so closely packed as to leave no room for the excess paper that had to be trimmed away if the stamps were to fit into the spaces allocated to them on the pages.

However, it is unjust to lay the blame only at the feet of Lallier. Much more often the ignorance of correspondents was the reason why non-rectangular stamps were trimmed close to their designs. Particularly is that the case with the 1854 issue of India where the 4-annas stamps still on cover are much more often than not cut to the shape of the design.

Within a very few years the accumulations of nothing more nor less than the printed designs began to lose favor, probably as being too crude and unsatisfying a form of collecting. But whether it was merely aestheticism, or the search for new worlds to conquer, or a desire to approximate scientific methods, or a combination of these reasons, whatever the reason that motivated the new trend is immaterial. It evidenced itself, flowed from logical France across the English Channel to Great Britain, and spread over the growing philatelic world.

It must not be thought, either here or elsewhere, that because a trend is mentioned as beginning or spreading it means that all or even the majority of collectors subscribed to the views of its promoters, or followed their example. Some examples were, seemingly, so obviously attractive that they almost immediately became well-nigh universally followed. Other trends, the majority probably, had to fight against ingrained custom and prejudice, even though these might have been of only a few years standing, and the old and the new co-existed side by side, and sometimes developed along diverging lines.

The new trend from France, in the search for differences between one stamp and the next, was not only to have regard for the design but also to inspect the backs, the edges and the hues or colors of stamps before being satisfied that an example could be classified correctly.

Beginnings of Study

It became implicit that good condition meant that the whole of the example should be readily available for inspection. No longer were margins to be trimmed: the difference between a perforated design and an identical design imperforate now meant that there were two collectible stamps where there had been only one before. Further, that difference necessitated there being sufficient paper around the printed design to make it self-evident that the example was, indeed, imperforate and not a perforated stamp that had been deperforated by having the perforations cut off.

Bringing the backs of stamps into review opened new oysters. The whole range of papers and incidents in their manufacture became subjects for record. As the differences between watermarked and unwatermarked paper were noted, so the numbers of collectible stamps increased. As collectors began to appreciate and look for the differences between colored and plain paper, and to record the varieties that were printed on wove or laid, on batonné or ribbed paper, so the numbers of stamps within the collectors' ken multiplied themselves many-fold.

Thus, good condition began, slowly, to import that the whole of the paper and watermark were present: for thinned stamps it could no longer be claimed that they were in good condition.

4

NEWLY-ISSUED STAMPS.

WE here present our readers with an engraving of the new Nicaraguan stamp referred to in our last number. Mr. H. Whymper (see advertisement) has for sale a few proofs of this really beautiful work of art. We have one now before us, and think it is admirable. Collectors unable to procure the original stamp, would do well to provide themselves with one of these fac-similes.

Collectors were advised to obtain "proofs" of this illustration if they could not procure the original Nicaraguan stamps. This is how the illustration appeared in *The Stamp-Collector's Magazine*, Vol. 1, Page 40 (April 1863).

As more and greater attention came to be paid to hue, tint or color, so it became of increasing importance that the whole of the design should be open to inspection. Thus more attention was paid to acquiring stamps that were unused or, if used, were lightly cancelled. And so, good condition, in a used stamp, came to mean that it was lightly, perhaps inconspicuously, cancelled. And as the issues came to be classified by, first major and, later, less conspicuous variations in color, so the numbers of collectible stamps grew and grew.

The different issues that had been made were unknown to collectors, and the great desideratum in the early days was a catalogue that listed all the known varieties. The universal aim of all collectors was to possess all these stamps, but the eager search for new varieties — new issues were enthusiastically hailed as "philatelic gains" — made that simple goal more and more difficult of attainment.

The proportionate increase of these varieties was enormous: for instance, in the second edition of a catalogue published in June 1862, 1,300 different varieties were listed, and in the third edition, published less than six months later, 1,700 different varieties were recorded; and the increase bore little relation to the number of new issues chronicled during that time. Nevertheless, it was still well within the bounds of possibility, in those days, to form a reasonably complete representative collection of the stamps of the world.

Early Scope

The early collectors cast their nets wide, and quite naturally their collections embraced government and private issues of postage stamps, adhesives and non-adhesives in the form of envelopes and other postal stationery. After seemingly slight opposition nearly all collectors sought for and obtained proofs and essays to include in their collections. At first it was unnecessary to distinguish between proofs as they are understood today and black prints of cuts or blocks used as illustrations for the current philatelic magazines. This was all of a piece with the idea behind the provision of facsimiles or imitations of those stamps of which it was difficult to obtain genuine originals. Collectors would openly accept the facsimiles as representative of those

placer dans son porte-monnaie, des timbres. Nous préférons faire
d'échelle
16 une hau
15¼ mètres,
15 une série
14½ suivant
14 différents
13½ de chaq
13 indiqué
12½ par deux
12 simplifie
11½ cherches
11 fait plai
10 pourront
9¼ emprunt
9 mètre,
7 ne tenons pas au nom, mais nou
petite mesure leur rendra de gra

The original "odontometre" (perforation gauge) as it appeared on Page 84 of *Le Timbre-Poste,* Vol. 4, October 1866.

stamps in order to approach the illusory goal of completeness. For example, the editor of *The Stamp-Collector's Magazine,* Vol. 1, Page 40 (April 1863), stated: "We here present our readers with an engraving of the new Nicaraguan stamp. . . . Mr. H. Whymper . . . has for sale a few proofs of this really beautiful work of art. . . . Collectors unable to procure the original stamp would do well to provide themselves with one of these facsimiles." Later the shadow was forsaken for the substance, and facsimiles were cast out as forgeries.

Essays in abundance appeared — with never an intention of their serving as designs for intended issues — made specially for collectors, and they were collected by many, naturally and in the normal course of events.

Anything that franked a message was, by analogy with the postage stamp, desirable; and, in time, collections included telegraph stamps. Revenue or fiscal stamps were collected with almost equal avidity. Newspaper stamps were admitted without question, as were newspaper tax stamps, and railway stamps.

The study of the peculiarities of stamps increased — "their history, their date, their formation, and their usual term of existence" to quote the words of Adelaide Lucy Fenton, one of the earliest advanced collectors; she was writing in *The Stamp-Collector's Magazine,* Vol. 4, Page 143 (September 1866).

Allied to the new interests of backs, edges and colors was an interest in the method of production. An ingenuous and inquiring reader of *The Stamp-Collector's Magazine* asked in April 1865 (Vol. 3, Page 63): "The Engraving of Stamps," how is it done? How were stamp designs produced by mechanical multiplication? From that time on, gradually greater and greater attention came to be paid to the methods by which stamps were printed, and the details recorded, often crudely, as often inaccurately, but the interest was there and the trend toward new fields of study had had its inception; with it came the necessity to distinguish between a design printed by one method and the identical design printed by another method, with the consequence that there were two desirable varieties where there had been only one before.

When Dr. J.A. Legrand invented and published in *Le Timbre-Poste* in October 1866 (Vol. 4, Page 84) the "odontometre" or perforation gauge for ascertaining the number of holes in each two centimeters of length caused by different perforating machines, a new method was added to those previously existing for classifying and differentiating between stamps, and the number of varieties grew by leaps and bounds.

Philately

In this manner, by stages, in a few years after the word "philately" had been coined and given to the world by M. Georges Herpin in *Le Collectionneur de Timbres-Poste* (Vol. 1, Page 20, November 1864), the term "philatelist" developed a current meaning as applied to one of a class interested in every facet of the production, issue and use of stamps. And with the increasing study, the number of collectible items continued to grow, quite independently of the stamps newly issued by an ever-increasing number of governments adopting the postage stamp as a convenient form of collecting payment for a service.

With an appreciation for good condition and the desirability of having the whole of the stamp available for inspection came the realization that it was no longer satisfactory to stick the stamp fast to the page by means of glue or even by three or four spots of rubber solution — practices which had been almost universal. M. Maury in his *Timbres-Poste Album du Collectionneur* mentioned a plan which the editor of *The Stamp-Collector's Magazine*, when reviewing the album in July 1868 (Vol. 6, Page 111), refers to as follows: "His plan is to gum a slip of paper on one side, cut it up into little bands, fold each band in the middle, keep the gummed side uppermost, and then attach one half of this gummed side to the stamp, and the other half to the page. This 'hinge' plan is very simple . . . and has the advantage of permitting easy reference to watermark &c., and of the removal of the stamp at any time without injury." The name of the initiator of the gummed hinge has been lost, but the trend toward hinging became very marked and widespread, and almost universally adopted by all but the least appreciative collectors. It is, perhaps, worthy of note that that hinge involved a more sophisticated idea than the one suggested on Page 16 of Vol. 7 of *The Stamp-Collector's Magazine* (January 1869). Under the heading "Answers to Correspondents" the editor stated:

M.L.B., Stroud, would like to know the best method for attaching stamps so as to permit of reference to the backs. Our present plan, and we find it to answer as well as any, is to cut up the margin of a sheet of stamps into little strips, of about half an inch long, and one fifth broad; double them cross-wise with the gummed side outwards, and attach one half of this side lightly to the stamp, and the other half firmly to the book.

A simple diagram with instructions illustrated the method.

Almost simultaneously with the hinge, the mount was introduced — a piece of paper or thin card slightly larger or smaller than the stamp; the hinged stamp was affixed to the mount which, in turn, was affixed to the album page. In *The Philatelist* for December 1869 (Vol. 3, Page 138), W. Dudley Atlee when writing about albums stated: ''The correct way of mounting adhesives so as to show their watermarks, is so well-known that it is almost a work of supererogation to mention it; but for the benefit of young collectors, we give a specimen properly mounted, as nothing is so satisfactory as ocular demonstration.'' And there, adhering fast to Page 138 of this early erudite magazine is to be found a mount upon which is hinged a stamp: in my copy of the magazine, the stamp is the Brunswick 1865 1 gr.

The First 'Specialists'

About the 1870s, the numbers of collectors throughout the world sharply declined; and what had been a furore, increasing too rapidly numerically for almost any universally accepted ethical and rational standards to obtain, died down. Those who remained in the ranks of collectors generally broadened and deepened their interests and studies. The natural result was a tendency to individual concentration upon special fields, and the term ''specialist'' was born.

The president of the National Philatelical Society of New York, at the September meeting in 1877 held in the United States Hotel, claimed as had others before him, that philately was entitled to rank as a science. He called attention to the fact that among ''collectors are specialists, some collecting postal cards only, some revenue stamps, and some the stamps of their own country''; he showed that ''this would result in a gain to philately.''

Mint or Used?

Great Britain 2d. 1840 Plate 2 with bottom sheet margin, including marginal inscription.

The great desire was, still, for a complete catalogue of the entire world of stamps, but it had been realized that this was almost certainly unattainable without the cooperation of specialists working either as individuals or in small groups concentrating upon the same subject. Specialist, in this connection, meant a person who set out to discover and acquire what different issues existed in his particular specialty. Moens of Belgium began the issue of his *Bibliothèque de Timbrophiles*, surveys of countries and groups of issues; in America compilation of a list of revenue stamps revealed more than 13,000 varieties; and in Britain the publication of the handbook on Spain by the Philatelic Society, London, underlined the trend toward specialization. But it was, in the main, specialization within the large ambit of general collecting, and the collector who restricted his collection to his specialty was, as yet, largely unknown.

There was still, as there had been in the earlier days and there is to some extent even today, an argument about what it was more desirable to collect — mint stamps or used. The proponents of "mint" stated that obliteration obscured the details of the printing and hindered the study of printing methods, while the opponents argued that, at any rate, a postage stamp had not performed the function that had called it forth unless and until it had passed through the post, franking postal matter and receiving the defacing mark. The trend, therefore, developed of collecting both mint and used examples of the same variety. No album published in those days made provision for the collection of more than one example of each stamp; and, therefore, the fashion grew of having two albums, one for used, and one for unused stamps.

It is worthy of comment, though, that even as early as February 1864, the editor of *The Stamp-Collector's Magazine* (Vol. 2, Page 30) in a book review suggested that the compiler of an album provided with guards should "offer for sale some loose leaves similar to those ruled in squares for the book" so that they could be gummed in to provide additional space where insufficient had been provided. The suggestion was acted on immediately and the compiler, Henry Whymper, wrote (Page 47, March), stating that the publisher would supply loose leaves at 9d. per dozen.

There had been argument, too, about the better method of collecting postal stationery, and after a time we find a well-known catalogue publisher, Oscar Berger-Levrault, writing in *The Stamp-Collector's Magazine*, Vol. 5, Page 124 (August 1867): "As to envelopes . . . amateurs take . . . two copies, one cut square and mounted in the album, the other kept entire and perfect." The trend, thus begun, of keeping the entire piece of stationery because it might tell more than the cut-square or cut-out, resulted eventually, as a natural development, in collectors preserving whole the items bearing adhesive postage stamps. These items could convey more information to the student than the stamp alone in the album, and thus perhaps add more scraps of information to those gathered in the insatiable thirst for knowledge about the production, issue and use of the stamp.

Restricting Begins

Broadly speaking it is accurate to state that the nineteenth century was, so far as stamp collecting is concerned, a period of expanding interests with the general run of collectors searching more and more widely with the objective of attaining completeness in representing the postal and fiscal issues of the whole world. It is only toward the end of that period that deliberate restriction of interests became widespread.

One of the earliest movements toward such limitations occurred soon after 1890, when some well-known collectors announced their intention of seeking after and collecting only the issues made during the first fifty years of use of postage stamps. That particular restriction at that time was short-lived and had, perhaps, little direct effect upon the majority of collectors.

That form of restriction again made itself manifest at the close of 1900, when there was a far more widespread and general trend toward collecting only nineteenth-century issues; but the majority of collectors, and particularly new recruits to the ranks, continued to collect the newly issued twentieth-century postal stamps.

However, at this time began the general period of and trend toward restriction or limitations of another kind. The tendency had been growing to collect only postal issues; fiscals and the like, if collected, had been segregated from the postal issues. At the end of the nineteenth century, segregation was under way, to be followed with some exceptions by almost relegation to the limbo of such postal issues as local stamps, particularly private locals, and postal stationery.

Another trend made itself manifest about that time. It was doubtless given momentum by the example set by the collector who later became H.M. King George V. Whereas collectors before had been content to acquire and retain single copies of stamps, following the royal lead, the tendency became to require a block of four of each stamp, and mount it either in lieu of or together with a single on the album page.

It is, broadly speaking, accurate to state that after the nineteenth century the period has been one of narrowing interests, with an almost universal concentration by individual collectors upon one or more special groups or classes of stamps, or restriction in one form or another.

Another movement toward a limitation, which cuts right across any restrictions imposed by date of issue, had got under way by that time, and was to come more and more into prominence — the trend toward restriction based upon geographical or political limitations. Collectors generally began to restrict their search for completeness to the issues of certain stamp-issuing countries or groups, to the exclusion of all others.

In the United States in particular, this trend was very marked, and it developed to the extent that the collectors of "foreign" postage stamps became the exception rather than the rule. In other countries the "nationalistic" trend was at first not so marked. However, with the passing of years the tendency became that the nationals of each country restricted their collections to the stamps issued by their own country and its possessions, if any; not, speaking generally, to the entire exclusion of other stamps, but to a considerable degree.

Student Specialists

These limitations brought with them the realization that the goal of completeness was far more easily attainable, and opened the door for the student-specialist — the collector and student who, within a self-imposed very narrow scope, set out to discover and record all the facts about an issue that intensive study of the stamps, postmarks and official documents could reveal. The "nationalistic" trend was a natural consequence arising from pride of country and because, of course, official documents of the postal authorities and, normally, of the printers were available in the country of the stamps' origin, and could be more conveniently studied by its nationals than by residents abroad.

It had long been appreciated and recorded that certain stamps, having been

A unique stamp.

individually engraved by hand upon the printing plate and therefore differing the one from the other, could be assigned to their correct positions on the sheet if a whole sheet were available. Also, that it was possible to reconstitute a sheet of stamps if sufficient multiples could be obtained and the characteristic stamps common to the multiples overlapped. Such reconstitution was called "plating." Students turned their attention to stamps that had been multiplied on to the printing plates by mechanical or semi-mechanical means, and discovered that these stamps could be plated.

Thus there began a trend, among certain collectors, to specialize and study intensely certain stamps or issues for the purpose of plating them, and thus forward the studies about the production of the stamps. Plating necessitated these students having innumerable copies of the same stamp in singles and multiples. As a result, these stamps, if obsolete, became more and more difficult and costly for the average collector to acquire. Because of this the tendency toward restriction of interests received a further impetus.

By the outbreak of World War I, the numbers of general collectors throughout the world who sought for and were capable of attaining substantial completeness representing all varieties of all issues were probably less than a score. Of course, in one respect not more than one collection could ever be complete, for there were several stamps of which only one example was known. This fact, however, did not deter the last few of the "Great Moguls," as these wealthy general collectors among others were called, and their insatiable quest for completeness was tempered, in some cases by thinking doubtfully about the authenticity or desirability of certain unique items they could not acquire.

By that time the International Philatelic Exhibition had become established as an event that set the standards for many of the more advanced collectors. The first exhibition of postage stamps as items worthy of interest and study had occurred as long ago as 1852 in a picture frame in a museum in Brussels, Belgium. No contemporary engraving exists of that remarkable early collection of stamps of various countries. However, its existence at the Vandermaelen Museum is well-documented and it is referred to with reverence by the pioneer Belgian dealer, J.-B. Moens, who wrote in his magazine, *Le Timbre Poste*, Vol. 1 (1867 reprint), Page 29, that before he became a dealer and was a "fervent amateur" he went to stand enraptured by the 100 or 150 stamps in their frame. He had eyes only for the stamps and would willingly have exchanged against them all the other earthly curiosities in the museum. A painting of that frame in the museum surroundings was made from memory by another pioneer collector, Adolph Reinheimer, in 1906. He exhibited his painting in a London exhibition that year. He presented it to the Earl of Crawford and it now forms part of the Bibliotheca Lindesiana in the British Library in London.

The first stamp exhibition as such had taken place at Dresden in 1870. It was an exhibition of the collection of Dr. Otto Carl Alfred Moschkau, the pioneer German collector and student. A report of the exhibition is to be found in *Deutsche Briefmarken-Zeitung*, Vol. 1, No. 2, Pages 3, 7 ([November] 1870), published at Dresden.

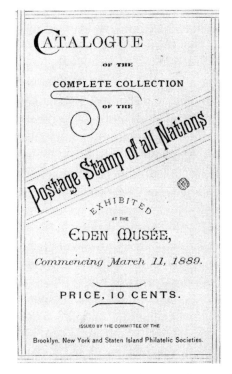

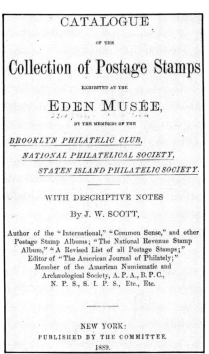

Cover and title page from catalogue of first major U.S. exhibition, 1889.

The first philatelic exhibition of any pretensions was held in Vienna, Austria, in 1881, November 13 through 20. Promoted by the Wiener Philatelisten-Club the exhibition was in effect the foundation stone of the modern internationals, attracting attendance by members of the Austrian Royal house and having the excellence or otherwise of the exhibits determined by a jury — a jury, not judges — a terminology which persists to the present day.

The first exhibition of importance in the United States had been at the Eden Musee in 1889. The International competitive exhibitions led to the collections being mounted and presented in more and more attractive forms, with great attention being paid to illustrating by means of elaborate and beautiful drawings the minute but important differences between varieties of an issue.

An early premium laid upon rarity led to a tendency, in some collectors, to what was termed "bloating" — the acquisition and display of several or numerous copies of the same stamp for no more reason than that it was rare. This trend started at the top, so far as the relative cost of the stamp was concerned, doubtless with a basis of so-called "sound 'cornering' economy," spread downward, and became widespread for a time.

The period after the end of World War I saw more and more collectors seeking for sidelines to their general collections, with the result that greater emphasis began to be laid upon special forms of collecting. Cancellations and other postal markings, in particular, attracted greater attention, and many

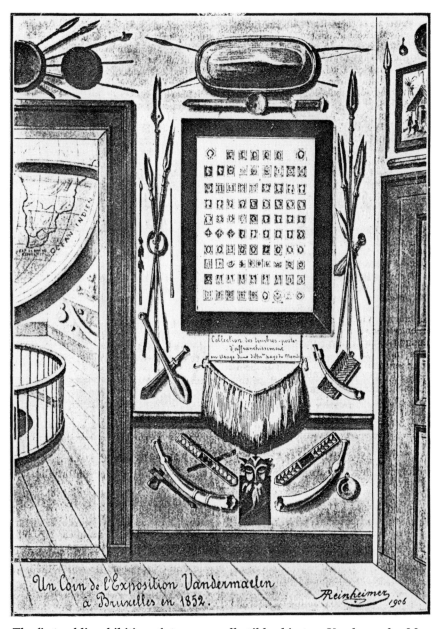

The first public exhibition of stamps as collectible objects — Vandermaelen Museum, Brussels, Belgium, 1852. A painting from memory by Adolph Reinheimer, 1906, is now in the British Library, London.

The Vienna Philatelic Exhibition of 1881 — an artist's impression.

collectors began to concentrate upon collecting stamps and covers that showed that they had been used upon some unusual route, or had performed some special service by rail or water.

The new collectors, beginning on the ground floor, concentrated on the issues made during the war and by the new stamp-issuing countries that appeared after the war. The stamps of "Neurope," as the then post-war Europe was called, enjoyed a vogue that amounted almost to a rage in the Old World and, to a somewhat less extent, in the New.

Sidelines and Branches

A new branch of collecting grew very quickly in the late 1920s and early 1930s, as special airmail stamps were issued by more and more countries to mark the initiation of airmail routes, and for franking mail carried on the ever-growing flying mail. The trend, the beginnings of which were discernible in the pre-war years, really began with the collecting of the special stamps, but veered quickly and generally to the acquisition of entire covers and cards carried by the aircraft and bearing evidence in the form of cachets, special postmarks, even pilots' and navigators' signatures that the mail had been so transported.

About that period another movement became discernible. The infinite variety of the subjects depicted in the designs of the stamps attracted greater and greater attention to the designs themselves, and the almost universal desire for some form of restriction in collecting interests led to the evolution of col-

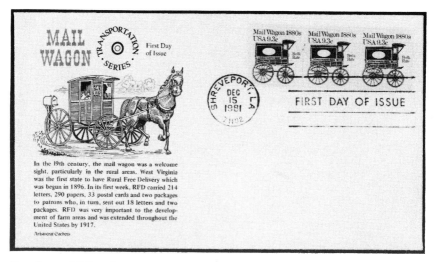

In the 19th century, the mail wagon was a welcome sight, particularly in the rural areas. West Virginia was the first state to have Rural Free Delivery which was begun in 1896. In its first week, RFD carried 214 letters, 290 papers, 33 postal cards and two packages to patrons who, in turn, sent out 18 letters and two packages. RFD was very important to the development of farm areas and was extended throughout the United States by 1917.

Aristocrat Cachets

One facet of "First Day Cover" collecting concentrates on the pictorial souvenir. Its adherents demand that the cover bear no trace of an address.

lections based upon a design subject, topic or theme. The trend began with the mere restriction to collecting every stamp that showed a part of the theme, then developed further and further away from that simple aim. Researches into the reasons why a particular subject appeared on a particular stamp led to the album pages becoming, in some cases, beautifully decorated with drawings and illustrations of the subject and its development, and to the searching out and acquisition of other details and items allied to the subject.

This pre-World War II period, too, saw the growth of another branch of collecting. Stamp-issuing countries had issued special stamps in connection with philatelic exhibitions and other events, and the stamps were printed in small sheets, sometimes of four or more and sometimes of two stamps and occasionally of one stamp only, provided with large margins, as a rule, bearing inscriptions relating to the event calling forth the issue. Numbers of collectors began collections limited to these specially issued commemorative miniature or souvenir sheets.

Another form of collecting associated with the obtaining of souvenirs and with stamp collecting had its inception about that period. The study of the use of stamps had laid emphasis upon the desirability of covers that were dated with a postmark used on the first date the stamps were valid for postage, such a cover being a document which told a story, so to speak, by itself. Over the years specialists in "foreign" countries had grown used to their "foreign" correspondents, in the normal course of events, mailing them a letter bearing a newly issued stamp; and from this basic idea spread the practice of indigenous collectors mailing to themselves new issues, in a variety of combinations, and usually vastly exceeding any possible appropriate postal rate, upon covers for the purpose of obtaining the postally applied first date of use. The practice grew, and "First Day Cover" collecting became a vogue, with some collectors restricting their collections to these items. Indeed, "First

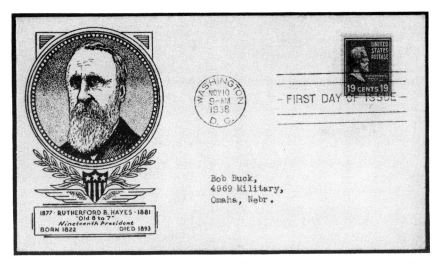

Other "First Day Cover" collectors view the cover as a postal document that requires an address to make it deliverable.

Day Cover" collecting developed at least two facets. One facet concentrated almost exclusively on the pictorial souvenir. So much so that collectors demanded that the cover bear no trace of an address. Even a lightly penciled address was considered to be anathema and the cover with it uncollectible. Another, less extreme, facet viewed the cover as a postal document which required an address to make the cover deliverable and so capable of having a postal function performed in respect of it.

Today's Approaches

In the years between that period and the present day, other movements and fashions have come and been interwoven in the fabric of stamp collecting. In the early 1860s, stamp collectors throughout the world could be numbered in their hundreds; today they are numbered in their millions; and it has become impossible, if it ever were possible, to make an exhaustive survey of the methods of collecting, and to set out rules that are not, probably, really the exceptions.

However, today, every sort of restricted collection is in vogue. Here I intend only briefly to mention some of these restrictions. It is, perhaps, necessary to state here that many individuals have more than one collecting interest, and probably the majority of collectors have more than one collection to which they are adding. There are, of course, many others who, desiring to concentrate upon one thing at a time, do so upon one form of restriction, then dispose of the collection and begin upon another in a different field.

"I have never sold a stamp in my life," used to be the boast of many collectors. That boast is rarely if ever heard today because of various factors, such as the almost infinite diversity of collecting interests, accommodation and taxation. One world-famous philatelist made an estimate, based on his considerable experience as a dealer and auctioneer, that the average time a collector retains a stamp is fifteen years, at all events in Great Britain. He then sells it, and the proceeds are applied either to a new collecting interest or to increasing another existing collection.

I think it desirable to emphasize that it will, of course, be impossible, in the headings that follow and in later chapters, generally to deal with more than the nature of restrictions and to indicate the innumerable permutations and combinations that exist and are possible. To attempt an exhaustive survey of current and past practices savours of the unattainable — the complete Encyclopedia of Stamp Collecting and Philatelic Knowledge has never been written and could not, I think, be compiled; if it could be compiled, it would run to more volumes than there are pages in this book.

It is doubtful whether, throughout the world today, there is any individual adult collector whose seriously pursued goal is the acquisition of all varieties of all issues. There are certain museums and institutions that have remarkably extensive collections and, in some cases, these collections are kept up-to-date with new issues, and acquisitions are made of obsolete stamps.

There are many collectors who collect generally, not with the idea of obtaining completeness in the world's issues, but with the aim of acquiring every different issue that comes their way and is within their means.

By far the majority of collectors limit their collections by definite pre-set bounds. These limited or restricted collections can be classified broadly according to the nature of the restrictions, although of course many exceptions exist. For example, the great majority of collectors today, in the first place, limit their collections to adhesive postage stamps, but there are others who collect not only other postage stamps but also stamps of other kinds.

Present-Day Restrictions

In this brief historical survey of philatelic trends I have already mentioned some of the ways in which collectors have limited or restricted their collections in the past. These restrictions are current today. Often one collection falls into a classification based on a restriction superimposed upon another or others in the historical-geographical-political groups. Other collections are formed within bounds set by considerations connected with the nature of certain stamps, or the reasons for their issue, or their use, or other considerations.

Almost any attempt at exclusive analytical classification would be defeated because some types of collections would fit equally well into one class as another. However, by listing alphabetically some of the classes of stamps and interests, I hope that the almost infinite combinations and permutations of collecting interests and restrictions will become appreciable.

Before I do so, however, I think it desirable here to add that, within most of the various classes of interests, there are collectors of every grade of advancement, from the tyro to the most intensive student.

Airmails. Not only stamps but all postal cards, covers and wrappers carried by air and bearing some indication of such carriage are collected.

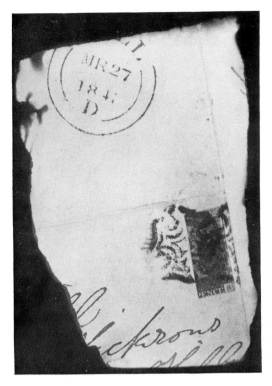

The first bisect (unofficial), Great Britain 1840 2d. used for 1d., at Lincoln. Received at Hull, March 27, 1841.

Adhesives. The majority of collectors limit their collections to adhesive postage stamps. The unqualified term includes not only postal but also fiscal stamps.

Balloon Posts. Stamps intended for mail, and mail, carried by balloon are frequently included in airmail collections, but separate collections of balloon mail exist.

Bisects. Officially authorized bisection of a stamp for use as half its value has occurred in many countries, and special collections have been restricted to such items (normally on cover or satisfactory piece), but usually such collections include other divisions such as quarters and eighths. The comprehensive term is "Splits."

Booklets Books of Stamps. Many countries have issued stamps for sale in small books, booklets or carnets, for convenience of carrying and use. This has attracted limited but widespread collecting interest.

Campaign Covers. Covers, whether bearing adhesives or not, used by members of armed forces on active service, have formed the subject of many collections, most of which are further restricted in some way, and sometimes include "Prisoner of War" mail emanating from both civilians and armed forces.

Cancellations. Defacements made by the authorities for the purpose primarily of preventing re-use of a postage stamp, but sometimes also to indicate the office of origin; cancellations are of many kinds, colors, and innumerable forms, and frequently the term is used synonymously with "Postmarks." Collections of cancellations are frequently restricted to country, issue or type.

Charity Stamps. Semi-postals of which the charge in excess of postage is devoted to a named charity or relief. Collecting charity stamps (as opposed to Charity Labels, which have no postal validity and are collected by some people) is widespread, but some collectors reject them.

Cinderellas. The bounds of Cinderellas have not been authoritatively established by definition other than by cataloguing categories. The initial definition was "stamps not listed in all the general catalogues." The inherent subtlety was too great for general acceptance because of the failure to appreciate that listing in any number less than all of the general catalogues constituted a Cinderella issue. A widely accepted definition of Cinderella issues is: "local stamps, telegraph stamps, fiscals, bogus and phantom issues, Christmas seals, registration labels, advertisement and exhibition labels — the so-called 'Cinderellas of Philately.' " That is the definition accepted by the Cinderella Stamp Club, established in London, England, in 1959. Collections of Cinderellas are often limited to one category and are frequently adjunct to Country collections. Locals are often considered to be regular postal issues of the countries in which the private undertakings operated.

Classics. Stamps of issues which, for some indefinable reason, enjoy positions of distinction among stamps. The term "Classics" is used, in its main sense, exclusively to refer to certain issues made between 1840 and 1875, but is used also, comparatively, for some more modern issues. The term has never been satisfactorily defined in regard to stamps, but collections restricted to classic issues are frequently made.

Combination Covers. Covers, each bearing (to signify *prepayment* of postage throughout by the sender) the postal issues of more than one country. They form the contents of many collections. Such collections are often restricted further, so that covers bearing only certain stamps in combination are included.

Commemoratives. Postal issues made to mark the occurrence of some event or anniversary, bearing facial indication of that reason for issue. There are many classes of such stamps, and collections of commemoratives are, usually, restricted further.

Country. Simple, single specimen collections are made; so are collections on advanced student-specialist lines; and between these two extremes, every variety of collection exists. Country collections, numerically, are among the most popular worldwide, as also are Topicals.

Covers. Envelopes, wrappers, and other outer wrappings of mail, and bearing adhesive stamps, form the contents of numerous collections restricted to such items, which normally include also postcards so franked. Many collections of covers are restricted to covers qualified by terms such as "Campaign," "Combination," "First Day," "Stampless," "Wreck."

Definitives. Postage stamps issued for normally permanent use and contrasted with provisionals, commemoratives, and other issues made with a particular object subsidiary to the collection of postage (and, sometimes,

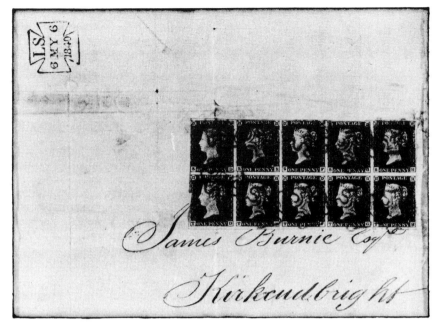

A first day of use cover of the first adhesive postage stamp, Great Britain, May 6, 1840, 1-penny black.

revenue). Definitives are regarded by many collectors more highly than are any other issues.

Errors. Popular collections have been formed of stamps differing from the intended normal stamps because of some unintentional mistake made during any stage of manufacture subsequent to designing and the production of the "die." Errors of design, or artists' errors, fall into a different category. Collections of both categories exist.

Essays. Essays, which are (printed) designs proposed but not adopted as proposed, are collected normally together with proofs and color trials.

First Day Covers. These are covers with postally applied official contemporary markings bearing the first date of officially authorized use. Collections of such covers are, normally, further restricted.

Fiscals. The collecting of fiscals, which are non-postal tax or revenue stamps, is widespread, but is often limited to certain issues.

Forgeries. Fraudulent imitations of stamp designs, overprints, surcharges, or cancellations, these are collected, usually, as part of a reference collection which includes other items such as fakes (genuine stamps or covers which have been tampered with, usually for a fraudulent purpose), bogus stamps, reprints, and genuine material for comparison. Two main categories exist: postal forgeries, that is, forgeries made with the intention of defrauding the revenue; and philatelic forgeries, that is, forgeries made with the object of defrauding collectors. Philatelic forgeries are, sometimes, called "private prints," because some legislation makes even possession of forgeries illegal.

21

Imperforates. Many collections have been formed restricted to stamps issued before the introduction of perforation within the countries concerned. These collections do not, usually, include stamps issued imperforate in error, or the comparatively few modern imperf issues.

Inverted Centers. These fall, usually, into the class of "Errors," but collections have been formed restricted to stamps with the center and frame inverted in relation to each other.

Issue. There are two main types of collections restricted to an issue: the highly specialized collection of one issue of one country; and the general collection of a world-wide commemorative series of issues, such as the "Victory" issues after World War II, often termed "omnibus issues."

Locals. Postage stamps with a franking validity limited to a town, district, or route. There are several classes of locals: government, semi-official, and private; and they have been issued in many countries. Frequently collected as part of a collection restricted to one country, locals form the contents of many collections restricted to them.

Maximum Cards. Pictorial postcards, pre-dating or reasonably contemporary with but not produced specifically for the purpose, duplicating the design of a stamp, with the stamp affixed to the pictorial side of the card and canceled with a postal marking relating as closely as possible to the picture. Some latitude has been tolerated in that some cards are considered by some collectors to be Maximum Cards even though maximum similarity to the stamp design is not achieved by the design of the card, or it was produced specifically for the purpose, or the postal marking is not the closest possible to the subject. Collections of Maximum Cards have acquired a degree of popularity and their collection has been recognized at competitive exhibitions with a class termed "Maximaphily."

Meter Postage Stamps. Franking marks applied by machine meters, either direct to the mail or to pieces of adhesive paper which are subsequently affixed to the mail. Numerous collections of Meter Postage Stamps exist. Comparatively recent introductions are adhesive items on public sale from coin-operated machines; they are termed "automatic stamps" and "Frama labels."

Officials. Adhesive postage stamps intended for use on mail by government departments. There are two main classes of official stamps: those intended for use by a special department ("Departmentals"); and those intended for use indifferently by all departments. These stamps are widely collected, and are known also as "Service Stamps."

Perfins. Postage stamps perforated with initials or devices of private origin but officially authorized have been issued in many countries, and are known also as "Branded Stamps" and "Spifs." Collections exist restricted to such private branding, or also including similarly branded "Officials."

Postal Stationery. Envelopes, letter-sheets, cards, wrappers, and other such items bearing officially applied non-adhesive postage stamps are collected by some, but rejected by the majority of collectors.

Postmarks. Markings applied by the authorities to mail in course of post, often dated and providing other information, have been the subject of much

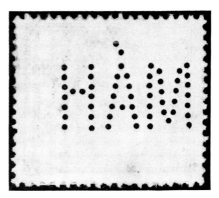

Perfins from the United States (left) and Czechoslovakia (below).

study and collection, frequently when on cover. There are many sub-divisions of "Postmark" and "Cancellation" collecting interests, such as "Ship Letters" and "Traveling Post Offices" marks.

Precancels. Stamps already canceled by machine printing or handstamp when issued, have been issued by several countries, and are widely collected either as part of another restricted collection, or by themselves, in which case it is usual to restrict the collection further.

Proofs. Impressions taken from the die or plate for the purpose of examining either the progress or state of engraving or manufacture, or else the color of the print (often called "color trials" or "color proofs"). Frequently proofs and essays form part of a specialized collection restricted in some other way but many collections exist restricted to proofs and essays generally.

Reprints. Prints taken from the printing base of issued stamps after they have gone out of use; the reprints, normally, differ in several particulars such as paper and color from the issued stamps. They frequently form part of reference or other collections.

Specimen Stamps. Some collections are restricted to samples of actual or suggested stamps, officially marked with the word "Specimen" or its equivalent by overprint, perforation, manuscript, or by inscription. Specimen stamps often form part of collections restricted to one country.

Telegraph Stamps. Adhesive or non-adhesive stamps used for the payment of telegraph charges. They are collected by few, but are most frequently encountered in specialized country collections. By definition they are "Cinderellas."

Topicals. Collections based on a subject, usually some feature in the design of stamps; but other collections, such as those restricted to covers addressed to a particular town, or issues printed by one firm, or stamps illustrating philatelic terms, also fall within this category. Topical collections, numerically, are popular, particularly as attracting new collectors, and are broadly divisible into two classes: subject collections, comprising political-chronological arrangements of stamps; and thematic collections, comprising themes as stories or histories illustratable by stamps and allied material. The swaddling clothes of topical collecting are to be found as early as, if not earlier than, a collection of Royal and other portraits on stamps formed by a contributor to *The Stamp-Collector's Magazine,* Vol. 7, Pages 108-109 (July 1870). Topical collections are referred to also as "Subject Collections" and "Thematics."

Used Abroad. Postage stamps used outside the country of origin, in possessions or post offices "abroad," identifiable as having been so used only by the cancellation or postmark on the stamp or the cover to which it is attached.

War Stamps. Postage stamps and semi-postals issued during war time are collected, often as separate groups by themselves, and frequently as sections of collections otherwise restricted.

Watermarks. Deliberate thinning or thickening of the substance of the paper made during its manufacture, and collections have been restricted to postage stamps bearing particularly paper-makers' watermarks.

2. Aims of Collecting

THE QUESTION that every person collecting stamps must ask at some time or another and in one form or another is: "What do I wish to achieve with my collection?"

That question is quite distinct and separate from the other question: "What do I want from my collection?" As with most fields of human endeavor, it is true that the more one puts into stamp collecting the more one gets from it. Most people, however, expect their collecting activities to provide them with pleasure in the form of relaxation and change from everyday work, even if the alteration consists merely in exchanging one form of study for another. Further, many people regard their collections as, at the same time, providing a form of investment — an investment not only in the sense that money is translated from cash into negotiable securities, but also in the sense that the cash so translated is tied up and linked with the pleasure of relaxation. Third — and this applies to possibly the majority of collectors — there is the feeling that perhaps the investment may produce a profit; a profit not only in the indefinable satisfaction that stamp collecting gives, but also in the hard cash that results from a good buy and an advantageous sale. Fourth, but not least nor last, is the satisfaction that comes from a sense of continuing achievement, and it is in this connection that the saying is most appropriate that the more one puts into the hobby or pursuit the more one gets out of it. For that reason — even if for that reason alone — it may be advantageous to formulate, precisely and distinctly, the question that is posed in the opening paragraph of this chapter.

Posed in other words, the question resolves itself into: "What goal shall I aim at?" That is followed, perhaps, by the further question: "Is the postulate necessary — do I need a goal at which to aim? Or, at all events, is anything more required than that I just meander along, acquiring any and every stamp that takes my fancy, with no more definite objective than the pleasure I derive from this?"

The answer to that question, "Is a definite goal necessary?" lies entirely with the individual. Philately is essentially go-as-you-please, and there are no dictators to say, "This shall be done by you," and no one can say, "This you shall not do." No one, that is, except the individual to, and of, himself.

However, if the individual believes that there is great satisfaction in achieving some objective, and also believes that the more one has to put into attaining an objective the more satisfaction one derives from its attainment, then the answer to the question, "Is a definite goal necessary?" is an unhesitating and emphatic "Yes." And this is in no way lessened by the thought that it is better to travel hopefully than to arrive. It is trite to state that anything worth doing is worth doing well.

The Extremes

What, then, are the present-day aims in stamp collecting in all its phases? The answer is that the individual goals are innumerable and infinitely varied, and stamp collecting today ranges between two extremes: *One,* the desire to acquire merely one example of each item that falls within bounds set by the individual collector; and *Two,* the intensive study of an issue, or one phase of it, to the end that the individual collector knows or seeks to know all the discoverable facts about that issue or phase. On the one hand there is the general collector, and on the other, the specialist; or, to state the matter differently, there is the restricted or selective collector, and the original-research student. While it is true that, nowadays, every original-research student is in that regard a restricted collector, it is equally true that not every restricted collector is an original-research student. The term "specialist" came to be identified almost exclusively with the original-research student, and later to others who followed the path beaten by him or her without contributing any newly allied facts to the available knowledge. Later usage of the term has tended to ally it with restricted collectors, and it will be interesting to see whether, in time, the term "specialist" ceases to have any significant meaning philatelically. Today, however, the unqualified term essentially signifies one who is a restricted collector in the sense that he or she limits the collection to the specialty *and* collects intensively within those limits with the object of discovering and demonstrating all the ascertainable facts of philatelic significance within the limits.

It was because the specialist pursued that goal, and because the general collector sought ever more widely and representatively that the phrases of an artist in word-imagery were applied to these collectors: "The specialist learns more and more about less and less until he knows everything about nothing, while the general collector learns less and less about more and more until he knows nothing about everything." It has, equally, been said that the general collector seeks "something of everything," while the specialist collector seeks to obtain "everything of something."

Completeness

The aphoristic idea behind these witticisms is completeness; and completeness is, probably, the universally pursued general aim in collecting today. Indeed, in all probability, it is and has been the only common factor among collectors throughout the world — not even excluding the stamps themselves, for many "philatelists" do not take account of adhesive stamps or postal stationery. It is in the striving for completeness, whether it be in representing the issues or items within a circumscribed group, or in acquiring knowledge of some particular aspect, that the extremes meet on common ground and share it with the multitudes between them.

It is because of this general aim of completeness that unrestricted general collecting — that is, the search after an example of every major variety of the stamps of the world — has decreased to vanishing point. In the past, and even today to a small extent, various devices have been adopted by some collectors to make the illusory goal of completeness seem attainable by playing on the words "major variety" and substituting for them such terms as "basic designs," and "representative issues," and omitting notice of every variation of color, paper, watermark, perforation and even overprint or surcharge. The question arose whether the substance of representative collecting had been lost in the striving to formulate bounds that made the shadow of completeness seem attainable. Quite apart from that question was the incontrovertible assertion that the bounds, whatever they were, postulated some form of restriction.

Reference to even the "simplified" catalogues of the world shows how hopeless is the task of attempting to form a complete or reasonably complete representative collection of the issues of the whole world, even with almost unlimited financial resources; and so the "simplified" collection was further restricted to countries or group of countries. And the days have long since passed when it was, if it ever was, true to state, as C. Stewart-Wilson and B. Gordon Jones stated in *British Indian Adhesive Stamps (Queen's Head) Surcharged For Indian Native States,* published in 1904: "The number of current stamps of any country (excluding the Seebeckised States) required for collections is to all intents and purposes the same, whatever that country be." It is no longer true because of the popularity factor and the ever-recurring animadversion against the escalation of new issues — re-echoed since the closing decades of the past century. The stamps of some countries are collected by far greater numbers of collectors than are the stamps of some other countries. Even the advent of the "New Issue Service" has not affected this. The days have long passed when, in order to obtain foreign stamps, it was necessary to have correspondents in the various stamp-issuing countries of the world or to write to local postmasters for the supply of each new issue. While dealers from the earliest days sought to and did acquire stamps from all over the stamp-issuing world, it was not until more recent times that any collector could obtain those stamps from the trade other than by going from one dealer to another.

The thrill of the jungle in the chase for newly issued stamps has been replaced by the comfort of the fireside armchair since the early years of the twentieth century saw the inception of the "New Issue Service." Under it, as a matter of course, many dealers will send newly issued stamps up to a specified face-value of specified countries to collectors ordering them by means of a standing order, thus providing an easy way of building up a collection of contemporary issues. In some countries, the post office has a philatelic bureau which will provide the post office's new issues against a standing order on a deposit account. The term "general collector" has come to mean today one who collects a single example of each major variety of the stamps of a country (or countries) according to their arrangement in one of the general catalogues. The term is wide enough to embrace collectors who include in such collections blocks of four and first day covers, but such collections are often termed "semi-specialized."

Three Highways

The courses available today to the individual collector can be summarized quite simply by stating that there are three highways open for choice. He or she may choose a certain and definitely circumscribed field about which to attain completeness in knowledge — for example, the production of the four adhesive postage stamps issued by the Suez Canal Company in July 1868.

The collector may choose a certain and definitely circumscribed field within which to attain completeness in representing issues — for instance, a single used example of each of the stamps issued by the United States during the twentieth century, which does not cost more than a certain amount, predetermined by the collector.

He or she may tread upon the *via media* — the broad and well-populated highway that runs between the two others — neither limiting himself or herself to one representative example and country, nor seeking to acquire all available knowledge about the items.

It is almost needless to add that these highways are not exclusive, and a collector can travel along all three at the same time with different collections.

The 5c. Suez Canal stamp.

Many collectors, perhaps the majority in organized philately today, do travel along more than one of the highways concurrently; and, of course, there are many collectors who have more than one collection on each.

The choices merit careful thought and adequate consideration before any selection is made.

The choice is there. How it is to be exercised depends upon factors peculiar to the individual, which vary almost to infinity. However, there are certain, general considerations which apply: and these are time, cost and space.

Three Factors

It is important to remember that a hobby is made for riding by the hobbyist, and not for him or her to be ridden by it. Therefore the choice made should be one compatible with the time which can be spared, the cash available and the space which can be provided for the collections and allied items.

A further important consideration is that it is necessary to choose a field in which success, if it cannot be complete, is at least within measurable distance. While it is desirable to aim high — if you aim for the moon you may not achieve it but might land on the summit of Everest, and that is no mean achievement — it is unwise to aim so high that there is no chance at all of success, for hopelessness is the bane of human existence. It would be futile, for instance, to set out to make a study of all the unused cut square examples of British Guiana 1856 1c. black on magenta, for none exists.

The ultimate aim of all philatelists is to be able accurately to classify, in one way or another, the items they study. It is toward this end that all study is directed. Without this ability in himself or herself, the collector must rely entirely upon the opinions of others, and is unable to take any intelligent interest in the subject collected.

Stamp Classifying

The philatelist with the widest knowledge is the person who is able accurately to classify within the narrowest limits the largest number of philatelic items.

The aim is apparent in the endeavors of all — from the veriest tyro to the most advanced student-specialist — it varies merely in degree. The youngster looking at the stamp, painstakingly spelling out the name of the country and searching through the stamp-finder to ascertain under what heading to place the stamp in his pocket-sized album, is just as truly applying methods of classification as is the research-student patiently solving the overlapping jigsaw of plating in order to ascertain from which position on the plate or from which plate the self-same stamp was printed. Equally, the topicalist searching for associations with his or her theme is as much "classifying" as is the stampless cover enthusiast digging among the records of a half-forgotten era in an attempt to solve a problem concerning the route along which the cover was carried. The artist sorting his stamps by color or design is just as much "classifying" them as are the members of the expert committee deliberating upon the genuineness or otherwise of the patients before them.

The unique British Guiana 1856 1c.

What, then, is the fundamental philatelic knowledge prerequisite in order that its possessor may be able to classify within narrow limits, if not every stamp that has ever been issued, at least a large proportion of the world's postal paper? The bare catalogue of headings under which that knowledge is ranged is a formidable one. Before embarking upon it I think it as well to state that no one person, and no small association of individuals today, possesses all the knowledge necessary to classify within the narrowest limits possible all the postal issues ever made. It is the sheer magnitude of the task that makes it an impossibility. Leonardo da Vinci was termed "the last master of all learning" — the master of all philately has never existed.

However, there are very many people in the world today so equipped with general principles and background knowledge that there is no branch of philately to which they could not turn and master. It is, then, the general principles and some of the background knowledge that I shall proceed to set out, omitting mention other than here for the time being of knowledge that enables most stamps to be assigned to the particular issuing authority.

Background to Classification

Stamp classification can be viewed from two standpoints. The one concerns itself with the reason for the stamp's existence; the other is connected with the production of the stamp. There is a third standpoint, applicable to many issues, and this is concerned with the actual use of the stamp.

It is necessary, in order to classify stamps according to the reasons for their existence, to have knowledge of what stamps have been issued. All collectors, to a greater or less extent, have acquired some of this knowledge, and much information about the world's postage stamps is readily available from the standard general catalogues and encyclopedias. For present purpose it will be sufficient to state that nearly all the issues of the world fall within

A United States twentieth-century rarity — the 5c carmine error — caused when a 5c transfer roll was used in re-entering three positions on Plate 7942 of the 2c stamps of the flat plate printings of 1917.

one of eight classes. (1) Government issues for the prepayment of postage on letters, which issues comprise: (a) normal services, and (b) special services. (2) Government issues for the post-payment of postage. (3) Government semi-postals. (4) Stamps for the payment of fees other than letter postage. (5) Local and private stamps issued for mail conveyance. (6) Stamps and labels for which no payment is required. (7) Stamps and labels of no validity. The further class is one which cuts right across the others: (8) Philatelic.

In order to classify a stamp according to its production, it is necessary to consider the constituent parts. It is no simple matter to define stamps by cataloguing their constituent parts: the following such definition covers most of the more common, philatelically considered: "A stamp is a piece of paper watermarked or unwatermarked and of a particular texture and with a particular finish, bearing a design applied by a particular process or particular processes in a particular color or combination of colors, with or without addition by the same or different process or processes and in the same or different color or colors, the whole being provided or unprovided with means of easy separation." Of course, a "postage" stamp requires further limitation, so do "used" and "unused" stamps; other limitations are appropriate in other circumstances, and certain purists will cavil at the description of a stamp as a "piece of paper."

From this definition it follows that under the heading of "paper," the philatelist requires some knowledge of what paper is, how watermarks are made, what are the various types of paper texture, from what processes they result, and how paper is treated by manufacturers after its substance comes into existence as paper. Under the heading of "design," he or she requires some knowledge of the types of design and of the terms used philatelically to designate the composite parts of the whole, and of any additions which may have been made to it. Such knowledge needs to incorporate details, at least in outline, of the various methods which, at one time or another, have been adopted to apply the design to the paper, and of the characteristics of certain printing inks. Further, the philatelist requires some knowledge of the methods used for enabling stamps in sheets to be separated easily and surely from one another. Also knowledge is requisite of adhesive substances used for stamps, and the characteristics resulting from their employment, or nonemployment as the case may be.

Having set out some of the headings of fundamental philatelic knowledge, I think it appropriate here to discuss the term "philatelist" in contrast with "stamp collector."

Philately and Stamp Collecting

Apart from so few exceptions throughout the world as to make little difference to the general accuracy of the statement, it is true to say that every amateur philatelist is a stamp collector but not every stamp collector is a philatelist. Many people use "philately" and "stamp collecting" indifferently, but there are others, probably the majority, who hold that the terms are not synonymous. So far as writers are concerned, and in speaking, the word "philatelic" is used to the exclusion of the barbaric sounding "stampic" and with somewhat different connotations.

The word "philately," as was briefly mentioned in Chapter 1, was coined by a Frenchman, Georges Herpin, who published his newly invented word in an anonymous article entitled "Baptême" that appeared in *Le Collectionneur de Timbres-Poste* for November 1864 (Vol. 1, Page 20). After stating that postage stamps had been studied and collected for the past six or seven years, and referring to "timbromanie" as impossible of acceptance to designate the pastime, he proposed "Philatélie" as expressing the idea that the odious term "timbromanie" endeavored to ridicule. He went on: " 'Philatélie' is formed from two Greek words: ΦΙΛΟΣ, friend, amateur, and ΑΤΕΛΗΣ (in speaking of an object), free, exempt from any charge or tax, franked; substantive ΑΤΕΛΕΙΑ. Philately therefore signifies: love of the study of everything relating to franking."[1]

From its inception, it will be seen, the term "philately" implied "study" in the mind of its coiner, and that implication was given to the world. The derived "philatelist" soon attracted the same implication; this is set out emphatically by the editor of *The Stamp-Collector's Magazine* in January 1868 (Vol. 6, Page 16), when replying to a correspondent: ". . . if our correspondent wishes to become a philatelist in the true sense of the word he must not be content with *buying* stamps and mounting them in his album — he must also study them."

The term did not find immediate and universal acceptance; for instance,

---

[1]The quoted translation is taken from *The Journal of the Philatelic Literature Society* for April 1915 (Vol. 8, Page 15).

although *The American Journal of Philately* was established in March 1868, and although the editor of *The American Stamp Mercury* had a "Philatelic Review" of 1867 (Vol. 1, Page 22), he inveighed against the word in July 1868 (Vol. 1, Page 63) in an editorial which began: "This is the new fangled term which a few egotists in Europe and a very few more in America have, in their self-sufficient wisdom, decided to be the term by which the science of stamp collecting shall henceforth and forever be designated." He went on to expound that a philatelist was really an "anti-taxationist" and stated that he himself was an anti-taxationist in respect of income rates, manufacturer's taxes and so on; he suggested that "timbrophily" was a suitable word to use, having been employed for some time past.

However, in spite of such active and also passive opposition, "philately" and its derivatives came into accepted use, and connoted strongly the leaning towards study which its early adherents had postulated as implicit. Indeed it was upon study that philately fed and waxed strong. Paradoxically the strength flowed from the one-time prevalence of forgeries, and the study that became necessary to enable the weeds to be distinguished from the flowers.

By careful study and by plating — that is, overlapping pairs and other multiple pieces, each including a stamp exhibiting identical characteristics, and repeating the process until no further extension was possible because the limits of the printing base had been reached — the exact pattern of the plates and dies of the genuine articles became known, and the stamps were susceptible of minute classification. The existence of forgeries acted as a spur to students, in presenting a challenge and a problem in this classification: until, for instance, every one of the New South Wales Sydney Views had been plated, because each hand-engraved stamp differed from the other, no one could be quite certain whether the piece of printed paper he or she owned was not a forgery. Similarly the studies of the other constituent parts of the stamps were all directed to the establishment of so minute a system of classification that no forgery, reprint, repaired or faked stamp or postal marking could escape the fine-mesh of the sieve of knowledge.

The American College Dictionary, in defining "philately" refers[2] to " . . . collection and study . . . "; Funk and Wagnalls *New 'Standard' Dictionary* (1946) places the emphasis differently, and the definition begins: "The study and collection. . . . "

It is questionable whether these authorities and others (not the least of which is the *Oxford English Dictionary*) despite the weight which is due to them, are entirely accurate in relation to "philately." There are many dealers whose general philatelic knowledge finds no parallel among amateurs, and who do not collect; those dealers are essentially and unquestionably philatelists. It may be stated that, in relation to philately, collection is not a *sine qua non.* One is left with study as being the essence of philately. Collecting is incidental and not essential to philately.

---

[2]According to J.B. Kaiser in *Bibliography The Basis of Philatelic Research* (1953). I have not seen a copy of this Dictionary.

Stamp Collectors, Philatelists and Specialists

Leaving aside the question whether the term "philatelist" has now acquired two meanings — the one specific, and the other general — the question of who are philatelists really resolves itself into one of degree and kind (or of kind and degree) of study by reference to its objects. Obviously no one who collects stamps intelligently can do so without, in some degree, studying them, even if only to ascertain, say, under what country to place them in the album.

"Stamp collecting," when viewed in contrast to "philately" has come to mean little more than the words imply in their ordinary sense, and a stamp collector is one who, with some knowledge of what stamps have been issued, seeks to obtain them in order to fill spaces in the album, to complete sets, or for other such reasons.

A "philatelist" — leaving the dictionary definitions on one side — is one who has as a prerequisite some of the knowledge of the stamp collector, and studies the stamps and the subjects which enable him to classify stamps according to their production and/or use.

A "specialist" is one who has as prerequisites the background knowledge of the philatelist, and who, by specially intensive study, has acquired detailed and particular knowledge of the subjects falling within the scope of the specialty. It is worth remembering that a specialist is not a specialist absolutely, but merely one within the scope of the specialty, and if he or she were to alter the object of study to another field, then he or she starts as a beginner, but one with the advantage of the background experience gained in the earlier specialty.

To conclude this part of the often hotly-debated subject of "Stamp Collecting" and "Philately," it is appropriate to set out two quotations. First, the words of A.J. Sefi in one of the most delightfully illustrated general philatelic books ever produced, *An Introduction to Advanced Philately* (1926), Page 5:

Modern Philately may be said to comprise the study of stamps from every possible angle of historical and philatelic interest. It includes enquiries into the reasons and circumstances leading up to an issue, and researches as to the essays and proofs for the stamps thereof; studies of all the different processes and methods of production used, and of any resultant varieties on the stamps themselves, and, finally, enquiries into all the uses or misuses to which the stamps, once issued, might be subject.

The second quotation was written by the late Stanley Phillips, in *Stamp Collecting*, the best and most comprehensive general introductory book ever written. After quoting A.J. Sefi's words which are quoted above, Mr. Phillips goes on to state (7th Ed., Page 27):

Within this definition is comprised the whole field of study which lies open to the collector who wishes to earn, in one way or another, the right to be called a serious philatelist. He need not attempt to cover it all, even in the case of one particular country or issue, but may deal with only one or two of the possible angles. . . .

That quotation of Stanley Phillips' words was elevated to citation in the introduction of the revision of the book by John Holman (1983, Page 8).

34

What Are 'Philatelic' Studies?

A question which, in one form or another, has from time to time been hotly debated throughout the world is: What studies allied to stamps earn for the students the right to be called seriously "philatelists"? There is no doubt that, from its inception, philately has been so intimately and widely associated with the postage stamp that it came to be identified with studies more or less closely connected with and arising from the postal services.

As an example: while at first fiscals and the like and their study were accepted unquestioningly under the umbrella, the time came when their position there was questioned because the objects of the study were not connected with the prime function of the posts. The beginnings of this questioning can be traced back as far as, if not further than, 1874 when J.-B. Moens of Belgium, the renowned dealer and publisher of *Le Timbre-Poste*, began publication of a separate magazine, *Le Timbre Fiscal*, wherein was published information relative exclusively to fiscals that had hitherto appeared in the pages of *Le Timbre-Poste*. The dissension increased, the students and collectors of fiscals accepted the distinction forced upon them but still maintained their close links in interest with the parent-body from which they had sprung. In 1892 the debate about status threw up *The Fiscal Philatelist*, a magazine whose title pinpointed the argument. After 1896 *Le Timbre Fiscal* ceased publication as a separate magazine and was merged with *Le Timbre-Poste,* and in 1900 *Morley's Philatelic Journal* first appeared, its sub-title being "A monthly paper for collectors of postage, revenue, telegraph and railway stamps"; in fact its contents were devoted almost exclusively to non-postal matters. By this time the argument had waned, and students of fiscals, not numerically great, were generally accepted again within the framework of philately.

However, in 1909, publication of Volume VII of the *Oxford English Dictionary* showed that the controversy was not at an end. This great authority, whose accuracy I have had the temerity to question above, defined "philately" (Vol. VII, Page 775) as: "The pursuit of collecting, arranging, and studying the stamped envelopes or covers, adhesive labels or 'postage stamps,' postcards, and other devices employed in different countries and at different times, in effecting the prepayment of letters or packets sent by post." There is no word anywhere in the definition that embraces the study of fiscal stamps. Webster's *New International Dictionary* (1928) defines "philately" (Vol. II, Page 1620) as: "The collection and study of postage stamps, stamped envelopes, or the like, of various issues." Applying legal principles of interpretation to this definition it is not (but loosely it is) sufficiently wide to embrace fiscals. Funk and Wagnalls *New 'Standard' Dictionary* (1946) defines "philately" (Vol. II, Page 1855) as: "The study and collection of labels or stamps, stamped envelopes and wrapper-stamps, issued by public authority to indicate prepayment or freedom from charge, payment due, or special service, as postage- or revenue-stamps, and also stamps of private telegraph and letter-carrying companies."

Similar controversies arose and waned in relation to postmarks, to precancels, to airmails, to stampless covers, to topical collecting and to maximaphily to name but six.

In connection with topical collecting, summarizing without exhausting the arguments advanced on one side, they may be stated as: philately concerns itself with the study of matters relating to the production, issue and use of a stamp as a stamp, and the subject of the design is merely incidental; whereas topical collecting concerns itself essentially with the topic, and the stamps are merely incidental.

Summarizing without exhausting the arguments on the other side, they may be stated as: all philatelic conditions are, by their very nature, collections within the subject of "philately." The choice of a topic is merely the choice of one form of restriction (the topic) rather than another (e.g. a country or an issue), and within that restriction there is scope for study about the chosen subject as well as other matters.

There are, let me hasten to add, other and probably more forceful arguments advanced on one side or the other as to the reason why topicalists, by virtue of the topical nature of their collections, respectively have not or have earned the right to be called seriously "philatelists." The question resolves itself into one of degree.

Until comparatively recent years many philatelists considered it inconceivable that a collection of items related to postal history and without adhesives could qualify for a place in a philatelic exhibition. The thought used to be that it was equivalent to the absurdity of including in a *philatelic* show items termed "pre-philatelic." By their very description, pre-philatelic items could have no legitimate place in a show which, by definition, was restricted to items that came into existence after the pre-philatelic items ceased to be current.

However illogical their inclusion might have seemed to the thoughtful and logical collector, the fact remained that they began to be accepted in even international exhibitions. Indeed, as time passed, special provisions were made for such items to be accepted as competing — in practice at least — on equal terms with adhesive postage stamps. That was so even though no true standards of direct comparison could possibly exist.

The answer to the paradox is that postal history embraces the whole history of the posts and that postage stamps form a part of the history of the posts.

Nevertheless, there exists a widespread misapprehension that it is possible for a collector to describe himself as collecting postal history. That is an obvious fallacy. Postal history is an intangible conception. It is, of course, possible to study postal history, just as it is possible to study stamps or philately. Collecting philately cannot be considered as a possible endeavor.

A philatelic collection can exist. A philately collection cannot. Nor can a collection of postal history. What can be the subject of endeavor is a collection of items concerned with or related to postal history.

The problem, in so far as it is a problem, is caused by the absence of a compound adjective equivalent in succinctness to "philatelic." Conceivably a postal-historic, or postally-historic, collection could have a separate existence, but the enunciation generally of the thought seems to present insuperable difficulties. Consequently one finds collectors, dealers and auctioneers stating that they collect, deal in or auction postal history.

3. Paper

ALL PAPER is a dried mat of interwoven fibers that have fallen from suspension in water. Except in a few special cases the fibers are cellulosic, obtained from a variety of vegetable origins. The problem of the paper-maker is to make this dried mat or felted web of requisite and uniform color, strength, surface, and thickness.

Papermaking can be divided into three stages. First, the preparation of the fibers from the basic material to form pulp, and their suspension in water to form what is called "stuff." Second, the spreading of the stuff and its treatment to form (a) the texture (the "wiremark"), and, possibly (b) the watermark, and its subsequent drying. Third, its finish and subsequent treatment.

Philatelists consider that readily appreciable and significant variations of paper are of interest and assistance in classifying stamps. Because of this it is necessary to have an outline knowledge of the processes of papermaking, and a more detailed knowledge of certain aspects. The varieties of widest interest to collectors in general occur during the second stage of papermaking. Of more recent years, however, increasing philatelic interest has been aroused by the third stage, with the greater study that has been devoted to tagging, which is considered later in this work in connection with inks and color.

Broadly speaking, all paper used for stamps can be divided into hand-made and machine-made, these terms referring to the operation of spreading the stuff. In a few cases the whole of the operations have been carried out by hand; and, therefore strictly speaking, so far as collectors are concerned there are three classes of papers:

(1) Hand-Made, where all operations are done by hand. About this class I shall say no more than that some stamps from some countries in the Far East, such as Japan and Nepal, have been printed on paper locally made by hand. Such paper varies greatly in thickness and texture. It is termed, philatelically, "Native Paper," but that term is sometimes used also loosely to embrace certain papers more properly falling within Class 2.

(2) Hand-Made, where the stuff is spread by hand operation. This class formed a large proportion of the paper used for postage stamps issued during the first few decades from 1840 onward.

(3) Machine-Made, where the spreading of the stuff and other operations are performed by machine. This is the class universally employed for postage stamps today.

The first stage of manufacture can be considered irrespective of whether the paper is to be hand-made or machine-made. But it must be remembered that what is about to be described here and later is the simplified outline of some operations, and that almost every paper mill has its own variations of the processes, and they differ in detail. **Moreover, it must be emphasized that, although the present tense is used throughout, the survey is historical; operations described obtained for many an issue long out of production and have been superseded in modern methods of papermaking.**

The Stuff

The cellulosic fibers can be derived from many basic sources that can be bleached, such as cotton, linen, hemp, manila, esparto grass, bamboo, and various trees — and, of course, old paper. Nearly all papers contain a mixture of two or more of the basic materials, to which various minerals or chemicals have been added. Certain papers contain a proportion of animal fibers, which cannot be bleached — silk, for example.

The finest papers used for stamps contain a large proportion of linen or cotton. These materials are not to any great extent used by the paper-maker in their natural state, and he obtains them in the form of rags. The rags are carefully sorted (Illustration A). During the sorting, such things as rubber, silk, nylon and other artificial fibers, buttons, pieces of wire and so on are removed. The rags are then chopped into small pieces, and boiled with chemicals until bleached (Illustration B). They are then beaten into pulp. Rag pulp looks like wet cotton wool (Illustration C).

A. In Britain, stamp paper is made partly from rags. Girls sort them carefully to exclude rubber, silk, art-silk, wool, nylon and other unsuitable fibers. The finding of rubber, especially dangerous in papermaking, earns a special bonus.

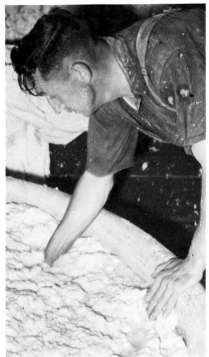

B. Removing rags from the boiler after they have been boiled in a solution of sodium hydroxide for eight to ten hours.

C. The fiber pulp, ready for the addition of water to make the stuff.

Pulp is made from other materials by putting them through various processes analogous to those used for rags. Wood pulp, for example, looks like porridge.

At the pulp stage the mixing of the various materials takes place. If the paper is to be colored throughout, dyes are added to the pulp.

Occasionally, bleached pulp is mixed with unbleached pulp to produce special effects. "Granite Paper" for example.

The materials from which paper is manufactured, and their proportion, is termed "the furnish," and there are several stamp papers that are known to collectors by names arising from the furnish, or by trade terms in certain instances. Some of these names appear in the alphabetical list at the end of this chapter.

The pulp is then put through certain other processes, and mixed with a very large amount of water to make the stuff. The stuff may be as much as, or more than, ninety-eight per cent water, and two per cent fibers. It looks like thin milk or paste, the color approximately that the paper will eventually be.

It is in the treatment of the stuff that the differences occur that have given rise to the terms "hand-made" and "machine-made" paper. Philatelically considered, there are common factors in the two classes of paper, and it is these common factors that provide the collecting world with the varieties of paper most frequently noted. The differences will be considered in turn. The varieties common and otherwise, will be listed later.

The stuff is made to flow into a vat, which is a container of convenient size, where it is kept in a perpetual state of agitation to prevent the fibers from settling to the bottom.

Hand-Made Paper

At the vat stands a vatman, who operates with a mould, which is a framework usually of mahogany, with struts supporting an arrangement of wire. The arrangement of the wire is important, and determines the texture — and watermark, if any — of the paper. (I shall deal with this at a later stage.) Over the mould fits a loose and detachable rim, called the "deckle." When the deckle is in position on the mould, it forms a shallow tray with a wire base.

The vatman fits the deckle over the mould, tilts it toward himself, and slides the two together into the stuff in the vat. At a moment he judges opportune he levels the mould and lifts it, now filled with stuff, from the vat. As he does so the water begins escaping through the wire. The vatman then deftly shakes the mould to interweave the fibers, and places it on one side, momentarily, to drain further. Some of the stuff has seeped between the mould and the deckle, thus causing the "deckle edge" characteristic of such paper.

After the deckle has been removed, the next operator, who is called the coucher, takes the mould. It now bears on top of the wire a soggy mat of interwoven fibers. He dextrously turns the mould over, and rocks the soggy mat or sheet from the mould on to a felt or blanket which lies on a stand before him. He covers the soggy sheet with another blanket, and is ready to accept another mould from the vatman and repeat the process.

When sufficient of these alternate layers of blankets and sheets have been put together, they form what is known as a "post." This is put in a press,

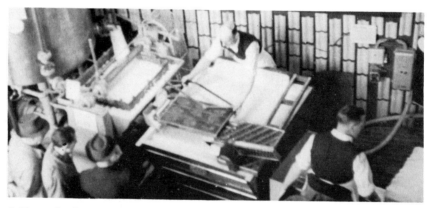

1. From the large and small parts of the installation at the left of the picture, fibers (about two per cent) and water (about ninety-eight per cent) are fed into the vat, center, where they are kept agitated. Facing the camera, with the vat before him, stands the vatman. On the bench over the vat is the mould. In the vatman's hands is the deckle, and he is about to fit it over the mould. To the right of the vat, with his back to the camera, stands the coucher, facing a stand. To his right is a pile of felts or blankets ready for use.

2. The vatman, having fitted the deckle over the mould, is preparing to dip it into the vat.

and heavily pressed to remove excess moisture. The sheets are then separated from the blankets. After further pressing and drying the sheets, which are known as "waterleaf" sheets, are treated with size and finished into sheets of paper (see Illustrations 1 to 9).

Because of the human element, one sheet of hand-made paper inevitably differs from the next in thickness. Indeed, because paper is sold by weight per ream, some sheets are made specially thick or specially thin to make up the correct weight of a ream. This fact accounts for some, but not all, varieties of stamps recorded as being on "thick paper," or "thin paper" — the adjectives being comparisons with the thickness normal for the stamps concerned.

Such variations in thickness must not be confused with varieties resulting from official experiments with or adoption of papers of different weights. For example, in Great Britain, the official standard weight of each ream was, in May 1840, thirty-one-and-one-half pounds; in June 1840, twenty-four,

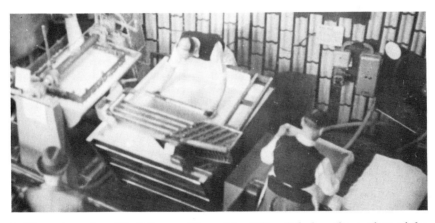

3. The vatman has tilted the mould, and is sliding it below the surface of the liquid.

41

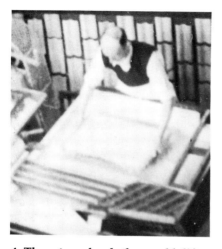 

4. The vatman levels the mould, lifts it clear, and shakes it skillfully to interweave the fibers. Excess liquid flows over the deckle and drains from the mould.

5. The vatman places the mould on one side to drain, and removes the deckle, ready to begin again with another mould.

6. In the meantime, the coucher prepares to receive the mould, by spreading a felt on the stand before him (see also picture No. 3). The mould has been stood upright, near his left shoulder, the water continuing to drain from the fibers on the wire.

7. The coucher, with his left arm outstretched, is about to take the mould, invert it and turn out a soggy mat of fibers on to the felt in front of him. He will then return the empty mould to the vatman, and cover the mat of fibers with another felt, ready to receive the contents of the next mould.

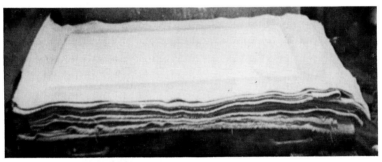

8. A mat of fibers (nearly recognizable as a sheet of paper) lies on top of a pile of alternate felts and sheets. This pile is the "post."

9. The post is pressed, hydraulically, to get rid of excess water. The sheets, called "waterleaf," are then separated from the felts and put through further processes of pressing, sizing, drying and glazing to result in finished paper.

twenty-six and twenty-eight pounds; and at the end of 1841, thirty-three to thirty-four pounds.

Machine-Made Paper

There is a type of machine that makes imitation hand-made paper in a series of traveling moulds. These moulds are filled, as they travel under sprays, with a predetermined amount of stuff. Subsequent operations are performed by hand.

There are two types of machines for making paper in the web — that is, in a continuous wide strip that may then be divided into convenient widths and rolled up into reels of convenient lengths.

Historically, so far as stamp collectors are concerned, the first type of machine (invented by John Dickinson) contains a perforated metal cylinder covered with finely woven wire. This cylinder revolves, partly submerged in a vat of stuff, very slowly, and picks up a film of fibers on the wire. These form a mat, and the superfluous water is carried away through the axle of the cylinder. The mat of fibers is a continuous strip and is led away over an endless web of felt, and subsequently pressed, dried, sized and finished. Such a machine, with refinements, was used to produce the paper on which the "Mulready" covers and envelopes of 1840 were printed.

The second type of machine is still known as the "Fourdrinier," after the man who first brought it into use in England during the early part of the nineteenth century. In this machine, the stuff is made to flow evenly on to an endless cloth of finely woven wire — something like ninety inches broad, and about sixty feet long — which has a sideways shaking motion at one end, to interweave the fibers.

At the same time this wire cloth moves forward. As it moves, the water drains away below, leaving the fibers on top. They are prevented from falling sideways from the wire cloth by deckle-straps, made of vulcanized rubber, which move independently but at the same rate as the wire cloth (Illustration D).

The web passes under a "dandy roll," a light hollow cylinder around which is an arrangement of wire. This arrangement of the wire, like that of the mould in hand-made paper, is important, and determines the texture — and watermark, if any — of the paper (and will be dealt with later) (Illustration E).

After passing under the dandy roll, which is of course carefully adjusted

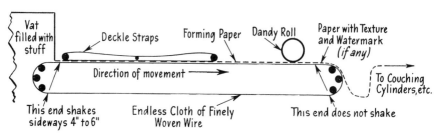

The "Fourdrinier."

D. The Fourdrinier machine. Stuff flowing on to the endless cloth of finely woven wire. Note the deckle straps passing over guide wheels at each side. The flow is shown from right to left in the picture.

to give correct pressure, the web of forming paper is led away from the endless wire cloth, between various sets of rollers which perform the operations of couching, pressing, drying and so on (Illustration F).

The rate at which paper can be made by machine varies enormously. In Great Britain normal stamp paper is made at about 100 to 120 feet per minute.

The Mould and the Dandy Roll

It has already been stated that the arrangement of the wires in the mould (for hand-made paper) and on the dandy roll (for machine-made paper) affects the texture of the finished paper and causes the watermark, if any.

The paper takes on the texture of the arrangement of the wires, rather in the manner that a cake will take on the pattern of a wire tray when placed on it from the oven to cool, or dried mud outside a garage bears the tire marks of the cars that drove over it when it was wet.

45

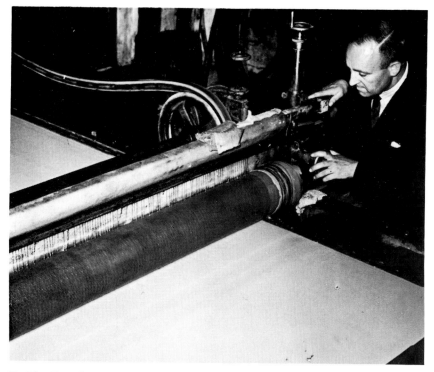

E. The Fourdrinier machine. The web passing under the dandy roll to be impressed with the paper texture (wove) and the British "Royal Cypher" watermark. The officer is making a careful adjustment. The flow is shown from left to right in the picture.

Where the fibers lay on the wire itself the paper will be slightly thinner than where they lay in the spaces between the wires. This texture can be appreciated by "looking through" the paper — that is, by holding it up to a strong light so that the paper acts as a screen between the light and the eye. The places where the fibers lay over each individual strand of wire will be appreciable as faintly lighter places in the paper than where the fibers lay between that wire and the next. It is possible, therefore, by examining the paper in this way, to tell what was the arrangement of the wires on the mould or the dandy roll as the case may have been.

This inevitable variation in the thickness of the sheet of paper is inherent in the very processes of manufacture. It was the fact that forming paper behaved in this manner that led to the introduction of "watermarks."

Watermarks (which are considered philatelically in the chapter devoted to them) are deliberate local variations in the thickness of an individual sheet of paper, caused by an intentional local variation in the surface of the mould or dandy roll.

Where the surface of the mould or dandy roll has been raised by a pattern, there the paper will be thinner according to the pattern raised. If the surface

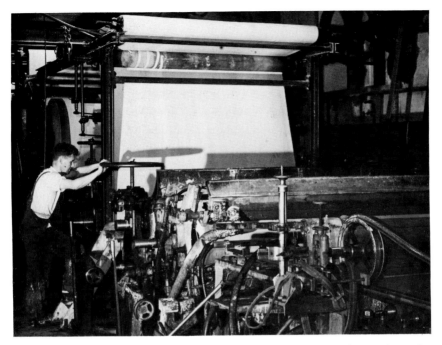

F. The Fourdrinier machine. Stamp paper in the web being led away from the endless wire cloth to various rollers that couch, press and dry the paper. The flow is shown from right to left in the picture.

of the mould or dandy roll has been lowered locally, there the paper will be thicker in the pattern sunk. Consequently, when a piece of paper so made is looked through, the watermark will be visible as a pattern additional to the texture of the paper, and appear lighter or darker than the surrounding paper dependent on whether the design has been respectively raised on or sunk in the mould or dandy roll. In the majority of cases, when a stamp has been printed on paper bearing a watermark, the watermark is much more readily appreciable than the texture of the paper.

It follows from what has already been stated, that there is a complete difference between hand-made and machine-made paper so far as the actual forming of the texture and any watermark is concerned. In hand-made paper they occur because the fibers lie on the wire, and are made in the underside of the manufactured sheet. In machine-made paper, the texture and watermark are made in the upper side of the manufactured web, because the dandy roll impresses them on that side.

Machine-made paper has a further characteristic, which is caused by the texture of the fine weave of the wire surrounding the cylinder (in the Dickinson machine) or of the endless wire cloth (in the Fourdrinier machine). This characteristic is, sometimes, referred to as the ''mesh''; it occurs, of course, on the underside of the paper. There is, in machine-made paper used for stamps, a clearly marked difference between the paper's upper side — which is comparatively smooth, and is normally used for the printing — and the underside, which is comparatively rough, and is normally used for the gum. However, this difference is often not appreciable because the gum masks the characteristics.

Broadly speaking, there is a further appreciable difference between hand-made and machine-made paper. When hand-made paper is looked through, it presents a generally cloudy appearance of small irregular blotches. In machine-made paper the clouding is not present, or rather, not present to so marked an extent.

Paper Textures

There are only two basic types of texture for paper; the other varieties are merely variations of the basic types. The basic textures are: "wove" and "laid."

WOVE: In wove wire, it has been closely interwoven like plain cloth — as, for example, in a pocket handkerchief. When looked through, wove paper presents no outstanding pattern. When closely examined, especially under moderate magnification, it reveals small light and dark dots, representing respectively the crossing of the fine wires and the spaces between.

Wove paper has been by far the most widely used of all paper textures for postage stamps. Examples of it are to be found in the issues of every country — from the Great Britain 1840 1d. and 2d. (hand-made) to the USA 1984 Christmas 20c multicolored (machine-made).

LAID: In laid wire, the individual wires have been arranged (or *laid* — hence the name) closely together in parallel lines, and supported at intervals of about one inch by other wires. The close wires are called the "laid wires"; the widely spaced wires are called "chain wires." When looked through, laid paper presents an outstanding pattern of alternate light and dark closely set parallel lines (called "laid lines") representing respectively the laid wires and the spaces between, crossed at right angles by a series of light lines (the "chain

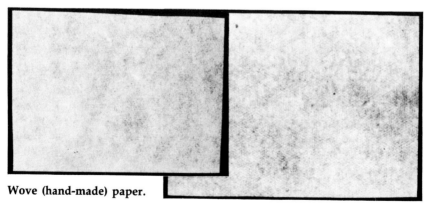

Wove (hand-made) paper.

Wove (machine-made) paper.

Hand-made wove paper. At right, back surface. (Great Britain, 1840, 2d.)

lines'') representing the chain wires, with about one inch between each chain line.

Laid paper has been frequently used for postage stamps and examples are to be found in the issues of many countries. Collectors acknowledge two main variations of laid paper, but the variations are caused by the use of the paper, not the papermaking itself. Where the laid lines run across the stamp, the paper is termed *Horizontally Laid*. Examples are to be found in, say, Moldavia-Wallachia 1862 (June 25) 3 paras to 30 paras. Where the laid lines run up and down the stamp, the paper is termed *Vertically Laid*. Examples are to be found, say, in Russia 1902-04 1k. to 70k. For stationery, at least, a further variation is noted: many officially issued envelopes are so printed on the paper that the lines run diagonally, and the term used is *Diagonally Laid*. Examples are to be found, for instance, in the USA 1853-55 issue of envelopes.

Texture Variations

The other varieties of paper texture combine the variation in thickness of paper inevitable in its manufacture, with deliberate thinning of the substance

Thin laid paper. At right, back surface. (Romania, Moldavia-Wallachia, 1862, 6p.)

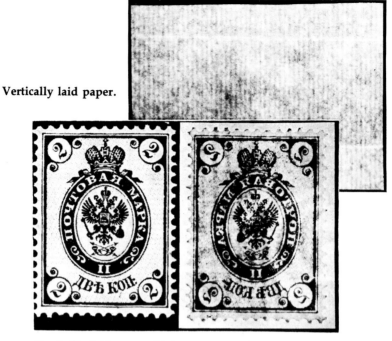

Vertically laid paper.

Vertically laid paper. Right, transmitted light shows pattern. (Russia, 1902-04, 2k.) This paper also has a watermark, a portion of which shows on the stamp.

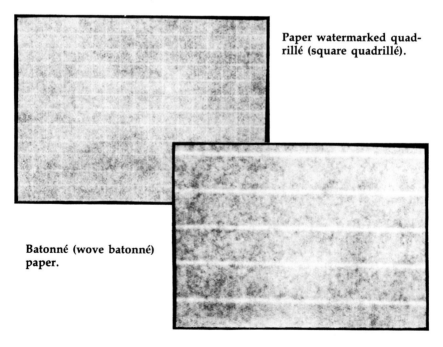

Paper watermarked quadrillé (square quadrillé).

Batonné (wove batonné) paper.

Wove batonné. Front and back. (Afghanistan, 1880-90, 2ab.)

of the paper, analogous to a watermark. Again, there are two main types: "batonné" and "quadrillé." There are other varieties, which are considered in the chapter devoted to watermarks.

BATONNE: In batonné paper, its substance has been deliberately thinned by raising comparatively thick and prominent wires, parallel to each other at intervals of about one-half inch between wires. The thinning of the paper is pronounced, and can be seen without looking through. This type of quasi-watermark was largely used and intended as a guide for writing.

There are two inevitable sub-types of batonné paper, which are the basic textures, "Wove Batonné," and "Laid Batonné." In *Wove Batonné* the spaces between the wide-set parallel lines are filled with wove paper. Only rarely has such paper been used for postage stamps. Examples are to be found in Poonch 1888. In *Laid Batonné*, the spaces between the wide-set parallel lines are filled with laid paper, the batonné lines being parallel with the laid lines. This type of paper, too, has only rarely been used for postage stamps. Examples are to be found in Afghanistan 1889-90 1a., and Guadalajara 1868 1r.

QUADRILLE: As a variety of paper texture, quadrillé paper was made in a mould in which a prominently raised pattern of thin wires was formed in the shape of rectangles each about one-eighth of an inch square. This results, as with batonné paper, in a quasi-watermark visible without looking through the paper. Examples of the use of such watermarked quadrillé paper are very

Laid batonné. Front and back. (Afghanistan 1880-90, 1ab.)

Quadrillé (oblong quadrillé) paper. At right, back surface. (Ecuador, 1865, 1r.)

rare in stamp production. Fiji 1870 Times Express stamps were printed on such paper.

The term quadrillé is applied also to paper upon which a rectangular pattern has been printed after the paper was made. (A familiar instance to many collectors is provided by certain types of album leaves printed with a pattern of light gray squares). So far as stamps are concerned there are two principal types of such paper. In the first type, the rectangular pattern consists of squares — the term *Quadrillé*, unqualified, designates "squares." Examples are to be found, for instance, in France 1892 (April) 15c. and Obock 1893-94 1c. to 1f. In the second type, the rectangles are oblong, and the paper is termed *Oblong Quadrillé.* Examples are to be found in Mazagan-Marakesh (Morocco) 1898 5c. to 1 peseta.

Paper Varieties

Quite apart from the varieties of texture in different papers, collectors note also the differences, often pronounced, arising from particular processes adopted during or after manufacture. Many of these paper varieties result from processes intended to afford greater security from forgery or cleaning and re-use of stamps with consequent loss to the stamp-issuing authorities.

Broadly, these varieties of paper can be classed under six headings. First, as was previously mentioned, are those deriving names, often of trade origin, from the furnish. Second are those arising because of deliberate additions to the pulp. Third are the continuous thread papers, the threads being introduced during the paper formation. Fourth are varieties resulting from surfacing or coating. Fifth are varieties caused by processes analogous to printing on the finished paper. And lastly, there are the varieties that are purely philatelic.

Apart from the foregoing varieties, paper is distinguished by watermarks, quasi-watermarks and pseudo-watermarks when they are present. Some of these have already been referred to, and the others are considered, philatelically, in the chapter devoted to watermarks.

Burelage, front and (right) design filtered out. (Estonia, 1928-35, 12s.)

Chalky surface paper. (Russia, 1913, 3k.)

Enamel coated paper. (Portugal, 1870-84, 15r.)

Chungking (local) Nov. 1894 4c showing variety "creased paper." Note the distortion of the rectangular shape of the stamp.

Granite paper. Front and back. (Austria, 1918-1919, 3k.)

Again, some materials bearing designs and used in stamp production are not, strictly considered, paper. They are the foils which are bonded to paper to form the base on which the color or ink is deposited. They are, perhaps, more logically considered in the main together with inks and color, as they are in this work. It is realized that an argument exists for considering them under "Paper."

The same applies to tagging — fluorescence, luminescence and phosphorescence. They, too, are considered mainly together with inks and color.

To ease somewhat the burden of locating the subjects generally some cross-references have been incorporated in the alphabetical list which follows in this chapter, but the surest way to locate an entry is to use the index.

No attempt has been made to sub-divide under the six headings the alphabetical list that follows, nor has any attempt been made to list every variety of paper. Omitted, for example, are the majority of papers known by the names of their suppliers, such as are, for instance, to be found frequently among the issues of New Zealand. On the other hand, included are a few terms associated with paper that are occasionally encountered.

I think it is desirable to add that the examples given of the issues for which the varieties of paper were used are no more than examples, chosen not quite at random, and do not pretend to be more than that. A catalogue of stamps,

Decal, resembling goldbeater's skin. Lowenberg patent. Front and back. (Prussia, 1866, 30sgr.)

54

On back of unfinished bank notes. Front and (right) back. (Latvia, 1919, 1r.)

listed under the varieties of paper could, perhaps, be compiled; it would be, doubtless, an interesting, expensive and wearisome philatelic task. However, the attentive observation of paper varieties is philatelically educative. Quite apart from the value of the interest to be derived from such observation itself, sometimes such knowledge is of more tangible value — especially so to the embryo specialist in countries where a variation of paper makes all the difference between a common stamp and a rare variety.

Aluminum Foil. Aluminum foil bonded to thin paper was used for Hungary 1955 (Oct. 5) Air, Light Metal Industries International Congress, Budapest 5f.

Art Paper. A highly glossed coated paper, similar to that used for the "glossy magazines." Examples are to be found in Kishengarh (India) issues from 1913 to 1936. Somewhat similar paper has been used by other stamp-issuing countries, for example: Uruguay 1908 (Aug. 23) Independence Commemorative 1c. to 3c.; and New Zealand 1925 (Nov. 17) Dunedin Exhibition Commemorative ½d. to 4d.

Joined paper. Great Britain 1953 2½d. The illustration shows how the variety appears when the joined paper is partly separated.

Blanket. This is the term sometimes applied to the felts used for hand-made paper, and the endless felt upon which machine-made paper is led after passing the dandy roll. Defective blankets can affect the appearance of the paper — varieties being "Blanket Marks" — sometimes resulting, for example, in apparently "Ribbed Paper."

Blued Paper. This is paper that, unintentionally, has turned blue, to a greater or less extent, owing to chemical reaction caused by a constituent of the furnish. Examples are to be found in: Great Britain 1854-57 1d. and 2d.; Barbados 1898 ½d. to 2s.6d. The French term *bleuté* is often used, as also is "bluish," which is sometimes employed when referring to "Blue Rag Paper."

Blue Rag Paper. An experimental paper, colored throughout, containing thirty-five per cent rag in the furnish, and used for a short while for USA stamps in 1909.

Blue Safety Paper. The name given to the paper, to the furnish of which prussiate of potash was added as a precaution against cleaning and re-use of the stamps, and used by De La Rue for Great Britain 1855-56 4d. and some fiscals.

Moiré overprinted paper. Front and (right) design filtered out. (British Honduras, 1915, 2c.)

Bond Paper. This is a trade term, of American origin, used for a thin tough paper with a smooth unglazed finish. Such paper was employed for proofs of, for example, USA Revenues, 1862-71 1c. Proprietary, dull red.

Burelage, Burele. These terms are used to designate a network pattern, usually printed in color, on the front or back of paper after manufacture. There are various types of burelage. Examples are to be found, for instance, in Alsace Lorraine 1870-71; Dominican Republic 1881; Estonia, regular issues of 1923 to 1933; Queensland 1895-96 ½d.; Venezuela 1932-38 5c. to 5b.

Card (board). Card or Cardboard, of various thicknesses, and white color, has been frequently used for USA plate proofs. It has been used also, for example, for certain quasi-stamps, such as Russia 1915 (Nov.) Currency Stamps.

Carton. This term is used, sometimes, as a synonym for "Card" or "Cardboard," to designate a thick, often soft type of paper, not very frequently employed for postage stamps. Carton may be found, for example, in some copies of Chile 1878-99 5c., Denmark 1875-1901 (1884) 3ö., and Portugal 1912-31 ½c.

Cartridge Paper. This is a trade term (derived from paper used for making ammunition) now used to designate a rough-surfaced, thick paper. Examples of its use for stamps are to be found in Trinidad 1853 1d. *on bluish cartridge paper.*

Chalk, Chalk-Surfaced, Chalky Paper. These are terms for paper coated with a solution containing a suspension of chalk, as a precaution against cleaning and re-use of the stamps. "Chalky" paper can be detected because when it is rubbed with silver it leaves a black mark. If the surface is wetted the design is ruined; further, almost equally disastrous results accrue from careless handling. Examples are to be found in many issues of the British Commonwealth between, say, 1902 and 1911. Other examples are to be found, for instance, in Angola 1886; St. Kitts-Nevis 1948 10s., £1. Paper covered with intersecting "chalk" lines, printed on it after manufacture, was used, for example, for Russia 1909-12.

China, Chinese Paper. These are synonymous for what is now termed "India Paper."

Coated Paper. This term is used, sometimes, to designate any paper that, after manufacture, has been given a surface by applying a coating mixture, in contrast to paper that has had a glazing mixture added to the pulp. Consequently there are many possible sub-divisions of the class, but the term is useful when it is unnecessary to distinguish between the various types of papers that have been processed during or after manufacture with the object of affording greater security from cleaning and re-use of the stamps. The more comprehensive term is "Safety Paper."

Colored Paper. Paper colored throughout because of addition of dye to the pulp, as contrasted with "Surface Colored Paper." Colored papers have been used frequently, and by many different stamp-issuing countries. As instances, examples are to be found in: Baden (Germany) 1851 (May 1) 1k. to 9k.; Great Britain 1887-92 2½d., 3d. and 6d.; and British Commonwealth, the blue, green, red and yellow papers of many issues. See "Pseudo-Colored Paper."

Creased Paper. This is a variety of printing rather than of paper, being caused by a crease in the paper before or during printing. When the crease is straightened the stamp is, normally, misshapen and bears an unprinted strip corresponding with the crease. Such varieties are inconstant, and take many forms. They must not, of course, be confused with "creased" stamps, where the creasing has occurred after printing.

Decal. See "Goldbeater's Skin."

Dickinson Paper. This is the term used to designate that particular type of "Silk Thread Paper" manufactured by John Dickinson, the inventor of the machine and process used for producing the paper used for Great Britain 1847-54 10d. and 1s., the unissued 1d. trial printing of April 1841, and the 1840 "Mulready" covers and envelopes, and later stationery.

Double Paper. This term has, philatelically, two distinct meanings: (1) "Duplex Paper," and (2) "Joined Paper." Therefore, when this term is used, its intended meaning should be made clear.

Duplex Paper. This term means, literally, two-ply paper, and such paper exists in several forms. It is manufactured by making two webs of usually different qualities of paper at the same time on two Fourdrinier machines and pressing the webs together under a common press after they passed under the dandy rolls. Such papers are referred to under "Safety Paper."

Dyed Paper. This is a term sometimes employed as a synonym for "Colored Paper."

Emergency Paper. This term is used sometimes as a synonym for "Palimpsest."

Enamelled Paper. This paper is somewhat similar to the "Chalk-Surfaced" papers, but has a slightly greyish tinge, and when looked through appears distinctly mottled. Examples are to be found, for instance, in: Angola 1893-94 10r. perf 11½; Portugal 1892-93 25r. green.

Error of Paper. This is referred to in the chapter devoted to watermarks.

Flaw. In relation to paper this term is sometimes employed strictly to refer to a blemish caused during the manufacture of the paper; but, usually, the market value of a stamp with a paper flaw is less than that of a perfect copy, irrespective of whether the flaw was caused during or after manufacture of the paper.

Fluorescent Paper. See Fluorescent Paper in the alphabetical list to the chapter entitled "Inks and Color."

Glazed Paper. This term is used to designate a paper that has been given a glossy finish by glazing with friction of applied heat, as contrasted with a paper

Pelure paper. Front and back. [Peru, Arequipa, 1881, (January) 10c.]

given a glossy finish by coating. It is used as a synonym for "Surfaced Paper." Such paper was introduced generally by the British Crown Agents for the Colonies in 1969 and was used, for example, for Antigua 1969 (September) printings of stamps perf 13½ that had been issued perf 11½ x 11 in November 1966.

Gold Foil. Two types of gold foil have been used for issues of stamps. The more common type is an artificial gold color bonded to paper — see "Foil Blocking" in the chapter on inks and color, and "Foil" in the alphabetical list to that chapter. The other type is actually gold leaf of, usually, fine gold so thin as to have very little metal value, bonded to paper and used for such productions as Staffa 1974 Original American States £6 and other high face value productions which have attracted comments adverse on the one hand and supportive on the other hand.

Goldbeater's Skin. This is a term applied to a tough paper, rendered transparent by saturation with resin or collodium. Examples of the use of such paper for stamps are rare, but are to be found in: Prussia (Germany) 1866 10sgr. and 30sgr.; and among USA fiscals, and revenue trial proofs, for instance, 1862-71 3c. Foreign Exchange in blue. When this type of paper is used, the printing is usually done in reverse on the back so that the design shows through the transparent paper. After they are affixed to a document, it is virtually impossible to remove these stamps without destroying the design. Such paper is termed, also, "Resinized Paper."

Grain. This term allied to paper is of modern philatelic inception, and is referred to under "Shrinkage."

Grande Consommation. The name applied to the poor quality greyish granite paper used by France for the issues of 1917-20.

Granite Paper. This paper, of which there are various types, has colored fibers of various lengths in its substance and showing on the surface, caused by mixing bleached and unbleached or dyed pulp, or by the addition of animal fibers to the vegetable fibers in the pulp stage of manufacture. Examples are to be found in: Austria 1918-19 2k.; Great Britain 1917 (May) 8d., which is colored throughout; Switzerland 1910.

Grill. A term used to designate a certain type of treatment of paper after manufacture and, usually, printing, for the purpose of affording greater security from cleaning and re-use of the stamps. There are several types and varieties of grill. Examples are to be found in: Peru 1874-79; USA 1867.

Hard Paper. A comparative term used, normally, to distinguish different papers employed for the stamps of one country.

India Paper. This is a tough thin opaque paper, often slightly toned, deriving its name from the fact that after it was first successfully made in England at Wovercote Mills it was used for Oxford Bibles, and was known as India Bible Paper. Originally the paper was introduced from China (about 1750), and is still, sometimes, referred to as "China Paper." India paper has often been used for proofs of dies and plates by many countries, including USA.

Japanese Paper. A native-made silky paper, used for the early issues of Japan.

Joined Paper. Where two different sheets (or webs) of paper have been stuck together end-to-end by overlapping after manufacture, and stamps printed on the paper so that part of the impression of the one stamp appears on both pieces of paper, it is referred to as being on "Joined Paper," or, sometimes, "Double Paper." Examples are to be found in: Peru 1871 (April) — printing from flat plates; USA — many rotary press printings.

Luminescent Paper. See "Luminescence" in the chapter on inks and color, and "Fluorescent Paper," "Luminescence" and "Luminescent Tagging" in the alphabetical list to that chapter.

Makeshift Paper. This term is a synonym for "Palimpsest."

Manila Paper, Manilla Paper. This term, used originally to denote paper made from Manila (note the single "l") hemp fibers, is now applied to a strong light paper of coarse texture and various colors, used for envelopes and wrappers. It is, usually, smooth on one side and rough on the other.

Mill Sheet. This is the term used to designate a sheet of paper as manufactured or sold by the paper mill. Such a sheet is often many times larger than the printed sheet, which in turn is often larger than the "Post Office Sheet" as sold to the public.

Moiré. This is a French term, meaning "watered," and used generally to describe the pattern of "watered silk." Philatelically it describes a similar pattern printed on paper, usually in color on the back of the stamp. Examples are to be found in: British Honduras 1915 — violet moiré; Mexico 1872 (definitive issue) — blue moiré.

Ordinary Paper. A term used, normally, when referring to the stamps of one

Safety paper. At right, stamp design partially filtered out. (Venezuela, 1932-38, 3b.)

Vertically ribbed paper. Front and (right) design partially filtered out. (United States, 1873, No. 158 with secret marks.)

country, to differentiate between untreated paper and paper such as "Coated," "Enamelled," and "Surfaced"; it is used, also, to differentiate between "Native Paper," and others.

Palimpsest. A palimpsest is "re-used parchment," and, in relation to paper, this term is used to describe those papers originally printed upon for some other purpose, and later employed for postage stamps. There have been such papers used by a number of stamp-issuing countries. Examples are to be found in: Latvia 1918 (December) — on German military maps, and later issues on various other papers; Mexico 1887 — ruled with blue lines; USA (Confederate States) Lenoir, N.C. — ruled with crossed orange lines.

Palladium Foil. Palladium foil bonded to paper was used for Tonga 1967 (July 4) Coronation of King Taufa'auau IV 1s. to 1p.

Pasing Paper. This term used to designate that particular type of "Silk Thread Paper" manufactured in Pasing, Bavaria, and used for Bavarian issues between 1849 and 1868.

Pelure Paper. This is a thin tough hard and sometimes brittle paper, semi-transparent and often of a bluish or greyish tinge. Famous examples of its use are the Hawaii 1852 Missionaries. A more readily acquired example is, for instance, Serbia 1905 3 dinars perf 11½; or, perhaps Arequipa (Peru) 1881 (January) 10c.

Phosphorescent Paper. See "Fluorescent Paper" in the alphabetical list to the chapter on inks and color.

Pinhole. In relation to paper, this term is used to designate a particular type of blemish, consisting of a usually small hole in the substance of the paper. See "Flaw."

Porous Paper. All paper is more or less porous. Generally speaking, the greater the amount of size with which the waterleaf has been treated, the less readily will the finished paper absorb moisture. The term "Porous Paper" is used to designate an absorbent paper, usually contrasted with a less absorbent paper used for the stamps of the same country. Examples are to be found in: Nicaragua 1877-78 rouletted 8½; USA special printing of, say, the 1875 issue printed by the American Bank Note Company. It is useful to remember that many stamps which have been

Thread paper. Front and back. (Bavaria, 1850-58, 6k.)

subjected to illicit cleaning reveal this because the cleaning removes the finish and size from the paper, rendering it more porous than an "undoctored" stamp of the same issue.

Pseudo-Colored Paper. This term is used to describe paper which unintentionally appears colored because of some occurrence after the manufacture of the paper and during the production of the stamps. For example see "Blued Paper." Also, the use of pitted or insufficiently polished printing bases will often result in pseudo-colored paper, and sometimes, too much moisture applied to the paper after printing causes the color to suffuse the paper.

Resinized Paper. See "Goldbeater's Skin."

Ribbed Paper. Paper with an uneven, corrugated surface, rather like exaggerated laid lines, but caused by passing the paper between ridged rollers. The same effect sometimes results from uneven or worn felts or blankets. It is said that while properly ribbed paper will remain so after soaking in water, accidental ribbing will disappear after such treatment. Sometimes the term "Repp Paper" is employed, and sometimes a distinction is drawn between it and "Ribbed Paper." Examples are to be found in: Argentina 1864 Rivadavias; Philippine Islands (Spain) 1859 (Jan. 1) 5c.; USA 1873 1c *on ribbed paper.*

Rice Paper. This is the term used to designate the thin hard white paper used for Salvador 1889 (July-August) 1c. special printing.

Ruled Paper. This term is used to designate the appropriate "Palimpsests."

Safety Paper. A comprehensive term used to designate any special paper of which the object was to prevent cleaning and re-use of used stamps. There are many different varieties of safety papers, such as "Chalk-Surfaced," "Duplex," "Enamelled," and "Silk Thread." They include, for example: Austria 1901-02 — paper printed with diagonal bars of shiny varnish; USA 1873 1c. and 3c. — printed on a patent (double) paper punched with the Fletcher Cog-Wheel Punch; USA 1881-82 1c. and 3c. — printed on Douglas patent (double) paper; and Steel's grill and patent (double) paper, as well as Dr. Francis's chemical paper.

Sheet. Sheets of paper associated with the production of stamps consist of: Mill Sheets, Printed Sheets, Post Office Sheets, and Miniature Sheets; and certain others, such as "Book" or "Booklet Sheets."

Shrinkage. All paper expands when wet, and then contracts unevenly in drying. The greatest expansion occurs not in the length but in the circumference of

Silk thread paper. Front and back. (Switzerland, 1854-57, 10c.)

each fiber. Because most of the fibers in each sheet or web of paper run in one direction, the expansion of the sheet or web is greatest across that direction, sometimes called the "grain." In many printing processes used for postage stamps, the paper has been dampened deliberately before printing — such printing is termed "wet printing." The subsequent contraction led to the belief among philatelists that some printing plates were smaller than they were in fact. Further, because of the irregular shrinkage of different sheets of paper, and also when both "wet" and "dry" printing took place from the same plates this (until the reason was known) led to the erroneous belief that more than one set of plates — or dies of different sizes — had been employed. The expansion of machine-made paper across the web or grain is very marked, and collectors of, for example, modern China sharply differentiate between stamps printed on paper "with the grain" and "across the grain." This expansion and contraction of paper led to great difficulties when Henry Archer was first experimenting (about 1848) with the introduction of perforation, and those difficulties find their echo in the strict temperature and humidity control exercised by modern stamp manufacturers.

Silk Paper. A term used to designate paper with comparatively short silk (colored) fibers in its furnish, as contrasted with "Silk Thread Paper." Silk Paper was used for some USA revenue stamps.

Silk Thread Paper. This term is used to designate paper which, during its manufacture, has had one or more continuous threads of twisted (colored) silk or cotton from reels introduced into its substance, so that the paper forms around the thread or threads. Two examples are: "Dickinson Paper," and "Pasing Paper." Other examples are to be found in Switzerland (Federal Administration) issues between 1854 (Sep. 15) and 1862 (Apr. 26).

Silver Foil. See "Foil Blocking" in the chapter on inks and color, and "Foil" in the alphabetical list to that chapter.

Soft Paper. This is a comparative term used, normally, to distinguish different papers used for the stamps of one country.

Surface Colored Paper. This term is used to designate paper colored on the (usually one) surface only, the color being applied intentionally after the normal processes of paper manufacture are complete, as contrasted with paper colored throughout. Examples are to be found in: many French Colonies; the British Com-

Varnish bands across face. Right, under ultraviolet light the varnish fluoresces lighter than the ordinary printing. (Austria, 1901, 1h.)

monwealth "white backs," which were the World War I substitutes for the colored papers previously used for these issues; Turkey 1863 (Dec. 1) 20 paras, 1 piastre. Distinguish "Pseudo-Colored Paper."

Surfaced Paper. This is a comprehensive term used to designate papers provided with a shiny smooth surface (both Safety Paper and others) as contrasted with paper unprovided with such a finish. The term is, normally, employed comparatively to distinguish different papers used for the stamps of one country.

Thickness. Usually the terms "Thick Paper," "Medium Paper," and "Thin Paper" are used comparatively to distinguish different papers used for the stamps of one country. The early issues of, say, Belgium, Iran, Liberia and Sweden provide examples. Sometimes micrometers are used to separate one issue from another. Some of the thinnest paper ever used for postage stamps occurs in Afghanistan 1880; some of the thickest in Poland 1919 Cracow issue.

Thread Paper. See "Silk Thread Paper."

Tinted Paper. This term is used as a synonym for "Toned Paper," and also to designate those papers referred to by the name of a color followed by "ish." Sometimes, careless wiping of a printing plate, or corrosion of a cylinder, produces effects, on the top surface at least, of "Tinted Paper." See "Pseudo-Colored Paper."

Toned Paper. This term is used to designate "off-white" paper, especially paper with a brownish or buffish tinge. Such paper has frequently been used for postage stamps. Examples are to be found in: Cook Islands 1892 (Feb. 29).

4. Watermarks

THE SUBJECT of watermarks may be conveniently considered under four heads, although the matters dealt with under these heads overlap somewhat. These four heads are: Types, Designs, Varieties, and Detection.

Apart from being classified this way, watermarks themselves may also be considered, as was briefly mentioned in the discussion of "Paper Varieties," in the chapter entitled "Paper," according to their nature: that is, (1) watermarks properly so called; (2) quasi-watermarks; and (3) pseudo-watermarks. Also, "phantom" watermarks fall to be considered.

There is little difference in effect between the first two of these classes. Watermarks properly so called, and quasi-watermarks both result from local variations in the thickness of an individual sheet of paper, caused by local variation in the surface of the mould or dandy roll or (in one particular instance) of the endless cloth of finely woven wire in the paper-making machine. Pseudo-watermarks are no more than the results of official application of a device to the paper after manufacture.

Broadly speaking, all watermarks are either (a) officially required, or (b) officially countenanced. Watermarks that are officially required owe their incorporation in the paper to the dictates of security, and are considered to be additional safeguards against successful forgery and consequent loss of revenue to the authority issuing the stamps. The stamp-issuing countries of the world can be divided into two main groups: those that consider this safeguard desirable and adopt it; and those that do not. Some countries have adopted it for a time or for certain issues, and then abandoned its use. As examples: Between 1840 and 1967, Great Britain never intentionally issued

Watermark thicker than surrounding paper — Russia.

65

Watermark thinner than surrounding paper — Chile.

any adhesive postage stamps on unwatermarked paper, except for the 1847 10d. and 1s. embossed; France has never issued stamps on paper incorporating officially required watermarks; the United States intentionally issued postage stamps on watermarked paper only for approximately twenty years, spanning the turn of the century.

Officially required watermarks comprise the majority of those known to the world of philately, and the majority of the stamps issued today on watermarked paper come from British Commonwealth countries.

Officially countenanced watermarks are those which, while not officially required, have been incorporated in paper upon which stamps are printed, and owe this incorporation to the choice of the stamp printers, or the suppliers or manufacturers of the paper — normally for the purposes of advertisement or identification. These are frequently known as "house watermarks" or "paper-makers' watermarks."

Usually, when paper is looked through, postage stamp watermarks appear lighter than the surrounding paper because the surface of the mould, or dandy roll has been raised locally in the pattern of the watermark, and the paper is therefore slightly thinner in this shape. Exceptionally, so far as philately is concerned, some stamps have been printed upon paper which, when looked through, presents a watermark appearing darker than the surrounding paper, because the paper in the pattern of the watermark is slightly thicker. This effect on Russia 1858 10 k., 20 k., and 30 k., was achieved by subjecting the forming paper to pressure from a smooth cylinder or roller upon which the watermark figures had been cut in recess, causing a slightly embossed effect which appears on the backs of the stamps.

In 1933 and later, Germany employed a paper which, when looked through, reveals both types of watermarks in the form of swastikas — that is, some devices appear lighter and some darker than the surrounding paper.

Usually, so far as concerns the paper used for postage stamps, the surface of the moulds or dandy rolls is raised to make watermarks by attaching to it pieces of bent wire or stamped-out brass in the shape of the required device. These pieces of wire or brass are referred to as watermark "bits," and they are usually sewn or soldered on to the mould or dandy roll in such formation as is required.

It follows from the processes inherent in paper manufacture that the "bits" on the mould (for hand-made paper) read normally from left-to-right, and the "bits" on the dandy roll (for machine-made paper) read reversed, that is, from right-to-left.

When watermarked paper is specially manufactured for postage stamps, the arrangement of the watermark is determined, *first* by the security requirements of the issuing authority, and *second* by cooperation between the stamp printers and the paper-makers.

Types of Watermarks

After the style and type of the watermark have been decided upon, not only have the repetitions of this watermark in the form of "bits" to be appropriately arranged on the mould or dandy roll, but also the mill sheets have to be so cut that eventually the printers can produce the stamps without undue difficulty of registration — which, in this case, is the coincidence of the printed design and the watermark in the paper. The paper-maker, when arranging the "bits" on the mould or dandy roll, or the authority responsible for giving him directions, has to bear in mind the limitations or characteristics of the printing method and, perhaps, also the machines to be used. Such considerations, being outside the scope of the present work, are no more than mentioned in passing.

Security requirements vary. How they have been met throughout the world

The twice-stretched garter.

has given rise to the different types and designs of watermarks, and the albums of collectors and students present interesting, if mute, commentaries upon the diverseness of human ingenuity in solving essentially similar problems in different ways. Later in this chapter reference is made, briefly, to some of the watermark designs used in postal issues worldwide.

It is obvious that the difficulties of registration are greatest when one watermarked device is to be incorporated in each individual stamp, the more so where part of the printed design is to be in register with the watermark. Examples of these types of requirements are frequently to be found on the early stamp issues. For instance, in the case of the first adhesive postage stamps ever issued, Great Britain 1840 1d. and 2d., the watermarked device of a crown was incorporated in every stamp; and in the case of Great Britain 1855 4d., the intention was that that part of the printed design which was the Queen's head should be surrounded by and enclosed within the watermark, which was a garter. In the second instance given, the enormous difficulties of registration resulted in the garter's being stretched twice, until the head could conveniently be accommodated — consequently there are three sizes of watermarked garter.

Single Watermarks

Such watermarks, that is, those so arranged that a single complete device or combination of devices is, or is intended to be, incorporated in every stamp, are termed philatelically "single" watermarks. This term should not be confused with "single-lined" watermarks, which is almost self-explanatory: the term "single-lined" is used to differentiate between, for example, the watermarked numeral "2" as used for Tasmania 1870-71 2d., and the same number as used for Tasmania 1857 2d., which watermarked numeral is referred to

Single-lined and double-lined numeral watermarks.

as "double-lined." Sometimes the term "unit" watermark is used.

A variation of this "single" watermark is to be found, for example, in Great Britain 1870 ½d., where the device — the words "half penny" in single-lined script characters — extends over three stamps, horizontally, repeated throughout the sheet of stamps.

A further variation, which may be conveniently considered under "single" watermarks, was used by the United States for postage stamps between 1895 and 1916, and consisted of the letters "U S P S" in various forms and sequences repeated throughout the sheets, and so arranged that at least portions of one or more of the letters were to appear on each stamp.

Usually, "single" watermarks (and some others) were set out on the moulds or dandy rolls so that the "bits" appeared in pane formation on the mill sheet. Each mill sheet "pane" consisted of the arrangement intended for each sheet. This arrangement on the mill sheet was adopted only for convenience in cutting the paper, and because the printed sheets of stamps usually had margins of unprinted paper. Sometimes around the printed sheet "panes" a special watermark device was incorporated.

Marginal Watermarks

For instance, the "Single Crown over C A" watermarked paper used for many British Commonwealth issues (including, for example, Jamaica 1903-4 1d.), the watermark "bits" of the crown and the letters "C" and "A" appeared 240 times for each printed sheet, in four panes of sixty, six across and ten down, each of these panes of sixty being surrounded by a frameline. These sixty-subject panes were arranged two above the others, with a space of about one-quarter inch between the vertical panes and about one inch between the upper and lower horizontal pairs of panes; the words "Crown Agents" appeared in the horizontal space; the wording "Crown Agents for" and "the Colonies" appeared outside each vertical pair of panes; there were, additionally, small watermarked crosses, known as "registration points," marking the centers of the margins.

Such watermarks outside the panes are referred to philatelically as "marginal" watermarks.

Although it was not usually the intention, nor indeed desired, sometimes stamps were printed on the sheets of paper with the watermark out of register, and the stamps from the outside rows or columns of such printed sheets are to be found with portions of one or more of these "marginal" watermarks. Further, because the marginal watermarks often do not occupy all the space available in the margins of the panes, some stamps thus printed incorporate no watermark at all.

Exceptionally, for example where printers are using paper specially prepared for stamps other than those they are printing, the displacement of the paper is deliberate, and the "marginal" watermarks appear quite normally in some sheets of stamps as printed. Examples are to be found in the stamps, for instance, of Gambia 1874, and in the "V over Crown" watermarks of the Australia-printed lithographed pictorials of Tasmania 1902-3.

A "mould mark" (the figure "1") in the sheet margin of Great Britain 1912-22, 2½d.

A "multiple" watermark from Ireland.

Mould Marks

One other matter, loosely connected with marginal "bits" may be conveniently mentioned here: that is "mould marks." Where there are several moulds or dandy rolls all similar, or where there are several repetitions of groups of watermarks in a sheet of paper as manufactured, paper-makers sometimes distinguish them by the addition, in an inconspicuous position, of a letter, numeral or combination "bit" which produces a watermark known as a "mould mark."

"Mould marks" are by no means universal, even with hand-made paper, but it has been claimed for them, with some justification, that they are the "plate numbers" of the paper-maker.

Multiple Watermarks

The difficulties caused by attempting to register each printed stamp with an individual watermark were rendered acute when the numbers of stamps required for normal use increased considerably. These difficulties were obviated by the introduction of the "multiple" watermark — that is, the device repeated closely throughout the whole of the sheet, so that only very small portions of paper are left without watermark.

Stamps printed upon such paper incorporate portions of several devices. Great Britain 1953 2½.d., for instance, provides an easily acquired example of this type of watermark. In such cases, the watermark "bits" are affixed all over the surface of the dandy roll, and this type of watermark is sometimes referred to as "all over" watermark.

A variation of such offically required "all over" watermarks consists of letters forming words or abbreviations of words and symbols repeated throughout the sheet. Such an "all over" watermark was used, for instance, for Brazil 1939 — "Casa + da + Moeda + do + Brazil."

Other "all over" watermarks are referred to under "Paper-makers' Watermarks" and "Quasi-watermarks."

A different variety of the "multiple" watermark appeared in Great Britain in 1912, and consisted of the device — a crown and royal cypher — in columns, the width of a stamp apart, so arranged that portions of two devices, one above the other, appear on each stamp. This watermark is termed "column," or sometimes "repeated," or "simple."

Sheet Watermarks

"Sheet" watermarks are watermarks incorporated in sheets of paper upon which stamps are printed so that the device, officially required, appears only once in the sheet, extending throughout more or less of the area of the paper. In many cases, a large proportion of the stamps in the sheet incorporate none of this watermark, and those that do incorporate any of it have only a small portion. Examples are to be found, for instance, in Cochin 1892 — an umbrella; and India 1854 — arms of the East India Company.

Other watermarks of this character are to be found, for example, in Romania 1900 — arms — where the watermark device extends over the space occupied by twenty-five stamps. As a further instance, in Tuscany 1851-52, the watermark device of a crown within framed borders is repeated twelve times in the area of the sheet upon which the stamps were printed.

One final instance may be quoted of the numerous variations of officially required "sheet" watermarks. In Fiji 1871 (December), the letters "Fiji Postage" occur across the center of the sheet, in single-lined sans-serif capital letters.

Paper-Makers' Watermarks

"Paper-makers' watermarks" are of many kinds, but the majority are similar to "sheet" watermarks, although instances occur of "all over" repetitions of letters, such, for example, as "Harrison & Sons, London," used for Ecuador 1943 Compulsory Postal Tax, and Maldive Islands 1933, and "W T & Co" used for Luxembourg 1935 (Nov. 15) Official.

In the early days of philately paper-makers' watermarks were, if not disregarded, looked upon as adventitious and of little account. This is clearly shown by the following extract from *The Stamp-Collector's Magazine*, Vol. V, Page 95 (June 1867), when the editor, in answer to a correspondent who had written inquiring about a letter and some figures[1] watermarked in the paper of some Newfoundland stamps, stated:

> The letters and figures are of the maker and date of the paper, and are not, in the sense philatelists use the term, watermarks; that is, they are not watermarks of the stamp or issue, but merely accidentally present in the paper used. They formed no part of the design or plan on which the stamps were made for emission. A similar and well-known case is the *T. H. Saunders* found on some sheets of the British Guiana stamps, and the *fleur-de-lys* in some of the Russian envelopes; both marks of the manufacture of the paper and not of the stamp.

The following month in the same magazine, *The Stamp-Collector's Magazine*, Vol. V, Page 103 (July 1867), Mr. (later Judge) F.A. Philbrick, when writing about the stamps of British Guiana and the watermark "T H Saunders" stated: "This is not a watermark properly so called, but an accidental variance in the fabric of the paper."

There was, of course, no accident about the incorporation of the paper-

---

[1]The "W" and "58" of what is now the well-known watermark "Stacey Wise 1858."

An all-over paper-maker's watermark
from Ecuador.

Watermark for first
issue of Tuscany.

All-over watermark, Brazil.

72

makers' watermark, which had been effected in the same manner as the officially required watermarks — by the deliberate affixing of "bits" to the mould or dandy roll — and they are, therefore, properly termed "watermarks." The real point of distinction, as the editor of *The Stamp-Collector's Magazine* had underlined in June, was that the watermarks were not officially required. Their occurrence had been noted and explained two years earlier in a series of well-illustrated articles, later published as a book, *Essai sur les Filigranes* by Dr. Magnus (Dr. J.A. Legrand) in *Le Timbrophile*, Vol. I, Page 47 *et seq.* (April to July 1865).

Later, with the development and advance of philatelic study, increasing attention and regard came to be paid to these watermarks, and they sometimes serve as the safest method of distinguishing between two otherwise apparently similar stamps — for example, those of the issues made by Rhodesia between 1890 and 1894. The popularity of paper-makers' watermarks seems never to have outgrown the early disregard of them, and H.R. Holmes, then editor of *The London Philatelist*, when writing about them[2] stated:

There can be few more intriguing philatelic studies than a collection of stamps showing the private watermarks of papermakers, and it is surprising that more collectors have not been attracted to the subject. The principal catalogues occasionally mention in footnotes that certain stamps are to be found with a watermark showing portions of letters that form part of the name of the papermaking firm, and in special cases some have attained a catalogue listing, for example, the Canadian stamps of 1868 and 1873, together with a price that indicates their undoubted rarity. . . .

What stamps exist with a papermakers' watermark? No complete list can be given. . . . A large proportion of the stamps that are listed in the catalogues as being on unwatermarked paper will be found to include isolated examples that show part of a papermakers' watermark, and many discoveries are awaiting the diligent searcher. The reason for this is that the papermakers' watermark invariably appears on only a portion of a sheet, and consequently the great majority of the stamps are without watermark. Furthermore the sheet of paper has usually to be cut into two or more pieces to fit the size of the sheet of stamps, and as a result only one sheet of stamps among many will show any trace of the papermakers' watermark.

In connection with the difficulty of finding these watermarks, Mr. Lees-Jones mentions in the paper he read before the Royal Philatelic Society, London, in October 1950 (for which he was awarded the Tilleard Medal) that on one occasion he was offered the pick of ten sheets of paper as used for printing the stamps of Mexico. He goes on to add: "The watermark in that case occurred in the corner, but of the ten sheets only three showed any of the three letters which composed the watermark; and of these three, only one sheet showed two letters. . . ."

Even finding one stamp with a part of a watermark is not the end of the search, one must still discover other stamps so that the whole watermark can be reconstructed. An interesting example of progressive discovery in this branch of philatelic study is provided by the watermark on the 1868 Canadian stamps. . . . It had long been known that stamps of the 1868 issue occasionally showed a watermark, and eventually the late John N. Luff succeeded in reconstructing (correctly, except for one letter) the whole watermark (see *American Journal of Philately,* Vol. VIII, 1895, pp. 77-79), which reads "E & C Bothwell Clutha Mills" in two lines.

---

[2]"Papermakers' Watermarks" — H. R. Harmer's auction catalogue for November 17, 1952.

Canada, 1868. "E. & G. Bothwell Clutha Mills" watermark.

In 1934 Mr. Lees-Jones and R. Roberts started enquiries about "E & C Bothwell," and found that no firm of that name had ever existed. They traced the watermark to the firm of Messrs. Andrew Whyte & Son Ltd., of Edinburgh, who were able to inform them that the watermark was an "artificial device," and that "E & G" (not C) stood for "Edinburgh and Glasgow," "Bothwell" for the street in which their warehouse was situated, and "Clutha" for "Clyde."

Quasi-Watermarks

When discussing "Texture Variations" in the chapter entitled "Paper," I stated that there were other instances of deliberate thinning of the substance of the paper like that occurring in *batonné* and *quadrillé,* analogous to watermarks. I term these "quasi-watermarks," although they are caused, basically, in the same way as those effects are more usually understood. Sometimes the term "continuous" watermarks is used in reference to them.

By quasi-watermarks I intend to include those arrangements of wires or "bits" that result in the appearance within the texture of the paper of straight or wavy lines, or dark and light shapes (additional to the wove or laid textures) but not in the more conventional designs of the single, multiple, sheet or paper-makers' watermarks.

Sometimes it is possible to describe the shapes shortly, as in the cases of "crossed lines," "wavy lines," and "mesh," but such descriptions give a very imperfect picture of the quasi-watermark as it appears. The editors of the principal catalogues long ago gave up the attempt to give word-pictures of any but the simplest of these shapes. They are illustrated pictorially, and referred to by number.

No point would be served here by attempting to describe them. They vary. The simplest forms consist of short straight lines parallel to each other. The most complicated forms defy short description. A study of the illustrations

Quasi-Watermarks

1, Japan; 2, Denmark; 3 and 4, Bavaria; 5, Spain.

6, Germany; 7, Lithuania; 8, Danzig; 9, Bavaria.

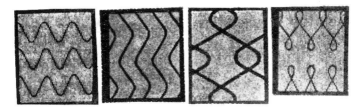

10, Bavaria; 11, Japan; 12, Lithuania; 13, Spain.

14, Danzig; 15, El Salvador; 16, Germany; 17, Colombia.

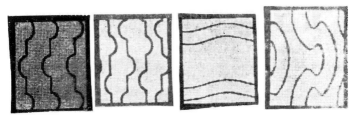

18, Japan; 19, Manchukuo; 20, Luxembourg; 21, Latvia.

of some of the representative quasi-watermarks which accompany this chapter will indicate the wide variation in types, patterns and shapes, and it will be seen that they are susceptible of rough grouping. They extend over the sheet and are, therefore, "all over" watermarks.

Stitch Watermarks

One form of quasi-watermark merits specific mention and discussion. That is the so-called "stitch" watermark.

A "stitch" watermark is, so far as it constitutes a thinning of the paper, unintentional, and is not caused by "bits." Two reasons account for its appearance in paper: *first*, the join in the "endless" cloth of finely woven wire in the Fourdrinier machine, or in the finely woven covering of the perforated metal cylinder of the machine invented by John Dickinson; and *second*, a repair of damage to these wire cloths. I do not know of any stitch watermarks caused by repair to the wire base of the mould used for hand-made paper, but their existence on postage stamps is a possibility.

The wire cloth for the machines used to be made in lengths, and the ends were joined by stitching with fine wire in order to make the cloth "endless," in the form of a band — something like ninety inches broad and about sixty feet long — which then was slipped over rollers that kept it stretched in position for working in the paper-making machine. The stitches caused a slight ridging across the whole width of this band — in the example quoted, ninety inches — and the paper which formed over this ridge was consequently slightly thinner than that formed on other parts of the wire cloth. Therefore, in a continuous web of paper, a line of quasi-watermark occurred right across the width of the web every time the ridge came around — which in the example quoted was every sixty feet. The width of the ridge varied somewhat according to the "sewing" or "stitching" process employed, and the stitch watermarks appear in the paper as a series of irregular, but mostly parallel, thin lines.

In some stamp-issuing countries, such as Great Britain, sheets bearing this type of stitch watermark were usually discarded, and not used for postage stamps. However, well-known instances of the occurrence of stitch watermarks exist — for example, Great Britain 1847 1s. embossed, and Rhodesia 1891 ½d.

Further, among the postage stamps of, for example, the United States, many issues have been found with

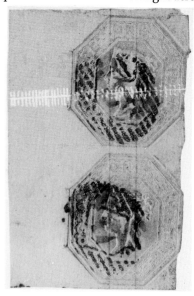

Great Britain 1847 1s., a "stitch" watermark.

At top, the Argentine Republic 1922 issue with the marking on the front; at bottom, the posthorn of Sweden, a numeral of Greece, the "N Z and Star" of New Zealand, and the Argentina "small sun."

stitch watermark and, the probability is, many other instances are awaiting discovery.

Pseudo-Watermarks

Pseudo-watermarks are not watermarks at all; they are not formed in the manufacture of the paper. They are devices, applied by the issuing authorities for reasons of security, in lieu and in the shapes of watermarks. Pseudo-watermarks are of several kinds: printed, embossed or impressed.

Printed pseudo-watermarks on stamps are of very long standing. The first instance of their occurrence is Greece 1861 "numerals on back." Twenty-five years later, another European country followed Greece's lead, and varied the theme; in Sweden 1886-91 there are instances of the application of a

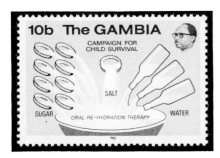

The Gambia, February 27, 1985, Campaign for Child Survival 10b. and pseudo-watermark.

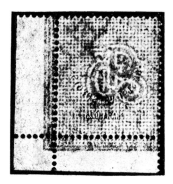

Pseudo-watermarks are not formed during the manufacture of the paper, but are printed, embossed or impressed for reasons of security and in the shapes of watermarks.

device, in that case a posthorn, to the paper on which the stamps were printed. In 1925, New Zeland similarly printed the device "N Z and Star" on three values.

A more recent example of pseudo-watermark occurs on stamps of The Gambia — for example, the February 27, 1985, Campaign for Child Survival 10b. to D 1.50, with a very pale blue-green pattern which could be described in non-technical terms as six wineglasses arranged in a sexagonal grid around a circular center. The official description is known as "C-Kurity" and "was printed on the reverse of the paper prior to gumming, was in the pattern of a snowflake and fluoresced under an ultraviolet light." The concept for the security paper was worked out between the suppliers and the Crown Agents.

In all the examples so far given, the printing of the pseudo-watermark was so effected that it appears on the back of the stamp.

One instance in which the pseudo-watermark was applied to the paper so that the design is visible from the front only, is to be found in Argentine Republic 1922 2 c., 5 c., and 20 c., where the sun with rays is printed in gray.

Embossed or impressed pseudo-watermarks on stamps are almost as old as printed pseudo-watermarks. Switzerland, in 1862, began the issue of stamps into the paper of which a device — a cross in an oval — had been impressed. Other instances of this type of pseudo-watermark are to be found in Argentine Republic 1892-95 (small sun) and Romania 1889 (arms).

A further instance of a pseudo-watermark may be mentioned; but in this case it was adopted in addition to, not in lieu of, a proper watermark. Czechoslovakia 1923 Fifth Anniversary Commemorative was an issue of four denominations — sold at double face value — and on top of the gum, which appears in small *quadrillé*, a monogram of the letters "C S P" was printed in brown.

For embossed "phantom" watermarks, see "Gum Watermark" in the alphabetical list to the chapter titled "Gum."

Designs of Watermarks

During the course of this chapter, of necessity, already reference has been made to numerous examples of watermarks and, incidentally, to their designs.

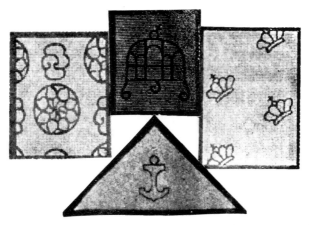

Ceylon (lotus flower); Hungary (crown); Greece (crowns);
Cape of Good Hope (anchor).

Spain (castle); China (Yin-yang); Argentina (sun); Germany (eagle); Albania
(eagle).

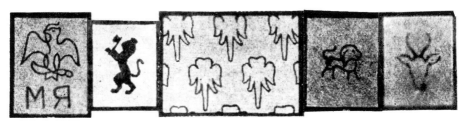

Mexico (eagle); Norway (lion); Burma (elephants' heads); Persia (lion); South
Africa (springbok).

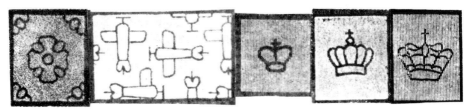

Iceland (rosettes); Luxembourg (airplanes); Denmark (crown); Sweden (crown);
Italy (crown).

As with the more limited field of quasi-watermarks, so with the others; no point would be served by attempting an exhaustive survey or catalogue of the various designs that, since 1840, have been used to watermark the paper upon which certain issues have been printed. Such a task would be equivalent to (if somewhat less than) an attempt to list the stamps themselves under the designs appearing on them. A work purporting — but unsuccessfully — to "present all watermarks found on stamps from all countries from the beginning of 'stamp time' through 1977" was *The Buxton Encyclopaedia of Watermarks* by B.H. Buxton (1977).

For the most part the single and multiple watermarks are reproduced more or less accurately in the principal catalogues, and are thus representatively available for the inspection and delight of the searcher.

The designs vary, and often reflect national characteristics. Sometimes, perhaps, they provide amusement, as though the person responsible for selecting them were enjoying a quiet joke at nobody's expense. It must be understood that the examples that follow are not more than merely a selection that does not pretend to be completely representative of either designs or issues, and no mention is made of any items that would be incorporated in the very long list that could be compiled of paper-makers' watermarks.

There are castles in Spain (the issue of 1876). There is mystery in the East, as exemplified by the Yin-yang of China (used for many issues from 1885 onward). There is a sun (Argentine Republic, 1892 onward), a crescent (moon) and star (Egypt 1867 onward), and other stars in profusion (Barbados, Grenada, New Zealand, Victoria).

There are birds — the swan of Western Australia (1854-60), the eagles of Germany (1930, *I posta*), Albania (September 1930), and Mexico (1897) — and beasts — the lion of Norway (1863-66), the elephant of Burma (1938), the curious animal of Persia (1915), and the springbok of South Africa (1913-21).

There are flowers — the lotus of Ceylon (1949), the rosettes of Iceland (1930 Air), and the myosotis of Lübeck (1859).

There are crowns of many shapes and sizes, anchors, aeroplanes, numerals, letters, wheels, crosses, circles, caps of Liberty, and a seemingly endless variety of combinations of other symbols and designs to meet the perceptive eye of the person who literally looks through a collection of stamps.

Watermark Varieties

All paper has what is known as a "good" side; this is the upper side — the side that is away from the mould in hand-made paper, and the side upon which the dandy roll presses in machine-made paper. This "good" side is the intended printing surface, and the watermarks are so arranged that, when paper is looked through from the "good" side, they read normally.

The "normal" watermark, from the point of view of the paper-maker, the printer and, in most instances, the philatelist, is the one that, when the paper is looked through from the face of the stamp, reads normally from left-to-right and with the watermark design upright (when it is of such form that it can be said to have a right way up) in relation to the design of the stamp.

Speaking generally, any variation from "normal" constitutes, philatelically, a watermark variety.

Philatelists are most used to examining a watermark from the back of the stamp than from its front; and, from the back, a "normal" watermark appears with the design reading reversed — that is, from right-to-left — although, of course, the watermark design remains the right way up.

It is quite elementary that, when a printer takes an individual sheet of plain paper to put into the printing press, there are four easily confused variations possible if the sheet is longer than it is wide (and only rarely are printed sheets of stamps square):

FIRST, he may put the sheet in as the paper-maker intended. This will produce a "normal" watermark.

SECOND, he may put the sheet in with the "good" side away from the printing base. This will produce a "reversed" watermark — that is, one reading from right-to-left when the stamp is looked through from the face, and from left-to-right when viewed from the back of the stamp.

THIRD, he may put the sheet in with the "good" side nearest the printing base but with the designs the wrong way up in relation to the designs of the stamps when printed. This will produce an "inverted" watermark — that is, one reading from right-to-left and upside down when viewed from the back of the stamp.

FOURTH, he may combine the abnormalities of *second* and *third,* and produce a watermark termed philatelically "inverted and reversed" — that is, one reading from left-to-right and upside down when viewed from the back of the stamp.

The foregoing are the simplest ways in which these varieties of watermark can be caused. However, when printing takes place from cylinders on to reels of paper, or "in the web," it is unusual for any variation from normal to occur.

Further, in some cases, an "inverted" watermark is caused deliberately. This is most usual where stamps are issued in small books, especially when the panes are stitched into the book's covers, as in Great Britain. For convenience in stitching and dividing the books, the sheets of stamps are printed so that alternate book panes are *tête bêche* — that is, upside down in relation to one another. (By this means it is necessary to have only half as many margins and more narrowly spaced sewing needles than would be the case if every pane were printed upright.) Because of the inversion of the alternate panes, one-half of the stamps incorporate an "inverted" watermark.

Because printed sheets are only very rarely square, it is not easy to insert a sheet sideways by error into the press, and the variety "sideways" watermark occurs only rarely by accident. A usual cause of such a variety is the using up of old paper, or the use of paper for stamps with upright formats intended for stamps with sideways formats. Another usual cause of the variety "sideways" watermark is the special printing of certain stamps for use in coils with delivery sideways.

There is one way in which a "sideways" watermark can occur through error, and this is thought to be the cause of that very rare variety of Great

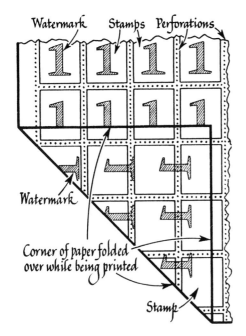

Watermark Stamps Perforations

Watermark

Corner of paper folded over while being printed

Stamp

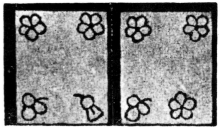

Above, at left, the normal "Emblems" watermark — two roses, a thistle and a shamrock. At right, the error — three roses and a shamrock.

Sketch shows how "sideways" watermark can occur by error — that is, a fold in the paper.

Britain (King Edward VII) 1911 ½d., printed by Harrison & Sons. If the corner of a sheet with a "normal" watermark is folded over at an angle of forty-five degrees and the sheet is then printed, that part of the sheet which is folded over will bear stamps incorporating "sideways" watermark. (Of course, the part of the sheet behind the fold will be unprinted, and the "sideways" watermark will be "reversed" as well. This type of error sometimes gives rise to the variety *printed on the gummed side*.)

Errors of Watermark and Paper

Errors of watermark are, in the main, errors of paper or printing, depending upon the view one takes of the cause. A true error of watermark would consist, for example, of the inversion of a "bit" in the mould, or the inclusion of a wrong "bit" on a dandy roll.

Deformed letters or designs are frequently encountered, but a true error is a rare occurrence. One well-known instance occurs among the stamps of Great Britain. In the watermark known as "Emblems" there are, incorporated in each design, two roses, a thistle and a shamrock. On one of these groups of "bits," the thistle fell away, and was replaced by another rose, giving rise to the watermark error *three roses and shamrock*. This error is found on Great Britain 1862 3d. (plate 2), 1865-67 3d. (plate 4), 6d. (plates 5 and 6), 9d. (plate 4) and 1s. (plate 4).

Another such instance occurs in the cases of several British Crown Colonies whose stamps were printed between 1950 and 1952 on "Multiple Script C A" paper. The crowns have a decidedly angular shape. Crowns fell away from the dandy roll in two positions on one roll or one crown fell away on each of two dandy rolls. As a result, some stamps exist with a crown missing in a row consisting of crowns only, and other stamps exist with a crown missing in a row consisting of Crown and C A alternately.

The errors of the missing crowns were noticed. In correcting the errors, further errors were made. Instead of replacing the missing crowns with the same angular-shaped crowns as had been used previously, they were replaced by crowns of a different, more rounded, shape — which is known as "St. Edward's Crown." As is to be expected, the error *St. Edward's Crown* occurs in the crown only row and also in the Crown C A row.

The error was first discovered on British Guiana Postage Due 1940-52 2 c.

By far the most common cases of what are termed philatelically "errors of watermark" occur because stamps are printed on paper intended for other values or issues. A well-known example occurs in the postage stamps of the United States 1938-43 Presidential Series $1. Normally this stamp was printed on unwatermarked paper, but unintentionally was issued printed on paper intended for revenue stamps and incorporating the watermark "U S I R." Two other instances of a similar error are to be found in the United States 1895 6 c. and 8 c. printed by error on revenue paper. Another well-known instance occurs in Transvaal 1905-9 1d. The paper intended for these stamps, and on which the majority were printed, is watermarked "Multiple Crown C A." By error one or more sheets of the stamp were printed on paper intended for the stamps of Cape of Good Hope, and incorporating the so-called "Cabled Anchor" or "Fouled Anchor" watermark of that philatelic country.

Many errors of watermark, where paper intended for one value was used for another, are to be found in the issues of some of the Australian States. For instance, in New South Wales 1866 6d. the watermark should have been

The "St. Edward's" crown watermark error. The error is at bottom left in the illustration of the 2c, and at bottom, center, in the 16c.

A portion of a sheet of the $1 Presidentials showing the spacing of the "U S I R" watermark, with a block of four superimposed.

a double-lined "6"; in July 1866 the stamp was issued with a watermark "5" intended for the 5d., and later in that year it was issued with watermark "12." Errors of a similar nature are to be found, for example, in Chile 1861-62 10 c., which should bear the watermark "10" in double-lined numerals but is also found, though rarely, with the watermark "20."

Errors of paper, akin to true errors of watermark sometimes occur because of a defect in the manufacture. For instance, the Dickinson paper used for Great Britain 1847 10d. and 1s. should contain two continuous silk threads; both these stamps are known on paper with only one such silk thread. A further instance of defective manufacture occurs in New Zealand 1924-25 1d. (on "Jones" chalky paper) where, because of the defect, the paper of one half-sheet was unsurfaced.

Instances are known of stamps that are printed by mistake on the wrong side of paper — one side of which is surfaced — thus giving rise to a variety on seemingly unsurfaced paper. An example is to be found, for instance, in Portugal 1885-87 20 r., rosine. This, of course, is the same type of mistake that gives rise to the variety "reversed" watermark and, as mentioned later, *printed on the gummed side.*

One type of instance of the use of a wrong paper is provided by Switzerland 1862 (Apr. 26) 2 c., where the paper should have contained green thread; by error paper with a yellow thread was used, as was paper with white thread. Similarly, Hankow 1894 (June) 2 c., usually printed on buff paper, was printed by error on yellow paper intended for the 5 c. of that issue. Another such instance occurred in Hungary 1913 60 f. which usually was issued on rose-colored paper; by error, some stamps were printed on uncolored paper. And in Portugal 1895-99 115 r. the normal paper was pink, but by error cream paper was used for some stamps of that value. Many other instances of such errors occur.

That certain stamps which usually should incorporate a watermark but fail to do so through misplacement of the paper when printing was mentioned earlier under the heading "Marginal Watermarks." Sometimes, however, stamps have been printed by error on sheets bearing no watermark, thus providing a true error of paper. One instance may be quoted: Great Britain 1912-22 5d., which should have incorporated the "simple Royal Cypher" watermark, is to be found, though rarely, on paper that reveals no watermark.

It is obvious that, in order to distinguish stamps that have fortuitously missed the watermark through misplacement of the paper when printing from those printed by error on unwatermarked sheets, it is desirable that the latter be represented by multiples — such as strips, or blocks of four — rather than by single examples.

The Detection of Watermarks

Some watermarks are much more apparent than others. The ease with which they can be appreciated depends upon many factors, among them being the texture of the paper, its finish, and some of the mechanics of manufac-

Above, "normal" watermark. Far left, "reversed" watermark. Left, "inverted and reversed" watermark. The "S U" is from a strip of United States 1902 2c carmine of the 1902 series; the "S P" watermarks are from pairs of United States 1908-1909 1c green imperforate.

ture, not the least important of which is the drying of the paper. A classic instance of drying affecting the prominence of the watermark in hand-made paper is on record in connection with the manufacture of the paper ordered from Stacey Wise by Perkins, Bacon and Company for the first issue of Western Australia. When the printers thought that the wire ("bit") of the swan was not sufficiently bold (prominent), and certainly not as bold as that used for the crown watermark of Great Britain, and complained to the paper-makers, the mould maker wrote to the printers on July 25, 1853, and stated:[3] "The *Swan* Water Mark is quite as *bold* a wire as the *Crowns* if not a little more. The reason that sheet does not shew so plain is because it was *dried* by Fire in haste."

With machine-made paper the prominence of the watermark, to some extent, depends upon how much of the weight of the dandy roll is permitted to bear on the forming paper, and the adjustment has to be made carefully. If too little weight is permitted to bear, the watermark will be insufficiently perceptible; this is especially liable to occur at the beginning of a "run" of the paper-making machine.

Not all postage stamp watermarks are readily apparent by unaided looking through the stamp. The extraneous light distracts and the color in which the stamp is printed hinders the eye. From early times philatelists have found that aids to the detection of watermarks were desirable. These aids today are of three principal kinds, all of which, of course, depend upon the greater transparency of thin than thicker paper.

One of the earliest devices, and one that still has much to commend it, is a plain card, a few inches square, with a small rectangle cut out of the center. The stamp to be examined is placed over this central hole, the card is held up to the light, and the stamp is looked through. The masking frequently renders visible watermarks that are otherwise imperceptible without such elimination of the extraneous light.

Watermarks are most easily seen in plain, unprinted paper, and the simple mask made no provision for neutralizing the design of the stamp. This can, of course, be effected quite simply, in the majority of cases, by looking at or through the stamp with the aid of a transparent glass or a film appropriately colored. The colored glass or film absorbs all the colors except the one used for coloring the glass or film, and that color is transmitted. A stamp printed in light blue ink upon white paper, if looked at through a similarly colored piece of glass, appears as a piece of plain light blue paper. An early commercial attempt to apply this well-known principle to philatelic watermark detection was made by W.S. Lincoln, a famous English dealer, who marketed a card with a series of circular colored windows made of film. The colors were pale but were chosen as approximating those in which many stamps had been printed. The "Lincoln" card was an improvement on the simple mask, but was insufficiently developed scientifically.

In more recent years a much more carefully and scientifically thought-out color-absorbent aid to watermark detection became available to philatelists.

---

[3] *Perkins, Bacon Records* (1953) Vol. I, Page 372.

This instrument has the trade name of "Philatector," and consists of a container in which there is a light source — a pocket lamp battery and bulb — over which a series and combinations of colored films can be centered. The stamp to be examined is placed in a transparent slide, which is so inserted in the container that the bulb, the colors and the stamp are in a line with a viewing aperture. With the aid of this instrument the majority of watermarks of monochrome stamps can be seen as though in plain paper. But, of course, black ink cannot be visually neutralized; and stamps printed in more than one color present certain difficulties.

It need hardly be stated that all these "watermark detecting" aids are useful also when examining paper for the purpose of determining the texture and its variations.

If a watermarked stamp is laid face-downward on a dark surface, the watermark will, in many cases, show up appreciably darker than the thicker paper. This effect led to the production of what is almost certainly the most popular and widely used type of "watermark detector" in use today. Simple and inexpensive, it is a black surface in the form of a shallow tray made either of glazed tile or in some plastic.

Not every watermark is readily visible merely by placing the stamp on the dark surface — something further is required to make the paper more transparent. Water will serve, but cannot be used for mint stamps without the gum being lost, and must not be used for any stamps printed in water-soluble inks or on safety papers.

For many years it has been known that highly volatile liquids — such as benzine, petroleum, and carbon tetrachloride — have the property of rendering paper transparent without damaging the gum of mint stamps, and drying by evaporation in a few moments, leaving the paper unaffected. Such liquids became very popular in use for detecting watermarks, and until roughly speaking forty years ago could be used with complete safety so far as the stamp was concerned. Of course, benzine and petroleum and similar liquids are highly inflammable, and prolonged inhalation of their fumes can produce, so medical authorities advise, discomfort and, possibly, serious toxic effects; inhalation of the vapors of carbon tetrachloride is, medically, dangerous. Therefore, when these liquids are used, elementary precautions are necessary — no smoking, no fires, no bad electrical contacts when using inflammable liquids — and, especially when using carbon tetrachloride, plenty of ventilation; preferably a draft of air.

Of more recent years such highly volatile liquids have ceased to be safe (so far as the stamp is concerned) with an increasing number of new issues. The ink of all stamps printed by photogravure or rotogravure is soluble in certain of these liquids, and they will destroy the design if the stamp comes into contact with them. (Brief experiment with a common stamp, for instance Great Britain 1953 2½d., will show how it can irretrievably be ruined philatelically when brought into contact with, for instance, cigarette lighter fuel.) Therefore, such stamps must not be allowed to come into contact with such liquids.

That problem and its solution are comparatively simple. Much more difficult is that occasioned by the fact that, particularly since World War II, certain constituents of some inks used for printing by other methods (including line-engraving) also are soluble in such liquids, and the stamps are adversely affected by contact with the liquids. The safe rule, therefore, is not to use them for any modern issues. Fortunately, with most modern papers, watermarks when present are comparatively prominent and fairly readily visible.

When these liquids are used in the detection of watermarks, it is not necessary to do more than place the stamp face-downward on the dark surface and allow a few drops of the liquid to fall upon the back of the stamp. It is unnecessary to have the tray full of liquid — indeed to do so usually hinders perception of the watermark. A philatelic accessory that has long been on the market, and which is useful and economical of the liquid, is generically known as a "benzine dropper"; it is a small, lipped bottle with a stopper that can be released so as to allow the liquid to escape drop by drop at the desired spot.

An accessory was marketed that combined the dark surface with optical principles. The accessory was sold under the name "The Macon Detector," and consisted of two parts: the base, which was the dark surface; and the top, which contained three optical "windows."

Photography and photographic papers provide useful aids to the detection and, particularly, illustration of watermarks. It is beyond the scope of this work to discuss in detail the photographic processes, normal, X-ray, and others, that are available to act as these aids. However, it may be useful to indicate that, except for special effects — such as photographing a postage stamp watermark as though on plain paper — a camera is unnecessary. All that is needed is some "contact" printing paper (without any faintly printed trade name on the reverse), the appropriate developer and fixer, and a printing frame.

The stamp is laid face-downward in contact with the paper in the frame, the printed side of the stamp in contact with the sensitive side of the paper. Exposure to light is made through the stamp, as though it were an ordinary photographic negative. Conditions and papers vary so much that it is almost impossible to give any guide to exposure, but about three seconds, three feet away from a single fifteen-watt electric light provides a useful starting off point for experiments which will soon reveal the best exposure. The paper is then developed, fixed and washed according to the manufacturer's instructions. This is then the "negative," bearing a reversed print of the stamp, and the watermark appears darker than the paper on which the stamp is printed; the design of the stamp appears darker under the design of the watermark than where there is none. This negative print may be all that is desired. If a "positive" is required, the negative print is placed, face-to-face, in contact with another piece of photographic paper, and another exposure to light is made, through the back of the "negative." This exposure will need to be considerably longer than the first. After the paper has been developed, fixed and washed, it will bear a positive print of the stamp, with the watermark appearing somewhat lighter than the surrounding paper. For many stamps and watermarks, photographic paper that is called "contrast" or "hard" will be found to be more satisfactory than the so-called "normal" paper.

Nowadays "contact" paper has given way almost entirely to "bromide" paper. Such paper is much more light-sensitive and the exposure time will be very short indeed, even five times as far away from the light source as mentioned for "contact" paper.

It is scarcely necessary to point out that such "photography" is possible only with loose stamps.

When searching for, or "detecting," watermarks, it is desirable where possible to have a fairly clear idea of the design which is to be detected. The principal catalogues are of invaluable assistance in this regard for most cases.

Another method by which it is sometimes possible to perceive a watermark is to look along the surface of the stamp held to light at eye level at an oblique angle. The substance of the paper being slightly thinner, it is, therefore, normally indented to a minute extent in the shape of the watermark, so that the surface of the paper undulates slightly, irrespective of the effect upon it of the ink and gum. If a completely regular surface is held to light at an oblique angle, the light rays are deflected regularly; but where the surface regularity is broken by a watermark, the light rays are deflected irregularly by the undulation, and the design becomes perceptible. This test is not infallible, and requires considerable experience before it is even useful in many cases.

The fact that the paper substance is thinner in the shape of the watermark has been known to philatelists for well over a century. Nevertheless, it is only of comparatively recent years that that fact has been exploited commercially for the benefit of collectors wishing to detect watermarks.

By an ingenious arrangement of glass, resilient plastic and ink, with pressure applied by a scraper or roller, a kit marketed under the name "Morley-Bright" enables the shallow depths of the watermark design to be seen darkly against a light background. Not only that, but by use of special ink a permanent record can be made of the design.

More recently a sophisticated instrument marketed under the name "Signoscope" has adopted the effect of slanting light to make the watermark visible. The stamp is placed face-down on a support and covered by a piece of thick glass in a holder, which is slipped into place and subjected to pressure, while light from a lamp is shone over the surface. The effect is that the watermark shows up dark against the remainder of the paper.

5. Stamp Design

WITH PURELY ARTISTIC considerations as they affect the stamp, the philatelist as such is not much concerned. However, there are some matters allied to the stamp's artistry that he or she requires to have knowledge of in general terms, and some of these matters will now be discussed.

Broadly speaking every stamp design falls into one of two classes. The first of these is what the artists or critics refer to as "formal"; the other is termed "proper." Again broadly speaking, it is true to state that the formal design depicts an abstraction or an idealized representation of a subject, while the proper design seeks a more realistic, a so-to-speak "photographic," representation of the subject. Compare, for instance, the "formal" representation of Queen Victoria on Great Britain 1840 1d. with the "proper" portrait of President Franklin Delano Roosevelt on Salvador 1948 12c.

It has been suggested that there are only four main types of stamp designs.

The first of these types is exemplified by the design of the first adhesive postage stamp ever issued — the Great Britain 1840 1d. just referred to. This type is called the *Formal Head Type*, and has been issued, at one time or another, by most of the stamp-issuing countries of the world. In the United States, from the issue of 1847 to the 1938-43 Presidents' Series, emphasis has been laid upon the tradition of a formal head. The early issues of France, Haiti, Luxembourg and the Netherlands, to mention only four countries, provide examples of this *Formal Head Type*.

The second of the types is termed *Formal Arms Type*. Here the head is replaced by arms or similar symbols of the issuing authority. The early issues of Austria, Liberia, Norway and Salvador, again to mention only four countries, provide examples of this *Formal Arms Type*.

The two foregoing types reveal clearly the historical origins and development of the postage stamp, in that the types have a strongly numismatic flavor. The people who were responsible for the first adhesive postage stamps had no precedent upon which to draw for size, shape, or design; and, as

Douglas B. Armstrong aptly stated, "the problem was solved, literally, by squaring the circle."[1] The heads of the sovereign and the arms which had, since the time-lost origins of coinage, appeared on the circular currency, were transferred to the rectangular pieces of paper. There have been, of course, numerous stamps that are non-rectangular, but the witticism is none the less valid on their account.

The third of these types, the most starkly utilitarian, is the *Numeral Type*, exemplified by the famous first issue of Brazil 1843 (July) Bull's Eyes, which had been preceded by Zurich (Switzerland) 1843 (March), and followed by, for instance Baden (Germany) 1851, and Sweden 1872 3 öre — yet again to mention specifically the stamps of only four countries. This *Numeral Type*, with its strongly fiscal flavor, is especially frequently encountered among the world's postage-due issues.

The fourth of the main types of stamp designs is the *Pictorial Type*. This, in its modern form evolved from stamp designs rather than developed directly from the coinage or fiscal labels. The first issue of Canada 1851 3d. portrays a beaver, the issue of the United States 1869 shows various pictures on five of the stamps, and there are many other stamps, such as the 1862 issue of Nicaragua, that bear formalized reproductions of scenes in nature or animals or other subjects. But such stamp designs are as far from the true pictorial as is the formal from the proper portrait. The first true pictorials, in the modern sense, appeared with North Borneo 1894, of which issue seven of the values were engravings of "photographic" representation. From that day until this, the *Pictorial Type* has become increasingly more popular, and there is scarcely a stamp-issuing country today that does not, in the main, have pictorial stamps.

Modern printing techniques, particularly photogravure, led to a revolution in stamp portraiture. A photogravure postage stamp was issued by Bavaria (Germany) on March 31, 1914. The stamps bore, for issues in those days, an astonishingly life-like portrait of King Ludwig III. That technique,

---

[1]*Approaches to Philately* (1950) — Page 133. The Art of the Postage Stamp.

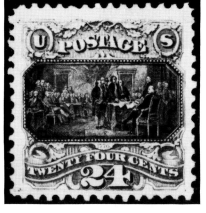

Natives. Photograph of plate from which the Post Office Mauritius stamps were printed.

perfected over the years, has led collectors to accept as almost commonplace on postage stamps, designs such as, to take but two instances, Guatemala 1937 (Postage) 1q., and, more recently, USA 1984 (June 6) John McCormack 20c.

There is a further type of stamp design, although to employ the term "design" is, perhaps, to dignify what is no more than the assemblage of pieces of print. This may be termed the *Inscription Type*, exemplified by Lithuania 1918, Parma (Italy) 1859, Sonora (Mexico) 1913 (May) and Wenden (Russia) 1863, once more to mention the stamps of only four countries.

Another term of artistic origins is frequently used by philatelists in connection with stamp artistry. That term is *Primitives* — almost self-explanatory as describing those crude productions of sometimes out-of-the-way and backward countries. Examples of *Primitives* (sometimes also referred to as *Natives*, to make a distinction between homemade and foreign-produced stamps) are provided, for example, by British Guiana 1850 "Cottonreels," Mauritius 1859 "Tête-de-Singe," New Caledonia 1860, Spain 1850, and Western Australia 1857.

Component Parts of Designs

The term "design," when applied to a stamp, is used often in the wide sense of meaning all the printing — incorporating as it often does, features more or less stringently enforced upon the artist by considerations of security, and also including additions made after the basic stamp has been in use. Even the most simple stamp design is composed of several parts, and these parts have names, or have been given them by philatelists who, in their studies and researches, have frequent occasion to refer to particular portions of the stamps in describing varieties, flaws, and the like.

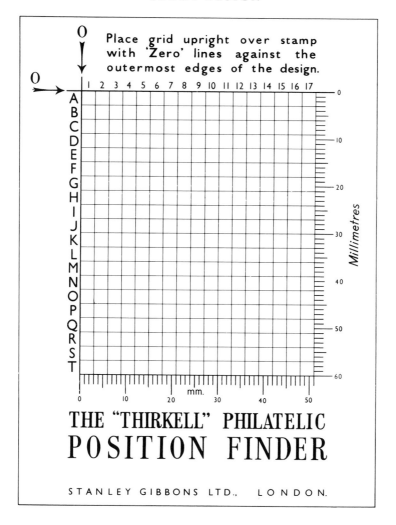

O

Place grid upright over stamp with 'Zero' lines against the outermost edges of the design.

THE "THIRKELL" PHILATELIC
POSITION FINDER

STANLEY GIBBONS LTD., LONDON.

In this connection, a useful philatelic accessory is on the market, and does away with the necessity for minute description of some artistic feature of the design. This accessory is called the "Thirkell" Philatelic Position Finder, and consists of a transparent grill divided into minute squares, identifiable by numbers and letters — thus enabling any detail of a design to be located and referred to with accuracy and certainty. In use, the "Thirkell" is keyed or zeroed on a spot — for example, the northwest corner of a rectangular design; by reference to this key spot, and the reference letters and numbers, all parts of the design can be easily and certainly identified on different copies of the same stamp.

Each division on the "Thirkell" is three millimeters square, and even closer location of a flaw may be made by laying the straight-edge of, say, a sheet of paper parallel with the ruled lines and against the millimeter graduations at the right or along the baseline of the position finder.

Errors and Freaks of Design

There are numerous instances of errors in design, or "artists' errors" as these pictorial anachronisms and other mistakes are often generically termed. Sometimes the fault is that of the stamp artist, sometimes it dates further back — to the designer or supplier of the original model incorporated by the stamp artist in the stamp design; and sometimes the mistake is that of the person responsible for the inscription.

Such mistakes, although often corrected in subsequent issues of stamps, are normal for the issues in which the mistakes occur; they appear in the design or die or its equivalent and in all stamps printed from it. Although these mistakes are popularly termed "errors," the use of the term in this connection is sharply differentiated from its use in other fields of philately, in which the term "error" signifies a stamp differing from the intended normal because of some unintentional mistake made during any stage of production subsequent to designing and the production of the die or its equivalent.

Numerous classes of so-called "artists' errors" exist, and I do not here attempt to mention more than a few of them.

Anachronisms, or apparent anachronisms, form one of these classes. A classic anachronism occurs in the badge of St. Kitts-Nevis, which pictures Christopher Columbus with a telescope to his eye although the explorer died years before the instrument appeared; this badge figured as the center of St. Kitts-Nevis 1901 ½d. and other values, and has been featured in many later issues of that stamp-issuing country. Another well-known anachronism — a Viking ship flying the Stars and Stripes at the prow and the flag of Norway at the stern — on USA 1925 Norse-American 5c., is accounted for by the fact that the model was a picture of a modern reproduction or copy of an ancient Viking ship excavated in 1880 at Gokstad in Norway, and the reproduction sailed across the Atlantic to the Chicago World's Fair in 1893.

The unintended incorporation of wrong models forms another class of these errors. An instance occurs in Australia 1947 Newcastle Sesquicentenary 2½d., which portrays the father instead of the son, Lieut. John Shortland. Another instance occurs in Philippines 1932 18c., which pictures the Vernal Falls, Yosemite Park, California, instead of the desired Pagsanjan Falls.

Solecisms in one form or another form a third class of such mistakes. A curious animal, the Tarsier or Tarsius is shown on Sarawak 1950 2c., where

it is ungrammatically described as ''The Tarsius.'' English titles of honor present certain difficulties, but Knights and Baronets are invariably referred to formally by the forename as well as the surname, as in ''Sir Edward Codrington''; yet on Greece 1927-28 Navarino Centenary 5d., he appears with the inscription ''Sir Codrington'' — later another stamp was issued correcting the solecism.

In many cases, where the detailed history of production has not been recorded, it is not known whether the artist or the engraver has been responsible for an error in detail in a design; and there are many instances of such

errors. Typical of an error in detail is Newfoundland 1928 Publicity 1c., where, on the map of that country, the geographical locations of Cape Bauld and Cape Norman were transposed, but corrected when the re-engraved design was issued the following year. The smiling peasant on Austria 1934 6g. would seem to have little to smile about, because some freak of drawing or reproduction has turned his ears backward; this anatomical vagary was rectified by a fresh issue in 1935.

Freaks of shading and contrast between different parts of the same design have often given rise to the appearance of probably unintentional features in a stamp. By far the largest number of these freaks results in profiles or other portraits or masks, and consequently this class is often termed "Ghost Stamps." No complete list of "Ghost Stamps" has been compiled, and while sometimes the apparition is reasonably clear for all to see, there are numerous instances where it is so only in the eye of the beholder.

One of the most readily perceived examples is to be found in Prussia 1861-65 1sg., the other values of the same issue, and the somewhat similar "eagle" design of the 1867 issue; when the stamp is inverted the area surrounding the eagle's head and between the outstretched wings resolves itself instantly into a silhouette of two quaintly attired or learned gentlemen engaged in earnest conversation or dispute. Another example, chosen at random, of a "ghost" visible when the stamp is inverted occurs in Iceland 1938-45 15a. where, to what is then the left of the main column of the geyser appears a smaller column (beginning about four millimeters below the letters "EY") that seems, with a little imagination, like a small, crowned head with a large flowing white beard. "Ghosts" and alleged ghostly portraits appear on many stamps, and another, final, example must suffice: it occurs in USA 1935 Boulder Dam 3c. When this stamp is turned sideways, with the inscription to the right, a shadowy mask or face (said to be that of the late President Franklin Delano Roosevelt) can be discerned in the shading of the hills.

Plagiarism in Stamp Design

Throughout the hundreds of thousands of stamp designs that have been prepared during the century and a half that have elapsed since the first issue

in 1840, it would be surprising if some unconscious arrival at a similar result had not occurred. However, some issues of different countries are so similar in design that the inevitable conclusion is that the artist of one stamp deliberately plagiarised the design of the other artist. Again, I do not attempt to mention other than two specific examples of such plagiarism.

An outstanding and early example is to found in Liberia 1881 3-cent Inland which, except for the central landscape, is a direct copy of Canada 1870-88 3 cents.

Equally obvious plagiarism occurs in Uruguay (Nov. 19) 1898-1899 Liberty 5 m., which, except in minor points of distinction without a difference, is a direct copy of Newfoundland 1890 3c.

Such copying is to be differentiated from the not unauthorized deliberate production of identical or virtually identical designs by the one printing house for different stamp-issuing authorities — for instance, Perkins Bacon & Company's Britannia design undenominated stamps for Trinidad 1851-56 and Mauritius 1854 (1858). Another such instance involves three issues, engraved by father and son. Jean Jacques Barre produced the design of France 1849-52 10c. to 1 fr. using an original framework enclosing the head of Ceres and altering first the head to President Louis Napoleon in 1852 and then altering the inscription from ''Repub Franc'' to ''Empire Franc'' in 1853 when Napoleon became Emperor of the French. That very frame design was used by Barre's son, Desire Albert, who succeeded his father as chief engraver to the Paris Mint, when producing the first issue of Greece 1861 (Oct. 1) 1 l. to 80 l. with the head of Hermes. He used the frame again, unchanged except as to inscription, for Romania 1872 (Oct. 15) 1½b. to 50b. with the head of Prince Carol, who became king in 1881.

Glossary of Design Terms

The alphabetical list that follows does not pretend to be a complete catalogue of the various terms that, from time to time, have been used to describe the features of various designs, nor are the examples quoted more than a choice of stamps bearing the features to which reference is made.

Background. The term used to designate the groundwork of lines, hachuring, shading, or of solid color against which an artistic feature — such as a head — is shown. Sometimes the term "background" is used in a particular sense to indicate such lines etc. printed in a separate color — for example, in reference to Russia 1883-88 1k. to 70k.

Center frame.

Center. Term used to designate the stamp's central, and usually most prominent, feature — whether a portrait, a picture, or a numeral. Sometimes the term *vignette* is used in reference to this feature.

Center Frame. A framework enclosing the center, usually forming only a subsidiary feature of the design. Center frames are of innumerable shapes. As instances: a round center frame is to be seen, for example, in USA 1940 Famous Americans Composers 1c., an oval in South Africa 1926 6d., an octagonal in Tasmania 1858 1s., while that in Mexico 1895 1p. cannot be described briefly.

Corner ornaments.

Check Letters. Letters in the corners of some of the Queen Victoria stamps of Great Britain — inserted as a precaution against successful forgery and the patching-up of uncanceled portions of several used stamps for the purpose of defrauding the revenue — instanced by 1870 (Oct. 1) ½d., and 1884 (Apr. 1) £1. Sometimes these letters are referred to as "Position Characters." Check Letters are found also in the early stamps of Victoria, for instance 1850 (Apr. 14) 2d.

Corner Letters. This term is used frequently as a synonym for "Check Letters."

Corner Ornament. A term used when referring to a feature, usually framed, in the extreme corner of a design — for example the northeast and northwest corners of USA 1928 Airmail, Beacon on Rocky Mountains 5c., or in all four corners of Hong Kong 1912-21 1c.

Corner Square. A term used to describe the feature that usually encloses and bears a corner ornament — as in the Hong Kong stamp referred to under the previous heading, and those stamps mentioned under "Check Letters."

Engine Turning. This term, and its synonym "Lathe Work," is used to designate the usually intricately interwoven lines of a design produced by a geometric lathe — for example, the entire background of Chile 1862 20c.

Format. This is a term (of French origin) used in reference to stamps in the sense in which it was originally employed in connection with books — that is, to designate the shape and size. The term is nearly always, necessarily, qualified by an adjective such as "horizontal," "large," "square," and "vertical."

Frame. The outer containing feature (of a design), often a single or double line, but sometimes an elaborate combination of features. When necessity arises for the line itself to be distinguished from a more elaborate artistic feature, the feature is sometimes referred to as the *Frame,* and the line as the *Frameline;* in the case of bi-colored stamps, especially, "the frame" is used, often to comprise all that portion of the design not included in "the center" — the color of the one portion being different from that of the other.

Free Form. A term applied to a stamp with an irregular and, usually, non-rectangular shape, the paper being trimmed to the design during production and adhering by pressure-sensitive adhesive to a silicone-treated base paper. The first free form stamps were produced by Walsall Lithographic Co. for Sierra Leone 1964 (Feb. 10) World's Fair, New York 1d. to 5s. postage and 7d. to 11s. air. The

Free form. The first free form stamp was an outline map of Sierra Leone issued Feb. 10, 1964, to commemorate the New York World's Fair.

Imprint. The two types of Peace and Commerce imprints.

free form shape had a vogue during the 1960s and '70s in the issues of Sierra Leone and Tonga in particular, with shapes varying from diamonds [Sierra Leone 1970 (Oct. 3) 1c. to 5c.] to bananas [Tonga 1978 (Sept. 28) 1s. to 5s.].

Hair Lines. This term is used correctly to designate only the fine uncolored lines diagonally crossing the outer corners of the colored backgrounds contained within the corner squares bearing check letters on certain stamps such as Great Britain 1862 4d.

Hidden Dates. See "Secret Marks."

Imprint. This term has several philatelic connotations, but when allied to the design of the stamp, it signifies the lettering, always in minute characters, usually outside and below the frame, comprising the name of the printers — for example, "Waterlow & Sons Limited" on Haiti 1950 (February) Port-au-Prince Bicentenary Exhibition 10c.; or of the designer and engraver — for example "J. Sage" and "E. Mouchon" on France 1876-81 (Peace and Commerce types); or of the printer and designer — for example "Courvoisier" and "B. Reber" on Switzerland 1947 (August) Railway Centenary 5c. Such imprints are often qualified by the appropriate adjective, that is to say, for example, "Engraver's Imprint," or "Printer's Imprint." Occasionally designs incorporate, in some inconspicuous position, some symbol, such as the initials of the engraver — for instance "J.B." (for "James Barnard") at the base of the neck in the renowned first issue of Mauritius 1847 Post Office. However, these savor more of "Secret Marks," and are referred to under that heading.

Inscription. The lettering comprising the name of the country, the value, and sometimes also including other lettering appearing as an inherent part of the design, as distinct from the portrait or other main and central feature.

Keytype. This is the term used to designate a design specially so prepared that

Above and top left, "Imprints." Bottom, left, "Keytype."

it can be used commonly for various countries by altering merely the inscription, and, sometimes, the value. Keytypes have been used widely for colonial issues; instances of such use are: by France, for example, for French Guiana 1892 1c. and Gaboon 1904-1907 1c; by Great Britain, for example, for Ceylon 1912-25 30c. and Seychelles 1917-20 25c; and by Portugal, for example, for Angola 1914 ¼c. and Inhambane 1914 ¼c.

Lathe Work. See "Engine Turning."

Legend. This term is used, sometimes, as a synonym for "Inscription."

Medallion. This term is used in two senses — first to designate an oval or circular frame enclosing, usually, a portrait; and second, to designate the portrait itself enclosed within such a frame, but in this case the better usage is to employ "Medallion Portrait." Medallions and Medallion Portraits are of many sizes, but the use of the term usually connotes that they comprise only a comparatively small proportion of the space occupied by the whole design. Examples of Medallions and Medallion Portraits are provided by Luxembourg 1927 (December) Child Welfare 10c. +5c., St. Helena 1934 Colonization Centenary 1d., and USA 1950 (July) Sesquicentennial of Indiana 3c. The term "Medallions" is used also as a sobriquet for Belgium 1850-65, to distinguish those stamps from the 1849 issue (which is nicknamed *Epaulettes*).

Name. In relation to the design, this term is used correctly to designate only the name of the stamp-issuing country.

Name Tablet. When, as is frequently the case, the name of the issuing country appears within a special frame in the form of a tablet, it is referred to as the *name tablet*. Fiume 1919 (January) provides an example of a design with a particularly prominent name tablet. In the designs of the postage stamps of Great Britain, no name tablet (nor any wording referring to the country of origin) has ever been used.

Ornament, Ornamentation. These terms, of vague significance, are frequently used to designate some particular part of the artistic make-up of the design. Sometimes they are positionally qualified, as in "Corner Ornament," when descriptive qualification of the ornamentation is normally unnecessary. Often, however, descriptive qualification is desired for clarity and ease of location, when almost self-explanatory (in the circumstances) terms are used, such as *comma-like, Greek-border, floreate,* and *star-like.* Ornaments and ornamentation used in stamp designs are almost infinitely diverse, and small purpose would be served here by quoting or illustrating examples.

Overprint. The term used to designate an addition to the face of a stamp after it has been printed. Sometimes the component parts of the stamp design are separately identified by referring to the "overprint" as such, and to the earlier printing as the "basic stamp." Overprints have many purposes, but the term should be compared with and distinguished from "Surcharge," which is a particular type of overprint. Occasionally one encounters the self-contradictory, paradoxical situation of a "manuscript 'overprint' " such as occurred in Newfoundland 1919 (April) 3c. Caribou with handwritten legend reading "Aerial Atlantic Mail J.A.R." for the Martinsyde abortive flight.

Plate Number. In relation to the design of the stamp, this term is used to designate the figures, often minute, and sometimes almost concealed in another feature, signifying the particular plate from which the stamps were printed. As examples: Great Britain 1858-64 1d. has either two or three numerals included in the engine-turning at both sides of the stamp; Great Britain 1872-80 6d. has the plate number (11 to 20) printed in a special feature, that is, a circle centrally set on both sides of the center frame. In Japan 1874 ½ sen to 30 sen the control or plate "numbers," in the form of Syllabic characters, appear at the foot, or immediately below the center design, or, in the case of the 6 sen, to the left of the

Position characters. In the lower corner squares of each stamp, the letters indicate the sheet position. The first letter indicates the row (S or T); the second letter indicates the position in the row (D to J).

buckle on the garter. The use of the term "Plate Number" in relation to the design is sharply differentiated in meaning from the same term in relation to the number of the printing plate from which the stamp was printed. Somewhat similar in appearance, but with a different significance are "Position Numbers."

Position Numbers, Position Characters. These terms are used to designate numeral or literal features that enable a stamp to be assigned to the particular plate position from which the stamp was printed. As examples: Uruguay 1882 1c. and 2c. have, at the foot of the center frame, an uncolored tablet bearing a number from 1 to 100. Great Britain 1840 2d. has, in each of the two lower corner squares, a letter; the left letter represents the horizontal row — lettered from "A" (the first such row) to "T" (the last such row), and the right letter represents the vertical column — lettered from "A" (the first such column) to "L" (the last such column); and such stamps bear combinations of these letters beginning with "A-A," which is the first (left-hand) stamp in the top row of the printed sheet, and ending with "T-L," which is the last (right-hand) stamp in the bottom row of the printed sheet. These letters are also termed "Check Letters" and "Corner Letters." In later issues of Great Britain these letters appear in all four corners, and the top letters are merely the lower "position characters" reversed; also with some of these stamps other combinations of letters occur.

Scroll. A term used to designate a feature, in the form of a strip or ribbon-shaped slip, often represented folded or curled, with letters inscribed. As examples: British Guiana 1931 Centenary of County Union 1c., the words "Demerara, Essequibo, Berbice" appear on a scroll, as do the words "Special Delivery" on USA Special Delivery Stamps 1925 20c.

Secret Marks. In relation to the design of the stamp, this term is used to designate those, often minute, indications introduced for the purpose of identifying particular craftsmanship, or to distinguish it from copies or counterfeits. Secret Marks take many forms. The letters "J.B." have already been referred to under "Imprint." As further examples: In Naples (Italy) 1858 ½ gr. to 50 gr., the dies were engraved by G. Masini of Naples, and in the outer borders of each stamp he engraved a different letter of his name. In USA 1873 issue, printed by the Continental Bank Note Company, the designs of the eleven values were almost identical with those of the 1870-71 issue, produced by the National Bank Note Company, with the exception that minute characteristics were added to each stamp of the eight lower values printed by the Continental Bank Note Company, to provide an easy and certain means of distinguishing that firm's products from those of the National Bank Note Company; these characteristics differ on each value, and, for instance, on the 1c., the secret mark takes the form of a crescent-shaped piece of shading immediately to the left of the ball representing the upstroke at the top of the figure of value "1." Somewhat similar in character to "Secret Marks" are the so-called "Secret Dates" or "Hidden Dates" that, in minute characters, are incorporated in Canadian stamps issued since 1935 when the year of issue does not form a prominent part of the design. These "Hidden Dates" take the form of four numerals representing the year in which the stamp was first issued. There is no standard position on the stamp in which these numbers occur — for example in Canada 1942-48 War Effort 50c., the numbers "1942" appear above the southwest numeral value tablet across the broadest part of the lowest leaf, and in Canada 1953 Definitives 3c. the numbers "1953" appear just above the bottom frameline at the southeast corner of the design.

Surcharge. The term used to designate an overprint that alters or confirms the face value of a stamp. As with the term "overprint," so with "surcharge,"

A surcharge and an overprint both appear on Morocco (Great Britain) French Zone 5c. on ½d.

sometimes the component parts of the design are separately identified by referring to the "surcharge" as such and to the earlier printing as the "basic stamp." The term "surcharge" is not synonymous with "overprint," and should not be so used; every surcharge is an overprint, but not every overprint is a surcharge. Frequently stamps bear both surcharge and overprint. Examples of surcharges that *confirm* the face value of the stamps are to be found in Great Britain 1883 (Jan. 1) 3d. and 6d. A surcharge that alters the face value of the stamp is exemplified by Colombia 1932 20c. on 30c. And an example of both surcharge and overprint on the same stamp is provided by Morocco (Great Britain) French Zone 1937 (June) 5c. on ½d. Some surcharges have been effected by manuscript — as examples: Hawaii 1857 "5" in manuscript on 13c. of 1853; and Trinidad 1882 (May 9) "1 d" in manuscript with a bar cancelling the original value on 6d. of 1876. Unlike the case of a manuscript overprint there is nothing paradoxical about a manuscript surcharge, except to the extent of the statement that every surcharge is an overprint.

Tablet. The term used to designate a feature (of a design) so framed that it appears as a panel upon which, usually, another feature — such as numerals or letters — is presented. Tablets, normally, are referred to with a qualification, such as "Name Tablet," and "Value Tablet." Because of the prominent name and value tablets in the design, the term "Tablets" has been used as a sobriquet for the Peace and Navigation keytype of the French Colonies, of which, for instance, French Congo 1892 (November) 1c. is an example.

Type. A term that has several quite distinct meanings philatelically. However, in relation to lettering within the design, the term "type" means "style," and what letterpress printers refer to sometimes as "face." Literally hundreds of different types, styles or faces of lettering have been used for stamps, and small purpose would be served by quoting or illustrating examples.

Value. The term used to designate that part of the inscription (numeral, literal, or both) that has reference to the monetary charge expressed and made for the service to be performed. Often the term, "Face Value," or simply "Face" is used. In the cases of charity and other semi-postal issues, the postal value of the stamp

107

Both the interior of the frame and the background of the central feature are vignetted on these stamps of British Honduras.

is often referred to as the "face value," and the additional charge as the "surtax" (*not* "surcharge").

Value Tablet. When, as is frequently the case, the face value of the stamp appears within a special frame in the form of a tablet, it is referred to as the "value tablet." French Congo 1900-04 1(c) provides an example of a design with a particularly prominent value tablet.

Vignette. This term is used loosely by philatelists to designate the central portrait or other main feature of a stamp, as distinct from the frame or framework. Actually the term "vignette" properly means a feature that has the edges shading off into the surrounding paper, as in the case of the background to the head of the Salvador 1948 12c. (previously mentioned as typical of a "proper" portrait), where the vignette is contained within a solid frame. This type of vignette is exemplified also, for instance, by Guatemala 1921 (August) UPU 1p. 50. The object of vignetting is to render less conspicuous the gaps which occur between different parts of the design when bi-colored printing is not in exact register. A frequent approach is to vignette both the interior of the frame and also the background of the central feature, as exemplified in British Honduras 1949 (Jan. 10) 150th Anniversary of Battle of St. George's Cay 1c. and 5c.

6. From Design to Issued Sheets

THIS CHAPTER surveys philatelically the steps preliminary to printing, briefly deals with printing generally and with some philatelic aspects of stamps in sheets and other multiples; a more detailed philatelic consideration of printing is to be found in the chapters devoted to printing and the various printing processes.

The detailed steps in the production of a stamp design in its final issued form vary almost infinitely, and depend on many factors such as local conditions, the requirements of the issuing authority, the practices of the printing establishment, and the process of printing to be adopted. It would be quite impossible — and it would be unnecessary to attempt — in a work of this nature to deal in detail with all variations of these steps that, from time to time, have been taken to produce stamps. Broadly speaking, the outline of the procedures may be summarized as follows:

1. The selection of details to be incorporated in the design.
2. The preparation of artists' drawings.
3. The production of the die or its equivalent.
4. The multiplication of the die or its equivalent to form the printing base.[1]
5. The transference of the design on the printing base to the paper.

During the course of the production of a stamp there necessarily come into existence a greater or less number of documents that are of great philatelic interest. In many cases these items never become generally available, and even their details are subject to security measures; in some instances, however, these documents do become available, and they are eagerly sought by many collectors.

The documents are produced stage by stage as the design evolves from its original conception, throughout any modifications that may be made to it, until there emerges a finished stamp. These items reflect, so to speak, the amicable arguments or interchanges of ideas that occur between the artists, the craftsmen, and the printers and issuing authorities during the processes that have as their goal the production of a stamp.

---

[1]The term "printing base" is used here and elsewhere for convenience and generically to include plates, cylinders, stones and other such material from which the stamp is printed.

| 1924-26. | 1934-36. |

It is necessary to emphasize that the steps and items mentioned below do not pretend to be completely comprehensive for every issue ever made; nor indeed are they all necessarily valid for any particular issue. The detailed steps in the production of many stamps have become known to philatelists generally by reason of the researches of numerous student-specialists; and it is only through research that the evolution of any specific stamp can be ascertained. Selected for mention here are steps and items from various processes and issues, and terms that the philatelist encounters, in some cases quite often, in others infrequently.

The details to be incorporated in a design, and the selection or approval of the design itself are the responsibilities of the stamp-issuing authority, which also determines the method by which the design is to be printed. Many interrelated factors have to be taken into consideration by the responsible authorities. For instance, a design to be printed by one process is rarely capable, without some modification, of being printed by another process. By way of brief illustration of this point may be instanced, say, Great Britain 1924-26 1½d. and 1934-36 1½d., where the change in printing method from relief[2] printing to rotary photogravure necessitated many minor amendments to the design — basically identical in both issues.

As between the stamp-issuing authority and the printers there is, of course, close cooperation in the production of a stamp, but there are, broadly speaking from the printer's point of view, only two kinds of approach: in the first, the printer is given a design and is instructed to print it; in the second, he is asked to suggest or prepare suitable designs, perhaps incorporating specified features. The United Nations Postal Administration, for instance,

---

[2]In this chapter, in referring to printing processes, I use terms less familiar, perhaps, to philatelists than to printers: I hope that the terms used, being in general descriptive of the printing base, are less likely to cause confusion than some others.

United Nations, 1954: Food and Agricultural Organization commemorative.

Bahamas: Sketch forwarded to
London by Governor C.J. Bayley.

provides the printers with a complete and "finished" design for the stamps
to be printed — by way of example may be mentioned the design of the 1954
(Feb. 11) Food and Agricultural Organization 3c. Again by way of example
chosen at random I may mention that the design of Bahamas 1859 1d. was
prepared by the printers from an impractical design, a sketch of a circular
frame enclosing a pineapple and conch shell, sent to London by C.J. Bayley,
the Governor of Bahamas (see illustration).

With such contractual details the philatelist has, usually, little concern; but
he or she has a philatelic interest in the genesis or evolution of the stamp
as finally produced; and, often to no less extent, in the designs and other
offshoots in production that never come to fruition as issued stamps.

The initial stage in the production of nearly every stamp design is the
preparation by an artist of a rough outline or sketch, often in pencil, of the
conception of the design. Such sketches, which rarely become available to

Great Britain, 1953, 2½d. Sketches by M.C. Farrer Bell.

Preliminary sketch by Irene Delano for the Puerto Rico commemorative of 1949.

Original drawing by Victor S. McCloskey Jr., based on Mrs. Delano's sketch.

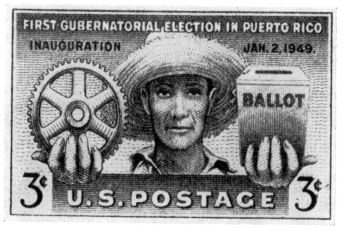

The finished stamp presenting the engravers' interpretation of tones and textures.

The late Edmund Dulac, stamp designer and artist in his studio. Note the "Artist's Drawing" of Great Britain 1948 Olympic Games 1s. near his left elbow.

philatelists, range in size from a square inch or two to many square inches. For instance, the preliminary sketch for USA 1949 Puerto Rico Election 3c. is in pencil on tracing paper, and the size of the frame is about nine inches by five-and-one-half inches; this document, the work of Mrs. Irene Delano, is now in the National Philatelic Museum, Philadelphia (see illustration). As a further instance I may quote the sketches of M.C. Farrer Bell in his search for a suitable design for Great Britain 1953 2½d. (see illustration).

After the design lay-out has thus been roughly sketched, the next step, often, is the production of a much more finished drawing or painting of the design, probably in color. Such a production (which eventually became Great Britain 1948 Olympic Games 1s.) can be seen in the accompanying picture of the late Edmund Dulac, photographed in his studio with the drawing near his left elbow in the picture. This picture gives a good idea of the relative size of the "artist's drawing," as such a production is often termed.

The artist's drawing is, usually, the document that is submitted to the authority responsible for accepting or rejecting designs. Different countries have different methods for obtaining the submission of designs from which choice can be made, and the practice is not even standard in any one country. For example, in Britain the usual procedure is that designs for postage stamps are selected from competitive entries submitted after invitation, by artists of repute or promise. These entries are judged by a panel whose members make recommendations. In some countries a particular artist is commissioned to produce a required design.

Sometimes competitions are held, open to the general public. The first competition of such a nature, but of far wider scope, was held in Britain in 1839 when the Treasury, in view of the impending postal reform in connection with the prepayment of postage, announced that before they could "decide upon the adoption of any course either by stamp or otherwise, they feel it will be useful that artists, men of science, and the public in general may have an opportunity of offering any suggestions or proposals as to the manner in which the stamp may best be brought into use." In that first competition more than 2,600 suggestions were received, and more than 250 designs for stamps were submitted. It is a matter of record that none of the competitive entries was considered satisfactory, and Rowland Hill negotiated with the firm that later became Perkins, Bacon and Company; between them they, empirically, evolved the classic beauty of the design of the world's first adhesive postage stamps. What was, probably, the first "designs" competition as such, resulted in the New South Wales 1888 Centennial issue. More recently a designs competition resulted in the Gold Coast 1948 issue. And India, in connection with celebrations to mark the centenary of the issue of postage stamps in that country, held a world-wide Gold Medal competition, open to children up to sixteen years of age, for stamp designs, the motif being "India as I see it."

The design or drawing of the artist often comprises entirely original features suggested and evolved by himself or herself. Frequently, however, an important or central feature of the stamp design is derived from an existing document. Thus, to refer again to the world's first adhesive postage stamps, Henry Corbould was commissioned to make a drawing of Queen Victoria's head as it appeared on the Guildhall Medal struck in honor of the Queen's Visit to the Corporation of the City of London on November 9, 1837. That drawing was used as a model for the stamps; the medal itself had been designed by William Wyon. As a further example, the central feature of USA 1901 Pan-American Exhibition 2c., the "Fast Express," was prepared from a photograph, by A.P. Yates of Syracuse, of Locomotive No. 938[3] drawing a train on the New York Central and Hudson River Rail Road. These are but two examples from hundreds that could be quoted; collectors and students have, for many years, been interested in tracing the original documents from which stamp designs have been evolved, and researchers have brought to light many curious facts in these connections.

After the production of the artist's drawing, the next step, often, is the production of a much more finished piece of work, that is sometimes referred to as the "model." Models vary according to the printing process to be employed; sometimes a model is a drawing in line — that is, with the light and shade represented entirely by lines, straight and curved, thick and thin, close together and spaced wider apart; sometimes it is in wash or continuous tone, like a watercolor painting that it often is. Sizes of models vary; a frequent practice is to make them something like ten times (linear) the size that the stamp will ultimately be.

---

[3]*Per* Allan M. Thatcher, in *Stamps* (New York), Vol. XIX, Page 287 (May 22, 1937).

Empire State Express of the New York Central & Hudson River Railroad (now the New York Central Railroad) used for the design of the U.S. 2c. Pan-American issue, 1901. The photograph was made by A.P. Yates of Syracuse, N.Y. It was found by Mr. Thatcher in the picture files of C.B. Chaney of New York, a railroad history enthusiast. Discovery of the photograph was first published by Mr. Thatcher in *Stamps* of May 22, 1937.

A further step, undertaken in many cases, particularly when the printing process involves the production of a die, is that the artist prepares a stamp-size drawing, sometimes in pen-and-ink, often in color, showing the design as it will appear when printed. The miniature works of art are, usually, unique, and are eagerly sought by collectors; and the terms ''artist's sketches'' and ''artist's drawings'' are often applied to them. Sometimes such miniatures are merely reduced photographs of the model. However regrettable it may be, there seems to be no adequately precise philatelic terminology to cope with all the different types of production prior to the die or its equivalent.

In miniatures, while it is often the case that one artist is responsible for the whole of the production, it is not by any means unusual for several artists to cooperate in the production of one drawing, each artist concentrating upon his specialty — for example, portrait, scene, lettering or framework.

Sometimes, the only step previous to the production of a die is the production of a miniature. This most frequently occurs when the new design incorporates an important or major feature that has previously been approved and used for an issued stamp. In such cases, a print of the previously used design is employed, and the part of the design to be substituted is cut out or pasted over and the new portion pasted on or drawn or painted in.

Essays

Up to this point, I have been discussing ''artist's sketches,'' ''artist's drawings,'' ''finished designs,'' ''models,'' and ''miniatures'' on the basis that a stamp resulted, and did so without there being any variation in design — this, in fact, is a comparatively rare occurrence. Philatelically a distinction is made between such productions, and similar productions that do not result in a stamp, or do not so result without variation. Such rejected productions, or those that are subsequently modified, are philatelically referred to as "essays." This term and its meaning merit a little discussion.

In the earliest days of philately, the term "essay" was in common use, being anglicized from the French "essai." *The Stamp Collectors' Review*, Vol. I, Page 20 (February 1863), reprinting an article from *The Leisure Hour*, ascribed the following meaning to the word: "The true 'essai' stamp . . . is that which has been printed for issue, but never got into actual circulation, such as the threehalfpenny label of this country, a great number of which were made a short time since." (The reference is to Great Britain 1860 1½d. in rosy mauve or lilac rose, *prepared for use but never issued;* stamps of the same value and design, but in rose-red or dull rose, were issued in 1870, long after the appearance in print of the article from which the quotation is taken.) Even in those days there was no general agreement as to the meaning of the term "essay," and Mount Brown quoted, in *The Stamp-Collector's Magazine*, Vol. II, Page 174 (November 1864), gives two meanings: "Stamps designed for issue but never circulated, and stamps printed in a different colour from those which have been, or are, in circulation." We may smile at these suggested meanings today, and Edward Loines Pemberton, that early, erudite and impulsive stalwart, in the same number and on the same page of that magazine, cavilled at indiscriminate collecting, and stated: " . . . this absurd and foolish practice of admitting every rejected design to be an essay. If we must collect essays let us confine ourselves to the collection of those which have been called forth by a necessity and not through the whim of an individual. A new issue of stamps is intended by the Belgian authorities, and designs are asked for; those which are rejected will be real essays because each one may be the design selected." The debate about the meaning of the term and the status of essays produced, in *The Stamp-Collector's Magazine*, Vol. II, Pages 189-190 (December 1864), the following statements that are accepted as accurate today: " . . . we must, of course, regard as an essay any engraving made and sent to the government for their approval, but not accepted by them. . . . It, therefore, follows that as soon as the government accepts the suggestion (so to speak) the engraving at once ceases to be an essay. . . ."

While those statements were accurate they were not all-embracing, and the exact meaning attaching to the term "essay" remained a matter of doubt, as, indeed to some extent, it still is, varying views having been expressed on both sides of the Atlantic Ocean. However, the following definition is that adopted by the Essay-Proof Society[4] and has gained a large measure of universal acceptance:

ESSAY — any design, or part of a design, essayed to or produced by a government (or established mail carrier) for a stamp, and differing in design in any particular from an officially issued stamp. There are die essays, plate essays, and forms of experimental essays, as well as unfinished or incomplete designs that may form part of a finally approved design.

---

[4]*Essay-Proof Journal*, Vol. I, Page 31 (January 1944).

German "sample stamp."   "Prince Consort" essay.

On the eastern side of the Atlantic, the term "essay" has, strongly, the implication of an attempt to show what the stamp would look like actually when printed. The American definition includes — and was intended by its authors to include — the large-size drawings or models.

Essays of designs can, *post hoc*, be divided into two classes; first those designs that, after modification, result in stamps in the modified design; and second those designs that are rejected and do not result in stamps. Sometimes a rejected design is modified and used for a different purpose.

Essays, as the definition connotes, are not restricted to handwork. Sometimes the persons or firms — particularly firms of printers — submitting designs for acceptance or competition, provide them in the form of printed paper so as to give the best idea of the intended stamp. These printed designs form by far the greatest class of essays encountered in philately.

Experimental essays include projects, in the form of stamps, submitted so that the issuing authority may judge of the type or standard of work, or other object of the essay. Such stamp-like productions often bear the name of the printer in the form of an inscription, like those of Harrison and Sons Ltd., produced in 1954 as examples of their printing in multicolored photogravure (see illustration). Sometimes these "stamps" are inscribed "specimen stamp" or "sample stamp" or their equivalents, as in the case of the German design illustrated. The terms "essay" and "specimen" are used, often as synonyms, for such productions; but the term "sample stamp" seems to have little philatelic employment, although its usefulness cannot be questioned.

Among the many thousands of all kinds of essays from all stamp-issuing countries, one of the most interesting is the so-called "Prince Consort Essay" of Great Britain. This relief-printed essay, which came into existence and was submitted to the authorities in 1850, was engraved by Samuel William Reynolds, printed by Robert Edward Branston, and fostered by Henry Ar-

Rough sketch (left) for French Olympic Games stamp and, above, the issued stamp.

cher, the inventor of stamp perforating, after he had experienced great difficulty in perforating the margins or gutters[5] of the then-current intaglio-printed stamps. The essay had three objects: first, to prove that relief-printed stamps could be produced at considerably less expense than intaglio-printed; second, that plates for relief printing were more regularly constructed than those then used for intaglio printing, and so provided more regular gutters for easier perforation; and third, the intention was, to print on dry paper and avoid the distortion resulting from the shrinking of dampened paper when drying, so ensuring uniformity in the size of the printed sheets.

It has already been stated that it is a comparatively rare occurrence for an artist's design to become a stamp unaltered. Usually the authorities suggest, or the artist himself or herself makes, alterations, and the suggested alterations are usually noted on the original design, or a copy of it. These notes often take the form of rough pencil or ink markings, as in the case of the essay that is illustrated for the stamp that became France 1924 Olympic Games 10c.

Basic Printing Methods

Before going on to consider the steps that are taken to produce the die or its equivalent, I think it will be helpful very briefly to survey the basic printing methods, philatelically considered, so that the ultimate object of copying the design on to the die may be envisaged.

All stamp printing falls under four main heads:

(1) INTAGLIO PRINTING, where the ink is held in and transferred to the paper from the incised and recessed areas of the printing base. The printing base consists, usually, of repetitions of the design represented by numerous grooves or cells; ink is applied to the whole of the printing base, which is then wiped, leaving the surface (the non-printing areas)

---

[5]The philatelic distinction between "gutters" and "margins" may be pinpointed by stating that gutters are the areas of paper between one unit and the next, while margins are those areas of paper surrounding a single unit.

clean, and the grooves or cells (the printing areas) charged with ink; paper is applied to the whole area of the printing base, and the ink in the grooves or cells is transferred to the paper by means of pressure applied through the back of the paper to the whole area of the printing base.

(2) PLANOGRAPHIC PRINTING, where the ink is held chemically separate on, and transferred to the paper from a uniformly surfaced printing base. This printing method basically relies upon the chemical fact that naturally oil and water will not mix, each having a natural antipathy for the other. The printing base consists of repetitions of the design represented by numerous lines, dots and other areas in greasy ink; the non-printing areas are wet with water; ink is applied to the whole of the printing base but is repelled by all except the printing areas; paper is applied to the whole area of the printing base, and the ink on the printing areas is transferred to the paper by pressure applied through the back of the paper to the whole area of the printing base.

(3) RELIEF PRINTING, where the ink is held on, and transferred to the paper from, the raised areas of the printing base. The printing base consists, normally, of repetitions of the design represented by raised lines, dots or other areas; ink is applied only to these raised areas, which alone come into contact with the paper; this is printed upon by pressure applied through the back of the paper.

(4) EMBOSSING, where the paper itself is distorted by pressure between the embossing plates to produce a design. The printing base is composed of two parts: the first part consists of repetitions of the design represented by recessed areas; the second part consists of repetitions of the design represented by relief areas that are the exact counterparts of the recessed areas on the first part of the printing base; embossing is imparted to the paper by placing it between the two parts of the printing base and exerting pressure, forcing the relief part of the printing base into the recessed part.

All these processes, and sometimes combinations of them, are capable of producing stamps in one color (monochrome), two colors (bi-colored), or more colors (multicolored). For monochrome printing, usually only one printing base is used. For most bi-colored and multicolored printing, as many different printing bases are used as there are colors in the finished product. However, a process was developed for intaglio printing whereby several different colors could be applied to a single sheet of paper on one pass under a single printing cylinder. This was effected by depositing ink on different parts of each image on the cylinder from appropriately cut out inking rollers — one roller for each color.

When multiplication of the design on to the printing base was necessary, all these printing processes, originally, necessitated manual or mechanical multiplication of the design; more recent developments led to the use of photography, sometimes, in this multiplication. Whatever printing process is employed, the first step is the production of a die or its equivalent. Broad-

BY APPOINTMENT
PRINTERS TO
THE LATE KING GEORGE VI

HARRISON AND SONS LTD

SPECIALISTS IN PHOTOGRAVURE

SPECIMENS

OF

PHOTOGRAVURE

3-COLOUR STAMPS

PRINTED BY HARRISON AND SONS LTD
LONDON HAYES AND HIGH WYCOMBE

Harrison & Sons Ltd. sample stamps, printed during 1954 as examples of multi-colored photogravure printing in blue, black, green, and mauve.

ly speaking, a die is produced when the design is to be multiplied mechanically; and where the design is to be multiplied by photography, the primary step is the production of a photographic negative that is the equivalent of the die.

Disregarding, for the moment, the photographic implications conveyed by the "negative," one may conveniently refer to the stamp design as being a "positive" — that is, reading usually from left-to-right — and view the various steps in the production of printing bases in the light of "positive" and "negative" — "negative" being something that reads reversed, that is, as though seen in a mirror. At the same time it is necessary to bear in mind that if the printing base is composed, for instance, of a surface bearing recesses, the recesses must be caused by something that has reliefs corresponding with the recesses.

Omitting any consideration of photography entering into the processes already referred to, they may be surveyed, simply, as follows:

INTAGLIO PRINTING. The design is cut into a die; the die is used to make a roller; the roller is used to multiply the design as many times as needed on to the printing base; the printing base is used to print on paper. Tabulated, the steps are: *Design:* Positive (flat). *Die:* Negative (recessed). *Roller:* Positive (raised). *Printing base:* Negative (recessed). *Stamp:* Positive (raised).

RELIEF PRINTING. The uncolored parts of the design are cut out of a die; the die is used to make moulds; as many moulds as are needed are grouped together; this group of moulds is copied to make the printing base; the printing base is used to print on paper. Tabulated, the steps are: *Design:* Positive (flat). *Die:* Negative (relief). *Mould:* Positive (recessed). *Printing base:* Negative (relief). *Stamp:* Positive (impressed).

PLANOGRAPHIC PRINTING: For planographic printing the original design may be specifically drawn on a flat surface, or special prints may be taken from a recessed or relief die, on special transfer paper; as many transfers as are needed are applied to the printing base; the printing base is used to print on paper. Tabulated, the steps (simplified) are: *Design:* Positive (flat). *Die:* Negative (flat, or recessed, or relief). *Transfer:* Positive (flat). *Printing base:* Negative (flat). *Stamp:* Positive (flat).

EMBOSSING: Simplified, the process is as follows: the areas to be raised are cut deeply in the die; the die is used to make a counterpart; both the die and the counterpart are copied as many times as needed to make the two parts of the printing base; these distort the paper placed between them. Tabulated, those steps are: *Design:* Positive (flat). *Die:* Negative (recessed). *Counterpart:* Positive (raised). *Stamp:* Positive (raised).

Having thus, briefly, surveyed the various basic printing processes, I now return to the place where I interrupted consideration of the course of the production of a stamp.

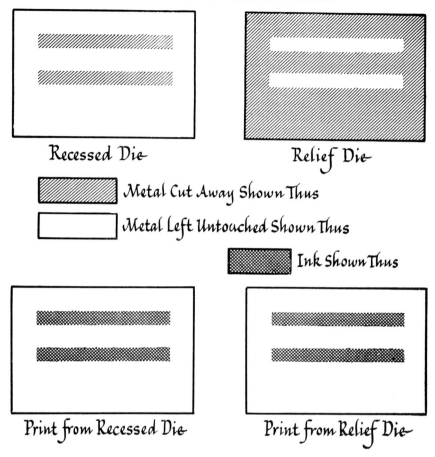

Recessed Die   *Relief Die*

Metal Cut Away Shown Thus

Metal Left Untouched Shown Thus

Ink Shown Thus

Print from Recessed Die   *Print from Relief Die*

Sketch showing comparative work on recessed and relief dies so as to produce the same area of print from both dies.

Dies and Die Proofs

After the design has been chosen and approved, perhaps subsequent to modification, the next step is the production of the die or its equivalent, depending on the printing process to be employed.

A die is a piece of metal, a small block or slip, usually steel, sometimes copper or other substance (and very occasionally other material, such as wood, ivory or plastic) on or into which the design is cut by hand, or in a combination of handwork etching or machine tooling. The equivalent of the die — used for certain printing processes such as photolithography and photogravure — is a photographic negative produced by means of a special camera.

The equivalent of the die calls for little discussion here, and may be dismissed by stating that it is usually upon glass, and results from exposing to the glass photographic plate either the drawing that the artist has made or a modification of it produced by the printer's artist who has borne in mind

An engraver working on a steel die, hand-cutting a design in recess.

the special characteristics and requirements of the printing process and the particular adaptation of it that the printer is about to use. From this photographic negative all subsequent productions stem.

Broadly speaking, there are only two types of die that are engraved. First, the recessed die, in which the lines and curves and dots that are to print are cut into the metal — that is, that metal is cut away or gouged out, and the printing takes place from the ink that is forced into the resultant hollows. Second, the relief die (a much more difficult production) in which the lines and curves and dots that are to print are left standing — that is, the surrounding metal is cut away, and the printing takes place from the ink that is applied to what has then become the apparently raised surface.

The differences in techniques and labor can readily be appreciated from the accompanying pairs of sketches, prepared to show what metal has to be cut away from each die for the purpose of producing merely two straight lines. In the case of the recessed die, only the two straight lines have to be cut away, leaving the rest of the surface of the die untouched. In the case of the relief die, all the metal surrounding and between the two straight lines has to be cut away, leaving only the surface of the lines themselves untouched. The diagrammatic prints from the two dies are intended to appear identical; they represent merely the areas of ink or color on the paper; in practice they would have the differences characteristic of the types of printing that

Newfoundland 1931. Series of twelve progress proofs showing stages in progress of the die. Each proof is dated — date, month, year — the first 15-7-31 (July 15, 1931). In No. 6, the inscription is outlined; No. 7, background lines have been added; No. 8, background hachuring has been added; and in No. 9, the background has been cleared and worked on until in No. 12, the finished die, dated 1-8-31 (August 1, 1931).

The issued stamp.

124

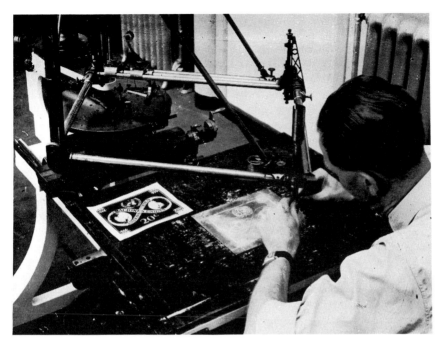

The pantograph in use. Note the reversal of the design (that is, right-to-left instead of left-to-right) on the specially engraved large copy of the design. Compare the crossing of the ribbon on this copy with that on the "model."

are referred to in the appropriate chapters later in this work.

The engraver is partly an artist, partly a craftsman who has served long apprenticeship. To some greater or less extent he "interprets" the model, and, within certain limits, modifies the design that he copies and cuts on to the metal, emphasizing a line here, or there making one less prominent, and determining by what depth and combination of lines to represent light and shade. The engraver always works with a magnifying glass to his eye, or with a binocular low-power microscope. His manual cutting tools are known as burins or gravers, and there are many shapes and gauges of them, each tool being ground, shaped and sharpened by the engraver himself.

The hand-cutting of a die is a lengthy process, demanding exactness and great patience. Sometimes many weeks of daily labor go into the production of the die of a stamp.

It is not unusual, as the work of cutting the die progresses, for an engraver from time to time to make prints from it in order that he may

The issued stamp.

judge how the work is shaping. These prints are known as "progress proofs," or sometimes as "working proofs," or "engraver's proofs," and they provide interesting commentaries on the day-to-day progress of the highly skillful labor that goes into the making of a stamp die. These progress proofs are often provided with the date they are taken. In the case of the series of twelve progress proofs illustrated — of the die from which Newfoundland 1931-37 3c stemmed — the dates run from July 15 (15-7-31) to August 1 (1-8-31), 1931. In spite of the loss of definition inevitable in half-tone illustrations (as are used in the present work) the, at times, nearly imperceptible differences between one progress proof and the next can be remarked; on the originals the differences are more pronounced.

Engravers, like artists, have their specialties of workmanship, some confining their work to portraits, others to vignettes, others to framework, and yet others to lettering. Only rarely is a specialist in one type of work adept in any other. it is more usual than not for a stamp die to incorporate the work of several engravers, each producing his own specialty.

Although, in many cases, the whole of the die consists of hand-work alone, it is frequently the case that it includes engine-turning or machine-ruling, applied mechanically. Frequently, too, assistance is derived from etching — that is, coating the surface of the die with an acid resist, then scratching part of the resist away and allowing acid to eat away that part of the metal that has been thus exposed, and so, in some cases, providing an outline or basis upon which the engraver then may work with his tools.

Sometimes a feature — particularly a portrait — sometimes the whole of the design in outline is marked or cut on the die through the medium of the pantograph. The pantograph as used for stamps is an instrument for the mechanical copying of a plane figure on a reduced scale, and consists of an arrangement of steel rods coupled to form a pointed parallelogram, on one extended arm of which is a stylus or tracing needle, while a cutting needle or diamond is attached to the juncture of one long and one short side of the parallelogram. By moving the stylus along the grooves of a specially engraved large copy of the design, the engraver, through the medium of the pantograph, cuts the design, proportionately reduced, on the die that is in contact with the diamond. The pantograph was used, for instance, in the production of the dies of the United Nations stamps printed by Thomas De La Rue and Company, Ltd., of which the 1951 20c. is an example. In the accompanying illustration, the engraver is seen using the pantograph in the preparation of the die of the stamp just mentioned. On the table before him is a "model" of the design, and also the specially engraved large copy of the design without the lettering. He holds the stylus between the forefinger and thumb of both hands, and is in process of moving the stylus along one of the grooves, from northeast to southeast. The die is seen in the center of the circular table, held in position by two clips that almost cover the northwest and southeast corners of the die. The diamond-pointed cutting needle is to the left of the clip at the southeast corner of the die.

If a stamp is to be printed in more than one color, usually a separate die must be produced for each differently colored part of the design. In the case

Evolution of Dies for Bi-Colored Relief Printing

No. 1. Unique die proof of the engraver from the official archives. In black, on card. Inscribed "Gravure — 1er etat."

No. 2. Similar to Number 1, inscribed "Gravure — 2e etat."

No. 3. Die proof of center only. In red. Surrounding metal not cut away.

No. 4. Die proof of center and frame. In red and blue. Surrounding metal not cut away.

No. 5. Final state of composite die. Die proof in issued colors. Surrounding metal not cut away but masked during printing.

Three items on card, from the official archives. At left: photographic miniature of artist's drawing, being an essay for 25c value. Next, a rough working (progress) proof from the die, with figures of value 30c, now termed an essay. At right: A proof from the then-finished die, also with figures of value 30c. (Note that inscription "Postes" appears in the center, low to the left of the athlete.) The word "non" ("no") signifies disapproval of this die, and therefore it is now termed an essay.

of a bi-colored stamp, such as USA 1938 Airmail 6c., two dies were required; in the case of a stamp printed in three colors, three dies are needed, and so on. By way of exemplifying the evolution of relief dies in two colors, I illustrate five items that came into existence during the production of the dies from which France 1924 Olympic Games 25c. stemmed.

After the engraving of the die has been completed, it is usual for prints to be made from it either upon India paper or upon thin, often surfaced card. Such a print is termed a "die proof." Because of the special care taken in making a die proof, and because it is made directly from the engraved metal, every line of the design shows with great clarity, and the engraving is seen to its best advantage.

Die proofs, usually, are made on paper appreciably larger than the die itself; and, because of the pressure exerted when printing, the shape of the block or slip of metal itself is, in the case of a recessed die, impressed into the paper (actually the paper is pressed round the outer edges of the die), giving the effect of a colorless frame surrounding the design of the stamp. Sometimes traces of color are to be found on the paper by this frame, caused by ink adhering to and printing from a slight and unintentional irregularity in the surface of the metal.

There is no universally standard practice about the color in which die proofs are printed. Often black is used because its intensity throws up most clearly every fine detail of the engraving on the die. However, frequently colors are used, and sometimes colors approximating those intended to be used for the stamp when issued.

The objects of making die proofs are to enable the engraver to see that his work reproduces as he intended, and for submission to the printers for technical approval, and to the issuing authorities for approval of the design as engraved on the die, and also for record purposes.

At this stage there often come into existence documents of very great philatelic interest; but they rarely become available generally, and even if they do become available they are, usually, unique so that only one person can own any one document. These documents are die proofs bearing annotations signifying either that the engraved die is approved as it is, or that certain corrections or alterations have to be made to the engraving. It follows from the definition of essay, which has already been quoted, that if an engraving is sent back for modification in any particular, what was a die proof becomes *ipso facto* and thenceforth an essay. This point is demonstrated by the accompanying illustration of the strip of three items of the design that ultimately became France 1924 Olympic Games 50c. Although the first item on the card was never anything but an essay, the other two items respectively at one time were properly called a progress proof (or working proof, or engraver's proof) and a die proof; but since the rejection of the design for the 30c. value and the alteration in position of the inscription and other modifications, these two items fall within the definition of, and are termed "essays." This point, in practice, does not cause any real difficulty to philatelists so far as terminology is concerned, because they hardly ever ac-

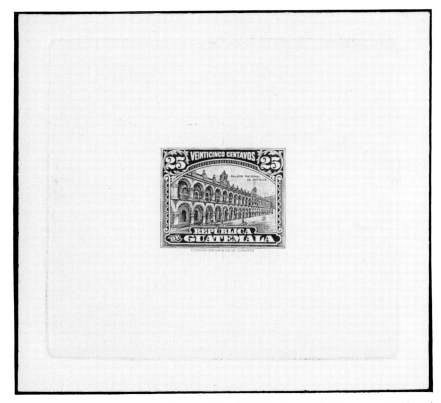

Guatemala: A posthumous die proof by Perkins Bacon & Company, Ltd., of the 1924 (August) 25c.

Feb. 13 1875   BEFORE HARDENING   Feb 19 1875   AFTER HARDENING

Feb. 19 1875   AFTER STRIKING

Royal Mail Steam Packet Company (Private Postage Stamp) 1875 10c. A set of die proofs from three stages of the relief die engraved for De La Rue & Company Ltd.

quire these documents until after the stamps have been issued, and therefore the designs of the stamps regulate the terms to be applied to the earlier documents.

A die proof that is made to enable the work to be judged, approved and recorded, and that is taken at the time when the work has just been completed, is sometimes designated by the term "contemporary die proof." This is to distinguish such a proof, philatelically, from a print from the die made at a much later date, often to supply the requirements of collectors. These late prints are sometimes termed "posthumous die proofs," because they are usually taken after the issue has gone out of use — that is, it is "dead" so far as the stamp-issuing authorities are concerned. Such posthumous die proofs do not have the same degree of interest as contemporary die proofs, but are accepted by many collectors as being legitimate objects of study, and representative of a particular stage of the development of the die. Sometimes posthumous die proofs are the only die proofs available of particular issues. Posthumous die proofs are often, but not necessarily, in color.

After a recessed die has been approved so far as the engraving is concerned the die is, usually, hardened in order that it may be used for the subsequent processes of making the printing base. Usually proofs are taken from the die after it has been hardened. Sometimes, but in rare instances, it is possible to find proofs of the same recessed die with manuscript or printed inscriptions indicating the state of the die, that is, "Before Hardening," and "After Hardening."

Similarly with relief dies; although, in these cases, the addition of "Before

Hardening'' or ''After Hardening'' to the die proof is more usual than not with certain printers. After the relief die has been hardened it is used for making the moulds, a process known as ''striking.'' Proofs from the die have been taken both before and after this process; and again, these proofs usually bear manuscript or printed inscriptions indicating the state of the die, that is, ''Before Striking'' and ''After Striking.'' It would seem that it should be possible to encounter proofs from the same die, each bearing markings of one of the four states, the proofs together making up a set of all four states. However, I cannot recall a single instance of the existence of such a set; three such markings are the most that I have encountered from any one die, either ''After Hardening,'' or ''Before Striking'' being missing from the potential set of four. The reason for this may be that these last two terms are used indifferently and, unless the printers suspected that damage may have occurred subsequent to the die having been proofed after hardening, there would be no point in proofing again before striking, as the die would have been subjected to no intermediate process. Very rarely, die proofs can be found marked ''After Hardening and Before Striking.'' Sometimes, but again in rare instances, a die proof taken ''After Striking,'' bears an indication of the number of moulds that have been struck from the die.

Plate Proofs, Color Trials, Color Proofs

After the dies have been finally approved, the printing bases are made. Various steps in their production, as it affects philatelic interest, are referred to in the chapters devoted to the printing processes. Later in the present chapter reference is made to some of the considerations that affect the make-up of, and the appearance of matter other than mere repetitions of the design on, the printing bases. For the present I continue a consideration of the documents that come into existence before the stamps themselves are printed. These documents are of three types: a print from a printing base — termed philatelically ''plate proof''; a print in a color other than that of the issued stamp — termed philatelically ''color trial''; and a print, for approval of the color, in the color of the issued stamp — termed philatelically ''color proof.''

After the printing base has been manufactured, one or more prints are taken from it in order that the actual result produced by the printing base may be checked and approved; such prints are termed ''plate proofs.'' It frequently happens that such proofs reveal that modification is necessary in a part or parts of the printing base before it will yield uniform and good prints. In these cases, indications of the work necessary are made on the proof by the approving authority; such marked proofs, of considerable philatelic interest, rarely become generally available and, if they are kept at all, form part of the permanent records of the printers.

After the correcting work has been carried out, final plate proofs in color are sometimes marked ''approved,'' or ''print,'' or with some similar authorization by the stamp-issuing authority. A sheet so marked is known as an ''imprimatur,'' a Latin term meaning ''let it be printed.'' In some countries imprimatur sheets are preserved as part of the archives of the stamp-issuing authorities.

It is unnecessary here to detail the steps leading to the production of color trials and color proofs, these terms being almost self-explanatory. However, about the term ''proof'' itself there has been no unanimity of opinion as to meaning, and it may be helpful to set out here the definitions adopted by the Essay-Proof Society:[6]

PROOF — Any impression from an officially approved design die, plate or stone, or a new plate made from the approved die in which the design is exactly like the stamp as officially sold to the public, regardless of the color, kind of paper or material on which it is printed, or any experimental treatment to which it was subjected and not used on stamps sold to the public. Proofs were not sold to the public.

---

[6]*Essay-Proof Journal,* Vol. I, Page 31 (January 1944).

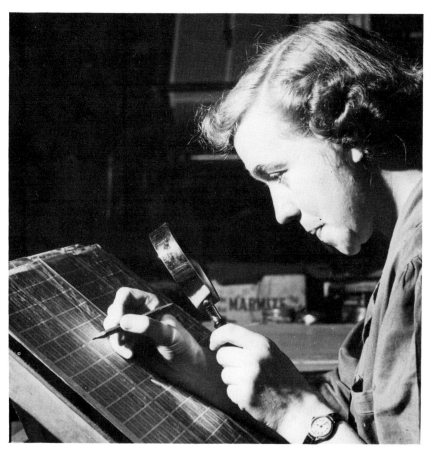

Scrutinizing a plate proof for defects and marking it so that the printing base may be retouched and defects removed. The proof is of a sheet of stamps for eventual issue in books (booklets).

TRIAL COLOR PROOFS — are impressions from the approved design die or plate in any color ink not normal to the issued stamp.

Printing Bases and Printed Sheets

The form, format and lay-out of the printing base depends not only upon the printing process used, but also, of course, upon the end product required by the stamp-issuing authority; such requirements may vary to a great extent and include, for instance, stamps in sheets of differing sizes, and books and rolls or coils of stamps, to mention but three main classes of requirements. In addition to the number and arrangement of the subjects[7] dictated partly by the requirements of the stamp-issuing authority it may also require or permit other matter to appear on the printed sheet. This other matter, which is referred to under the comprehensive term "Plate Markings," may be classified as follows:

1. Markings applied by the printers (a) as a necessary part of the printing or production processes, and as guides; or (b) for the purposes of identification or advertisement.

2. Markings applied by requirement of the stamp-issuing authority (a) as security checks on (i) sheets, or (ii) what would otherwise be areas of unprinted paper; or (b) to assist the postal officials in handling and selling the stamps; or (c) as directions to the users of the stamps; or (d) for advertisement.

The make-up of the printed sheets and printing bases of almost any philatelic country comprises a complete study in itself, and no standard practice obtains. Therefore it is clearly impossible in a work of this nature to deal in detail with every one or even the majority of the different arrangements of stamps on the printing bases and with the devices in addition to stamps that have appeared either joined to or between the stamps themselves or in the margins of the sheets. The most that can usefully be done in this connection is to mention some of the arrangements and types or classes of devices or plate markings that occur; and to list alphabetically some of the terms in use in this connection; thus providing some indication of the existence and extent of such matters generally, together with reasons for the existence of some of those specifically mentioned.

It has been stated, and truly, that many collectors rarely see a complete sheet of stamps; however, not only are sheet and printing base formations of interest, and knowledge of them essential to the student-specialist interested in every facet of stamp production, but some such knowledge in general will often be the means of solving an apparent problem where a collector

---

[7]The term "subject," as referring to a unit of the design on the printing base, does not seem to have wide philatelic employment, but when printing bases generally are being referred to this term has, in my opinion, advantages that are not possessed by terms with specific and limited meanings, such as are "cliche," "electro," "entry," "stereo," and "transfer." The term "subject" is used here and elsewhere in this connection for convenience and generically, irrespective of the process that resulted in the appearance of the design on the printing base, and irrespective of the nature of the printing base itself.

encounters a stamp with an attached or a separate piece of paper perhaps in the form of a stamp and bearing some strange device unlike any stamp ever issued. It is only in very rare instances that philatelists have direct access to a printing base itself for study; the arrangement and lay-out of the subjects and other matter on the bases have been, usually, deduced by students from either whole sheets of the stamps as issued, or reconstructions built up by means of plating and, in some instances, with the aid of information supplied by the printers. In the cases of the older issues of stamps, of which whole sheets were not available, such knowledge had to be pieced together bit by bit, but with more recent issues the collector-conscious stamp-issuing authorities have in many cases made the information readily available when it has not infringed the prime need of security.

A printed sheet is often too large to be handled conveniently; therefore it often comprises several units, and is cut up before delivery to the stamp-issuing authority into these units which are then in the size as sold to the public, and are termed, philatelically, "Post Office Sheets" (or, sometimes — but confusingly — "panes"). The usual post office sheet consists of a regular number of stamps between which are gutters and the whole arrangement is surrounded by margins, known as "Sheet Margins." Many of the markings applied by the printers or by requirement of the stamp-issuing authorities occur in the sheet margins, and are known to philatelists by the generic term "Marginal Markings."

In many instances, post office sheets, instead of comprising stamps set solidly within the sheet margins, are divided into smaller units within those margins; often each smaller unit represents one-quarter the value of the whole sheet. These smaller units are referred to philatelically as "Panes." Often each pane is divided from the next by a space equivalent in height or width to a row or column of stamps; such spaces are termed, philatelically, "gutters," or "pane gutters" and, sometimes, "pane margins."

As a rule the number of stamps in the printed sheet bears a relation to the coinage system of the country issuing the stamps. That is, for instance, in countries using the decimal system, the sheet will contain multiples of ten; for example, the printing bases of USA stamps have been composed of 100, 200, 300 and 400 subjects. And, as another instance, in countries, such as some of those of the British Commonwealth, where the monetary system comprised pence, shillings and pounds, the printing bases of the lower denominations of stamps usually contained a number of subjects to make up one pound (240 pence) or a convenient multiple or fraction of it; for example, the sheets of all the low-value definitive stamps of Great Britain contained 240 stamps. This rule is not universally invariable, and sometimes the reasons for departure from it are unknown or obscure. For example, to quote one instance specifically of such departure: Suez Canal 1868 1c. to 40c. were printed in Paris for use by the French company in Egypt; yet the printing bases for each value contained 120 subjects, and the sheets each comprised 120 stamps; the reason for this is unknown, but the fact has provided an interesting and, perhaps, insoluble puzzle for students.

Usually each sheet or pane contains stamps so arranged in rows and col-

Book or booklet leaf, Great Britain 1954, showing 1d stamps se-tenant with requests to the public.

umns as completely to fill a rectangular area. Sometimes, however, the sheets or panes contain an unusual arrangement of stamps, and in such cases the rows and columns are made regular either theoretically by leaving blank spaces or practically by complementing them with another device. Again to quote specifically one instance: in 1850 the Austrian currency was 60 kreuzer to 1 gulden, and for convenience of accountancy it was therefore decided that the stamps should be issued in units of sixty, and the sheets of Austria 1850 1k. to 9k. each contained sixty stamps. Probably overall printing convenience demanded that the arrangement of subjects should not be six by ten; the units (actually they were "panes") on the printing base each contained eight by eight; so that there were seven complete rows of eight subjects, and the eighth row contained four subjects and four complementary devices each in the form of a diagonal cross; the device occupying what would otherwise be blank paper, and printed in the color of the stamp, is known, in English, as "St. Andrew's Cross." The devices were incorporated for two reasons: to avoid the temptation to forgers afforded by the issue of blank, official paper; and to assist in balancing the inking roller during printing, and so avoid technical printing difficulties.

Similar considerations have led, in many cases, to the incorporation of printed devices in pane gutters.

Many countries issue stamps in small books or booklets, for which special printing bases have to be prepared to meet convenience in production processes. Mention has already been made of this, when I discussed "inverted" watermarks under Watermark Varieties in the chapter entitled "Watermarks." As these books are usually made up to sell at a convenient price, it is often necessary to provide for an odd number of stamps in a booklet page. Frequently, therefore, two measures are resorted to: the booklets sometimes contain stamps of different denominations printed on the one page, and sometimes a page will contain not only stamps but also devices in the form of advertisements or printed matter consisting of advice or memoranda to the public. For example: Great Britain 1954 book of stamps selling at 2s.6d. contained a page comprising three 1d. stamps and three labels, perforated and gummed

135

like the stamps, reading "Please Post Early in the Day," printed in the same color ink and at the same time from the one printing base.

In Belgium, Denmark and Italy, to mention specifically only three other countries, frequently stamp-size advertisements attached to stamps appear on the booklet pages, printed in either the colors of the stamps themselves, or in different colors. Advertisements, in some countries, sometimes appear also in the margins of the post office sheets.

Frequently the printing bases for rolls or coils of stamps, used in vending

Austria 1858, 5 soldi showing the four St. Andrew's crosses. The sheet is in the Austrian Postal Museum at Vienna, the only known sheet of this kind. Also in the Vienna Museum are sheets of the 1850 issue, 240 stamps in four panes of sixty, plus four crosses.

Coils: A machine that separates the columns of stamps in the printed reel of paper and rolls them into coils.

and affixing machines, are specially made, and the stamps are printed in reels instead of in sheets with margins. As coils may contain anything up to about 1,000 stamps, the study of a single coil will often provide a clue to the lay-out of one dimension of the printing base.

Plate Markings and Stamps in Multiples

The alphabetical list that follows contains terms that are in philatelic use mainly in connection with what are known as "plate" markings — that is, markings that appear between stamps or in the margins of the sheets as printed or issued, resulting usually from additions made to the printing bases, whether flat, curved or cylindrical. Plate markings are of differing sizes, and often occupy, in one dimension, more space than a single stamp. It is usual, if the marking is collected and it is marginal, for it to be shown unsevered from the contiguous stamp and either with sufficient adjoined stamps and marginal paper to exhibit the fact that the marginal marking does not appear in the margin beside each stamp, or else to show the complete marginal marking if it extends marginally beyond one stamp. Further, it is the frequent practice to show the position of the marking in relation to the lay-out of the sheet itself; this is accomplished by proving its position — that is (where the marking itself does not appear in one corner of the sheet) by not limiting the stamps and contiguous marking to merely sufficient to show the complete marking but by leaving unseparated a sufficient number of stamps and marginal paper to extend to the nearest corner of the sheet itself. These practices more often than not involve the representation of stamps in multiples; it has, therefore, been thought convenient to include in the alphabetical list that follows, philatelic terms in use in connection with stamps in multiples. It is desirable, again, to emphasize that the list that follows does not pretend to be exhaustive; especially is this so in regard to the terms applicable to plate markings; and I am conscious of the fact that there are few references to specific stamps or issues. Further, in more than a few cases, there are sharp and consequently confusing differences in meanings attached to identical words as used in different English-speaking countries.

Account Letter. A term used to designate a letter, usually forming part only of a combination of letter and number — for instance "A 24" as printed in the color of the stamps in the bottom or left-hand sheet margin of ½d. to 1s. stamps of Great Britain issued between 1887 and 1947 — in connection with public accounting. When in addition to the letter a number appears, the number consists of the last or the last two figures of the year during which they were applied to the sheet. In Britain the letters, or letters and numbers, are more usually termed "Controls" or "Control Letters."

Account letter and number. A positional pair from southwest corner of the sheet, exhibiting "Control" A 11 and coextensive Jubilee line.

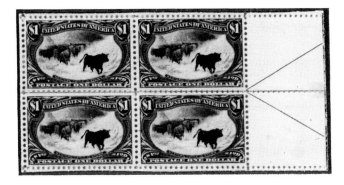

An arrow block.

Arrow. A term used to designate a mark, sometimes three pronged (consisting of two diagonal marks forming an angle bisected by a third mark), sometimes two pronged (diagonal marks only), and sometimes without any diagonal marks, printed in a sheet margin as a guide or register mark for printer or cutter or perforator, or as a guide to dividing or folding the sheet into a convenient fraction.

Block. This is a term used to designate an unseparated group of three or more stamps in more than a single column or row, and comprising less than a pane or paneless sheet. When the block is not regular or square it is properly qualified as "irregular block." Precision demands that, in use, the term be qualified numerically. If the number of stamps in the block is a prime, it must be irregular — for example, "block of three," "block of seven." If the number of stamps is stated to be an even number, the implication is that the block is not irregular. Often the term "block" has been used without justification as though synonymous with "block of four." Other qualifications are often applied to the term "block"; as examples: "Arrow Block" — with attached margin exhibiting an arrow; "Center Gutter Block" — a block centrally incorporating parts of the two wide spaces quartering the printed sheet into panes; "Center Line Block" — a block centrally exhibiting in the gutters parts of the center lines and their point of crossing; "Guide Line Block" or "Line Block" — a block centrally exhibiting in the gutters a part

**Block of three.
Suez Canal
1868 5c.**

of either the vertical or horizontal guide line (see "Guide Mark"); "Traffic Light Block" — a block with attached margin bearing color checks termed "Traffic Lights."

Book, Booklet. Terms used variously by different stamp-issuing authorities to designate the small cotton- or wire-stitched books in which stamps, usually of several denominations, are sold for convenience in carrying and use. Each stamp page comprises, usually, six stamps or a combination of stamps and advertisement or other devices.

Booklet Leaf. Term used to designate a stamp page from a book or booklet. "Booklet Pane" is used as a synonym for "Booklet Leaf," but see "Pane" and "Sheet."

Booklet Sheet. This term is used correctly to designate the unsevered sheet as printed for intended use in books or booklets. Booklet sheets are laid-out differently from the sheets intended for eventual issue as "Post Office Sheets." Booklet sheets of normal size stamps of USA were printed in panes of twenty across and three down with gutters between; the sheets contain either three or six such panes that are destroyed (as panes) when the sheets have been assembled and are cut into booklets.

Center Lines. Term used in connection with the stamps of USA to designate those printed lines, vertical and horizontal, that quarter the printed sheet, and the term has particular reference to their point of crossing — see "Guide Mark."

Center Line Block. Term used in connection with the stamps of USA to designate a block of stamps exhibiting in their gutters the point of crossing of and parts of the "Center Lines."

Column. Term used to designate a vertical strip of stamps, as contrasted with a horizontal strip, which is referred to as a "row." Normally, use of the term "column" in relation to a strip implies that it is of the greatest length possible from a pane or paneless sheet.

Column Totals. Term used to designate the marginal inscription printed on the post office sheets of some countries — Germany, for example — consisting of the face value of the columns of stamps. Usually the first total is that of the left-hand column, the second total above the next column is of the first two columns aggregated, and so on across the sheet.

A center line block.

Consecutive number.

Consecutive Number. This term is used to designate a number or number and letter printed or struck in the margin of a sheet in order to count and distinguish it individually. The term "Sheet Number" is used synonymously with Consecutive Number. In some countries, such as Spain, the Consecutive Number is endorsed on every stamp in the sheet.

Control, Control Letter and Number. The term "Control" has two separate meanings: *first,* especially in Britain, as a synonym for "Account Letter," for which "Control," or the plural "Controls" is usually employed; *second,* as a generic term signifying any security measure in the form of overprinting, endorsement, or perforation employed for the purpose of counteracting pilferage. When used in its second sense, the term is often qualified as "Private Control" to distinguish private from official measures.

Corner. This term, particularly in combination with "block," is used to designate one of the four corners of the pane or paneless sheet. Use of the term "Corner Block" implies that the marginal paper is unsevered from the stamps.

Current Number. Term used, in reference to the stamps of the British Commonwealth, to designate a number appearing on and printed by the printing base, indicating the particular place occupied by that particular printing base in one main sequence of printing bases, irrespective of the face value of the stamps, their purpose, or country of intended use. The Current Number often appears within a frame. Compare and contrast "Plate Number," and distinguish "Account Letter" and "Consecutive Number."

Cylinder Number. The number that appears, for example, in small size figures in the left-hand sheet margins of the stamps of Great Britain printed by rotary photogravure; the number, in the color of the stamps, serves to identify the cylinder from which particular sheets are printed, and also the portion of the cylinder, for the number appears with or without a period which identifies the half of the cylinder, there being more than a single post office sheet on each sheet-printing cylinder. Cylinder Numbers are the equivalent of "Plate Numbers," and where bi-colored or multicolored rotary photogravure printed stamps are issued, two or more cylinder numbers appear in the sheet margins, one for each cylinder, and in the stamp color it prints.

Electric Eye Markings. Term used to designate those particular marginal marks that are made on the printing bases and printed on the sheets of some stamps of USA for the purpose of actuating an electronically controlled mechanical device coupled to or incorporated in the machine that perforates the stamps after they have been printed. The Electric Eye Markings serve mainly to center the perforations in the stamp gutters, and take the form on the printed web of vertical dashes (so-called), or horizontal dashes (called "lines" or "bars"). The terminology of "Electric Eye Markings" has been standardized by reference to their appearance on the printed web irrespective of whether the marking is vertical or horizontal on the post office sheets as issued, and a special dictionary entitled *Electric Eye Terminology* has been published by the Bureau Issues Association.

Guide Line — see "Guide Mark."

Guide Mark. Term used generically to indicate any line, dot, cross, circle, or other symbol serving as a guide during the process of printing or perforating the stamps, or cutting the sheets. In Britain, the terms "Guide Dot" and "Guide Line" both imply that they were made for the purpose of guides during processes preliminary to the actual printing, whereas the object of a "Guide Mark" is to act as a guide during or subsequent to the actual printing. "Register Mark," unqualified, is a synonym for "Guide Mark." In connection with the stamps of USA, "Guide Lines" is used to designate vertical or horizontal lines, in the color of the stamps, that extend wholly or partly across the sheet and often terminate with arrows — see "Arrow."

Gutters. The spaces between the design of one unit and that of the next (whether the unit be a stamp, a pane or a sheet) but only while the units are unsevered. Thus it is possible, in the cases of some printed-sheet formations, to have "Stamp Gutters," "Pane Gutters," and, even, "Sheet Gutters"; but "Printed Sheet Gutters" cannot exist. Often the term "Gutter," unqualified, implies only the spaces between stamps normally and closely set. Compare and distinguish "Margins."

Gutter Dashes. Used, sometimes, to designate those guide marks that, in some cases, appear between panes as guides in separating the panes.

Gutter Ornaments. Term used to designate the ornamentation, often elaborate, always in the color or colors of the stamps, printed in the pane gutters to avoid the issue of substantial quantities of official paper unprinted. See also "Pillar."

Imprint. This term has several philatelic connotations but when allied to the printed sheet, "Imprint" means the name of the printer or the place of printing that appears in the sheet margin. Imprints vary greatly in style and presentation; often the name appears within a framework.

Inscription. In reference to the printed sheet this term, often qualified by "Marginal," is used as a synonym for imprint.

Irregular. In reference to stamps in multiples this term is used to qualify "block," as meaning that the block is not regular or square — see "Block."

Electric eye markings.

Imprints.

Gutter ornament.

Joint Line. This term is used specially to designate the line that results in the stamp gutters because of the ink collecting at and printing from the juncture of two plates curved to form a cylinder.

Jubilee Lines. This term is used to designate the lines in the color or colors of the stamp that appear in the margins of panes or sheets of certain relief printed stamps of Great Britain and the British Commonwealth. Jubilee Lines, when introduced, surrounded each pane, and their purpose was to protect the edge of the subject on the printing base from damage by the inking roller. There are two types of Jubilee Line: continuous, that is, unbroken; or coextensive, that is, a series of short lines, each of the contiguous stamp dimension. The name ''Jubilee'' derives from the sobriquet applied to Great Britain 1887 issue that appeared during the year of but not specially to commemorate Queen Victoria's Jubilee, and the Jubilee Line first appeared with stamps of that year — actually first, experimentally, in a plate of the 1d. of 1881. Similar seeming lines appear in upper and lower margins of sheets of rotary photogravure printed stamps of Great Britain, the purpose being to ensure even inking of the stamps. Modern usage favors employment of the term ''Marginal Rule'' for such markings.

Leaf. Term used to designate a page (of stamps) from a stamp book or booklet.

Line. Term used, generically, to designate any printed linear plate marking. In connection with the stamps of USA this term is an abbreviation of ''Guide Line,'' for which see ''Guide Mark.''

Margins. The area of paper surrounding the design of a detached unit, whether a stamp, a pane or a sheet. Sometimes the term is used as a synonym for ''Gutters,'' especially when qualified in ''Pane Margins.'' ''Gutters'' become ''Margins'' when the units are detached from each other. When pane gutters are perforated by a single central line of perforations and the panes are separated from each other, each of the pane-marginal stamps will have an extended margin, termed ''Wing Margin.'' Compare and distinguish ''Gutters.''

Marginal Marking. Term used generically to refer to any marking printed in the margin of the sheet. Usually the particular type of mark is qualified, as in ''Marginal Guide Marks,'' distinguishing them from guide marks in gutters. Often the word ''Marginal'' is used to qualify other terms, as in ''Marginal Inscription.''

Marginal Rule. Modern usage favors employment of this term to designate what used to be referred to as ''Jubilee Line.'' The modern usage springs from the fallacious concept that the sole meaning of ''line'' was its mathematical sense of a length without breadth or thickness and entirely disregarded the many other uses including ''a long and narrow stroke or mark, traced with a pen, tool, etc. upon a surface.'' Sometimes the term ''Printer's Rule'' is used as though it were a synonym for the term ''Marginal Rule'' in its modern usage.

Millesime. Term used to designate the figure or figures signifying the year in which the stamps were printed. Millesimes appear usually in pane gutters or sheet margins. With stamps manufactured in France, the millesime, consisting of the last figure of the year, appears in the gutters between panes,

Millesime.

or in the lower sheet margin. The term is synonymous in meaning with the figures referred to under "Account Letter."

Miniature Sheet. This term is now used to designate a souvenir specially printed, and usually with wide margins specially inscribed, containing one stamp or a small number of stamps, issued or put on sale, usually to commemorate some event. "Commemorative Sheet" and "Commemoration Sheet" and "Souvenir Sheet" are synonyms. Such sheets are not to be confused with printers' sheets or post office sheets that contain few stamps because of production difficulties or postal requirements, and sometimes termed by stamp collectors "Sheetlets."

Multiple. This word is used as a convenient generic term for referring to a group of stamps unseparated from each other. Usually the smallest multiple is two stamps; in exceptional cases, such as Switzerland (Geneva) 1843 10c. (Double Geneva), and Mecklenburg-Schwerin (Germany) 1856 4-4s., a unit contains a multiple of the fractional stamp.

Pair. Term used to designate two adjacent stamps so printed and not separated from one another. The term is often qualified in use, but unless "vertical pair" is specified, the use of the term "pair" implies "horizontal pair." Further, other qualifications are often applied to such a multiple; as examples: "Joint Line Pair" — a pair exhibiting part of the joint line; "Line Pair" — a pair exhibiting part of the guide line (see "Guide Mark"); "Paste-Up Pair" — a pair exhibiting part of the "Paste-Up."

Pane. This term is used in Britain to mean, exclusively, a multiple forming a unit that (depending upon the printed sheet lay-out) is either surrounded by pane gutters or has a pane gutter on at least one side, and the unit forms part only of a sheet as issued; when a pane is detached from a sheet, if the pane is philatelically complete it must have margins on all sides including (depending upon the printed sheet lay-out) at least one pane margin. In USA the term "pane" is used irrespective of whether the printed sheet contained pane gutters, or the detached pane has any pane margin, and refers to a portion of a sheet as cut for sale at the post offices; so that a pane may be a fraction of a paneless sheet — see "Paneless." Similarly most stamp booklets in USA are printed in sheets containing a certain number of panes that are destroyed during the cutting process, and a leaf from a booklet in USA is termed a "(Booklet) Pane."

Paneless. A term used to designate that form of issued sheets that contains no pane formation, the stamps appearing in continuous rows and columns broken only by the stamp gutters, and forming a unit as sold by post offices. The stamps of USA that are printed from 400-subject plates are printed in paneless sheets that are then cut up into four and sold by post offices in paneless sheets of 100 each; in USA these "sheets" of 100 are termed "panes." See "Booklet Sheet."

Vertical paste-up pair (both sides).

Plate number. Bermuda 1937 Coronation 1d. A corner block of four showing plate number 1B, with register mark in left margin.

Paste-Up. A term used to designate overlapping paper at each place where sheets printed from flat plates have been pasted or gummed together so as to make a long strip that is subsequently rolled into coils or rolls of stamps.

Perforation Guide. Term used to designate any plate marking, marginal or otherwise, that is printed on the sheet for the purpose of assisting registrations during the subsequent perforating process. Perforation guides take many forms; the earliest form was a mere dot or cross, termed ''Pin Mark''; later forms became more complicated in shape, such as the hollow square of Great Britain, and the ''Electric Eye Markings'' of USA.

Pillars, Pillar Blocks. These terms are used to designate a particular type of ornamentation, in the form of repetitions of a narrow, lined, rectangle (hence ''pillar''), printed, for example, in the pane gutters of certain stamps of Great Britain and India partly as a security measure — that is, to prevent unprinted, watermarked paper being readily available for use by forgers.

Plate Markings. Term used generically to designate all markings, marginal or otherwise, that are printed on the sheet by the printing base from which the stamps are printed, irrespective of the object for which particular markings have been made.

Plate Numbers. In relation to plate markings, the term ''Plate Number'' is used, in reference to stamps of the British Commonwealth, to designate the *marginal* number applied to the plate and printed on the sheet that indicates within the country of issue the particular place occupied by that particular plate in the sequence of printing plates made for the particular denomination of stamp for which the plate was made; in this connection, compare and contrast ''Current Number.'' ''Plate Numbers'' on the sheets of stamps of USA are defined in *Scott's Catalogue of United States Stamps Specialized* as ''serial numbers assigned to plates, appearing on one or more margins of the sheet or pane to identify the plate.'' Often, in the cases of stamps printed in more than one color, a separate plate number identifies each plate used in the production of the stamps. See ''Cylinder Number.'' The term ''Plate Number'' has reference also to a feature in the design of some stamps — see the alphabetical list in the chapter entitled ''Stamp Designs.''

Positional Block, Positional Stamp. These terms are used generically to designate any stamp or block that, whether by reason of undetached marginal paper or otherwise, proves its position on the sheet.

Post Office Sheet. Term used to designate a sheet of stamps as sold by the stamp-issuing authority to the public. For a synonym in USA see "Pane."

Printed Sheet. Term used to designate a sheet of stamps as printed. Sometimes the term "Printer's Sheet" is used as a synonym for "Printed Sheet." In the cases of some stamps, printed from cylinders in the web or on continuous reels of paper, no "Printed Sheets," as such, ever exist.

Printer's Imprint — see "Imprint."

Printer's Rule — see "Marginal Rule."

Register Mark. Term used, generically, to designate any marking, marginal or otherwise, that is printed or made on the sheet for the purpose of assisting registration of the sheet in any production process or part process subsequent to the one during which the Register Mark is made. These are three main classes of Register Marks: (1) Printing Register Marks, to ensure correct registration of a second or subsequent color where the stamps are printed in more than one color — such marks often take the form of a short, marginal line; (2) Cutting Register Marks, indicating the places where the printed sheet is to be cut to make up, say, the post office sheets; and (3) Perforation Register Marks — for which see "Perforation Guide." Sometimes the terms "Registration Mark" and "Registry Marking" are used as alternatives to "Register Mark."

Registration Mark, Registry Marking — see "Register Mark."

Rotation Number. Term used to designate the number applied to the sheet for the purpose of checking the sheets of stamp paper. In many cases the Rotation Number is placed on the sheet before it reaches the printer; in other cases the Rotation Number is applied, as the sheet is printed, by an attachment to either the press or the cylinder. Often the term "Sheet Number" is used as a synonym for "Rotation Number," as also is "Consecutive Number."

Row. A horizontal strip of stamps, as contrasted with a vertical strip which is referred to as a "column." Usually, use of the term "row," in relation to a strip implies that it is of the greatest length possible from a pane or paneless sheet.

Selvedge. Term used to designate sheet margins or pane margins of perforated stamps.

Se Tenant. This term, a French expression, means joined to one another, and is used to designate, usually, two different stamps or two different varieties of the same stamp unseparated. In use, the expression is employed, usually, after the word "pair," as in "The 5c. and 2c. in pair *se-tenant.*"

Sheet. In USA this term is used to designate, according to *Scott's Catalogue of United States Stamps Specialized,* in single-color printings, the impression from a plate, and a sheet of bi-colored stamps requires the impressions from two plates. The term "sheet" has several meanings philatelically, and precision demands that in use the term be qualified, as in "Post Office Sheet" and "Printed Sheet." In Britain the use of "sheet" unqualified usually implies "Post Office Sheet," and such sheets may either contain "Panes" or be "Paneless." See also "Miniature Sheet."

Sheet Margin — see "Margins."

Sheet Number — see "Rotation Number."

Tête-bêche.

Single. The expression "a single" is often used in speech and writing when emphasizing the unit of a stamp contrasted with multiples.

Strip. Term used to designate three or more unseparated stamps from the same column or row. Unless "vertical strip" is specified, the use of the term "strip" implies "horizontal strip." Precision demands that, in use, the term be qualified also numerically, as in "vertical strip of four."

Subject. Term used sometimes to designate a stamp in a sheet; and also to refer to the number of stamps in the sheet — as, for instance, in the phrase "400-subject sheets."

Tête-Bêche. This term, a French expression, means head-to-tail, and is used to designate a unit (stamp or pane) so printed that it is inverted in relation to at least one other and adjacent unit. The minimum number of whole stamps that can exhibit the variety *"tête-bêche"* is two — that is, a vertical or horizontal pair, for if the pair is separated, two normal singles result. The variety *tête-bêche* can exist in a strip or a block. A stamp that is only partly inverted in relation to its adjoined neighbor is sometimes referred to as "semi *tête-bêche,*" but is often more accurately described (if, for instance, in pair) as "pair, one stamp sideways."

Traffic Lights. Collectors' term for color check dots intended to assist the printers' checkers in noticing whether all the colors have been printed — one color dot for each color used in printing. Traffic lights were first used in sheet margins of Great Britain 1962 (Nov. 14) National Productivity Year 2½d., 3d. and 1s. 3d. As many as seven traffic lights are not unusual.

Traffic lights.

7. Printing Problems and Varieties

THIS CHAPTER briefly surveys the philatelic interest and problems involved generally in printing, and deals with some philatelic and other terms and varieties that are either common to all printing processes or may be encountered in any printing process. Chapters that follow deal with the types of printing, their characteristics as revealed by the stamps, certain of the printing processes in greater detail, and some of the philatelic terms and varieties peculiar to each process.

Except in special cases, printing is the art or practice of mechanically impressing designs on paper or other material, and the special problem of the stamp printer is to reproduce a small design many times consistently and faithfully, the object being to forestall successful forgery. The philatelic interest in printing lies in its being one of a series of processes used in the production of the stamp. Each printing method, and many of the separate and particular steps involved in each method, present certain characteristics on the printed stamp, and the philatelic problems involved in printing may be stated to comprise:

First: an identification of the basic printing method.

Second: an identification of the particular steps involved in any particular method used in the production of any particular stamp.

Third: an identification of the cause of any apparent variation from the norm.

In this respect a philatelist may be likened, loosely, to a diagnostician who observes certain effects and ascribes, or seeks to ascribe, causes to those effects. Dependent on his or her knowledge, studies, perception, experiences and ability, so he or she will be more or less successful in accurately determining the causes of the symptoms displayed by the stamp. Generally speaking, philatelic problems of printing and their solution require a general knowledge of all printing methods as used for stamps, and also a minute and detailed knowledge of certain processes and part processes.

Within his special problem of reproducing a small design many times consistently and faithfully, the stamp printer labors to produce a good, workmanlike product. He realizes that, in certain processes, some variations between one subject and another are inevitable, and consequently they are to him unobjectionable and of no account. To the philatelist, however, such variations are of considerable importance: Being the inevitable results of the use of the process, they reveal the process itself. Further, the standard of excellence set by the printer and the stamp-issuing authority is based on considerations of security; within narrow limits some variations are permissible and tolerated, and their causes comparatively unimportant. Yet these same variations, viewed from the standpoint of the philatelist and collector, who prizes abnormality above the norm, are not only of interest but also, in some cases, of enhanced value.

Saying that the philatelist and collector prizes abnormality above the norm must not be understood to be saying that he or she regards every variation as of equal interest. Scientifically it is probably true to state that no two stamps, even those contiguous in the sheet or printed consecutively from the same part of the same printing base, are absolutely identical. However, some variations are constant — that is, they are variations in the subject itself — and appear on the printed stamps because the stamps are printed from the subject that varies from the norm, and will continue so to vary either throughout the life of the printing base or until it undergoes some modification; and some variations are inconstant — that is, they are variations caused during the printing from a subject that (for the purposes of this illustration) is a norm, but appear on the printed stamp because of some irregularity during the process of applying the ink, paper or pressure to the printing base.

Within the class of regularly issued stamps, varieties of greatest interest to the student are those which are constant and the result of processes involved in the production or subsequent history of the printing base — for instance, the doubling of the whole or part of the subject, or the inclusion of a wrong subject. Within the same class of stamps, varieties of less interest, with a few exceptions, are those that are inconstant and caused during printing — for instance, a slight movement of the paper resulting in a fortuitous blurring or doubling of the impression. Minute, casual and inconstant imperfections in printing are of no account or interest except in so far as they reveal the printing process used, when that cannot be perceived otherwise.

At the same time there is, often, little relation between, on the one hand, philatelic interest from the point of view of printing, and, on the other hand, market value of the stamp. A common stamp, readily available in large quantities, may make an absorbing and intensely puzzling study for anyone who sets out to discover the full history of its complicated production. A rare and costly stamp may have its simple production so well documented and recorded that little remains to be discovered. An error of color, regularly issued, is prized greatly because of its existence; and it matters little whether the error was the result of carelessness in applying the wrong color ink to the printing base, or of carelessness in including one or more wrong subjects in the printing base. An inverted frame, regularly issued, has its value based on its appearance, not whether it was caused by the inversion of the sheet when the second color was applied, or because the maker of the printing base inserted a subject or part subject upside down. Similarly, certain striking abnormalities, regularly issued, have their values as freaks because of their very conspicuousness.

It cannot be over-emphasized that mere size alone of a variation bears no relation to the philatelic interest. A half-hidden dot the size of a pinpoint may, on some stamps, be of intense interest as providing a clue to one or more of the detailed steps employed in producing the printing base. In other stamps, a dot of the same size, or very much larger and more prominent, is completely insignificant and, therefore, of no philatelic interest whatever. Only study and experience can teach what varieties are significant.

The philatelist, the student-specialist, the intelligent collector, assesses, evaluates, and appreciates each such variation and, for sufficient reason, devotes his or her collection to significant variations only; freaks, if they figure at all in the collection, are labeled for what they are. The uncritical collector seeks to copy the form of such collecting without realizing or bothering to inform himself or herself about the reasons that lie behind the form, and includes in the collection indiscriminately numerous variations insignificant in size and cause — with the result that such collectors have attracted to themselves and their mode of collecting epithets such as "fly marks," "flyspeck," and "dotty." This uncritical searching for and acquisition of flyspecks has led inevitably, in some cases, to enhanced prices being paid for insignificant variations.

One of the problems facing the would-be philatelist, and to some extent even the student-specialist, is how to sort the wheat from the chaff, and how to distinguish between the variation that is significant and the casual printing flaw. Many flaws cannot be other than casual printing flaws; many other variations cannot result from irregularities in printing. Some of these are, as classes, so self-evident that they cannot cause confusion to anyone with even a rudimentary knowledge of printing processes and effects. Others are not so self-evident, and require more detailed knowledge before their causes can be ascribed to them. In other cases, the effects of widely differing causes are similar; and in these cases it is true to state that it is impossible to say, from the study of only a single stamp bearing the variation, what its cause was.

In other words, the problem is one of degree, and many matters that puzzle the tyro cause no hesitation in the mind of the experienced student; and each unexplained variation from the norm presents its own problem that can be solved, if it can be solved at all, only after a consideration of all the relevant facts; and they can be ascertained, often, only by the process known as "plate study" — which begins where "plating" leaves off, and is referred to later in this work.

It may be stated that, to discuss the *effects* of the production as seen on the stamps is to deal with what is readily apparent or self-evident, and calls for an ability to perceive what is visible. Accurate observation is a necessary prerequisite in the student. However, to be able to account for those effects, to deduce accurately or to diagnose their *causes*, is to deal with what is then invisible, and calls not only for a background knowledge of printing processes generally and detailed knowledge of certain steps in those processes, but also, in some cases, a power of logical reasoning. There is no short cut to such learning; if it is to be acquired at all, it is acquired by application and study — as much application and as much study as, in other fields, qualify many people for academic honors.

Modern Influences in Printing

Although there are only four basic printing methods, three if embossing is excluded, there are many variations of them, and many subsidiary variations in the steps taken to construct the printing bases. Some of the comparatively modern variations are of general application, and may be conveniently mentioned, briefly, here. These are: dry printing, rotary printing, and photographic multiplication of the design.

Wet Printing and Dry Printing. These terms refer to the state of the paper at the moment when it is printed. For centuries it was the practice of printers to dampen the paper immediately before printing, the effect being to give a better impression. More modern methods, resulting originally from the need for greater speed in working, dispense with the necessity for printing on dampened paper. The two terms, although seemingly confusing, are simply understandable. The chief philatelic importance of these facts is allied to the shrinking of dampened paper — as mentioned under "Shrinkage" in the alphabetical list to the chapter entitled "Paper." The inevitable variation of paper stock, the variation in the amount of moisture applied to different batches of printing paper, the absence of or inadequate humidity and temperature control and the consequent uneven shrinkage of sheets of stamps (all in fact printed from one printing base) resulted in the stamps varying in size, sometimes one millimeter or more in twenty millimeters. Occasionally, the same printing base has been used for both wet and dry printing, and the resultant stamps, of course, exhibit the differences of size. It should be noted that a stamp produced by wet printing is smaller than a stamp from the same printing base used for dry printing — damp paper is larger than dry paper; the shrinkage occurs, across the grain, during drying.

Flat and Rotary Printing. These terms refer to the characteristics of the printing base. In flat (or "flat-bed" or "flat press") printing, the printing base is flat, and in rotary (or "rotary press") printing, the printing base consists either of one or two plates that have been curved to fit on or around a hollow cylinder, or else of a metal cylinder that rotates during the printing. With flat press printing it is possible to print only on sheets of paper; with rotary printing it is possible to print either on sheets of paper or continuously on the web or reel of paper.[1] For rotary printing from plates, the

---

[1]Exceptions to the generality of these statements exist. For example, over many years, the coil stamps of Great Britain were printed on a web eighteen inches wide by a flat-bed machine specially constructed by Grover, working on a principle similar to that adopted in harrow perforation of stamps perforated "on the web," whereby the web moved a predetermined distance between impressions.

plates are treated after the subjects have been applied. The treatment varies, but in the cases of comparatively thick and steel plates, they are rolled between shaping rollers that impart the desired curve. Because the outer surface of the plate stretches during this curving treatment, any subject on the plate at the time of curving is similarly affected, and each subject increases in dimension along the direction of the curve. Consequently, after a plate has been curved, each subject is appreciably either longer or wider (depending upon its relation to the curve) than it was when first applied to the plate. This increase in dimension is, of course, imparted to the subsequent stamps. There have been many cases in which the same die has been used for constructing both types of printing bases — flat plates, and also plates that have been subsequently curved for rotary printing — and, because of the increase in dimension, the resultant stamps can easily be separated. This difference is well-known in the United States, where many designs have been intaglio printed by both methods. The difference in dimension does not occur when the subject is applied direct to a cylinder or to a pre-curved plate.

Manual or Mechanical and Photographic Multiplication of the Design. In rare cases a design has been drawn or engraved by hand on the printing base separately, as many times as there are stamps on the printed sheet. Apart from those cases, the one-time invariable method of multiplying the design was to undertake the steps that are briefly surveyed in the discussion of the basic printing methods in the chapter entitled "From Design to Issued Sheets": If the stamps were to be intaglio printed, the design was multiplied mechanically by means of the transfer roll; if the stamps were to result from planographic printing, the design was multiplied by the repeated taking of lithographic transfers; and if the stamps were to be relief printed, the design was multiplied by the repeated making of moulds. These processes of mechanical multiplication are all still in widespread use today. However, photography has come more and more into use to replace mechanical multiplication of the design, and is employed in all the basic printing methods. One basis of photographic duplication is the step-and-repeat projection camera, an ingenious instrument of micrometric accuracy, by which an image can be projected on to a large photographically sensitive plate as many times as necessary, with predetermined spacing and alignment. The instrument steps out the necessary exposures for a complete row, alters the vertical position, and then repeats the whole process until the plate is filled. The photographically sensitive plate, after development, contains the repetitions of the designs, and is then used in combination with etching to make a metal printing base. By varying the photographic and etching processes, printing bases can be made for intaglio, planographic and relief printing. In cases in which the same photographic plate is used for the production of different printing bases of the same stamp, the possibility exists that a flaw occurring on the photographic plate will be reproduced on these different printing bases, giving rise to the class of variations termed "photographic master flaw" or "photographic master variety."

Terms and Varieties of Printing Generally

It is important to appreciate the scope of the alphabetical list that follows. No attempt is made to deal with terms and varieties that are peculiar to individual printing processes — those terms and varieties, or some of them, will be found in the later, more restricted, chapters. The list that follows here deals, in the main, with generalities — that is to say, with terms and varieties of general application so far as printing is concerned. Some of the terms are common to all the printing processes, and examples of stamps with the variations listed may readily (or rarely) be encountered as products of any of the processes. All of the terms are common to at least two different printing processes.

Even within the limits of its scope, the alphabetical list that follows does not pretend to be complete but includes the majority of such terms and varieties most likely to be encountered in a reasonably long philatelic life.

Albino. This term, unqualified, is used to designate a complete impression uninked. Such an impression can occur in various ways: because printing takes place when no ink has been applied to the printing base; because two sheets of paper are fed into the press at the same time, and only one sheet receives the ink from the printing base, the other sheet receiving only the pressure of the design through the thickness of the paper. Usually, albino impressions are errors, and are most frequently encountered in embossed stamps that should be partly colored — especially in postal stationery; but albino impressions from most of the printing processes are known of stamps, overprints and surcharges — see "Double Impression." An instance of an intaglio albino impression deliberately printed and issued occurs in France 1942 (Oct. 12) Tricolor Legion 1f.20+8f.80, where the stamps were printed in sheets containing rows of five impressions each, the top two rows blue, the center row albino and the bottom two rows red. Many instances are known of partial albino impressions of sheets and stamps, where corners of sheets have been folded over, or pieces of paper have become interposed between the printing base and the sheet of paper, have partly masked the

Partial albino. A "confetti" variety, showing both the stamp partially albino, and the scrap of paper (bearing the portions of the design missing from the stamp) that caused the variety. Note that this scrap of paper bears printing in both colors, proving that the "confetti" adhered to the sheet while both colors were applied, and became detached afterward.

design, and have then become detached from the stamp; examples of such partial albino impressions, called *Confetti* varieties (because of the circular shape of the errant paper — which came from the sheet margin and was punched out to make a perforation register aid), are to be found on many British Commonwealth stamps, including, for instance, South-West Africa 1937 Coronation 6d. See also "Center Omitted," "Value Omitted." The term "albino" is used only in cases such as those quoted; in many embossed stamps at least part of the design is intentionally uncolored, and the term used for such cases is "embossed in colorless relief."

Background Inverted. This term, almost self-explanatory, is used to designate stamps exhibiting the printing of the background or groundwork inverted in relation to the rest of the stamp. Instances are to be found, for example, in Russia 1883-98 2k. Usually the inversion of the background is through error. Omissions of background are known.

Bi-Colored. Term used to designate a stamp so printed that the design is composed of two parts, each in a separate color. For stamps of which the design is composed of two parts, one in color, the other colorless, the term most aptly used in this connection is "printed from double plates."

Blanket Print — see "Set-Off."

Block. In relation to printing bases, the term "block" is used sometimes as a synonym for "subject," but is used more precisely when qualified, as in "line block" and "half-tone block," to designate a subject made by photo-etching processes for relief printing.

Center Inverted. Term used to designate an error in which the center appears inverted in relation to the frame. The error occurs mainly in bi-colored stamps,

Center inverted. Jamaica 1919-21 1s, so-called "center inverted." Specialists contend that the variety is "frame inverted" because the watermark is upright in relation to the center, which was printed first.

Center omitted. Virgin Islands 1867-68 1s. "Missing Virgin."

**Center inverted. USA 1918 Air 24c.,
Inverted Jenny.**

and the term is often a misnomer because, in the majority of cases, the center was printed first, the frame having been applied from a second printing base; in such cases, the error is that of the printer inserting the partly printed sheet upside down in the press for the second operation. Because of their striking appearance, and usually because few sheets escape the vigilance of the printer's checkers, such errors mostly command very high prices. Numerous instances occur, and are to be found, for example, in USA 1869 15c., USA 1918 Air 24c. and India 1854 4a. Inverted Head to mention only two philatelic countries that have issued classic "inverted centers" as these errors are often termed. Because of their doubtful status and ample supply, Haiti 1904 Independence Centenary 2c. to 50c. *center inverted* are inexpensively available, as are Nyassa 1901 2½r. to 300r. *center inverted.* A classic and exceptional instance of inversion in a monochrome stamp occurs in Western Australia 1854 4d. Inverted Swan, where the inversion resulted from the faulty workmanship of the lithographer who placed the frame the wrong way up when preparing a fresh printing base. See also "Frame Inverted" and "Inverted."

Center Misplaced. This term is used sometimes to designate the result of faulty registration during bi-color or multicolor printing where the center does not fall within the usually narrow limits intended for its accommodation on the face of the stamp. Usually the term is a misnomer because, in the majority of cases, the center is printed first, the frame being applied from a second printing base — as was the case, for random example, with Great Britain 1902-11 1½d. Small variations in registration are of frequent occurrence and no importance, but occasionally wide divergences are encountered, having escaped the vigilance of the printer's checkers, and are sought after as freaks.

Center Omitted. This term is self-explanatory. Because the omission is so strikingly obvious, such varieties comprise printer's waste, or, occasionally, proofs. The most common cause of the variety is a sheet partially albino because of the interposition of extraneous paper. A classic instance of such a variety (not a partial albino) attaining catalogue rank is to be found in Virgin Islands 1867-68 1s. *central figure omitted* (the so-called "Missing Virgin"), but that value was never thus issued.

Center Transposed. This term is used to designate a very rare type of error, the printing on to a sheet (already containing a part of a design) of a center or frame, as the case may be, intended for a different stamp, so as to produce a stamp with a center not intended for the frame. One instance of such transposi-

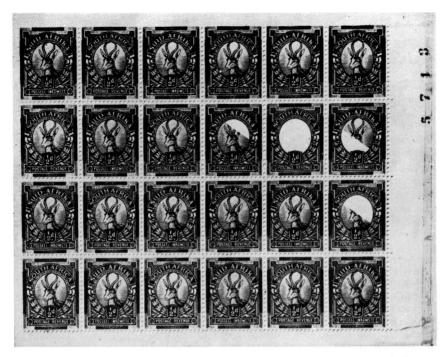

Center omitted. South Africa ½d. A block of stamps illustrating a partial albino of the printing for the centers, pinpointing how the variety "Center Omitted" (row 2, stamp No. 5 in this instance) is sometimes caused. The centers of three of the adjacent stamps bear partial albino impressions, and it is possible clearly to envisage the shape of the strip of extraneous paper that became interposed between the sheet and the printing base when the centers were printed.

tion is to be found in Canal Zone 1909-21 5c. (where the overprint occurs on Panama 1909-15 5c.) with the head of Hernandez de Cordoba intended for the 2c., instead of the head of Justo Arosemena intended for the 5c. A similar error occurs in Sardinia (Italy) 1861 Newspaper Stamp where the 1c. frame is known with the central numeral "2" and the 2c. frame is known with the central numeral "1." Another, somewhat more recent, example exists in Falkland Islands 1964

Center transposed. Falkland Islands 1964 (December 8) 6d. with center transposed and showing *HMS Glasgow* of the 2½d. together with normal 6d. showing *HMS Kent*.

(Dec. 8) 50th Anniversary of the Battle of the Falkland Islands 6d. picturing not, as it should, *HMS Kent* but *HMS Glasgow*, which was normal for the 2½d. The centers were printed first and the frames afterward, and a sheet intended for the 2½d. stamps became mixed up with the sheets intended for the 6d. stamps.

Cliche. Term used, loosely, to designate a subject on a printing base, and often synonymously with "Subject." It is used correctly to designate only a subject produced by polytyping for relief printing.

Confetti. A particular type of partial albino — see "Albino."

Cracks. This term, or its singular, is used to designate the effect on stamps caused by printing from a base that has developed a flaw in the form of a crack in the printing surface. The flaw appears on the stamps as a colored line in intaglio printing, and an uncolored line in relief printing, or as a group of such lines. Cracks develop from many causes, of which some have generic characteristics, enabling the cause to be deduced; some cracks are caused by faulty material, some by faulty processing or surfacing, and others by physical damage to the printing base. Stamps exhibiting such varieties are of interest in that they reveal part of the history of the printing base. Often the term "cracked plate" is used as a synonym for "cracks."

Damage. This term, of vague significance when employed in connection with the design of a stamp, is used to designate any flaw resulting from external force or inherent defect in a printing base, causing abnormality in the stamp as printed. The use of the term implies that the effect occurs on every similarly positioned stamp printed subsequent to the damage having happened to the printing base until it is repaired — see "Repair." Damage takes an infinite variety of forms — see "Cracks," which is one form; see "Scratches," which is another. According to the printing method used, and the stage in the process at which the damage occurred, the stamp will exhibit colored or colorless flaws in the design. Such varieties must not, of course, be confused with "damaged" stamps, where the damage to the stamp has occurred after printing. See also "Flaw."

Design-Type — see "Die" (3).

Die. This term has several quite distinct meanings philatelically. (1) In its primary sense, die, unqualified, means the piece of metal or other material on which appears the engraved or otherwise applied design, subsequently multiplied to form the printing base. In the cases of issues where the individual stamps differ from each other, so far as design is concerned, only in the denomination, the first die to be produced is, sometimes, one without any symbols of value, called an "undenominated die." This die is termed, so far as production is concerned, the "master die," the "mother die," the "original die," or the "parent die." From this master die, reproductions are made: in their undenominated state, these are sometimes termed "slips"; when the symbols of value have been added, the dies are, often, termed "duty dies," "subsidiary dies," or "working dies," and from these stem the printing bases for the various stamps. Sometimes the term "intermediate die" is used, and this is often the case where the original die was denominated; the intermediate die is undenominated, and from it the subsidiary dies are made.

(2) When the term "die" qualifies the term "flaw," it signifies a flaw or variation necessarily present on every multiplication from that die because the flaw or variation was present on the die itself, thus forming an integral, although perhaps unintended, feature of the design.

(3) When the design on a die or a reproduction from it has been subjected to minor amendment and subsequently used to multiply the amended design on

___2d Great Britain 1912-22___

Die I. Inner frameline at top and sides close to solid of background. Four complete lines of shading between top of head and oval frameline.

Die II. Inner frameline farther from solid of background. Three lines between top of head and oval.

another printing base, stamps printed from it are often referred to as from a "re-engraved die"; and sometimes the two, slightly differing, designs are referred to as "Die I" and "Die II." Broadly speaking, the term "re-engraved die" is used where substantial differences are apparent, and "Die I, Die II" is used where the differences are only very slight — but see "Recut," etc. Numerous examples of such variations are to be found; as instances: Great Britain 1912-22 2d. Die I (issued in August 1912), and Die II (issued in September 1921); and Jamaica 1929-32 1d. Die I and Die II. Sometimes such variations are termed "Type I and Type II," in the sense of meaning "Design Type I" etc. — but see "Type." Occasionally, minor amendments to the printing base give rise to varieties that are misnamed "sub-die," or are given a letter following the die number; for example, Australia 1937-49 3d. Die I, Die Ia (where the white flaw joining the letters "TA" of "POSTAGE" was retouched manually on every subject on the printing base, and therefore, the use of "die" in the term "Die Ia" is strictly inaccurate), and Die II.

Double Impression. This term has several meanings philatelically. (1) In its widest sense it is used to designate a stamp that exhibits linear duplication in all or some part of the design, irrespective of the cause of such duplication. Such duplication can result from any one or more of many different causes, and in most cases it is impossible accurately to diagnose the cause from examination of a single example of a stamp unless the particular cause on that particular stamp is known. Therefore, the term double impression in its widest sense is useful when it is unnecessary, undesirable, or impossible to diagnose the cause of the duplication and to state whether it occurred on the printing base or during the process of printing.

(2) In a more restricted sense, "double impression" is used to designate a stamp that exhibits linear duplication in the design because the stamp has been actually

Double impressions. India 1882-87 2c. and Mauritius 1848 2d.

printed twice instead of once. Sometimes this occurs through the printer erroneously passing the sheet twice through the press. Usually, however, the sheet is passed through the press deliberately on the second occasion, the reason being that the impression on the first occasion was out of register or too lightly inked or too faintly printed to provide a satisfactory stamp; it is, therefore, printed again to save paper. Often the cause is apparent on the finished stamp — one impression is light, the other normal, and the whole stamp appears darker than a stamp normally printed. Instances of such double impressions are numerous; three examples are to found in USA 1873 3c, India 1882-87 ½a., 2a., and New Zealand 1900 6d. Instances occur where the first impression is albino and the second impression is normal — for example, Pakistan 1952 (August) Centenary of Indian Postage Stamps 3a., in which the albino impression is inverted in relation to the normal impression. See also "Printed Both Sides." In this sense, "double impression" is not limited to duplication of the entire design; in bi-colored stamps either the center or the frame can be double, and very numerous instances are known of double overprints. An instance of a double impression of a center, the second impression being normally inked, the first being lightly printed and inverted in relation to the second, is to be found, for example, in Romania 1869 50b. In use in this sense of the term, double impression varieties should be distinguished from varieties resulting from a flapping, cockling or movement of the paper during printing — see "Slurred Print." However, this (because of the difficulty of diagnosis) is sometimes a counsel of perfection, and the standard catalogues fail to distinguish between the various causes. See also "Set-Off."

Double Plates. Term used to designate two printing bases used to produce a monochrome or bi-colored stamp. Sometimes the printing bases are of the same printing method — for example, relief printing as used for the British Commonwealth keytypes; sometimes the printing bases are of different printing processes — for example, relief printing and embossing as used for Sardinia (Italy) 1861 Newspaper Stamps 1c. and 2c.

Double Print. (1) This term, in a particular sense, is used specially to designate Sweden 1872-77 20ö., where the stamp was printed originally in a pale orange or dull yellow color that faded badly, and the sheets were printed for a second time in vermilion over the first color, being issued in 1876; so carefully was this second printing applied in register over the first that the variety was not discovered until years after it was issued. (2) In a more general sense "double print" is used indifferently with "Double Impression" in its secondary or more restricted meaning.

Dry Print. This term has the adverb "too" ("excessively") implied at the beginning of the phrase, and is used to designate a stamp exhibiting uncolored lines, spots or other areas, caused by wet printing upon paper insufficiently dampened. The term must be sharply distinguished from "dry printing" — that is, printing upon intentionally dry paper; see "Wet Printing and Dry Printing." Such varieties are inconstant, and they vary greatly in appearance in individual cases. Accurate diagnosis is, often, extremely difficult. See "Peeled Ink."

Electro. This term, an abbreviation of "electrotype," is correctly used to designate a subject or group of subjects made by depositing copper galvanically in a mould of wax or other material.

Entry. This term is correctly used to designate a subject made by rocking a transfer roll on to a printing base, usually for intaglio printing, but sometimes for relief printing.

Error of color. Thailand (Siam) 1940, a 5s subject in the printing base of the 3s value.

Error. In connection with printing, the term "error" is used to designate any accidental and marked deviation from the intended norm, and *inter alia* includes: "Background Inverted," background omitted, "Center Inverted," "Center Omitted," "Center Transposed," " Error of Color" of stamp or overprint, "Error of Value" or inscription caused through accident or oversight in any stage subsequent to designing, "Frame Inverted, "Frame Omitted," "Inverted" subject resulting from mistake, "Overprint (or surcharge) Omitted," "Substituted Subject," "Transposed Subject" and "Value Omitted."

Error of Color. This term is, broadly speaking, used to designate a stamp printed in a color intended for a different stamp. There are two principal ways in which this can occur: (1) The inclusion of a wrong subject in a printing base. This forms the largest class of errors of color, and they can be found in many countries. Classic examples occur in Cape of Good Hope 1861 Woodblocks 1d. and 4d., where a wrong subject was incorporated in each printing base; another well-known example, USA 1917 5c. in the color of the 2c. is illustrated earlier in this work in the chapter entitled "Aims of Collecting"; a third instance is to be found, for example, in Thailand (Siam) 1940 5s. in the color of the 3s. (2) The inking of a printing base with the wrong color and the consequent printing of a sheet or more in the wrong or an undesired color; for example Tobago 1896 1s. in brown orange instead of olive bistre. In Heligoland 1873 ¼s., a bi-colored stamp, an error of color occurred when those parts of the design that should have been printed in rose were printed in green and *vice versa*, giving rise to the variety *colors reversed*. (3) A third manner in which an apparent error of color can occur is that, occasionally, a stamp has been specially printed in a color different from the regular stamp in order to provide a distinctive stamp to be overprinted as a provisional; for example South Australia 1867-79 4d., usually printed in violet, was printed in deep blue or ultramarine for issue in 1879 surcharged "3 Pence"; by error, the surcharge was omitted on some of these blue stamps, resulting in an apparent error of color, but being actually the error "surcharge omitted."

Error of Value. Term used to designate a rare class of error, wherein through oversight a stamp has two different face values. This has been caused by the incorporation in the printing base of a differently denominated subject that has been only partly amended. As instances: in Sweden 1876-78 20ö. *Tretio error*, one damaged subject on the printing base was replaced by a subject in which the figures "30" had been removed and "20" substituted, but the words of value,

Error of value. Left, Sweden
1876-78 20 öre *Tretio error.* Right,
Lubeck 1859 2s *Zwei ein halb*
error.

"Tretio Ore," were left unamended; in Lubeck 1859 2s. *Zwei ein halb error,* when
the printing base of the 2s. stamp was constructed, by error two subjects of the
2½s. value were incorporated, the figures "2½" were replaced by "2" but the
words of value "Zwei Ein Halb" were left unamended; and in Santander
(Colombia) 1886 10c. *Cinco error,* during the preparation of the printing base for
the 10c., a transfer of part of a design for that value was completed by error with
the transfer inscribed "cinco centavos" instead of "diez centavos." Stamps printed
from double plates exist with the center value differing from that of the frame
— see "Center Transposed." Sometimes the more compendious term "Error of
Inscription" is used to designate such errors, but this term covers equally gram-
matical errors and other mistakes and misprints such as occur, as instances: in
British Guiana 1898-99 2c. surcharged "Two Gents"; and Niue 1903 1s. *"Thief
error,"* where what should be the surcharge "Taha e Sileni" (one shilling) appears as "Tahae Sileni" (thief shilling).

Flaw. A term of vague significance that has several quite distinct meanings
philatelically. A. When employed in connection with the design of a stamp, "flaw"
is used to designate any blemish in the stamp's design resulting from or occasioned by the process of printing — see "Variety" (3). In this sense of the term,
the flaw does not adversely affect the collectible condition of the stamp. Flaws
are constant and non-recurring, or recurring, or inconstant.

(1a) Constant flaws result from damage to or inherent defect in the printing
base or as result of some defect in the process of constructing the printing base,
and reproduce on every sheet printed from the plate until their cause is remedied.
When a constant flaw occurs in only one position on the printing base, the term
"non-recurring" is employed; and in this sense the term "flaw" is sometimes
appropriately used synonymously with "Damage," and the term is often qualified
to "plate flaw." Plate flaws are infinitely various, some prominent, some minute;
they are particularly popular with collectors when the flaws result in some oddi-
ty or seeming error in wording or figures on the stamp, such as occurs, for instance, in Great Britain 1912-22 1½d., where the words of value appear as "Three
Halfpencf" instead of "Three Halfpence," and in Germany 1948 700th Anniversary of Cologne Cathedral 12pf. +8pf. where the dates appear as "1948-1948"
instead of "1248-1948."

(1b) The term "flaw" is used also synonymously with the characteristics of
"Type" in its sense of designating the blemishes occurring in a design when
multiplied by certain printing processes. In this sense the term "recurring" is
employed. When the particular origin of these flaws is known, the term is often
qualified in use for precision; for example, "primary flaws" when they result
from the first multiplication of the die or its equivalent; "secondary flaws" when
they result from multiplication of the unit that comprises the first multiplication
of the die or its equivalent, and aggregate with the primary flaws; and "tertiary
flaws" when they result from multiplication of the unit that contains the second-

Plate flaw. A constant flaw that alters the figure "2" to "9" on the lower right-hand stamp.

ary flaws and primary flaws. And, independently of these (primary, secondary and tertiary), those constant flaws that occur for the first time on the printing base are termed, for precision "(constant) printing flaws" — see "Repair."

(1c) The term "die flaw," or more shortly "die," is used in a particular sense — see "Die" (2).

(2) It is substantially correct to state that inconstant flaws do not reproduce on any except the sheet on which they occur, and result from adventitious circumstances causing some irregularity during the process of applying the ink, paper or pressure to the printing base; such circumstances include, for example, unwelcome presence of dust or grit that causes minute, extraneous and casual areas of color on a sheet of stamps; and the casual presence of pieces of paper that cause partial albino impressions; and the presence of oil or grease spots that cause parts of the design not to reproduce; and air bubbles that have similar effects. Some non-recurring flaws are neither entirely constant nor entirely inconstant — that is, they appear on several or numerous sheets printed consecutively, and then, on later sheets, either become fainter and fainter or do not appear at all. Flaws of this nature (for example, caused on a recess-printing plate by a scratch that becomes less prominent because the surface of the plate is slowly worn away by the abrasive action of wiping; or on any plate by impacted dirt or dried ink that is subsequently removed) are termed "semi-constant."

B. When employed in a wider sense, the term "flaw" includes any blemish in a stamp resulting from or occasioned by any process of production of the stamp. Normally such blemishes adversely affect a stamp's collectible condition, because they usually result in some damage to the stamp itself, as distinct from damage to its design before or during printing.

C. The term "flaw" is used also, distinctly, in relation to a stamp's collectible condition, as designating some blemish after production.

Frame Inverted. This term is correctly used to designate a stamp of which the frame is inverted in relation to the frames and centers of the other stamps in the

Frame inverted. Western Australia 1854 4d, with frame inverted — the famous Inverted Swan, of which only fourteen examples are known.

sheet, constituting a variation on the printing base. In bi-colored stamps, where the frame and center are inverted in relation to each other because the sheet has been placed incorrectly in the press for the second operation, it is usually the centers that are printed first, but these varieties are usually termed "center inverted" although "frame inverted" would be technically more accurate — see "Center Inverted," where an example of a true *frame inverted* in a monochrome stamp is quoted. Examples of bi-colored stamps with inverted frame as errors are: Spain 1865 12c. *frame inverted,* and 1867-68 25m. *frame inverted;* and Brazil 1891 100r. *frame inverted.*

Frame Omitted. This term is self-explanatory. Because the omission is so strikingly obvious, such varieties comprise printer's waste, or, occasionally, proofs. The most common cause of the variety is a sheet partially albino because of the interposition of extraneous paper. Instances are to be found, for example, in Union of South Africa 1930-45 1d. *frame omitted.*

Impression. This term, nearly always qualified, is used in appropriate cases to designate the effects that result from printing from separable states of wear of the same printing base. Where a printing base is subject during printing to wear that shows progressively in the stamps printed from it, the stamps are referred to by comparative classifications applied to the printing base. By way of illustrating such use of the term, I instance the four classes into which have been grouped Mauritius 1848 Post Paid 1d. and 2d. — that is "earliest impressions," "early impressions," "intermediate impressions," and "worn impressions"; as wear is gradual, and printing bases are, normally, continuously printed from, the classes usually overlap. See "State." Often the term "plate" is used in place

Impression. Mauritius 1848 Post Paid 2d. From left to right: Earliest impression, early impression, intermediate impression, worn impression.

of "impression," as in "worn plate." In many cases only one comparative term is used, and its choice depends upon what is normal for the particular stamp; use of the term implies that the other state is more usually encountered; for example, USA 1898 *Regular* 5c. *worn plate*, Great Britain 1840 1d. *worn plate*. In a similar manner the term "impression" is often qualified by terms such as "good," "clear," "coarse" and "poor" — for example Greece 1870, 1876 (Paris print), 1876 (Athens print) and 1889-95, respectively. Compare and distinguish "Printing" in its secondary sense.

Inverted. This term in use nearly always qualifies some other term such as "Background," "Center," "Frame," "Overprint," which are referred to in this alphabetical listing under those headings. Often the varieties and errors are referred to in speech and writing by placing the word "inverted" before the appropriate noun, as in "inverted center," "inverted head" and "Inverted Swan." Other instances of inversion within designs occur: such as that of the side panels in Egypt 1874-75 5p. (which are normal — that is, they occur on all stamps) and the stamp of Spain 1876 4/4c. of which examples are known showing one-quarter stamp inverted in relation to the other three-quarters (and these examples are abnormal, that is, the inversion occurred through error). Inversions occur of whole subjects on the printing base, giving rise to the varieties "Tête-Bêche" in pairs at least. Apart from cases where the inversion is of large numbers of subjects deliberately made to meet some production demand, as for making stamp books (or because the press was not large enough to accommodate a full sheet of paper — as, for example, in New South Wales 1850-51 Sydney Views 2d.), there are cases where the inversion has been unintentional, occurring in only one or two subjects on the printing base; such inversions are often termed "errors," whether or not the inversion was the result of mistake, and are keenly sought after in pairs or larger multiples by collectors. Among the instances of such inversion may be mentioned as a classic example of an error Finland 1875-85 20p. tête-bêche pair, and as a classic example of deliberate inversion, France 1849-50 20c. tête-bêche pair. A rare case of an inversion by error occurs in Sweden 1920-34 Coil Stamps 10ö tête-bêche pair. There the stamps were printed from a cylinder composed of two curved plates joined to make the cylinder; by mistake one of these plates was inserted the wrong way around, giving rise to two different types of tête-bêche pairs, one with the lions head-to-head, the other with them tail-to-tail, each pair exhibiting a joint line.

Kiss Print. This term is used, sometimes, to designate a variety exhibiting linear duplication in the design caused by the paper flapping against the inked printing base either before or after impression; and, in this sense, is used synonymously with the more striking effects of "Slurred Print." This sense of the term must be sharply differentiated from "kiss printing," which is used by printers to designate a mode of printing whereby the paper is only lightly pressed on to the printing base, the two being brought into as light contact as possible consistent with satisfactory impression (see Page 201).

Lay-Out. This term is used in reference to the arrangement of the subjects on the printing base, and, consequently, the overall appearance of a printed sheet — see "Printed Sheet." In reference to individual sheets, such as "Post Office Sheets," sometimes the terms "Lay-Out," "Make-Up" and "Setting" are used synonymously in the general sense of overall arrangement. See "Subject."

Make-Ready. This term is used in reference to the preparation made by the printer, after the printing base has been fitted in the press, to ensure that a satisfactory impression results over all the printed sheet when the press is operated. Make-ready comprises local adjustments of pressure; these adjustments are effected in various ways: by placing packing, sometimes a whole sheet of paper, sometimes only a scrap, often more than one layer thick (a) under a mounted plate (to bring it up to printing height) — termed "underlay"; (b) between a plate and its mount — termed "interlay"; and (c) between the back of the paper to be printed and that part of the press that provides the pressure — termed "overlay"; other forms of "make-ready" include the use of a blanket of felt or other material to provide some resilience in the pressure.

Make-Up — see "Lay-Out."

Matrix. This term is used to designate a counterpart, usually of the die, sometimes of the printing base. In intaglio printing, the roller die is sometimes referred to as the matrix; in relief printing, the mould or subject-punch is the matrix. See "Punch."

Mirror Print. Term used to designate an impression so made that it reads from right-to-left instead of from left-to-right. Very few instances of true mirror prints are known where the cause was the result of error. Prussia (Germany) 1866 10sgr. and 30sgr. and other instances mentioned under "Gold-beaters' Skin" in the alphabetical list to the chapter entitled "Paper," are examples of true mirror prints deliberately so made. Other examples are to be found in Turkey 1863 1p. *design reversed;* in Mafeking (Cape of Good Hope) 1900 3d. *design reversed;* and in USA Confederate States Mount Lebanon 5c.; in all of which cases the mirror printing was the result of error. Partial mirror prints are known, such as New-foundland 1910 Guy 6c. Type I, with the "Z" of "Colonization" reversed. Most set-offs are mirror prints in the sense that they are reversed — see "Set-Off."

Mirror print. Turkey 1863 20p, design reversed.

Monochrome. Term used to designate a stamp printed in a single color, irrespective of the number of operations involved, and irrespective of whether the center was printed at the same time as the frame. For stamps printed in two operations, the term most aptly used in this connection is "printed from double plates."

Multicolored. Term used to designate a stamp so printed that the design is composed of three or more parts each in a separate color. Some stamps have been printed in many colors: as instances — Colombia 1947 Orchids 1c. to 10c. mostly in five colors each; Dominican Republic 1946-47 Waterfall 1c. to 50c. in which each value contains different arrangements of the same five colors; Honduras 1937 150th Anniversary of U.S. Constitution 46c. in five colors; and Tikhvin (Russian Zemstvo) 1891 in six colors. Many modern issues of USA and Great Britain among other stamp-issuing countries are printed in multicolor.

Offset. This term is used correctly to designate a printing process in which the designs are printed first on to a rubber-covered cylinder from which they are printed on to the paper. Sometimes the term is used loosely as a synonym for ''set-off'' — see ''Set-Off.''

Overprint Omitted. This term is self-explanatory. The main cause of the error is misplacement of the sheet during overprinting so that some stamps escape the overprint while it appears elsewhere, where it was not intended — for example, in the sheet margins. In cases in which the overprinting is done to only part of the sheet at an operation, and then the sheet is moved so that another part may be overprinted, misplacement may result not only in the error ''overprint omitted,'' but also in the complementary error ''overprint double.'' Instances of both these errors are to be found, for example, in Cyprus 1880 1d. (plate 208); of course, because the basic stamp was that of Great Britain, the only satisfactory method of showing the error of omission, unused, is to have it in at least a vertical pair, one stamp with the overprint omitted, the other stamp with the overprint normal — if it were detached, the error would appear no different from the normal stamp of Great Britain 1864 1d. (plate 208). In the case of the Cyprus errors, the overprint was omitted from the first row (lettered AA to AL) and appears double on the eleventh row (lettered KA to KL). Similar circumstances account for similar errors of surcharge; for example St. Helena 1868 1s. *surcharge omitted,* and the same stamp with *surcharge double.*

Palimpsest. In relation to printing this term is used generically to designate a stamp that exhibits characteristics showing that the printing base was previously used for a different subject, which was imperfectly removed from the printing base. Instances of such palimpsests are to be found, for example, in Union of South Africa 1930 ½d. on booklet stamps printed from a particular portion of the cylinder and exhibiting duplications of the Springbok's horns and ears; in Suez Canal 1868 1c., 5c. and 40c., nearly every type shows part of the figures of value ''20,'' proving the palimpsest-like origin of these designs; in Great Britain 1941-42 2½d. from cylinder 146, the control O/44 reveals traces of an imperfectly removed ''N/43.'' Further, for example, in Mexico 1874-83 25c., some stamps show quite clearly traces of the 10c. design, and thus that the plate had previously contained stamps of that denomination; and in Mexico 1884 1c. on some stamps appear traces of designs that had previously been entered at right angles to the stamps — one of the most extraordinary cases of ''palimpsests'' on record.

Overprint double. A vertical strip exhibiting two errors — the topmost stamp shows ''surcharge double,'' the lowest stamp shows ''surcharge omitted.''

Peeled ink. Switzerland 1941 80c. line-engraved. The lower frameline, which should be solid color, has uncolored patches in it, so have the upper parts of the right diagonals of the letters "V" and "A" of "Helvetia." The extreme outer framelines at the left and right should be solid color (as they are at their upper extremities), but they, too, have uncolored patches in them; and, particularly near the lower frameline each appears as two thin, separate lines. Those colorless patches have been caused by ink which has failed to adhere to the paper. Varieties such as this are inconstant.

Peeled Ink. Term used to designate a variety exhibiting an uncolored flaw or uncolored flaws resulting from non-adherence to or blistering or peeling from the stamp as printed of ink that should have been present. The term is used generically to describe such varieties when the cause is uncertain — and the causes are often difficult to diagnose. Peeled ink varieties are inconstant, and vary greatly in appearance, but often take the form of a series of comparatively small uncolored spots, frequently within the width of a single line that should be solid color. See "Dry Print" and "Wet Print." Sometimes the term "Stripped Color" is used loosely as synonymous with "Peeled Ink" to designate a class of uncolored flaws, but the better usage is to distinguish the terms, reserving "Stripped Color" for a class of colored flaws. See "Stripped Color."

Photographic Master Flaw or Variety. These terms are used to describe a class of variation from the intended norm that occurs on the large photographic plate bearing the photographic repetitions of the design, either positive or negative, used in many different modern processes for producing printing bases — for example, the diapositive of photogravure, or the multinegative of some photolithographic procedures. As a class such variations include, for example, "Double Exposure" that results in the thickening of the numeral on South Africa 1948-49 postage due 2d. (interior cylinder 28, row 16, stamp No. 5); the "Diapositive Flaw" that results in the uncolored area to the right of the head on Great Britain 1952 1½d. (cylinder 15, stamp No. 217); and the "blister" that results in the excess of color below the "S" on USA 1918-20 3c. ("offset printing" plate 8799, upper right pane, stamp No. 6). In numerous instances, the photographic master is used during the production of many different printing bases, with the result that the identical flaw appears on all the different plates and cylinders — unless the photographic master is photographically retouched, in which event printing bases made subsequently may, and usually do, reveal the effects of the photographic retouching, in the form of a different sort of variation from the intended norm; for instance, compare the effects, with the examples given above, of stamps from the same positions on G.B. cylinder 6 and USA plate 9289.

Plate. This term unqualified is often used as a synonym for "printing base," irrespective of whether it is flat, curved or cylindrical. Sometimes, when terms such as "plate flaw" and "plate variety" are employed, the word "plate" is used irrespective of the material of which the printing base is composed. Use of these terms implies that the abnormality, being present on the printing base, will continue to be reproduced until it is altered or repaired. In some processes, a plate is made and then reproductions are made from it; in such cases, the first is called the "master plate" (which, in some instances, is not used for printing), and the reproductions are called "working plates" and are used for printing. The term "faced plate" is used to designate a plate that has been given a thin protective coating of hard metal (or "surfacing") to resist wear during printing — for example, steel, nickel and chromium have been used. Sometimes the term "plate" is preceded by a qualifying term, the two being used to designate stamps printed from a printing base in a certain condition — for example "cracked plate," when it designates "cracks"; "worn plate," when it used in the sense referred to under "Impression"; "cleaned plate," when it designates stamps exhibiting a clear, fine impression as a result of printing after the printing base has had removed from it the dried ink and dirt that have accumulated from previous use — instances of such varieties are to be found in Greece 1868-69 (Athens Print from cleaned plates) 1 l. to 60 l.

Plug. This term is used in two senses: (1) to designate a piece of metal or other substance (bearing part of a design) that can be fitted into and removed from, usually, a die for use as required — as in the case of multiplying a design for stamps in a series, where one stamp differs from another in the series only in symbols of value; for example, Australia 1913-48 1d. to 1s.; or Great Britain 1873-79 3d., plates 11 to 20, where each stamp differed from the other merely in having different corner letters and different plate numbers; and (2) to designate a piece of metal used to fill a hole drilled in a die or subject for the purpose of retouching — when the retouch is termed a "plug retouch." See "Retouch."

Printed Both Sides. This term is used to designate a stamp that bears a print of the design on the front and the back of the paper. Both impressions must, of course, be normal in the sense that they read from left-to-right, as distinct from one normal and one reversed, that is, reading from right-to-left — see "Set-Off." The usual cause of the variety is that the sheet when first printed was out of register or too lightly inked to provide a satisfactory stamp; the sheet is, therefore, turned over and printed again to save paper. Usually the impression at the back is misplaced in relation to the impression on the front. Numerous instances of the variety are known: for example USA 1861-66 2c. (Black Jack) variety *printed both sides*, and USA Confederate States General Issues 1861 10c. variety *printed both sides* and Great Britain 1881 1d. (16 dots) variety *printed both sides*, and Mexico 1861 2r. variety *printed both sides*. A rare class of printed both sides variety is instanced in Venezuela 1880 issue, in which the 5c., 10c. and 25c. were all printed in yellow; the 25c. is known with an impression of the 5c. on the back, and the 50c. is known with an impression of the 25c. on the back. Occasionally the variety printed on both sides occurs by error, the sheet being put through the press twice by accident, and the variety occurs in overprints and surcharges; an example, chosen at random, is to be found in Chile 1900-01 5c. on 30c. *surcharged on front and back*. Occasionally only part of the design is found on one side of the paper, and the other part of the design on the other side. Salvador 1911 Centenary of Insurrection 5c. (with watermark) is known with the head printed on the back of the stamp.

Printer's Waste. Term used to designate sheets faultily or only partly printed that ought to have been rejected either by the printers or printer's checkers and ought not to have been allowed to get into circulation. In its widest sense, the term includes most of the major errors and varieties. However, philatelically a distinction is drawn between, on the one hand, those items which, having escaped the vigilance of the checkers, have been issued and sold by the stamp-issuing authorities as normal stamps in the normal way over the post office counter, and, on the other hand, such items that have come on to the market through other channels. The regularly issued items are highly regarded and eagerly sought after; the others are held in low regard. Occasionally real doubt exists whether a particular item falls into one class or the other; but, especially nowadays, regularly issued major errors and varieties are usually so well-publicized by their fortunate discoverers that the mere existence of doubt is a ground for suspicion that the item has become available through other than regular channels in the normal course of sale.

Printing. This term, in its primary sense, is used to designate the art or practice of mechanically reproducing a design on paper; and, in special rare cases, the production of stamps by photographic printing. In its secondary sense, "Printing" is used to designate the aggregate number of sheets or items produced as a batch, or, perhaps, consignment. In this secondary sense, different printings are, in many cases, distinguishable by slight and sometimes considerable variation in color of the stamps; and they are sometimes referred to by qualifying the term with an appropriate adjective, such as "early printings," "late printing." Compare and distinguish "Impression."

Printing Base. This is used as a convenient term when it is unnecessary to distinguish the form or composition of the material from which the actual printing takes place, and the term embraces cylinders, plates, stones and other such material, and assemblages of blocks, clichés, etc.

Punch. A term used generically in reference to a tool employed for applying by direct pressure (as distinct from rocking) part of a design to a piece of metal prepared to receive it. In stamp manufacture, widely differing forms of punches have been employed. They may be classified as follows: (1) for use as a step in producing a die — in which case the punch usually takes the form of a counterpart of the whole or part of the design (as opposed to lettering) and comprises a "die-matrix" specially made for use during manufacture of the die, and coming into existence before the die is completed; (2) for use as a step in multiplying the design after the die has been completed, and comprising a counterpart of the die, being a "subject-matrix" — see "Matrix"; (3) for use in adding, usually, letters to an incomplete design, and comprising a "letter-punch." Perhaps the most frequent use has been made of letter-punches, which were employed, for instance, in Great Britain 1840 1d. for punching recesses into the lower corners of each subject on the plate to form the colored corner letters, and, for example, 1867-73 1s., plates 4 to 7, for punching recesses into the four corners and the center frame of each subject on the plate to form uncolored corner letters and plate numbers.

Recut, Redrawn, Re-Engraved, Retouched. In connection with the die or its equivalent, these terms are all of vague significance, and are used for designs that differ more or less in detail because, after a printing base has been produced and stamps have been printed from it, either (1) the die from which that printing base stemmed has been altered by manual or mechanical work (or the manual or mechanical work is effected to a reproduction made from that die or its equivalent), or (2) an entirely new die or its equivalent is made, and the altered or new die is used to produce a new printing base from which stamps are printed. These terms, as used in the principal catalogues, do not reflect the amount or nature of the work carried out to effect the differences in the various dies, and

170

in different cases the terms are used as though they were interchangeable and synonyms which, in the main, they must now be regarded as being when used in connection with the dies. If any distinction is to be found, it is that the term "redrawn" is used mainly where there are substantial differences caused by omission or alteration of some subsidiary feature of the design; as, for instance, in Argentine 1935-51 1p. issued in 1936 and issued redrawn the same year. Also, the term "re-engraved" is frequently used when all the lines of the design have been affected, while "recut" and "retouched" are often used when only some of the lines have been affected. These uses of the terms "recut" and "retouched" must be sharply distinguished from their uses in connection with alterations or repairs effected to a particular subject on the printing base. Compare and distinguish "Repair."

Registration. In relation to printing, this term is used mainly to designate the positioning of a part of a design in relation to another part of the same design, when the two parts have been printed on the paper at different operations or by different cylinders on a web passing between sets of them in banks of massive, modern, multicolor presses. Questions of registration during printing arise usually in bi-colored and multicolored stamps, and the question arises for each color subsequent to the first. When a part of the design falls within the usually narrow limits left and intended for its accommodation, the stamp printing is said to be "in register"; if any part is outside those limits, it is said to be "out of register." See "Center Misplaced." Occasionally a question of registration arises in monochrome stamps — that is to say, when double plates are used and the center is printed separately from the frame; for example, Straits Settlements 1937-41 2c. (Die I), printed from double plates. See also "Register Mark" in the alphabetical list to the chapter entitled "From Design to Issued Sheets."

Repair. In relation to printing, this term is used to designate a stamp exhibiting the effects of remedying damage to the printing base or a subject or subjects on it; compare and distinguish "Recut, etc." The terms "recut" and "retouch" are often used synonymously with "repair," but have wider connotations in that a "recut" or a "retouch" may be made to remedy a flaw resulting from causes other than damage. See "Damage"; see also "Flaw," "Plug" and "Repaired Impression." Just as there are numerous different effects resulting from damage and there are many kinds of flaws, so there are many different effects on stamps resulting from different kinds of repairs; and in each variation of each different printing process, various kinds of repairs and retouches are made. These uses of the term must, of course, be distinguished from its use in connection with the stamp itself. A "repaired" stamp has had the repair effected for the purpose of improving its apparent condition or to disguise some defect that renders the stamp less desirable as a collectible item.

Repaired Impression. This term is used by some students to designate the stamp resulting from a subject that has been restored some time after the printing base has been used for printing stamps. This excludes from the category of repairs all operations carried out on the printing base before such printing, and implies the existence of at least two states of the stamp under consideration — a first or original state before repair, and a second state following repair. See "State."

Retouch — see "Recut etc."; "Repair."

Scratches. This term, or its singular, is used to designate the effect on stamps caused by printing from a base that has developed a flaw from being abraided with a sharp instrument or by a piece of grit so that a fine line is scored across the printing surface. Use of the term implies that the effect occurs on every similarly

171

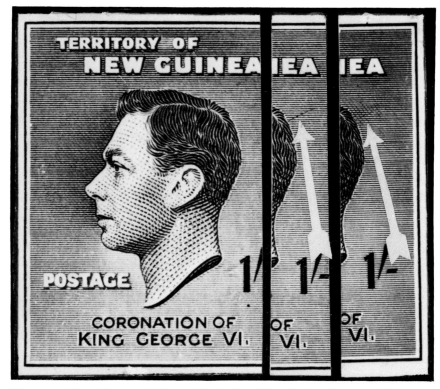

Damage and repair — typical examples in intaglio printing, discovered by H.F. Johnson in 1937. This illustration shows parts of stamps printed from three states of a printing base — that used for New Guinea 1937 Coronation 1s., subject 21 on sheets printed from plate 1B. At the left is the first state, showing the stamp as first printed; in the center is the second state, after damage had occurred to the subject in the form of a line standing out diagonally from the back of the head; at the right is the third state after the subject had been repaired. The effect of the damage has been reduced, parts of the horizontal lines of the background have been thickened, and several diagonal lines have been emphasized (they are otherwise almost invisible) across what remains of the damage. On the actual stamps, further damage, which was not repaired, can be traced in the hair, beginning about three millimeters above the earhole, and extending diagonally upward toward, but stopping short of, the back of the head. A further state, intermediate between the first and the second, was discovered also by H.F. Johnson; in this intermediate state, what later becomes the diagonal line of the second state is no more than a dot or very short line projecting from the back of the head. (The photographs from which the illustration was made vary minutely in size.)

positioned stamp printed subsequent to the scratch occurring, until the printing base is repaired; but, in intaglio printing, a scratch may disappear from the printing base, as printing proceeds, because of the abrasive action involved in wiping. Often the term "scratched plate" is used as a synonym for scratches. In intaglio printing, a scratch appears in color on the stamp; in relief printing, a scratch appears colorless on the stamp; in planographic printing, a scratch usually appears in color on the stamp.

Set. In relation to printing this term is used with numerical qualification to indicate the number of subjects on the printing base — for example "240 set" indicates a printing base comprising 240 subjects. Sometimes the term "set solid" is used as a synonym for "Paneless," and to distinguish such a formation from one set in panes. See also "Setting."

Set-Off. This term is used correctly to designate an additional unintended impression or part impression of the stamp design on the face or back of a stamp, caused by wet printing ink coming into contact with the surface that bears the additional impression. Most commonly a "set-off" appears on the back of a stamp, and the most frequent cause is that the sheet has been forced into close contact with another sheet of freshly printed stamps before the ink is dry. It is a characteristic of most set-offs that the design is reversed, that is, it reads from right-to-left — compare and distinguish "Printed Both Sides"; also see "Mirror Print." Frequently a set-off is slightly out of register or key with the normal impression. It is readily understandable that, in the case described above, the set-off would occur on the back of the second sheet, the ink coming from the face of the first sheet. However, if a part of the second sheet became folded outward before it came into contact with the first sheet, a double set-off might occur — that is, the ink from the outward folded part of the face of the second sheet would set-off on to the corresponding part of the face of the first sheet, while the ink from the face of the first sheet would set-off partly on the back and partly on

Set-off. The word "Nigeria," the upper frameline and part of the crown appear, reversed, almost centrally on a diagonal (southwest to northeast) of the normally printed stamp. The set-off is partly masked by the cancellation.

Set-off. Great Britain 1959-68 2s,6d printed by De La Rue. A remarkable example, from the northeast corner of the sheet, of the design completely set-off so that the reversed image seems to come from the northwest sheet corner. The set-off is on the gummed side of the paper and slightly out of register with the design printed on the proper side of the paper. [Photo: Phillips, London (Auctioneers)]

the face (the outward folded portions) of the second sheet; and in such a case the set-offs on the faces of both sheets would be out of alignment with the normal impressions, depending upon the nature of the fold in the second sheet.

Another frequent cause of a set-off is that, by error, the press operates without a sheet of paper in it, and the ink prints upon the tympan material or backing of the press, normally masked by the sheet of paper to be printed; when the press is then operated with a sheet of paper in position it acquires two impressions — the one normal, from the inked subjects on the printing base, the other abnormal (reversed, reading from right-to-left) from the ink inadvertently deposited on the tympan material or backing. Such a set-off is sometimes termed a "blanket print"; and it is characteristic of such a blanket print that both it and the normal impression are in absolute register or key, but, of course, on different sides of the paper. On rare occasions this blanket print itself gives rise to a set-off on the sheet previously printed, and this type of set-off, exceptionally, reads normally — that is, from left-to-right; because of this characteristic, the first sheet bears one normally printed impression and one normally reading set-off blanket print; and it is very difficult, sometimes impossible, to distinguish such a variety from a "Double Impression" or a "Slurred Print." Sometimes the term "offset" is used loosely as a synonym for "set-off." See "Stripped Color."

Setting. Term used primarily to designate a particular arrangement of individually identifiable subjects on a printing base, but also correctly used to identify any particular arrangement of subjects. Most frequently the term is used in reference to the arrangement of the printing base when it is composed of separate units (such as a separate *stereo* of each design, or separate castings of each overprint) that are clamped together in a form. Although the particular arrangement of the units may be upset by their being removed from the form, they remain individually identifiable, and can be reassembled; and then, the arrangement being different, they would be referred to as "in a different setting," or the reference would be that "the plate was subject to re-setting." Frequently, the particular arrangements are referred to as "first setting," "second setting," and so on; or "Setting I," "Setting II," etc. In its secondary sense, the term is used synonymously with "Set," as in "the setting was in two rows repeated three times in the sheet" in a reference to the arrangement of the surcharge for Rhodesia 1917 (August) ½d. on 1d. See "State"; see also "Lay-Out."

Slurred Print. Term used to designate a stamp exhibiting in all or part of the design linear duplication caused by the paper cockling, flapping or moving during the actual printing. Slurred prints sometimes exhibit smudging of the ink, and in such cases diagnosis is usually easy and certain. Often, however, doubling is readily apparent, and diagnosis difficult — see "Double Impression." The term "slur" is used often as a synonym for slurred print. Slurs are, of course, not confined to basic stamps, and are often encountered in overprints and surcharges.

State. Term used in referring to separately identifiable conditions of a printing base; employed particularly when referring to stamps printed from these separately identifiable conditions. For example: if a printing base is printed from, then a subject on it is damaged and subsequently repaired — the first state of the printing base is the undamaged state; stamps exhibiting the effects of the damage are referred to as having been printed from the second state; and those exhibiting the results of the repair are referred to as being printed from the third state. If a subsequent repair is made to the same subject, a fourth state occurs; and so on. See also "Impression," "Repair," "Repaired Impression," and "Setting."

Stereo. This term, an abbreviation of "stereotype," is correctly used to designate a subject or group of subjects made by casting metal in a mould of *papier-maché*, or plaster or other material.

Stripped Color. This term is used precisely to designate a variety exhibiting an area or areas, usually blurred or indefinite, of unusual color caused by the wet or damp ink of previously printed stamps being deposited upon some part of the machine producing them (for example, the perforating head), and being subsequently re-deposited in part upon a different portion of the same or another sheet or reel of stamps. Sometimes such depositing ("stripping") and re-depositing results in the appearance of a shadowy outline of part or all of the design. Sometimes a comparatively clear "impression" is made by the stripped color, as in the cases of certain United States stamps printed on the presses incorporating precancel overprinting units, where the stripping occurs usually on a brass roller, but is removed from this by a felt pad, occasionally removed for replacement during a run of the machine, when the ink of either or both the precancel and stamps is re-deposited on the web. Such impressions are sometimes termed "set-offs" — see "Set-Off." Stripped color varieties are inconstant and fortuitous, but because of their cause may appear repeatedly. Sometimes the term "stripped color" (colored flaw) is used loosely as being synonymous with "Peeled Ink" (uncolored flaw), doubtless because of the analogy between stripping and peeling, but the better usage is to distinguish the terms.

Subject. In relation to printing, this term is used to designate a unit of the design on the printing base, irrespective of the process that resulted in the appearance of the design on the printing base and irrespective of the nature of the printing base itself. The term "subject" embraces a "cliché," an "electro," an "entry," a half-tone block, a line block, a "stereo," a "transfer" and other such units. The term is used also in connection with multiples of stamps — see the alphabetical list in the chapter entitled "From Design to Issued Sheets."

Substituted Subject. This term is used to designate the replacement on the printing base of a, usually damaged, subject by another. "Substituted Subject" gave rise to the Swedish *"Tretio error"* — see "Error of Value." Often the terms "substituted cliché" and "substituted transfer" are used; usually the substitution is properly made by the printer, and no error occurs, but the fact that the substitution has been effected can be remarked because stamps printed subsequently from the relevant position on the printing base differ from those printed earlier, either as being in a different type [see "Type" (1)], or otherwise.

Transfer. This term has two quite distinct uses, apart from its use as a verb. In relation to intaglio printing, the term is used in connection with the roller, as in "transfer roll," the disk of metal used for the purpose of multiplying the design on to the plate or cylinder. In relation to planographic printing, the term is used in connection with the special paper that receives the design from the original die or its equivalent; the paper is called "transfer paper." When it bears the design it is called "a transfer"; and sometimes also the subject or group of subjects on the planographic printing base is termed "a transfer," or "a group transfer." See "Bloc-Report."

Transposed Subject. This term is used to designate a rare class of error in which a subject for one printing base is inserted by error in another printing base. The most frequent effect of such an error is that a stamp of one value is printed in sheets of a different value — see "Error of Color" (1). Another effect of the error of transposition is that a stamp of one country is printed in sheets of a different country; in such cases usually the error can be recognized as such only if it is se-tenant with the normal stamp. Examples are to be found in Cape Verde 1877 40r. *se-tenant* with Mozambique, and Turkey 1881-84 1pi. *se-tenant* with Eastern Rumelia. Similar occurrences account for some errors of surcharge; for example Morocco (Great Britain) Spanish Zone 1935 10 centimos on 1d. *se-tenant* with the same basic stamp similarly overprinted but surcharged "10 centimes."

Type. This term has several quite distinct meanings philatelically. (1) In relation to the philatelic study of printing processes, the term "type" is used to designate a stamp exhibiting flaws or characteristics that, in certain processes, result from multiplication of the design — see "Flaw," **A** (1b). In this sense, types occur for example in lithography and electrotyping and stereotyping, when the printing base is built up in stages by multiplying a unit that itself consists of multiplications of the original. The primary flaws give rise to "types"; the secondary flaws give rise to "sub-types"; and the tertiary flaws give rise to "sub-sub-types." In this sense, the term "type" is inappropriate to line engraving, in which such types do not occur, nor do they occur when the design is multiplied photographically by step-and-repeat exposures of one and the same photographic image. However, in some cases (as in Cape of Good Hope 1853 6d. for line engraved stamps, and in Great Britain 1935 Silver Jubilee 1½d. for photogravure stamps), multiplication of the design is effected from a roller or master negative that itself comprises more than one subject, and each such subject bears identifiable characteristics. In such cases, exceptionally, the term "type" is, sometimes, used to classify the multiplications — being used in sense (2). (2) In a more general sense, the term "type" is used synonymously with a particular sense of "die"; see "Die" (3). (3) In a still more general sense the term "type" is used to designate a representative design, such as a "Keytype." (4) The term "type" is used also in the special sense of style of lettering — see "Type" in the alphabetical list to Chapter 5, "Stamp Design."

Value Omitted. This term is self-explanatory. Because the omission is usually so strikingly obvious, such varieties often comprise printer's waste or, occasionally, proofs. The most common cause of the variety is a sheet partially albino because of the interposition of extraneous paper; an example of a variety so caused and regularly issued is to be found, for instance, in Netherlands 1926-39 (9c) *value omitted.* Other examples of stamps with value omitted are to be found, for instance, in Cook Islands 1902 (2d.), Gibraltar 1889 (10c.), and Gold Coast 1883-91 (2d.). Occasionally, as in the case of the monochrome stamp of Victoria 1850 Half Length (2d.) *value omitted,* the omission results from a defective subject on the printing base.

An unusual occurrence accounts for Great Britain 1976 (June 30) Roses — Royal National Rose Society centenary, "Sweet Briar" (13p) *value omitted.* The stamp was printed by photogravure in six colors by Harrison & Sons Ltd. That involved use of a separate printing cylinder for each color.

The denomination was printed from the black cylinder and, so far as concerns the stamp design, that cylinder bore 200 repetitions in two double panes of fifty of only the denomination "13p" and the words "Sweet Briar." The cylinder was chromium-plated.

After some printing had been carried out, and while the cylinders were at press, a flaw developed on the black cylinder near the denomination on the ninth stamp in the first row of the upper pane. The printers' method of correcting the flaw — described as "a spot (that) came up" — was to deposit copper into the recessed cells near the flaw, thus filling the chromium-plated cells of the denomination to non-printing height, and then to correct the flaw.

Transposed subject. Above, Cape Verde 1877, 40r, se-tenant with Mozambique. Right, Morocco (Great Britain) Spanish Zone, 1935, 10 centimos on 1d se-tenant with error "10 centimes."

Value omitted. Bottom left, the result of a partial albino, Netherlands 1926–39 (9c) se-tenant with normal. Above, Cook Islands, 1902 (2d). Top left, Gibraltar 1889 (10c).

Value omitted. Great Britain 1976 (June 30) Roses, "Sweet Briar" (13p) *value omitted* with normal stamp at right for comparison. (Photo: B. Alan Ltd.)

Ideally, the copper deposited into the cells is removed before a cylinder thus treated is returned to press. However, the black cylinder was returned to press with the copper still filling the cells of the denomination. Printing continued, with the result that some sheets contained one valueless stamp. When the error was noticed, the offending stamp was removed by hand from most sheets. Nevertheless, a few sheets escaped scrutiny, and the three recorded examples provide philately with examples of an unusual oversight. (For details of cylinder preparation, see Chapter 9, Intaglio Printing — II: Gravure.)

Variety. This term has numerous different philatelic meanings. (1) In relation to stamps generally the term is used as a synonym for ''stamp,'' and in several other of the normal dictionary meanings. In this sense, the term ''major variety'' is often used to designate every officially approved and issued stamp; to distinguish other variations and distinctions that have been noted by philatelists, the comparative term ''minor variety'' is often used.

(2) In relation to particular stamps the term ''variety'' means a stamp that differs from the norm; and in this sense ''variety'' includes every error — that is to say, all errors are varieties, but not every variety is an error.

(3) In a special sense in relation to printing, the term ''variety'' means any stamp that differs from every other stamp because of characteristics imparted by the method and process of printing; in this sense, varieties are sharply differentiated into ''constant varieties'' and ''inconstant varieties.'' A constant variety is one that occurs on every stamp printed from the particular position on the printing base that gives rise to the variety; and includes, for instance, all recurring flaws — see ''Flaw,'' **A** (1a). An inconstant variety is one that occurs because of some temporary circumstance affecting only the particular stamp or sheet of stamps on which the inconstant variety appears; and includes, for instance, all inconstant flaws — see ''Flaw,'' **A** (2) — and other variations from the norm such as ''Albino'' (all partial albino impressions), ''Center Inverted'' and ''Frames Inverted'' (in bi-colored stamps), and ''Printed Both Sides.'' Broadly it may be said that to the student of production, constant varieties are of importance however insignificant their abnormality, while inconstant varieties are of no more than passing interest, no matter how striking their appearance. The terms ''major variety'' and ''minor variety'' and ''error'' are used loosely and inexactly to give a semblance of grading to stamps, and they cannot be related to the terms ''constant variety'' and ''inconstant variety''; for example, Jamaica 1919-21 1s. *frame inverted* is an inconstant variety, but it is an error and is termed a major variety. Broadly (and in contradistinction to the viewpoint of the student of production in relation to constant and inconstant varieties), it may be said that to the collector, major varieties are of importance and desirable while minor varieties are of no more than passing interest.

Wet Print. This term has the adverb ''too'' (''excessively'') implied at the beginning of the phrase, and is used to designate a stamp exhibiting uncolored lines, spots or other areas caused by wet printing upon paper excessively dampened. The term must be sharply distinguished from ''wet printing'' — that is, printing on normally dampened paper — see the explanation of ''Wet Printing and Dry Printing'' earlier in this chapter. Because the paper is dampened too much, the oil in the ink is repelled by the excessive moisture, and particles of color fail to adhere, although traces are sometimes visible as stains where they were pressed into the paper. Sometimes the excessive moisture causes the color to suffuse the paper, resulting in ''pseudo-colored paper.'' Such varieties are, of course, inconstant, and they vary greatly in appearance in individual cases. Accurate diagnosis is, often, extremely difficult — see ''Peeled Ink.''

8. Printing Characteristics

IN THE PREVIOUS CHAPTER, I stated that, of the philatelic problems involved in printing, the first is an identification of the basic printing method. The basic printing methods, which are briefly surveyed in the chapter entitled ''From Design to Issued Sheets,'' are four in number: intaglio, planographic, relief and embossing. These printing methods will be considered in greater detail in subsequent chapters; for the present, attention is devoted to the characteristic appearances of stamps printed by the different methods.

Intaglio Printing

Historically the first printing method used for postage stamps was intaglio printing. In the days of 1840, intaglio printing was confined to line engraving, that is, printing from recessed portions of the plate, the recesses having been cut or engraved line-by-line, dot-by-dot into the substance of the metal of the die. This method is still in very great and widespread use today; for example, the majority of U.S. adhesive stamps have been produced by it.

Modern developments of intaglio printing are the photogravure and rotary photogravure processes, in which the ink is held in and transferred to the paper from cells of varying depths — the cells having been made on the printing base by a combination of photography and etching. This process, historically, was first used for government-issued postage stamps in 1914 by Bavaria, then for French Morocco 1923-27; and since the mid-1920s has been the method used to produce very many postage stamps throughout the world.

Intaglio printing has, thus, two main branches: line engraving on the one hand, and photogravure and rotary photogravure on the other. The characteristic appearances of the stamps produced by these branches of intaglio printing, however, have nothing in common.

A line-engraved stamp is readily identifiable as such because the ink in the lines of the design is proud, that is to say, it stands up from the surface of the paper. Also, to a greater or less extent, the paper at the back of the stamp is indented in the colored lines of the design because the paper has been forced by pressure into the recesses of the printing base. The outlines of each line or colored portion of the design are usually definite, clear and sharp. However, nowadays, the one-time unique characteristic of proudness of design of a line-engraved recess-printed stamp is no longer by itself a sure guide to that printing method. A technique known as ''thermography'' (heat printing, or heat raising) enables a design to be raised from the paper surface.

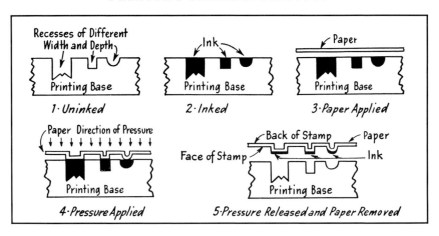

Recesses of Different Width and Depth

Printing Base

1· Uninked

Ink

Printing Base

2· Inked

Paper

Printing Base

3· Paper Applied

Paper Direction of Pressure

Printing Base

4· Pressure Applied

Back of Stamp   Paper

Face of Stamp   Ink

Printing Base

5· Pressure Released and Paper Removed

Line engraving.

Nevertheless, thermography does not result in the paper distortion at the back, and the raised lines lack the sharpness of those resulting from line engraving. Consider also the characteristics imparted by die stamping.

Under magnification the colored portions of a line-engraved recess-printed stamp can clearly be seen to be standing up from the paper, and in the cases of most such stamps, this proudness can actually be felt if the fingernail is lightly passed across the surface of the paper. Indeed, if a piece of thin metal foil is placed over such a stamp and rubbed lightly with the finger, part or all of the design will be taken up by the foil. (This practice is not recommended, as stamps are delicate things, and their collectible condition may be impaired by the discoloration resulting from pressing the foil onto the face of the stamp.)

While these characteristics obtain with every line-engraved stamp, they are more or less prominent in individual issues. The proudness of the lines is less marked, for instance, with some of the early issues of, say, the United States, than in the case of a stamp such as, for example, Antigua 1949 75th Anniversary of the Universal Postal Union 1s., where the prominence of the ink is very marked. Similarly with the indentations in the paper when viewed from the back of the stamp. In the case of the Antigua stamp, for instance, the distortion of the paper is very pronounced, especially in the name tablet, and gives the appearance, almost, of embossing; this effect is heightened by the unusual (but not, of course, unique) instance in this UPU issue of a stamp produced by that process having colored letters on an uncolored ground in the name tablet.

Generally speaking, it is true to state that in line-engraved stamps resulting from dry printing, the distortion of the paper apparent is greater than in such stamps resulting from wet printing. The reason for this is that with dry printing the stamps are printed on to paper already gummed, and the indentations are not, as in wet printing, lessened by the subsequent processes. In wet printing, the stamps are printed onto dampened paper that is, usually, ungummed, and the printing ink has to dry before the paper is gummed; incidentally the paper, too, dries; the gumming again dampens the paper, and this, because of the expansion of the fibers of which the paper is composed, lessens the amount of apparent indentation.

Further, it is, generally speaking, true to state that a stamp produced from a die into which each recess has been cut by hand will show the lines of the design more sharply defined than will a stamp produced from a die on which the recesses have been created by etching.

The accompanying sketches show, in section, the cause and effect of the main characteristics of printing. In the sketches, both the cause and the effect are exaggerated.

Photogravure

Many photogravure printed stamps are, generally speaking, readily identifiable as such because, if the design is examined closely, especially under magnification, it will be seen to be composed of innumerable dots or minute squares of the same size but of different intensity. These dots are the effect of the cells of which the printing surface of the plate or cylinder is composed.

While the dot formation can be remarked throughout the design, the formation is most clearly perceptible in the lighter parts of the design, and in fine details, particularly along the edges of a dark line on a light ground, or vice versa.

Viewed in another light, such photogravure-printed designs consist of ink of different intensity, criss-crossed by thousands of minutely thin uncolored lines that are most readily perceptible in those areas of the design bearing little color. The uncolored lines cannot, of course, be seen in the uncolored areas of the design itself.

Excellent examples of these types of characteristics are provided by Great Britain 1952 2½d. where, in the lighter parts of the background within the center frame, the cell or uncolored line formation is very readily to be remarked. Within, for example, the letters "E" and "R" no such lines appear, but around the edges of these letters the dots are clearly visible.

The "screen" (that is, the dot or uncolored line formation) on these stamps is termed "diagonal," the uncolored lines, which cross at right angles, running diagonally in relation to the rectangular outlines of the stamp design.

In other, and particularly comparatively early, photogravure-printed stamps — such as, say, some printings of Egypt 1927-34 1m. — the screen is upright; that is, the uncolored lines run parallel to the vertical and horizontal outlines of the stamp design.

In certain photogravure-printed stamps no regular screen is apparent, the cells being of irregular sizes as well as of different depths. In such cases the whole design has a granular or irregularly grained appearance, as opposed to the regularly striated appearance imparted by the use of a screen. These grained photogravure-printed stamps are sometimes termed "screenless" or "unscreened." These terms are encountered, for example, in connection with some issues of the Union of South Africa — for instance, the frame of 1945-46 2d. purple and slate-black.

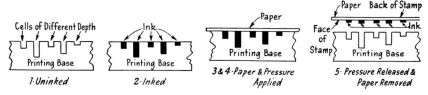

Cells of Different Depth — Printing Base — *1·Uninked*

Ink — Printing Base — *2·Inked*

Paper — Printing Base — *3&4·Paper & Pressure Applied*

Paper   Back of Stamp — Face of Stamp — Ink — Printing Base — *5· Pressure Released & Paper Removed*

Photogravure (screened).

In some cases, the ink in which a stamp is printed tends to mask the screen, and the stamp presents the appearance of being screenless. A good example of this occurs, for instance, in Italy 1950 (October) Provincial Occupations issue, of which all the lower values are printed in rotary photogravure; the screen is clearly visible on most of the stamps in the highlights, but on the 20-lire blue violet, can hardly be remarked.

Although in photogravure-printed stamps (as in line-engraved) the intensity of tone depends upon the depth of the recess in which the ink is held, the different nature of the photogravure ink and the minuteness of the cells result in neither perceptible proudness of ink nor indentation of the paper corresponding with that resulting from line engraving. To all appearance, even under considerable magnification, the surface of a photogravure-printed stamp is smooth, and velvety-matt to the touch.

In the cases of some photogravure stamps, particularly those printed since 1956 — for example, Federation of Malaya 1958 (Aug. 31) First Anniversary of Independence 30c. — multicolor printing has been used in which several colors are printed in close register. In spite of the close register involved, the effect of the photogravure screen is visible throughout the design, with the screen lines running diagonally in the same direction irrespective of color. In more recent developments, the screen is rotated to different angles for different colors, and stamps so produced are to be seen, for example, in USA 1984 (Sept. 26) Crime Prevention 20c. and Papua New Guinea 1985 (May 1) Ceremonial Structures 15t. to 60t.

Relief Printing

Stamps produced by relief printing present, usually, two characteristics that enable the basic printing method to be identified. Because the only parts of the printing base that come into close contact with the paper are the raised portions in the shape of the design, it may be stated that a relief-printed stamp is impressed into the paper, and this impression has two effects. First, in many cases, when the stamps are viewed from the back, a more or less slight distortion of the paper is visible in the design of the stamp. This distortion is the reverse of that obtaining with a line-engraved stamp; that is to say, in the line-engraved stamp the paper is distorted (in the colored portions of the design) toward the observer when viewing the *face* of the stamp, while in the relief-printed stamp the paper is distorted (in the colored portions of the design) toward the observer when viewing the *back* of the stamp. Printers consider such distortion of the paper in relief printing to be a fault, and make

182

great efforts to minimize it, with more or less effect. Nevertheless, it is usually perceptible, and especially so around the edges of an outer frameline.

The second characteristic also flows from the pressure of the lines of the design on to the paper. Because of this pressure, the ink covering the surface of each line or other area in contact with the paper is squeezed outward, toward the edges of the line or area. The color is, therefore, more intense at the edges than along the central area of each line.

Another factor contributes to an excess of color along or outside the edge of a line or area of a relief-printed stamp. This factor is termed ''ink squeeze'' by printers, and occurs because, however nicely the ink roller is adjusted, when it passes over the surface of each relief, slight compression of the roller occurs and some ink is deposited over the edge of the vertical ridge of metal comprising the relief. When the paper is pressed against the relief, the excess ink over the edge is transferred to the paper. The noticeability of this characteristic varies from issue to issue, almost from stamp to stamp in the sheet, but it can nearly always be remarked under fairly strong magnification.

A further characteristic that is frequently apparent in relief-printed stamps is the actual impression of the lines of the design into the paper when viewed from the face of the stamp. This characteristic, the ''bite'' as it is sometimes called, is most apparent around the edges of letters in an otherwise blank tablet, as obtains, for instance, in the case of the word ''Hongkong'' in Hongkong 1938-46 5c.

One other characteristic of some relief-printed stamps may be visible under magnification, and be of use in determining the method of printing. It must be borne in mind that a line of color in relief printing consists of ink transferred by pressure from the relief surface of the subject to the mat of fibers that comprises the paper. Uncoated paper, when examined under a magnification of X20 or greater, reveals the fibers lying on the surface, creating the appearance of mountains and valleys. Unless great pressure is used in print-

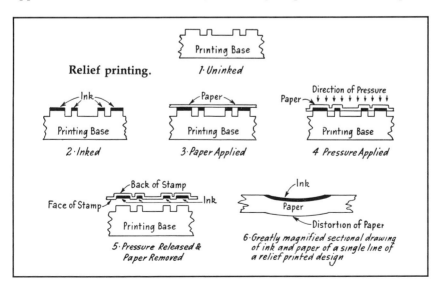

Relief printing.

1. Uninked

2. Inked

3. Paper Applied

4. Pressure Applied

5. Pressure Released & Paper Removed

6. Greatly magnified sectional drawing of ink and paper of a single line of a relief printed design

ing, these mountains are not squashed flat; the ink, therefore, is transferred to the mountains but fails either completely or partly to be imparted to the valleys. As a consequence, if a relief-printed line is examined under adequate magnification, the uninked or under-inked valleys are visible, in the form of interruptions to what should be continuous areas of color.

The designs of some relief-printed stamps incorporate a "screen" used for the purpose of reproducing some pictorial feature — economy being the reason for this method of reproduction, it being cheaper to use a photograph than to employ an engraver. The screen is used during a photo-mechanical engraving process, and the design is reproduced on the printing base by a combination of photography and etching, as in the case of photogravure stamps. Unlike that of the photogravure design, however, the screened relief-printed design consists of innumerable dots of different sizes, but all, of course, of the same height. In the lighter parts of the design, the dots are minute and quite separate from one another; in the darker parts of the design, the dots are larger and, sometimes, coalesce. This variation in size gives the appearance of tone. Unlike the photogravure design, in which the different intensity of tone results from the different depths of the cells, the different intensity of tone in the screened relief-printed design flows from the different areas of the dots.

In relief printing, the screen is known as the "half-tone screen," and it is the normal process used for illustrating photographs and stamps in the present work. Historically, its first use in stamp production may be stated to begin with Uruguay 1908 (Aug. 23) Declaration of Independence 1c., 2c. and 5c., of which the centers, depicting the cruiser *Montevideo* and a gunboat, were printed from a half-tone block. The use of half-tone blocks in relief printing of postage stamps has been widespread but not great; among other relief-printed issues, half-tone blocks may be seen, for instance, in Afghanistan 1927 (Feb. 26) 8th Independence Anniversary 10p., the so-called "Dotted Background," Latvia 1937 (Jul. 12) Monuments series, and Kishengarh (India) 1913 ¼a.

In the cases of some relief-printed stamps for which a half-tone screen has been used in the design, the stamps have been printed in multicolor, a process-color separation method having been employed. Examples of such stamps are to be found, for instance, in the local and private issues of the Central Pacific Cocoanut Plantations Ltd. for Christmas Island (Pacific Ocean) 1924 5c. It is characteristic of prints made from process-color separated plates that the prints present the appearance of many different colors being used in the printing, whereas only three, or four, colors are usually used — yellow, red, blue, and perhaps black. The many-colored effect is obtained by printing dots of different colors close together in varying amounts. In order to prevent the dots printing exactly on top of each other, the screen is rotated to a different angle when each separate color-plate is made. The result of this is that if a stamp printed from process-color separated plates is examined closely, the dots of different colors will be seen to present an effect resembling a "rose," and this effect is repeated throughout the design.

Planographic Printing

The main characteristic of a stamp produced by any of the planographic processes is that it is quite flat, having neither the proudness of the line-engraved nor the impression of the relief-printed stamp. The tendency of the edges of lines printed by these planographic processes is slightly toward unsharpness, but in many stamps printed by them, thinner lines occur than in any others except finely executed line engravings. In the comparatively modern photo-lithographic and offset-lithographic processes, there is a tendency toward a multiplicity of minute uncolored flecks throughout the whole design, but this characteristic is not of universal occurrence.

Photo-lithography and, sometimes, offset-lithography involve the use of photography in the processes leading up to the production of the printing base, and, in general, stamps printed by these methods reveal a noticeable lack of sharpness. Sometimes, for the purpose of reproducing a feature with gradations of tone, a "screen" is used in combination with these methods. This screen, so far as its general characteristic appearance is concerned, presents results identical with the half-tone screen of relief printing, but the photo-lithographic and offset-lithographic stamps are quite flat, and do not present the impression characteristics of the relief-printed stamps. Such a screen was used, for instance, in producing the center of Spanish Post Office in Morocco 1948 (Jan. 2) 2c., and Israel 1949-50 15 (p.).

Many multicolored planographically printed stamps are printed from printing bases produced with the aid of process-color separation. In these cases the "rose" effect is clearly visible, and used to be of assistance in differentiating between this form of printing and photogravure — in which the "rose" effect did not occur until recently.

One other characteristic of some planographically printed stamps may be visible under magnification, and be of use in determining the method of printing. It is substantially true to state that a line printed by lithography, from a stone or a plate, consists of minute round drops of ink squashed flat. Under a magnification of X10 or greater, a line or the edge of an area of color gives the appearance of an irregular string of beads. This characteristic is not necessarily observable throughout the design, but occurs almost unfailingly in some part of every lithographically printed stamp, particularly in such stamps printed before about 1920. The size of the beads varies from issue to issue: for example, in France 1870 Bordeaux 20c., and in USA 1918-20 2c. offset printing, the beads are very small; in Suez Canal 1868 20c., the beads

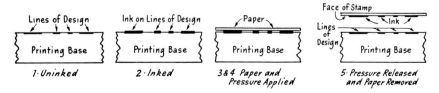

Planographic printing.

185

are medium-sized; and in Colombia 1937 (May 14) Postal Tax 5 (c), the beads are large.

This "string of beads" characteristic must be distinguished, on the one hand, from the serrated edges of lines in screened photogravure, and on the other hand from the irregularity of line edges produced by small accumulations of ink, or "ink squeeze," in relief printing.

Further, in offset printing, the transference of the ink to the paper takes place from a resilient rubber surface. As a consequence, the rubber adapts itself to the mountains and valleys of the paper, and the ink-starving of the valleys (observable in relief-printed stamps) is absent from offset-printed stamps.

Embossing

The characteristics of embossing are so well-known as scarcely to merit their description. The use of this method of production for adhesive postage stamps has been comparatively infrequent, but it has been and is widely employed in the manufacture of postal stationery. The chief characteristic of embossing is a high colorless relief or distortion of the paper in the shape of the embossed features of the design; this distortion of the

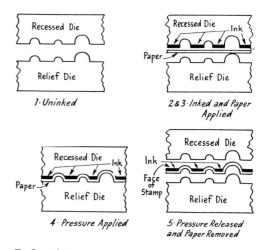

Embossing.

paper is equally apparent from the front and back of the stamp. The paper is distorted in one direction only — that is, toward the observer viewing the face of the stamp. Color, when it is present, lies on the natural surface of the paper.

Comparing the Processes

In the cases of a very large number of issues printed by each of the various processes, the characteristics are outstanding, and the identification of the basic printing method can be readily made after only a little experience based on informed observation. However, in some cases, the characteristics imparted by the basic printing method are, for one reason or another, masked. This is most likely to occur in the cases of planographic and relief printing, and to present difficulty to the unaided eye. This difficulty is usually resolved by the use of a fairly powerful magnifying glass, but there have been occasions when even practical and master printers have expressed themselves as being unable with certainty to identify the method used for producing certain stamps. However, such instances are rare, and should not discourage generally the solution of the first philatelic problem involved in printing.

This design was recess-printed. The same design appeared printed by lithography and also relief-printed. These stamps are useful in providing comparisons for study of the effects of these different printing methods.

This stamp was printed from a hectograph.

This stamp was printed from plates made by electrotyping.

This stamp was printed by photography.

This stamp was printed from plates made by stereotyping.

This stamp was printed by offset lithography.

This stamp was printed from a copper printing base.

The greatly magnified photographs used in the accompanying illustrations have been specially produced to exhibit, so far as is possible by photography, the appearance presented by stamps printed by selected processes. The photographs for the illustrations lettered "A" to "F" on the following pages were made for me by the late W.H.S. Cheavin, FRMS, FRPSL, by means of the philatelic microscope that he specially designed in 1913. The photographs for the illustrations lettered "G" to "I" were taken by me by means of a copying camera, and the enlarged portions of these represent photographic enlargements of the resultant negatives.

Some issues of some countries provide ideal starting points for comparison of identical or very similar designs printed by different methods. Tasmania, for instance, is outstanding in this respect; for example the 1d. design showing Mount Wellington was first recess-printed and so issued in 1899 (December); then it was lithographed and so issued in 1902; later that year, in October, the design was relief-printed and so issued. Other values in the designs first issued in Tasmania (December) 1899-1900 series as recess-printed stamps later appeared as lithographs and relief-printed.

The United States provides well-known examples of identical designs printed from line-engraved plates and by offset lithography: the head of Washington, which, with numerals in the lower corners, first appeared in the series of 1908-09 was issued recess-printed for many years — and in 1918 was issued printed by the offset process.

A comparison of line engraving and photogravure can be made in Union of South Africa in the, for example, 2d. design showing the Government Buildings at Pretoria. This design, first issued recess-printed in 1927, was slightly altered and printed in rotary photogravure, being so issued in 1931. The Union of South Africa provides further examples for comparison of the effects of different printing methods. For instance, the ½d. design showing the Springbok's head was first issued in 1926 relief-printed; in September 1935, the design was issued in sheets printed in unscreened rotary photogravure; and in 1947, in screened rotary photogravure.

Terms Used in Describing Printing Processes

The alphabetical list that follows embraces terms used in describing printing processes. Philatelists often use many of these terms synonymously, while printers usually sharply distinguish these same terms, with the consequence that, on many occasions, philatelists and printers are incomprehensible to each other — using the same words but, so to speak, "talking a different language." I am especially conscious of this, and further realize that there are, in some cases, great differences in meanings attached to terms by the printing trade on different sides of the Atlantic. I have sought to set out the meanings attached to the terms in philately, and have attempted to indicate the trade significance. This list does not pretend to be complete. This is particularly so in regard to trade names of processes, and has been compiled with emphasis on the terms relating to the basic printing processes.

A.

Great Britain 1952 2½d, and a microscope photograph of part of the design. This stamp was printed by rotary photogravure, the screen being diagonal, and 175 lines to the inch. Note the clearly defined colorless lines, and that the dots (that is, small squares) are all of the same size. The different intensities of color result from the different depths of the cells. In the darkest parts of the design, the striations are lost. Differentiate between the effect of this screen and the half-tone screen in Illustrations C and D.

B.

Great Britain 1887 3d, and a microscope photograph of part of the design. This stamp was printed by relief printing from plates made by electrotyping a group of lead moulds, each struck from an engraved die. Note especially the characteristic "squeezing of ink," especially prominent in the top line of the northeast corner square, which gives the line the appearance, almost, of being split in half horizontally. Note also the characteristic small accumulation of ink at the northeast of the tablet to the left outside this corner square.

190

C.

Kishengarh (India) 1913 ¼a., and a microscope photograph of part of the design. This stamp was relief-printed from a half-tone block produced by photographing the design through a diagonal screen of about 120 lines to the inch. Note that, in the lighter portions of the design,

the dots are quite separate and that they run together and form a confused mass in the darker portions of the design, which, because of the great enlargement, is hardly recognizable. (If this illustration is held at arm's length or more, the details in the microscope photograph become recognizable as part of the design.) Note that, in many cases, the ink has been "squeezed" to the outer edges of the colored areas, giving the effect almost of circles in outline; this effect in this instance is partly accounted for by the semi-art surface of the paper on which this stamp was printed. Compare the effect of this screen with the similar effect in Illustration D, and differentiate between the effects of these screens and that in Illustration A.

D.

Spanish Post Office in Morocco 1948 (Jan. 2) 2c, and a microscope photograph of part of the design. This stamp was printed by planographic printing, and during the course of the production of the printing base for the center, a diagonal half-tone screen was used. This screen contained thirty more lines to the inch than did that used in the production of the stamp pictured in Illustration C. Note the comparative solidity of the dots, and the more even appearance of the print of this stamp (when compared with that of Illustration C). In this instance, the design of the microscope photograph is still recognizable, even though the degree of enlargement is the same as that for Illustration C; this is accounted for partly by the smaller mesh of the screen, and partly by the method of printing. Distinguish between the effects of the half-tone screens of Illustrations C and D, and the effect of the screen in Illustration A.

E.

United States 1917-19 2c, and a microscope photograph of part of the design. This stamp was intaglio-printed from a line-engraved flat plate. Note that each line of the design is clear cut, and note also the definite and regular pattern in the background at the upper left. Note the fineness of the top line of the toga, and the varying thickness of its other lines visible in the microscope photograph. Note the finely tapering end to the scroll at the left. Compare this example with Illustration F.

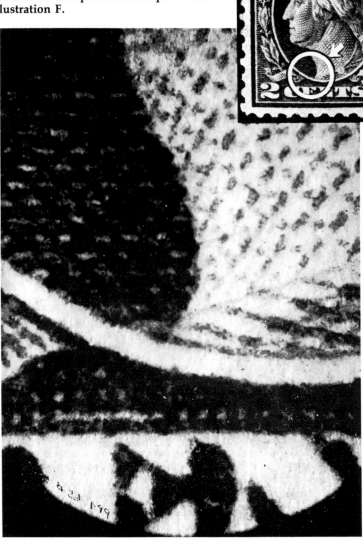

F.

United States 1918-20 2c, and a microscope photograph of part of the design. This stamp was printed by the planographic process of offset lithography. Compare this with Illustration E. Note the comparative coarseness of the lines, and the blotched irregularity of the pattern in the background at the upper left. Note the coarseness of the top line of the toga and its other lines visible in the microscope photograph. Note the blunted end to the scroll at the left, and the bulbous end to the contained lines. Note also the "string of beads" effect visible in the lowest line of the toga above the letters "EN."

G.

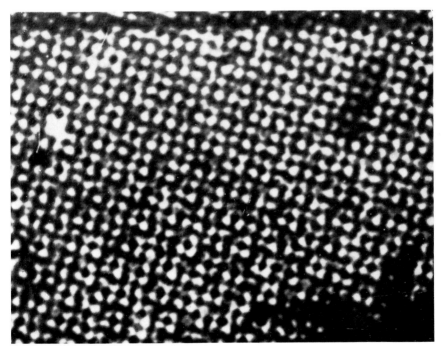

Christmas Islands (Pacific Ocean) 1924 5c., and a photographic enlargement of part of the design. This stamp was relief-printed from process-color separated half-tone blocks in three colors: yellow, red and blue. Note the "rose" effect of the dots in the enlarged portion of the design, caused by a rotation of the half-tone screen to a different angle when each half-tone block was made.

H.

Federation of Malaya 1958 First Anniversary of Independence 30c., and a photographic enlargement of part of the design. This stamp was printed in multicolor photogravure in five colors: yellow, red, brown, green and blue. Compare this with Illustration G, and note the absence of the "rose" effect. Compare this with Illustration A, and the effect of the screen on a monochrome stamp.

I.

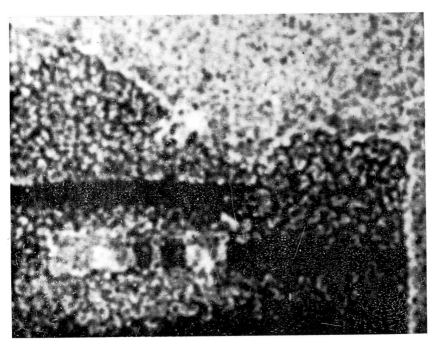

Poltava (Russian Zemstvo) 1912 (Jul. 13) 1(k), and a photographic enlargement of part of the design. The center of this stamp was printed by collotype. Note the irregular granulated appearance of the enlarged portion of the design, and contrast this with "grained" or "screenless" photogravure illustrated in Chapter 9, Part II.

Chalcography. Engraving a design in recess on a copper plate and printing direct from the plate; e.g. Mauritius 1847 (Sept. 20) Post Office 1d. and 2d.

Chromolithography. Term used to designate lithography in more than one color on one sheet of paper. The earliest use of chromolithography for stamps occurs in Zurich (Switzerland) 1843 (March) 4r. and 6r., where the design in black was lithographed over a previously lithographed background of red lines. See "Color Separation."

Collogravure. The trade name of Harrison & Sons Ltd. for "Photogravure."

Collotype. A planographic printing process, sometimes called "photogelatin" in USA. A photographic negative is made of the design. A sheet of plate glass is given a slightly rough surface by grinding, is then coated with albumen or gelatine, covered with potassium bichromate, and dried in the dark. The plate glass is then exposed to light through the photographic negative; the bichromated gelatine is hardened in direct proportion to the amount of light the negative permits to pass, and the plate glass is developed in warm water, the unhardened gelatine being dissolved away. The plate glass is dried, allowed to mature for some hours, and immersed in glycerine and water. The plate is then ready for the press, being rolled with greasy ink that adheres to the gelatine in proportion to the amount of light that acted upon it. Collotype has been used widely for high-grade illustrations, only rarely for postage stamps. Poltava (Russian Zemstvo) 1912 (Jul. 13) 1(k) bears a central design printed by collotype. Among the illustrations produced in collotype is, for example, the souvenir sheet distributed at the London International Stamp Exhibition 1950 and bearing reproductions in color of Cape of Good Hope 1855-58 4d., Ceylon 1857-59 4d., Great Britain 1840 1d., New South Wales 1860 Sydney Views 1d., and Nova Scotia 1851-53 1s.

The difficulty experienced sometimes in attempting to diagnose "Collotype" as the printing process involved in production of some issues may be instanced by my experiences relating to the issue of Great Britain's National Telephone Company Ltd. 1884 (December) 1d. to 1s. stamps. The central portrait is remarkably lifelike, almost a photographic likeness. The philatelic records revealed that the printers were Maclure, Macdonald & Company of Glasgow and that the stamps were "engraved" by the printers. Because the printing method was obviously neither intaglio nor relief but planographic, and the other processes had equally obviously played no part in the production, the word "engraved" must have been used in a very special sense. Close examination under a considerable degree of magnification failed to reveal any trace of screen or reticulation. Being unable to satisfy myself about the printing method used, I approached two of the leading firms of security printers — of course, sending them the stamp issue in question. Both enlisted the services of their experts. One firm was adamant that the stamps

Collotype (?). Great Britain's National Telephone Company Ltd. 1884 (December) 1s. stamp. The exact printing method was not recorded at the time in the philatelic press. Nowadays, the experts of two of the greatest security printing firms worldwide are in conflict about the printing process used — one says "direct lithography from stone," the other, "collotype." Where does this leave the philatelic student?

had been printed by direct lithography from stone. The other firm was equally adamant that the stamps had resulted from collotype.

Color Separation. The technique whereby the colors of a bi-colored or multi-colored original are sorted out so that each part of the design to be printed in one color appears on only one printing base. Two methods of color separation have been employed in stamp production:

(1) Mass separation, or "flat color," whereby separate areas of color are printed from as many different printing bases as there are colors. The colors are printed on the paper to give the effect of two (bi-colored) or three or four or sometimes more (multicolored) distinct colors; this form of mass separation is by far the most frequently employed in stamp production, and has been used for each of the three main printing processes — for example, intaglio printing, line engraving (USA 1869 15c. brown and blue); intaglio printing — gravure [Singapore (Straits Settlements) 1955 25c. orange and plum]; planography — lithography (India 1854 4a. red and blue); planography — offset-litho. [Great Britain 1985 (June 18) Safety at Sea 17p. black, azure, emerald, ultramarine, orange-yellow, vermilion, bright blue and chrome yellow]; relief printing (Gold Coast 1899-1902 ½d. lilac and green). Exceptionally, intaglio printing from certain line engravings can be multi-colored when only one printing cylinder is used. This involves applying different colors to appropriate parts of each subject on the cylinder by use of a special element in the press — as with the Serge-Beaune patent and the Giori press. Early examples of stamps so printed are provided, for instance, by France 1953 Dress-making Industry 30f., blue-black and violet, and USA 1957 Wildlife Conservation 3c., blue, orange and green.

(2) Process separation, or "process color," whereby the colors of the original are split up, photographically, into the primary colors (red, yellow and blue) and are printed on to the paper in minute dots so blending as to give the effect of many different colors; the many-colored effect and the design depend upon the frequency and size of the dots in three colors (sometimes also incorporating an extra printing in black or gray) in any given area. The first use of process color for postage stamps occurs in Christmas Island (Pacific Ocean) 1915(?) 5c.; more modern instances are to be found, for example, in the center of Germany 1952 (Apr. 15) Fifth Centenary of the Birth of Leonardo da Vinci 5p., and in the backgrounds to Dominican Republic 1957 Olympic Games 1c. to 7c.

Cyclostyle — see "Mimeograph."

Copper Plate Engraving, Copper Plate Printing. Terms widely used among printers for designating engraving and intaglio printing from a plate or cylinder where the design has been cut into it by hand or by a combination of handwork and mechanical processes. The terms derive from the copper printing base that, for many years, was the invariable and only available medium. Although the steel plate or cylinder has, in many cases, replaced the copper, the original terms remain, and are frequently used irrespective of the composition of the printing base itself. Philatelically, the use of the terms is infrequent, the term line engraving being preferred. Mauritius 1848 Post Paid 1d. and 2d. are true instances of stamps produced by copper plate engraving, as are, among many others, Norway 1914 Centenary of Independence 5 ö to 20 ö.

Delacryl. Trade name of De La Rue & Company Ltd. for a trade secret "lithographic printing" process, specially developed for printing stamps and first marketed about 1966. Stamps printed by the Delacryl process include, for example, Great Britain 1969 (Oct. 1) Post Office Technology 5d. to 1s.6d.

Die Stamping. Term used for the process of raising colored reliefs on an uncolored ground by means of a recessed die in a stamping press. On Sierra Leone 1964 (Feb. 10) World's Fair, New York, 1d. and the remainder of the issue, the raised portions of the designs in black, red and other colors were applied by die stamping, according to the printers, Walsall Security Printers Ltd.

Direct Plate Printing. Term used by printers to designate intaglio printing from engraved plates where the design appears on the printing base, usually of steel but often of other material including copper, as the result of the combination of handwork and mechanical processes. The term is used as an antonym for offset printing. The use of the term philatelically is infrequent, the term line engraving being preferred.

Electrotyping. This term is used to designate a method of copying a design or group of designs by depositing copper galvanically or electrolytically in a mould of wax or other material. Electrotyping has been and is used to produce printing bases for intaglio and relief printing. Sicily 1859 (Jan. 1) ½g. to 50g. are instances of intaglio-printed stamps produced by electrotyping; as an instance chosen at random, British Honduras 1913-17 1c. to 5c. are examples of relief-printed stamps so produced.

Embossing. Distortion of the paper by raising reliefs from the non-relieved surface with or without color in the non-reliefs or on the reliefs. The trade terminology varies widely to designate the processes for producing different effects — see the chapter entitled "Embossing." Modern stamps incorporating embossing in the design include, for example, Gilbert Islands 1979 (Jan. 15) Bicentenary of Captain Cook's Voyages 1768-79 45c., in which the portrait and medallion frame were produced by embossing in colorless relief.

Engraving. This term properly refers to the action of cutting metal away by hand in producing a die or, even, plate for ultimate use in any of the printing processes. Loosely, the term is often used synonymously with line engraving.

Epargne. This term, from the French *en épargne* which means "in relief," is used to designate that form of engraving employed for producing a die to be used in relief printing, where the non-printing surface is cut away.

Etching. This term is used to refer to the process of eating away metal by a mordant. Etching has been used to produce substantially the whole of a design drawn by hand, but is usually used only as an aid to the engraver; it plays an important part in the modern photo-mechanical printing processes. Germany 1935 6(pf.) depicting Heinrich Schütz is an example of a portrait produced by etching.

Flat-Bed Printing. Term used to refer to the process of printing by pressure applied to the paper on a plate held flat on the bed of a press, as opposed to "Rotary Printing," which is used in reference to printing by pressure applied to paper against a cylindrical printing base. A "cylinder" press is a flat-bed press, the printing surface being flat, the pressure being applied by a cylinder. In a "rotary" press, both pressure and printing obtain from cylinders. See "Rotary Printing."

Galvanotyping. A synonym for "Electrotyping," and its philatelic use is infrequent.

Glyphography. Term used in reference to the process for which a patent was granted in 1842 to Edward Palmer of Newgate Street, London (British Patent 9927 of 1842). By his process he could, and did, produce printing surfaces in relief or recess irrespective of whether the original engraving was in relief or in recess, with the result that intaglio and relief plates could be made from one engraving. Glyphographic originals were used, for example, for Saxony (Germany) 1855 (Jun. 1) to 1856 (Apr. 24) ½n. to 10n.

Gold Process. A process by which a relief die can be made from a recess-engraved die. A copper electrotype is taken from an engraved die; the sunken portions of the copper electrotype are filled with gold; the surface copper is then dissolved away, leaving the gold in relief, and the gold reliefs then form the "die," which is copied and multiplied by means of moulds and electrotypes. The Austrian State Printing Works used the gold process in connection with, it is thought, Hungary 1871-72 2k. to 15k. The adhesive stamps were intaglio-printed from line engravings, and some of the postal stationery in the same design was relief-printed.

Gravure. This term, which omits any prefix, is sometimes used to embrace the processes of photogravure and rotary photogravure; sometimes it is loosely and equivocally used as though it were synonymous with either.

Hand Engraving. This term, strictly used, refers to the process by which printing bases are produced solely by handwork, such as, for example, Japan 1876 (Mar. 19) 5s., Mauritius 1847 Post Office 1d. and 2d., and United States (Confederate States) Grove Hill, Ala. Often the term is used as though it were synonymous with line engraving in intaglio.

Handstruck. Term used to designate stamps printed by striking the printing base (consisting normally of one subject) by hand upon paper. Although sometimes used to embrace stamps such as Scinde District Post (India) 1852 and Great Britain 1847-54 6d., 10d. and 1s., the term is usually employed as referring exclusively to the productions of relief-printing bases. It has a widespread use also in relation to postal markings and pre-adhesive stamps. Burma 1942 (Jun. 1) no value, bearing the seal of S. Yano, is a comparatively recent example of a hand-struck postage stamp.

Hectograph. A planographic process of printing and a print made from special ink containing an aniline dye held on a gelatine printing base to which the ink has been transferred from a drawing on special paper. The paper bearing the drawing in the special ink is laid face-down on the gelatine; the dye transfers itself to the gelatine in a few seconds, and the drawing paper is then removed. Clean paper pressed against the gelatine will receive some of the dye and thus become a hectograph. The hectograph process was used in the production of, for example, Arzamas (Russian Zemstvo) 1886-90 5(k), and Telsiai (Lithuania) 1920 (Jan. 10-14) no value expressed.

Heliogravure. A trade name for rotary photogravure, which stems from the firm of Helio-Vaugirard, the French printers.

Hologram — see "Tridimensional."

Intaglio. This term, an Italian word meaning "engraving, engraved work, or a carving," is used to designate printing from recesses, as opposed to relief printing. The term "Recess Printing" is used synonymously with "printing in intaglio."

Kiss Printing. This term is used by printers to designate a mode of printing whereby the paper is only lightly pressed on to the printing base, the two being brought into as light contact as possible consistent with satisfactory impression. Kiss printing can be effected only on cylinder and rotary presses. It has as its object the elimination of distortion by pressure of the paper, and the reduction to a minimum of "ink squeeze" — the term used by printers to designate the

Cyclostyle. Matabeleland (Rhodesia) Reuter's Telegraph Service 1894 (March) 2s.6d., 5s. and 10s. These stamps were produced by "Cyclostyle" in sheets of eighteen (six across, three down), the top row containing the 10s. value, the middle the 5s. value and the bottom the 2s.6d. Only fifty sheets were printed. They prepaid a postal service by runners from Buluwayo to the destinations inscribed on each stamp. The stamps were canceled in indelible pencil with the date and initials.

small accumulations of excessive ink along the edges of a line caused by the ink roller depositing ink not only on the surface but also slightly over the edge of each relief line or area on the printing base. Compare "Kiss Print," Page 165.

Letterpress. Term used, mainly by printers and occasionally by philatelists, to designate all relief printing, irrespective of the processes used for constructing the printing base.

Letterpress-Printed. The effect of printing from an assemblage of printer's type made for use on, often, one occasion only, the assemblage usually being distributed after use. In this sense, the term is a synonym for typeset — see "Typeset." Contrast with "Plate-Printed."

Line Engraving. Philatelically this term, unqualified, is used loosely to designate the process that results in a stamp of which the design on the paper appears in lines, dots or other areas of color in relief. Synonymously so used, sometimes, are "Engraving" and "Recess Printing." Strictly, the term "line engraving" is applicable to all engraving, whether the printing is effected from recesses or reliefs, and sometimes the terms "Recess Engraving" and "Relief Engraving" are used in an attempt at precision. (The difficulty with this attempt at distinction is that, in both cases, the engraver cuts recesses; however, for intaglio printing, the recesses he cuts represent the colored areas in the print, and for relief printing, the recesses he cuts represent the uncolored areas in the print.) Sometimes "line engraving" is used strictly to differentiate between dies on which all the design has been incised into the metal by hand or machine and dies in the production of which etching has been employed.

Lithography. This term, strictly, refers to printing from stone. Loosely the term is used synonymously with "Planography," irrespective of the material of which the printing base consists. The term is abbreviated to "Litho." British Central Africa 1897 (August) 1d. to £10 are examples of stamps printed by lithography.

Mechanical Mezzotint. Term sometimes used to designate "Photogravure."

Mimeograph. This term, in its original use, designates an apparatus invented by Edison for producing stencils of written pages, from which stencils many copies may be obtained. The stencil sheet comprises a porous tissue covered with a coating impervious to ink. Drawing with a sharp instrument, or typing on the stencil disturbs the coating locally and exposes the porous tissue. If the stencil is then stretched on a frame, a piece of paper placed beneath and in contact with it, and an ink-charged roller run over the surface of the stencil, the ink will be permitted to pass in those areas and lines that have been disturbed, and so cause a design to appear on the paper. A similar effect is obtained by "Cyclostyle," by which a pen with a small toothed wheel cuts minute holes in specially prepared paper that is then used as a stencil. Philatelically considered, the use of these processes is rare. The mimeograph was used for Kume Island (Ryukyu Islands) 1945 (Oct. 1) 7s. Cyclostyle was employed for Matabeleland (Rhodesia) Reuter's Telegraph Service 1894 (March) 2s.6d., 5s. and 10s.

Offset, Offset Lithography, Offset Printing. These terms, in reference to a printing process, are used to refer to a planographic process in which the printing base prints impressions on to a rubber-covered cylinder or "blanket" from which they are transferred (that is, "offset") on to the paper. The abbreviation "offset-litho." is sometimes used. In a different sense, the term "offset" is used loosely as a synonym for "Set-Off" — see the alphabetical list to the chapter entitled "Printing Problems and Varieties." As examples chosen at random, Iceland 1930 Parliamentary Millenary Celebration 3a. to 10k. are instances of stamps produced by offset-lithography; so are Singapore 1985 (Aug. 9) Public Housing: 25 Years of Achievement 10c. to 75c.

Photo — see "Rotary Photogravure"; distinguish "Photography" and "Photo-Lithography."

Photography. This term is properly used to designate the processes used for producing a very limited number of stamps — for example, Mafeking Siege stamps 1900 1d. and 3d. The abbreviation "photo." is *not* in normal philatelic use to designate such productions; see "Rotary Photogravure."

Photogravure. Often this term is used to refer to the process by which intaglio prints are made from flat plates having an irregular groundwork or grain, as opposed to a "screen." Sometimes the term is used to embrace the flat plate and also the rotary photogravure processes, and sometimes, in this sense, the abbreviation "photo." is used.

Photo-Lithography. This term, a compound of "photographic" and "lithography," is used to designate a process in which the subjects are reproduced direct on to a planographic printing base by a photo-mechanical process. The further abbreviation "photo.-litho." is often used. The abbreviation "photo." does *not*, as such, apply to "photo-lithography." Stamps produced by photo-lithography include Australia 1985 (July 17) Australiana: Children's Characters 5c.

Planographic Printing, Planography. These terms designate printing from a surface that has neither the raised subjects of "Relief Printing" nor the recessed subjects of "Intaglio," but is uniform; the surface is, or may be, flat only in that sense, for the printing base is often curved to make a cylinder. Planographic printing embraces "Lithography," "Offset Lithography" and "Photo-Lithography"; in one sense, also, it embraces "Collotype," "Hectograph," "Mimeograph" and "Photography."

Plate-Printed. Printed from a continuous-surface plate made for use on more than one occasion. Contrast with "Letterpress-Printed."

Recess Engraving — see "Line Engraving."

Recess Printing — see "Intaglio." Strictly speaking "recess printing" embraces "Line Engraving," "Photogravure" and "Rotary Photogravure," but frequently the term "recess printing" is used as though it were synonymous with line engraving only.

Relief Engraving — see "Line Engraving."

Relief Printing. Term used to designate printing from a printing base of which those areas that are to appear in color on the stamps are raised above the non-printing areas, and only the color-producing areas come into contact with the paper at the moment of impression or printing. Often the term "Surface Printing" is used synonymously with relief printing.

Relievo, In Relievo. These are the Italian equivalents of "relief," used to distinguish this method from "Intaglio."

Rotary Photogravure. Term used to designate intaglio printing from cylinders on which the subjects appear in the form of hundreds of thousands of minute cells, either regular ("screened") or irregular ("unscreened"). The abbreviation "photo." normally signifies "Rotary Photogravure." Compare "Photogravure."

Rotary Printing. Term used to refer to the process of printing in which pressure is imparted by an impression cylinder to the paper against the printing cylinder. See "Flat-Bed Printing."

Rotogravure. An elision of the two words comprising the term "Rotary Photogravure."

Spitzertype. Term used in reference to the relief-printing process for which a patent was granted to Edmund Spitzer (German Patent 161911 of Dec. 10, 1901, and 194586 of Feb. 3, 1905). A copper plate, coated with a layer of bichromated gelatine or glue, is exposed to light through a continuous tone negative and then immediately etched with solutions of iron perchloride, which causes granulations to form in the light-affected gelatine and so control the degree of etching of the copper. After cleaning, the copper plate comprises the printing base. Spitzertype was used in the production of Bulgaria 1907 (Aug. 28) 5s., 10s. and 25s.

Steel Engraving. Term used normally to differentiate engraving in steel from "Copper Plate Engraving." Many relief designs are steel-engraved, but often the use of the term steel engraving implies that the design is intaglio-printed.

Stencilling — see "Mimeograph."

Stereotyping. Term used to designate a method of copying a design or group of designs by casting metal in a mould or matrix of plaster of paris or other heat-resistant material. Stereotyping has been and is normally used to produce printing bases for relief printing, especially nowadays for overprints and surcharges. Norway 1883-84 3 ö. is an example of a stamp produced by stereotyping.

Surface Printing. This term is used, philatelically, as synonymous with "Relief Printing."

Taille Douce. This is a French term, the equivalent of "Intaglio."

Thermography. A technique whereby a resinous compound is dusted on to ink remaining wet on parts of normally printed subjects and then passed under heat, which causes the compound to swell and stand proud of the paper. Compounds can be of various colors. On New Caledonia 1985 (Feb. 27) Shells 55f. and 72f., the shell designs were raised by thermography.

Thermography. New Caledonia 1985 (Feb. 27) Shells 55f. and 72f. The shell designs were raised by thermography.

Tridimensional. Printing intended to present the appearance of a three-dimensional view or object. The first stamps so intended were Italy 1956 (Dec. 29) First Anniversary of Admission of Italy to U.N.O. 25 l. and 60 l. Slightly divergent images of an outline globe were lithographed in red and green on tinted paper. When the stamps are viewed through red and green spectacles (one color before each eye), the globe seems to stand out from the paper. During the 1960s and early 1970s, many tridimensional stamps were marketed with the names of Middle East and Far East countries. The designs, in multicolors, were offset-printed in reverse on a flat-surfaced transparent plastic, which was then bonded to white paper. The upper surface of the plastic was finely ribbed vertically and had a pattern of horizontal bars. When viewed normally (without colored spectacles), the design has a strong tridimensional appearance. Among such stamps, chosen at random, is Bhutan 1970 (Jan. 19) Famous Paintings 15 ch. picturing a painting of Napoleon. *Scott* relegates the issue to "For the Record" and *Stanley Gibbons* similarly places it in the "Appendix." The printing technique has been misnamed "holography" and the result a "hologram." U.S. patent No. 3241429 was taken out by Visual Impact Inc., of Gardner, Kansas, for tridimensional printing. A true hologram produced by means of a laser beam was incorporated in Austria 1988 (Oct. 18) Austrian Export 8s. by bonding stamped foil bearing the hologram to the paper. The hologram depicts a solid cube bearing

Tridimensional. Austria 1988 (Oct. 18) Austrian Export 8s. The cube and logo portrayed against the colorless rectangle comprise a hologram on foil bonded to paper.

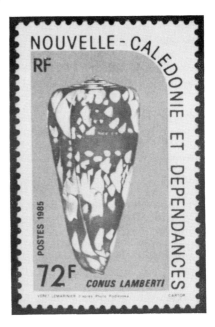

a logo of an "A," with "AUSTRIA" as the cross bar against a colorless rectangle.

Typeset. Term used to designate the effect of printing from pieces of printers' type, ornaments and rules, assembled to make a printing base composed of several or many repetitions of the same or somewhat similar assemblages. Antioquia (Colombia) 1901 1c. is an example of a typeset postage stamp. See "Letterpress-Printed."

Typographed, Typography. Philatelically these terms are widely used synonymously with "relief-printed" and "relief printing." In this sense, the term "typographed" is often abbreviated to "typo." Outside philatelic circles, "typography" signifies the art of choosing and displaying type faces to their best advantage, and most typographers would probably indignantly and certainly justly deny any suggestion that they are printers.

Woodblock, Woodcut, Wood Engraving. Self-explanatory, these terms are rarely encountered in philately, the processes having been very infrequently used to produce postage stamps. Paradoxically, the most frequent use of the term "Woodblock" is in connection with a misnomer — Cape of Good Hope 1861 Woodblocks 1d. and 4d. printed in fact from stereotypes of a steel die hand-engraved in relief. Engraving or cutting wood to produce relief-printed stamps was used, for example, for Haiti 1881 (Jul. 1) 1c. to 20c. and for Victoria 1854-58 6d. Technically, a woodcut differs from a wood engraving in that a woodcut is made on the plank by cutting with a knife, whereas a wood engraving is engraved with a graver on the end-grain of hard wood.

Xylography. Printing from woodblocks or woodcuts.

Zincography. Printing from zinc plates.

9. Intaglio Printing — I: Line Engraving

INTAGLIO PRINTING is printing from the recessed portions of the printing base, so that the intensity of the design printed on the paper is in direct proportion to the depth of each recess on the printing base. This characteristic alone is common to gravure and other recess-printing processes.

Copper plate engraving and printing, direct plate printing, engraving, hand engraving, line engraving, recess engraving and printing, steel engraving and *taille douce* are among the more common of the terms employed to denote the processes used for the production of stamps of which the lines of the design recessed in the plate stand up from the surface of the paper. The term most frequently used compendiously is "line engraving," and the stamps are often referred to, simply, as "engraved."

The principle of recess engraving is: into smooth metal are cut channels and holes — recesses; ink is forced or dabbed into them, but none is allowed to remain on the surface of the metal; then paper is pressed into contact with the metal and forced into the recesses; when the paper is taken away, it sucks out the ink, which lies on the paper in ridges and humps corresponding to the channels and holes in the metal. If the channel or hole in the metal is deep and large, the corresponding ridge or hump on the paper will be high and large; similarly a narrow and low ridge results from a narrow and shallow channel. The deeper the channel, the more intense the color of the ridge. A line-engraved design in the metal consists of a series of channels and holes varying in depth and width; a recess-engraved design on the paper consists of a series of ridges and humps, varying in height, width and intensity.

Line-engraved printing may take place directly from a printing base engraved by hand (or any combination of handwork, etching or machine work), or from a printing base produced only after many processes subsequent to the original engraving.

Direct Hand Engraving

Printing by the most crude and simple form of line engraving, termed "chalcography," was used in the production of, for example, Mauritius 1847 Post Office issue. A single design of a value of a stamp was cut by hand into a copper plate by gouging out the metal with an engraving tool known as a burin or graver. The copper plate, which bears two subjects, one for the 1d. and the other for the 2d. value, can be seen pictured in the chapter entitled "Stamp Design." This copper plate formed the printing base, and the stamps were printed one at a time from it. Such printing was, of course, wasteful of labor in actual printing. It is usually not resorted to in stamp production except for the making of proofs and essays, to which reference was made in the chapter entitled "From Design to Issued Sheets."

In order to produce a printing base bearing repetitions of the design, its multiplication may be carried out by hand, mechanically, galvanically or photographically.

Multiplication of the Design by Hand

Multiplying the design on the printing base by hand involves the separate cutting of not one but as many repetitions of the subject as are required either by hand engraving alone or in combination with etching and, perhaps, the assistance of a pantograph. Each of the plates for Philippines 1854 5c., 10c., 1r. and 2r. contained forty subjects separately engraved by hand.

In some instances, such hand-engraved plates contained combinations of values; for example, the plate of U.S. Postmasters, Providence, R.I., 1846 contained twelve subjects, eleven of them being of the 5c. value, the other subject being the 10c.

The plate of, for example, Nevis 1861 1d. bore twelve subjects, three across and four down, engraved by hand, probably with the assistance of a pantograph.

Because it is impossible, even with the assistance of the pantograph, absolutely identically to reproduce an engraved design by hand, each subject separately engraved differs from every other subject so engraved; and, therefore, the stamps each bear the corresponding differences. While this fact is of philatelic interest and value in that it enables the stamps to be assigned to their original positions on the sheet, it is undesired by the issuing

Philippine Islands 1854 10c. This stamp was printed from a plate bearing forty subjects, each separately engraved by hand.

authority, which normally requires comparative identity of subjects to minimize the risk of successful forgery. Also, such printing is wasteful of labor in actual engraving.

A method that has been adopted to multiply a design for recess printing is the preparation of a flat die that is hammered into a flat copper plate in as many different positions as required. Such a process was used for Tasmania Postal Fiscals 1863-64 3d. to 10s. and Brazil 1881 (July 15) 50r., 100r. and 200r.

Multiplication of the Design Mechanically

The basic steps involved in the mechanical multiplication of the design in order to produce line-engraved printing bases are universally taken; but it is, broadly speaking, true to state that the intermediate steps vary widely, and nearly every printing establishment has its individual variations of steps in the process. It would be quite impossible, in a work of this nature, to attempt to include every such practice past and present.[1] The most that can be attempted is to give an outline of the basic steps involved in the process which is known, familiarly, as the Perkins Die and Mill Process — named after its patentee and user, Jacob Perkins of Massachusetts, who together with his partner Joshua Butters Bacon was later responsible for so many of the early classic stamps.

Depending upon the discovery that the same piece of steel can be made comparatively soft or hard at will, this process when reduced to its elements involves the following steps:

1. Softening a small block of steel — the "die."
2. Engraving the design in recess on the die.
3. Hardening the recess-engraved die.
4. Softening a mill or roll (a small cylinder) of steel.
5. "Taking up" the design on to the periphery of the roll by pressing the soft roll into contact with the hardened die under great pressure and, with a rocking motion, forcing the metal of the roll into the recesses of the die, resulting in a "relief" of the design on the periphery of the roll.
6. Hardening the roll — with its relief termed the "roller die."
7. Softening a comparatively large sheet[2] of steel — the "plate."
8. "Laying down" or "rolling in" the design on the plate (in as many different positions as required) by pressing the relief on the hardened roll into contact with the softened plate under great pressure and, with a rocking motion, forcing away the metal of the plate, resulting in recesses on it corresponding with the relief of the roller die and the recesses of the die.

---

[1] Each line-engraved issue when studied must be studied by reference to the particular processes used in its production; and it is quite unsound to use the practices of one printing establishment as standard and to refer exclusively to it for the purpose of diagnosing with certainty the cause of variations found in the products of a different printing house. This statement holds true, of course, for any other of the printing processes, and cannot be too strongly emphasized.

[2] Although in this outline of the process I employ the term "sheet" of steel, and refer to "the plate," other forms are used, so are other metals, to which reference is made later in the discussion of "The Printing Base."

These three stamps show how the printers rung the changes, using the frame and head for different designs, altering the inscriptions.

9. Printing from the plate.

This method of engraving on steel is termed siderography; the engravers and workmen are termed siderographists.

The Die

The first step is the production of a flat die, a small block of steel that has been softened comparatively by being decarbonated, and has been given a highly polished working surface. In its simplest form, a die for this type of printing consists of such a piece of steel that has had the design cut into its substance manually by one engraver. However, it is rarely the case that an engraved subject consists solely of handwork; also many designs contain one or more features that have been taken from other designs, and many stamps incorporate the results of the work of several engravers.

Closely spaced parallel lines are often the result of what is termed "lathe work," being marked or cut by the stylus of a machine constructed for that purpose, and patterns of intricately woven lines, referred to as "engine turning," are similarly made by a geometric lathe. Such effects are found on very many stamps. As an instance, in the illustration captioned "Damage and Repair" in the chapter entitled "Printing Problems and Varieties," the parallel lines of the background to the whole stamp were thus mechanically ruled; and further by way of single instance, in U.S. 1931-32 Postage Due series, the portion surrounding the central numeral of value provides an excellent example of one type of the product of the geometric lathe.

Such mechanical work is rarely effected directly to the piece of steel that the engraver has handworked; use is made of the principles of the process to "take up" work from several different dies, and, after removing — usually from the roll — the parts unwanted for the particular design in hand, to "lay down" the requisite parts[3] on to a composite die, which then becomes the original die for the particular design in hand. Exemplification of this is provided, for instance, by three stamps: Ceylon 1857-59 4d., Tasmania 1858 6d.,

---

[3] Sometimes the term "subsidiary die" is used in reference to the piece of metal bearing a design forming part of a composite die.

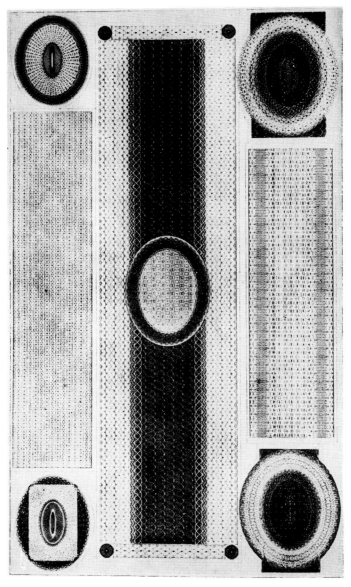

Engine turning. Examples of the effects produced by an early geometric lathe. This complete design was submitted about 1822 to the Bank of England by Jacob Perkins and Charles Heath as suitable for the reverse of a bank note. Part of the dark central strip was used, with additions, as the background for Great Britain 1840 1d. and 2d., and was later incorporated in several other postage stamps, including Cape of Good Hope 1853 1d., 4d.; 1855-58 1s.; Victoria 1856 (October) 1d.; 1858 (November) 6d.; St. Vincent 1880-81 5s., and New Zealand 1915-22 1½d. to 1s.

211

Geometric lathe. USA 1931-32 Postage Due 30c., and Chile 1862 20c. These two designs illustrate some aspects of the product of the geometric lathe.

and Ionian Islands 1859, where the changes were rung on the frame and background, and head.

In numerous cases one design differs from another merely in denomination. In such cases, frequently, one die is engraved containing one value. This die is termed variously "master die," "mother die," "original die," and "parent die." From this master die a roller relief is then made; from the relief the symbols of denomination are removed, and then as many new dies are laid down as required; these new dies are termed sometimes "subsidiary dies," and sometimes "working dies." On each subsidiary or working die, the required symbols of value are engraved; and each die then becomes the basis from which new roller reliefs and, subsequently, the printing bases are made; and these dies are then, sometimes, referred to as the "original dies" for the respective values. Sometimes the original engraving bears no symbols of value, and as many reproductions are made from it as are required, and the denominations are engraved for the first time on these reproductions. Instances of such procedures are provided by Rhodesia and Nyasaland 1954 ½d. to 1s., of which the designs differ only in the symbols of value.

A classic instance of a single engraving subsequently employed for the stamps of more than one country is provided by the Britannia design, originally engraved with a blank tablet, and first used for Mauritius 1849-58 (no value expressed) *prepared for use and never issued,* and later used for Barbados 1852 (½d. to 4d.).

As a further instance: for Great Britain 1955 2s.6d., 5s., 10s., and £1, one die was engraved for the head; one undenominated die was engraved for the framework; four dies were engraved for the centers. Four composite dies were then made by laying down from roller reliefs the head, frame, and center, and on these dies the denominations were engraved; from the then-completed composite dies stemmed the printing bases of each value.

212

These designs both stemmed from a single engraving incorporating a blank uncolored tablet. Upon dies comprising copies of the engraving, the letters were engraved and from these dies the printing plates stemmed.

After it bears the required design, the die is hardened. Details of the hardening process vary, but a widespread practice is to heat the die for a predetermined length of time in a furnace and on a bed of cyanide maintained at a certain temperature, and then to dip the hot die in a liquid. Sometimes,

Great Britain 1955 2s.6d., 5s., 10s. and £1. In the production of these stamps, one die was engraved for the head, one undenominated die for the framework and four dies for the castles; four composite dies were then made from these engravings by transference, and on the composite dies the values were engraved.

213

to assist in handling, the die has had one or two holes drilled through it — of course well away from the center where the design is to be engraved.

The Roller Die

After the flat die has been hardened, the next step is the production of the relief on the roll. This is effected through the medium of what is termed a "transfer press."

The hardened flat die is placed in the bed of the transfer press; the roll (termed variously the "transfer roll," "transfer roller," "transfer cylinder," and "mill"), which is comparatively soft, is held in the press so that part of the polished periphery is in close contact in a tangential line with the surface of the flat die. The transfer press is capable of exerting very great pressure, in the order of thirty tons, between the flat die and the roller, and is constructed so that, under such pressure, the surfaces of the die and roller can be moved in relation to one another in what is termed a "rocking" motion. By reason of the very great pressure, the metal of the roll on its periphery is distorted and forced into the recesses engraved on the die at the tangential line of contact; and because of the rocking motion, the line of contact can be varied back and forth until the whole area of the design has been covered and the corresponding area of the periphery forced into the recesses.

When the rocking operations are completed, the transfer roller bears on part of its periphery a copy of the design on the die. As was tabulated in the chapter entitled "From Design to Issued Sheets," the design on the flat die is negative and recessed, and the design on the roller is positive and raised. There are, in fact, no recesses on the roller; the design stands out from the periphery, and is termed a "relief" or "relief transfer"; philatelically the roller and relief are termed "roller die," and, sometimes, "matrix die." The operation of translating the recesses on the die into the reliefs on the roller is termed "taking up" or "picking up."

The operation of taking up a relief from a steel die to a steel roller is a lengthy process, involving numerous rockings; and a whole working day may well be required for the production of two reliefs. Nevertheless, the softness of the steel, and its liability to be affected by extraneous circumstances, are quite remarkable. For example, it is in my experience that a human hair, interposed between the roller and die, will leave an impress deeply on the soft steel; indeed, the interposition of four or five such hairs caused the transference of the design itself to cease until they had been "rolled in" to a depth sufficient to overcome the impediment which they, as reliefs, presented to the operations of the siderographist.

It is in the use or misuse of the roller, after it has been hardened, that most philatelic varieties occur, and these, or some of them, are referred to later, where "The Printing Base" is discussed. However, certain occurrences to the relief before it is hardened have philatelic importance, and may conveniently be dealt with here.

An unhardened roller bears a relief that is susceptible to damage by careless handling. The lines of the design that are eventually to print in color are minute ridges on the roller, and a blow with an instrument such as a spanner

Great Britain 1955 £1. Showing the flat die in the bed of the transfer press, and the roller with the relief taken up. Because of the lighting, the recesses on the flat die appear lighter than the surface of the die. Note the design on the flat die is reversed, and the design on the transfer roll is normal. Again because of the lighting, the surface of the roll appears darker than the relief lines, thus giving the design on the roll the appearance of being negative — on the printed stamps the lines that appear light on the roll are printed in color; and the areas that appear dark on the roll are uncolored on the printed stamp. Note the hole drilled through the flat die to make for ease in handling when the die is heated for hardening. Note also the reference number on the flat die.

The transfer press. Showing how the flat die for Great Britain 1955 £1 was adjusted in the transfer press for taking up the relief on the roll.

Damaged relief. Netherlands 1852 (Jan. 1) 10c. Horn on Forehead — showing on all stamps from the plate. The damage takes the form of an uncolored mark, like a horn apparently projecting from the forehead. The mark was caused by damage to the relief, on the roll, of the ridges comprising the background.

or screwdriver or the placing of the periphery of a roller on a flat or uneven surface are sufficient to damage one or more of the ridges. Unless such damage is detected and remedied, every stamp resulting from use of that particular relief will bear the signs of the damage, in the form of an uncolored or lightly colored mark where there should have been intense or intenser color. A well-known instance of such damage is to be found in Netherlands 1852 (Jan. 1) 10c., the so-called Horn on Forehead variety, which appears on every one of the 100 stamps in the sheet, and shows an uncolored mark in what should be the dark background to the right of the forehead.

Because the design on the roll consists merely of ridges, it is comparatively simple to remove a portion of the design, if desired, and it is usually from the roll that, for example, figures or words of value are erased when undenominated dies are required from an original die bearing such figures or wording. The removal is effected by the siderographist, who scrapes or stones away the undesired ridges so as to leave the periphery unraised over the desired area, which is then polished. A relief so treated, or one on which damage has been repaired, is referred to as an "altered relief."

It has been and still is widespread practice to take up more than one relief on the transfer roll; the circumferences of different rolls vary, and they are usually large enough to accommodate from three to seven separate reliefs. Often these reliefs are all of the same die and design, but instances are recorded of the one roller bearing reliefs from different dies and different values — for example, Switzerland 1943 (Feb. 26) Centenary of First Cantonal Postage Stamps 10(c.) was produced by use of a roller bearing side-by-side reliefs of a 4(c.) and 6(c.) design.

After the reliefs have been taken up on the roller, it in turn is hardened in the same manner as the flat die.

The Printing Base

After the transfer roller has been hardened, the next step is the preparation of the printing base to receive the subjects. In its original form, the Perkins Die and Mill Process involved the use exclusively of a flat plate to form the printing base, and this flat plate was initially of unhardened steel. Later developments of the printing process involved the use of plates that were curved into half-cylinders, and still later developments involved the use of printing bases comprising entire cylinders. Substances other than steel have been used, and surfacing with hard metal, such as chromium, has in some cases replaced the case-hardening process of the furnace and cyanide or its equivalent. Philatelic varieties arising subsequent to the hardening of the transfer roller can be found commonly in the products of all three types of printing bases, and it is convenient to consider them in historical order.

The Flat Plate

Every one of the world's first adhesive postage stamps, the Penny Black and Two Pence Blue of Great Britain 1840 and many thousands more designs, have been printed from flat plates. The plate is a sheet of comparatively soft steel, with a highly polished surface; its size is chosen as convenient for the work in hand, and the thickness varies from plate to plate.

The subjects are applied to the plate by a process exactly similar to that used for taking up the relief on the roller. That is, the roller and plate are put in a transfer press, and the operations gone through in as many different positions on the plate as are desired; the transfer press used in this step of the process may be a much more massive piece of apparatus than that used for transferring from die to roller.

Before the plate is ready for the bed of the transfer press, much preliminary work has to be done; this work consists of preparing the plate so that the subjects can be placed in alignment. Before the days of perforation, exact alignment of the subjects was not essential, and if single watermarked paper was to be employed, alignment was guided by that consideration and the limits of the plate. After the introduction of perforation, and the necessity for having the perforation holes in the gutters between stamps, exact alignment of subjects on the plate became a matter of precision, demanding more and more technical development and care.

Different devices have been used to ensure correct alignment. Usually, for varying reasons, the working area of the plate is marked with several series of dots, dashes and even continuous lines. The process of applying the dots and lines is termed ''laying-out the plate.'' All these markings, which are made after careful measurement, are made with the object of guiding the siderographist where to make the entries. Normally the intention would be that none of the markings should appear on the printed stamp — they should either be hidden by a feature of the design or obliterated by it, or else later

Guide dot. Great Britain 1841 1d. showing a guide dot or position dot in southeast corner square. The dot was marked on the printing plate as a guide to show the siderographist where to enter the relief, and was intended to be obliterated by the lines of the corner square.

be removed from the plate. However, many instances are known of stamps bearing such dots, termed ''guide dots'' or ''position dots,'' and lines, called ''guide lines,''[4] usually within the edge of a design — in color, for, of course, the dot or line on the plate is in the form of a slight recess.

Sometimes dots of this nature may be encountered in a sheet margin, and each such dot occurs there because it denotes a positioning place of a centering device termed a ''side point.'' This consists of a pointer fixed to the mandrel of the transfer roller, and use of a side point involves that the appropriate dot on the plate does not occur within the area of the entry located by reference to that dot. The position of each such dot, not only in the sheet margin but also over the whole printing area of the plate, has been located only after several series of calculations and measurements, followed by markings, each of which has resulted in other dots, dashes or lines on the plate. Philatelic terminology is not standard in reference to these various markings, and the terms ''guide dot'' and ''position dot'' are sometimes used synonymously and generically. The term ''side point dot'' does not seem to have any wide philatelic use, but would appear to be unequivocal in meaning,

---

[4] But see that term in the alphabetical list to the chapter entitled ''From Design to Issued Sheets.''

Guide line. Great Britain 1841 1d. showing a guide line in northeast corner square. The line was marked on the printing plate during a series of operations for making a guide to the siderographist where to enter the relief, and was intended to be obliterated by the frameline at the right.

and is available for use when the precise character of a particular dot can be ascertained.

After the plate has been laid out it is placed in the bed of the transfer press; the roller die is brought into close contact with the plate under pressure and the rocking operation takes place. This rocking, when perfectly done, covers the whole area of the relief on the periphery of the roller, and the hardened steel relief forces itself into the comparatively soft metal of the plate, making recesses that are exact copies of the recesses on the flat die; the design on the plate is negative and recessed.

The process of translating the reliefs on the roller into the recesses on the plate is known as "rocking in," or "entering the relief"; a backward and forward movement of the plate and roller in relation to one another and covering the whole area of the design is termed a "pass"; and the subject on the plate is termed, philatelically, an "entry," and, sometimes, a "transfer."

How many passes are necessary before an entry is made satisfactorily is a matter for the judgment and skill of the siderographist. Because the roller relief displaces, or forces away, only some of the relevant metal in the plate during any pass, it is sometimes necessary to make as many as 100 or more passes before a sufficient depth has been reached to yield satisfactory prints.

After each entry has been made to the satisfaction of the siderographist, the plate is moved, and an entry made in a new position until the plate bears the required number of subjects.

There are many stages during the rocking in at which something short of perfection can be achieved, and thus cause varieties of philatelic interest. For instance: the precise axial line at which the relief and the plate first come into contact for any design is a matter for the judgment of the siderographist; this line is frequently at one extremity of the relief, but sometimes is at other places. Further, imprecision in the mechanism or in judgment may result

Dropped roll. Cayman Islands 1946 Victory 1½d. showing marked duplication or thickening of the lines of the design throughout a vertical area embracing the first "S" of "Islands." The duplication or thickening is more marked at the top than at the bottom of the stamp.

in an attempt to begin rocking in under pressure at a wrong place; if this attempt almost immediately ceases, and an entry is then properly made, the resultant stamp may bear little or no effect of the false start — but the effect may be present, and it is present, for example, on Cayman Islands 1946 Victory 1½d., stamp No. 45 on sheets printed from plate A1, where the thickening of the lines of the design vertically throughout the stamp in a narrow area embracing the first "s" of "Islands" can clearly be remarked, more especially at the top of the design. Such a variety is sometimes termed "dropped roll."

Again, the exact amount of pressure to be used in each pass, and the speed at which the pass is carried out are matters for the siderographist, who has to take into account the plasticity of the unhardened steel plate. Because of this plasticity, if too much pressure is applied, or if the pass is made too quickly, a minute wave of steel is pushed forward by the roller on the surface of the plate. If an entry has been partly made before the excessive pressure or speed is employed, the minute wave of metal will carry on it the lines already entered, while the roller will impress new lines during the pass it is making. This will result in duplication of the lines of the design in the resultant stamp, and is termed a "shift" or "shifted transfer." Such duplication almost invariably occurs at the extremity of a design, and a repetition of faulty judgment may cause such duplications at both extremities.

Duplications of the lines of line-engraved stamps result from many causes; and most causes have no characteristically peculiar effects. For these reasons, accurate and certain diagnosis of the cause of an effect on a particular stamp frequently cannot be made; the most that the careful and accurate student can do, when the cause cannot with certainty be deduced, is to describe the effect, leaving the cause perhaps to be established in the light of further discovered facts, and perhaps never to be established beyond doubt. For this reason, some terms that are used philatelically are of great value, being descriptive of duplications or more multiplications of the lines of such stamps; such terms include "double transfer," "triple transfer," and, in its widest sense, "double impression."[5] These terms are, of course, wide enough to embrace the effects of "dropped roll," "shifts," and many other causes.

The continued use of even a hardened roll may result in part of the relief breaking away and, consequently, that portion of the design being missing from the resultant entry and subsequently printed stamp. Often such breaking away is progressive, so that less and less, say, of a line appears on following entries. When this occurs, the order of entering the relief can be ascertained, by noting the progression of the break in relation to the stamps on the printed sheet. Stamps bearing such varieties are said to result from a "broken relief."

A comparative effect is sometimes caused by failure to enter a relief to a sufficient depth to yield good prints; the term used to describe such an effect, where fine lines fail to reproduce on the plate, is "incomplete transfer." How-

---

[5] See the alphabetical list to the chapter entitled "Printing Problems and Varieties."

Fresh entry. New Zealand 1855-72 1d. showing duplications in the design because of fresh entry. The lines of the original entry are visible in "NE" of "New," above the top frameline, in "ONE PENNY," in "POST-AGE," outside the left frameline near the foot, and elsewhere in the design.

Non-coincident re-entry. New Guinea 1937 Coronation 5d., showing an outstanding example of non-coincident re-entry, with all lines of the design doubled laterally.

ever, incomplete transfers lack the progressive element possible in broken relief.

A transfer incomplete in the sense that the lines of the design are missing at one or both of its extremities can be caused by failure to rock in the complete relief; stamps exhibiting such varieties are referred to as "short transfer."[6] However, short transfer usually results from a cause different from incomplete rocking, as is mentioned below.

After the entries have been made to the satisfaction of the siderographist, the plate is examined and, probably, proofed; and much work may be necessary before the plate is passed as satisfactory.

For example, in the case of an incomplete transfer, the plate would probably be returned to the transfer press, and the relief entered again at the offending position. The keying of the transfer relief with the recesses of the entry is normally accomplished without difficulty by the almost uncanny skill of the siderographist, who is said to "feel" the relief into place. When perfectly done, this operation — which is referred to as "re-entry" — leaves no effect on the plate to denote what has been carried out. In the vast majority of cases when re-entry is carried out — and it is effected innumerable times as a matter

---

[6] *Scott's Catalogue of United States Stamps Specialized* instances as a good example of short transfer United States 1851-56 1c. Type III, with the top and bottom curved lines outside the duty and value labels missing in the middle.

221

of course and everyday practice in the production of line-engraved printing bases — it is perfectly done. However, it sometimes happens that exact keying of the relief with the original entry does not take place; therefore, when the re-entry is completed, some or all of the lines of the design are doubled, and this reveals itself on the resultant stamps. Such varieties, for precision, are referred to as "non-coincident re-entries." Such a set of circumstances, with a slight lateral movement of the plate or roller, gave rise to such a variety in New Guinea 1937 Coronation 5d., stamp No. 22 on sheets printed from plate 2A, where every line of the design shows clearly doubled, laterally to the right.

Of course, the non-coincidence of lines in re-entry is undesired. Re-entry takes place in other circumstances for the purpose of repair, to which reference is made below.

Again, it sometimes happens that an entry is made so out of alignment with the other subjects in the column or row or both that it is considered unsatisfactory, and amendment of the plate is needed. It is necessary to erase the offending entry from the plate. This is done by a lengthy combination of processes to the plate — burnishing, scraping, perhaps drilling the plate from the back and hammering the back of the plate to cause the plasticity of the metal to fill in the lines — all with the object of preparing a completely flush surface which is polished and is then ready to receive a newly made entry in alignment with the others. This process is termed "fresh entry."[7]

When all the processes are perfectly carried out, there is nothing in the resultant stamps to show what has occurred. However it sometimes happens — relatively more frequently than in the case of re-entry — that fresh entry does leave some signs visible on the resultant stamps. For one reason or another some of the lines of the original entry escape complete erasure or obliteration, and the lines of the resultant stamp reveal seeming duplication; sometimes, but by no means invariably, this duplication is a comparatively large distance away from the line or lines duplicated.

It is clear that the greatest this distance can be is equivalent to half the width or height or both of the stamp itself, and such extremes have been recorded in, for instance, the early stamps of Ceylon and New Zealand. However, these extremes are very rare occurrences, and the usual misplacement is to be measured on the millimeter rather than the centimeter scale. These circumstances accounted for the double transfer to be found, for example, on New Zealand 1855-72 1d., stamp No. 12 in row 14, where the duplications can be traced outside and in many parts of the design.

Of course, in fresh entry, the non-coincidence of the new and the original entries is intentional; what is undesired is that any of the lines of the original entry should print.

Other amendments to the design that can take place after the plate has been entered initially is manual work to any part of one or more subjects.

---

[7] Some students and authorities use the term "fresh entry" to denote any noticeable amendment made by another application of the transfer relief to the plate before it is printed from, irrespective whether such application was made to effect re-entry or fresh entry, and limit the use of the term re-entry to corrections to the plate after it was put to press.

Recut. Brunei 1952 10c. The frame of every stamp in the sheet of this value was re-cut, particularly at the left about the ornamentation which takes the form of the normal upright "2." A value for which the frame was not recut is shown at right, for comparison.

This normally occurs when re-entering will not effect a desired improvement — for instance, if the original engraving has yielded a die that does not transfer well, or the relief does not transfer well, or perhaps some other combination of circumstances. Such handwork with the engraver's tools is termed "re-cutting,"[8] and evidence is available that re-cutting is by no means limited to older issues. For instance, in Brunei 1952 1c. to 50c., the common design of the frame exhibits extensive handwork on the plate of nearly every value, and, for instance, on the 10c., the frame of every stamp in the sheet has been re-cut, particularly at the left about the ornamentation that takes the form of the normal upright figure "2."

The entering of a relief, and manual re-cutting also, cause the metal outside the actual area of operations to lift and sink, resulting in what is termed "burr," and in an area that could hold ink, print, and leave undesired and unsightly marks. This burr is, normally, removed manually by scraping, burnishing and polishing, but sometimes is incompletely removed, resulting in areas of color, usually outside the framelines of the design.

After all necessary amending work has been done to the plate, and it is approved, the back of the plate is, in some instances, rocked over by a narrow roll to level up the spaces between subjects, and the plate is then hammered, further treated and polished. In some cases, printing has taken place from unhardened plates.

After a plate has been printed from for some time, it may wear, and begin to yield unsatisfactory impressions; because the surface wears away, the recesses become less deep and do not hold sufficient ink. In such cases, and for other reasons, a decision might be taken to repair the plate.

---

[8] Some students and authorities use the terms "re-cut" and "retouch" as synonyms.

Repair may be effected by the process of manually re-cutting, particularly framelines and the outer portions of designs, or by re-entry, or by other work. The effect of such re-cutting is identical with any such operation carried out before the plate is printed from.

An illustration of repair to damage of a subject on the plate accompanies the alphabetical list to the chapter entitled "Printing Problems and Varieties."

A further and outstanding instance of repair to damage is provided by China 1948 (Jun. 24) Air $10,000 surcharged on 1940-41 Air 30c., plate BC1.7, stamp No. 94, which can be found in three states. The first is the undamaged state. The second state exhibits extensive damage in the form of a colored line, resulting from a scratch, on the left-hand part of the design; the scratch passes in a northeasterly direction through the numerals, up the mountain and approaches the plane, then in a northwesterly direction the scratch passes through the wing and to the upper frame of the stamp. In the third state, the effect of this damage has been reduced by retouching, visible as a series of additional markings in the mountain, but traces of the scratch are still visible in the numeral and at the top frameline.

Repair by re-entry, when it does not key perfectly with the original entry, results in double transfer, and is referred to for precision as "non-coincident re-entry." The fact that it is a repair to a partly worn plate instead of an amendment to a plate not yet printed from (as in the case of non-coincident re-entry resulting, for example, from deepening or completing an originally incomplete transfer) can be deduced philatelically by the existence of stamps from the same position on the plate in different states, respectively without and with the double transfer.

When the repair by re-entry has been effected in perfect key with the original entry, the fact that re-entry has occurred requires more acute philatelic observation than is the case with non-coincident re-entry. There are no duplications of lines to catch the eye, and the fact that re-entry has taken place can be deduced only from other circumstances, such as the greater clarity or intensity of impressions that can be proved to have been made after, than those that can be proved to have been made before a certain period of use of the plate. For this purpose, copies of stamps bearing dated cancellations or on dated correspondence provide useful but not conclusive evidence. These matters are among those relevant to the ultimate in the philatelic techniques of the research-student of production — plate study.

The operations of re-entry and fresh entry can lead to startling errors; for instance, an error of color. In United States 1916-17 2c., flat-plate printings, on plate 7942, re-entry was effected to three positions on the 400-set plate. The siderographist used the wrong relief, that of the 5c. design instead of the 2c., with the result that about 50,000 of the sheets printed between March 9 and April 1, 1917, each bore three errors of color, the 5c. in the color of the 2c. carmine. More than 130,000 of the errors survived the government's attempt to recall them. A block of nine, imperf, with the error as the middle stamp, is pictured in the chapter entitled "Aims of Collecting."

Such a variety is sometimes colorfully termed "errant entry," or, sometimes, "foreign relief."

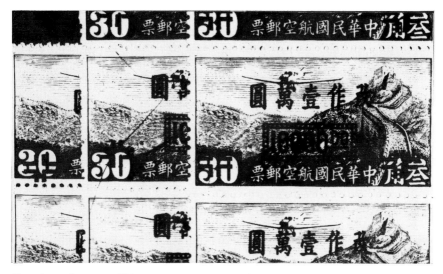

Repair to damage. China 1948 (Jun. 24) Air $10,000 surcharged on 1940-41 Air 30c., plate BC1.7, stamp No. 94 in three states. At the left is the first state, showing the stamp as first printed; in the center is the second state, after damage had occurred to the subject, by a scratch that passes upward in a northeasterly direction through the "3," the mountain, and sky, and then curves northwesterly, passes through the tip of the wing of the plane, and so to the upper frameline. At the right is the third state after the subject had been repaired — the effect of the damage has been reduced, and additional, short lines of shading have been added to the mountain; parts of the scratch can still be seen, notably through the "3" and by the upper frameline. The same scratch has affected also the subjects below and above stamp No. 94.

Errant entry is of comparatively rare occurrence, but a well-known example occurs in New Zealand 1915-22 4d., stamp No. 10 in row 4 of plate 20, where the value tablet at the top left bears clear marks of the partly obliterated figures "2½d.," mute testimony to the fact that the relief of the 2½d. stamp had been entered for that subject, and the errant entry partly corrected. A further instance is to be found, for example, in United States Revenues, second issue, 60c. (Scott No. R116), where traces occur of the 70c. design.

Another well-known instance of a double transfer consisting of more than one value exists in Canada 1888-97 6c., where a repair effected to the plate resulted in one stamp bearing traces of the upper part of the 5c. design; the portions of the 5c. design are considerably displaced vertically downward from the upper limits of the 6c. design, and there is doubt whether the variety owes its origin to an attempt to repair that subject with the wrong relief, or to an over-rocking (of the transfer roller containing reliefs of both designs) during a repair to the subject vertically above the one exhibiting the errant entry. To many Canadian specialists, the variety is known as "the 5 on 6c. re-entry"; less dogmatically, it is referred to as "the 5 on 6c. double transfer."

Over-rocking of the relief roller and also rolling the back of the plate can produce the effect of weakening the lines, or some of them, of an entry already

Errant entry. Canada 1888-97 6c. Unique block of six, containing "the 5 on 6c. double transfer" — the center stamp in the lower row. The lines that are the upper portion of the 5c. design can be traced most clearly through the letters "ANA" of "Canada" and "AG" of "Postage."

Short transfer. The stamp above the double transfer exhibits the variety short transfer, the outer frame to the curved tablet bearing "Canada Postage" being partly missing, and the other portions of the top extremity of the design being faint or missing.

made. Because of the plasticity of the metal, these two operations tend to fill in the lines of adjacent subjects, causing them to yield unsatisfactory prints in the parts affected. Many instances of "short transfer" and "incomplete transfer" result from these causes, termed "ironing out."

Very frequently, before they were printed from, the steel printing plates were hardened by being carbonated. This resulted in longer working life of the plate. Alterations to plates have been made after they have been hardened, and *Perkins Bacon Records* contains reference to the softening of the plate in order to effect repair by re-entry.[9] However, repairs to hardened plates have been carried out by local etching, and such repairs are, sometimes, referred to as "retouches"[10] to distinguish them from recutting in which the engraver's tools are used.

---

[9] *Perkins Bacon Records*, Vol. 1, Page 396.

[10] Some students and authorities use the term "retouch" to denote repairs made to a plate after it has been put to press, confining the term "recut" to amendments made before the plate is printed from.

Great Britain 1955 £1. The curved printing plate, showing how the subjects have been entered in two panes of forty, each pane being surmounted by a security scrollwork pattern. The plate (reference) number appears in positive at the base; and at the top, between and beneath the two scrollwork patterns, the same plate (reference) number has been engraved in reverse and recess. Note the holes and slots machined through the plate to hold it in the press. The stamps were issued in sheets of forty, the printed sheet being appropriately divided and trimmed.

In many instances, the surfacing of plates by electro-deposition of a wafer-thin chromium deposit has replaced case-hardening. This process is termed "facing," and the deposit can be stripped. If the metal plate beneath the facing has been damaged by, for example, a blow, the plate may be repaired, and re-surfaced.

The Curved Plate

In certain presses it is necessary to use the plate in the form of a half-cylinder; and some presses use two such plates placed together in the form of a cylinder.

In some cases, for use in such presses, after the flat plate has been completed it is put into a machine that bends the plate into a semi-circle, with the subjects on the outside. This bending process actually stretches each subject along the direction of the bend, and causes a slight lessening of the depth of each recess. This results in the stamps being longer (about one millimeter in twenty millimeters) than they would have been if printed from the plate when flat.

After the bending, the inner side of the plate is provided with slots, known as gripper slots, or other means whereby the plate may be held in the print-

Joint line. 1½c. Presidential coil. The line between these stamps results from ink collecting in one of the gaps between the two plates curved to form a cylinder.

ing machine. Sometimes in use the strain placed on this slotted part of the plate is so great that a crack develops there, which reproduces on adjacent stamps, and is known as a "gripper crack."

When two plates are used in one press to form a cylinder, two lines are formed where the junctures occur, leaving minute gaps between the two plates. During printing, these gaps sometimes fill with ink, which prints in the gutters or sheet margins, giving rise to "joint lines."

In some processes, the plates are curved before the subjects are entered. Curved plates are, normally, hardened and surfaced.

The Cylinder

For the preparation of line-engraved printing cylinders, such as are used, for example, in Switzerland, the preparation of the die and transfer roller proceed in the same manner as for the production of flat plates.

However, after the roller has been hardened, it is put in a different type of transfer press — one constructed to enable the roller and cylinder to be brought together under pressure and to be given a reciprocating motion. This transfer press is a large machine of great precision, with the transfer roll suspended above the cylinder to be entered, and with an adjustment enabling the lateral positions of the roller and cylinder to be varied.

Tête-bêche. Sweden 1920-34 coil stamps 10 öre. These stamps were printed from a cylinder comprising two curved plates; by error, one plate was inserted the wrong way 'round, giving rise to two different varieties of tête-bêche: head-to-head (illustrated) and tail-to-tail. Note the joint line.

228

Line-Engraved Postage Stamp Production in Switzerland

Switzerland 1949 20c. depicting Reservoir at Grimsel.

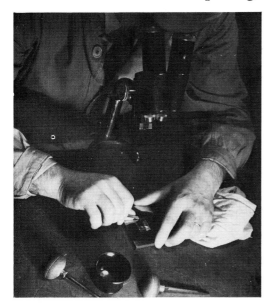

Engraving the flat die. The engraver at work, viewing his operations through a binocular low-power microscope. In his right hand is a burin, which he is guiding with his thumb and forefinger, gouging out the metal. On the table before him are other tools, called lozenge and scorper. Note the hole in the die (another hole is hidden by the engraver's left forefinger), drilled for ease of handling later.

The flat die completed. Note that the design is reversed. Because of the lighting, the recesses appear light and the surface of the die dark in the picture. Both holes are visible.

Hardening the flat die. The heated flat die is being removed from the furnace where it has been heated on a bed of cyanide to a temperature maintained at 850° Centigrade. Note the use to which the two drilled holes have been put: wire is passed through them and looped over the rod, enabling the die to be handled.

The roller die. The transfer roll with relief. Note that the design is normal, but because of the lighting the lines protruding from the periphery of the roll appear light and the surface of the periphery dark in the picture — on the printed stamp these lines appear in color, and the areas of the stamp corresponding with the surface of the periphery of the roll appear uncolored. Note the other reliefs (of the same value), parts of which are just visible in the picture equidistant to right and left of the complete design.

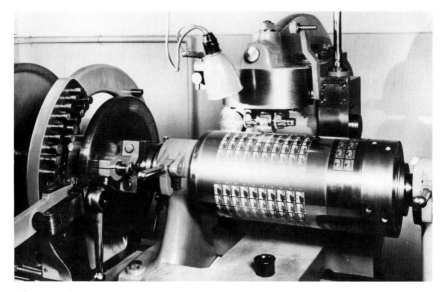

The transfer press, showing the relief being entered directly on to a cylinder.

The completed cylinder ready for the press. Note that the subjects have been entered in panes of fifty (five across, ten down on the pane, but ten across, five down on the cylinder).

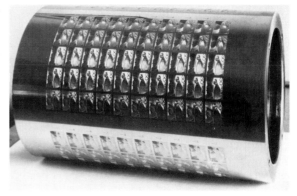

When entries are made directly on to the cylinder, there is no difference in size between the design on the die and that on the cylinder. Because no bending takes place, no stretching of the subject occurs.

After all the entries have been made on the cylinder, it is, usually, surfaced.

Multiplication of the Design Galvanically

The galvanic process of electrodeposition has had long and widespread use for the production of printing bases employed in intaglio printing, although it is more frequently associated with those used for relief printing. Among the earliest postage stamps printed from plates made by the electrodepositing of copper were Sicily 1859 Bomba Heads. The process has had two main applications in intaglio printing: first, the copying of a matrix plate made mechanically by taking impressions from a line-engraved die; and second, the copying of an entire plate made by the die and mill process.

In order to obtain the matrix plate, the recessed die was impressed into soft metal, thus making a mould or matrix, the design being in relief on the mould or matrix. This process was repeated until the required number of moulds was made. These moulds were then grouped together to make the matrix plate. The matrix plate was then suspended in an electrodepositing bath, and a shell of copper grown on the face of the plate. (In the case of the Bomba Heads, five days were required to grow the copper shell, but modern methods have reduced the necessary time to one of hours and minutes rather than days.) The matrix and adhering shell were then removed from the bath, and the copper separated in one piece from the matrix. The copper then bore the required number of subjects, each in reverse and recess,

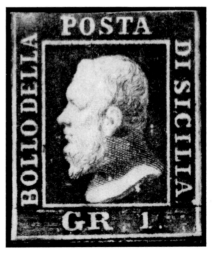

Master plate. Bermuda 1910-36 Ship Type. The plates from which these stamps were printed were electrotypes made from the master plate.

Sicily 1859 1gr. The plate from which this stamp was printed was made by electrotyping a matrix made by pressure from the line-engraved die.

copies of the recessed die. This copper shell was strengthened at the back, and put to press. A similar process was, it is thought, used by Thomas De La Rue & Company Ltd. in the production of Falkland Islands 1904-12 ½d. to 5s.; the matrix for each value consisted of the requisite number of separate pieces of lead (each impressed with one subject) suitably arranged and mounted together on an iron base.

Variations of this process involve the suspension of the engraved die itself in the electrodepositing bath, and the growing of a copper shell over the face of the die. This copper shell, when removed, bears a relief copy of the design, and is termed an ''alto.'' After the desired number of altos have thus been grown, they are joined together and placed in the bath again, a new shell being grown over this alto plate. When this new shell is removed it bears intaglio copies of the design, and is called a ''basso.'' This basso may be used after strengthening for printing, or else it is used to obtain further altos to a required number to form a master alto plate which serves as the base for growing fresh large bassos to be used for printing.

Copying of an entire plate (called the ''master plate'') made by the die and mill process can be effected in two ways. First, it is possible to make a soft metal (usually lead) matrix of the master plate, by bringing the surface of the master plate into close contact with a sheet of the soft metal and pressing the two together in a hydraulic press, causing the soft metal sheet to take up reliefs from the subjects on the master plate; this soft metal matrix is the alto upon which metal is grown in the electrodepositing bath, so providing the printing base. Second, it is possible to place the master plate itself into the electrodepositing bath and to grow an alto, which in turn is placed in the bath to grow the printing plate — or as many printing plates as are required. Of course, this process reproduces any varieties that the master plate may contain; it was used, for example, for Bermuda 1910-36 Ship Types. Further varieties, in the form of retouches, occur on many of these stamps, reflecting work carried out on the plates after they were grown. In the cases of these stamps, the denominations were pantographed on to the printing plates.

Multiplication of the Design Photographically

Multiplying a design by photography involves the use of the step-and-repeat camera to produce a large glass plate bearing the required number of subjects as photographs, in the extreme form of clear glass and dark areas and gradations between the extremes. This glass plate is then brought into contact with a metal plate having a specially prepared and coated surface that becomes insoluble in water directly in proportion to the amount of light allowed to fall on the surface of the metal plate. Exposure to light is then made through the glass plate; after preliminary treatment, the metal plate then bears areas of coating that are acid-resistant and correspond with the clear parts of the glass plate, other areas in the lines of the design — some that are uncoated and therefore are not acid-resistant and correspond with the dark areas of the glass plate, and others that are partly coated and, therefore, are partly acid-resistant. The metal plate is placed in an etching bath where the etching fluid eats away the surface in proportion as it is uncoated, forming recesses of different depths comprising reversed copies of the design. The plate is then faced, and forms the printing base.

When a step-and-repeat camera is not available, other, more primitive methods have to be adopted to obtain the necessary repetitions of the design in the required arrangement. For example, in the cases of Liechtenstein 1920 (May 6) Syndicate 5h. to 10k., and 1920 Madonna 50h. to 2k., photographic copies of the original, undenominated drawings were mounted at predetermined positions on card; the denominations were then affixed in position on each subject; the assemblies comprising the ultimate sheet arrangements were then photographed on to large glass plates, and these were used for the exposures of the coated metal printing plates.

Monochrome and Sequent Color Printing

So far in this chapter, I have discussed the processes of producing line-engraved printing bases for the printing of monochrome stamps. Until comparatively recent years, the invariable practice in the production of line-engraved postage stamps to be printed in more than one color was to produce a separate printing base for each color required, and to apply the different colors to the paper one after the other at separate operations; and this is perhaps the general rule today. Where all the colors are to be applied to the paper from line-engraved printing bases, this involves going through each of the nine steps described above and producing a flat die, a roller relief and a printing base for each color, with the exception that it is not necessarily requisite that each part of the design be manually engraved on a separate flat die. Just as a composite die may be made by transferring the required portions from other dies, so it is possible to transfer a required portion from a complete design on to an otherwise blank die, from which then stems the printing base for the appropriate color.

Because, during the production of any line-engraved printing base, the possibility exists of varieties occurring which will reproduce on the resultant stamps, it follows that the possibilities of a variety occurring on any stamp are multiplied by as many times as there are colors in it.

Until comparatively recent years, line-engraved postage stamps printed in more than one color were invariably printed on sheets of paper — the second and any subsequent color being printed by returning the partly printed sheet, after the ink was dry, to the press for a second or subsequent impression in a different color.

Line-Engraved Principle of Printing

The basic principle of printing from all line-engraved printing bases is adhesion of the ink coupled with the distortion of the paper under pressure. By pressing heavily a yielding substance into contact with the whole of one surface of the printing base covered with paper it is forced into the recesses in that surface; and, as the recesses contain ink, the paper is pressed into contact with the ink, which adheres to the paper and is sucked out of the recesses when the paper is removed.

The yielding surface is provided by a blanket of felt or other substance either detached from or covering a metal cylinder forming one of a pair or more by means of which the pressure is applied.

Because damp paper can be distorted more easily than dry paper, the use of damp paper for line-engraved printing requires the employment of considerably less pressure than does the use of dry paper. The majority of line-engraved postage stamps have been produced by printing on dampened paper, but use is made of machines where the working pressure is so heavy that paper wetting is unnecessary. This enables the stamps to be printed conveniently on paper already gummed. In some cases where printing takes place on a reel of paper, or "on the web," it is already gummed, and moisture is applied to only the printing surface of the paper; this necessitates the intercalation of sheets of, usually, tissue paper between the printed sheets as they are delivered at the end of the machine after the web has been guillotined, in order to prevent the sheets sticking together as a result of this moisture.

Printing from Line-Engraved Printing Bases

From time to time many methods have been developed to put the basic principle of line-engraved printing into practice. Such methods vary to a great extent in detail. It is, broadly speaking, true to state that no two types of presses are identical in their application of the principle, and it would be quite impossible in a work of this nature to deal specifically with every type of press, much less with every one of the types of machines which have been aggregated into complex units for the production of postage stamps. In the descriptions which follow, I have attempted to outline, and to do no more than outline, some of the methods that have been adopted in printing from line-engraved printing bases.

Printing from Flat Plates

In printing from line-engraved flat plates, which are kept warm to assist working the comparatively stiff inks used for this type of printing, the printer covers the printing surface of the plate with ink, either by means of a dabber, which is a cloth pad, or with an ink roller. The ink is not only made to cover the surface of the plate but is forced into all the recesses of the designs by working it in. Then the printer removes all the surplus ink from the surface of the plate. First he does this by means of a wiping cloth, which he rubs briskly over the surface, removing from it all but a thin film of ink. Then he removes this by polishing; that is, he covers his hands with whiting and rubs them over the surface of the plate, repeating the operations until no trace of ink remains on the surface, but the ink remains in the recesses.

These wiping and polishing processes are highly skilled. They sometimes give rise to two well-known but philatelically unimportant varieties: "pseudo-colored paper" and "scooped color."

If the printer should fail to remove the film of ink from the non-printing surface of the plate — that is, from the non-recessed surface — this ink will be deposited upon the paper, and in some cases this has the appearance of being suffused with that color, the resultant stamps being sometimes

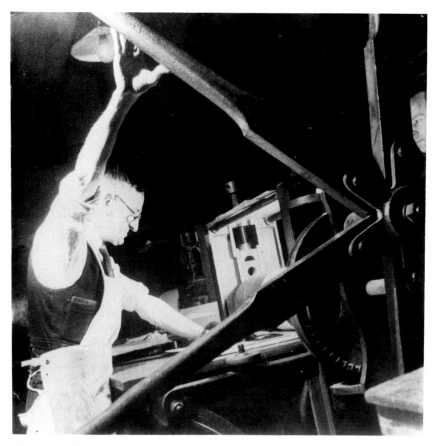

Line engraving. A hand-operated press used for printing from line-engraved plates. The press is being used actually for taking a proof from a flat die. The inked, wiped and polished flat die, partly covered by the small piece of paper upon which the impression will be made, can be seen on the traveling bed of the press, being placed in position by the operator with his left hand. The impression cylinder (in the picture visible to the right of the die) is partly covered with a light-colored "blanket." By pulling on the large spoked wheel, the operator causes the bed to travel, and carry with it the die and its covering paper.

smudged and printed on what, at first glance seems to be, but is not, surface-colored paper.

Scooped color results from a too vigorous or careless polishing of the plate, causing the removal from some of the recesses of some or all of the ink that should have been allowed to remain in them. On the resultant stamps the areas affected have either partly or entirely missing lines or else very faintly colored lines.

After the plate has been polished it is covered with the paper and the "blanket," and is passed between cylinders which provide the pressure necessary to force the paper into the recesses. These cylinders are termed "impression cylinders." After this passage between the impression cylinders,

Line engraving. Rotary printing from metal cylinders. The picture shows the complex printing, perforating and cutting machine manufactured in Switzerland, as used by the Swiss PTT Administration in the production of line-engraved postage stamps such as 1949 3(c) to 70(c). The machine prints on dry, gummed paper "on the web"; part of the reel of unprinted paper can be seen on its spindle near the center of the picture. The paper is led over rollers, to the left in the picture, down and between the impression and plate or printing cylinders. The operator at the left is adjusting the ink feed, and the printed paper can be seen leaving the plate cylinder, the sheet gutters being clearly visible. The paper is led from the plate cylinder to the top of the machine, and then travels to the right in the picture, under "blowers" which force a stream of hot air over the printed paper, and toward the perforating head, indicated by the five pairs of springs in front of the operator standing on the platform. The stamps, still "on the web," are perforated by a "harrow" machine — a whole (eventual) sheet at one descent of the head. The paper is then led again under "blowers," which force a stream of cold air over the paper, to a cylinder with blades, called the "cross cutter," which cuts the web into sheets. The sheets are delivered on a rack to the operator at the extreme right.

the paper is removed from the plate. As has already been mentioned, in some cases the blanket forms part of one of the cylinders; in other cases, the blanket is a separate piece of felt or other yielding substance.

The most simple form of press for printing from line-engraved flat plates is operated by hand, the plate, paper and felt being placed on a traveling bed which, by means of a ratchet coupled to a large spoked wheel, the operator forces between the impression cylinders. All the early line-engraved stamps issued, for example, by Great Britain, were printed from flat plates in hand presses.

Line engraving. The Swiss machine. The inking rollers and printing and impression cylinders. At lower left, ink can be seen in the duct, from which the
inking roller is fed with ink by means of intermediate ink-spreading rollers.
The paper is led downward, at the right in the picture (where the gummed side
is visible), around the impression cylinder, and comes up between it and the
plate or printing cylinder. The lowest part of the paper bearing impressions in
the picture is immediately after the axial line at which the printing has taken
place; the printing cylinder operates counterclockwise.

There are machines which print from a single flat plate, in some of which
the inking, wiping and polishing, paper application, printing and subsequent
cleaning of the plate are all effected mechanically.

Some presses employed for stamp printing necessitate the use of four identical line-engraved flat plates. The usual procedure in such cases is for only
one plate to be made by the die and mill process, and from this plate (sometimes called the "master plate") three electrotype copies are made. The master
plate and the three electrotypes are then used in the press together.

The four plates are simultaneously in use; while one plate is being printed
from, another is being inked, another wiped, and the fourth is being polished.
The four plates, fixed face upward, are rotated counterclockwise through the
machine, and each plate undergoes the necessary sequence of operations.
The inking operation is effected by the machine; rollers, which operate automatically, deposit a carefully adjusted amount of ink on to the plate. Wiping,
too, is automatic, and is performed by a vibrating felt pad, over which is tightly stretched a length of clean wiping cloth fed from one roll on to another
and mechanically wound on after each plate has been wiped. The polishing
operation is carried out by hand in the usual manner. After each plate has
been polished, the dampened paper is placed in position by hand, and after
the plate and paper have passed between the impression cylinders, the paper
is removed by hand from the plate.

Line engraving. The Swiss machine. The perforating head. In the picture the web is emerging, with the (eventual) sheets perforated, and passing under the "blowers," which blow cold air, toward the "cross cutter."

Rotary Printing

Increasing demands for speed in production led to the development of rotary printing from line-engraved printing bases. With flat plates, whether the press is hand-operated or power-assisted, it is possible to print on sheets of paper only; with the introduction of the rotary printing press, printing on reels, or "on the web," became available, but rotary presses for line-engraving printing are, broadly speaking, divisible into two classes: sheet-fed and web-fed.

238

Line engraving. The Swiss machine. The "cross cutter" and sheet delivery rack. The "cross cutter" revolves, the blades and the revolutions being adjusted to sever the web in the sheet gutters.

Sheet-fed presses use either one plate curved around part of a cylinder, called the "plate cylinder" or "printing cylinder," or else two or more such plates which together make a continuous printing surface on the plate cylinder. This is in contact with one side of the paper, and the paper is squeezed heavily between the plate cylinder and the impression cylinder, which is in contact with the other side of the paper. All operations, except in some cases the actual feeding of the sheets, are automatic, and some machines print on dry paper.

In web-fed presses, every operation except the preliminary feeding of the web around the various parts of the machine is fully automatic. Web-fed presses are of two types: those using two or more curved plates joined on the machine to make the plate cylinder, and those which use a hollow continuous cylinder of steel, bronze or other metal. Two curved plates were employed, for example, in the Stickney Rotary Web Press used for many

United States issues. In the machine used in producing many line-engraved issues of Switzerland, the printing surface is provided by a hollow metal cylinder.

Such presses are often incorporated in machines which effect all the operations necessary to turn a reel (or roll) of paper into printed, perforated, numbered, counted and trimmed sheets of gummed stamps.

Sequential Color Printing on the Web

Line-engraved sequential color printing on the web was instituted by the Imprimerie Belge de Securité, a subsidiary of Waterlow & Sons Ltd. of London, who put into use a machine perfected after many years' research and experiment. In this machine the cylinders are of steel, and there are as many printing cylinders as there are colors in the finished stamp — each cylinder bearing the appropriate portion of the design, of course, repeated as many times as there are subjects to be printed at one revolution of the cylinder. Dry and already gummed paper is used, and the colors are applied one after the other in sequence as the paper travels from cylinder to cylinder. All printing operations, including the inking, are effected mechanically, and the surplus ink is removed by means of a doctor knife. The machine also perforates the stamps and delivers them cut into sheets and interleaved with tissue paper to avoid spoilage. The machine could be used also for other methods of printing, and could, of course, be employed for producing monochrome stamps. Examples of some of the first postage stamps printed on this machine are Rhodesia and Nyasaland 1955 1d. coil stamp perf 12½ x 14, with the figure of value denoted by crossed lines, and Nigeria 1956 2d.

The security printing division of Waterlow & Sons Ltd. was taken over by De La Rue & Company Ltd. on January 9, 1961, covering among other things the designing and printing of postage stamps by all processes. De La Rue & Company Ltd. did not take over the Imprimerie Belge de Securité.

Color Printing from a Single Cylinder

The French postage stamp printers, by means of a patent process, were able to print monochrome, bi-colored and multicolored stamps from a single printing cylinder. The ingenuity of the machine enabled the printers to effect, during a single revolution of the cylinder, not only the inking and the wiping processes, but also the printing of the stamps. The ingenuity of the press lies, mainly, in the three ink feeds and rollers, and the wiping arrangements. Each inking roller has a slightly plastic surface, extends the full width of the printing cylinder, and is the same diameter as the length of a sheet of stamps; the surface of each roller has been routed so that it is raised appropriately, and ink is applied to only the desired portion of each subject on the printing cylinder. As the printing cylinder revolves, it is inked in turn by each roller, and every subject has been inked completely during the course of part only of a single revolution. During the course of the same revolution, the surface of the printing cylinder then comes into contact with another roller or cylinder which, with a to-and-fro movement, acts like a razor and removes the surplus ink from the surface of the printing cylinder, without removing any from the recesses and without mixing the colors. Immediately afterward, the surface of the printing cylinder comes into contact with the paper, fed around the impression cylinder. These French stamps were wet printed on paper which had already been gummed; the paper was dampened on only the printing surface, the gummed side being kept dry; but because of the dampening, the machine has a special attachment incorporated which intercalates the cut sheets of printed stamps with other sheets, fed from a supplementary reel, and thus prevents the adhesion which would inevitably follow from the damp surfaces coming into contact with the gummed. The multicolored stamps printed by this machine include, for example, 1954 Sesquicentenary of St. Cyr 15f.

The USA, by using the Koebau-Giori press for printing postage stamps, adopted the process of color printing from a single cylinder with 1957 Flag Issue 4c. This massive machine worked on essentially similar principles to the French press (a "Rotative Chambon en taille-douce" with the Edouard-Lambert adaptation incorporating the Serge-Beaune patent) but, unlike the French press, printed on to sheets of paper, and printed from two plates that were curved around the printing cylinder and occupied about half its circumference. These plates were electrotype copies of the plate normally rolled-in from a transfer roll bearing the complete design. The inking rollers were routed by a machine incorporating the principle of the pantograph, and from every subject on each roller was removed substantially every piece of its surface representing the color or colors that that roller was *not* to ink.

It is characteristic of most stamps printed in more than one color that difficulties of registration on the paper are encountered when it is passed through the press during the printings of colors subsequent to the first. This has the result that, sometimes, to a greater or less extent, gaps occur in the design; a stamp from one sheet appears to differ from a stamp from another sheet in that the variously colored portions of the design occupy relatively different areas of paper. See "Registration" in the alphabetical list of terms to the

USA 1957 Flag Issue 4c. and Jamaica 1960 (Jan. 4) Postal Centenary 1s. These two issues represent milestones in postage stamp production in the USA and British Commonwealth, respectively, each being the first issues printed on the Giori press.

Koebau-Giori Press at Washington

Color printing from a single cylinder. Routing an inking roller. The routing machine operates on the principle of the pantograph, and the operator is shown guiding the stylus that controls the cutting head that is poised over the roller. The roller bears the designs used for USA 1957 Flag Issue 4c., and from the surface of the roller have been routed the areas corresponding to the red color. The roller represents the one used for applying the blue ink to the plates for printing those stamps.

INTAGLIO PRINTING — LINE ENGRAVING

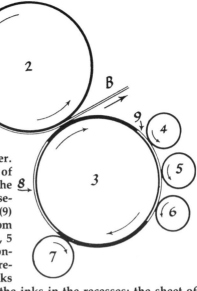

A-B. *Path of paper travel.*

1. *Paper feed.*
2. *Impression cylinder.*
3. *Plate cylinder.*
4. *Ink roller i.*
5. *Ink roller ii.*
6. *Ink roller iii.*
7. *Wiping cylinder.*
8. *Plate (inked in three colors, wiped, and ready for printing).*
9. *Plate (in process of being inked in three colors).*

Three-color printing from a single cylinder. The Koebau-Giori press at the Bureau of Engraving and Printing, and a diagram of the printing and inking arrangements. The sequence of operations is: the clean plate (9) receives ink in the appropriate positions from each of the three inking rollers in turn (4, 5 and 6); the fully inked plate comes into contact with the wiping cylinder (7), which removes all the surplus different colored inks from the non-printing areas, and leaves the inks in the recesses; the sheet of paper has been led by the paper feed (1) around the impression cylinder (2) and is pressed into contact with the inked and wiped plate on the plate cylinder (3). In the picture, (A) is the pile of sheets of gummed, unprinted paper, and the numerals correspond with those in the diagram. Beyond the steps in the picture are the ink fountains, the delivery pile for the printed sheets, and other portions of the massive and complex press.

chapter entitled "Printing Problems and Varieties." On stamps printed in colors from a single cylinder at one operation, such variations in registration cannot occur, and every portion of each design is always the same relative distance from every other, no matter in what colors they are printed.

However, one form of variety that can, and does, occur in stamps printed in colors from a single cylinder at one operation is termed "misapplied color," and consists in the printing of some lines of the design in one color on stamps from some sheets, and in a different color on stamps from other sheets. On stamps printed in different colors from separate plates, such a variation is of major importance and signifies the use of different dies and plates. On stamps printed in colors from a single cylinder at one operation, these varieties are unimportant except as instances of what can occur, and result merely from a slight misapplication of ink intended for one portion of the design but applied to another; they are caused by something short of absolute perfection in the synchronization of the inking rollers with the plate.

Although the Koebau-Giori press is capable of printing in three or more colors at one operation, not every design permits full use to be made of these capabilities; some designs are "compatible" — and for those which were not, three colors involved that the paper had to be passed through the press more than once, with consequent varieties of color registration. For example, USA 1957 (Aug. 31) Champion of Liberty Magsaysay 8c. was not "compatible," nor were the other multicolor stamps in the same series. On the other hand, USA 1957 (Nov. 22) Wildlife Conservation 3c. was printed in three colors at one operation.

With Jamaica 1960 (Jan. 4) Postal Centenary 2d., 6d. and 1s., Waterlow & Sons Ltd. began printing postage stamps on the Giori press, those being the first British Commonwealth stamps so printed.

Varieties and Terms in Line Engraving

The alphabetical list that follows includes some of the terms and varieties appropriate to line-engraved stamps. It does not in the main, and is not intended to, incorporate those varieties which, although encountered in line-engraved stamps, occur also in other printing processes, being varieties of printing generally rather than those occasioned by the productions from a specific kind of printing base. Those general printing varieties, or some of them, are to be found in the alphabetical list to the chapter entitled "Printing Problems and Varieties." A few of the terms that follow refer to varieties of printing, but they are confined to effects peculiar to printing from line-engraved printing bases, or have special significance in this application. The varieties listed consist in either the presence or else the absence of color where it should be respectively absent or present on the normal stamp. Where unusual color is present, the variety is referred to as "colored flaw"; "uncolored flaw" signifies the absence of color which normally appears. Colored flaws result from many causes, some giving rise to constant varieties, other causes resulting in merely inconstant varieties. The same statements hold true with regard to uncolored flaws. Further, both of these classes of flaw — colored and uncolored — can occur either as the result of happenings, during its manufacture or use, to the printing base, or as the result of happenings during printing. In diagnosing the cause of an abnormality it is, therefore, not possible to draw any general rules based on either the presence or the absence of color. Furthermore, some colored and uncolored flaws are caused by happenings for which the philatelist and, indeed, the printer have no short identifying term. In such cases, the procedure adopted by some students is to note the flaw as colored or uncolored, as the case may be, and follow that notation either with a summary of the events leading up to the flaw's occurrence, or with "cause unknown," or "cause uncertain," as appropriate.

Broken Relief. Uncolored flaw. A line-engraved stamp exhibiting a variety caused by a broken relief presents an uncolored area (corresponding with the break in the relief) where there would be color if the relief had not been broken, or damaged. The variety "broken relief" is constant; it occurs on the subject on the printing base, and reproduces on every stamp printed from that subject until it is repaired, if ever. Usually where broken relief occurs, the variety is found on more than one subject on the same printing base, and may be found in progressive form on different subjects on the same printing base or on printing bases subsequently produced from the same transfer relief. Broken relief is caused by damage to a line or other area of the roller-relief, or by inherent weakness, causing the relief to break down under the stress of repeated transferring to the printing base. Instances of broken relief are to be found, for example, in U.S. 1909 Alaska-Yukon Pacific Exposition Issue 2c., where the lower line of the ribbon appears broken over the "T" of "Cents"; and in Great Britain 1840 and 1841 1d., plates 7, 8, 9 and 10, in the form of the so-called "O flaw" or "ON flaw," where the first letter of "ONE" simulates "Q" and in later stages of the relief break appears joined to the "N." The term "Damaged Relief" is used synonymously with "broken relief." See "Roller Flaw."

Burr. Colored flaw. Burr is a rough ridge of metal which holds ink, and results from use of the engraving tool or transfer roll; the ridge reproduces as an indefinite mark in color. Usually burr is removed from the printing base before printing takes place; but, particularly in the cases of repair by recutting or re-entry, the removal may not be completely effected for fear of damaging, during the scraping, burnishing and polishing necessary, the repaired or an adjacent subject. Burr is frequently most noticeable in the stamp margins or gutters. The variety is constant in that it occurs on or outside the frameline of the subject on the printing base, and will reproduce on every sheet until removed specifically or by reason of wear of the printing base. Many instances of burr, or "Burr Marks" as these varieties are sometimes termed, are to be found, for example, in Great Britain 1841 1d. and 2d.

Corrosion. Colored flaw. When the metal of the printing base has been attacked by rust, the pitting on the surface will hold ink and reproduce as an area more or less indefinite of minute colored spots. Sometimes this pitting simulates the lines of the design, resulting in seeming "Double Transfer." Marks of corrosion on the plate may be found in many stamps; instances are to be encountered, for example, on some stamps of Great Britain 1841 2d., plate 3.

Damaged Relief. Uncolored flaw. This term is used synonymously with "Broken Relief" — see "Broken Relief."

Double Letter. Colored flaw. Term used mainly in reference to early line-engraved stamps of Great Britain which bear letters in the corner squares. These letters were individually applied to the printing plate by the operator using a letter

Line engraving. Corrosion. Great Britain 1841 2d., plate 3, stamp lettered "K E." In the southeast corner square, containing the letter "E," the dark patches above and to the right of the letter are caused by corrosion attacking the metal of the printing plate. Under considerable magnification, the corrosion can be seen as innumerable minute dots, reproduced in the color of the stamp itself.

punch held in position by hand and struck by a hammer. A double striking of the punch, or the correction of a wrongly entered letter, resulted in duplication to a greater or less extent of the letter. An instance is to be found in Great Britain 1841 1d., plate 20, stamp lettered S J, where the "S" is the "double letter."

Double Transfer. Colored flaw. Term used to designate a line-engraved stamp bearing duplications in some part or all of the design resulting from duplications appearing on the printing base. It is to be noted that the term is descriptive of what is apparent, and makes no pretense at any diagnosis of the cause of the duplication except that it occurs on the printing base. Many causes give rise to "double transfer" — for example, "Dropped Roll," "Foreign Relief," "Fresh Entry," "Non-Coincident Re-Entry," "Shifted Transfer."

Dropped Roll. Colored flaw. Term used to designate a line-engraved stamp exhibiting in the design duplications, usually throughout a narrow band extending usually the whole width or, as the case may be, height of the design, caused by the transfer relief coming into contact with the printing base accidentally in unintended position, either because the transfer roll was "dropped" on to the printing base or because the siderographist applied pressure momentarily before the printing base was properly aligned in the transfer press. In "dropped roll" only one entry was ever complete, the accidental entry never being more than a partial entry; this distinguishes "dropped roll" from "Fresh Entry" and "Non-Coincident Re-Entry." A "dropped roll" variety is constant. An example is to be found in Cayman Islands 1946 Victory 1½d., plate A1, stamp No. 45.

Dry Print. Uncolored flaw. Because the paper is insufficiently dampened, it is not sufficiently forced into all the recesses on the printing base, with the result that ink does not adhere in some portions of the design, causing uncolored flaws. Sometimes the ink adheres for a time, and then blisters and peels off, resulting in similar flaws. Such varieties are, of course, inconstant, and they vary greatly in appearance in individual cases. Accurate diagnosis is, often, extremely difficult. See "Peeled Ink" in the chapter entitled "Printing Problems and Varieties."

Entry. Term used sometimes to designate a subject on the printing base, occurring there as the result of the application of the transfer roller. The term is, often, qualified in use. See "Original Entry."

246

Errant Entry. Colored flaw. Term used to designate a line-engraved stamp exhibiting in the design a double transfer caused by either the original or the subsequent entry being made from the relief of a different value or design. The variety is rare as a class. The terms "Foreign Relief" and "Parasite Transfer" are used synonymously with "errant entry." The variety is constant. An instance occurs in U.S. 1911 (Jan. 5) 2c. imperf, with the 1c. design as the errant entry. Among other instances are: Canada 1888-97 6c. with part of the 5c. design as the errant entry; Iraq 1941-43 3f., 4f. and 5f., with part of an unissued design as the errant entry; and New Zealand 1915-22 4d. plate 20, row 4, stamp No. 10, with part of the 2½d. design as the errant entry.

Foreign Relief. Colored flaw. A synonym for "Errant Entry."

Fresh Entry. Colored flaw. Term used philatelically to designate a line-engraved stamp exhibiting a double transfer resulting from the following causes, that is to say, where an original entry has been made faultily or out of alignment, has been only partly erased from the printing base and a new (fresh) entry made correctly. A fresh entry is made on what is intended to be a smooth surface on the printing base, but the surface is sometimes not smooth because of failure to eliminate all traces of the original entry, which failure gives rise to the duplications. Sometimes, early prints do not reveal the duplications, which begin to show only after the surface of the printing base has begun to wear. Philatelically the term is, for all practical purposes, limited to varieties exhibiting duplications; from the printer's point of view the operations of fresh entry do not by any means invariably result in double transfer — but they sometimes result in the fresh entry being out of alignment. Sometimes the term "fresh entry" is used to designate any noticeable amendment of the printing base made by another application of the transfer relief to the printing base *before it is put to press,* irrespective of whether such subsequent application was made to effect fresh entry as described above or to effect "re-entry" — see "Re-Entry." The variety "fresh entry" is constant.

Guide Dot, Guide Line. Colored flaws. Terms used to describe respectively a minute dot or a faint horizontal or vertical line appearing, usually, just within or just outside the design of a line-engraved stamp. The dots and lines were marked on the printing base either directly to guide, or with the eventual object of guiding the siderographist where to make the entries, and normally should have been either obliterated by the entries or else erased from the printing base before it was put to press. The term "Position Dot" is sometimes used as a synonym for "guide dot." A centering device, consisting of a pointer attached to the mandrel of the transfer roll, is known as a "side point," and its use involves that the appropriate dot on the plate does not occur within the area of the entry located by reference to that dot. The position of each such dot is determined by several series of measurements and markings of dots, dashes or lines. Philatelic terminology is not standard in reference to these various markings; the term "side point dot" does not seem to have any wide philatelic use, but would appear to be unequivocal in meaning. The varieties are constant. The term "guide line" is used also in a different sense — see "Guide Line" in the alphabetical list to the chapter entitled "From Design to Issued Sheets."

Incomplete Transfer. Uncolored flaw. Term used to designate a line-engraved stamp exhibiting a variety in which lines that should have appeared in color are entirely or partially absent, resulting from insufficient rocking of the transfer relief in depth ("Shallow Transfer") or in height or width of the design ("Short Transfer"). The variety is constant.

Malburin. Colored flaw. Term used generically to designate a variation from the intended design caused by a slip or mishandling of the engraving tool (burin).

Line engraving. Malburin and double transfer. Canada 1908 Quebec Tercentenary ½c., plate 1, stamp No. 44. The lowest line of the subject on the printing base was manually recut, and the engraving tool slipped in two places during this operation; the first slip has resulted in a prominently divergent line outward, most noticeable beneath the letters "RE" of "Centenaire"; the second slip resulted in a less divergent line outward, visible as a marked thickening beneath the letters "EB" of "Quebec." The colored flaws of the double transfer are most prominently visible as spots in "08" of "1608," and dots and a line in "CANAD" of "Canada."

If this slip or mishandling occurs during the engraving of the die, the malburin will reproduce on every subject and stamp resulting from the use of the die; if the slip or the mishandling occurs during recutting or repair to a particular subject, the malburin will appear on stamps printed from only that subject. Malburins take many forms, but are usually denoted by a more or less wide deviation from normal in a line. They occur frequently on subjects upon which other repair has been effected. An instance is to be found, for example, in Canada 1908 Quebec Tercentenary ½c., plate 1, stamp No. 44, which shows a double transfer and also a malburin where the engraving tool slipped on the lowest line of the design.

Misapplied Color. This term, philatelically considered, is of comparatively recent introduction, and is limited in use to stamps bi-color or multicolor printed from a single cylinder on the Koebau-Giori press and others incorporating the Serge-Beaune patent, as in the cases, for example, of Argentine Republic 1949 (Nov. 19) 75th Anniversary of Universal Postal Union 25c., Finland 1957 (Dec. 4) Ida Aalberg 30m., France 1953 (Nov. 28) Sports 20f., and USA 1980 (Oct. 9) Architecture 15c. The term signifies that color intended for one part of the design has been misapplied to another part of the design, with the result that on stamps from some sheets an area appears in one color while on stamps from other sheets the same area appears in a different color. This occurs, usually, where the colors adjoin one another, and is caused by something short of perfection in the syn-

248

chronization of the inking rollers and printing plate. Except as instances of what can occur with this method of printing, such varieties are philatelically unimportant — unlike the case of a similar effect in printing from separate plates or cylinders, where it would signify the use of different dies and plates or cylinders.

Non-Coincident Re-Entry. Colored flaw. This term is used philatelically with precision to designate a line-engraved stamp exhibiting in the design a double transfer resulting from the repair of a subject by a further application of the transfer relief, where the lines of the subsequent entry fail to key with those of the original entry. The duplication may extend throughout or may be limited to a part or parts of the design. The variety is constant. See "Re-Entry."

Original Entry. Term used to designate the first entry made for a particular subject on a printing base, occurring there as a result of the application of the transfer roller. This term is used particularly in differentiating between the first and the subsequent entries in double — or more — transfers resulting from "Fresh Entry" and "Re-Entry."

Parasite Transfer. Colored flaw. A synonym for "Errant Entry."

Position Dot. Colored flaw. This term is sometimes used as a synonym for "Guide Dot," and is sometimes used in the sense of "Side Point Dot."

Recut. Colored flaw. In connection with a stamp printed from a subject on a line-engraved printing base, this term is used to designate a variety resulting from manual amendment of a line or lines of the design by means of an engraving tool or with etching fluid. Lines recut in this manner invariably reproduce more intensely than similar lines not recut, and often complete coincidence between the recut and the original lines is not obtained. In many cases, recutting is effected to strengthen a frameline, and the variety is termed "Recut Frame"; an instance is to be found, for example, in United States 1928 Air 5c. The term "recut" is sometimes used in a narrow sense as denoting a manual amendment made to a subject on a line-engraved printing base before it is printed from, and in cases of such use, the term "retouch" is employed to distinguish a manual amend-

Line engraving. Recut frame. Great Britain 1841 1d., plate 76, stamp lettered "D E." On the printing plate the subject from which this stamp was printed was recut with an engraving tool, the four sides being strengthened. Note the boldness and intensity of the dark line at each side beyond the engine turning, and compare these lines with the corresponding positions on the stamps illustrating "Corrosion" and "Roller Flaw."

ment made after some printing has been effected. Often the terms "recut" and "retouch" are used as synonyms in connection with line engraving. See "Retouch." Some students have suggested that the term "retouch" be used exclusively for amendments made to subjects on planographic and relief printing bases, and that "recut" be reserved for such amendments to line-engraved printing bases. The variety is constant. These uses of the terms in relation to a subject on a printing base must be distinguished from their uses in connection with "die" — see "Recut, etc." in the alphabetical list to the chapter entitled "Printing Problems and Varieties."

Re-Entry. When perceptible, colored flaw. This term is used philatelically with precision to designate a variety, not necessarily a double transfer, resulting from a second or subsequent application of the transfer roller to a particular subject on the printing base for the purposes, *inter alia,* of deepening or repairing the original entry. Re-entry may be effected (1) before the printing base is printed from, and may result in (1a) perfect coincidence of lines, or (1b) non-coincidence of lines (double transfer), or (2) after the printing base has been printed from, and may result in (2c) perfect coincidence of lines, or (2d) non-coincidence of lines (double transfer). In the case of (1a), there is nothing observable in the resultant stamps to enable any deduction to be made that re-entry has occurred, yet in practice this forms by far the greater proportion of re-entries made by the siderographist. Re-entries in the class (1b) will exist on all sheets printed until the printing base is repaired, if ever. Because they exist in the very earliest state of the use of the printing base, such re-entries are sometimes termed "fresh entries" by those students who differentiate between fresh entries and re-entries by reference to the question of whether the printing base has been put to press, and who ignore, for this purpose, the reason why the transfer relief was applied on the subsequent occasion — see "Fresh Entry." In the case of (2c), the re-entry can be deduced philatelically by comparing stamps printed before the repair with stamps printed after the repair; the subsequently printed stamps will present much clearer lines and, usually, more intense color than those printed before the repair. In the case of (2d), the duplications of lines in stamps resulting from a subject previously yielding unduplicated lines enables diagnosis to be made philatelically — see "Non-Coincident Re-Entry." The variety is constant. Sometimes the term "re-entry" is used as though it referred to *duplications* in a line-engraved design, but such use of the term is not recommended, and causes confusion — the term "Double Transfer" is adequate to describe undiagnosed duplications, and, among others, terms such as "Fresh Entry" and "Non-Coincident Re-Entry" are precisely available when certain diagnosis has been made.

Retouch. Colored flaw. In connection with a stamp printed from a subject on a line-engraved printing base, this term is used to designate a variety resulting from amendment of a line or lines of the design, and is often used synonymously with "recut" — see "Recut." Sometimes the term "retouch" is used to denote an amendment made by local etching, and in such cases the term "recut" is used as meaning manual amendment with the engraving tool. Sometimes the term "retouch" is used in a narrow sense as denoting a manual amendment made to a subject on a line-engraved printing base only after it is printed from, and in cases of such use, the term "recut" is employed to distinguish a manual amendment made before any printing has been effected. Some students have suggested that the term "retouch" be used exclusively for amendments made to subjects on planographic and relief printing bases, and that "recut" be reserved for such amendments to line-engraved printing bases. These uses of the terms must be distinguished from their uses in connection with "die" — see "Recut, etc." in the alphabetical list to the chapter titled "Printing Problems and Varieties."

Line engraving. Retouch and malburin. Australia 1949 ½d. The stamp of which a portion is visible at the left of the picture was printed from a subject which on the printing base had been considerably retouched by hand. The whole of the colorless area (on the normal stamp wholly visible in the picture) surrounding the head has been filled with lines, and other lines representing the sky have been strengthened. The actual retouching extends over more of the stamp than is represented

by the portion pictured, and results in the hill at the back of the kangaroo being tonally indistinguishable from the sky. The left frameline was recut, and the engraving tool slipped on two occasions inward into the design. The more divergent line is most prominently visible just below the point at which the skyline of the hill meets the frameline; the less divergent line has resulted in a thickening of the frameline opposite and extending over a distance equivalent to that between the mouth and ear of the kangaroo.

Roller Flaw. Colored or uncolored flaw. This term is used generically to designate any flaw resulting from impacted metal (colored), or damage to the relief (uncolored) on the transfer roller. In the case of "Broken Relief," the uncolored flaw may be progressive, and occurs on every entry made from the flawed relief. In the case of impacted metal, the progressive element is usually absent from the resultant colored flaw, which will occur on only some of the entries made subsequently if the impacted metal becomes detached from the relief. Such flaws are constant.

Line engraving. Roller flaw. Uncolored. Great Britain 1841 1d., plate 10 (in red), stamp lettered "L E." The "ON flaw," being a later stage of the "O flaw." The dark background at the lower right of the "O" of "ONE" has not reproduced, and that letter apparently protrudes to the right and joins the left serif at the foot of the left upright of the "N." This flaw was caused by damage to the transfer relief, which (probably because of weakness caused by impacted metal in the flat die) broke down under the strain of repeated transferring, and failed to impress a recess that should have been present where the color is lacking.

Scooped Color. Uncolored flaw. Term used to designate a variety caused by the excessive wiping or polishing of an inked line-engraved plate, whereby color is removed from recesses, resulting in an absence of a colored line or other area that should appear in color on the stamp. The extent of scooped color varies in individual cases. The variety is inconstant. An instance of "scooped color" occurring on Mauritius 1848 Post Paid 2d. is illustrated as the left-hand stamp under the heading "Impression" in the alphabetical list to the chapter entitled "Printing Problems and Varieties," where the scooping is particularly prominent at the left around the word "Paid."

Shallow Transfer. Uncolored flaw. See "Incomplete Transfer."

Shift, Shifted Transfer. Colored flaw. Term used to designate a line-engraved stamp exhibiting a variety seemingly of double transfer in the form of duplication at the end or ends of a design, but resulting from the use during the rocking-in of a transfer of excessive speed or pressure, causing a minute wave of metal to travel in front of the roller, the wave bearing the lines of, and so stretching, an entry partly made, the duplications occurring because the relief impresses new lines on the stretched metal which already bears the extended lines of the partly made entry. Shifts can occur at either or both extremities of the design; and, in those cases in which the rocking-in begins with an axial line about the center of the design, shifts can occur about the center of the design. The variety is constant.

Short Transfer. Uncolored flaw. See "Incomplete Transfer."

Side Point Dot. Colored flaw. See "Guide Dot."

Transfer. This term is used sometimes as synonymous with "entry" — see "Entry."

Wiping Mark. Colored flaw. Term used to designate a variety exhibiting a colored mark or colored marks caused by the failure to remove all the ink from and properly to wipe clean and polish the surface of the printing base before printing takes place from line-engraved printing bases. Wiping marks are, of course, inconstant, and take many forms. Sometimes such failure results in the stamp being printed on what is seemingly surface-colored paper; this is especially liable to occur during the very earliest impressions from modern line-engraved printing bases used in machines where the wiping is done mechanically — such varieties being referred to, sometimes, as on "Pseudo-Colored Paper." Sometimes, in bi-colored wet-printed line-engraved stamps, the paper is pseudo-colored with a tint of one of the colors in the stamp, this being caused by the printed color "running" when the paper is dampened again for the printing of the second color; in such cases it is possible, with a fair degree of certainty, to deduce which of the colors was first printed — it being that which has suffused the paper. See "Pseudo-Colored Paper" in the alphabetical list to the chapter entitled "Paper."

9. Intaglio Printing — II: Gravure

THERE ARE TWO TYPES of gravure printing — from flat plates and from curved plates or cylinders. Strictly the term "photogravure" applies to both; printing from curved plates or cylinders is properly called "rotary photogravure," but this does not necessarily involve printing only on reels or "on the web." Some rotary photogravure machines have been used to print stamps on sheets of paper.

In the essentials, the production of the recesses or cells is the same, whether on the flat plate or on the cylinder, and both processes rely for their effect upon the varying depth of the cells, whether they are regular, as in "screened" photogravure which is the newer process, or irregular as in "unscreened," "screenless" or "grained"[11] photogravure.

The intensity of the design printed on the paper is directly proportionate to the depth of the recess, a deep cell resulting in strong color and a shallow cell resulting in weak color; this characteristic alone is common to the line-engraving and the gravure printing processes — of course in conjunction with the fact that the ink is deposited on to the paper from recesses in the printing base, these recesses being below its non-printing surface which, at the moment of impression, is or should be entirely free of ink.

Collogravure (a trade name of Harrison & Sons Ltd.), gravure, Heliogravure (a trade name of Helio-Vaugirard), mechanical mezzotint, photogravure, rotary photogravure, and rotogravure are all terms employed to denote the processes used for the production of stamps of which the design is composed of cells of varying depth. Philatelically, the term most frequently used compendiously is "photogravure," and this is often abbreviated to "photo." That is regrettable because that abbreviation is used not infrequently also in connection with photographic-lithography — an entirely different process — and such use is a potential source of confusion. When abbreviation is necessary in relation to photogravure, the less objectionable use would have been to employ "gravure." However, perversely, common usage seems to have become to drop "photographic" and its abbreviation "photo." from the doubly abbreviated term "photo.-litho.," so that "photo" is used to designate "photogravure," while "litho" is then used to signify "photographic-lithography."

---

[11] Some writers and authorities use the historical term "screen-grain," but the better usage would seem to be to limit the use of the term "grain" so that it contrasts with the regularly striated effects produced by the use of the grid.

Photogravure. Model and negative. Great Britain 1952 2½d. The "model" (or "design," or "original design"), upright on a stand in the picture, has been photographed to produce a negative which is being carefully examined and compared with the model by a photographic retoucher who holds, in his left hand, a magnifying glass and, in his right hand, a "spotting brush" as used in photographic retouching. It is often the case that spotting (the application of retouching paint to minute areas of clear glass) is necessary, as also are the strengthening of highlights and the separation of tonal values.

Gravure printing is, so far as stamps are concerned, a comparatively new process. Its first recorded[12] use for a government-issued[13] postage stamp was for Bavaria (Germany) 1914 (Mar. 31) — 1919 2 pf. to 80 pf. However, its application can be traced as far back as 1858, and it was commercially used in Lancaster, England, at the end of the past century under the name ''Rembrandt'' process, although details were kept secret until about 1907. During the subsequent eighty years of progress and improvement, many differing methods have been evolved for applying the basic principles of the process, and the procedure varies in detail from country to country and from printer to printer. It would be impossible in a work of this nature to discuss all these variations, and such a course would be undesirable; the most that can be attempted is an outline of the processes.

The problem involved in producing a gravure printing base for postage stamps may be stated to be: the production photographically of the requisite number of subjects in a medium capable of being conveniently handled (so that the subjects may be transferred to the printing base) and which will act proportionately as a resist (so that through it the printing base may be appropriately etched) and result in a printing base of which the printing areas are below, and the non-printing areas are on, the surface having a grain or a screen to act as a bearer for a wiper or doctor knife. The multiplication of the design is effected by photography; the medium used in transferring the subjects to the printing base is ''carbon tissue'' — light-sensitized gelatine which, when exposed to bright light, becomes insoluble in water in direct proportion to the amount of light allowed to fall on the gelatine, and which also acts as an etching resist in direct proportion to the amount of gelatine not dissolved away; the printing base consists of copper, and the etching fluid is ferric chloride. The grain is applied mechanically; alternatively, the screen is applied photographically.

Broadly speaking, the outline of the steps involved in the production of a gravure printing base may be summarized as follows:

1. Producing a finished master negative.
2. Producing a diapositive or multipositive.
3. Applying the ''grain'' or ''screen'' as the case may be.
4. Producing the ''carbon tissue'' print.
5. Transferring the image to the printing base.
6. Etching the subjects.
7. Cleaning the etched printing base and preparing it for printing.
8. Printing from the printing base.

---

[12] There is a suggestion, based on the recollection of an employee of F.A. Bruckmann of Munich, that postage stamps were printed by that firm in photogravure for Romania as long ago as 1909. Otto M. Lilien, who provided me with this information, stated that he was informed that no archives exist to confirm the employee's recollection; all the firm's records, if indeed they existed of such governmental postage stamps, are said to have been destroyed in air raids during World War II.

[13] The Bavarian issue was printed by Bruckmann on a machine made by John Wood in Ramsbottom, Lancashire, England.

The Master Negative

The original from which the master negative for a monochrome stamp is made is a single specially prepared painting, photograph, lithograph or drawing, often in continuous tone or wash, but sometimes in line. This is, usually, much larger than stamp size, often as much as ten times linear — that is, one hundred times the area — and is sometimes referred to as "the model" or "the design," or "the original design." Perhaps, more often than not nowadays, the "model" consists of several photographs on transparent film, each of differently colored elements of the design. These are superimposed to form a composite model.

The model is photographed in a special camera, adjusted with great precision, usually on to a glass plate to make a first negative. This is a true photographic negative, with reversals of the tonal values and the design, including of course the legend. The size of this first negative varies according to the practice which varies from time to time in the works of different printers; for example, the practice of Waterlow & Sons Ltd. was to make this first negative four times stamp size; in other cases, the first negative is a same-size copy of the model; and the practice of Harrison & Sons Ltd. was to use a model four-and-one-half times stamp size and a negative twice stamp size,

Rotary photogravure. India 1948 (Aug. 15) First Anniversary of Indian Independence 12a. Produced in screened rotary photogravure by Courvoisier. Photographing "the model" or the original design to make the first negative. The model is secured by swivelling clips to the vertical easel, the light being supplied by electric lamps in reflectors mounted on stands diagonally in front of both sides of the easel. The camera is mounted on a trolley running on rails. The operator is making a critical adjustment of focus of the image projected by the lens on the fine ground glass screen at the back of the camera. In his left hand he is holding a magnifying tube through which he is viewing the effects of the adjustment he is making to focus and alignment with his right hand.

Rotary photogravure. India 1948 (Aug. 15) First Anniversary of Indian Independence 12a. Produced in screened rotary photogravure by Courvoisier. Photographically retouching the master negative. Note that this negative has been "reversed" — that is, although the tonal values are truly negative, the legend reads normally from left-to-right, unlike a more usually encountered photographic negative, in which the legend would read from right-to-left. This "reversal" is necessary because of the subsequent uses to which the photographic image is put, and can be accomplished either by a special arrangement of  lenses in the camera or by stripping and turning the photographic emulsion. If any flaw escapes or is caused by retouching, it will be reproduced on every subject and resultant stamp. This master negative is the equivalent of the "die" in line engraving and other processes; but, as can be seen, it differs from a true die in being many times greater in size than the stamps that will result from its use.

linear. From the first negative the master negative stems, either directly or, more usually, indirectly.

The master negative consists of a reversal of tonal values only, the design reading normally from left-to-right. Before the master negative is ready for use, the photographic image will have been photographically retouched at one or more stages of production. This retouching is, normally, limited to the correction of photographic flaws, such as may be caused by pinholes, scratches, dust, or air bubbles during the processes of photographic exposure, development, fixing, washing and drying; the object being the production of a flawless photographic image with the full tonal values, reversed, of the model.

The size of and the number of subjects which appear on the finished master negative depend upon the practice of the particular printers involved. Often the finished master negative comprises only a single subject; but, for example, Waterlow & Sons Ltd. used a master negative consisting of a strip of five or ten subjects of stamp size.

The master negative consisting of a single subject is the equivalent of the die in other printing processes in which the design in multiplied mechanically, and from this master negative all the subjects stem. It follows that any flaw or variation from the intended norm will reproduce on every stamp, and such a flaw would properly be referred to as a "master negative flaw" or, perhaps, "die flaw." Such a flaw exists, for instance, on Seychelles 1938-41 2.25 r. in the form of an uncolored small patch or nick at the extreme lower portion of the design beneath the left extremity of the last letter of "Seychelles."

Rotary photogravure. Master negative flaw. Seychelles 1938-41 2.25r. Produced in screened rotary photogravure by Harrison & Sons Ltd. The flaw takes the form of an uncolored small patch, like a nick, in the extreme lower portion of the design beneath the left extremity of the last letter of "Seychelles." This "nick" is present on every stamp in the sheet of sixty of this value. The flaw does not occur on any stamp in the sheets of the four other values with the same design, sufficiently proving that the flaw was not present on "the model" or original design from which the master negative was made.

However when, as for example in the case of Waterlow & Sons Ltd. previously mentioned, the master negative consists of five or ten separate subjects, or any other number, the master negative is in effect the equivalent of an "intermediate transfer" as used frequently in multiplying a design lithographically; and in such cases the possibility exists that any or all of the master negative subjects may differ from the intended norm and from each

Rotary photogravure. Different "dies" — varieties resulting from the use of different master negatives. Great Britain 1935 Silver Jubilee 1½d. Produced in screened rotary photogravure by Harrison & Sons Ltd. The variations in design can be seen in the two lines above "Silver Jubilee." On the top stamp these lines are prominent throughout their length; on the middle stamp these lines are weak throughout their length; on the lowest stamp the lines are weak but there is a pronounced thickening of the upper line above "JU." The top stamp came from a post office sheet; the other two stamps came from books or booklets, the middle stamp having an inverted, and the lowest stamp a normal watermark. These varieties are constant for all such stamps emanating from these sources, and result from different degrees of photographic retouching to three separate photographic images. The master negative used for the production of the booklets comprised four photographic images, two of the lowest design — upright — and two of the middle design — inverted; the photographic retouching having been effected at an earlier stage.

other, and thus give rise to "types" recurring regularly throughout the printed sheet.

It is no unusual course for more than one master negative to be made for any design. Although the processes used in the production of a master negative are mainly photographic, and therefore complete identity of photographic images of the same model could reasonably be expected to exist on the master negatives, variations have occurred, and instances have been recorded of photogravure stamps exhibiting differences equivalent to those which occur in, say, line engraving when different dies are used. One of the first of such instances recorded philatelically occurred in Great Britain 1935 (May 7) Silver Jubilee 1½d., where study of the stamps revealed that those printed in sheets differ slightly in design from those printed in books or booklets; and, further, the stamps in the books vary in that those with inverted watermarks are slightly different in design from those with normal watermarks. (The differences are visible in the lines above the words "Silver Jubilee.") From these facts, the inference is that one master negative was used in the production of the stamps issued in sheets (the probability being that this consisted of a single subject); and that for the production of the books (which contain blocks of four stamps and of which the printed sheet formation was alternate pairs of columns *tête bêche* with a wide gutter between each group of four columns[14]), a master negative was used consisting of four subjects in two pairs, one pair upright and the other pair inverted, each pair having been made from a separate first or subsequent photographic negative of the model. Similarly, slight differences in design have been discovered in Great Britain 1952 2½d., which show that a different master negative was used for stamps in sheets and books of stamps; but in this case, no difference has been recorded between the designs of book stamps with inverted and with normal watermarks.

Philatelists have still not come to grips with the terminological problems set by varieties occurring in the various stages of photogravure production, and no standard practice obtains. However, because the master negative is the equivalent of the die (and, indeed, it is sometimes referred to as the "die negative"), there seems to be little reason against referring to designs of the same stamp, which differ minutely because of the use of different master negatives, as emanating from Die I, Die II, etc.,[15] as obtains with stamps printed by other processes, and so long as it is emphasized that, in the cases of gravure stamps, the "die" is a master negative produced photographically.

For stamps intended to be printed in more than one color, a master negative must be made for each color to be separately printed on the finished stamps.[16] This normally involves a complicated series of processes connected with col-

---

[14] See the illustration, of a different issue, accompanying the chapter entitled "From Design to Issued Sheets" where plate proofs, color trials and color proofs are discussed.

[15] See the term "Die" in the alphabetical list to the chapter entitled "Printing Problems and Varieties."

[16] This procedure sometimes obtains in the case of a monochrome stamp printed from "Double Plates" — see that term in the alphabetical list to the chapter entitled "Printing Problems and Varieties."

or separation, to determine how much of the design is to appear on each master negative, and later involves difficulties of registration throughout the subsequent processes; however, these complications apart, the production of a master negative of only part of the design is precisely similar to that of one for a monochrome stamp.

The Diapositive or Multipositive

The diapositive, as the alternative name multipositive suggests, consists of multiple repetitions of the design, with the tonal values of the model positively represented but the legend reversed. The diapositive is made from the master negative, and, in the cases of stamps to be printed in more than one color, a separate diapositive must be prepared from each master negative.

The diapositive is a large quarter-inch thick photographic glass plate — at least as large as, and usually larger than, the eventual printed sheet of stamps — and the images are produced photographically with the aid of a "step-and-repeat" camera.

There have been, and are, numerous varieties of step-and-repeat cameras marketed under different trade names. They are all developments of the idea of projecting an image many times on to different positions of the same photographic plate, with refinements that ensure the exposures shall be of identical duration and that enable the spacing between different images to be regulated to a minute degree of accuracy. Unlike the more usually encountered camera, the step-and-repeat camera used for gravure operates by *projecting* a negative image — that of the master negative — which is illuminated from behind.

Except in the cases of entirely automatic control of light source, exposure and spacing, the multiple exposures and movements of the step-and-repeat camera provide potential sources of variations from standard. For example, unless the voltage to the lamps is rigidly controlled, it may fluctuate; if it does, the diminution or increase of light resulting will cause the eventual stamps to be respectively darker or lighter, so that different stamps in the one sheet differ in intensity of color. Similar results will flow from variations in the length of exposure. Further, when the movement of the multipositive plate from position to position depends upon hand control, the possibility exists that, despite the accurate gearing, the movement will not be made to exact limits — or that, perhaps, the operator may forget having exposed at one position and expose again at the same or at a nearly identical position, giving rise to the variety "double exposure," to be encountered, for example, in South Africa 1932-40 Postage Due 2d., row 5, stamp No. 6, where the numeral appears thicker than usual because the two exposures did not exactly coincide.

Some idea of the care taken to secure the accuracy of the spacing between images and their regularity is afforded by the statement that Harrison & Sons Ltd. had its step-and-repeat camera bedded in fourteen feet of concrete to avoid vibration, and that the camera is accurate to one two-thousandth part of an inch. The accuracy and regularity of spacing is dictated by the need to perforate the eventual stamps.

Gravure. Diapositive flaw, double exposure. South Africa 1948-49 Postage Due 2d., interior cylinder 28, a block of six, comprising row 16, stamps Nos. 4, 5 and 6, and row 17, stamps Nos. 4, 5 and 6, exhibiting in row 16, stamps Nos. 5 and 6, the variety "Double Exposure." The stamps were printed from two cylinders, one for the frame and one for the denomination. The master negative for the denomination comprised a block of four subjects; the step-and-repeat camera was hand-operated. By error the operator doubly exposed the diapositive to the master negative for the denomination at one position, and by a further error the two exposures did not exactly coincide. As the result, four positions on the sheet (of which only two are shown in the illustration) exhibit marked thickening of the figure "2" and the "D," in which the central uncolored area is much thinner, and a pronounced oval appearance of the stop.

As has been stated, Harrison & Sons Ltd. used a master negative twice stamp size, and this necessitates a reduction by two when the image is projected through the lens of the step-and-repeat camera; the reduction is effected photographically, by means of accurate adjustment and focus. In cases in which larger images are used on the master negative, the proportionate reduction in size is consequently greater.

The number of separate exposures made by the step-and-repeat camera is dependent upon two factors: the number of images on the master negative and the number of subjects there are to be on the sheet as printed — or, in the cases of stamps printed in continuous reels, the number of subjects to

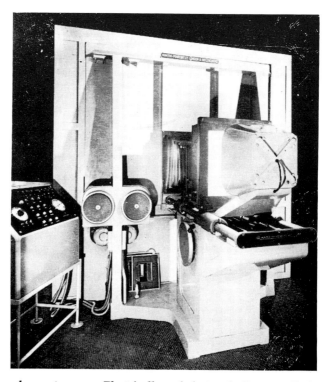

The step-and-repeat camera. Electrically and electronically controlled. Since 1957 a hand-operated step-and-repeat camera at the works of Harrison & Sons Ltd. has been superseded by electrically and electronically controlled apparatus; the one pictured is described as "The 'H.P.' Auto Step-and-Repeat Projector Incorporating Automatic Focusing and Entirely Automatic Step Movement," manufactured by Hunter-Penrose Ltd. (British Patent 663175). The movements were controlled by an arrangement that enabled a circuit to be closed or opened at predetermined intervals, dictated by slots punched out of control charts made of stout paper fed around revolving metal drums, the circular ends of which can be seen between the camera bellows and the control box panel. Once the control charts were prepared and inserted, the operator merely pushed a button, and the apparatus did the rest; a 480-subject diapositive was completely exposed in about two hours, as compared with eight to ten hours in a hand-operated camera. Exposure times were electronically controlled by a light meter that automatically corrected any variations of light intensity. Among the earliest stamps to be produced with the aid of this camera are Ghana 1957 (Mar. 6) Independence Commemoratives 2d. to 1s.3d.

appear on the printing cylinder. These factors vary with individual printers, with individual issues and, indeed, with the intended form of issue of particular stamps; for example, the printing arrangement of stamps intended to be issued in rolls with sideways delivery will almost certainly vary from that for the same stamp intended for issue in post office sheets. By way of example: Before 1960, it was believed that, for the low value stamps of Great Britain, including, for instance, Great Britain 1953-60 3d. for issue in sheets,

Great Britain 1953-60 3d. blocks showing beneath stamp in southeast corner the marginal variety "Phantom R" in two states: as originally discovered; and partly retouched.

the master negative consisted of a single image, which was projected 480 times by the step-and-repeat camera to make the diapositive. This was believed to bear 480 images only, and it was further believed that the blank spaces for sheet gutters and margins were created by adjusting the step-and-repeat camera. The fact that the multipositive contained many more than 480 images was established philatelically by a marginal variety which my late brother, Maurice, and I were delighted to discover by chance when buying some 3d. stamps from the Exhibition Post Office at the London International Stamp Exhibition 1960 held in the Royal Festival Hall. In the lower sheet margin beneath each stamp is a bar of color which assists in uniform inking — called a "Jubilee" line. It is made by masking part of the multipositive with a narrow strip of tape. Underneath the last stamp in the sheet — it was printed from cylinder No. 41, no dot — part of the strip had torn away before the cylinder was etched. Revealed, when the cylinder was printed from, was a shadowy "R" that exactly matched the "R" in the stamp's upper-right spandrel. Obviously, the "Phantom R" — as we immediately named the variety — had emanated from a stamp image on the multipositive below the last one on the sheet. That proved that the multipositive bore more stamp images than merely the 480 reproduced on the sheets — 240 in each of the pairs of post office sheets, one sheet with a cylinder number without dot and the other with a dot after the cylinder number. Later, the "Phantom R" was discovered in retouched states and from a different cylinder.

After it has been photographically developed, fixed, washed and dried, the diapositive is subjected to a critical examination in order to eliminate the effects of any flaws which may have been caused by pinholes, scratches, dust blisters or air bubbles. These flaws are remedied, or efforts to remedy them may be made by photographic retouching of the diapositive — the latest stage of the process at which purely photographic retouching can be effected.

Any flaw caused or not eliminated by retouching at this stage will reproduce on the resultant stamps; however, unlike a flaw on the master negative which reproduces on every resultant stamp, a flaw on the diapositive will be reproduced on only the particular subject affected. Such flaws are of not uncommon occurrence, but their allocation definitely to the diapositive is not always possible. Philatelic proof of their origin depends upon the ability to eliminate other possible sources, which may include (as will be mentioned later) the carbon tissue, the "screen" plate, and manual retouching to the printing base.

In some instances, elimination of most if not all of the other possibilities can be accomplished, as in cases where a particular flaw is repeated on a subject which can be proved to have been printed from a different printing base produced with the aid of a screen plate exhibiting characteristics different from those exhibited by the screen plate used in the production of the original flawed subject. Examples of the use of the one diapositive to make more than one printing base are well-known, for instance, in the rotary photogravure issues of the Union of South Africa, and a random instance of a flaw occurring on the diapositive and reproduced on more than one printing base and the resultant stamp is provided by Union of South Africa 1930 ½d., the so-called "Snail on buck's neck" variety, occurring on cylinders 1 and 2, row 1, stamp No. 12.

Further instances of the use of the same diapositive for making different printing bases occur among the stamps of Great Britain, for example, 1952 1½d. cylinders 1 to 14 (except 3 and 7), all of which stemmed from the same diapositive. On this 480-subject diapositive, the subject corresponding with stamp No. 217 on the right "pane" of the printed sheet was damaged after cylinder 1 had been prepared. The damage took the form of a disturbance of part of the darkened emulsion to the right of the head, level with the ear, leaving an irregular patch of clear glass. This diapositive damage was photographically retouched before cylinder 2 was prepared, but the retouching was imperfect, and stamps from position No. 217 from cylinders 2., 4., and 5. exhibit an uneven background in the area corresponding with the damage. The retouching deteriorated before cylinder 6. was prepared, and stamp No. 217 from cylinder 6. exhibits a small white flaw. A further retouch was made to the diapositive, and this retouch lasted, in the form of uneven background, throughout cylinders 8 to 13. Stamp No. 217 from cylinders 14. and 15. once more exhibits a white flaw, but progressively larger.[17]

In cases of certain diagnosis, philatelic terminology for such varieties presents no problem: "diapositive flaw" or "multipositive flaw" or

[17] On cylinders 6., 14., and 15., retouching was carried out to the cylinders themselves, with the result that stamps from these cylinders are to be found in two states — with the flaw, and with the manual retouch peculiar to the cylinder from which the stamps were printed.

Rotary photogravure. Diapositive flaw. Great Britain 1952 1½d., cylinder 6., stamp No. 217, and the same stamp from cylinders 14. and 15., exhibiting the effects of a diapositive flaw that was retouched photographically on more than one occasion.

"retouch," as the case may be, is sufficiently unequivocal and precise to meet the most exacting requirements.

In the case of stamps to be printed in more than one color, the work on the diapositives is not limited to a critical examination of each diapositive, but involves also what the technicians term "montage" or "setting up" — that is, the careful checking of the diapositives superimposed to ensure that, photographically, perfect superimposition and registration have been obtained of all the different parts of all of the subjects. Details of this checking vary from printer to printer, as do the registration markings applied to each diapositive, but the examination is invariably carried out under a low-power microscope and parallax correcting viewer.

The Carbon Tissue Print

The carbon tissue print comprises a reproduction of the images on the diapositive, transferred to the light-sensitized gelatine by exposure to strong light. No visual changes occur in the gelatine, which is later "developed" in plain warm or hot water. The carbon tissue print, before development, contains latent multiple repetitions of the design, with the tonal values of the model negatively represented, but the legend reading normally from left-to-right.

The carbon tissue itself consists of a paper backing upon which is spread with exact accuracy a film of gelatine of precisely constant thickness. The gelatine is normally colored red, and the word "carbon" is of historical significance, being a carry-over from the days when the color was black, and lamp-black was used to provide that color. The object of the coloring is to enable the technicians easily to observe the limits and amount of gelatine during later processes, which would be a difficult matter if gelatine in its naturally colorless state were to be used.

Gelatine normally is soluble in warm water; however, as has already been indicated, gelatine which has been treated with potassium bichromate in solution has the property of being affected by light. Where light falls on gelatine so treated, it becomes insoluble in water, and becomes insoluble in direct proportion to the amount of light falling on any part of the gelatine.

Consequently, if the amount of light allowed to fall on an area of treated gelatine is primarily regulated by careful timing and further regulated by being passed through, for example, a photographic image consisting of varying tonal or light values, the gelatine will become insoluble in proportion as the photographic image consists of clear emulsion. Where the emulsion is clearest, there the greatest amount of gelatine will be insoluble; where the emulsion is darkest, there the gelatine's solubility will be substantially unaffected; and the gradations between these extremes will be dependent upon the other light values obtaining in the photographic image.

As a result, after exposure in this manner and after development in warm or hot water (which washes away the gelatine in proportion to the extent to which it has been affected by light), the gelatine which remains is thickest where the greatest amount of light fell — that is, in the parts corresponding with the areas of clear emulsion of the photographic image — and there are other areas of diminishing thickness of gelatine corresponding with the intermediate light values of the photographic image, until only a trace of gelatine remains in those areas where the photographic image was darkest.

The sizes of the carbon tissue sheets used in the production of postage stamps vary in individual cases, but depend upon the measurements of the printing base to be used; the measurements will be the height and width of the printing plate, or the width and circumference of the printing cylinder.

The carbon tissue and diapositive are carefully adjusted in a special glass-fronted printing frame, the gelatine face of the treated carbon tissue and the emulsion side of the diapositive being brought into contact. Because the air normally present between the surfaces of the carbon tissue and the diapositive would present an impediment to perfect contact over the whole area, the frame is made airtight and this air is drawn off by means of an attachment. Such a frame is termed a "vacuum printing down frame."

Exposure to extremely bright light is then made for a carefully calculated period of time.

After the carbon tissue has been exposed to light through the diapositive, the gelatine is transferred to the printing base. However, the sequence of operations depends upon the method which is adopted for providing the printing base with the necessary "grain" or "screen," and these aspects of the processes are referred to under that heading later in this chapter.

Philatelically constant flaws can occur during the course of making the carbon tissue print. As has been stated, this consists of the latent images in light-affected gelatine, and they should be no more and no less than perfect reproductions of the images on the diapositive. However, the undesired presence of dust and grit, flaws on or damage to the glass plate at the front of the vacuum printing down frame, minute imperfections in or damage to the carbon tissue itself, and the difficulty, even with the use of the vacuum printing down frame, of obtaining exact contact over the whole of a large area, all contribute to the possibility of varieties occurring as a result of making the carbon tissue print.

Nevertheless, certain diagnosis of the cause of such flaws on the resultant stamps is, philatelically, extremely difficult. It can be accomplished only by a process of elimination, and this process can be applied to finality only on rare occasions: for example, when proof is possible that certain constant flaws are not diapositive flaws (for instance, in cases in which the same diapositive can be shown to have been used in the production of more than one printing base; one carbon tissue print can never be so used because it is destroyed during the subsequent processes), and were not caused by the use of a flawed screen plate or by damage or inherent defect or repair during any of the subsequent steps in the reproduction of a particular gravure printing base.

Grain and Screen

The ability of the gravure processes to reproduce continuous tone subjects rests on the grain or screen which splits up the design into a mass of recessed cells of varying depth. Without this cell formation, the liquid ink used in this form of printing could not be controlled sufficiently, and would overflow from the deeper to the lighter etched portions of the design, resulting in smeared impressions.[18] The minute cells, with their walls at surface height, ensure that the ink escapes mainly on to the paper direct from each cell.

A purpose of applying the grain or screen is to make these cell walls at non-printing height, that is at surface height in order to act as bearers for the wiper or doctor blade which scrapes the non-printing surface free of ink. But, even with the addition of this controlling factor, the ink during rotary printing does tend to overspill and spread, particularly in the darker portions of the design, and so mask what would otherwise be colorless areas corresponding with the tops of the cell walls. This characteristic is utilized by the producers of gravure stamps for the purpose of improving the appearance of the darker portions of the design, to make them more solid.

The grains, or the lines of the screen, act as an etching resist, so that below each individual grain or line the surface of the printing base is unaffected by the etching fluid; between the grains or the lines, the etching fluid affects the printing base to the extent permitted by the light-affected gelatine of the carbon tissue print of the diapositive.

Until comparatively recent years, a certain difference in procedure during gravure production was that grain was applied mechanically and directly to

---

[18] Photo-etching, without the addition of grain or screen, is used in the production of some printing bases for intaglio printing; this is for line subjects, and in such cases comparatively stiffer inks are employed than are usual for printing from line-engraved plates, with the result that the ink is contained within the etched lines. See the chapter entitled "Intaglio Printing — I: Line Engraving," where "Multiplication of the Design Photographically" is discussed.

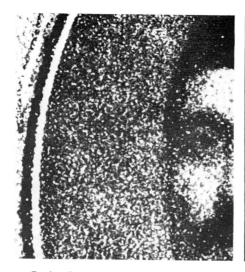

Grained rotary photogravure. Coarse grain. Egypt 1923-24 20 m. and a photographic enlargement of part of the design, showing the effect of a coarse grain formed by powdered bitumen or resin — "corn grain." Note the irregular sizes of the ink patches, and the blotched or mottled effect produced by the irregular and different sized cells. Note also that, even in the darkest portions of the design, colorless areas are pronounced.

the printing base, and screen was applied photographically and directly to the carbon tissue. Nowadays, however, a simulation of grain can be applied photographically to the carbon tissue, and screen may be introduced at a stage as early as the master negative.[19]

Grained rotary photogravure. Union of South Africa 1937-40 Hyphenated 6d., a photographic enlargement of part of the design, showing the fine colorless lines that assist in bearing the doctor blade, and prevent the removal of too much ink from the surrounding portions of the design.

The essence of a grain, or "corn grain" or "mosaic" as it is sometimes termed, is that it produces cells of different size.[20] The cells not only are different in size but also are irregular in shape and application.[21]

Grain

Mechanically applied grain consists of innumerable small particles of bitumen or resin, which are attached to the printing base — comprising a flat plate which may later, for printing, be curved around a cylinder. Various methods have been employed for applying such grain. One method is to flow an aquatint ground over the plate, covering it evenly with a solution of shellac in alcohol; as this dries, the shellac "crazes" or cracks into minute pieces; each piece adheres to and serves as a protection for a corresponding portion of the surface of the plate, and is surrounded by, so to speak, minute fissures or crevices, leaving those parts of the plate unprotected (except for the protection later afforded by the carbon tissue print of the diapositive) and ready to be acted upon by the etching fluid. Another method is to allow grains of finely powdered bitumen or resin to settle on the plate and then to affix them to it by heating it.

A simulation of grain can be applied photographically to the carbon tissue by means of a specially prepared grain plate. A grain plate consists of minute areas of alternatively clear and dark glass in no regular pattern. A carbon tissue print of the grain plate is made by exposing the carbon tissue to bright light through the grain plate for a carefully calculated period of time, thus hardening the sensitized gelatine under the areas of clear glass, and leaving the gelatine unaffected under the areas of dark glass. This exposure to the grain plate is made, usually, before the carbon tissue is exposed to the diapositive.[22]

The effect of the grain on the resultant stamps, when examined under magnification, is that the design consists of small and irregular blobs or blotches of color, giving the areas a mottled appearance; minute colorless areas are visible throughout, often including the dark portions of the design.

---

[19] Therefore, as in so many instances that occur throughout the study of stamp production, it is unsound to take any one practice as standard, and to refer exclusively to it for the purpose of establishing the sequence of events or of drawing purported certain deductions in relation to any particular issue. Each issue must be studied by reference to the particular practice obtaining in its particular production.

[20] In this respect only, is the effect of the grain somewhat analogous to the effect of the half-tone screen, use of which results in dots of different size. However, there is no true analogy between the two; in gravure printing, light and shade depend upon the depth of the respective cells resulting in differing intensity of ink according to depth — and the varying size of the cells does not at all affect the representation of light and shade; in half-tone screen work, light and shade and intensity depend solely upon the respective sizes (areas) of the dots, each of which is covered with a film of ink to the same depth — no question of varying depth of ink arises.

[21] In this respect, also, the effects of the grain differ from the effects of the half-tone screen, use of which produces regular (but, sometimes, coalescing) dots arranged in a definite pattern.

[22] This procedure — that is, the employment of a grain plate — gives rise to the possibility of identical flaws occurring on completely different issues, such flaws — "grain plate flaws" — being identical in character and origin with "screen plate flaws."

Usually, the outline of the design, such as the edge of a frameline, is sharply defined.

An early philatelic use of grain was made by Harrison & Sons Ltd., for Egypt 1923-24 1 m. to £1. In this instance the grain appears coarse, and colorless areas are prominent even in the darkest portions of the design.

A less coarse grain was used in the production of Russia 1945 Relief of Stalingrad 60k. and 3r.

In the Union of South Africa a fine grain is used to produce the so-called "screenless" or "unscreened" gravure-printed issues.[23] The use of the fine grain more or less effectively eliminates the minute colorless areas in the dark portions of the design, they being covered by ink overspill and spread. Nevertheless, under magnification, these dark portions of the design present a blotched or mottled appearance, caused by varying intensity of color.

In some of the more clearly printed examples of some grained gravure stamps of the Union of South Africa, in portions of the design that seem solid color, a series of very fine diagonal colorless lines can be seen. These lines are very thin indeed, and are visible only under considerable magnification and in good light. They are spaced variously at about one millimeter or one-half millimeter apart, and appear, usually, diagonally upward from left to right. The purpose of these lines, at non-printing height on the cylinder, is to assist in bearing the doctor blade (which is flexible) and so prevent the removal of too much ink from the surrounding portions of the design. The lines may be seen, for example, on Union of South Africa 1935 Silver Jubilee 1d. around the words "South Africa" and "Suid Africa," and in 1937 Coronation 1d. around the words "Coronation" and "South Africa" and their Afrikaans equivalents. These fine lines are not to be confused with the colorless crossing lines of a screen.

Screen

The essence of a screen, or "grid," or "mesh," or "cross-line screen," as it is variously termed, is that its use results in cells of the same size throughout the design on the printing base; but, in the heavier inked portions of the printed design, the cell formation is, usually, masked by ink overspill and spread.

The photogravure screen consists of plate glass upon which appear myriads of minute dark rectangles regularly spaced in vertical and horizontal columns and rows. Viewed in a different light, this "screen plate," as it is termed, consists of dark glass upon which appears a series of closely spaced lines of clear glass crossing one another at right angles.[24]

In cases in which the screen is applied to the master negative, the original design is first photo-reduced to the correct size through the screen, to make the original negative. The master negative, therefore, bears the screen formation as part of its design, and this screen is reproduced automatically on every subject on the diapositive which stems from the original negative.[25] It follows that, should any flaw occur on the portion used of the screen plate, the flaw will be reproduced on the master negative, and will be a "master negative flaw," which is the equivalent of a "die flaw."[26]

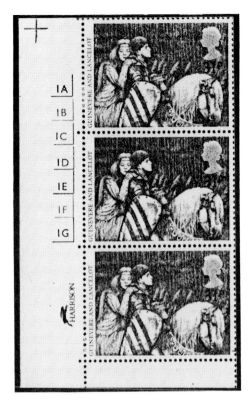

Great Britain 1985 (Sep. 3) Arthurian Legend 31p. with two different screen sizes: 250 for main design and 400 for inscription vertically at left. Cylinder numbers 1E and 1G are both gray-black; cylinder number 1A is black.

In cases in which the screen is applied direct to the carbon tissue, a carbon tissue print of the screen plate is made by exposing the carbon tissue to bright light through the screen plate for a carefully calculated period of time, thus hardening the gelatine under the lines of clear glass and leaving the gelatine unaffected under the dark rectangles. This exposure to the screen plate is made, usually, before the carbon tissue is exposed to the diapositive.

---

[23] In that country the Government Printer has used both grain and screen concurrently; and has, indeed, produced individual issues by a combination of the two processes. For example, in Union of South Africa 1937 Coronation ½d. to 1s., the frames are grained and the centers screened — of course, the printing base for the frames was different from that for the centers.

[24] Basically the grid or mesh of the photogravure screen is similar to that of the half-tone screen — but there is an important difference. The half-tone screen is the "negative" of the photogravure screen. The photogravure screen may be likened to a series of minute doors in clear glass, and the half-tone screen to a series of minute windows in dark glass. A further difference between the two screens is that, in the photogravure screen, the "doors" are wider than the spaces between them, while in the half-tone screen the "windows" and spaces are the same width.

[25] This process, it seems, was used by Thomas De La Rue & Company Ltd. for gravure postage stamps — see "How Stamps Are Made" *De La Rue Journal* Stamp Centenary Number, Page 22 (June 1955.)

[26] See the term "Die" (2) in the alphabetical list to the chapter entitled "Printing Problems and Varieties."

Screen plates vary in several ways. The size of the plate depends upon the stage of the process at which it is to be used; a screen plate for use at the master negative stage need be only the size of the master negative; but in cases in which the screen plate is to be used directly on the carbon tissue, the screen plate is large — at least as large as the sheet of carbon tissue, which will be as large as is necessary to accommodate the number of subjects required on the printing base. Other variations between different screen plates occur in relation to the number of lines to the linear inch, and the relation of the width of the line to the width of the cell. However, philatelically speaking, perhaps the most prominent variations in the appearance of the resultant stamps arise not from any of these causes but from the manner in which the screen plate is applied in relation to the design — that is, whether the screen plate lines appear on the printed stamp as upright and horizontal ("upright screen"[27]), or diagonally ("diagonal screen").

The number of lines to the linear inch on the screen is, usually, employed to characterize the screen. The number of such lines varies greatly, but the most usually encountered screens, philatelically, range between about 150 to 300. It follows that, per square inch of the design, the number of cells for a "250" screen is 62,500, for a "150" screen is 22,500, and so on. A comparatively coarse screen was used, for example, for Belgium 1954 Definitive 4f., Mozambique 1929 Compulsory Tax 40c., and Slovakia 1939 5h.; while a fine screen was used, for instance, for Belgium 1949 (Nov. 15) 50th Anniversary of the Death of Guido Gezelle 1f.75c. + 75c., Congo 1949 75th Anniversary of the Universal Postal Union 4f. and Liberia 1938 Air 1c.

However, sometimes a different screen size is used for particular parts of a design in order to obtain special effects. For instance, in Great Britain 1985 (Sep. 3) Arthurian Legend 17p. to 34p., the normal screen of 250 lines was used for all the design except the lettering at the left. The lettering, with the serifs, was so fine that the effect would have been lost with the normal screen. Thus, a 400-line screen was employed for the lettering — of course on a different printing cylinder. That is the reason why each of the stamps, for which seven colors were used, had two identically colored "traffic lights" and cylinder numbers — namely, gray-black from cylinders 1E and 1G in each case. The 17p. stamp had six colors and only cylinder 1E was printed from gray-black ink. In the cases of the seven-colored stamps, one of the gray-black colors was used within the design and the other was used for the inscription.

Philatelically, precise accuracy about the number of lines per linear inch on the screen plate is unimportant, and fairly difficult of ascertainment. The differences are usually important only when they help to distinguish between stamps resulting from different printing bases; and for this purpose, the qualifications "coarse screen" and "fine screen," or "— mesh," are, normally, sufficient. Such differences, with the same design, occur, for example, in some stamps of the Union of South Africa — for instance, Union of

---

[27] Sometimes the terms "horizontal screen" and "vertical screen" are used in this connection.

Screened rotary photogravure. Upright screen. Egypt 1927-37 10 m. and a photographic enlargement of part of the design, showing the effect of an upright screen. (The screen is not entirely upright; it is tilted slightly counterclockwise.)

South Africa 1942-44 War Effort (Bantams) 2d. printed from cylinder 6931 "coarse screen" ("150" screen), and printed from cylinder 39, "fine screen" ("200" screen).

Usually in photogravure screens there is a considerable difference between the width of the line and the width of the cell, the cell being wider than the line. The relation varies with individual screens — anything from about one-and-one-half to one to four to one being normal; there is, of course, no variation in the same screen. This difference affects the apparent detail visible in the design, and the apparent coarseness of the screen.

As has been stated, an "upright" screen, or a "diagonal" screen results merely from the relative positions of the screen lines and the design; and, provided the overall size of the screen plate is sufficiently large, there is little difficulty in making the same screen plate serve to produce either effect on different carbon tissue prints and the resultant printing bases and stamps. The differences on the stamps between "upright" and "diagonal" screens are well-illustrated by the issue of Egypt 1927-37 1 m. to 200 m., produced by the Survey of Egypt when experimenting with the then, in Egypt, novel method of stamp production. Several of these stamps, including for example the 1 m., 2 m., 4 m. and 5 m., can be found with either an "upright" or a "diagonal" screen. A characteristic difference between the two is that the frames and outside edges of the solid portions of the design of the stamps with "upright" screen are comparatively sharp and straight, while these same

273

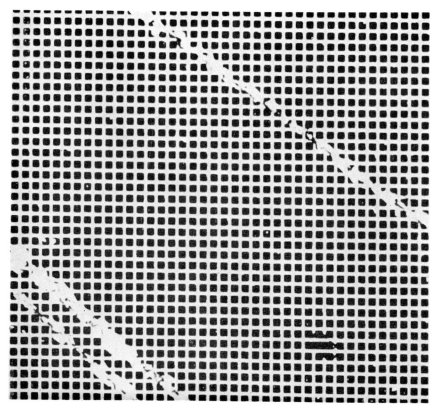

Screened rotary photogravure. Screen plate. A photographic enlargement made by transmitting light through part of a screen plate of a "175" screen, and then making a positive print. (Enlarged about twenty-two times linear.) The ruled surface of the screen plate has been damaged by scratching with a hard substance, and some of the dark rectangles have been disturbed. Such an occurrence accounts for the variety to be found on Union of South Africa, for example, 1954 (Feb. 23) Orange Free State Centenary 4½d., row 20, stamp No. 3. (Note the flaw in the screen plate where the ruling of some of the colorless lines was interrupted, leaving comparatively large rectangles of dark glass.)

parts of the design of the stamps with "diagonal" screen are serrated; under considerable magnification, the saw-tooth effect is pronounced.[28]

This serration of, particularly, horizontal and vertical edges of a design is a characteristic of all diagonally screened gravure stamps; the finer the screen, the closer the serrations.

A "screen plate" is not subject to wear in any ordinary sense of the term, and its life is indefinite, depending on the hazards attendant upon any comparatively large sheet of plate glass subject to repeated handling. It is a costly piece of equipment, and is carefully treated. It is used over and over again,

---

[28] This difference is a useful guide in determining whether Union of South Africa stamps are "grained" or "screened" — in the "grained" stamps, edges are usually sharply defined.

for different stamps and different issues. It is, however, capable of being damaged and the dark rectangles disturbed locally, for example, by scratching; and instances have been recorded of several different stamps exhibiting the same or nearly identical flaws which are attributed to damage to the screen plate. The flaws vary, but the most prominent flaw takes the form of an elongated area showing marked lack of color. Among these stamps are: Union of South Africa 1953 (Jun. 3) Coronation 2d., cylinder 98 or 66, row 2, stamp No. 1 (or 11); 1953 (Sep. 1) Cape Triangular Centenary 4d., cylinders 66 and 86, row 20, stamp No. 7, and cylinders 106 and 90, row 11, stamp No. 5; and 1954 (Feb. 23) Orange Free State Centenary 4½d., row 20, stamp No. 3.

Transferring the Carbon Tissue Print to the Printing Base

As has been stated, after the carbon tissue has been exposed to light through the diapositive, the next step in the gravure process is to transfer the carbon tissue print to the printing base. The sequence of the operations depends upon whether the carbon tissue does or does not bear (of course, latently) the screen or grain.

The carbon tissue will bear the screen or a simulation of grain if this has been applied photographically. And this can be effected either by exposing the carbon tissue to a screen plate or grain plate as a separate operation before exposure to the diapositive, or else by having the screen incorporated in the images on the diapositive, because the screen formed part of the design on the master negative. The carbon tissue will not bear screen or grain unless it has been so incorporated; and, in that event, the carbon tissue print will be in continuous tone or line depending upon the character of the model.

If the carbon tissue print does incorporate screen or grain, the next step

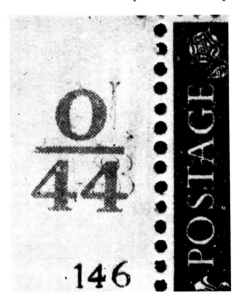

Screened rotary photogravure. Palimpsest (re-used cylinder). Great Britain 1941-42 2½d., cylinder 146, control O/44, showing the outline of control N/43 also, because of defective erasure of the earlier control for which the cylinder was previously used.

Rotary photogravure. H.L. Palmer etching a printing cylinder at the works of Harrison & Sons Ltd. The cylinder was later used for printing Great Britain 1937-39 7d. Note the dark outlines of the varnish which has been applied to the sheet gutters and the sides of the cylinder.

is to apply the carbon tissue to the printing base — which may be either a flat plate or a cylinder. If the carbon tissue is in continuous tone or line, the next step is to provide the printing plate with the grain by one of the mechanical methods mentioned, and after that to take the step of applying the carbon tissue to the plate.

Gravure printing bases are of copper; the cylinders usually comprise a steel core upon which has been deposited a coating of copper; and plates are usually thin sheets of copper.

The surface of the copper is made true by turning and polishing.[29] If any scratch or flaw in the metal should escape or be caused by these turning and polishing operations, and the cylinder be used, such a scratch would reproduce on the resultant stamps as a line of unusual color.

Printing bases may be used for more than one production, and palimp-

---

[29] In cases of mechanically applied grain, the polishing is effected before the grain is applied.

Rotary photogravure. Transferring the carbon tissue print to the printing cylinder at Harrison & Sons Ltd. The highly polished printing cylinder can be seen in the center of the picture. The operator at the right is directing a gentle stream of water from a hose onto the surface of the printing cylinder. The operator at the top left is holding, at the extreme edge, one end of the sheet of carbon tissue, and is guiding it into the machine. The other end of the sheet of carbon tissue is passing between a rubber-covered roller and the printing cylinder and is being pressed or squeegeed into close contact with the printing surface. The operator at the lower left is turning a wheel to operate a worm drive which imparts a revolving movement to the printing cylinder. As this cylinder revolves, so the sheet of carbon tissue progressively covers the surface. All these operations must be carried out with great care and accuracy.

Rotary photogravure. Carbon tissue applied out of true. Great Britain 1950-51 2d., a strip from a coil. The strip illustrates the variety which results if the carbon tissue is applied slightly out of true when being squeegeed onto the printing cylinder. Unless the initial line of contact between the carbon tissue and the cylinder is parallel with the center of the cylinder, the leading and trailing edges of the carbon tissue will not meet properly, and the rows of stamps will be not quite horizontal, resulting in irregularity where the rows begin and end. The strip shows where the edges of the carbon tissue sheet met, at the gutter between the third and fourth stamp; the three stamps at the left appear to be set slightly higher than the three at the right, the most pronounced difference occurring between the third and fourth stamp. (There are twenty-five stamps around the circumference of the cylinder.)

sests have been recorded. One of these occurs among the issues of the Union of South Africa; this consists of Union of South Africa 1930 ½d. in booklets printed from a particular portion of the cylinder.[30] Others are known among the issues of Great Britain, but only in the sheet margins where the control appears; for example, on Great Britain 1941-42 2½d. from cylinder 146, by the control O/44, a faint outline of the control "N/43" can be clearly discerned, because of defective erasure of that control for which the cylinder was previously used; "erasure" in this case involved stripping the chromium surfacing of the cylinder and filling in the cells with metal; an appropriately exposed piece of carbon tissue was then applied locally, and local washing and etching resulted in the new control on the cylinder, which was then resurfaced with chromium.

The carbon tissue print is transferred to the printing base by squeegeeing the gelatine face of the carbon tissue to the printing surface of the printing base. This is effected by directing a stream of water over the surface of the printing base and applying the carbon tissue under carefully regulated pressure. All the operations involved in this step of the process demand great care and accuracy, and, for cylinders, are carried out by a team of operators on a complex machine. The sheet of carbon tissue is fed between a roller and the printing cylinder, which revolve in counter directions and are so adjusted that the correct pressure is imparted, causing the paper-backed gelatine to adhere to the polished surface of the cylinder.

---

[30] The variety is referred to in the *Handbook/Catalogue Union of South Africa Stamps*, published by The Philatelic Federation of Southern Africa (1952), Page 166, as follows: "The first rotogravure booklets were produced in 1930. On some of the ½d. panes of this issue will be found certain additional portions of the Springbok's horns and ears. These are simply traces of images which had previously been etched on this particular cylinder, but inadvertently out of register with the corresponding images on the accompanying frame cylinder, and not completely erased prior to . . . (re-etching) the . . . (subjects) correctly."

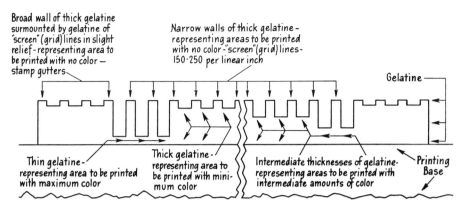

Broad wall of thick gelatine surmounted by gelatine of "screen" (grid) lines in slight relief - representing area to be printed with no color — stamp gutters

Narrow walls of thick gelatine - representing areas to be printed with no color -"screen"(grid) lines - 150·250 per linear inch

Gelatine

Thin gelatine - representing area to be printed with maximum color

Thick gelatine - representing area to be printed with minimum color

Intermediate thicknesses of gelatine - representing areas to be printed with intermediate amounts of color

Printing Base

The initial line of contact between the leading edge of the carbon tissue sheet and the cylinder must be accurately determined, and this edge of the carbon tissue must be applied to this line with great accuracy; otherwise the leading and trailing edges of the carbon tissue sheet will not meet in a straight line, but may partly overlap and partly not meet, and the subjects will not lie in parallel columns and straight rows on the cylinder. This may lead to difficulties at later stages of production, especially in the cases of bi-colored or multicolored stamps, in which one color would be out of register, and also when the stamps (even if they are monochrome) come to be perforated.

So far as sheets of monochrome stamps are concerned, minute variations from absolute accuracy may be tolerated, and would be philatelically indiscernible, except, perhaps, to this extent — that stamps at one end of the sheet would be well-centered, while at the other end of the sheet the stamps would be slightly off center; any overlap and gap between the leading and trailing edges of the carbon tissue would occur in the stamp sheet margins, and so would not be visible. However, in the cases of stamps printed for use in coils, often the cylinder bears no spaces for sheet margins, and the images extend to the edges of the carbon tissue. For such stamps, even minute variations from accuracy can be discerned philatelically, and the inaccuracy is marked by the irregularity of alignment that recurs throughout the coil strip. This characteristic is useful for determining the lay-out of the cylinders from which coils were printed.

After the carbon tissue has been applied to the printing base, the two are allowed to "rest" for a time. Then the printing base and the adherent carbon tissue are treated by bathing in warm or hot water. The water penetrates the paper, and dissolves that gelatine which has been unaffected by light, enabling the paper backing to be stripped away. The bathing with water is continued until all the unaffected gelatine is dissolved. This treatment is termed "developing the gelatine print."

When this development is complete, the printing base bears, adhering to its polished surface, a very thin film comprising all the light-affected gelatine, representing the sheet margins (if any), the gutters (if any), and the requisite number of subjects, with the designs reading from right-to-left.

At this stage (if the eventual stamp is to have uncolored margins, and if the, for example, screen has been applied photographically), each subject on the printing base is represented as follows:

(1) The subject is surrounded by broad walls of thick[31] gelatine, representing the stamp gutters. These areas were, of course, affected by the exposure of the screen plate, and at that primary stage on the carbon tissue comprised merely a fine grid — the grid lines being of insoluble gelatine, and the contained rectangles of soluble gelatine. Then the diapositive exposure was made. The areas representing the stamp gutters were of clear glass, and thus passed all the light, and rendered insoluble also the gelatine in the contained rectangles. However, because more light has affected the gelatine under the lines of the screen than anywhere else, the top of this wall bears, in slight relief, the gelatine representing the grid lines.

(2) Within these broad walls, the design itself is represented by a fine grid of thick gelatine, representing the lines of the screen plate, and forming narrow walls surrounding myriads of rectangular spaces, representing the minute dark rectangles of the screen plate as affected by the additional exposure to the diapositive. In these minute rectangular spaces, the thickness[31] of the gelatine varies. Where much light was passed by the diapositive (that is, in those areas of the design to be printed with little color), the gelatine is thick; where no light was passed (that is, in those areas of the design to be printed with much color), the gelatine is thinnest;[31] and the thickness of the gelatine in the other spaces corresponds with the amount of light passed by the intermediate light values of the diapositive.

Again, at this stage — that is, when the development of the gelatine print is complete (if grain has been applied to the printing plate at a separate operation) — the printing plate bears the individual irregularly spaced and sized grains, and, superimposed on them and the spaces between, the gelatine of varying thickness. The gelatine will be thickest in the areas representing the highlights, and thinnest in the areas to be most deeply colored.

Gelatine Flaws

The next stage in the gravure processes is to prepare the printing base for etching the subjects. However, it is convenient here to consider some of the philatelic varieties that result from some types of flaw that can occur during the handling of the carbon tissue and the gelatine on the printing base.

The gelatine surface of the carbon tissue and the gelatine on the printing base, particularly when wet, are especially liable to damage from the slightest mishandling. Such damage will reflect itself on the resultant stamps.

A thinning of the gelatine caused, for example, by a slight gouge will be represented on the resultant stamps by unusual color. Such an effect is well-illustrated by Union of South Africa 1937-40 Hyphenated 6d., the so-called "Phantom Ladder" variety, occurring on the stamp inscribed in English, printed from interior cylinder 52A, row 5, stamp No. 10, and issued in October 1937.

---

[31] The term "thick" is used to indicate the depth of the gelatine standing up from the surface of the printing base; so also the comparative terms.

Grained rotary photogravure. Gelatine flaw. Union of South Africa 1937-40 Hyphenated 6d., "Phantom Ladder" variety, interior cylinder 52A, row 5, stamp No. 10. The appearance of the "ladder" results from local over-etching of parts of the horizontal lines of the background, resulting from an insufficiency of gelatine in the area affected.

"Gelatine shifts" can occur — that is, a portion of the gelatine from one part of the design may be removed and be deposited on another portion of the design. This will result in unwanted color appearing at the place from which the gelatine was removed, and the absence of color at the place where this gelatine was deposited. Such a cause accounts for Union of South Africa 1933-45 Hyphenated 5s., the so-called "Broken Yoke Pin" variety, occurring on the stamp inscribed in English, printed from interior cylinder 6929, row 18, stamp No. 5, and issued in October 1933. On well-registered copies of this bi-colored stamp, the place from which the gelatine was removed can be seen in the form of a colored (black) mark immediately above the left-hand figure of value; on badly registered copies of this stamp, this mark is more difficult to see, being masked by the green ink of the frame. This piece of gelatine lodged on the cylinder coincident with the yoke pin, filliing what was a depression in the gelatine, and so resulting in a seeming break in the design.

In diagnosing the cause of gelatine flaws it is important to bear in mind that thinning of the gelatine results in more color than desired on the corresponding portion of the resultant stamp — and that if the resultant stamp exhibits an absence of color because of a gelatine flaw, the color is absent because the corresponding portion of the gelatine was thickened.

Etching the Printing Base

After the development of the red pigmented gelatine print is complete, the printing base with its adherent thin film of gelatine is allowed to dry. The next stage in the process is to paint on by hand an etching resist — a varnish — to those parts of the printing base corresponding with those parts of the printed sheet upon which no color at all is to appear.

Areas such as sheet margins and, sometimes, the stamp gutters themselves

Screened rotary photogravure. Varnishing flaw. Great Britain 1934-36 2½d., cylinder 8, control Y/36, row 20, stamp No. 1 and part of the adjoining sheet margin, showing a varnishing flaw — the edge of the varnished area. The varnishing should have protected the whole of the sheet and stamp margin from the action of the etching fluid. But, because the varnish was not sufficiently applied, the etching fluid penetrated the gelatine and formed shallow cells that held ink and printed a wedge-shaped area of faint color in which the screen lines appear.

are so treated. In the cases of stamps to be printed in more than one color, this work of painting for each cylinder may be greater than on the single cylinder for monochrome stamps, and every part of each printing base, except those parts of it bearing the relevant portion of the finished design, may be covered with varnish.

This varnishing is necessary, often because, if it were not done, undesired color would appear — the color coming from the shallow cells which result from the screen lines being in slightly thicker gelatine than the thickest gelatine of the design and margins.

Because this etching resist is applied by hand, there is always the possibility that the varnish will not cover all that it was intended to cover; and, if it does not, the result will be reflected in the stamps. Many instances occur in which the screen lines can be seen in parts of the sheet margins and stamp gutters. For example, on Egypt 1947 Air 3m., with control A/47, the sheet margins show clearly the edge of the varnished-out area. And on Great Britain 1934-36 2½d., cylinder 8 with control Y/36, row 20, stamp No. 1 and the adjoining sheet margin exhibit a wedge-shaped area of screen where the varnish was not applied to the cylinder.

After varnishing (and, if necessary, the addition of any marginal markings applied by hand) the printing base is ready for etching.

Etching is carried out by ferric chloride solution made up in various strengths; the stronger the solution, the less fluid it is, and so the strongest solution is able to penetrate only the thinnest parts of the gelatine. The various solutions are applied in turn by the etcher, who has to judge to a nicety when the etching fluid has completed its work. He pours the etching fluid over the printing base, taking care to see that it is completely covered. Local control can be exercised by dabbing on the solution with cotton wool.

Cleaning and Finishing the Etched Printing Base

After the etching is complete, the printing base is thoroughly washed and cleaned. In the process of cleaning screened cylinders and plates, the cleaning removes the gelatine and varnish; with plates bearing mechanically applied grain, the cleaning removes the grain as well as the gelatine and varnish.

Usually, the printing base is then proved — that is, a proof sheet is printed from it, and the sheet is examined for faults. If any faults are found, and are considered of sufficient importance to merit attention on the printing base, it is then retouched by hand.

There are two classes of fault. The one produces colored flaws because of an undesired depression in the surface of the printing base; the other produces uncolored areas because of the absence of a desired depression in the surface of the printing base.

Both these classes of fault can be remedied on the printing base; the uncolored flaw by manually cutting away the copper by use of a burin or graver; the colored flaw by filling the depression with metal and subsequently touching up as necessary with the burin.

Such work, of course, demands great care, and skill comparable with that of the steel-engraver.

Many instances of such retouching have been recorded on postage stamps. An example, chosen at random, is to be found on Great Britain 1934-36 2½d., cylinder 8 with control Y/36, row 18, stamp No. 1. The panel at the left of the stamp should have been etched more deeply than it was; it appeared almost colorless on the proof. But part of this panel was retouched by hand in a manner to simulate the lines of the screen, and the effect of this retouching is clearly visible on the printed stamp.

Examples of such retouching abound on modern issues. It is at its most obvious on monochrome stamps. When several or many colors are used in printing one design, retouching is less prominent, because it usually tends to be masked by the other colors.

After the printing base has been finally approved, it is, usually, surfaced with chromium, and is then ready for the press.

Printing from Gravure Printing Bases

Most gravure printing takes place on rotary machines, either from a plate bent around a cylinder or from a cylinder. In printing from plates around a cylinder, the printing must be effected on to sheets of paper, but in printing from cylinders, either sheets or, more usually, reels of paper are used.

The curved plate or cylinder is placed in the machine and rotates, being supplied with ink by a roller or by rotating in the ink trough. The ink floods the surface of the printing base, filling the cells and covering the non-printing surface. As the printing base continues to rotate, it comes into contact with a doctor blade which scrapes the ink from the non-printing surface, but does not disturb the ink in the cells.

The doctor blade (or "doctor knife" or "ducteur knife" as it is sometimes called) is a thin, flexible strip of finely ground steel, somewhat longer than

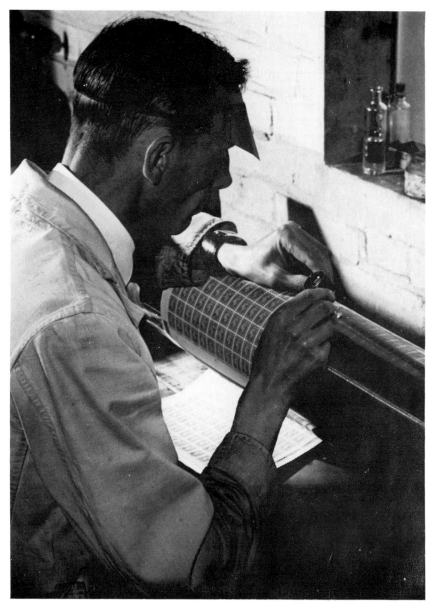

Rotary photogravure. Retouching a printing cylinder at the works of Harrison & Sons Ltd. From the cylinder a proof has been printed; this proof, suitably corrected and marked, can be seen wrapped around the cylinder by the left arm of the engraver, who is studying the corresponding portion of the cylinder through a magnifying glass held in his right hand. With his left hand, he is retouching one of the subjects; the end of the tool he is using can be seen below the middle finger of his right hand. Other marked proofs can be seen on the workbench, above which the cylinder is resting, and which bears other retouching tools.

Screened rotary photogravure.
Retouch. Great Britain 1934-36 2½d.,
cylinder 8., control Y/36, row 18, stamp
No. 1, and (i) a photographic enlargement of part of the design showing a
retouch to the panel at the left of the
stamp, and (ii) a photographic enlargement of a normal panel, for comparison. The retouch was effected to
deepen the apparent tone of the panel,
which had not been etched deeply
enough; the retouch simulates the
screen.

(i)   (ii)

the width of the printing base. A clamp in the machine holds the doctor blade,
which is set at a tangent to the curved surface of the printing base, and the
two are in close contact. The doctor blade bears on the non-printing surface,
which comprises the unetched portions — that is, for example, the sheet
margins and the screen lines or grain. A slight sideways movement, alternately from left-to-right and right-to-left, is imparted to the doctor blade by
the machine, so that, as the printing base revolves, any particular point along
the edge of the doctor blade traces a slightly diagonal and zig-zag path over
the face of the printing base.

The doctor blade gives rise to philatelic varieties termed "doctor blade
flaws." Such flaws have two causes.

First, although the doctor blade is firmly set in the machine in close contact with the printing base, instances occur of the doctor blade vibrating temporarily. This has the effect of moving the blade minutely out of contact with
the non-printing surface of the printing base, and of allowing ink to pass
along a series of lines, each line representing the distance traveled by the
surface of the printing base while it and the doctor blade were out of contact. This distance is minute in each case, and the effect is that a series of
lines of color appears on the stamps at right angles to the direction of travel
of the surface of the printing base. That is, if the subjects were set on the
cylinders so that, for example, a sheet was printed from top to bottom, a
"doctor blade flaw" caused by vibration occurs across the sheet from side

Rotary photogravure. The doctor blade on a printing machine at the works of Harrison & Sons Ltd. The doctor blade can be seen in contact with the printing cylinder, being held in place on the machine by being bolted between the clamping plates on which the hand is resting. In the picture, the paper is being fed from above; the printing surface is visible. The paper is traveling downward between the printing cylinder (which is turning clockwise) and the impression cylinder, part of which is just visible at the right of the picture below the large cylinder guiding the paper. Beneath the doctor blade the surplus ink can be seen falling back into the ink trough. This machine produces the equivalent of 5,000 sheets an hour.

to side. Often such doctor blade flaws are accompanied by an excess of color on the face of the stamps, giving rise to the variety "pseudo-colored paper." Such varieties are, of course, inconstant.

Second, the edge of the doctor blade in contact with the printing base is finely ground, and is liable to damage. Grit in the ink or from elsewhere could make a nick in the edge of the blade, and this would have the effect of permitting a minute quantity of ink to pass on the non-printing surface; such ink will continue to pass until either the nick is reduced by wear (the chromium facing of the cylinder being harder than the steel of the doctor blade), or the doctor blade is reground. Such ink appears in the form of a, usually, very thin line of color, and this is set slightly diagonally over the

Screened rotary photogravure. Doctor blade flaw (uncolored). Great Britain 1952-54 4d. The lightly colored, almost vertical streak extending from below the "A" of "Postage" through the ear and above was caused by a piece of soft dirt becoming lodged under the doctor blade and removing some of the ink. Note that the shallower cells (that is, the less colored portions of the design) have been most affected by the scooping action caused by the additional local pressure.

stamps because of the sideways movement of the doctor blade. Such varieties are inconstant, but they may well occur throughout more than one sheet.

Grit or other impurities during rotary photogravure printing can cause other effects.

A slight piece of dirt, lodged under the doctor blade, may cause too much pressure at that place, with the result that ink is removed not only from the surface but also from some of the shallower cells, resulting in a light mark through parts of the design. These marks are, characteristically, set slightly diagonally, revealing their source of origin as being the doctor blade. Such

Screened rotary photogravure. The completed cylinder. Great Britain 1948 Silver Wedding £1, produced in screened rotary photogravure by Harrison & Sons Ltd. The picture shows the chromium-faced cylinder ready for the press.

287

Rotary photogravure. Monochrome printing. One of the photogravure stamp printing machines specially built for Harrison & Sons Ltd. by Timsons Ltd. The paper in the web has been printed, and, at the left of the picture, is being led to the top of the machine; the paper then hangs in festoons while the ink dries, and is then led, at the right of the picture, down over rollers where it is re-reeled before being removed for cutting into convenient sized sheets for perforating and trimming.

varieties are, of course, inconstant, but they will continue to occur until the piece of dirt is dislodged. This type of variety is known on several issues of Great Britain, including 1952-54 2½d. and 4d., and 1953 Coronation 1s.6d.

Grit or dirt impacted into the cells on the cylinder may result in a colorless flaw on the resultant stamp; if such grit or dirt is at non-printing height, the action of the doctor blade will scrape off the ink, and no color from that portion of the printing base will reach the paper. This is thought to have caused Great Britain 1948 (Jul. 29) Olympic Games 3d., the so-called "Flaw on Crown" variety on cylinder 1, row 20, stamp No. 2. Such varieties are inconstant, but they may occur on many sheets, until the impacted dirt falls off or is removed. The stamp just mentioned can be found from later printings without the colorless flaw and with the crown slightly misshapen.

After the non-printing surface has been scraped free of ink, the printing base encounters the paper which is pressed heavily into contact by an impression cylinder; the paper sucks the ink from the cells, and thus the stamps are printed. The pressure is very great but, because of the minuteness of the cells, no palpable distortion of the paper occurs.

Rotary photogravure. Multicolor printing. Switzerland Pro Juventute 10(c.) + 5(c.). Produced in screened rotary photogravure by Courvoisier. Printing a further color. In the picture, the web of paper bearing the partly colored designs is being fed downward on the right (where the gummed side of the paper is visible) and under a guiding roller toward the left, where the paper passes underneath the ink trough and then upward between the next set of printing and impression cylinders, which add a further color to the designs. The paper can be seen leaving this printing cylinder, and the impression cylinder is just visible above.

In the case of monochrome stamps printed on the web, no further printing is necessary. However, in the cases of stamps printed in more than one color, the web is led to the next set of impression and printing cylinders in the machine, and the colors are applied sequentially.

In the length of a web of paper it is not unusual to find places at which the paper has broken and been repaired by overlapping the edges of the whole width of the web at the point of breakage, causing the paper to be doubly thick at that point. Should this portion of the web pass through the machine without being noticed, the result will be that some stamps will be printed on "joined paper." A variety of this nature on a rotary photogravure stamp — occurring on Great Britain 1952-54 2½d. — is illustrated in the alphabetical list to the chapter entitled "Paper."

The sharp edge of the double thickness of paper may damage the printing cylinders and it is usual to release the pressure on the machine, so as not to print on the web where any join occurs; and for this purpose the edge of the reel is, usually, marked by a colored "flag" to inform the operator when to release the pressure. When pressure is thus released, part of the web will be unprinted, or only partly printed. Stamps thus imperfectly printed are, usually, removed during checking; but instances have been recorded where such stamps, having escaped notice during checking, have been issued.

Diagnosing the printing method of some modern designs often causes difficulty. This can be especially the case with photogravure ("photo" or, preferably, "gravure") and photographic-lithography ("photo.-litho." or, as the common usage frequently is, "photo.").

However, the effects of the two different processes vary considerably, quite apart from the differences of screen which are visible under substantial magnification. The gravure-printed stamps are vivid in their contrast between the lighter and darker portions of the design; the photo.-litho. printed stamps lack that sharp contrast, and the central feature or portrait stands out with less apparent clarity. Excellent opportunities for comparing the differences in the overall visual effect of a monochrome stamp design printed by photogravure and exactly the same design printed by photo.-litho. are presented by some of the low values of the definitive series of Great Britain popularly referred to as the "Machins" because the Queen's portrait is based on a photograph of a sculptured plaque by Arnold Machin. One specific instance of such productions is provided by Great Britain 1971-85 2d. green printed in photogravure by Harrison & Sons Ltd. and the same design printed in photo.-litho. by the House of Questa.

Varieties and Terms in Gravure Printing

The alphabetical list that follows includes some of the terms and varieties appropriate to gravure-printed stamps. The list is not intended to be exhaustive, and to it may be applied the generality of the remarks preceding the alphabetical list to the chapter entitled "Intaglio Printing — I: Line-Engraving." Varieties in gravure printing may be considered as falling into three classes:

(1) "Cylinder" or "plate" varieties, appearing as either colored or uncolored flaws, caused by (a) damage to or inherent defect in the printing base, or (b) some variation from the intended norm in one or more subjects on the printing base, occurring because of some irregularity during any stage of one or more of the steps during its preparation, or (c) repair or retouching of (a) or (b). A variety of this class is constant — see Variety (3) in the alphabetical list to the chapter entitled "Printing Problems and Varieties."

(2) Doctor blade varieties — that is, varieties resulting from the use of the doctor blade; such varieties are, usually, colored, but may appear as the absence or partial absence of color; a variety of this class is inconstant.

(3) Printing varieties in the special sense of excluding doctor blade varieties; a variety of this class is inconstant, although its cause may (in the case, for example, of impacted dirt) give rise to damage, resulting in a "cylinder variety," class 1(a).

Philatelists generally have not come to grips with the terminological problems set by varieties occurring on gravure-printed stamps; and to the student these problems are not made any the easier of solution by the fact that, in diagnosing the cause of an effect upon a gravure-printed stamp, it is often

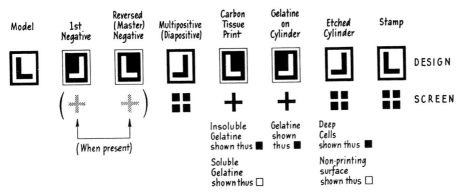

Variations from positive to negative and from left-to-right and right-to-left the image undergoes during various stages of production of a gravure printing base.

difficult to be accurate and more precise than to place the flaw generally in one of the three classes of "cylinder" flaws, doctor blade flaws, and printing flaws. The study of gravure-printed stamps is, in large measure, concerned with minute flaws; and, during any attempt at diagnosis of the cause of an effect, it is essential to bear in mind the numerous variations from positive to negative and from left-to-right to right-to-left which the image undergoes during the various stages of production of a gravure printing base.

Photogravure and photo.-litho. Great Britain 1971-86. Machin 2p. At left, the photogravure printing by Harrison & Sons Ltd.; at right, the same stamp printed photo.-litho. by House of Questa; exhibiting the visual difference between the results of the two printing methods.

Carbon Tissue. Term used to refer to the paper-backed sheet of gelatine, made sensitive to light by immersion in a solution of potassium bichromate, and used in transferring the photographic images from the diapositive to the printing base. The gelatine is, usually, colored red, the term "carbon" being a reminder of the early days when lamp-black was used instead of red pigment — see "Pigment Paper."

Carbon Tissue Flaw — see "Gelatine Flaw."

Coarse Grain, Coarse Screen — see "Grain"; "Screen."

Corn Grain — see "Grain."

Cross-Line Screen. Term used as a variant of "screen" to signify the crossed colorless lines appearing on some gravure-printed stamps. The term "cross-line" is used to emphasize the difference between the regular striations produced by use of the screen, and the irregular effect of grain. See "Screen"; "Grain."

Cylinder Flaw. Colored or uncolored flaw. In the cases of gravure-printed stamps this term is used generically to denote a constant flaw which results on a stamp because of some defect on or damage to the printing base. Often the term "cylinder flaw" is used irrespective of whether the printing base was a cylinder or curved plate. The term is only partly diagnostic, and signifies little more than that the flaw is constant, being used in the sense of distinguishing such flaws from those occasioned by use of the doctor blade, and from printing flaws. Because of its imprecision, the term is useful in those many cases when the cause of the defect on the printing base cannot be established; for example, defects on the printing base occurring there because of, say, damage to the carbon tissue or the diapositive may properly be referred to as producing "cylinder flaws" on the stamps; but doctor blade flaws cannot properly be referred to as "cylinder flaws." Use of the term "cylinder flaw" implies that the flaw is constant. Colored cylinder flaws are caused by depressions in the cylinder; uncolored cylinder flaws are caused by the absence of depressions in the cylinder.

Diagonal Screen — see "Screen."

Diapositive. Term used to refer to the completed photograph comprising the base, usually plate glass but sometimes a sheet of film, supporting the developed photographic emulsion containing the images of the design repeated the requisite number of times. Often the variant term "Multipositive" is used. The photographic images on the diapositive are positive in the sense that they directly reproduce the light values of the original design or model, but they are reversed in that the design reads from right-to-left.

Diapositive Flaw. Colored or uncolored flaw. In the cases of gravure-printed stamps this term is used to denote a flaw on the stamp resulting from some defect on or variation from intended norm in a subject or subjects on the diapositive. If the defect consists of the presence of unwanted color, such as a speck of dirt on the diapositive, the flaw on the resultant stamp will be colored; if the diapositive defect consists of the absence of color, such as an air bubble or pinpoint of missing emulsion, the flaw on the resultant stamp will be uncolored. Such flaws can, of course, result from or be remedied by photographic retouching of the diapositive. See "Cylinder Flaw." The use of a diapositive is often not limited to the making of a single printing base, and diagnosis of a variation from intended norm as the effect of a diapositive flaw depends, usually, upon the ability to prove the existence of the same flaw on more than one printing base. An instance of a colored diapositive flaw is to be found on Great Britain 1934-36 1½d., cylinder

Rotary photogravure. Switzerland 1947 (Aug. 6) Railway Centenary 5c. Produced in screened rotary photogravure by Courvoisier. Checking the diapositive. The technician is examining, through a low-power microscope and parallax correcting viewer the ''montage,'' ''setting up'' or superimposition of the diapositives of which there are three, one for each color, to ensure correct photographic registration, and to eliminate this as a possible source of error that might become manifest at later stages of production. The registration tests and adjustments are made after each diapositive has been individually examined for possible photographic faults and flaws, and any necessary photographic retouching has been effected.

116 and 119 (control W/35), row 20, stamp No. 1, where the flaw takes the form of a pronounced dot in the upper margin of the stamp about one-and-one-half millimeters to the left of the cross on the crown. An instance of an uncolored diapositive flaw is to be found on Great Britain 1934-36 1½d., cylinder 116 and 119 (control W/35), row 19, stamp No. 1, where, at the right of the stamp, above and to the right of the ''1'' of ''½,'' the flaw appears as a thickening of the curve of the inner frame. See ''Double Exposure.''

Die Negative. In gravure printing, this term is used synonymously with ''Master Negative.''

Doctor Blade, Doctor Knife, Ducteur. These terms are used to denote the long, thin, flexible strip of finely ground steel which scrapes the excess ink from the non-printing surface of the printing base. Use of the term, and the doctor blade itself, is not limited to the gravure printing processes; some variations of line engraving incorporate the use of a doctor blade — for example, see ''Sequential Color Printing on the Web'' in the chapter entitled ''Intaglio Printing — I: Line Engraving.''

Doctor Blade Flaw. Colored or uncolored flaw. In the cases of gravure-printed stamps this term is used to designate a flaw caused by some happening affecting the proper working of the doctor blade. (1) There are two types of colored doctor blade flaws: (a) the first type consists of horizontal lines across stamps printed from top to bottom, and is often accompanied by pseudo-colored paper; such flaws are caused by vibration of the doctor blade, which permits ink to pass across the line of travel of the printing base; (b) the second type consists of fine lines

293

slightly out of perpendicular over stamps printed from top to bottom; such flaws are caused by nicks made in the finely ground edge of the doctor blade by grit or other impurities, permitting ink to pass along the line of travel of the printing base. These types of colored flaws are the equivalent of those referred to under "Wiping Mark" in the alphabetical list to the chapter entitled "Intaglio Printing — I: Line Engraving." (2) There is one type of uncolored doctor blade flaw, consisting of a pronounced line of insufficient color visible, usually, only in the more lightly colored portions of the design, and set slightly out of perpendicular on stamps printed from top to bottom; such flaws are caused by some soft substance becoming lodged between the doctor blade and the printing base and wiping too much ink from the cells. This type of uncolored flaw is the equivalent of those referred to under "Scooped Color" in the alphabetical list to the chapter entitled "Intaglio Printing — I: Line Engraving." Doctor blade flaws, whether colored or uncolored, are inconstant.

Double Exposure. Colored flaw. This term is used to denote a rare class of flaw occurring when the step-and-repeat camera is manually operated and, by error, the operator exposes the diapositive more than once in the same or nearly identical position. Unless the two exposures are in identically the same position, the effect is that the subject presents thickened or doubled lines — for example, as in South Africa 1948-49 Postage Due 2d., interior cylinder 28, row 16, stamps Nos. 5 and 6. If the double exposures are in identically the same position, the effect is, or may be, that the subject as printed will exhibit an excess of color because the excess light results in greater opacity on the diapositive, consequently insufficient hardening of the bichromated gelatine of the carbon tissue, less mordant-resisting gelatine on the printing plate or cylinder, excessive etching of the plate or cylinder, causing deeper cells that hold more ink.

Fine Grain, Fine Screen — see "Grain"; "Screen."

Gelatine Flaw, Gelatine Shift. Colored or uncolored flaw. In the cases of gravure-printed stamps, these terms are used to designate the effects caused by damage to or irregularity in the gelatine of the carbon tissue. If the damage or irregularity consists in the local thinning of the gelatine, the flaw will appear colored on the stamp; and if the gelatine is thickened locally the flaw will appear uncolored. The term "gelatine shift" is limited in use to cases where the gelatine from one portion is deposited on another portion of the gelatine image, so that the colored flaw has a corresponding uncolored flaw, usually on the same subject. Such varieties reproduce on the printing base, and are constant. See "Cylinder Flaw." An instance of a colored gelatine flaw is to be found on Union of South Africa 1937-40 Hyphenated 6d., interior cylinder 52A, row 5, stamp No. 10, where the flaw takes the form of an emphasis over a diagonal area of the horizontal lines of the design, the so-called "Phantom Ladder" variety. An instance of a gelatine shift with the colored and corresponding uncolored flaws is to be found on Union of South Africa 1933-45 Hyphenated 5s., interior cylinder 6929, row 18, stamp No. 5, where, at left of the stamp, the colored flaw is to be found above the figure of value, and the corresponding uncolored flaw is in the form of a seemingly missing portion of the design, the so-called "Broken Yoke Pin" variety.

Grain. Term used to designate the irregular pattern or mottled appearance imparted to all parts of the design of some gravure-printed stamps by the use of grains of powdered bitumen or resin on the printing base, or of a grain plate to which the carbon tissue is exposed — see "Grain Plate." The term "grain" is used in contradistinction to "screen," and the terms "Corn Grain," "Mosaic," "Screenless," and "Unscreened," are used as synonyms for "grain." A characteristic feature of grained gravure-printed stamps is that the edges of, for

294

example, straight lines are comparatively sharply defined, and do not present serrations as in the cases of most screened gravure-printed stamps. The grain in individual issues varies; it is classified, when necessary, as "coarse" or "fine." An instance of a coarse-grained gravure-printed stamp is to be found in Egypt 1923-34 1 m. An instance of a fine-grained gravure-printed stamp is to be found in Russia 1945 Relief of Stalingrad 60k.

Grain Plate. Term used to denote a special photographic or other plate so made that if the carbon tissue is exposed to the grain plate the eventual stamps have the appearance of having been printed from a printing base to which grains of powdered bitumen or resin have been directly applied.

Grid. In gravure printing this term is used synonymously with "Screen."

Horizontal Screen — see "Screen."

Master Negative. Term used to denote the photographic negative (bearing an image reading from left-to-right) used for the production of the diapositive. The master negative is the equivalent of the die in printing processes involving the mechanical multiplication of the design — see "Die (1)" in the alphabetical list to the chapter entitled "Printing Problems and Varieties." The term "Die Negative" is used as a synonym for "Master Negative."

Master Negative Flaw. Colored or uncolored flaw. In the cases of gravure-printed stamps, this term is sometimes used to designate a variation from the intended norm, occurring on the master negative. However, because such a variation occurs on every stamp resulting from the use of the master negative, the variation in itself constitutes the norm for all these stamps, and is the equivalent of a die flaw — see "Die (2)" in the alphabetical list to the chapter entitled "Printing Problems and Varieties." An instance of an uncolored master negative flaw is to be found on Seychelles 1938-41 2.25 r., plate 1, where, on every stamp in the sheet of sixty subjects, the flaw takes the form of a small patch or nick at the extreme lower portion of the design beneath the left extremity of the last letter of "Seychelles." An instance of a colored master negative flaw is to be found on Great Britain 1934-36 1½d., on stamps from sheets, where, beneath the value tablet, in the lower margin of all stamps, appears a slightly diagonal line extending beneath most of the letters of "Threehalfpence."

Mesh. In gravure printing this term is sometimes used synonymously with "Screen."

Model. Term used to denote the photograph, drawing or painting that is photographed to make the original negative which, when reversed, comprises the master negative.

Mosaic. In gravure printing this term is sometimes used synonymously with "Grain."

Multipositive. In gravure printing this term is used synonymously with "Diapositive."

Negative — see "Master Negative"; "Original Negative."

Original Negative. Term used to denote the photographic negative made by exposing the photographic plate to the model. The original negative (sometimes called the "First Negative") is reversed to make the master negative.

Pigment Paper. In gravure printing this term is supplanting "Carbon Tissue." The paper no longer has any connection with carbon, and never had anything to do with tissue.

Plate Flaw. Colored or uncolored flaw. In the cases of gravure-printed stamps this term is rarely used, whatever the form of the printing base. Usually the term used is "cylinder flaw" — see "Cylinder Flaw."

Retouch. Colored or uncolored flaw. In the cases of gravure-printed stamps this term has two possible meanings: (a) a flaw resulting from photographically retouching any one or more of the various photographic plates which come into existence during the intermediate stages of the production of a gravure printing base; (b) a flaw resulting from an alteration or repair effected to a particular subject on the printing base. While retouches made at any stage of the process before the diapositive will reproduce on every stamp, being master negative flaws, and are thus simple to diagnose, it is often difficult accurately to determine at which stage later retouching flaws came into existence, but their nature is usually self-evident on closer examination. Assistance in diagnosis may sometimes be obtained from the presence or absence of "screen" within the area of the retouch; if "screen" is absent, the inference is that the retouch was to the subject on the printing base. An instance of a retouch is to be found on Seychelles 1938-41 6c. plate 1, stamp No. 48, where, about two millimeters below the first "L" of "Seychelles" the retouch takes the form of a patch of seemingly irregular inking, the flaw being both colored and uncolored. Gravure printers limit the meaning of the term "retouch" to (a) above; for (b) above they usually employ the term "repair."

Screen. Term used to denote the crossed colorless lines appearing on some gravure-printed stamps. These lines occur because of the use of a screen plate. The screen in individual issues varies, depending upon the screen plate used; this variation is, mainly, in two respects: size, and direction. (1) Size is measured by reference to the number of lines to the linear inch, 150 to 300 being the sizes of screens often encountered philatelically. Philatelically, classification of screen sizes by number is, normally, unnecessary; comparisons are made by using the terms "coarse screen" and "fine screen," or "coarse mesh" and "fine mesh." An instance of a coarse screen is to be found on Belgium 1954 Definitive 4f. An instance of a fine screen is to be found on Liberia 1938 Air 1c. (2) Direction has reference to the appearance of the lines in relation to the outlines of the stamp design. Usually these lines appear diagonally, the term used being "diagonal screen." On some stamps the lines appear vertically and horizontally, or nearly so, the terms used being, variously, "horizontal screen," "upright screen," and "vertical screen." A characteristic feature of diagonally screened gravure-printed stamps is that the edges of, for example, horizontal lines in the design have serrated edges. This characteristic does not obtain on stamps with an upright screen. An instance of a diagonally screened gravure-printed stamp is India 1953 (Oct. 2) Conquest of Mount Everest 2a. An instance of an upright screen is to be found on Egypt 1927-34 1 m., with control A/26.

Screenless. This term is used to denote stamps printed in grained gravure — see "Grain."

Screen Plate. Term used to designate the glass plate bearing the pattern which results in the colorless lines on screened gravure-printed stamps. The screen plate pattern consists of minute rectangles of dark glass arranged in regular columns and rows separated by thin lines of clear glass. The number of these thin lines occurring in the linear inch determines the "size" of the screen — see "Grain."

Screened rotary photogravure. Screen plate flaw. Union of South Africa 1953 (Jun. 3) Coronation 2d., cylinder 98, row 2, stamp No. 1; and 1953 (Sep. 1) Cape Triangular Centenary 4d., cylinders 66 and 86, row 20, stamp No. 7; and 1954 (Feb. 23) Orange Free State Centenary 4½d., cylinder 104, row 20, stamp No. 3; each showing an identical flaw resulting from a defect on the screen plate. (On the picture, the flaw has been made more pronounced than it appears on the stamps.)

Screen Plate Flaw. Uncolored. In the cases of gravure-printed stamps, this term is used to designate a flaw that can be proved to have originated on the screen plate. A screen plate is susceptible to damage; if it is damaged by, for example, a scratch affecting some of the minute rectangles of dark glass, this will cause a flaw to appear on the printing base and the resultant stamp or stamps; such flaw will, of course, appear each time that the flawed screen plate is used, and the use of a particular screen plate is not limited to any one issue. A screen plate flaw is constant. Examples of different issues bearing the same screen plate flaw are provided by Union of South Africa 1953 (Jun. 3) Coronation 2d., cylinder 98, row 2, stamp No. 1 (or No. 11); 1953 (Sep. 1) Cape Triangular Centenary 4d., cylinders 66 and 86, row 20, stamp No. 7, and 1954 (Feb. 23) Orange Free State Centenary 4½d., cylinder 104, row 20, stamp No. 3.

Step-and-Repeat Camera. Term used to refer to the massive and complex electrical, mechanical and photographic apparatus which produces the diapositive by projecting images of the master negative repeatedly on to a large photographic plate. Sometimes exposure and spacing are effected automatically by pre-set controls, but hand-operated cameras have been used in the production of many issues. The use of the step-and-repeat camera is not limited to gravure printing; it is employed also in producing some printing bases for line engraving, relief printing and planographic printing. See "Photographic Master Flaw" in the alphabetical list to the chapter titled "Printing Problems and Varieties."

Unscreened. This term is used to denote stamps printed in grained gravure — see "Grain."

Upright Screen — see "Screen."

Varnishing. Term used in referring to the manual operation of painting an acid resist to all portions of the printing base that need to be protected from the etching fluid. Such portions include, for example, the back of a printing plate, and the areas corresponding with the sheet margins.

Varnishing Flaw. Colored flaw. In the cases of gravure-printed stamps, this term is used to designate a flaw caused by defective or insufficient varnishing, which has resulted in the surface of the printing base not being sufficiently protected against the action of the etching fluid, and which has allowed etching to be effected where not intended. Normally such flaws are to be found only in the margins, but may be found in the design on stamps printed in more than one color. A varnishing flaw is constant. An instance of a varnishing flaw is to be found in Great Britain 1934-36 2½d., cylinder 8 (control Y/36), row 20, stamp No. 1 and the adjoining sheet margin, where the flaw takes the form of a wedge-shaped area of lightly printed screen.

Vertical Screen — see "Screen."

10. Planographic Printing

FROM THE POINT OF VIEW of the stamp printer, the term "planographic printing" is limited to the mechanical transference to paper, in lithographic printing ink from a printing base with a substantially uniform surface, of a design placed there by a combination of manual, mechanical or photographic and chemical processes. Philatelically, however, it is convenient here to bracket under this heading not only such productions but also the few issues that have been produced by other processes such as photography and stenciling. Logically also this is convenient, for these issues were produced from uniform surfaces of the equivalent of printing bases.

Photography

The issues produced by photography include Mafeking (Cape of Good Hope) 1900 1d. and 3d.; Regensburg (Germany) semi-official Air 1912 (Oct. 11-13) 10 pf. and 20 pf.; Chile, 1919 semi-official Air, Figueroa 5p. issued for

Siam (Thailand) Intra-Palace Locals, 1887 (?) on thin yellowish paper, perf 11½ (clean-cut). These stamps, produced by photography, are sepia. The color resulted from the use of daylight printing paper, then the normal type of photographic paper.

Siam (Thailand) Dusittanos issue, 1919 (?). These stamps were produced by photography. The blue color resulted from use of a ferro-prussiate printing process used for producing blueprints.

299

Regensburg (Germany) Semi-
Official Air 1912 (Oct. 11-13).

the Valparaiso-Santiago flight; and Siam (Thailand) Intra-Palace Locals 1887(?) undenominated, perf 11½ (clean-cut) and Dusittanos 1919(?) 3 satang perf 14½ x 15 (rough). These stamps resulted from solely photographic processes, by use of which the multiplication of the design and the printing were effected.

The Mafeking stamps, and also the Dusittanos, are blue in color, resulting from a ferro-prussiate ("blueprint") process of photographic development. In the case of one variety of Mafeking 1900 3d., a very rare class of error occurs — a mirror print — in which the design is reversed because, by error during the making of one exposure or more, the wrong side of the photographic plate was placed in contact with the photographic printing paper.

The Regensburg 20 pf., and the Intra-Palace Local stamps are sepia, and result from a sulfide toning process of a print originally black, or from daylight printing paper being used.

The Regensburg 10 pf. is black, and represents the normal development of the silver salt in the photographic printing paper.

Printing in a mechanical sense, but from a photographic plate, is termed collotype printing and has been used for stamps. See "Collotype" in the alphabetical list of "Terms Used in Describing Printing Processes" in Chapter 8.

Kume Island (Ryukyu) 1945 (Oct. 1) 7s. This is the only recorded issue produced by mimeographing a wax stencil cut on a typewriter. The central characters (Japanese) were overprinted by handstamp after the mimeographing.

Stenciling

One of the few uses of stenciling for producing postage stamps occurs in Kume Island (Ryukyu Islands) 1945 (Oct. 1) 7 s., issued under the authority of the United States Army which, after taking the island from the Japanese, re-established the postal system that had operated during the war.

The wax stencil was cut, as a matter of record, by Yeoman 2/c R.A. Crutchfield, on a standard Underwood typewriter, there being twenty-four subjects (three across, eight down) in the sheet. The stamps were mimeographed in black on sheets of cream-colored paper. Afterward each subject was impressed with a seal in vermilion, bearing Japanese characters signifying "Seal of the Postmaster Kume Island." About 3,100 stamps were produced, and they were issued ungummed and imperforate.[1]

Lithographic Processes

Planographic printing, or printing that involves the use of the principles of lithography, is different from every other method of printing. In the other methods, the printing effects are obtained only by mechanical means and from printing bases bearing either recesses or reliefs; in planographic printing, the printing effects are obtained by chemical as well as mechanical means and from printing bases having substantially uniform surfaces — that is, having neither the recesses of intaglio nor the reliefs of relief printing bases. In planographic printing, the intensity of the design printed on the paper is in direct proportion to the size of each area of color, and the depth of the film of ink does not, or should not, vary. This characteristic is common to stamps produced by planographic and by relief printing, but in planographic printing, the effect of deeper intensity is sometimes produced by hachuring, or cross-hatching, which is never the case with relief printing.

Terms used in relation to various methods of planographic printing which involve the use of the principles of lithography include: lithography, offset, offset lithography, offset printing, photographic lithography (abbreviated to photo-litho), and photo-litho-offset. Frequently the term "lithography" is used compendiously, and when it is unnecessary to distinguish finely between the variations of the processes. For a brief discussion of lithography in more than one color, see "Chromolithography" in Chapter 8. For a more extended discussion, see "Chromolithography" later in this chapter.

The Principles of Lithography

Four principles are involved in lithography, and upon them depends the ability of the printer to reproduce designs that are "stone writing" — which is a translation of the two Greek words the term is derived from: *lithos* (a stone) and *graphein* (to write). The basic or foundation principle is that

---

[1]For the circumstances of issue and use of this unusual postage stamp see *The Mimeographed Postage Stamp of the Island of Kume* by R.P. Alexander (1952). See also "Mimeograph" in the alphabetical list of "Terms Used in Describing Printing Processes" in Chapter 8.

limestone or any other calcareous stone has a natural porosity and a natural affinity for grease, and the two substances combine to form oleo-margarate of lime, which is insoluble in water or spirits, and, even under considerable friction, is very durable. This principle is easily demonstrable by a simple experiment,[2] the requisites being pieces each of slate, glass, lithographic stone, soap and cloth, and some turpentine and water. Having thoroughly washed the slate, glass and stone with water and allowed them to dry, mark each of them with soap and allow to stand for about thirty minutes. Then, with the cloth wetted with the turpentine, rub the three surfaces. The grease is easily removed from the slate and glass, but no amount of rubbing with the turpentined cloth will remove the film of grease marked by the soap on the stone; this film remains impervious to even boiling water. It can be removed by giving the stone a new surface — for example, by grinding its face with sand and water, and afterward polishing it with a very fine stone.

The second principle is that grease and water repel each other. Consequently, because the porous limestone can, at any one part, receive either grease or water, those parts which have received grease will repel water; and those parts which are damp, after treatment, will repel grease.

The third and fourth principles are concerned with the treatment of the stone, to enable the non-greased parts to repel grease present in the printing ink. The third principle is that dilute nitric acid affects the stone in a particular manner to enable it to receive gum. The fourth principle is the chemical action of a solution of gum arabic on the surface of the stone prepared by dilute nitric acid; the gum fills up the pores of the stone, and the arabic acid in the gum combines with the limestone to form a grease-repelling film.

Consequently, after a stone has been prepared with a design, consisting of lines and other areas of grease, and the other parts of the stone have been rendered grease-repelling, if water is applied to the whole surface of the stone, the design will repel the water, and the other areas will absorb it; if, then, greasy ink is applied to whole surface of the stone, the damp areas will repel the ink, but the greased areas will accept it. If, then, paper is placed over the stone and pressed into contact, by a scraper passing over the paper, the side of the paper in contact with the stone will pick up the surplus ink from the subject, and will thus be printed; from the damp, non-greased areas of the stone, the paper will receive a certain amount of moisture but no ink.

These principles were applied by Aloys Senefelder, who discovered and developed the process of printing from stone near the end of the eighteenth century.[3] He discovered that the design not only could be drawn directly upon the stone but also could be transferred to it from paper that he specially prepared, and further could be transferred from stone to stone by means of the special paper. Thus, not only did it become possible to print, at one operation, single copies from a single drawing or ''original'' on a stone, but also it became possible, by printing many transfers of a single original and

---

[2]See *Handbook of Lithography* by David Cumming. 3rd ed. (1946) Pages 5-6.
[3]Stones for use in a lithographic press are bulky and weighty; not only must the stones be of sufficient area to accommodate the subjects required, but also they are some three to four inches thick.

Lithography and offset lithography. Yugoslavia 1919 30 h. printed by lithography, and 1920 30 h. printed by offset lithography. The differences in characteristic appearance resulting from the use of these processes are well-demonstrated by these two stamps. (In the illustration, the differences are not as pronounced as in actual examples of the stamps.)

Lithography from stone. Zurich (Switzerland) 1843 (March) 4r. and 6r. These were the first postage stamps to be printed by lithography. They were printed direct from stones.

then transferring these to stone, to produce on it as many reproductions of the original as required, and, at a single operation, to print on the paper all the reproductions on the stone. This simple method of multiplying an original was the basis of the production of some lithographed postage stamps. However, by using not one but two stones, the labor involved in taking numerous transfers of a single original was obviated; and if, for example, five reproductions of a single original were transferred to one stone, only twenty re-transfers of these five would be necessary to produce a stone capable of yielding 100 reproductions at a single printing operation. This method of transferring and re-transferring has been employed in the production of most lithographed postage stamps.

For many years lithography remained a process involving the use exclusively of stone as the printing base, and the transfer paper as the only satisfactory method of multiplying the design on the stone. However, with developments during the nineteenth and twentieth centuries, the bulky and weighty stone was replaced by convenient, thin, specially treated aluminum, iron, zinc and bi-metallic[4] plates, and the camera was introduced as a means of multiplying the design; further, the flat-bed printing process, a necessary incident in the use of a stone, gave place to rotary printing from metal plates; and, with the introduction of a rubber-covered cylinder or "blanket" between the stone or plate and the paper, the printing became the "offset" process.

Classifying the Processes

While the details of lithographic printing and procedure vary widely between different printers and in the production of different issues, the lithographic printing processes can be regarded, broadly, from two different standpoints: first with reference to the multiplication of the design, which may be effected by the transferring process or by photography; and second with reference to the printing, which may be direct or offset. The transferring process may be used in multiplying the design either to stone or to metal plates. Photography is used to multiply the design, usually, for metal plates. The printing from stone or metal plates may be either direct or offset.

It is rarely possible, from an examination of an individual stamp itself, to determine what particular lithographic process has been employed in manufacture. However, broadly speaking, it is true to say that stamps printed from stone, because the stone has a polished surface, present cleaner im-

---

[4]Printing from bi-metallic plates by the "Pantone" process depends for its effect upon the fact that chromium will not amalgamate with mercury, and that mercury repels the printing ink. A copper plate is thinly surfaced with chromium. Upon the chromium the design is then applied, photographically or otherwise, and made acid-resistant, protecting the printing areas. The plate is placed in an acid bath, and the chromium dissolved from the non-printing areas, which are then silvered and treated with mercury; the acid resist is cleaned from the printing areas. The plate is then inked; the ink adheres to the chromium, but is repelled by the amalgam of silver and mercury. Paper pressed into contact with the plate picks up the ink, and is thus printed. Other processes involving bi-metallic plates depend for their effects upon similar but varying principles, the ink or water being repelled by one but accepted by the other metal.

pressions and finer lines than do stamps printed from plates; and that stamps printed from plates, because the plate necessarily is grained (to simulate the natural porosity of the stone), reflect this graining so that very fine lines tend to break up into a series of dots. Further, stamps printed by the offset process, because the film of ink is very thin, tend toward a flatness of tone and lack of contrast between the colored and uncolored portions of the design.

The characteristic differences between the natures of the impressions of lithographed and offset printed stamps of the same design and color are well-illustrated in pronounced form, for example, by Yugoslavia (issues for Slovenia) 1919 30 h. pink (litho) and 1920 30 h. pink (offset litho), both printed at Ljubljana.

Lithography from stone. French Morocco 1943 Tour Hassan. One of the more recent examples of postage stamps printed direct from stones.

The older issues of lithographed postage stamps, beginning with Zurich (Switzerland) 1843 and including, for example, Suez Canal 1868, were printed direct from stones. Modern issues rarely are, but an exception is to be found, for instance, in French Morocco 1943 Tour Hassan issue. Nevertheless, stones are still used to a considerable extent by some printers for the production of originals and transfers before the printing bases themselves are produced.

Summary of Manufacturing Differences

The principal difference in manufacture between stamps produced by lithography and those produced by photo-lithography lies in the method used to multiply the original. In lithography, as has been stated, the design is multiplied by the transferring process; in photo-lithography, usually, the multiplication is effected by use of different adaptations of the step-and-repeat camera. In photo-lithography, two main variations of procedure have been used in producing the printing base: As a preliminary, the design may be multiplied on to a large photographic plate, or else the design is multiplied photographically directly on to the printing base.

When the process adopted involves the use of a large photographic plate, the design is photographed; then, by means of a step-and-repeat camera, such as the Uhertype machine which was used by Waterlow & Sons, Ltd., multiple exposures are made on to the photographic plate, which is then processed photographically. Such a photographic plate may be used, usually in a vacuum printing down frame, to make a contact print, either (1) on

305

The Hunter-Penrose Auto Step-and-Repeat Machine, by means of which any number of image repeats could be stepped and printed down on to the printing plate without further attention by the operator after he had registered the unit photographic plate in the carrier, inserted the lithographic printing plate and punched and mounted charts which electrically controlled spacing and exposure. He inserted the light-sensitized printing plate at the left of the machine, lifting the cover by the two handles; the unit photographic plate was inserted in a carrier beneath the domed head toward the right of the machine, and this also contained the light source. When the machine was operated, the plate traveled under this head for the vertical spacing, the head itself moved for the horizontal spacing. The machine spacing was accurate to one one-thousandth of an inch. The machine could be used also to produce multiple images on a large photographic plate or film.

photo-lithographic transfer paper which, after processing and inking, may be employed to transfer the designs lithographically to a stone or metal plate printing base; or (2) directly on to a light-sensitized metal plate which is then processed and used as the printing plate.

When the process adopted does not involve the use of a large photographic plate, the design is photographed; then, by means of a step-and-repeat printing down machine, for example the ''Auto Step-and-Repeat Machine'' of Hunter-Penrose Ltd., multiple exposures are made on to a light-sensitized metal plate which is then processed and used as the printing plate.

Other and technical differences exist between lithography and some photo-lithographic processes. In photo-lithography from metal plates, where an ''albumen'' process is used to effect the light-sensitizing of the plate, the basic principle of lithography (the combination of grease with stone or metal) has no application, and the subject consists merely of a hardened skin of albumen minutely in relief on the face of the plate. And, in the ''deep'' offset proc-

The "Uhertype Machine"
used by Waterlow & Sons
Ltd. in the production of
photo-litho. stamps.

ess, the blanket receives ink from areas that are, almost imperceptibly, recessed below the non-inked areas of the plate.[5] Usually, also, where the design is multiplied photographically, the nature of the original design differs from that of one to be multiplied by the transferring process in being a specially prepared large-scale line drawing or a "halftone," instead of a same-size drawing or even line engraving as is the case with lithography.

The principal difference between direct and offset lithography (apart from the use of the rubber-covered cylinder or "blanket") is that on the stone or plate used in direct lithography the subjects are reversed, that is, they read

---

[5]This process, sometimes termed the "offset intaglio" process, is the modern equivalent of engraving on stone, such as was used for New Caledonia 1860 (January) 10c., which was printed directly from a stone into the protected surface of which Sgt. Triquera cut the lines of the design with a pin.

307

from right-to-left, while in offset lithography the subjects on the stone or plate are not reversed, that is, they read normally from left-to-right, so that when printed on to the blanket they read reversed, and when offset on to the paper they read normally.

Flaws

In lithography, perfect identity can never be obtained in reproducing an original by the transferring process. Every time a transfer is made flaws, more or less minute, occur; and these flaws then become part of the design on the stone. So that, if a re-transfer is made, two sets of flaws[6] occur on the reproduction: the flaws created during the re-transfer that aggregate with the flaws created during the first transfer.

As a consequence, careful study of a sheet of stamps printed by lithography, whether direct or offset, will enable the various steps in transferring to be deduced. Further, because the final transfer to the printing base inevitably gives rise to particular flaws, it follows that each subject in the sheet bears individual flaws that are characteristic of that subject alone; therefore, by reference exclusively to these final flaws, every subject in the sheet can be identified and located. Also, given adequate material (such as a complete sheet, or sufficient multiples that can be overlapped by reference to individually characteristic stamps), even single examples of the stamps may be assigned to their original positions in the sheet — that is, "plated."

In photo-lithography, generally speaking, no flaws equivalent to those caused by transferring and re-transferring occur.[7] Nevertheless, more or less minute flaws inevitably occur during the final processes in the production of the printing base, and such flaws similarly enable the perceptive student to "plate" such stamps.

Transferring: Variations in Procedure

Lithography and the transferring process are readily adapted to the alteration of major or minor details of a design, and to the production of a printing base containing the many repetitions of the design requisite for the printing of a sheet of postage stamps. The processes lend themselves to wide variations in practice, and many different procedures are available to multiply a design; many more variations are available when it is necessary to produce not only a single value but a whole series of values differing the one from the others merely in details. It would be quite impossible in a work of this nature to discuss every such variation in the transferring process that has been employed from time to time by different lithographers for the produc-

---

[6]The philatelic nomenclature adopted in reference to these flaws and others is dealt with later in this chapter.
[7]Exceptions exist in some cases: if, in the step-and-repeat camera, a photograph is used not of a single design but of, say, a strip or block of designs (all intended to be identical but in fact presenting some slight difference), any flaw on any design will recur or repeat on the printing base as many times as differently positioned exposures are made in the step-and-repeat camera.

tion of different postage stamps. The most that can be done is to give an outline of some of the practices and to indicate others.[8]

In connection with lithography generally, philatelic nomenclature presents difficulties of a nature encountered in no other process. These difficulties are occasioned by the fact that numerous different procedures have been used to produce printing stones by the transferring process, and the significance of a term in one procedure may be different from the significance of the same term in another procedure. Furthermore, no universal standard usage of terms obtains among philatelic students; and unless, in each individual case, the closest attention is paid to the particular sense in which a particular student has employed a term in a particular study, the reader may be hopelessly at a loss to understand the significance attached to that term by that student in that study. This difficulty is not in any way lessened by the fact that printers themselves use similar terms in different circumstances to mean different things — and, paradoxically, different terms to signify the same thing.[9]

The following paragraphs of this chapter indicate some of these terminological difficulties, and in the addendum to this chapter, "Illustration of Multiplying the Design by the Transferring Process," I attempt to survey some of the terms that, from time to time, have been used by different students and writers.

Multiplying the Design

The crudest form of multiplying a design for lithographic printing is for an artist separately to draw on stone or transfer paper the requisite number of copies of the design to appear in the sheet, and for prints to be made from the stone so prepared. Such a stone is an "original stone," and it is also the "printing stone." This unusual and crude form of multiplication has been used for postage stamps — such as Afghanistan 1875 1s. — but it takes no account of the benefits conferred by the use of the transferring process in multiplying the design. Each such hand-drawn design inevitably differs from every other, and each different subject on the stone is termed a "type."[10]

One stage more advanced is for the artist to produce a number of different

---

[8]Each lithographed issue when studied must be studied by reference to the particular steps taken in its production as revealed by the evidence provided by the stamps; it is quite unsound to use the practices employed for any one issue or by any one printer as standard and to refer exclusively to it for the purpose of drawing purported certain deductions in relation to any other particular issue.

[9]For example, the term "intermediate stone" strictly used signifies a particular stone intermediate between an original stone and a printing stone, where "original stone" signifies the stone that first bears a lithographic impression of a design not itself an original drawing or engraving but a modification of an original drawing or engraving, and "printing stone" signifies the stone from which the stamps are printed. However, the term "intermediate stone" is, frequently, used to signify an "original stone" in the above sense, and it is, therefore unsafe invariably to infer from the mere use of "intermediate stone" that the previous step in the process was an "original stone" — it may have been an original engraving, or something else. Also, the term "transfer stone" is used as a synonym for "original stone" and "intermediate stone."

[10]More specifically, "design type."

Lithography. Hand-drawn stone. Afghanistan 1875 1s. These stamps were printed from stones upon which the fifteen subjects were separately drawn by hand.

drawings of the same design in a group, either on or transferred to a small stone (the "original stone"), from which a sufficient number of prints on transfer paper (termed, generically, "pulls," or, more specifically, "re-transfers" or "stone-to-stone transfers") are produced. The excess paper around the group of designs is trimmed away, and the stone-to-stone transfers may be dealt with in different ways. Either (a) they are placed on a piece of paper (termed a "patching sheet") in pre-arranged and, perhaps, marked[11] positions and affixed there by special paste or by "stabbing" — that is, by piercing the superimposed transfer and patching sheet with a needle point in several places outside the colored areas of the design. This process is termed "patching up." The patching sheet is then applied face downward on, and the designs are transferred to, a large stone (termed the "printing stone"), which is then used for printing the sheets. Or else (b) the stone-to-stone transfers are placed in pre-arranged and, perhaps, marked[11] positions directly on the printing stone and transferred to it.

Either of these processes is termed "building up the printing stone," and the transferring of a design or group of designs to a stone is termed "laying down." For example, the first lithographed postage stamps — Zurich (Switzerland) 1843 4r. and 6r. — were produced in this manner, the artist making a strip of five separate drawings for each value, and twenty transfers of each strip of five being laid down on each printing stone. Of course, in each case, the five drawings differed from each other because of the hand-drawing, and each different drawing is termed a "type." Consequently each "type"[12] recurs or repeats twenty times on the printing stone. In addition, each subject on the printing stone has individually characteristic lithographic flaws that enable each stamp to be "plated." This form of procedure uses only partly the benefits of multiplying the design by use of the transferring process.

More advanced still is the case where the artist prepares a single drawing of a design either on or transferred to a stone (called the "original stone"),

---

[11]The marking often takes the form of ruled complete rectangles, or, sometimes, merely short crosses denoting the extremities of the rectangular spaces. These markings may or may not reproduce on the subsequently printed stamps. If they do reproduce, the mark-ings provide obvious guides to the steps taken to multiply the design, because the mark-ings will occur in the gutters representing the extremities of each group of designs.

[12]The illustration of these stamps that appears earlier in this chapter shows the "types" which resulted from this procedure, and the strip of each value represents the appropriate five original drawings.

from which a few stone-to-stone transfers are pulled and transferred in a group to a second stone (termed a "primary stone"). On this "primary stone" each separate subject in the group bears lithographic flaws (termed "primary flaws") identifying each separate subject as a "type." From the "primary stone," other stone-to-stone transfers are pulled, and used for a third stone (called a "secondary stone"). On this "secondary stone" the "types" will be repeated, and, in addition, each subject will bear additional lithographic flaws (termed "secondary flaws") identifying each subject as a "sub-type." The "secondary stone" in turn yields two or more stone-to-stone transfers for a fourth stone, that is, the printing stone (termed, alternatively, in this instance, the "tertiary stone"). On this "tertiary stone," the "types" and "sub-types" will be repeated and, in addition, each subject will bear further lithographic flaws (termed "tertiary flaws" or "printing stone flaws"[13]) identifying the "sub-sub-types" and enabling the stamps to be "plated."

The most complex procedures for building up printing stones obtain where, for a series of stamps of which the designs differ, for example, merely in figures of value, the artist prepares, for instance, a single drawing of the design, and drawings for only the other figures of value. In such cases the least complicated procedure would be for the lithographer to pull a number of stone-to-stone transfers of the design. Some of these pulls he would use unaltered to transfer to a "primary stone" (which will then bear the "types" for that value); and from the "primary stone" the printing stone would be built up by convenient stages. For each of the other values in the series, he might take a convenient number of pulls; from each of these transfers he would cut out those parts of the design consisting of the figures of value, and he would then paste or affix the incomplete transfers to a patching sheet; then he would take an appropriate number of pulls of the new figures of value, trim away the excess paper, and paste or affix the pieces of transfer paper bearing the figures of value to the patching sheet in the positions left incomplete in the designs because of his previous cutting out. When the patching up is complete, the lithographer would have a patching sheet on which are assembled and to which are affixed, perhaps, some hundreds of small pieces of transfer paper. This assemblage of designs would be transferred complete to a stone (in this instance called the "original stone"), which will bear the "types" of the new value, represented by the "primary flaws" on the "original stone." From this "original stone," the printing stone would be built up by convenient stages.

Originals

So far I have discussed only cases in which the first stage of the lithographic process is a drawing by an artist in lithographic ink on transfer paper or stone

---

[13]Sometimes a distinction is drawn between the terms "tertiary flaw" and "printing stone flaw" — the term "tertiary flaws" being limited to the flaws occurring initially on the printing stone as a result of the transferring, while the term "printing stone flaws" is used to denote not only "tertiary flaws" but also flaws occurring on the printing stone as the result of some damage or retouch first occurring after some printing has taken place.

Lithography. Original engraving. Exeter College, Oxford (Great Britain), 1882 (November) (no value expressed). A proof from the copper "die," line-engraved in recess. From this "die," six plate-to-stone transfers were printed, and transferred to an "original stone" in a block of six, producing six "types" (1, 2, 3 over 4, 5, 6). From the "original stone," sixteen re-transfers were taken and laid down on the printing stone.

— that is to say, multiplication of an original drawing. However, multiplication can be effected lithographically from an original that is engraved in recess or relief or set up in printer's type; and it is from such engravings that many lithographic printing bases have been built up.

The most usual first step is the line engraving, often on copper, of a recessed die (termed by lithographers "the original engraving," or "the plate"). Such engraving was the invariable practice, for instance, of Waterlow & Sons for the lithographed issues they produced — and was used, for example, for British Guiana 1852 (January) 1c. and 4c., which were the first postage stamps printed by that firm. From the engraved dies, as many transfers (termed "plate-to-stone transfers") were printed as were necessary, affixed to a patching sheet, and transferred to the printing stone. The printing stone, therefore, bore no "types,"[14] but each subject differed from every other by reason of its individually characteristic lithographic flaws on the printing stone.

A variation of this procedure was followed, for instance, by Emberlin & Son, who produced Exeter College, Oxford (Great Britain), 1882 (November) (no value expressed). From the engraved copper die,[15] six plate-to-stone transfers were printed and laid down on an "original stone," which, therefore, bore six "types"; from the "original stone," sixteen stone-to-stone

---

[14]In fact, in the case of the issue mentioned, two designs of each value were engraved, and both of these engravings were used, giving rise to what are termed "Type I" and "Type II"; more specifically, they are termed "Design Type I" and "Design Type II."

[15]Proofs from this die are known, and a picture of a die proof is shown above.

XXIV CENTS.   XLVIII CENTS.

Lithography. Original engraving. British Guiana 1863 6c., 24c. and 48c. A proof from the engraved "die" bearing the 6c. design complete and the value inscriptions for 24c. and 48c. From this "die," complete plate-to-stone transfers were made for the 6c. value, arranged on a sheet of paper, and transferred to the printing stone. For the other values, the value tablet was removed from the transfers, and replaced by transfers from the appropriate inscription.

transfers were pulled and laid down on the printing stone, which, therefore, bore sixteen repetitions of the six "types," and each of the ninety-six subjects bore individually characteristic lithographic flaws, enabling each stamp to be "plated."

As with original drawings, all the permutations of the transferring process are available for use with original engravings. An illustration is provided by Suez Canal 1868 1c., 5c., 20c. and 40c. The four stamps were produced by Chezaud & Tavernier of Paris. The original engraving was on copper, and was of the 20c. design complete with figures of value in all four value circles.[16] For the 20c. value, 120 separate plate-to-stone transfers were printed, affixed to a patching sheet by stabbing, and transferred to the printing stone. There were, therefore, no "types" on the printing stone, but each subject bore individually characteristic lithographic flaws, enabling each stamp to be "plated." For each other value, four plate-to-stone transfers were printed and laid down on an "original stone," which, therefore, bore four "types"; they were in a block of four, Types A and B over Types C and D. The figures of value were more or less effectively removed from each group of sixteen value circles, and the new figures of value were inserted, possibly hand-drawn on the "original stone." From each of the three "original stones," thirty stone-to-stone transfers were pulled, stabbed on to a patching sheet, and transferred to the printing stones, each of which thus bore 120 subjects, comprising the four "types" recurring regularly thirty times; in addition, each subject bore individually characteristic lithographic flaws, enabling each stamp to be plated.

---

[16]No die proof is known, and the die has not been found in the archives of the Compagnie Universelle du Canal Maritime de Suez. The procedure has been deduced from an examination of the evidence provided by the stamps.

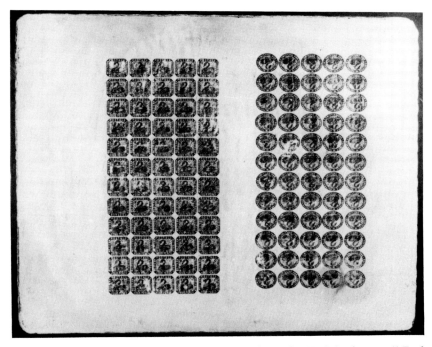

Western Australia 1854 4d. and 1s. — a print from the "original stone." Each group of sixty subjects originated from a plate-to-stone transfer from an intaglio plate produced by Perkins, Bacon & Company in London. The appropriate surrounding portion of each design was erased by use of a brush dipped in acid. The frames were then added from locally drawn transfers. Later, on the 4d. in the position corresponding with stamp No. 1 in row 8, the frame transfer was inverted, thus giving rise to the (misnamed) "Inverted Swan."

Similarly, a procedure involving patching of part of the design was followed, for example, by Waterlow & Sons in the production of British Guiana 1863 6c., 24c. and 48c., and a proof is known of the die bearing the 6c. design complete, and the additional inscriptions "XXIV CENTS" and "XLVIII CENTS."

Original intaglio engravings to be multiplied by the transferring process for postage stamps have been made not only on metal but also on stone — for example, Trinidad 1852 (1d.).

On some occasions, lithographed postage stamps have been printed from stones to which the subjects have been transferred by a single plate-to-stone transfer made from the entire printing area of a plate previously used to produce stamps by line engraving — for example, Nevis 1876 1d. to 1s. In such cases, any variety occurring on the printing plate is reproduced on the stone, and diagnosis of the cause of the variety will demand a knowledge not only of lithography but also of the original printing process.

Occasionally plate-to-stone transfers have been made from only part of a previously used printing base — such as in the case of Western Australia 1854

4d. and 1s. For the 4d., a plate-to-stone transfer of sixty subjects from the London-made line-engraved 1d. plate was used and an appropriate portion of the frame of each of the sixty subjects was erased from the stone with acid — see "Substituted Transfers" later in this chapter. Stone-to-stone transfers of the locally drawn new frame were fitted around each subject of the plate-to-stone transfer; the sixty composite subjects were accordingly laid down on an "original stone," there being, therefore, sixty "types"; these types were repeated four times on to the printing stone, on which each of the 240 subjects bore individually characteristic lithographic flaws, enabling each stamp to be plated. A similar process was used for the 1s. value. In fact, the sixty subjects of each of the 4d. and 1s. appeared on the same "original stone," which was discovered in 1978.

On some occasions, lithographed postage stamps have been printed from stones built up from plate-to-stone transfers taken from relief-printing bases.

Transferring to Stone

From what has been written, it will be appreciated that no single standard practice obtains in building up a printing stone for postage stamps. However, whether it be initially for the purpose of making a stone-to-stone transfer of a single subject, intermediately for laying down a "secondary stone" by means of a patched-up sheet, or finally for making a single plate-to-stone transfer of a group consisting of many subjects, the common factor is the actual transferring to the stone and its preparation for printing. As has been stated, the transferring process inevitably gives rise to flaws, and perfect identity can never be obtained by this method of reproduction; such flaws are inherent in the lithographic process. Other flaws may occur because of defective transferring and attempts made to remedy it.

Before I discuss in greater detail certain aspects of the transferring to stone, the preparation of the stone for printing, and the causes of some of the flaws and other varieties, it will be helpful if the steps taken by the lithographer are briefly summarized. Here it may be stated again that no one practice is standard for these steps, and the processes are subject to variation in detail. However, they may be summarized as follows:

1. Transferring the design.
2. Adding to, removing, or completing defective lines or areas — "touching up."
3. Gumming the stone.
4. Inking the design.
5. The first "etch."
6. Cleaning up the stone.
7. Re-inking the design.
8. Protecting the inked design.
9. "Etching" the stone.
10. Washing and re-gumming the stone.
11. Washing out "the work."
12. Re-inking and re-gumming.

The object of all the steps from No. 3 onward is to render the non-inked areas of the design on the stone resistant to grease, so that the grease present in the printing ink may be rejected by those areas.

Transferring the Design

In order satisfactorily to transfer a design to stone, the lithographer requires it to have a finely polished surface and to be reasonably free from blemishes affecting that surface. Polishing is effected by grinding the surface of the stone with fine sand, and then finishing it off with a very fine stone known as "snakestone."

Numerous different natural and minute blemishes or defects can occur in stones, and these blemishes account for many of the flaws inevitably occurring as a result of transferring. These blemishes will have one of two effects upon the resultant stamps, dependent upon whether the blemish accepts or rejects grease. Each blemish will result in either the absence of desired or the presence of undesired color in the position and area corresponding with the blemish.

In the simplest instance of transferring, the lithographer, having obtained his polished stone, washed and dried and warmed it and placed it in the press, will take his transfer. When he first obtains it, the transfer will be dry, and will bear on its face the design drawn or printed in a greasy ink. If the print is from a recessed die or plate, the ink will be of a sufficient hardness to withstand pressure, which would otherwise cause the lines of the design to spread, and the lithographer will use a cold stone.

If necessary, the lithographer will trim away with scissors any excess paper around the design.

He will then dampen the transfer and apply it face downward on to the dry polished stone. Alternatively, he will apply a dry transfer to a slightly damp stone; but, in this event, he must carry out the next steps very quickly, after damping the stone.

He will cover the transfer on the stone with one or two sheets of paper and a leather cover or "tympan," and will operate the press. The press is so constructed that the stone with its covering travels under and in contact with a "scraper" — that is, a ridge of boxwood or polished steel — and the scraper can be adjusted to bear down on the tympan with greater or less pressure.

He operates the press a few times, with carefully adjusted pressure. Then he lifts the tympan and covering sheets, damps the back of the transfer with a sponge, covers the transfer again, and operates the press a few more times with greater pressure on the scraper. This process is then repeated.

Once more the back of the transfer is uncovered; the operator now takes the sponge filled with water, and thoroughly soaks and rubs the transfer with the sponge and his hand. When the transfer is entirely limp, he lifts the paper away, leaving the ink impression on the stone.

He then cleans from the stone, with water, the composition facing of the transfer paper — a mixture of gelatine, starch, gamboge, and other ingredients. The stone is then laid aside for further preparation.

In many cases, the lithographer, before transferring, must first prepare his patching sheet with the requisite number of pieces of transfer paper affixed in position. He places this face downward on the stone, and his subsequent operations are similar to those that he carries out for a transfer bearing a single complete design. However, half way through the process, he uncovers the back of the patching sheet and removes it from the stone; he leaves adhering to the stone the individual pieces of transfer paper. He then continues his operations, eventually removing each individual piece of transfer paper, and cleans the stone, which is afterward laid aside for further preparation.

Lithographic Varieties

If the preparation of the patching sheet has been properly carried out, and if it (or, as the case may be, the transfer) has been laid properly on the stone and the transferring efficiently done, the designs will appear on the stone free from any flaws except those inherent in the lithographic process. However, the preparation of the patching sheet or the transfer, and the transferring itself present opportunities for something less than perfection in workmanship, with the result that varieties may occur that are of philatelic interest.

Many different kinds of mistakes can be made by a lithographer when patching up a sheet of transfers, and these mistakes will reproduce on every stamp or multiplication of the erroneous design. Among the most striking of such errors are those that result in, for example, an "Error of Value,"[17] caused by the lithographer patching-in a transfer or part of a transfer from, perhaps, another pile on the bench in front of him. Such an error on the stone of one value does not necessarily lead to a compensating error on the stone of the other value, because it is the almost invariable practice to pull some spare transfers to anticipate the effect of loss by spoilage. Other errors can result, for example, in "Frame Inverted" and "Tête-Bêche," to mention but two.

As has been stated, the lithographer trims away the excess paper around the design or designs on the transfer preparatory to affixing it to the patching sheet. If he cuts carelessly, he may infringe the design itself, with the result that the design on the stone will be incomplete, as will the printed design of the resultant stamp or stamps. Such a variety is termed a "trimmed transfer" or "clipped transfer," or, sometimes, a "cut transfer," and is to be found, for example, in Suez Canal 1868 40c., stamp No. 26, where the right frameline tapers to the base instead of being an even width throughout. Such trimming can occur at any stage of building up the printing stone.

---

[17]See "Error of Value" in the alphabetical list to the chapter entitled "Printing Problems and Varieties."

Lithography. Double transfer. Bolivia 1897 5c. exhibiting doubling in the letters NCO of CINCO. This doubling occurs on all stamps of this design, and the "Double Transfer" is not a variety of this stamp, but is a lithographic variety.

However, in the case of the Suez Canal stamp, it occurred on a transfer from the "original stone"; although the "trimmed transfer" is in fact on "Type B," the tapering frameline is not a "type" characteristic, and the variety occurs only once on the printing stone.[18]

When the lithographer is patching and stabbing the transfers, he must be careful to avoid stabbing through the colored part of the design; if he does not avoid this, he will prevent the grease at this spot from coming into contact with the stone, and consequently the resultant stamp will exhibit a colorless area where color should be present. Such a variety is termed "stabbed transfer." The Suez Canal 1868 40c., stamp No. 26, provides a clear example of a "stabbed transfer" variety, in the form of a colorless area between the right and bottom framelines. Because he had trimmed away all the marginal transfer paper and some of the design, the lithographer could not stab around it, and, for some reason, did not stab in the uncolored area of the value circle that was available to him.

When the lithographer first lays a transfer face downward on the stone, he must take care to see that the printed side of the transfer comes into close and immovable contact with the surface of the stone. The surface of the stone is very sensitive to grease, and the design on the transfer is, of course, in greasy ink. Consequently, any flapping or movement of the transfer may

---

[18]In fact, part of the same careless cut is visible at the top right of stamp No. 38, which is immediately below stamp No. 26 in the sheet, and formed part of the same "original stone pull," being "Type D."

Lithography. Trimmed transfer and stabbed transfer. Suez Canal 1868 40c., stamp No. 26, and an enlargement of the southeast corner of the design. The frameline at the right tapers to the base because the lithographer cut away part of the design when trimming the excess paper from the transfer before affixing it to the patching sheet, causing the variety "Trimmed Transfer."

When stabbing the transfer to the patching sheet, the lithographer failed to avoid stabbing a colored portion of the design, thus causing the colorless area resembling a break between the right and bottom framelines, and resulting in "Stabbed Transfer."

These characteristics are not representative of the "type" (C) — there are four "types," A and B over C and D, regularly repeated in the sheet of 120 subjects — and occur only on stamp No. 26.

Lithography. Folded transfer. Western Australia 1854 4d., the unique "Peice" variety, and a reconstruction of the transfer fold. The fold has resulted in a squeezing up of the "N" of PENCE, an obliteration of part of the background and the body and neck of the swan, a squeezing up of the "T" of POSTAGE and a narrowing of the space between T and A; and this stamp measures 21.25 mm. wide, as against the 22.25 mm. width of a normal stamp. This variety occurred on the third subject of the fifth horizontal row (subject 27) of the "group transfer," and originally occupied on the printing stone one of the four positions 83, 88, 93 or 98 on the sheet. The transfer was early corrected on the stone, and only one example of the "Peice" variety is known to exist.

result in its yielding part of its ink in an unintended position, and the remainder of its ink at the desired position. A stamp bearing duplications of the lines of the design resulting from such a cause is referred to as exhibiting a "(lithographic) double transfer." Such a "double transfer" variety is to be seen, for example, in Bolivia 1897 5c., where the letters NCO of CINCO appear clearly doubled, probably because the strip of transfer paper bearing the words of value buckled momentarily when the transfer was first applied.

"Double transfer" varieties can occur at any stage of the building up of the printing stone. When they occur at the first stage, the variety is, of course, "die"[19] as in Bolivia 1897 5c. If the "double transfer" occurs on the "primary stone," the doubling will be characteristic of the "type" produced as, for instance, in the case of Victoria 1850 (1855-56) Half-Length 3d., Campbell stone D, Types 22 and 24. If the "double transfer" occurs first on the printing stone, the doubling will be characteristic only of the particular subject or subjects affected, and will be a "plating" characteristic — as, for instance, in Victoria 1850 (1854-55) Half-Length 3d., Campbell stone A, Type 10 (? 319).[20] "Double transfers" are difficult to distinguish from "slurred prints,"[21] and

[19]See "Die (2)" in the alphabetical list to the chapter entitled "Printing Problems and Varieties."
[20]See *The Half-Lengths of Victoria* by J.R.W. Purves (1953).
[21]See "Slurred Print" in the alphabetical list to the chapter entitled "Printing Problems and Varieties."

Lithography. Folded transfer. Romania 1866 2 p., stone C, stamp No. 104, exhibiting at the northwest corner the effects of a transfer fold. This variety occurs on only one position on the stone, thus proving that the variety results from a printing stone flaw caused when the assembled "group transfers" were laid down on the printing stone. The printing stone for this value was built up by transferring from an "original stone" bearing six "types." The stamp illustrated is "Type 3," but the transfer fold is not characteristic of the "type."

several copies of each stamp generally are required before certain diagnosis of the doubling can be made.

Failure to ensure that the whole surface of the printed side of the transfer comes into close contact with the surface of the stone may have other effects, and give rise to the variety "folded transfer" or "creased transfer." Usually the transfer is damp when it is applied to the stone, and damp paper is difficult to handle. Further, when transferring is effected not of a single piece of transfer paper but of an assemblage of many pieces of paper on a patching sheet, if the "grain"[22] of the transfer paper is not parallel with the "grain" of the patching sheet, buckling will occur because the papers after dampening will stretch in different directions. For these and other reasons, the transfer or part of the transfer may become creased or folded, with the result that an incomplete design is laid down on the stone. Examples of "creased transfer" are to be found in many lithographed postage stamps. A striking example occurs among many others in Western Australia 1854 4d. in the unique "Peice" variety, where the crease has resulted in the stamp being one millimeter less wide than normal, and, *inter alia*, instead of PENCE the word reads PEICE. Another readily perceived instance occurs, for example, in Romania 1866 2p. Stone C, stamp No. 104, where the frame at the upper left is folded, distorting the corner square.

The sensitivity of the lithographic stone to grease is not limited to the grease present in the transfer ink. The lithographer must guard against touching the stone, or, indeed, the transfer itself, carelessly with his fingers, for the grease exuded from the skin will leave its tell-tale mark. Such fingerprints are not unknown to students of lithographed stamps, and an instance of a

---

[22]See "Grain" in the alphabetical list to the chapter entitled "Paper."

Lithography. Primary stone touch-up. Suez Canal 1868 1c., "Type B," exhibiting a "Touch-Up" and (at left) an untouched-up "type" for comparison. The touching-up has resulted in a marked thickening of the left frameline near the southwest value circle. This thickening recurs regularly and identically thirty times on the printing stone of 120 subjects, and is characteristic of "Type B," proving that the "touch-up" was effected to the "original stone," which contained four "types," A and B over C and D.

"fingerprint variety" is to be encountered, for example, in Victoria Postal Fiscal 1884-96 (1879) 3s. violet on blue, in the upper part of the left of the stamp, by the scroll bearing the name. (On this stamp, the "fingerprint variety" occurs on Type 1, there being six "types" — three across, two down — repeated in the sheet of eighty.)

Touching Up

When the stone is dry after the transferring is completed, and before it is prepared further, the lithographer will examine the designs and decide whether it is necessary for him to remedy any defect by handwork. The surface of the stone is still sensitive to grease, and if any line or other area has failed to transfer in part, the lithographer may complete it with a pen or a fine brush and greasy ink.

The effect of such handwork is often referred to philatelically as a "touch-up" (to distinguish it from "retouch," which is the term used to refer to handwork after printing has taken place from the stone). A clear instance of "touch-up" occurs in Suez Canal 1868 1c., in the form of a marked thickening of the left frameline of the stamp near the southwest value circle. The "touch-up" is a characteristic of "Type B" and recurs identically thirty times on the printing stone, proving that the touching-up was effected to the "original

Lithography. Fingerprint. Victoria
(Postal Fiscal) 1884-96 (1879) 3s. Two
stamps and an enlargement of a portion of the right-hand stamp showing
a lithographed "Fingerprint" — the
colored horizontal lines which are particularly visible as they cross the uncolored vertical inner frameline at the
left. This class of variety is limited to
lithography, and is caused by the
lithographer's carelessness in allowing
his finger to come into contact with the
sensitized stone or transfer. The grease
exuded by the skin is transmitted to the
stone, and later receives ink that causes
the "fingerprint" to print as part of the
design of the subject affected.

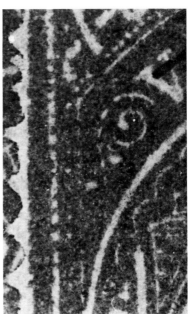

stone," that is, the "primary stone"; and such a variety is alternatively termed a "primary (stone) retouch."

Touching-up is not limited to the addition or completion of areas that should be colored, and may take the form of removal of an unwanted area of color, where undesired grease has come on to the stone. Such areas may be removed by scraping with a steel blade or by rubbing with snakestone. There are other methods of removal of unwanted color, notably by use of acid, and more detailed reference to that method is made later in this chapter, in connection with "substituted transfer." Acid on a brush was used to effect deletions, for instance, it is thought, in Suez Canal 1868 1c., 5c. and 40c. on each "primary stone," removing the figures "20c." in the sixteen value circles before the other figures "1c.," "5c.," and "40c." were added; and was used, for instance, it is thought, on Victoria 1850 (1854) Half-Length 3d. White Veils on the "primary stone," where part of each of the twelve subjects was touched-up to remove the shading from the veils on both sides of the head; the same "primary stone" was previously used in building up the Shaded Veils of this stamp, in use between 1853 and 1854.

Sometimes the term "touch-in" is used to denote the addition of color, and the term "touch-out" is used to denote the removal of color.

Such touching-up can occur at any stage of the building up of a printing stone; and retouching can, of course, occur after printing has taken place from the stone.

Preparing the Stone

After the lithographer has transferred the designs and carried out any touching-up that may be necessary, he prepares the stone for printing. As has been stated, the steps taken vary among different printers, but the preparation of a stone for printing is a complicated process.

First the stone is freely covered with a solution of gum arabic; this is spread with a wide camel-hair brush; and the stone is then tilted to allow the surplus solution to drain off. The gum is repelled by the greasy areas of the design. The stone is then allowed to dry, and to stand for some hours. The gum seals the uninked portions of the stone and prevents the lines of the design from spreading, while the ink of the design penetrates into the stone. This penetration is considerable, and sometimes accounts for the duplication encountered in "Palimpsests," which are discussed later in this chapter.

The stone is then cleaned with water, left damp, and rubbed over by the lithographer with, in one hand, a piece of cloth bearing a small amount of printing ink, and, in the other hand, a sponge containing gum. This process, known as "rubbing up," is continued until the whole of the design appears quite black. Then the lithographer takes an ink roller charged with ink, and rolls it over the damp stone, adding more ink to the colored areas of the design. This strengthens the design on the stone.

Next the stone is covered with a thin solution of gum arabic containing a small amount of nitric acid. After this the stone is "cleaned up," that is, unwanted areas of color are removed by a steel blade or by polishing with snakestone.

Then the stone is dampened, the colored areas of the design are fully charged with ink, and powdered resin or asphaltum is dusted over the stone. The powder is an acid resist and adheres to the ink-charged colored areas of the design, protecting them against the action of the acid during the next step in the process.

Next the stone is "etched" with a stronger solution of nitric acid and gum arabic or, sometimes, with a solution of nitric acid in water. This has the effect of giving the colored areas of the design an almost imperceptible relief on the stone. The stone is then washed with water, covered with a good coating of gum arabic, and allowed to dry. The effect of these steps is that the acid opens the pores of the stone, making it more receptive of the gum, the application of which forms a grease-resistant surface on those portions of the stone not covered with the acid resist.

Then the gum and acid resist are washed off the stone, and the lithographer washes out "the work," which is the term he uses for the designs on the stone. Washing out consists of rubbing the work with a turpentined cloth to remove the ink from the design, leaving only the grease on the stone, the designs being invisible.

With the stone dampened again, the lithographer charges the designs fully with ink, then he re-gums the stone. When he is ready to print from the stone, he washes off the gum, and leaves the stone damp.

Philatelic varieties of special interest occur in lithography, although they are not limited to this method of printing; such varieties are termed "Substituted Transfers" — see "Substituted Subject" in the alphabetical list to the chapter entitled "Printing Problems and Varieties."

Substituted Transfers

A "substituted transfer" comprises the replacement of a subject by another on a stone or patching sheet. Such substitution need not be limited to a single subject. Usually the substitution occurs because the original subject is damaged on the stone, or the transfer will not yield a satisfactory result.

That the substitution has occurred can be deduced philatelically by variation in alignment or by the disturbance of the regular repetition of "types."[23]

---

[23]That the "types" do not repeat regularly in any particular sheet of stamps does not necessarily imply that substitution has occurred. In some cases the "types" appear in no particular order of regularity — as an example chosen at random, in Wei-Hai-Wei (Great Britain, Chinese Treaty Ports) 1899 (January) 2c. and 5c., the "types" occur at random in the sheet. Further, for some issues, "group transfers" were used, and the number of subjects on the printing stones was not a regular multiple of the number of subjects in the "group transfer," or the stones were not of an area capable of accommodating merely repetitions of the "group transfers" unaltered; consequently, in such cases, several "group transfers" were used whole, and the printing area of the stone was completed by portions cut from other "group transfers," with the result that the "types" recur regularly throughout part of the sheet but are irregularly or not at all represented in other parts of the sheet. Such an instance is to be found, for example, in Tierra del Fuego Popper's Post 10 centavos, where the sheet of 100, lithographed by Kidd & Company Ltd. of San Martin, consists of six repetitions of a group of twelve transfers and portions of three other such group transfers.

As is implicit, "substituted transfers" are of two classes, and can be the result of operations at different stages of the lithographic processes.

The first class of "substituted transfers" comes into existence during the building up of the printing stone. In such cases, the most frequent cause of the substitution is that, on some "group transfers," one of the subjects on the "primary stone" does not yield an impression that would transfer well. Consequently, after the "group transfers" are printed on the transfer paper, the unsatisfactory subjects are cut out of the appropriate "group transfers," and the spaces on the patching sheet are completed by subjects cut from satisfactory portions of another "group transfer." Such an operation gives rise to what is termed a "primary substituted transfer." Such substitution can occur at any stage of the building up of the printing stone, and may result in the printing stone bearing several "substituted transfers." Usually, a characteristic of a "primary substituted transfer" is that it occurs more than once on the printing stone, in the same relative position with reference to the other "types."

The second class of "substituted transfers" first occurs on the printing stone itself, and is, characteristically, usually limited to one position, having been rendered necessary by damage to the subject originally occupying that position. Various methods are available to the lithographer for re-sensitizing the stone to effect the substitution. One method involves the use of acid and is termed "gumming out."

The lithographer carefully protects the satisfactory parts of the stone, first by inking and then by covering the satisfactory subjects with powdered resin or asphaltum. Then he carefully gums over the parts that are to remain with a good coating of gum, which is allowed to dry. This coating of gum covers the greased as well as the non-greased areas protected on the stone. Next he "washes out" the unsatisfactory subject by rubbing it with turpentine to which has been added about ten percent of carbolic acid. This weakens the work so washed out. The lithographer then "etches" the stone with nitric acid solution, and this removes the unsatisfactory subject, while leaving the gummed and powdered parts of the stone unaffected. If necessary, the vacant space is then polished with snakestone, a fresh subject is transferred, and the uninked portions are rendered grease-resistant in the normal way by subjecting the stone to the processes necessary to prepare it for printing.

Such an operation gives rise to what is termed a "secondary substituted transfer."

Both "primary substituted transfer" and "secondary substituted transfer" occurred in the case of the Western Australia 1854 4d. "Inverted Swan." The substitutions were effected in two stages. At the first stage, as was suggested in *Western Australia: The 4d. Lithograph 1854-1864* by Brian Pope (1984), after some printing had taken place from the printing stone, it was damaged so that re-transferring became necessary. When the stone bearing the sixty subjects was inspected, the frame of one subject was found to be defective. The damage was corrected by erasing the frame and transferring a new frame in its place. By mistake, the new frame was inverted but unnoticed. That was the "primary substituted transfer." From that stone, four stone-to-stone transfers were made and laid down on a printing stone. It, therefore, bore four subjects — "primary substituted transfers" — with inverted frames, and 236 subjects with upright frames. The errors were unnoticed and ninety-seven sheets were printed. Later, when a new printing became necessary, the inversions on the printing stone were noticed by a newly appointed lithographer. He, therefore, erased the four subjects exhibiting the error and replaced — that is, substituted — each one of them with a transfer that had a normal upright frame. They were the "secondary substituted transfers" and they resulted in normal stamps, even though the substituted subjects were appreciably out of alignment.

Palimpsests

After printing has been carried out from a stone, it may be re-used to print different work; however, before it is so re-used, the stone must have the original work removed. This removal is usually effected by grinding away the surface of the stone to the depth to which the grease has penetrated. The surface of the stone is ground with fine sand and water, and is afterward polished with snakestone.

The grease penetrates the stone to a relatively substantial depth, and the degree of penetration is not always standard over the whole area of the stone. Consequently, areas of clear stone have to be ground away if all the grease is to be removed; often, the fact that some grease is present is not easily perceptible because it is uncolored. However, unless all traces of grease are removed, they may accept ink and print when the stone is brought into use again, and so cause areas of unwanted color on stamps resulting from subsequently applied subjects.

Such stamps are termed "palimpsests," because they exhibit characteristics showing that the printing base was previously used for a different subject. "Palimpsests" are

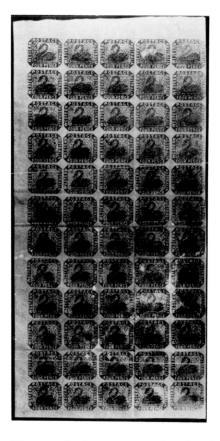

Photograph of one-quarter of a printed sheet of 4d. stamps exhibiting out-of-alignment stamp correcting "Inverted Swan" (the eighth stamp in the left-hand column).

327

Lithography. Primary palimpsest. Suez Canal 1868 5c. "Type D," bearing evidence of the earlier use of the "original stone" for a subject containing the value "20c." This is particularly prominent in the northwest value circle, where parts of the figure "2" can be seen to the left of the "5," and the remains of the earlier "c" and the hollow stop can be seen to the right. Traces of the earlier value can be seen also in the three other value circles. Such traces are visible on all stamps of the 5c. sheet of 120 subjects, and occur on the four "types" in varying degrees, proving that the "palimpsest" occurred on the "original stone," which contained four "types," A and B over C and D. Similar traces can be seen on the 1c. stamps, and, to a less marked extent, on the 40c. stamps — see the illustrations captioned "Lithography. Primary Stone Touch-Up" and "Lithography. Trimmed Transfer and Stabbed Transfer."

not limited to cases in which the earlier design has been removed by grinding.

During the course of this chapter, reference has been made on several occasions to Suez Canal 1868 1c. to 40c., as exhibiting varieties of philatelic interest. That issue provides also instances of two classes of "palimpsests." As with "substituted transfers" so with "palimpsests"; in lithography, they may be classified into "secondary" and "primary" according to whether they first occur respectively on the printing stone or at an earlier stage.

Examples of "primary palimpsests" are provided, for instance, by Suez Canal 1868 5c., where every "type" and, consequently, every stamp bears evidence of the earlier use of the "primary stone" for subjects containing the value "20c." This is especially prominent on "Type D."

Examples of "secondary palimpsests" are to be found on, for instance, Suez Canal 1868 40c., where many stamps (including, for example, stamp No. 104) exhibit many marks extraneous to the design, in the form of a series of parallel vertical dotted lines — as though the stone had previously been used for printing billheads or invoices.

Transferring to Metal

So far I have discussed transferring to stone for direct printing, and the varieties resulting from such transferring.

As has already been stated, use for direct printing has been made not only of stones, which are rarely employed nowadays for printing stamps, but also of thin metal plates. These plates are usually of zinc or aluminum. Historically, zinc was used first. It was not until about the year 1891 that aluminum was patented in New York as a printing plate and rotary lithographic printing became more widely adopted.

Plates are much used for rotary offset printing — see "Offset Rotary Printing" later in this chapter. If offset printing is to be used, the original engraving or drawing, instead of being reversed so that the wording reads from right-to-left (and a print reads normally from left-to-right), must be a straightforward, direct representation of the finished print; that is to say, the engraver must reverse his usual procedure, and cut his design directly into the metal, so that the wording reads normally from left-to-right (and a print from the die is a mirror image of the finished print).

Lithography. Offset printing. Die proof. Bolivia 1930 (Jul. 24) Air, an intaglio-printed proof from the recess-engraved die of which the design was actually used for the 5c., 35c., 1b. and 3b. values. The design in the print from the die reads reversed because the die was engraved direct, this being necessary because the printing method to be adopted was offset.

Drawing on or transferring to metal is carried out substantially in the same manner as is the case with stone, but with variations in the composition facing of the transfer paper and the amount of pressure upon the scraper of the press. The principles of lithography are involved; the grease combines with the metal, and, according to some authorities, penetrates into its substance to some degree. However, the degree of penetration is far less than with stone. If the penetration of the metal were the same as that of stone, the design would be seen coming through the plate on the back.

Although some printing has taken place from smooth plates, the almost invariable practice in more recent times has been to use plates that have been given a grain.

The plate is placed in a tray that is shaken mechanically with a circular motion; the plate is covered with marbles and fine sand or carborundum or other powder, and water is introduced. The motion and abrasion of the damp sand or powder and marbles raises a grain on the surface of the plate. This greatly increases the surface area of the plate, gives a larger area for the ink to adhere to, and, in the non-inked areas, has the effect of simulating the natural porosity of the stone, thus enabling the plate to retain the moisture applied by the dampening rollers during printing.

After the designs have been assembled on a patching sheet and transferred to the plate by use of the press, any necessary touching-up can be effected to them. The completion of areas unintentionally uncolored can be carried out with a fine brush or pen and greasy ink. The removal of areas of unwanted color presents greater difficulty, because the surface of the plate cannot be scraped locally with a metal knife without damaging the grain at that place. However, such removal may be effected by a pumice stick used lightly with a circular motion; alternatively, the unwanted ink may be removed from the plate by means of a benzine-moistened piece of rag wrapped around a wooden point, and the removal of the design may be completed by the "etching" to which the plate is later subjected in preparing it for printing.

This preparation for printing broadly follows that adopted for stone. The lines and other areas of the design are protected by an acid resist, and the plate is "etched," if of aluminum with a solution of phosphoric acid, and if of zinc with a different acid solution.

Plates can be re-sensitized, and corrections, such as retouches or secondary substituted transfers, can be made to the plate. While practices vary widely and in detail, a method of effecting substitution on zinc plates is to wash off the ink from the unsatisfactory subject with petrol (gasoline) or benzine, and apply a strong solution of caustic soda, care being taken not to allow it to come into contact with other parts of the work. After the caustic soda has been allowed to remain on the plate for about two minutes, the solution is removed by means of blotting paper. The clear part of the plate is then lightly scoured with pumice powder on cotton wool, and the plate is washed with a nitric acid and alum solution that has the effect of re-sensitizing the plate, which is then washed with water and is ready to receive the "substituted transfer." With aluminum plates, strong sulfuric acid is used in place of caustic soda, and a weak oxalic acid replaces the nitric acid and alum solution.

Examples of stamps printed from metal plates, on to which the designs were multiplied by the transferring process, are to be found, for instance, in Bolivia 1930 (Jul. 24) Air 5c. to 3b. These stamps were printed by Perkins Bacon & Company Ltd., and comprise two designs for the various values: the 5c., 35c., 1b. and 3b. depict an airplane flying over a bullock cart, and the 15c., 20c., 50c. and 2b. show an airplane over a steamer on Lake Titicaca. All values except the 35c. were printed in sheets of fifty (five across, ten down); the 35c. was printed in sheets of 100, consisting of two panes of fifty (each five across, ten down). In each value there are three "types," and on each "original stone" the "types" appeared, probably, in a vertical strip. The arrangement of "types" on the "original stone" is suggested by the arrangement of "types" in the sheets. Although the "types" do not repeat regularly, the arrangement substantially is that each of three adjoining horizontal rows in the sheets comprises one of the three "types," and this arrangement is repeated three times, with the tenth row in the sheet con-

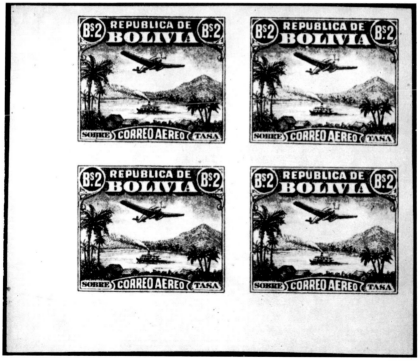

Lithography. Transferring to metal plates. Bolivia 1930 (Jul. 24) Air 2b. variety imperforate. Produced by Perkins Bacon & Company Ltd., these stamps were offset lithographed from a grained zinc plate. There are three "types" repeated in the sheet of fifty subjects. The printing plate was built up by the transferring process from an "original stone" of three subjects ("types") in a vertical strip.

taining all three "types." The arrangements of the two panes of the 35c. differ from one another in such a manner as to prove that the one pane did not result from a re-transfer of the other pane complete, but that both were separately built up from transfers taken from the "original stone."

Re-Use of Plates

As is the case with a stone, a plate can be used again and again for different subjects. The old subjects must be removed, and the plate regrained. Again, practices vary widely and in detail, but one method of removal is for the ink to be removed from zinc plates with turpentine or naphtha, and the designs destroyed with a strong solution of caustic soda rubbed over the surface of the plate with a block covered in felt.

In the case of an aluminum plate, after the ink has been removed, the designs are destroyed, usually by nitric or sulfuric acid.

The plate is then washed and regrained, and is ready to receive new subjects.

The removal of old designs from a metal plate differs in an important respect from such removal from stone. Where the surface of a stone is reground and polished, the operations result in the removal from its depth of a thickness of stone amounting to the thickness of a thin metal plate. In the case of a plate, regraining leaves the thickness of the metal substantially unaffected. As a consequence, palimpsests do not noticeably occur with metal plates.

Photographic Lithography

Photographic lithography, which is usually abbreviated to "photolithography," or "photolitho," is a combination of processes involving the principles of photography and some of the principles of lithography.

Usually photography is used to multiply the subjects, and in the later stages of producing the printing base as well. However, that is not invariably the case, and instances are known where the subjects have been multiplied by mechanical means, and a single photograph taken of the designs arranged as they are to appear on the sheet when printed.

The various steps taken in the production of two issues exemplify these differences. The two issues are: USA 1918-20 1c., 2c. and 3c. offset printing (photographic multiplication of the design), and Union of South Africa 1925 Air 1d., 3d., 6d. and 9d. (mechanical multiplication of the design).[24]

With minor variations, the steps taken for the production of the printing plates for the issue of the United States were the same for all values. From the line-engraved original die (used in the production of the earlier recess-printed stamps) a proof was recess-printed in the usual manner. This proof

---

[24]For the purposes of this illustration, dealing only with the multiplication of the design, it is unimportant that on the lithographic printing plate, the subjects of the issue of the United States appeared with the design reading normally — that is, from left-to-right — as did those of the issue of the Union of South Africa.

Lithography. Multiplication of the design by photography. USA 1918-20 1c. "offset printing." A photographic negative of this design was used in a step-and-repeat camera to make a glass multipositive bearing 400 subjects. From this multipositive a photographic print on celluloid was made, and used when the sensitized printing plates were exposed to light.

was then photographed, and a greatly magnified photographic enlargement was carefully retouched photographically, so that every colored line was entirely clear-cut and sharp and the uncolored areas were completely clean. This retouched enlargement was then photographed in reduced format, so that the resulting photographic negative was the required size.[25]

The negative was then placed in a step-and-repeat machine or projection camera, by means of which the design was multiplied the requisite number of times on to a large photographic glass plate. This photographic glass plate, after development, formed the "master (photographic) positive," from which contact prints were made photographically on film coated with a photographic emulsion. Marginal markings were added to the images on the film, and the films were then used to make the printing plates.[26] These were of zinc, and they were prepared for printing in substantially the same manner as that adopted for Union of South Africa 1925 Air 1d. to 9d.

For Union of South Africa 1925 Air 1d. to 9d., the steps taken in the production of the photographic plate involved photography only as the ultimate step. The first step was the hand-engraving in recess on copper of a single undenominated design, about four times larger than the size of the eventual stamp; also engraved on copper, and in the same proportionate size, were the figures to be incorporated in the value circles. Prints from the copper engraving were then made on transfer paper in special transfer ink, by the process usual for recess printing. For each value, a group of four designs was prepared, and the appropriate figures of value were patched in each of the eight blank value circles.

The patched-up designs in the group of four were then transferred to stone

---

[25]For the purposes of this illustration, the actual size of the image on this negative is unimportant — such negatives may vary, for different reasons and with different printers, between actual stamp size and about four times, linear, magnification.

[26]*The United States Postage Stamps of the Twentieth Century* by Max G. Johl (1937), Vol. I, Pages 118, 173-74, 216-26, 241-45.

Lithography. "Mechanical" multiplication of the design. Union of South Africa 1925 Air 1d. An enlarged recess line engraving on copper was made of this design, undenominated; the figure of value was engraved separately. Recess prints in transfer ink on transfer paper were then made, and the figures of value were patched in place. Four composite designs were transferred to stone. Lithographic prints were made from the stone and arranged on card. The card was photographed, so that the designs were stamp size. Two of these photographic negatives were used when the sensitized printing plates were exposed to light.

in a lithographic press, there being one "original stone" of a group of four for each value. From the stone, lithographic prints were made in black ink. For each value these prints were trimmed and mounted in pre-determined positions on large cards; each card bore sixty subjects (ten across, six down). After the sheet-marginal markings had been placed in position, each card was photographed twice — the first time with the marginal markings at the top and at the right of the group of sixty subjects, and the second time with them beneath and at the right of the group. The distance between the camera and the cards was so adjusted that the resulting photographic images were stamp size. Each pair of photographic negatives was then used in the preparation of the printing plate for each value.

The plates were of grained zinc, and each was coated with a solution of bichromated albumen. Each pair of photographic negatives was brought into close contact at pre-determined positions with one of the zinc plates in a special photographic printing frame, and exposed to bright light for a calculated period of time.

This exposure to light had the effect of rendering insoluble the albumen beneath the areas of clear emulsion of the photographic negative, while leaving unaffected the albumen shaded by the darkened areas of the negative. This exposure of the albumen-coated plate to light through the photographic negative is termed "printing down."

After printing down was complete, the albumen on each zinc plate was given an all-over thin coating of a special mixture of transfer ink. The ink adhered to all the albumen, both soluble and insoluble. Each plate was then immersed in or sprayed with water, with the result that the soluble albumen dissolved away, carrying with it its inky coating, while there remained adhering to the zinc the insoluble albumen covered with the special ink. Thus, each subject on the plate was then represented in the following manner: the areas to be printed in color consisted of albumen, minutely in relief, and covered with ink — they would receive further ink from the inking rollers; the areas to appear uncolored on the paper consisted of clear zinc, of which the grain would retain the water from the dampening rollers, and repel the greasy ink from the inking rollers.

Afterward the plates were carefully washed again, and subjected to further treatment that rendered them ready for use in the press.

For an instance of the use of photographic transfer paper employed lithographically in intermediate stages of stamp production, see "Multiplying the Design" in the chapter entitled "Relief Printing" and Footnote 103 to that chapter.

Halftones

So far I have discussed only one class of design that can be reproduced by photolithography — the "line" subject, which consists of clearly defined colored and non-colored areas, even in those parts where some gradation of tone has resulted from deliberate variations in the thickness of the lines, from cross-hatching, or from breaking the line into short dashes or dots.

The other class of design is the "continuous tone" subject, such as a wash painting or a photograph. While such a tonal subject cannot be faithfully reproduced by any method other than photography, a representation and appearance of continuous tone can be effected by breaking up the design into minute colored and non-colored areas, of which the relative proportions cause the illusion of varying strengths of tone. This is termed "halftone." This breaking up of the design is carried out by exposing a photographic plate to the subject through a cross-line screen, termed a "halftone screen."

The halftone screen consists of clear glass or film upon which appears a series of closely spaced dark lines crossing one another at right angles. Viewed in a different light, the halftone screen consists of dark glass or film upon which appear myriads of minute clear rectangles regularly spaced in vertical and horizontal columns and rows.[27]

Halftone screens vary in the number of lines to the linear inch, and this number is used to characterize the screen. For different work the number of such lines varies greatly, but the most usually encountered halftone screens, philatelically in lithography, range between about 150 and 300. Philatelically, precise accuracy about the number of lines per linear inch of the halftone screen is unimportant, and fairly difficult to ascertain. Usually it is sufficient to differentiate between "coarse screen" (in reference to a screen with comparatively few lines per linear inch), and "fine screen" (in reference to a screen with comparatively many lines per linear inch). Examples of different screens

---

[27]Basically the grid or mesh of the halftone screen is similar to that of the photogravure screen — but there is an important difference. The photogravure screen is the "negative" of the halftone screen. The halftone screen may be likened to a series of minute windows in dark glass, and the photogravure screen to a series of minute doors in clear glass. A further difference between the two screens is that, in the halftone screen, the "windows" and spaces are the same width, while in the photogravure screen, the "doors" are wider than the spaces.

are to be found, for instance, in Iran (Persia) 1942-46 5d. to 200r., and Uruguay 1949 Fourth Regional American Conference of Labor 3c. and 7c.

It is characteristic of a halftone screen that the width of each line is equal to the width of each space, unlike the photogravure screen in which there is a considerable difference between the width of the line and the width of the space.

The effect of using a halftone screen is that the design, as it passes through the screen, is broken up into a pattern of dots of different sizes, each clear rectangular space in the screen acting as a sort of subsidiary lens.

The photographic emulsion behind each window will be acted upon according to the amount of light passed by that window, and the amount of light is dependent upon the tonal or light value of the corresponding portion of the design. The result is that where much light passes through the windows of the screen, the light spreads and overlaps the lines of the screen, leaving only parts of the photographic emulsion unaffected by light, and resulting in small clear dots spaced comparatively far apart. Where only a very small amount of light passes through the windows of the screen, the effect upon the photographic emulsion is negligible, so that it is unaffected by the light; no, or very little, spread occurs, and the emulsion is further protected by the lines of the screen, so that there are large areas of clear dots spaced close together. Between these extremes, the sizes of the resulting dots will vary according to the amount of light passing through the other windows. This effect is termed ''dot formation.''

The resulting effect on the photographic emulsion is that it is either clear or opaque — there is no half-way house — at any particular point, and the whole design is made up of clear or opaque emulsion in small or large areas. There is, in fact, no ''tone,'' but tone is simulated by the varying areas of clear and opaque emulsion. This effect and the dot formation can be clearly remarked by examining under magnification any of the pictures of stamps or apparatus in the chapters of the present work. As a specific example, the picture of the Hunter-Penrose Auto Step-and Repeat Machine earlier in this chapter has been reproduced with a dot formation resulting from the use of a ''120-line'' halftone screen.

Photolitho Varieties

Whenever a printing base is produced with the aid of photographic processes, the possibility exists that blemishes peculiar to photography will occur, and something less than perfection may be attained in the photographic processes. Such peculiarly photographic blemishes, unless noticed and remedied, will have the effect of causing a flaw to appear on the resultant stamp or stamps — and sometimes the remedying itself will be imperfect, with the result that its occurrence can be deduced philatelically.

Whether the flaw is colored or uncolored will depend upon various factors. The factors are: whether the blemish resulted, at the exposure stage of the printing plate, in the passage of too much or too little light; whether the printing plate was exposed to light through a photographic negative or

Lithography. Halftone screen. Persia (Iran) 1942-46 2r. The center design of this stamp bears a dot formation produced by use of a "halftone screen."

positive; and whether the printing areas or the non-printing areas were (even minutely) in relief.

It would be impossible in a work of this nature to survey all the causes and effects of photographic blemishes.[28] The most that can be attempted is to refer to some causes and to indicate others. Whenever an attempt is made

---

[28]See "Photographic Master Flaw or Variety" in the alphabetical listing to the chapter entitled "Printing Problems and Varieties."

Lithography. Halftone screen. Uruguay 1949 Fourth Regional American Conference of Labor 3c. The center design of this stamp bears a dot formation produced by use of a "halftone screen."

Lithography. Halftone screen. A photographic enlargement made by transmitting light through part of a 175-line screen, and then making a positive print — enlarged about twenty-two times linear. Compare this screen with the screen illustrated for "Screened rotary photogravure. Screen plate," in the chapter entitled "Intaglio Printing — II: Gravure." Note that in the "halftone screen," the lines and spaces are of equal width, and in the "photogravure screen," the lines are narrower than the spaces.

to diagnose the cause of a photographic variety occurring on a photolitho stamp, the various factors already mentioned must be borne in mind. Each issue, when studied, must be studied by reference to the particular processes used in its production. Practices vary widely and in detail between different printers and from time to time. And it is quite unsound to accept one practice or series of steps as standard and to refer exclusively to it for the purpose of drawing purported certain conclusions about the cause of any variety on any issue except one produced by that practice or series of steps. Certain

338

diagnosis, philatelically, of flaws cannot always be made. Indeed, if only one printing plate is manufactured from a photographic plate or film bearing many subjects, certain diagnosis can rarely be attained; however, if several or many printing plates stem from the same photographic plate or film, accurate diagnosis becomes a reasonable possibility, because the flaw will (unless steps are taken to eliminate it) occur again on the affected subjects similarly positioned on the various printing plates.

In any photographic process, the possibility exists that the photographic emulsion may be inherently defective or damaged.

A common form of inherent defect is a small pocket of air trapped when the emulsion is spread so that it does not adhere to its glass or film support at the place where the pocket occurs; such a pocket is termed ''a blister.'' Blisters vary in size from pinheads to several square millimeters in area. The usual result of a blister is that, after the photographic plate or film has been processed, the emulsion over that area breaks away completely from the support, leaving clear glass or film at that place. The consequence is that, unless the defect is remedied, too much light will be passed when light is exposed through the plate or film.

Another cause of an emulsion-free area is careless handling when the plate or film is wet. During photographic development the emulsion is very soft and very susceptible to damage by even the slightest mishandling, such as scratching or gouging with a fingernail or implement.

Among other causes of photographic imperfection are air bubbles during processing. For perfect processing, the developer or fixer must come into contact evenly with the entire surface of the emulsion for a calculated period of time. Sometimes a bubble of air will adhere to the photographic plate or film, and so prevent, at that place, perfect processing. If such a bubble adheres during development, development will be impeded at that place, and the result will be a circular area of underdeveloped emulsion, in the form of entirely or comparatively undarkened emulsion. If such a bubble adheres during fixing, the result will be an area of overdarkened or opaque emulsion.

The desire of the photographer is to produce a perfect plate or film by development and fixing. Should that ideal not be attained, various processes may be resorted to for the purpose of remedying defects considered as meriting attention. These processes are termed ''(photographic) retouching.'' Printers who employ photographic processes in the production of printing bases use the term ''retouch'' to signify amendment exclusively of a subject on a photographic plate or film — and use the term ''repair'' when referring to amendment of a subject on a printing base. Philatelically, the term ''retouch'' connotes amendment not only of a photographic plate or film but also, and perhaps primarily, of a printing base. In order to avoid confusion, philatelically, in reference to a photographic amendment, the term ''retouch'' may be qualified as in ''(photographic) retouch.''

Photographic retouching has two main effects: the lightening of an overdarkened area, and the darkening of an insufficiently darkened area.

The lightening of an overdarkened area may be effected in two principal

(text continues on Page 342)

On the Facing Page:

Photolithography. Blister and (photographic) retouch. USA 1918-20 3c. offset printing (design type IV). At top, an unflawed stamp, and enlargement of detail to show the design. At center, stamp No. 6 from upper-right pane of plate 8799, and enlargement of detail showing "blister." At foot, stamp No. 6 from upper-right pane of plate 9289, and enlargement of detail showing "(photographic) retouch." (NOTE: the stamp and enlargement illustrated at top are not from the same pane and stamp position as the lower two pairs of illustrations, and are included merely for the purpose of comparison.)

These stamps were offset-printed from grained zinc plates, with the design represented on the printing plate by hardened albumen minutely in relief for the colored areas, and by clear zinc for the uncolored areas. To obtain the designs in this form on the printing plates, each plate was coated with light-sensitized albumen, and then exposed to light through a 400-subject photographic negative, upon which those parts of the designs eventually to be printed in color were represented by clear photographic emulsion, and darkened photographic emulsion represented those parts of the designs eventually to appear uncolored. After exposure, the printing plate was covered with ink, the unhardened albumen was dissolved in water, and the plate was then etched and prepared for the press.

Blister. On the photographic negative on one subject (upper-right pane, stamp No. 6) appeared a flaw caused by a "blister" — a piece of photographic emulsion that broke away from the transparent support after the photographic images had been processed because a bubble of air had been trapped at that position when the photographic emulsion was originally spread over the support. Because of this "blister," the negative at that position was entirely undarkened, instead of being partly darkened and partly undarkened. Consequently, when the printing plate was exposed to light through the negative, all (instead of only part) of the albumen beneath the "blister" became hardened, and that area of the stamp was eventually printed in color (instead of part color and part without color). The "blister" occurs on all plates used between 8720 and 9270, in the form pictured at center.

(Photographic) retouch. Later, by handwork with a fine brush and photographic retouching "paint," the missing darkened emulsion was simulated on the photographic negative by painting in the areas to appear uncolored on the stamp when printed. The "(photographic) retouch" occurs on all plates used between 9278 and 9599, and appears pictured at bottom.

NOTE: On the same subject from other plates, the "blister" shows; and on the same subject from yet other plates, the effects of "(photographic) retouch" are exhibited.

ways: by scraping away the emulsion itself with a sharp, fine blade until a sufficient depth has been removed; and, by the local application, by brush, of a bleaching agent, termed "a reducer." The darkening of an insufficiently darkened area is effected by painting, with a fine brush, sufficient of an appropriate "paint" either on to the emulsion or on to the glass or film, until the desired depth of tone has been attained.

The effects of scraping or reducing are permanent, and last the lifetime of the photographic plate or film on which such retouching has been effected. However, when the photographic retouch consists of the addition of tonal value by "paint," the retouch may be impermanent, and, in time, may flake off. It this should happen, the defect will reappear, usually in its original form. The same defect may be subject to further photographic retouching from time to time if the need should arise.

An example of a "blister" is to be found on USA 1918-20 3c. offset printing, on some stamps from one subject of Type IV,[29] and other, similarly positioned stamps also provide instances of photographic retouch. The varieties occur on all plates used from 8720 to 9933, and the subject affected is upper-right pane, stamp No. 6. The area affected is situated beneath the "S" of "U.S." In its initial stages on the stamps, the flaw consists of an excess of color appearing roughly triangular in shape; it presents the appearance of an interruption of the horizontal uncolored lines of the background, and a shortening of the top of the left-hand leaf of the wreath.

The printing plates were of grained zinc, coated with light-sensitized albumen, and were exposed to light through photographic negatives bearing 400 subjects. On the photographic negative the flaw consisted in the absence of photographic emulsion caused by a blister. Part of the missing emulsion was darkened, corresponding with the uncolored portions of the design, and part was undarkened, corresponding with the colored portions of the design, within the area of the blister. As a consequence, when the printing plate was exposed to light through the negative, this blister allowed too much light to pass within its area where there should have been darkened emulsion; that undarkened emulsion was missing had no importance. This caused albumen, which should have remained soluble, to become insoluble and to remain on the printing plate when the soluble albumen was dissolved away; consequently, the blister formed part of the design of that subject, and the flaw appeared on the resultant stamp. Either the blister on the photographic negative was not noticed, or it was considered as not meriting attention, and each U.R. 6 subject printed from all plates used between 8720 and 9270 show the flaw in its initial stage.

Later, photographic retouching was carried out, and this resulted in subsequent U.R. 6 stamps showing the effects of this retouching, in the form of a partial absence of the excess color previously appearing in the area affected. The main effects upon the stamp of the photographic retouching are that, below the "S," the top horizontal colored line of the background appears rough and uneven, while the next colored line diagonally joins the leaf, and

---

[29]More specifically, "Design Type IV."

the leaf has lost its outline at the top. This photographic retouching carried out on the photographic negative within the area of the blister comprised the painting of color on the areas corresponding with the subsequently un-colored portions of the resultant stamp. More than one retouch was, in time, carried out to the same subject,[30] and, on some U.R. 6 subjects printed from some later plates, the blister appears again.

Producing Plates, Stones and Transfers

Many different processes have been employed from time to time to pro-duce transfers and stones or plates bearing the requisite number of subjects for printing. Each process has, for one reason or another, been adopted, and each possesses its own peculiar advantages and disadvantages in producing the particular work required. Reference has already been made in this chapter to a number of these processes. It would be impossible in a work of this nature to survey them all in detail. The most that can be attempted is to refer to some, and to indicate that others exist.

As is the case with every printing method, some fundamental steps are common to all the varying procedures adopted to put that method into use.[31]

Passing mention has already been made earlier in this chapter to the proc-ess of engraving upon stone and to its modern counterpart, the ''deep'' off-set process.

Engraving upon stone is carried out by coating the smoothly polished sur-face of the stone with gum, washing off most of the gum, and rubbing the surface with powdered lampblack to make a ground upon which to work. The design is then cut into the stone with a fine point, such as a needle or a diamond;[32] the lines of the design appear white on a black background. These lines are then filled with oil, which is allowed to stand for a short while. Then the oil is washed off, and ink is dabbed over the surface of the stone, in the manner of inking a line-engraved plate.[33] The excess ink is wiped off, and damp paper is laid on the stone and pulled through the press. New Caledonia 1860 (January) 10c. provides an example of a stamp printed directly from engraving upon stone. Trinidad 1852, 1853 and 1855-60 (1d.), and France 1870-71 Bordeaux 1c. to 80c. (Yon engravings) provide instances of designs engraved on stone and then printed from stones that were built up by transfers from the engravings.

---

[30]Per Dr. David M. Berest.

[31]It is to these fundamentals that much philatelic study is devoted — but these fundamentals do not necessarily constitute a norm; and, so far as concerns the study of a particular stamp or issue, it is unsound to use the practices of one printing establishment at any one time as standard and to refer exclusively to it for the purpose of diagnosing with certainty the cause of variations found on products at a different time or of a different establishment. The only safe rule is to establish, by reference to the stamp or issue itself, and by such other means as may be available — including the possibilities and limitations of the printing method and its variations — the actual steps undertaken in the production of that particular stamp or issue.

[32]Or a pin — as was used by Sgt. Triquera.

[33]See ''Printing from Flat Plates'' in the chapter entitled ''Intaglio Printing — I: Line Engrav-ing.''

Lithography. Photolitho. "deep" off-set. Israel 1950 (Oct. 1) Third Mac-cabiah 80p. This stamp was printed by the "deep" offset process in which the colored portions of the design are slightly recessed below the surface of the plate; the surface represents the un-colored portions of the design. The ink held in the recesses is deposited on the blanket which offsets the ink upon the paper.

Lithography. Engraving upon stone. New Caledonia 1860 (January) 10c. This stamp was printed directly from a stone upon which the design had been engraved by hand.

For the "deep" offset process, the printing plates are made by exposing a zinc plate with a light-sensitized coating to a photographic positive of the design. The exposure has the effect of rendering insoluble on the printing plate areas of the coating corresponding with the non-printing areas of the

Lithography. Engraving upon stone. Trinidad 1852 (1d). France 1870-71 Bordeaux 2c. These stamps were printed from stones built up by lithographic transfers taken from a stone upon which the design had been engraved by hand.

344

design. After exposure, the coating of the plate is reinforced to withstand etching, and the coating representing the colored areas of the design is dissolved away, leaving clear zinc in those areas. The plate is then etched, the etching solution being able to affect only the non-coated areas of the plate. Consequently, these areas become minutely recessed into the plate. After etching, the plate is dried and inked. Then the coating is washed away from the non-printing areas of the design by a solution of soda. The plate is then made ready for use in the press. As has been stated, the colored areas are only minutely recessed into the plate — to the depth of the thickness of a layer of ink. The "deep" offset process was used, for example, to produce Israel 1950 (Oct. 1) Third Maccabiah 80 pr.

Relying upon somewhat similar principles is the "Vandyke" process, in which the coated zinc plate is exposed to light through a drawing or tracing of the design. Afterward, the soluble parts of the coating are washed away, leaving the design represented by clear zinc, and the background by insoluble coating. The plate is then dried, and the design filled with ink; after this the hardened coating is chemically removed, and the plate is prepared for the press.

Other processes, such as the "Typon," involve the making of a negative print of a drawn design upon special photographic paper, through which the printing plate with a light-sensitized coating is exposed to light.

Chromolithography

So far in this chapter I have discussed the processes of producing lithographic printing bases for the printing of monochrome stamps. Many lithographed stamps are bi-colored or multicolored, and in such cases production involves the making of a separate printing base for each color required, and the printing of the different colors one after the other at, substantially, different operations — although, in modern presses, the operations are carried out very soon one after the other, that is, the paper travels, often, less than thirty-six inches between the different color cylinders.

Chromolithography, as lithographic printing in more than one color on the same sheet of paper is termed, involves numerous interrelated operations in the production of the various printing bases in order that the colors on the stamp may be in register.

In lithography from stone by the transferring process, very great care must be taken to ensure that, on the various stones, the different parts of the designs are accurately spaced in relation to each other; in photolithography the same accuracy is required, but the technique of spacing is rendered comparatively simple by the step-and-repeat camera or step-and-repeat printing down machine. Instances of chromolithographed stamps printed from stone are, for example, India 1854 4a., and chromolithographed stamps printed from plates are, for example, Peru 1951 (December) Air, San Marcos University Foundation 5s.

Various methods have been used for preparing a set of stones to be used for chromolithographic printing. These methods vary in detail, and no useful purpose would be served in attempting to survey them all.

Lithography. Chromolithography. India 1854 4a. This stamp was printed at two operations from two (color) stones — a blue stone and a red stone.

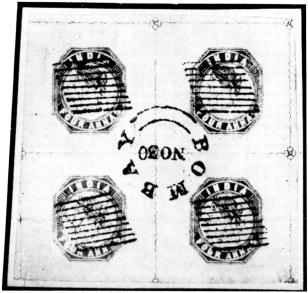

The basis of accurate color register is termed "the key." The key comprises an outline of the design, clearly defining all the areas of color. The key, together with specially drawn rectangular register marks outside the corners of the design, is transferred to a stone. This stone serves two purposes. First it is used to make re-transfers that are affixed to a patching sheet in predetermined positions and transferred to another stone, termed "the key stone." Second it is used to make as many other transfers as there are colors; and upon each of these transfers the lithographer completes, with greasy ink, the portion of the design to appear in the relevant color, and also fills in part of the register marks.

After the lithographer has thus completed all the color transfers — each with its relevant portion of the design and of the register marks — they are transferred, each to a separate stone. Each stone bears only a portion of the design, together with only a portion of the register marks. From each of these stones, a sufficient number of transfers is printed for patching on a sheet termed "the key sheet."

The key sheet consists of a print from the key stone, and contains the requisite number of subjects appropriately spaced in the form of the eventual sheet of stamps. The key sheet is used sequentially for each color.

To each subject on the key sheet, the lithographer affixes by stabbing or with special paste the transfer for one color, registering the partial design by means of the register marks. When each design bears its transfer of that color, the partial designs of all the subjects on the key sheet are transferred, in the usual manner,[34] at one operation to the printing stone for that color.

---

[34]See "Transferring the Design" earlier in this chapter.

Lithography. Chromolithography. Peru 1951 (December) Air, San Marcos University Foundation, 5s. This stamp was chromolithographed by Thomas De La Rue & Company Ltd., in black, blue, gold, green, red, silver and yellow.

The lithographer then uses the key sheet in a similar manner for another color, and a similar transfer is made to another printing stone.

These operations are repeated until there is a separate printing stone for each color to appear on the finished stamp.

For registering the paper on each stone one after the other during the printing of the sheets, various devices have been adopted. One device is to mark a cross at each side of the key stone and to transfer these crosses to each color stone during the operation which transfers the color. At the center of each cross, on all color stones except the first, a fine hole is drilled to receive a needle; after the first color is printed on the sheet, a needle is pierced through each cross printed on it, and the sheet is then placed in position on the next stone by fitting the needles into the holes; the sheet is held lightly in position, the needles are removed, and the next color is printed. These operations are repeated until all the required colors appear on the sheet. Another device is to make a rectangular mark on the stone and to lay one corner of the sheet coincident with the mark.

So far I have been discussing chromolithography based on the separation of one mass of color from the other, the number of different colors in the resultant stamp stemming from the number of different stones or plates used for printing. Such color separation is termed ''mass separation'' or ''flat color'' — see ''Color Separation (1)'' in the list of ''Terms Used in Describing Printing Processes'' in Chapter 8.

The other form of color separation used for the production of some planographically printed stamps enables an apparently unlimited number of colors to be represented from no more than three or four printing bases, and is known as ''process color,'' ''process separation,'' ''three-color process,'' or, if four printings are involved, ''four-color process'' — see ''Color Separation (2)'' in the list of ''Terms Used in Describing Printing Processes'' in Chapter 8. The colors are separated photographically and, by use of the halftone screen (see ''Halftones'' earlier in the present chapter), each printing base contains subjects that comprise myriads of dots of different sizes apparently spaced at varying distances apart. The screen is rotated to a different angle for the making of each different printing base, so that the dots do not occupy exactly the same positions on any of the printing bases. Consequently, when the prints are made on the same piece of paper, the dots

347

of different colors occupy different positions. The multicolor effect results from an optical illusion, the colored dots blending to produce an infinite variety of color, depending upon the inks used for printing. This method of process-color separation is discussed in somewhat greater detail in connection with relief printing, under "Three-Color Process," later in this work. Among the planographically printed issues for which process-color separation has been used are, for example, the vignette of Germany 1952 (Apr. 15) Fifth Centenary of the Birth of Leonardo da Vinci 5(p.), and Montserrat 1985 (Feb. 8) National Emblems $1.15 depicting "The Mango," where the inscriptions in black are unscreened but the picture consists of a blending of blue (or cyan), yellow and red (or magenta) to give a multicolored effect. One of the characteristics which enable this form of color separation to be identified is that, if the medium tones of the stamp are examined closely, the dots of different colors present a "rose" or "reseau" effect, somewhat resembling a Tudor rose.

Color separation. Three-color process. Montserrat 1985 (Feb. 8) National Emblems $1.15 bearing a multicolor picture printed planographically from plates (or cylinders) made by the three-color process, incorporating the halftone screen set at a different angle for each of the three colors, blue (or cyan), yellow and red (or magenta). The inscriptions and devices are printed in black from unscreened plates or cylinders.

Color separation. Three-color process. Germany 1952 (Apr. 15) Fifth Centenary of the Birth of Leonardo da Vinci 5(p.), bearing a multicolor vignette printed planographically from plates made by the three-color process, incorporating the halftone screen set at a different angle for each of the three colors.

Printing from Lithographic Printing Bases

All lithographic printing depends upon the principle of the mutual antipathy of grease and water, and all such printing is carried out from a stone or plate that has first been dampened and then charged with ink. The process of damping and then inking is repeated for each sheet of paper that is fed through the press or for each time the printing surface is printed from; and this is so, regardless of whether the printing is direct to the paper, or first onto the rubber-covered blanket cylinder for offset printing.[35] Failure to ensure that the stone or plate is sufficiently dampened will result in the printing base picking up ink in areas intended to be uncolored, and will lead to the occurrence of varieties.[36]

With the passage of time since lithography was first discovered, many methods have been developed for putting the principles of lithographic printing into practice. Such methods vary to a great extent in detail, and it is, broadly speaking, true to state that no two types of presses are identical in their application of the principle.

As has already been indicated earlier in this chapter,[37] the presses may be divided into two main classifications — flat-bed and rotary — and they may be viewed from two standpoints, whether the printing is direct or offset. Another consideration is whether the press is hand-operated, power-assisted, or power-operated.

Historically, the first lithographic presses were flat-bed and hand-operated. The first development was the application of power to assist the operation of the press. Rotary printing by power-operated presses followed and, with its introduction, the speed of printing increased. The modern press evolved from the introduction of offset printing. The offset press represented a great advance in the technique of lithographic printing, one of the reasons being that this press enabled a great variety of paper to be used.

Before the introduction of the offset press, it was necessary, in order to obtain good impressions, to use, exclusively, paper with a smooth or glazed printing surface, or to squeeze the paper surface flat by great pressure in the press — there being on the surface of the stone or plate no recesses into which to force the paper so that it might pick out the ink, or no reliefs to force the ink into the substance of the paper. However, the rubber covering of the blanket cylinder of the offset press is resilient, and adjusts itself to minute irregularities in the paper. Because of this, paper with a mat or, even, rough surface will yield good impressions by this method of printing.

Therefore, when an attempt is being made, philatelically, to determine the process used in the production of a planographically printed stamp, if the paper has a comparatively rough surface and bears a good impression with the ink evenly distributed over the fibers of the paper, these factors are of

---

[35]A method has been developed of inking lithographic plates without dampening them.
[36]See " 'Scum' or 'Dry Print' " later in this chapter.
[37]"Principles of Lithography."

assistance in arriving at the conclusion that the offset method of printing was employed.

The advent of a new class of press did not mark the end of use of the other classes. Indeed, the flat-bed direct and flat-bed offset machines were used long after the rotaries came into existence. Until recent times, the knowledge and techniques of handling metal plates were very much in their infancy; and until these times stones gave far sharper and cleaner results. This, for special quality work such as postage stamps, was considered of greater importance than mere speed of production.

It would be quite impossible in a work of this nature to deal with every type of planographic press made by different manufacturers throughout the world. In the descriptions that follow, I have attempted to outline, and to do no more than outline, some of the methods that have been adopted in printing from lithographic printing bases.

Direct Printing from Stone

The lithographic hand press, such as was used for example in the production of India 1854 ½a., 1a. and 4 as., and Zurich 1843 4r. and 6r., is similar in general principles to its equivalent for printing from line-engraved plates. It consists of a bed that can be made to travel under a part of the machine that imparts pressure — in the case of the lithographic hand press, the "scraper," which is a wooden or steel blade.

The stone, with the gum washed off, is placed on the bed of the press. The stone is then damped and inked with appropriately charged rollers. Paper is then laid in position on the stone; to protect the paper, it is covered by a tympan. The tympan consists of a sheet of, usually, cowhide leather stretched on a frame that is hinged to the bed of the press, and may be raised to permit the paper to be placed in position and removed, or lowered to cover the paper on the stone. The back of the leather is lubricated to reduce friction. The stone, with its covering of paper and tympan, is then passed under the scraper which bears down under pressure. The pressure causes the ink applied to the subjects on the stone to be transferred to the paper. After passage under the scraper, the tympan is raised, and the printed paper is removed from the stone, which is then ready for damping and inking again.

In a power-assisted press, such as was used, for instance, by Maclure, Macdonald & Company, which produced, for example, Sarawak 1869 3c. and Uruguay 1866 (Jan. 10) 5c, 10c, 15c and 20c, the passage of the stone under the scraper, and sometimes the damping and inking, were carried out under power provided by a machine.

Later developments in lithographic presses resulted in the scraper being replaced by an impression cylinder and the paper being applied to and removed from the stone mechanically. In such machines, the slight resilience afforded in the hand press by the tympan was replaced by a "blanket"[38] on

---

[38]This type of "blanket" — that around the impression cylinder — is common to all impression cylinders, whatever the method of printing, and is to be distinguished from the rubber-covered "blanket cylinder" of the offset press.

Offset lithography. Monochrome printing. A "Baby" Mann — Demyfolio — single-color, sheet-fed press. This picture, from about 1930, is of an obsolete type which would be made now only to special repeat orders. Union of South Africa 1925 Air 1d. to 9d. were printed on a "Baby" Mann.

the impression cylinder. The pressure of the impression cylinder upon the stone was some tons in weight.

Direct Rotary Printing

The essential requirement of a direct rotary lithographic printing machine is that both the printing and the impression cylinders should be carefully ground to give true surfaces and perfect circumferences, because there are no springs allowing any elasticity in the pressure, and very heavy pressure is necessary in this form of press.

The sheet of paper is fed into the machine, held by grippers and led between the printing and impression cylinders. Around the printing cylinder (or "plate cylinder" as it is sometimes called) the printing plate has been clamped. As it revolves, it comes into contact first with one or more rollers that damp it, then it meets another set of rollers that ink it; next it meets

351

Diagrammatic Representation of the Various Kinds of Presses

① FLAT BED DIRECT

A-HAND PRESS

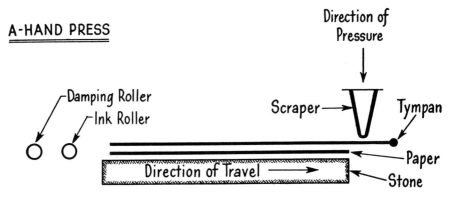

B-POWER ASSISTED PRESS

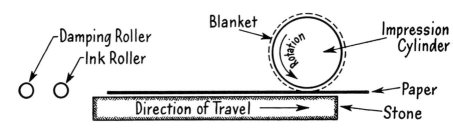

② FLAT BED OFFSET

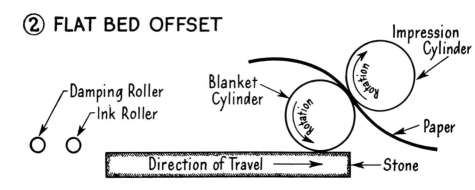

③ ROTARY DIRECT

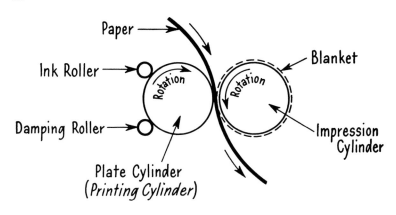

④ ROTARY OFFSET

A-ONE COLOR

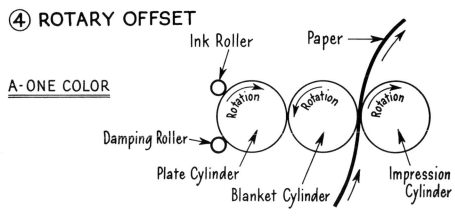

B-TWO COLORS

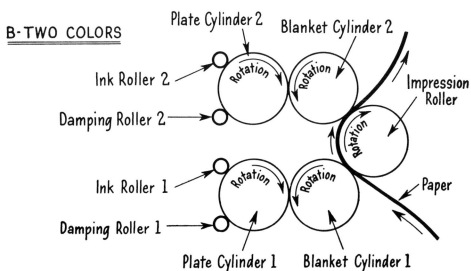

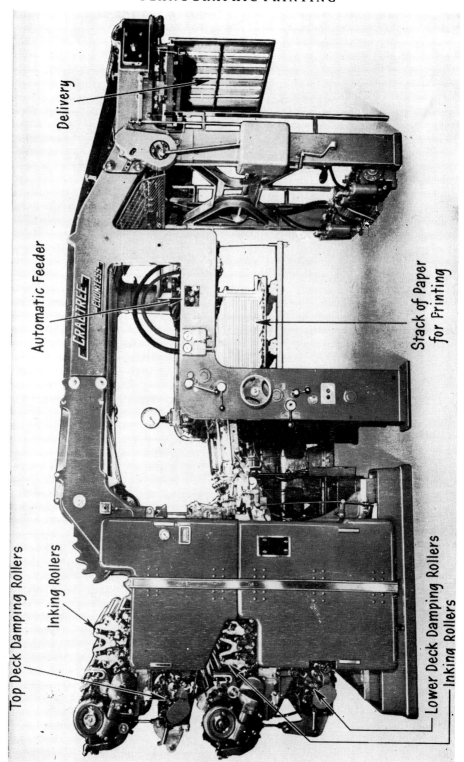

Delivery

Automatic Feeder

Stack of Paper for Printing

Top Deck Damping Rollers

Inking Rollers

Lower Deck Damping Rollers
Inking Rollers

Offset lithography. Bi-color printing. A Crabtree Mark 4 two-color, sheet-fed press. Many of the world's offset lithographed postage stamps are printed on Crabtree presses. The picture shows a press capable of printing two colors on to a sheet of paper each time it is passed through, and the two colors can be registered not only with each other but also with previously printed designs on the same sheet of paper. Precise accuracy of registration and identical positioning on the sheets are obtained — these are essential requirements for subsequent division and perforation of the sheets. Either gummed or ungummed sheets may be fed into the press, which can operate at speeds of up to 6,000 sheets per hour. In the picture, the casing at the left of the machine hides the upper and lower sets of plate and blanket cylinders and the impression cylinder that is positioned between the two blanket cylinders. (See diagram of rotary offset presses.) The paper is fed around the impression cylinder and led to a "taking-off" drum that passes the paper to straps or strings at the top and so on to the delivery board at the right of the machine.

---

the paper which is pressed into heavy contact by the impression cylinder that has a covering, a "blanket," of yielding material.

If this blanket should be out of adjustment, and distorted, the pressure in the machine, after it has been running for a while, may cause the blanket to sag somewhat along part of its length or width and to come into contact with the inked printing cylinder; this will cause the blanket at that place to pick up some ink and deposit it on the underside of the paper, giving rise to a set-off — see "Set-Off" in the alphabetical list to the chapter entitled "Printing Problems and Varieties."

After the paper has been printed as a result of the pressure imparted during its passage between the printing and impression cylinders, it is led away over another cylinder (called a "taking-off cylinder") and on to an arrangement of strings or straps which carries it to the delivery board.

Offset Rotary Printing

The offset rotary press, such as was used in the production of, for example, USA 1918-20 1c. offset printing, Burma 1938-40 3p., Indian 1950 (Jan. 26) Inauguration of Republic 2a., and most modern "litho"-printed issues, is unique among printing presses in that the printing on to the paper takes place not, as in all other classes of press, direct from the printing base but from a "blanket cylinder"[39] upon which the ink has been deposited from the plate cylinder. This is effected by (and the main difference between a direct rotary press and an offset rotary press lies in) the introduction of the blanket cylinder between the plate cylinder and the impression cylinder.

The plate cylinder, as it revolves, comes into contact first with one or more rollers that damp it, then with another set of rollers that ink it. Continuing its revolution, the plate cylinder next meets the blanket cylinder; the two cylinders revolve in contact with one another and in opposite directions. The ink from the designs on the plate cylinder is transferred to the surface of the

---

[39]Also termed, sometimes, "blanket," and sometimes "transfer cylinder."

blanket cylinder in the same way as, in a direct rotary press, the ink is transferred to the paper from the plate cylinder.

In the single-color rotary offset press, the sheet of paper is led over the impression cylinder and pressed into close contact with the surface of the blanket cylinder bearing the ink from the designs, and is then led away to the delivery board.

The two-color rotary offset press differs from the single-color press mainly in the provision of an additional set of damping and inking apparatus and an additional plate and blanket cylinder. The sheet of paper is led over the impression cylinder and pressed by it into close contact in turn with the first blanket cylinder and the second blanket cylinder. The paper, having received a different color from each blanket cylinder, is then led to the delivery board.

Flat-Bed Offset Printing

Viewed from some standpoints, the introduction of the flat-bed offset press was a retrograde step because it involved dispensing with the convenient thin metal plates and re-introducing the clumsy and bulky stone, with attendant difficulties in handling; and allied to these difficulties was the fact that the flat-bed press was slower in operation than the rotary. However, the compensating advantages, the greater sharpness and cleaner results, were considered by many printers to outweigh the disadvantages, especially when quality rather than speed was demanded.

In one type of flat-bed offset press, the stone passes under the blanket cylinder, and the paper is pressed into contact with the blanket cylinder by the impression cylinder. In another type of flat-bed offset press, known as a "proving" or "proofing" press, the stone is placed in position at one end of the press and the paper rests on a support at the other end of the press; the blanket cylinder is mounted on a moving head, and rolls first over the stone (picking up the ink from the designs) and next over the paper (depositing the ink upon the paper).

The Blanket Cylinder

The blanket cylinder comprises a metal support around which is stretched a rubber covering. The construction of the support and the arrangements for stretching the rubber covering around the support vary from machine to machine. However, the correct adjustment and tension of the rubber covering are important matters to the printer; as also is the correct amount of pressure between the blanket cylinder and the plate and impression cylinders. These factors sometimes give rise to varieties of which the diagnosis, philatelically, causes difficulty.

Philatelically outstanding among varieties caused by maladjustment of the blanket and pressure are "double impressions"[40] — that is, duplications of lines of the design. Sometimes such duplications appear of the same inten-

---

[40]See "Double Impression (1)" in the alphabetical list to the chapter entitled "Printing Problems and Varieties."

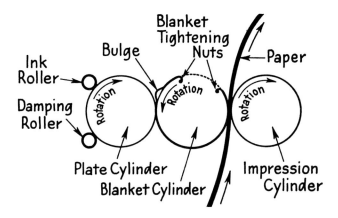

sity of color, and sometimes the design appears normally printed and the duplications faintly printed. All such duplications are, of course, printing varieties; and, philatelically considered, are inconstant, although they may occur on successive sheets until the cause is remedied.[41]

At least three causes may account for the blanket thus bearing ink traces of more than one design where there ought to be only one, and consequently depositing upon the paper excess ink in the form of linear duplications of the design: first, a distorted blanket which has caused a slight bulge to occur at part of the leading edge where it is secured and held in tension on the support; second, excessive pressure which has thrown the printing and blanket cylinders out of true relation; and third, a slight and unlooked for sideways movement between the plate cylinder (or the stone) and the blanket cylinder.[42]

Imperfections in the surface of the rubber covering itself may give rise to a further series of flaws resulting in the appearance of more or less minute areas of color or the absence of color. Like the duplications to which reference has been made, these other flaws are printing imperfections, and may occur on successive sheets until the cause is remedied. A hollow patch in the blanket will result in the absence of color; the presence of grit or impacted dirt will result in the presence of unwanted color.

'Scum' or 'Dry Print'

There is one class of constant variety that is found on the products of lithographic printing alone of all the printing methods, but may occur in all the various forms of printing from lithographic printing bases. This variety consists in the presence of unusual color on the stamp, and occurs on the printing base by reason of the chemical actions involved in these processes of printing.

---

[41]See "Flaw A (2)" in the alphabetical list to the chapter entitled "Printing Problems and Varieties."

[42]Sometimes, maladjustment of the pressure or blanket may result in a stamp bearing traces, more or less prominent, of many different inkings of the same subject.

Photolitho offset postage stamp production in Israel

Israel 1952 (Apr. 13) Taba Airmail 100p. and 120p. Top, left, photographing the designs. After a separate drawing has been made for the differently colored parts of the designs, a separate photograph is made of each drawing. Top, right, retouching. Later, multiple photographic plates or films are made, bearing the required number of repetitions of the design — twenty in this case. These are photographically retouched to remove any flaws.

Center, left, printing on to the printing plate. The multiple photographic plate or film, or a copy of it, is used in a step-and-repeat printing down machine to print the designs on to a light-sensitized zinc or aluminum printing plate. Center, right, developing the printing plate. After five exposures in the step-and-repeat printing down machine in different positions, the printing plate is developed, and deep etched. It is closely examined for imperfections.

Bottom, left, printing by offset. The plate is placed around the printing cylinder of the offset machine, a Mann Double Crown automatic offset. The operator is checking a proof sheet, with a freshly inserted offset cylinder, or blanket cylinder, in position. Bottom, right, perforating the printed sheets. Each printed sheet contains five post office sheets, and after perforation the printed sheets are severed into post office sheets.

In order for the intended non-printing areas of the stone or plate to reject ink, they must be kept sufficiently damp. If the stone or plate should be insufficiently dampened, part of the intended non-printing areas may pick up grease from the ink — or, as the printers say, the plate begins to "catch"; and, once this happens, the grease at those areas will continue to attract ink and deposit it on the paper by reason of what is, in effect, a plate flaw. In certain circumstances, if the defect is not remedied, the grease will become as firmly attached to the stone as are the subjects themselves, and will form a permanent feature of any affected subject.

However, particularly in the case of a plate, the defect can sometimes be remedied by, as the printers term it, "giving the plate an etch" — that is, by swabbing the affected portion of the plate with an appropriate etching solution and then preparing the plate again for printing. This process the printers term "clearing the plate"; and it may be carried out without removing the plate from the press. The term used philatelically to designate a variety caused in this manner is "scum"; sometimes, because of the reason for its appearance, the variety is termed "dry print."

If the plate is "cleared" after some printing has taken place with the scum in evidence, the same subject may be found from two or more "states" of the plate, depending upon when the defect first appeared. An instance of scum is to be found on Israel 1952 (Sep. 3) New Year 110p., plate 53, row 3, stamp No. 1; on this stamp, in the earlier printings, the line representing the left of the left reed is interrupted near the center, and the line representing the right side of the left mount is interrupted near the junction with the right mount; in later printings these defects are absent, the plate having been "cleared."

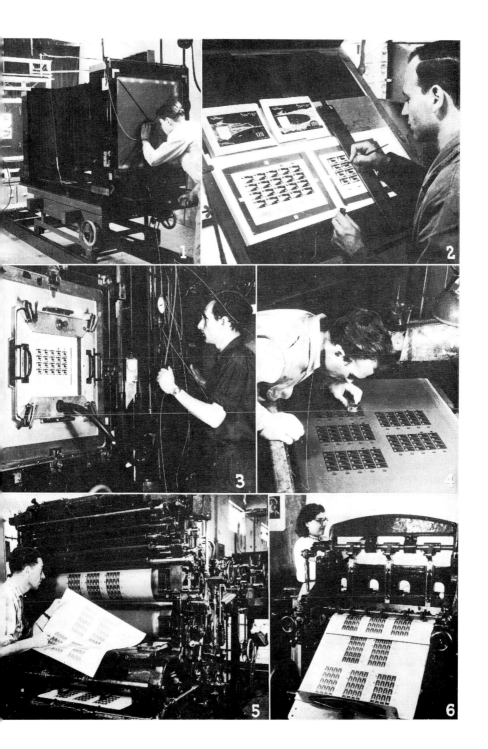

Varieties and Terms in Planographic Printing

The alphabetical list that follows includes some of the terms and varieties appropriate to stamps printed by lithography direct and offset from stones and plates. The list does not pretend to be exhaustive, and to it may be applied the generality of the remarks preceding the alphabetical list to the chapter entitled "Intaglio Printing — I: Line Engraving." As has been indicated, in connection with lithography generally, philatelic nomenclature presents unusual difficulty — see "Transferring Variations in Procedure" earlier in this chapter. Because of this difficulty, I have thought it helpful to insert many cross-references in this alphabetical listing.

Base Sheet. In reference to lithography the term "base sheet" is used to designate a sheet of usually stout paper upon which are arranged, and to which are affixed, pulls from either an original engraving or from an original or intermediate stone, for the purpose of enabling a transfer of several whole or composite designs to be made to stone at a single operation. See "Intermediate Stone"; "Pull"; "Original Engraving"; "Original Stone." The term "Patching Sheet" is used synonymously with "base sheet," because the designs are said to be "patched" or "patched up" on the sheet — see "Patching"; "Stabbing."

Blanket. (a) In reference to printing generally, the term "blanket" is used to designate a covering comprising a relatively yielding surface that is affixed to an impression cylinder to assist in obtaining a good impression. (b) In reference to offset lithography, the term "blanket" is used to designate a rubber-covered cylinder which, in the press, deposits the ink upon the paper, so causing it to bear the designs. The blanket receives the ink from the printing plate, and deposits (or "offsets") the ink upon the paper. In rotary offset presses, the blanket revolves in contact, at one point, with the lithographic printing plate bearing the inked designs and dampened non-printing areas, and, at another point, with the paper which is pressed into contact by an impression cylinder. The blanket sometimes gives rise to varieties — see "Blanket Variety." (c) In reference to papermaking, see "Blanket" in the alphabetical list to the chapter entitled "Paper."

Blanket Variety. (1) Colored flaw. In reference to offset lithographed stamps the term "blanket variety" is used to designate a colored flaw consisting of duplications of the lines of the design. At least three different causes produce such duplications: (a) a slight bulge in the blanket resulting from imperfect adjustment of the rubber covering on the cylinder; (b) excessive pressure that throws the blanket cylinder and impression cylinder out of true relation; and (c) a slight sideways movement between the plate cylinder and the blanket cylinder that causes the blanket to receive ink at slightly different places, from which it is imparted to the paper — see "Blanket." (2) Uncolored flaw. Should damage to the blanket result in a depression, an uncolored flaw will result.

Blister. Colored or uncolored flaw. In reference to any printing method in which photographic processes have been employed during the production of the printing base, the term "blister" is used to designate a flaw resulting from a particular type of defect occurring on a photographic plate or film. The defect consists in the local absence of photographic emulsion, causing unimpeded transparency within the area affected, and is occasioned by the breaking away of the photographic emulsion at that place, and results from the trapping of air or fluid when the photographic emulsion was spread over its transparent support; the effect of such trapping is, technically, termed "a blister." The flaw resulting from a blister may, according to various factors, be colored or uncolored; the factors

360

are: (a) whether the blister occurred on a photographic positive or negative; (2) whether the printing base was exposed to light through a photographic positive or negative; (c) whether the printing areas are in fact (even minutely) in relief or recessed. A well-known instance of a blister occurs on USA 1918-20 3c. offset printing all plates used between 8720 and 9270, upper-right pane, stamp No. 6. See "Photographic Master Flaw or Variety" in the alphabetical listing of terms in the chapter titled "Printing Problems and Varieties"; compare "Master Negative Flaw" in the alphabetical listing of terms in the chapter titled "Intaglio Printing — II: Gravure."

Bloc-Report. In reference to lithography the term "bloc-report" (which is French for "Group Transfer") is sometimes used in English philatelic writings in a special sense to designate an assemblage of designs on a patching sheet, when each subject comprises two or more separate pieces of transfer paper, each bearing part of the design to be transferred. See "Group Transfer"; "Patching Sheet"; "Transfer."

Clipped Transfer. Uncolored flaw. In reference to lithographed stamps the term "clipped transfer" is used to designate a stamp bearing a design more or less incomplete because the lithographer trimmed or clipped away part of the design on the transfer paper when cutting away the excess paper around the design (preparatory to assembling the transfer upon the patching sheet), with the result that the subject was incomplete on the stone — see "Base Sheet"; "Transfer." The terms "Cut Transfer" and "Trimmed Transfer" are used synonymously with "clipped transfer." The variety is constant. Examples of clipped transfer are to be found, for instance, in Suez Canal 1868 40c., stamp No. 26, where the clipping has resulted in a tapering frameline at the right of the stamp; and in Victoria 1850 (August-November 1855) 1d. Half Length Campbell and Ferguson stone 3, Type 20.

(Color) Stone. In reference to chromolithography the term "(color) stone" is used to designate each separate stone upon which appears the portion of the subjects to be printed in the color which designates the stone. The term "stone" is qualified by the appropriate color, as in "yellow stone," "blue stone," "red stone."

Creased Transfer. Uncolored flaw. In reference to lithographed stamps the term "creased transfer" is used to designate a stamp bearing an incomplete or distorted design because, at the time when the lithographer was transferring the design from the transfer paper to the stone, the transfer paper stretched or buckled or cockled and became folded or torn, with the result that that part of the design within the fold failed to transfer, or the tear resulted in a gap or overlap, and the subject was incompletely or misshapenly represented on the stone. The terms "Folded Transfer," "Squeezed Transfer," "Torn Transfer" and "Transfer Fold" are used synonymously with "creased transfer" — see "Transfer." The variety is constant; and, as a class, is frequently encountered in stamps printed from stone. Examples of creased transfer are to be found, for instance, in Romania 1866 stone C, stamp No. 104, where the frame at the northwest is folded over, distorting the corner square; and in Western Australia 1854 4d., stamp No. 157, where the letters "Western" appear squeezed down and only one-and-one-half millimeters high.

Cut Transfer. See "Clipped Transfer"; contrast "Transfer Cuts."

Double Transfer. Colored flaw. In reference to lithographed stamps the term "double transfer" is used to designate a stamp bearing duplications in some part

Lithography. (Lithographic) double transfer. Victoria 1854 2d. Queen on Throne, Campbell stone (?8), stamp No. 10 showing "(lithographic) double transfer." The doubling occurs in the northeast corner, and extends to about half-way down the column at the right. The duplications are constant, and prove that the variety occurred on the lithographic stone, thus distinguishing this variety from a "slur" or "slurred print" for which it might be mistaken.

or all of the design because the duplications appeared on the printing base — see "Transfer." The variety is constant. It is to be noted that the term "double transfer" is descriptive of what is apparent, and is only partly diagnostic. Such duplication can result from several causes, such as the failure of the lithographer to ensure close and immovable contact when the transfer paper is applied to the stone or plate for the purpose of transferring the design, or because of a double exposure in a step-and-repeat camera, or in the circumstances of a palimpsest of a similar design — see "Palimpsest." In the case of a double transfer caused by cockling or movement of the transfer paper, the doubling results from causes similar to those giving rise to slurred print (see "Slurred Print" in the alphabetical list to the chapter entitled "Printing Problems and Varieties"); in such a case diagnosis is especially difficult, and several copies of the identical stamp are required to confirm that the doubling does not vary from stamp to stamp, and that the variety is not merely a slurred print. When greater precision is possible, the term "double transfer" may be qualified in use: "Primary (stone) double transfer," as in Victoria 1850 (1855-56) Half-Length 3d. Campbell stone D, Types 22 and 24; and "Printing stone double transfer," as in Victoria 1850 (1854-55) Half-Length 3d. Campbell stone A, stamp (?319 — lower pane stamp ?159).

Dry Print. Colored flaw. See "Scum."

Extrinsic Flaw. A flaw resulting from the processes of lithography as opposed to a flaw resulting from some other plate-making process. The term is rarely used, and only when a lithographic printing base has been built up from transfers made from the plate resulting from the other plate-making process. In such cases the term used to designate flaws resulting from the other plate-making process is "Intrinsic Flaw," which is used, strictly in the sense of "Design-Type" — see "Design-Type." "Extrinsic flaw" and "intrinsic flaw" are apt in use, for example, in reference to the various flaws which are to be found on the central portions of Western Australia 1854 4d. which resulted from transfers of a portion (sixty subjects out of 240) of the steel plate made by Perkins, Bacon & Company for the 1d. value; the flaws resulting from the Perkins die and mill process are reproduced in the lithographs (intrinsic flaws), which bear also flaws resulting from lithography (extrinsic flaws).

Final Flaw. Colored or uncolored flaw. In reference to lithographed stamps the term "final flaw" is used to designate a flaw first occurring upon a printing stone as a result of transferring; a final flaw does not repeat because no re-transfers are made from the printing stone. (See "Flaw"; "Printing Stone"; "Re-Transfer"; "Transfer Flaw.") The term "final flaw" is used in a special sense to distinguish such a flaw from lithographic flaws arising during transferring at earlier stages in the process of building up the printing stone, in which case for any such earlier flaw the term "intermediate flaw" is used in its generic sense — see "Intermediate Flaw." In this special sense, and dependent upon the number of steps taken to build up the printing stone, the term "final flaw" is synonymous with "tertiary flaw" or "quaternary flaw" — see "Quaternary Flaw"; Tertiary Flaw"; "Printing Stone Flaw."

Fingerprint. Colored flaw. In reference to lithographed stamps the term "fingerprint" is used to designate a stamp exhibiting a fingerprint printed from the stone or plate because the lithographer carelessly allowed his finger to come into contact with the face of the transfer or the sensitized printing base at the time of transferring the design, thus causing the grease exuded by the skin to affect the printing surface, and so causing the fingerprint to become part of the subject affected. See "Transfer." Examples of fingerprints are to be found, for instance, in Victoria Postal Fiscal 1884-96 (1879) 3s. violet on blue, on some stamps of Type 1.

Flaw. See "Flaw" in the alphabetical list to the chapter entitled "Printing Problems and Varieties." Every lithographed stamp exhibits several or numerous flaws more or less minute, and one of the problems involved in a study of lithographed stamps of which the subjects have been multiplied by the transferring process is to determine the nature of the various flaws that are inevitably present; and, by deductions based upon the incidence and frequency of the flaws, to deduce the steps undertaken in building up the printing stone or plate — and, as a necessary incident, to separate the flaws into such of the classes as are appropriate — compare "Intermediate Flaw," "Primary Flaw," "Printing Stone Flaw," "Quaternary Flaw," "Secondary Flaw," "Tertiary Flaw," and "Transfer Flaw." It is, broadly, true to state that, in the study of a lithographed stamp, if a particular flaw occurs on only comparatively few stamps, it is likely to be a printing stone flaw, quaternary flaw, or tertiary flaw; and if a particular flaw occurs on comparatively many stamps, it is likely to be a primary flaw. (See "Type.") In diagnosing the causes of other constant flaws occurring on a stamp printed by lithography and where photographic processes have been used in preparing the printing base, two factors particularly have to be borne in mind: (a) that a flaw — whether colored or uncolored — can result from diametrically opposite causes at different stages when photographic negatives and positives are concerned; and (b) in some photolitho and offset processes the colored areas of the design are represented on the printing plate by hardened albumen minutely in relief, while the non-colored areas are equally minutely recessed from the colored areas; in other offset processes ("deep" offset), the ink for the colored areas of the design is held in minutely recessed areas of the plate, while the non-colored areas are equally minutely in relief from the colored areas. Therefore, for example, the absence of height will, in the albumen process, result in an uncolored flaw, and will, in the "deep" offset process, result in a colored flaw. See also "Extrinsic Flaw."

Folded Transfer. Uncolored flaw. This term is used synonymously with "creased transfer" — see "Creased Transfer."

Group Transfer. In reference to lithography the term "group transfer" is used to designate a transfer printed, usually, from a stone bearing a group of subjects as distinct from a single subject — see "Transfer." The term "Multiple Transfer" is used synonymously with "group transfer," as sometimes is "bloc-report" in a special sense — see "Bloc Report." Group transfers are used, sometimes, in multiplying a design to build up the printing stone through the medium of a secondary stone; and group transfers are used, sometimes, in multiplying a design to build up a secondary stone through the medium of a primary stone. See "Primary Stone"; "Printing Stone"; "Secondary Stone."

Intermediate Flaw. Colored or uncolored flaw. In reference to lithographed stamps the term "intermediate flaw" is used generically to designate any lithographic flaw arising during the transferring of a design at any stage subsequent to the first multiplication of the design — see "Flaw." The term is also used, sometimes, in reference to any such flaw arising at any stage of transferring subsequent to the original or the original engraving — see "Original"; "Original Engraving." In this latter sense, the term "intermediate flaw" is used to distinguish such a flaw from a final flaw — see "Final Flaw." Because of its imprecision the term is sometimes useful, but its use is liable to cause confusion unless the particular sense in which it is employed is made clear. When used strictly, "intermediate flaw" has the implication of "an intermediate stone flaw." See "Secondary Flaw"; "Tertiary Flaw"; compare "Final Flaw"; "Primary Flaw"; "Printing Stone Flaw." See also "Intermediate Stone."

Intermediate Stone. In reference to lithography the term "intermediate stone," strictly used, designates either (a) a stone bearing the first multiplication of the design if the design itself appeared on stone; or (b) a stone intermediate between an original stone and a printing stone — see "Original Stone"; "Printing Stone." In the production of some stamps two or more intermediate stones have been used for successive multiplication of the design, and they are then, strictly, termed "first intermediate stone" (bearing the several transfers taken from the design on stone), and "second intermediate stone" (bearing the several transfers taken from the first intermediate stone), etc. Sometimes the term "intermediate stone" is used imprecisely in reference to any stone intermediate between an engraved design and a printing stone; because of its imprecision when used in this sense, the term is sometimes useful, but its use is liable to cause confusion unless the particular sense in which it is employed is made clear. See "Primary Stone"; "Secondary Stone"; "Tertiary Stone." Sometimes the term "Transfer Stone" is used as a synonym for "intermediate stone" — see "Transfer Stone."

Intermediate Transfer. In reference to lithography the term "intermediate transfer" is occasionally used in reference to a lithographic print on transfer paper made at any stage of the transferring process subsequent to a transfer direct from an original engraving or an original. The term is, of necessity, imprecise in meaning, and the terms "original stone pull," "primary stone pull," and "secondary stone pull" are available for use. See "Original"; "Original Engraving"; "Original Stone"; "Printing Stone"; "Pull"; "Secondary Stone." See also "Transfer."

Intrinsic Flaw — see "Extrinsic Flaw."

Key. In reference to chromolithography the term "key" is used to designate an outline of the design clearly defining all the areas of color. The key, together with specially drawn register marks usually forming right angles outside the design, is transferred to a stone from which re-transfers are made to the key stone. See "Key Stone"; "Re-Transfer"; "Transfer."

Key Sheet. In reference to chromolithography the term "key sheet" is used to designate a sheet of usually stout paper (sometimes mounted on thin zinc) upon which appears a print from the key stone — see "Key Stone." The key sheet is used in turn for each color. To the relevant portion of each subject on the key sheet the lithographer affixes the transfer for one color, and, when each subject bears its transfer for that color, the partial designs are transferred at one operation to the color stone for that color — see "Color Stone." The same procedure is carried out for each different color.

Key Stone. (a) In reference to chromolithography the term "key stone" is used to designate the stone upon which appear re-transfers of the key arranged as required — see "Key"; "Re-Transfer." Sometimes the key stone is used for printing on the finished sheets, to mask any slight deviations in the register of the other colors — see "(Color) Stone." (b) In reference to lithography the term "key stone" is occasionally used synonymously with "Transfer Stone."

Laydown. In reference to lithography the term "laydown" is used philatelically to refer to an arrangement of subjects transferred to a stone or plate.

Matrix Stone. In reference to lithography the term "matrix stone" is a misnomer, because "matrix" means "a mould by or in which something is cast or shaped," and has no application in lithography. However, the term "matrix stone" is sometimes used philatelically to refer to a primary stone — see "Primary Stone."

Multiple Transfer — see "Group Transfer."

Original. In reference to lithography the term "the original" is used to designate a drawing in lithographic ink; in photolithography the term is used in reference to a drawing used to make a photographic plate or used directly for exposure to the light-sensitized printing plate. Compare "Original Engraving"; "Original Stone"; see "Transfer."

Original Engraving. In reference to lithography the term "original engraving" is used to designate a subject produced otherwise than by lithographic drawing or photography. Often an original engraving is a line engraving in recess upon copper, or, sometimes, on stone; but relief engravings have been used. Rarely the term is used in the sense of embracing also a drawing. In its general sense the original engraving is the equivalent, philatelically, of the die — see "Die (1)" in the alphabetical list to the chapter entitled "Printing Problems and Varieties." When appropriate, the term "the plate" is used synonymously with "the original engraving" — see "Plate (a)." Prints are made in special ink from an original engraving, and, sometimes, these prints are used to build up an original stone; sometimes such prints are used to build up the printing stone. Compare "Original"; "Original Stone"; see "Printing Stone."

Original Stone. In reference to lithography the term "original stone" is used to designate a lithographic stone upon which appears the first multiplication to stone of a design when the multiplication is effected (a) by separately hand drawing each design, (b) by plate-to-stone transferring, or (c) by patching up transfers of composite parts of the design — see "Plate-to-Stone Transfer"; "Patching"; "Transfer." Sometimes the term "transfer stone" is used as a synonym for "original stone" — see "Transfer Stone." Strictly, the term "original stone" is *not* employed in reference to a lithographic stone bearing the first multiplication, unaltered, of a design previously appearing singly on another lithographic stone; in those circumstances, the terms "intermediate stone" or "first intermediate stone" are used as appropriate — see "Intermediate Stone." To avoid confusion caused by the nicety of these distinctions, the term often used for the stone that bears the first multiplication of the design is "primary stone" — see "Primary Stone."

Palimpsest. Colored flaw. In reference to lithographed stamps the term "palimpsest" is used to designate a stamp that exhibits characteristics showing that the stone was previously used for a different subject which was imperfectly removed before the stone was used again. Usually stones are prepared for re-use by grinding off the printing surface to the required depth by abrading the stone with sand and then polishing the new surface with a specially fine stone, a "snakestone." Unless the grinding is effected to the greatest depth to which the grease of the ink has sunk into the printing stone, grease will remain in the stone, and this grease will again attract ink and will print subsequently. When greater precision is possible, the term "palimpsest" may be qualified in use: as instances, "Primary Palimpsest" as in Suez Canal 1868, for example 5c., where every "type" reveals in the value circles evidence of the earlier use of the primary stone for subjects containing the value "20c."; "Secondary Palimpsest" as in Suez Canal 1868 40c., for example stamp No. 104 which reveals vertically in the center of the design a number of flaws consisting of dots or circles, being part of a series of parallel dotted lines, remaining from an earlier use of the stone for, perhaps, invoices. This latter stamp combines both classes of palimpsests. See "Palimpsest" in the alphabetical list to the chapter entitled "Printing Problems and Varieties."

Parent Stone. In reference to lithography the term "parent stone" is used occasionally by philatelists in a generic sense to designate any stone from which one or more printing stones were built up.

Patching, Patching Up. In reference to lithography the terms "patching" and "patching up" are used to designate the process of assembling transfers, comprising whole or part designs, upon a base sheet for the purpose of transferring the aggregate or composite subjects at one operation — see "Base Sheet." The subjects or part subjects are lightly affixed in position on the base sheet either by a special paste or by stabbing — see "Stabbing."

Patching Sheet. This term is used synonymously with "base sheet" — see "Base Sheet."

Plate. In reference to lithography the term "plate" has two main meanings: (a) sometimes it is used to refer to the piece of metal upon which appears an original engraving — see "Original Engraving"; and (b) sometimes it is used to designate the actual printing base when this consists of a metal plate — and such use is usually limited to distinguishing the metal from the rubber-covered offset cylinder (the "blanket") when one is used — see "Blanket."

Plate Flaw. Colored or uncolored flaw. In reference to lithographic printing the term "plate flaw" is rarely used, whatever the form of the printing base. Usually the term used is "(printing) stone flaw" — see "Flaw."

Plate Transfer. In reference to lithography the term "plate transfer" is used to designate a transfer printed in special transfer ink from a metal plate, usually an original engraving but sometimes a printing base previously used for a different printing process — see "Transfer." As examples: in the production of (a) Suez Canal 1868 20c., 120 separate plate transfers from the line-engraved die were used in building up the printing stone; (b) Western Australia 1854 4d., a single plate transfer of sixty subjects of the line-engraved 1d. plate was used in making an original stone for the 4d.

Plate-to-Stone Transfer. In reference to lithography the term "plate-to-stone transfer" is used to designate a plate transfer specially made to be, and in fact, transferred to a stone — see "Plate Transfer"; "Transfer"; compare "Stone-to-Stone Transfer."

366

Primary Flaw. Colored or uncolored flaw. In reference to lithographed stamps, and when appropriate, the term "primary flaw" is used to designate a lithographic flaw arising during the transferring of the design to the primary stone — see "Primary Stone." Primary flaws characterize each subject on the primary stone, and repeat at every subsequent multiplication from it. Primary flaws identify the "types" — that is, each "type" exhibits several or, perhaps, many different primary flaws which certainly in aggregate and in fact individually are peculiar to that "type" only — see "Flaw"; "Type." Often primary flaws are the least conspicuous of the flaws present on an individual stamp; on a sheet of stamps on which primary flaws appear, they occur more often than any other class of flaw except "die flaws" — as often as each "type" is repeated in the sheet.

Primary Palimpsest — see "Palimpsest."

Primary Stone. In reference to lithography the term "primary stone" is used, generically, to designate a lithographic stone upon which appears in a group of subjects the first multiplication of the design, irrespective of whether the stone is, in fact, an intermediate stone (in the strict sense of that term) or an original stone — see "Intermediate Stone"; "Original Stone." Upon the primary stone first appear the primary flaws that identify the "types" — see "Primary Flaw."

Primary Substituted Transfer — see "Substituted Transfer."

Printing Plate — see "Plate (b)."

Printing Stone. In reference to lithography the term "printing stone" is used to designate the lithographic stone from which the printing takes place. The term "Working Stone" is used synonymously with "printing stone." The printing stone may be the first and only stone that comes into existence (as in the case of, for example, Afghanistan 1875 1s., where the stamps were printed direct from the stone upon which the designs were hand-drawn) or may be several stages removed from the first stone (as in the case of, for example, India 1854 ½a., where the design was, as a preliminary, engraved on copper then transferred and re-transferred and multiplied through the medium of more than one stone intermediate between the first stone and the printing stone). In appropriate cases, sometimes the terms "Tertiary Stone" or "Quaternary Stone" are used synonymously with "printing stone." Sometimes, but confusingly, the term "Secondary Stone" is used synonymously with "printing stone" when the printing stone is built up by re-transfers from a primary stone — see "Intermediate Stone." The printing stone is said to be "built up" by the steps undertaken in obtaining the necessary number of subjects for it — see "Transfer Stone."

Printing Stone Flaw. Colored or uncolored flaw. In reference to lithographed stamps the term "printing stone flaw" is used to designate a flaw first occurring on the printing stone — see "Flaw"; "Printing Stone." The term "Working Stone Flaw" is used synonymously with "printing stone flaw." The term "printing stone flaw" often includes, as appropriate, tertiary flaw or quaternary flaw — see "Tertiary Flaw"; "Quaternary Flaw." However, sometimes a distinction is drawn, and in such a case the term "printing stone flaw" is limited in meaning to a flaw occurring on the printing stone as a result of wear, damage, or retouch first happening after some printing has taken place, and excluding tertiary flaws or, as the case may be, quaternary flaws — see "Transfer Flaw"; in such cases, the printing stone flaw will appear only on later printed stamps, and at least two states of the printing stone will exist — see "State" in the alphabetical list to the chapter entitled "Printing Problems and Varieties." The lithographic flaws present on the printing stone comprise the aggregate of those that first appear on the printing stone (printing stone flaws) and those that are repeated on to it because of the use of such original and intermediate stones as were employed in building up the printing stone. Often the printing stone flaws are the most conspicuous of the flaws present on an individual stamp. It is important to remember that a printing stone flaw is constant and (after it has occurred and until such time as it is remedied, if at all) will occur on every sheet printed, whereas mere printing flaws are inconstant and occur substantially only on an individual sheet — although printing flaws may consist in the presence or absence of color and appear similar in form to printing stone flaws or other lithographic flaws.

Pull. In reference to lithography the term "pull" is used generically to designate a print in transfer ink upon transfer paper irrespective of whether the print is made from a plate or a stone — see "Transfer." When greater precision is necessary, the term may be qualified in use, as in "Primary Stone Pull," "Secondary Stone Pull," etc.

Quaternary Flaw. Colored or uncolored flaw. In reference to lithographed stamps, and when appropriate (which is rarely the case), the term "quaternary flaw" is used to designate a lithographic flaw arising during the transferring to the quaternary stone — see "Quaternary Stone." The quaternary flaws are the initial individual characteristics of each subject on the quaternary stone, and enable each stamp to be plated. In appropriate cases, on every stamp quaternary flaws aggregate with primary, secondary and tertiary flaws — see "Primary Flaw"; "Secondary Flaw"; "Tertiary Flaw." The term "quaternary flaw" is used synonymously with "transfer flaw" and to distinguish "printing stone flaw" — see "Printing Stone Flaw"; "Transfer Flaw."

Quaternary Stone. In reference to lithography the term "quaternary stone" is used to designate a lithographic stone upon which appears multiplications of the group of subjects that first occurs in that group on the tertiary stone — see "Tertiary Stone." The quaternary stone bears a laydown of re-transfers from the tertiary stone, and comprises a re-re-re-multiplication of the design — see "Laydown"; "Re-Transfer." Upon the quaternary stone appear the quaternary flaws that identify each subject in the sheet — see "Quaternary Flaw." The quaternary stone is the printing stone — see "Printing Stone"; contrast "Transfer Stone." Quaternary stones were used in the production of, for example, India 1854 ½a., Die I.

Report. In reference to lithography the term "report" is used rarely and as an anglicization of "bloc-report" — see "Bloc-Report."

Redrawn. Colored flaw. In reference to lithographed stamps the term "redrawn" is used to designate a stamp exhibiting evidence that an amendment has been made to part of a subject on stone for the purpose of improving a feature in the design. Frequently the term "Touch-In" is used synonymously with "redrawn" — but usually "redrawn" signifies a relatively substantial amendment, while "touch in" may include a relatively minute addition. An example of redrawing is to be found, for instance, in Sarawak 1875 (Jan. 1) 4c., right pane, stamp No. 67, where the frameline at the foot has been redrawn and appears uneven.

Retouch. Colored or uncolored flaw. Generally in reference to lithographed stamps the term "retouch" has two possible meanings: (1) in a generic sense, a flaw resulting from an alteration or repair effected to a particular subject on a printing stone or plate, or a stone used at an earlier stage during the building up of the printing stone or plate — in this sense, the term "retouch" embraces "touch-in," "touch-out," and "touch-up"; (2) a flaw resulting from photographically retouching any subject on any of such photographic plates or films as may come into existence during the production of a photolitho printing plate. In cases in which the subjects have been multiplied by the transferring process, and photography has played no part in building up the printing base, the question of photographic retouching does not arise in attempting to diagnose the cause of a flaw caused by retouching. However, in such cases — that is, when the question of photographic retouching does not arise — a distinction is sometimes drawn between (A) alterations or repairs effected before the printing base is printed from (in which case the flaw is normal for the subject affected), and (B) alterations or repairs effected after some printing has taken place (in which case, at least two states of the same subject may be encountered). The terminological distinction sometimes made is to restrict the use of the term "retouch" to designate an alteration or repair effected after some printing has taken place, and to use "touch-up" for pre-printing amendments. When greater precision is possible, the term "retouch" (or "touch-up") may be qualified in use, as in "primary (stone) retouch" (or "primary stone touch-up") and "secondary (stone) retouch" (or "secondary stone touch-up"), etc. — see "Touch-Up." It will usually be impossible with certainty to determine the stage at which a retouch was made on a photolitho printing plate if only one such plate came into existence; however, the fact of its occurrence is an indication that the

Lithography. Redrawn and touch-in. Sarawak 1875 (Jan. 1) 4c. At top: right pane, stamp No. 67. At center: right pane, stamp No. 77. At bottom: left pane, stamp No. 77.

"Redrawn." At top, the stamp shows the variety "redrawn." The frameline at the foot of this subject was redrawn, and appears uneven on the stamp.

"Touch-in." At bottom (only part of the stamp is visible), the stamp shows the variety "touch-in." The top line of the southwest corner square appears thickened at the left where the lithographer touched-in to complete the line. Above this, the base of the trelliswork column appears crudely finished where the lithographer touched-in to complete the missing portion.

At center, this stamp shows no variety, and is provided for purposes of comparison only, being the same "type" as that upon which the touch-in appears.

retouch has a photographic origin, because amendments to a photolitho printing plate are rarely made. In cases in which more than one printing plate was made from the same photographic plate, accurate determination is reasonably possible; because, if the retouch has a photographic origin, the retouch (or some other evidence) will appear on subjects similarly positioned on sheets printed from the different plates. Retouching may result in the presence of excess color ("touch-in") or the absence of color ("touch-out") on the resultant stamp, depending upon (i) in lithography, the nature of the operation — for example, (a) the drawing or painting in of broken or missing lines ("touch-in"), or (b) the removal of an unwanted area of grease ("touch-out"); and (ii) in photolithography (c) the bleaching of darkened emulsion, or the painting on a photographic plate or film of an opaque or darkening retouching medium, *and* (d) the stage of the process at which the retouching is effected — see "Touch-In"; "Touch-Out." Occasionally, during the same process of retouching, a touch-in follows a touch-out. See also "Repair" in the alphabetical list to the chapter entitled "Printing Problems and Varieties" and "Retouch" in the alphabetical list to the chapter entitled "Intaglio Printing — II: Gravure."

Re-Transfer. In reference to lithography the term "re-transfer" is used to designate the process or result of transferring from a subject that itself has been transferred — see "Transfer." A re-transfer on stone is at least two, and may be several, stages removed from the original.

Scum. Colored flaw. In reference to lithographed stamps the term "scum" is used to designate a stamp that exhibits color in what should be an uncolored portion of the design because, during printing, insufficient moisture was applied to the stone or plate before it was inked, with the result that the grease in the ink adhered to what should have been a damp portion of the stone or plate. Because of the cause of the variety, sometimes the term "Dry Print" is used synonymously with "scum." Such varieties can occur both on ordinary and "deep" offset plates. The unwanted area of grease can usually be removed from the plate by subjecting it to a further etching; if the scum is removed after some printing has taken place, at least two states of the plate will result: (a) with scum; (b) scum removed. Philatelic diagnosis of the cause of such a variety can rarely be made with certainty. An instance of scum is to be found on Israel 1952 (Sep. 3) New Year 110p., plate 53, row 3, stamp No. 1 where, in the earlier printings, the line representing the left of the left reed is interrupted near the center, and the line representing the right side of the left mount is interrupted near the junction with the right mount; in later printings both these defects are absent.

Secondary Flaw. Colored or uncolored flaw. In reference to lithographed stamps, and when appropriate, the term "secondary flaw" is used to designate a lithographic flaw arising during the transferring to the secondary stone — see "Secondary Stone." Secondary flaws characterize each subject on the secondary stone, and repeat at every subsequent multiplication from it. Secondary flaws identify the "sub-types" — that is, each "sub-type" exhibits several or, perhaps, many different secondary flaws which certainly in aggregate and in fact individually are peculiar to that "sub-type" only — see "Flaw"; "Type." In appropriate cases, any stamp bearing secondary flaws bears also primary flaws — see "Primary Flaw." On a sheet of stamps on which secondary flaws appear, they occur more frequently than any other class of flaw except primary flaws and "die flaws" — as often as each "sub-type" is repeated in the sheet.

Secondary Palimpsest — see "Palimpsest."

Lithography. Scum or dry print. Israel 1952 (Sep. 3) New Year 110p., plate 53, stamp No. 11 (row 3, subject 1), early printing showing variety caused by "scum" or "dry print," and the same stamp from later printing with normal design. The stamps were printed by the "deep" offset process.

In the early printings, in the left-hand reed the left line is interrupted near the center (below the wing), and the line representing the right slope of the left mount is interrupted near the junction with the right mount. The variety was caused (probably during the initial preparation of the plate for printing) because the plate was insufficiently dampened, and what should have been an uninked area of the plate picked up grease present in the ink and, via the blanket, deposited it on the paper.

The variety was corrected when the plate was "given an etch" — that is, while on the press, the plate (or part of it) was wiped over with a sponge damp with an appropriate acid solution; this had the effect of removing the unwanted grease. The plate was then given further treatment, and the subsequent printings reveal no trace of the "scum" or "dry print."

Secondary Stone. In reference to lithography the term "secondary stone" is used to designate a lithographic stone upon which appears multiplications of the group of subjects that first occurs as a group on the primary stone — see "Primary Stone." The secondary stone bears a laydown of re-transfers from the primary stone, and comprises a re-multiplication of the design — see "Laydown"; "Re-Transfer." Upon the secondary stone first appear the secondary flaws that identify the "sub-types" — see "Secondary Flaw." The secondary stone sometimes bears regular repetitions of the "types" appearing on the primary stone; but sometimes the repetitions are irregular — see "Substituted Transfer"; "Transfer Cuts." Use of the term "secondary stone" to designate a printing stone built up solely by re-transferring from a primary stone is inapt — see "Intermediate Stone"; "Printing Stone"; "Transfer Stone."

371

Secondary Substituted Transfer — see "Substituted Transfer."

Squeezed Transfer. Uncolored flaw. This term is used synonymously with "creased transfer" — see "Creased Transfer."

Stabbed Transfer. Uncolored flaw. In reference to lithographed stamps the term "stabbed transfer" is used to designate a stamp bearing a design incomplete because of an uncolored flaw occurring as the result of the lithographer's stabbing through an area of grease on the transfer when patching up subjects or groups of subjects on a base sheet — see "Base Sheet"; "Patching"; "Stabbing"; "Transfer." The variety is constant. An example of stabbed transfer is to be found in Suez Canal 1868 40c., stamp No. 26, where the stabbing has resulted in a break between the vertical and horizontal framelines at the southeast corner.

Stabbing. In reference to lithography the term "stabbing" is used to describe the process whereby a lithographer lightly affixes transfers in position on a base sheet by pushing a needle point through the superimposed transfer and base sheet — see "Base Sheet"; "Patching"; "Transfer." Because stabbing disturbs the substance of the transfer paper and its surface, the lithographer must be careful not to stab through an area of grease; if he does not avoid all such areas, the grease will not transfer to the stone, any affected design will be incomplete, and a stabbed transfer will result — see "Stabbed Transfer."

Stone. In reference to lithography the term "the stone" is sometimes used as synonymous with "the printing stone" — see "Printing Stone"; see also "(Color) Stone."

Stone-to-Stone Transfer. In reference to lithography the term "stone-to-stone transfer" is used to designate a stone transfer specially made to be and in fact transferred to a stone or a lithographic printing plate — see "Transfer"; "Stone Transfer"; compare "Plate-to-Stone Transfer." A stone-to-stone transfer may be a pull from a primary, secondary or tertiary stone, as the case may be.

Stone Transfer. In reference to lithography the term "stone transfer" is used to designate a transfer comprising a pull from a stone — see "Pull"; "Transfer."

Substituted Transfer. In reference to lithographed stamps the term "substituted transfer" is used to designate a stamp bearing flaws or the absence of flaws that, in combination with other evidence, prove that a transfer of a subject was replaced by another either on a base sheet or on a stone — compare "Substituted Subject" in the alphabetical list to the chapter entitled "Printing Problems and Varieties"; see "Transfer"; "Base Sheet." The other evidence referred to above will depend upon the steps taken to prepare the printing base and the stage at which the substitution occurred. A substitution may occur: (a) during the building up of the printing base — this is termed "Primary Substituted Transfer"; or (b) after the printing base has been built up, and, perhaps, printed from — this is termed "Secondary Substituted Transfer." A primary substituted transfer is brought about by the lithographer cutting out from a group transfer a defective subject and replacing it by a satisfactory subject which is then patched in place on the base sheet — see "Base Sheet"; "Group Transfer"; "Patching"; "Transfer." That substitution has occurred can be deduced when the regular repetition of the "types" or "sub-types" is disturbed in the position affected — but see "Transfer Cuts." In the case of primary substituted transfer there is not, on that account, more than one state of the printing base — see "State" in the alphabetical list to the chapter entitled "Printing Problems and Varieties." A secondary substituted transfer is brought about by the lithographer replacing on the original or printing stone a subject which is defective or has become damaged — see "Printing Stone." That this substitution has occurred may be deduced by variation in alignment or, perhaps, disturbance of the regular repetition of the "types" or "sub-types" at the position affected. If printing has taken place from the printing base before the substitution was made, at least two states of the printing base will have resulted. Examples of secondary substituted transfer are to be found, for instance, in Western Australia 1854 4d., stamp Nos. 141, 146, 151 and 156 which replaced the "Inverted Swans" that previously occupied those positions and that resulted from four stone-to-stone transfers of a bloc-report of sixty subjects in which the "Inverted Swan" occupied one position.

Sub-Type — see "Type."

Tertiary Flaw. Colored or uncolored flaw. In reference to lithographed stamps, and when appropriate, the term "tertiary flaw" is used to designate a lithographic flaw arising during the transferring to the tertiary stone — see "Tertiary Stone"; "Transfer." Tertiary flaws characterize each subject on the tertiary stone, and repeat at every multiplication from it. In cases in which multiplications are made of the group of subjects as a group from the tertiary stone (see "Quaternary Stone"), tertiary flaws identify the "sub-sub-types" — that is, each "sub-sub-type" exhibits several or, perhaps, many different tertiary flaws which certainly in aggregate and in fact individually are peculiar to that "sub-sub-type" only — see "Flaw"; "Type." In appropriate cases, any stamp bearing tertiary flaws bears also secondary and primary flaws — see "Primary Flaw"; "Secondary Flaw." In cases in which no multiplication is made of the group of subjects as a group from the tertiary stone, and the tertiary stone is used as the printing stone, the term "tertiary flaw" is used synonymously with "transfer flaw" and to distinguish "printing stone flaw" — see "Printing Stone Flaw"; "Transfer Flaw."

Tertiary Stone. In reference to lithography the term "tertiary stone" is used to designate a lithographic stone upon which appears multiplications of the group of subjects that first occurs in that group on the secondary stone — see "Secondary Stone." The tertiary stone bears a laydown of re-transfers from the secondary stone, and comprises a re-re-multiplication of the design — see "Laydown"; "Re-Transfer." Upon the tertiary stone first appear the tertiary flaws that identify the "sub-sub-types" — see "Tertiary Flaw." The tertiary stone bears, usually, regular repetitions of the "types" and "sub-types" appearing on the secondary stone; but sometimes the repetitions are irregular — see "Substituted Transfer"; "Transfer Cut." Sometimes the tertiary stone is the stone from which the stamps are printed; it is then the printing stone, and the use of the term "sub-sub-type" to designate an individual subject in the sheet is unnecessary in most cases — see "Printing Stone"; "Tertiary Flaw." Sometimes the tertiary stone is an intermediate stone — see "Intermediate Stone (b)"; "Quaternary Stone." In such cases, the term "transfer stone" may be used in reference to the tertiary stone — see "Transfer Stone."

Torn Transfer — see "Creased Transfer."

Touch-In. Colored flaw. In reference to a lithographed stamp the term "touch-in" is used to designate a colored flaw present because of retouching at some stage of the lithographic or, as the case may be, photographic processes used in the preparation of the printing base — see "Retouch"; "Redrawn." It is to be noted that the term "touch-in" is descriptive of what is apparent, and is only partly diagnostic. Accurate determination of the nature of the operation and the stage at which it was carried out depends upon the possibility of determining the steps undertaken in the preparation of the printing base — see "Flaw." An instance of touch-in is to be found, for example, in Sarawak 1875 (Jan. 1) 4c.,

Lithography. Touch-in. Suez Canal 1868 20c., stamp No. 91, showing "touch-in." The "touch-in" occurs above the letters DE and consists of a pronounced curved mark where the lithographer attempted to complete the extremity of the center, and so mask the colorless flaw in the sea and the break in the frame of the center. (No attempt was made to remedy the defect that caused the north-west corner of that "E" to be missing.)

left pane, stamp No. 77, where, in the southwest corner, the touch-in takes the form of an uneven line completing the base of the column of trelliswork, and of supplying the left half of the top line of the corner square. Another instance of touch-in is to be found, for example, in Suez Canal 1868 20c., stamp No. 91, where, above "De," the touch-in takes the form of a pronounced curved dash completing the outer extremity of the center, and masking a colorless flaw in the sea and the break in the extremity of the center.

Touch-Out. Uncolored flaw. In reference to a lithographed stamp the term "touch-out" is used to designate an uncolored flaw present because of retouching at some stage of the lithographic or, as the case may be, photographic processes used in the preparation of the printing base — see "Retouch." It is to be noted that the term "touch-out" is descriptive of what is apparent, and is only partly diagnostic. Accurate determination of the nature of the operation and the stage at which it was carried out depends upon the possibility of determining the steps undertaken in the preparation of the printing base — see "Flaw." An instance of touch-out is to be found, for example, in Victoria 1850 (1854) Half-Length 3d. White Veils, where the shading from both sides of the veils was removed by retouching each of the twelve subjects on the primary stone. Another instance of touch-out is to be found, for example, in USA 1918-20 Offset Printing 3c., plate 9278, upper right pane, stamp No. 6, where the touch-out resulted in the absence of color (the "addition" of uncolored lines) in a colored flaw beneath "U.S.," the appropriate photographic retouching medium having been applied to the relevant photographic plate or film that was flawed because of a blister in the photographic emulsion — see "Blister."

Touch-Up. Colored or uncolored flaw. In reference to lithographed stamps the term "touch-up" is used generically to designate a touch-in or touch-out made at any stage of the preparation of the printing stone or plate before any printing has taken place from it — see "Touch-In," "Touch-Out"; compare "Retouch"; see also "Printing Stone." When the stage at which a touch-up was effected can be ascertained, the term may be qualified in use, as in "Primary (Stone) Touch-Up," "Secondary (Stone) Touch-Up," etc.

A, B, C etc. = Types

1, 2, 3 etc. = Sheet Positions

——— = Transfer Cuts

A	B	C	D	E
F	G	H	I	K
L	M	N	O	P
Q	R	S	T	U
V	W	X	Y	Z

Transfer stone (twenty-five subjects).

Printing stone (144 subjects). Twenty-five types in sheet.

A 1	B 2	C 3	D 4	E 5	A 6	B 7	C 8	D 9	E 10	A 11	B 12
F 13	G 14	H 15	I 16	K 17	F 18	G 19	H 20	I 21	K 22	F 23	G 24
L 25	M 26	N 27	O 28	P 29	L 30	M 31	N 32	O 33	P 34	L 35	M 36
Q 37	R 38	S 39	T 40	U 41	Q 42	R 43	S 44	T 45	U 46	Q 47	R 48
V 49	W 50	X 51	Y 52	Z 53	V 54	W 55	X 56	Y 57	Z 58	V 59	W 60
A 61	B 62	C 63	D 64	E 65	A 66	B 67	C 68	D 69	E 70	C 71	D 72
F 73	G 74	H 75	I 76	K 77	F 78	G 79	H 80	I 81	K 82	H 83	I 84
L 85	M 86	N 87	O 88	P 89	L 90	M 91	N 92	O 93	P 94	N 95	O 96
Q 97	R 98	S 99	T 100	U 101	Q 102	R 103	S 104	T 105	U 106	S 107	T 108
V 109	W 110	X 111	Y 112	Z 113	V 114	W 115	X 116	Y 117	Z 118	X 119	Y 120
A 121	B 122	C 123	D 124	E 125	L 126	M 127	N 128	O 129	P 130	V 131	W 132
F 133	G 134	H 135	I 136	K 137	Q 138	R 139	S 140	T 141	U 142	X 143	Y 144

Transfer cuts. A typical arrangement of "types" resulting from building up a printing stone of 144 subjects from a transfer stone of twenty-five subjects.

Transfer. — See "Transfer" in the alphabetical list to the chapter entitled "Printing Problems and Varieties." In reference to lithography the technical meaning of the term "(lithographic) transfer" is anything that is capable of being transferred to a stone or a metal plate for the purpose of printing. There are two main classes of transfers: (a) transfers prepared or drawn by hand; and (b) transfers printed with transfer ink. A transfer drawn by hand, after being transferred, forms what is technically termed an "original" — see "Original." Printed transfers, usually, are used to build up a printing stone or plate — see "Plate Transfer"; "Re-Transfer"; "Stone Transfer."

Transfer Cuts. In reference to lithography the term "transfer cuts" is used to designate the disseverance of group transfers, sometimes rendered necessary because the next intermediate stone or the printing stone was not of an area capable of accommodating merely repetitions of the group transfers unaltered — see "Group Transfer"; "Intermediate Stone"; "Printing Stone." In such a case several group transfers were used whole, and the remaining printing area of the stone was filled in with appropriately shaped portions cut from another group transfer or other group transfers. In this manner, a stone might comprise, for example, 144 subjects (twelve across, twelve down) composed of four repetitions unaltered of a group of twenty-five subjects (to make ten by ten) with the remaining subjects supplied from two group transfers; the transfer cuts resulting in four groups of ten subjects (two being five across, two down, and two being two across, five down), with the remaining four subjects derived from two horizontal or vertical

375

pairs out of the two strips of five — all that remained from the six group transfers that were originally printed. In such a case the stone thus built up would show, for example, (a) in the top row, a regular repetition of "types" for subjects 1 to 5 and 6 to 10, with, probably, two of those "types" again repeated in subjects 11 and 12; (b) in the left-hand column a regular repetition of "types" for subjects 1, 13, 25 etc. to 109, with, probably, two of those "types" again repeated in subjects 121 and 132; (c) the block of four subjects in the southeast corner would comprise four "types" combined vertically or horizontally in a manner found nowhere else on the stone. In other cases group transfers have been dissevered for other reasons, and the transfer cuts have resulted in no regular order of "types" anywhere on the stone.

Transfer Flaw. Colored or uncolored flaw. In reference to lithographed stamps the term "transfer flaw" is used generically to designate a lithographic flaw arising from transferring at any stage of the process of building up a printing base — see "Flaw"; "Transfer." The term "transfer flaw" is, sometimes, used to draw a distinction between such a flaw and one arising from damage or repair to or inherent defect in a stone or plate — see "Printing Stone Flaw."

Transfer Fold. Uncolored flaw — see "Creased Transfer."

Transfer Squeeze. Uncolored flaw — see "Creased Tranfer."

Transfer Stone. In reference to lithography the term "transfer stone" is used generically to designate a stone to which have been transferred designs for the purpose of their being re-transferred to another stone or other stones — see "Intermediate Stone"; "Original Stone"; "Re-Transfer"; "Primary Stone"; "Secondary Stone"; "Tertiary Stone." From the transfer stone, directly or intermediately, the printing stone is built up. Printing stones, being large, were costly, and their use was rarely limited to one issue or printing of a stamp; consequently it was a frequent occurrence for the designs to be removed, and the printing stone to be used for some different work. In such cases, the transfer stone would be carefully preserved for future use in re-transferring the designs it bore, so that when necessary a new printing stone might be built up. Such practices account for the occurrence, in some cases, of identical or almost identical "types" or, as the case may be, "sub-types" from demonstrably different printing stones; and also, when combined with variations in transfer cuts, account for the occurrence of different settings. See "Transfer Cuts"; "Setting" in the alphabetical list to the chapter entitled "Printing Problems and Varieties." Occasionally the terms "key stone," and "original stone" are used synonymously with "transfer stone" — see "Key Stone"; "Original Stone."

Trimmed Transfer. Uncolored flaw — see "Clipped Transfer."

Type. See "Type (1)" in the alphabetical list to the chapter entitled "Printing Problems and Varieties." In reference to lithographed stamps the term "type," strictly used, is applied only to a stamp that differs from another stamp because of lithographic flaws arising during the primary stone stage of building up a printing stone — see "Flaw"; "Primary Stone"; "Printing Stone." Often the term "type" is used loosely and applied to a lithographically printed stamp that differs from another because each design was separately drawn or engraved; but the better usage is to distinguish such variations by the term "Design-Type." Sometimes, also, the term "type" is applied to each subject on a printing stone built up directly by separate transfers from a single subject, but the better usage is to refer to such a printing stone as having only one "type" repeated the relevant number of times. In many cases a printing stone has been built up in stages by use of a primary stone, secondary stone, and, occasionally, tertiary stone; in such cases the "types" are characterized by the lithographic flaws first occurring on the primary stone; the lithographic flaws first occurring on the secondary stone characterize the "sub-types" (see "Secondary Stone"); the "sub-sub-types" are characterized by the lithographic flaws first occurring on the tertiary stone (see "Tertiary Stone").

Working Stone — see "Printing Stone."

Working Stone Flaw — see "Printing Stone Flaw."

10. Addendum

Multiplying the Design by the Transferring Process

Stage 1, the 'Original'

STAGE 1 CONSISTS of either (a) a stone bearing a design drawn either directly upon the stone or else upon transfer paper and then transferred to stone, and is termed by printers "the original," or "the original stone"; or (b) an original engraving on metal, or sometimes on stone, or a relief-printing surface, either specially made for the purpose or previously used for a different purpose, and is termed by printers "the original engraving" or "the plate," and by philatelists "the die."

Any flaw, colored or uncolored, or variation from the intended norm on this original in fact forms part (albeit an unintended part) of the design itself, and will recur at every subsequent multiplication from Stage 1. Such flaws or variations from intended norm are referred to as "die flaws," or, more shortly, "die" — see "Die (2)" in the alphabetical list to the chapter entitled "Printing Problems and Varieties." Such flaws have no philatelic significance in relation exclusively to stamps resulting from such an original or original engraving. However, in a wider connection, such flaws may be philatelically significant — such as where two similar but minutely differing designs have as their respective originals or original engravings that themselves derive from a common origin anterior to Stage 1 in this illustration. In such a case, the minutely differing designs are, sometimes, separately identified as "Die I" and "Die II," or by some other appropriate identification. In view of the significance attaching to the term "type" (see Stage 2), that term unqualified is usually avoided by students in reference to Stage 1, but is sometimes used, qualified, as in "Design Type I," etc. However, the standard general catalogues do not make this distinction; and, in cases where such variations are noted, the unqualified terms "Type I," etc. are used in the sense of "Design Type I," etc. — see "Type (2)" in the alphabetical list to the chapter entitled "Printing Problems and Varieties."

Stage 2, the Primary Stone

Stage 2, *the first intermediate stone*, is a stone that bears the first multiplication of the design, and results from the transfer of prints on lithographic transfer paper to this stone. Philatelically these prints are referred to generically as "pulls." The steps taken to obtain these pulls depend upon the nature of Stage 1; and, strictly speaking, the term applied to the stone at Stage 2 varies with the steps taken to obtain the pulls. They may be obtained by (i) lithography, or (ii) intaglio or relief printing in special transfer ink.

(i) The pulls (for Stage 2) are obtained by lithography when Stage 1 resulted in a stone bearing a lithographic design. Printers refer to such pulls as "re-transfers" (for the obvious reason that they are transfers of transferred designs), and, in this event, refer to the stone at Stage 2 as "the intermediate stone," or, in the series of operations occurring in this illustration, "the first intermediate stone," or, sometimes, "the transfer stone."

(ii) The pulls (for Stage 2) are obtained by intaglio or relief printing when Stage 1 consists not of a stone but of an original engraving on metal or stone, or a relief-printing surface. Printers refer to such pulls as "plate transfers," and, in these events, refer to the stone at Stage 2 as "the original stone."

Although philatelic usage is not standard in reference to the stone at Stage 2, the term "primary stone" is widely employed philatelically in this connection, and avoids the difficulties arising from the varying uses of and meanings attaching to "original stone."

Most of the excess paper around the design on each pull is trimmed away, and the trimmed pulls are, usually, arranged and affixed face upward to a piece of paper of convenient size. This arranging and affixing of the pulls is termed "patching," and the piece of paper is termed a "base sheet," or "patching sheet." The pulls are affixed to and kept in position on the patching sheet either by a special paste, or else by a process known as "pricking through" or "stabbing" — that is, at several positions on each pull (of course, usually avoiding the colored portions of the design), a needle point is pushed through the superimposed transfer paper and patching sheet and then removed, leaving the two pieces of paper adhering to one another. This assemblage, for which a short descriptive term in English is wanting, is termed in French "bloc-report." The patching sheet with the adherent pulls is then turned face down on to the primary stone, and the designs are transferred to it in the press.

This transference or printing of the pulls on to the primary stone is called "laying down," and the group of subjects on the primary stone is, sometimes, termed "a laydown." Printers refer to the transference as a "stone-to-stone transfer," or as a "plate-to-stone transfer," depending upon the nature of Stage 1.

The printing of these pulls and their subsequent transference to the "primary stone" inevitably give rise to flaws, colored and uncolored, which recur or repeat at every subsequent multiplication from the "primary stone." These flaws are termed, philatelically, "primary flaws." Sometimes a flaw is of such a nature as to warrant correction or attempted remedy by

378

retouching, and this may be carried out directly to the "primary stone"; the effect of such retouching is termed a "primary (stone) retouch," or a "primary (stone) touch-up." The individual characteristics of each subject on the "primary stone" are the distinguishing characteristics of the "types."

Philatelic usage is to refer to the "types" by number or alphabetically as they would appear on a print from the "primary stone," and not in the order in which they appear on the stone itself; and this usage has been adopted in the drawings for this illustration (Page 383).

Stage 3, the Secondary Stone

Stage 3, *the second intermediate stone,* is a stone that bears the first multiplication from Stage 2 and, consequently, the re-multiplication of the design, and results from the transfer to the stone at Stage 3 of pulls from the stone at Stage 2. The term applied by printers to the stone at Stage 3 depends upon their terminology for the stone at Stage 2. If Stage 2 comprises an "intermediate stone," Stage 3 is termed "the second intermediate stone"; if Stage 2 comprises an "original stone," Stage 3 is termed "the intermediate stone," or, sometimes, "the transfer stone."

Again, although philatelic usage is not standard in reference to the stone at Stage 3, the term "secondary stone" is widely employed in this connection, and avoids the necessity for numerical qualification when "intermediate stone" is used.

A short descriptive term in English for an individual pull from the stone at Stage 2 has not acquired any wide philatelic use. Sometimes the terms "group transfer" and "multiple transfer" are used, and sometimes the French term "bloc-report" is employed. Attempts have been made to equate the French *report,* anglicized to "report," with the "bloc-report." Sometimes the phrases "intermediate stone pull," "intermediate transfer," and "primary stone pull" are used.

The "primary stone pulls" are arranged and affixed to a patching sheet, and the assembled designs are transferred to, or "laid down on" the "secondary stone."

Again, the printing of each re-transfer comprising a "primary stone pull," and the subsequent transference of the designs on the assembled "primary stone pulls" to the "secondary stone" inevitably give rise to a new set of flaws, colored and uncolored, termed philatelically "secondary flaws," which aggregate with the "primary flaws," and will recur and repeat at every subsequent multiplication from the "secondary stone." These "secondary flaws" are the individual characteristics of each subject on the "secondary stone," and are the distinguishing characteristics of the "sub-types." Consequently, each subject on the "secondary stone" will exhibit (a) "primary flaws" ("types"), which enable the arrangement of the "primary stone" to be deduced, and which, in this illustration at Stage 3, are identically repeated on four subjects — for instance, I i, I ii, I iii, and I iv; or II i, II ii, II iii and II iv; etc.; and (b) "secondary flaws" ("sub-types"), which enable each of the otherwise identical designs (for instance, I) to be allocated to its group (i, ii, iii or iv).

If the printing and patching of the "primary stone pulls" is satisfactorily carried out, the "secondary stone" will bear the "types" regularly repeated and recurring in the order in which they appear on the "primary stone" — as in this illustration. However, should any subject on any pull be unsatisfactory, it can be cut out from the pull, and the vacant space on the patching sheet be filled by a subject cut from an additional pull. This procedure of substituting a transfer gives rise, in this instance, to a "secondary stone substituted transfer." If this is of a different "type" from the one it replaces, it follows that, on the stone at Stage 3, the regular order of "types" will be disturbed, and that at the position affected they will appear, for example, as IV, II, III, IV; in the other positions, the normal order will obtain. Even if such a "secondary stone substituted transfer" is of the same "type" as the one it replaces, the likelihood is that its alignment will differ, perhaps only minutely, from that of the one it replaces, and so the substitution can be detected philatelically. Of course, such substitution need not be limited to only a single subject.

Any retouching at Stage 3 will result in a "secondary stone retouch," or "secondary stone touch-up."

Stage 4, the Printing Stone

Stage 4 is the stone that is used for printing, thus "the printing stone." The printing stone results from the transfer to it of pulls from the stone at Stage 3. The printing stone bears multiplication from Stage 3, and, consequently, re-multiplication from Stage 2, and re-re-multiplication of the design. The printing stone is termed also "the working stone," and, sometimes, "the tertiary stone."

The "secondary stone pulls" (for Stage 4) are arranged and affixed to a patching sheet, and the assembled designs are transferred to, or "laid down on" the printing stone.

The preceding processes of transferring and re-transferring and patching, which result in the printing stone, are referred to as "building up" the stone.

Once again, the printing of each re-transfer comprising a "secondary stone pull" and the subsequent transference of the designs on the assembled "secondary stone pulls" to the printing stone inevitably give rise to a new set of flaws, colored and uncolored, termed philatelically "tertiary flaws," which aggregate with the "secondary flaws" and "primary flaws," but which will not repeat and recur, as no subsequent multiplication is made to stone of the designs on the printing stone. These "tertiary flaws" are the initial individual characteristics of each subject on the printing stone, and are the distinguishing characteristics of the "sub-sub-types." Consequently, each subject on the printing stone will exhibit: (a) "primary flaws" ("types"), which will enable the arrangement of the "primary stone" to be deduced, and which, in this illustration, are identically represented on eight subjects (at Stage 4), for instance, positions 2, 4, 6, 8, 18, 20, 22, and 24; (b) "secondary flaws" ("sub-types") which will enable the arrangement on the "secondary stone" to be deduced, for instance, positions 2, 4, 18 and 20; and (c) "tertiary flaws" ("sub-sub-types") which enable each of the otherwise identical designs (for instance II i, II ii, II iii, and II iv) to be allocated to its group (A or B). Thus, for example, the subject numbered 24 in this illustration is "sub-sub-type B of sub-type iv of Type II of the design." Sometimes these tertiary flaws are termed "final flaws," and the primary and secondary flaws are termed "intermediate flaws."

By reference exclusively to the "tertiary flaws," the subjects may be "plated" (given adequate material), but the manner in which the printing stone was built up can be deduced only if regard is paid to the "primary flaws" and "secondary flaws."

Thus, in this illustration it will be seen from the drawings at Stage 4 that, if the subjects were to be cut out and detached from each other, the most frequently occurring feature would be the star representing the design, or "die." Upon the assumption that all that is available for study is a large number, say 800 of these individual subjects, and that no circumstances of the production are known except that the printing method has been identified as lithography, the possible deductions and reasons are as follows:

Further examination of the individual subjects would reveal that the next most frequently occurring features are the "primary flaws" so that the subjects can all be assorted into four groups, each limited to one "Type," and each group containing 200 subjects. From this and a knowledge of lithographic procedures it can be deduced that, during the lithographic production, there was a stone bearing four copies of the design. From a comparison of the designs on each of the subjects, and by noting that each subject differs from the others not in the essentials of the design but in lithographic flaws, it is possible further to deduce that the four copies stemmed from a single original — whether a drawing or an engraving is immaterial for this purpose. What cannot be deduced at this stage (or at any other stage without material other than singles) is how the four copies were arranged on the stone — whether in a vertical or horizontal strip or in a block, or their order.

Upon further examination of each of these four groups it would be seen that each group can be divided into four, by reference to the "secondary flaws," each of these groups containing fifty subjects. There are, therefore, sixteen groups of fifty subjects each. It is possible to deduce that there was a further stone bearing four reproductions of the arrangement on the stone, each bearing the four copies of the design; but again it is impossible to deduce either arrangement.

Yet further examination of each of these sixteen groups would reveal that each group can be divided into two, by reference to the "tertiary flaws," each group containing twenty-five subjects. There are, therefore, thirty-two groups of twenty-five subjects each. It is possible to deduce that there was yet a further stone bearing two transfers, the one reproducing the arrangement on the other; but yet again no actual arrangement can be deduced.

Yet more examination of each of these thirty-two groups would reveal that they cannot be further divided into groups, and the implication is that the sheets contained thirty-two subjects.

No further progress can be made with individual subjects. The steps in the process have been deduced, but before any other inferences can be made it is necessary to have multiples in sufficient number to enable the arrangement on at least part of the printing stone to be ascertained.

It is most unlikely that, in the practical study of a lithographed stamp, material would be limited to singles; usually multiples are available to assist in deducing the transferring procedures that were used. The most frequently encountered flaws are the "primary flaws" (when, indeed, they are present), and, broadly speaking, the most prominent flaws are the "tertiary flaws" (which are always present). However, it is, generally speaking, not safe to make, about the procedure, deductions based alone on the numbers of stamps exhibiting particular flaws.

NOTE: This illustration is no more than an outline of one of the ways in which a printing stone may be built up, and of some terms and varieties that may be encountered in philatelic writings.

The procedures that have been adopted in building up different stones vary widely; as instances — some consist merely of a "plate transfer" from a line-engraved plate direct to the printing stone; others comprise a bloc-report of the requisite number of "plate transfers" from an engraved die direct to the printing stone; and still others involve bloc-reports in which each subject consists of portions of different transfers assembled to make the design.

Furthermore, the illustration shows a regular repetition of all the types. By no means does this invariably obtain. In many cases printing stones have been built up from "group transfers" that sometimes contain all the "types" and sometimes are divided in various ways before being attached to a patching sheet; so that, for example, a horizontal strip of, say, six stamps might contain Types I, II, I, I, III and III in that order — not because of "substituted transfers" but because the "group transfers" were, for one reason or another, cut unevenly.

Also, although some varieties have been referred to in this illustration, no mention has been made here of numerous others that occur in the lithographic processes of building up a stone, nor of the varieties that can occur on the printing stone itself either before or during its use.

Each lithographed stamp or issue must be studied by reference to the evidence presented by the stamps themselves about the particular steps undertaken in its preparation. And when attempts are made to diagnose the cause of a variation from the norm, that evidence must be considered in the light of the possibilities and limitations of the lithographic method of printing.

Multiplying the Design
by the Transferring Process

▶ STAGE 1
(The Original)

▶ STAGE 2
(The Primary Stone)   The first intermediate stone.

▶ STAGE 3
(The Secondary Stone)   The second intermediate stone.

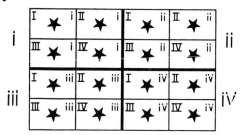

▶ STAGE 4
(The Printing Stone)

A				B			
I ★ i A 1	II ★ i A 2	I ★ ii A 3	II ★ ii A 4	I ★ i B 5	II ★ i B 6	I ★ ii B 7	II ★ ii B 8
III ★ i A 9	IV ★ i A 10	III ★ ii A 11	IV ★ ii A 12	III ★ i B 13	IV ★ i B 14	III ★ ii B 15	IV ★ ii B 16
I ★ iii A 17	II ★ iii A 18	I ★ iv A 19	II ★ iv A 20	I ★ iii B 21	II ★ iii B 22	I ★ iv B 23	II ★ iv B 24
III ★ iii A 25	IV ★ iii A 26	III ★ iv A 27	IV ★ iv A 28	III ★ iii B 29	IV ★ iii B 30	III ★ iv B 31	IV ★ iv B 32

KEY: I, II etc. = Primary flaws : "Types"
i, ii etc. = Secondary flaws : "Sub-types"
A, B   = Tertiary flaws : "Sub-sub types"
1,2,3,4,5 etc.= Sheet positions

11. Embossing

PHILATELICALLY CONSIDERED, the term "embossing," which involves distortion of the paper in the shape of the design or part of it, is used generically in reference to several processes that are known variously by printers under a variety of names. These processes may be divided into two broad classes: (1) embossing without the use of color at the moment when the reliefs are raised, termed "die plain"; and (2) embossing with the use of color at the moment when the reliefs are raised, termed "relief stamping." Relief stamping comprises two effects: (a) where the reliefs are colorless, which is, frequently, termed "cameo stamping"; and (b) where the reliefs raised are in color, which is, frequently, termed "die stamping."

Both broad classes have been used for stamp production, and each class may comprise either the production of one subject at one operation of the press, or the production of a sheet of subjects at one operation of the press. Philatelically speaking, when the subject is uncolored, the term usually employed is "embossing in colorless relief." Sometimes technical works devoted to graphic arts define die stamping as "a form of printing with all characters in relief," and embossing as "raising above the surface of the paper letters or designs previously printed." However, so far as stamp production is concerned, the actual embossing is almost invariably uncolored, and, when color is present, it lies on those portions of the paper that are not distorted upward when viewing the face of the stamp.[1] In that sense, therefore, stamps are, almost invariably, embossed in colorless relief, whether or not color has been used in their production. The subject of terminology is further discussed later in this chapter under the heading "Terminology."

Philatelically considered, by far the greatest use of embossing is to be encountered in postal stationery, especially in envelopes. But many issues of adhesive postage stamps have been produced either by embossing alone, with or without color, or by embossing upon previously printed paper. Among these issues may be mentioned, by way of examples: Bavaria (Germany) 1876-79 3pf. to 2m.; Czechoslovakia 1918 (October) Scout Stamps 10h. and 20h.;[2] Gambia 1869-87 Cameos; Germany (Federal Republic) 1954 St. Boniface 1200th Anniversary 20(pf.); Great Britain 1847-54 6d., 10d. and 1s.; Natal 1857 (Jun. 1) 3d. to 1s.; Peru 1862 (Nov. 18) 1d.; Portugal 1853-84; Sar-

---

[1]See diagram "Embossing" in the chapter entitled "Printing Characteristics."
[2]*Scott's Standard Postage Stamp Catalogue* does not list these stamps, but they are listed in *Stanley Gibbons Priced Postage Stamp Catalogue* Part 5 as Czechoslovakia Nos. 1 and 2.

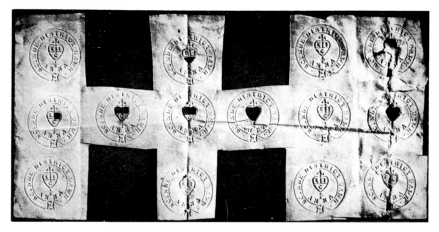

Embossing in colorless relief (die plain). Scinde (India) 1852 (Jul. 1) District Dawk ½a. white. Embossed, one impression at a time, upon sheets of paper. This irregular block of fourteen is the largest multiple known of the white stamp. (Eight stamps are damaged because the embossing caused pieces of the paper to break away — other stamps are imperfect because of creasing subsequent to embossing.)

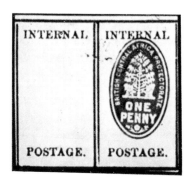

Embossing with color (cameo stamping). Nyasaland Protectorate (British Central Africa) 1898 Check Stamp 1d. se-tenant with error, center omitted.

Embossing in colorless relief (die plain). Natal 1857 (Jun. 1) 6d.

Embossing in colorless relief (die plain). Scinde (India) 1852 (Jul. 1) District Dawk ½a. scarlet. Embossed, one impression at a time, to form round wafers. Only singles of these stamps are known.

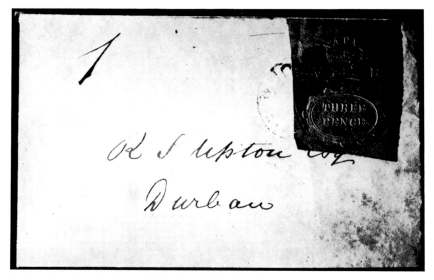

Embossing in colorless relief (die plain). Natal 1857 (Jun. 1) 3d. Probably the finest known example of this stamp used on cover.

dinia (Italy) Newspaper Stamps 1861 1c. and 2c.; Scinde (India) 1852 (Jul. 1) District Dawk ½a. white, blue, scarlet; Venezuela 1957 (Oct. 9) 125th Anniversary of the Death of Bolivar 5c. to 50c.; and Germany (West Berlin) 1982 (Apr. 15) Berlin Philharmonic Orchestra Centenary 60pf.

Many different methods have been employed in the production of embossed adhesive postage stamps — from the individual stamping of a small seal [as used for Scinde (India) 1852 (Jul. 1) District Dawk ½a. scarlet] to the stamping out of individual subjects from strips of paper [as used for Magura (Hungarian Hotel Posts) 1911 4f.]; from the stamping of impressions on long, narrow strips of paper [as in the case of Peru 1871 (April) 5c.] to the stamping of individual impressions one at a time upon a sheet of paper (as in the case of Great Britain 1847 1s.); and from the printing and embossing from one plate of a small sheet (for example, of fifteen subjects, as in the case of Gambia 1886-87 Cameos ½d. to 1s.) to the printing in two operations followed by embossing [as in the case of Schleswig-Holstein (Germany) 1850 (Nov. 15) 1s. and 2s.].

Nevertheless, all these various methods have this in common: that, at some period of time, the paper is pressed between either two dies — one in recess, and the other in relief — or a recessed die and a resilient or moulded surface, for the purpose of distorting the paper upward (toward the viewer of its face) in those portions of the design that are to be embossed. Very frequently, the height of the distortion is intended to be, and is, uniform throughout the design; occasionally, and particularly in the cases of portraits, the height of the distortion varies.

For many years, embossing was a "lost art" to the collector of adhesive postage stamps, but its use remained (and remains) widespread and frequent

Embossing with color (cameo stamping). Magura (Hungarian Hotel Post) 1911 4f. used in combination with Hungary 1900-1904 10f. on cover. The Magura stamp was produced by a process that punched the stamp from the paper, giving the effect of rouletting in color, so that only singles are known. A similar process was used in the production of Czechoslovakia 1918 (October) Scout Stamp 10h. and 20h.

Embossing with color (cameo stamping). Great Britain 1848 10d. impressed one at a time in sheets of twenty-four on a color embossing press (supplied by Dryden Brothers), with the spacing between impressions controlled by hand only. This often resulted in irregularity of alignment and overlapping of impressions. These four stamps are reasonably well-spaced.

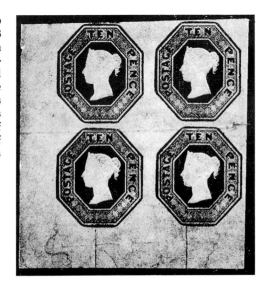

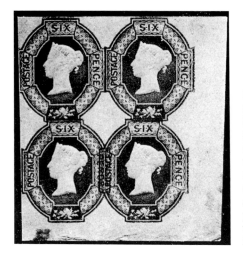

Embossing with color (cameo stamping). Great Britain 1854 6d. impressed one at a time in sheets of forty on a color embossing press (supplied by Dryden Brothers), with the spacing between impressions controlled by hand only. This often resulted in irregularity of alignment and overlapping of impressions. Multiples of this stamp with spaces on all four sides of each impression are not encountered.

in connection with postal stationery. However, in comparatively recent years there has been a recrudescence of embossed issues, stemming from the State Printing Works of Germany; and while the intricacies of this form of production may remain of interest primarily to the student of what are widely regarded as "classic" issues (no less than to the student of postal stationery), the collector of new issues also will find matters of interest in embossing — which first saw the light of day (philatelically speaking) on an adhesive postage stamp as long ago as Basel (Switzerland) 1845 (Jul. 1) 2½r. Basel Dove.

Various Types of Dies

In some cases, only a single engraving has been made and used directly for embossing, with or without color, in conjunction with what is termed a "force" or "counterpart" composed of metal or some plastic substance. More usually, however, the die from which the actual embossing and printing take place results from a more complex form of procedure — and many variations in procedures are possible. Therefore, before I go on to consider some of the embossing processes in greater detail, it will be convenient here to outline the steps undertaken in the production of a series of dies all having some features in common — such as are used, for example, in the production of several stamps with different face values.

What follows does not pretend to be a factual account of the steps undertaken in the production of a particular set of dies for a particular issue of either adhesive stamps or stationery. Little more is done than outline the processes, because variations in procedure inevitably occur in particular instances; and some of these variations are referred to when some of the embossing processes are discussed in greater detail. The accompanying diagrams and chart will make some of the possible variations readily appreciable.

Three main and one subsidiary type of die have to be considered: (1) the "master" die;[3] (1a) the "sub-master" die, or the "supplementary-master" die; (2) the "hub" or "hob" die; and (3) the "printing" or "working" die. Additionally, for the actual embossing and printing operation, some "force" or "counterpart" is required to work in conjunction with the printing (or working) die.

Of these types of dies, the master, the sub-master (or supplementary-master) and the printing (or working) die are, as a rule, recessed; the hob (or hub) die is in relief, as, almost invariably, is the force (or counterpart).

The Master Die

Before engraving, the blank master die comprises, usually, a cylinder of soft steel with one end highly polished ready to accept engraving; sometimes this end has been squared-off. Into this end, the engraver cuts the design in reverse and in deep recess — that is, he operates in a manner somewhat similar to that of the engraver of a die for intaglio printing line engraving, but with a different technique and cutting more deeply.

Further, generally speaking, what the engraver of an embossing die cuts away at this stage will eventually (if color is to be used in the production of the stamps) be uncolored and in relief, and what he leaves untouched will appear in color and on the unraised surface of the paper. To the generality of these statements there are exceptions; and, at later stages of the production, modifications can result in the intentional appearance of color in areas cut away by the engraver of the master die, and in the intentional absence of color in areas he has left untouched.

These exceptions apart, when the engraving of the master die is complete, the die represents the printing surface of those portions to be incorporated in the eventual printing (or working) die.

Proofs may be printed from the master die, either for the purpose of judging the accuracy of the colored areas — in which case, all that is necessary is to ink the unrecessed surface and print as for relief printing — or for the purpose of judging the progress of the engraving — in which case, it is necessary to make a special "force" of plaster of paris, leather, or some other substance. Sometimes the engraver will judge the progress of his work, not by taking proofs in the accepted sense, but by viewing the result of modeling wax forced into and removed from the die.

The master die often comprises only a feature that will be common to several different designs; only rarely will the master die contain the whole design.

Only on very rare occasions will further engraving work be done on the actual piece of metal that comprises the master die. When additions or modifications have to be made to the design, they are, almost invariably, carried out on a copy of the master die — that is, on a supplementary-master die.

---

[3]Because, usually, these dies are engraved in recess, it would seem more logical that the term "mother die" or "matrix" be used in this instance, and that, for "sub-master" and "supplementary master," some female rather than male connotation should be indicated. However, I follow the practice.

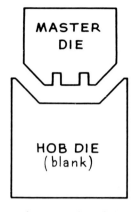 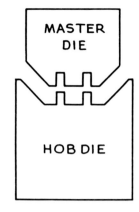

Before transfer of design. After transfer of design.

Sometimes a master die is an original engraving, as in the procedure outlined above; sometimes, however, the master die of a whole series of stamps comprises merely the transfer of a single feature from a previously existing die, the unwanted portions of the previous design having been removed by intermediate processes. In such cases, the better designation for the series-master die would seem to be "sub-master die."

When the master die has received all the intended portions of the design, the die is hardened by heat in the manner described under the heading "The Die" in the chapter entitled "Intaglio Printing — I: Line Engraving." The hardened master die is then used for making a hob die.

The Hob Die

The blank hob die is a large, usually cylindrical, piece of soft steel with a shallow depression in one end, into which the master die is placed. At first the unrecessed surface of the master die is in close contact with the flat surface at the base of the depression, and between that flat surface and the engraved areas of the master die are air spaces. However, the design is taken up on the hob by forcing the two dies into closer contact with one another, thus filling the air spaces with the soft metal of the hob, while the flat surfaces of the two dies remain unaffected.

Transference of the design from one die to another is effected, frequently, by presses similar in most respects to coining presses. The pressure involved, and the consequent alteration in metal structure, often result in the hob die becoming prematurely hardened, with the result that the hob die has to be annealed several times before the transference can be completed.

After the design has been fully taken up, the hob die is, or should be, an exact counterpart of the master die, the recesses of the master die being represented by corresponding reliefs on the hob die, and the design on the hob die reading normally from left-to-right. It is not unusual that the pressure involved in translating the recesses of the master die into the reliefs of the hob die should result in some surplus metal being squeezed up, so causing

(text continues on Page 394)

Diagrammatic Representation of Stages in Embossing and Printing Dies

STAGE I
Master Die

STAGE 2
Primary Hob Die

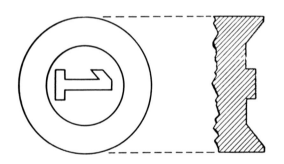

STAGE 3
Sub-master Die
(blank)

STAGE 4
Sub-master Die with
additional engraving
(completed)

STAGE 5
Hob Die
(blank)

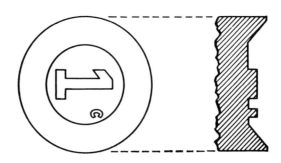

STAGE 6
Hob Die with some
reliefs removed
(completed)

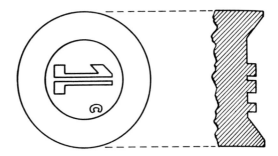

STAGE 7
Working Die
(blank)

STAGE 8
Working Die with
additional engraving
(completed)

STAGE 9
"Force" or "Counterpart" and
representation of embossed
and printed stamp, the uncolored
areas being in relief

certain imperfections in the design on the hob, and thus causing it not to be an exact counterpart of the master die. In such instances, it will be necessary for an engraver to work over the design on the hob, cutting away surplus metal and clearing up the imperfections. Such handwork inevitably leaves its traces visible; so that, not only are there minor differences between the hob and the master, but (where more than one hob is made from the same master) minor differences exist between one hob and another. These will be transmitted to the stamps resulting from the use of different hobs.

Proofs cannot be printed from hob dies.

Hob dies may be considered as falling into two classes: (a) primary hob dies, used for the production of sub-master or supplementary-master dies, and being the equivalent of the die matrix in relief printing; and (b) hob dies used for the production of working dies — often as many as or more than 100 — and being the equivalent of the subject matrix in relief printing.[4]

No engraving in recess can be carried out to the design on the hob die. However, additions and modifications may be made to the design by removing some of the reliefs, leaving the surface of the hob die unraised at those positions. The effect of such removal is to create, in the resultant stamp, a colored area where no color would have appeared (if the stamp is embossed and printed in color), or merely to cause the absence of part of the design (if the eventual stamps are embossed in colorless relief). The removal of reliefs from the hob die has often been effected for the purpose of adding colored letters to a ground bearing uncolored engine-turning. Such removal can be effected by cutting the metal away with engraving tools, or, sometimes, by the use of special letter-punches.

The usual manner of making a sub-master die that incorporates only one feature from a previously existing die is to make a hob die from the previously existing die, and then to remove from the hob die all the unwanted reliefs, leaving on it only those reliefs that will be required to make the recesses in the sub-master die. Further, it is not unusual for several hob dies to be made, and for certain features only to be removed from different hobs, so that they yield supplementary-master dies differing in design.

When the hob die has reached the required stage of transference, with or without the removal of reliefs and unwanted metal, it is hardened by heat in the manner described under the heading "The Die" in the chapter entitled "Intaglio Printing — I: Line Engraving." The hardened hob die is then used for making either one or more sub-master or supplementary-master dies, or else the required number of printing dies. If the hob die is to be used for making working dies, it is usual for more than one hob die to be made from the same master, the reason being that a hob die so used is subjected to oft-repeated very rough treatment. Although the hob die is massive and strong, it does eventually wear out or break down, so that the provision of spare hob dies is a normal precautionary measure. However, it is not usual for duplicate primary hob dies to be made, because they are used for comparatively few sub-masters.

---

[4]See "Punch" in the alphabetical list to the chapter entitled "Relief Printing."

Chart Representing Derivation
of Embossing and Printing Dies

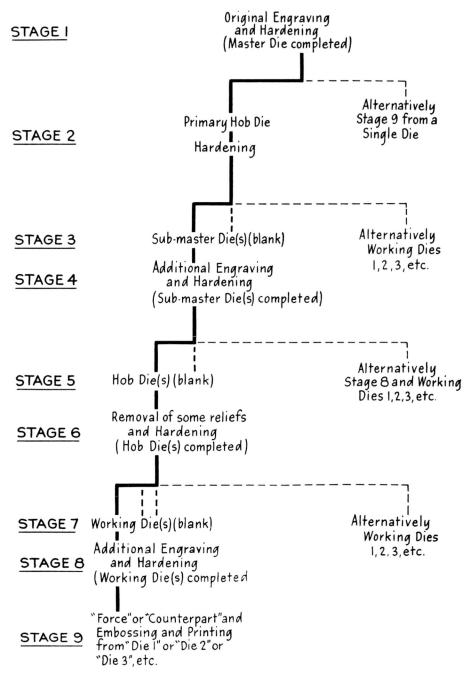

STAGE 1 — Original Engraving
and Hardening
(Master Die completed)

STAGE 2 — Primary Hob Die
Hardening

Alternatively
Stage 9 from a
Single Die

STAGE 3 — Sub-master Die(s)(blank)

STAGE 4 — Additional Engraving
and Hardening
(Sub-master Die(s) completed)

Alternatively
Working Dies
1,2,3,etc.

STAGE 5 — Hob Die(s)(blank)

STAGE 6 — Removal of some reliefs
and Hardening
(Hob Die(s) completed)

Alternatively
Stage 8 and Working
Dies 1,2,3,etc.

STAGE 7 — Working Die(s)(blank)

STAGE 8 — Additional Engraving
and Hardening
(Working Die(s) completed

Alternatively
Working Dies
1,2,3,etc.

STAGE 9 — "Force"or"Counterpart"and
Embossing and Printing
from "Die 1"or"Die 2"or
"Die 3",etc.

The Sub-Master Die

The blank sub-master die is, usually, a flat piece of soft steel, shaped so as to fit into the shallow depression of the hob die, and having one surface highly polished, ready to receive the transference of the design from the hob.

The first stage is to fit the sub-master die into the shallow depression; the polished surface of the sub-master rests on the reliefs of the design on the hob die, with air spaces between the unraised portions of the hob and the rest of the polished surface.

Next, pressure is brought to bear, applied in many cases in a coining press, and the reliefs of the hardened hob push into the soft metal of the sub-master. As in the case of the master and the hob, so in the case of the hob and sub-master, the pressure involved often results in the sub-master becoming prematurely hardened, so that it has to be annealed before the transference of the design can be completed.

The design on the sub-master die is reversed, and those portions that are to be uncolored and embossed are recessed, the colored portions being unrecessed.

Additions and modifications to the designs can be made on the sub-master die by engraving in recess for the purpose of adding uncolored or raised portions to the eventual stamps. Neither color nor unraised portions can be added to the design at this stage. Indeed, what has already been stated in reference to the master die applies equally to the sub-master die in regard to engraving and the taking of proofs, the main difference being that it is in no way abnormal for additional engraving to be carried out on a sub-master die.

When the design on the sub-master die has reached the required stage, it is hardened in the usual manner, described under the heading "The Die" in the chapter entitled "Intaglio Printing — I: Line Engraving," and is then used to make a hob die or several hob dies from which the working dies are made. Except for the additional portions of the design, such hob dies are exactly similar to primary hob dies.

The Working Die

The blank working die is similar in shape and properties to the sub-master die, and may be subjected to all the same treatments, with the same limitations. It is by no means unusual for additional engraving to be carried out directly to the working die, particularly in the form of adding (of course, uncolored) figures and letters either of value or to distinguish the die as one in a series.

The design on the working die is reversed, and those portions that are to be uncolored and embossed are recessed, the colored portions being unrecessed.

The precise shape and form of the working die will depend on the manner in which it is to be used, and the press for which it is intended; the die may itself be type high, or may be much thinner and mounted on a support to attain that height; alternatively it may be of a thickness bearing no relation to type height but determined by the requirements of the stamping press in which the die is to be used.

The Force or Counterpart

The force or counterpart, which is essential for the production of the embossing of the paper, is sometimes made of metal, but frequently consists of pasteboard (termed "force card"), leather, plaster or wax, and sometimes is merely a resilient material. As its name suggests, the counterpart or force is a counterpart of the die — the recesses of the die are represented by reliefs on the counterpart — and, often, the two are referred to as being, respectively, the "female die" and the "male die."

Frequently, for metal male dies, copper is used, and the male die is made by striking the female die on to a piece of semi-fused metal held in a collar, the striking pressure being applied by a drop hammer.

When pasteboard, cardboard or leather is used, the force is made by striking the female die repeatedly on to the material of the force so that it is made to take up the design.

For each working die, a separate or, rather, individual force is required.

Terminology

Having outlined the steps undertaken in the production of a series of dies having some features in common, I now turn to a closer consideration of some of the embossing processes. At this point, it is, perhaps, desirable to devote further attention to some aspects of terminology in connection with those processes.

By no means, even in the printing trade, is there unanimity in regard to definitions of the processes. What is accepted as axiomatic in practice by some houses is not understood in the same sense by others — and printers, die-stampers and embossers in general, usually, have to be at pains to make themselves unequivocally understood when referring to any special aspect of the different processes that the philatelist refers to, generically, as "embossing." Especially so is the corollary the case, and a philatelist speaking to a printer, die-stamper or embosser must be extremely careful to ensure that the terms employed are not used in a conflicting sense by the other party to the conversation.

Reference has already been made to some definitions of "embossing" and "die stamping" in technical works devoted to graphic arts; and, generally speaking, the primary difference between embossing and relief stamping consists in, respectively, the absence or presence of color in or on the female die. However, that is not the whole story, and similar and closely allied but distinct procedures are involved in a consideration of these embossing processes. They are: embossing, relief stamping, cameo stamping and die stamping.

Embossing comprises the raising of reliefs without the use of color at the time the reliefs are raised. Both die stamping and cameo stamping comprise the raising of reliefs including the use of color at the time the reliefs are raised;[5] but in die stamping, the color appears on the *reliefs*, and in cameo stamping, the color appears on the *non-reliefs*. In this sense, die stamping and cameo stamping bear exactly the same relationship to one another as do intaglio printing line engraving and relief (letterpress) printing,[6] the color being applied to the same respective areas. In die stamping, the color is applied to the whole die, is wiped from the surface, and is permitted to remain only in the recesses from which transference to the paper occurs; in cameo stamping, the color is applied only to the non-recessed surface of the die from which transference to the paper occurs.

One form of distinction sometimes made in definitions is that embossing comprises the raising of plain or printed surfaces between dies, that die stamping comprises the forcing of plain material into a die containing ink in the recesses, and that cameo stamping comprises the forcing of plain material into a die bearing ink on the non-recessed surface. These suffice, broadly, to describe the processes, but are liable to cause confusion because of exceptions to the rules, and because similar effects can be produced by different processes. Broadly speaking, from the point of view of the philatelist, five main effects have to be considered.

Different Effects

First, and simplest, is a colorless relief on an uncolored ground of uncolored paper. This effect can be obtained singly by individually stamping the impressions one at a time in a single position on a sheet of paper, and is exemplified, for instance, by New South Wales 1838 stamped covers. The effect, individually, is no different from a relief and ground of the same color, which can be produced singly by the same method. A similar effect can be produced with multiple impressions on a sheet (a) by moving the sheet after each subject has been embossed; or (b) by embossing multiple subjects from a special arrangement of female working dies and forces or male dies in a special press — as was done, for instance, upon blue paper in Sardinia (Italy) 1853 (Oct. 1) 20c.

The second effect to be considered is a monochrome (or colored) frame[7] without reliefs containing a center[8] comprising a colorless relief on an un-

---

[5]The matter of terminology is further confused by the fact that it is not unusual in the trade to refer to embossing (that is, to the raising of reliefs without the use of color at the time when the reliefs are raised) as "die stamping, die plain," "embossing, die plain," "plain die" or "plain stamping." To avoid confusion in the present work, the unqualified term "embossing" is used in the sense indicated in this paragraph of the text.

[6]Indeed, sometimes an effect of cameo stamping is produced (deliberately) on relief-printing presses by adjustment of the ink feed and the employment of a special type of make-ready coupled with printing pressure heavier than that usually used in relief printing. Further, sometimes the effect of embossing is produced by the use of uninked intaglio-printing plates — for example the center row of the sheets of France 1942 (Oct. 12) Tricolor Legion 1f.20 + 8f.80. See "Albino" in the alphabetical list to the chapter entitled "Printing Problems and Varieties."

[7]See "Frame" in the alphabetical list to the chapter entitled "Stamp Design."

[8]See "Center" in the alphabetical list to the chapter entitled "Stamp Design."

Embossing. The raising of colorless reliefs on an uncolored ground of uncolored paper. New South Wales 1838 stamped cover. Covers such as this, officially designated "stamped covers," were sold, as from Nov. 1, 1838, by the General Post Office of New South Wales at the charge of 1s.3d. a dozen. Their function was, to quote the post office notice, ". . . to envelope Letters, which being posted in Sydney, would exempt such Letters from any further charge, to the full limits of the Two-penny Post delivery." The embossing was effected singly on individual sheets of paper.

colored ground. This effect is, almost invariably, produced at two entirely separate operations, the first having no relation at all to the embossing process. For instance, the frames were printed by lithography in Neapolitan Provinces (Italy) 1861 (February) ½t. to 50g., and the heads were later embossed in colorless relief; further, the frames were line-engraved and intalgio printed in Germany 1955 (May 9) Schiller 40p., and the heads were later embossed in colorless relief. Another instance of this form of procedure is provided

Embossing with color on letterpress (relief-printing) machines. Gambia 1868 Cameo 6d. This stamp, and its companion 4d., printed and embossed by Thomas De La Rue & Company in sheets of fifteen subjects, was the least costly of the issues produced by the printers — who charged, for engraving and finishing two embossing and printing dies and plates, each containing fifteen multiples, only £10 — that is, £5 each, as compared with approximately £100 for the die and plate for a relief-printed stamp.

Embossing with color (cameo stamping). Portugal 1853 100r. impressed one at a time in sheets on a color embossing press (supplied by Dryden Brothers), with the spacing between impressions controlled by semi-mechanical means, ensuring ample spacing between subjects in the sheet.

by, for example, Poland 1960 (Jun. 15) Olympic Games 60g., in which the designs are reproduced by offset litho. and the colorless figure representative of the "game" is embossed in relief. Clearly, therefore, whatever the particular steps taken for raising colorless reliefs in instances such as these, there is essentially no difference in the actual embossing processes that may be used to produce such instances and the most simple effect. The production of such stamps is merely made more complex by the necessity for registering the center within the frame — a necessity that is frequently encountered in all the usual stamp printing methods.

Third is a monochrome frame without reliefs containing a center comprising a colorless relief on a monochrome ground of the same color as the frame. This effect is presented, for instance, by many issues of Germany and German States including, for example, Germany 1875 (Jan. 1) 10p., which was produced in sheets at one operation of a specially constructed press in the

Embossing with color on letter-press (relief-printing) machines. Bavaria (Germany) 1874 (Aug. 5) 1m. printed and embossed in sheets on letterpress machines at the mint in Munich.

Prussian State Printing Works. The frames and the center ground were relief-printed, and the eagles were simultaneously embossed.

Fourth is a monochrome frame with embossed colorless reliefs[9] containing a center comprising a colorless relief on a monochrome ground of the same color as the frame. This effect epitomizes cameo stamping, but can be produced either simultaneously or at two operations. When produced at one operation, as instanced by, for example, Great Britain 1847 (Sep. 11) 1s., the stamp results from cameo stamping proper; and such stamps produced one at a time may result in multiple impressions on the same sheet of paper, as in the instance just quoted, or in single subjects by individually stamping an impression in a single position on a sheet of paper, such as an envelope blank, as is the case with many "embossed" envelopes. Also, production at one operation may result in sheets of multiple subjects, in which event the female "die" comprises an assemblage of female working dies clamped together in a chase, after the manner frequently encountered in relief print-ing.[10] In such cases — instanced, for example, by Switzerland 1881 Sitting Helvetia 5c. — the counterpart or force comprises, usually, a plaster or mould-ed continuous surface with appropriate reliefs made directly from the chase, and so reproducing exactly all the characteristics of each subject. When stamps are thus produced by two operations, as instanced by, for example, Gambia 1887 ½d. (even though only one plate is used both for printing and as the assemblage of female working dies), such a stamp results from a combina-tion of processes essentially similar to those involved in producing a monochrome stamp with a monochrome frame without reliefs containing a center comprising a colorless relief on a uncolored ground — that is to say,

---

[9]Sometimes these reliefs comprise letters; at other times, the reliefs consist of the spaces surrounding the letters.

[10]See "Chase" in the alphabetical list to the chapter entitled "Relief Printing."

the production really comprises no more than the colorless embossing of already-printed paper, and the production is made complex merely by the necessity for registration of the embossing within the uncolored frame. In other words, these forms of printing and embossing bear, of course, a close similarity to those quoted above in relation to the second type of effect.

Fifth, and most visually striking, is the effect produced by a bi-colored stamp with a center comprising a colorless relief on a monochrome ground of the color in the frame. This effect is presented, for example, by Heligoland 1867 (Apr. 15) 6s., printed at two operations from two assemblages of different subjects — one assemblage for the spandrels and centers, and necessitating the use not only of the usual form of make-ready[11] but also of the appropriate number of forces; and the other assemblage for the frames, necessitating the use merely of the usual form of make-ready. In the case of this value, the frame was printed first in green, and then the spandrels and center ground were printed in rose simultaneously with the colorless relief embossing of the heads. In the case of, for example, the ½s. of the same issue, the frames and the center grounds were printed in green simultaneously with the colorless relief embossing of the heads, and at a second operation the spandrels were printed in red, this second operation being carried out from an assemblage of subjects each of which had a hollowed-out oval in the center to prevent the embossing from being squashed flat.

Die Stamping

Die stamping is a form of graphic art comparatively frequently encountered in note-paper headings. It presents some of the characteristics of line-engraved and intalgio-printed work, with the reliefs on the face and the indentations on the reverse more accentuated and, almost invariably, a pronounced shine on the ink. Further, an examination of the paper held obliquely to the light usually reveals, both on the face and on the reverse, an outline in the shape of the force, which is usually cut only slightly larger than the overall area covered by the ink.

Although affording reasonable facilities in security, die stamping has been only very rarely employed in connection with the production of postage stamps — indeed I do not know of an instance in which an adhesive stamp has been so produced. The reason for this lack of use is, possibly, the somewhat circumscribed size of the dies, and the consequent limitation upon the number of subjects that could be produced at one operation of the press. However, die stamping has been used in the production of some surcharges and overprints — for example in Czechoslovakia 1925 International Olympic Congress overprinted on 1923 Fifth Anniversary of Republic 50h., and in Salvador 1937 Air 30(c.) on 1935 Habilitado on 1935 (Mar. 16) Third Central

---

[11]See "Make-Ready" in the alphabetical list to the chapter entitled "Printing Problems and Varieties."

Die stamping. The raising of reliefs in color. Salvador 1937 Air 30(c.) on 1935 Habilitado on 1935 (Mar. 16) Third Central American Games 55c. The surcharge, "30," was die-stamped. (This stamp presents three different printing methods: the basic stamp was line-engraved and intaglio-printed; the word "Habilitado" was overprinted by relief printing; and the surcharge was die-stamped.

American Games 55c.[12] If these stamps are held obliquely to a good light, the shape of the force can be seen with reasonable clarity both on the face and on the reverse.

Individual Subjects

A form of cameo stamping occasionally encountered among adhesive postage stamps results in the production of individual subjects; multiples of the stamps are unknown because they never existed, each subject being, virtually, stamped out of the paper at the time the impression was made. Among such issues may be mentioned Czechoslovakia 1918 (October) Scout Stamps 10h. and 20h.; Dresden (German Local) 1887 Control 50p. and 1888 Control 10m.; Frankfurt (German Local) 1888 (June) 10th Anniversary of the Founding of the Frankfurt Philatelic Society 1p., and Magura (Hungarian Hotel Posts) 1903, 2f. and 4f., and 1911, 2f. and 4f.

Such stamps resulted from a normally engraved cameo-stamping die — that is to say, a die cut in reverse with the portions to be uncolored cut in recess — but with a special cutting edge incorporated in the die. To create this cutting edge, the engraver first outlined it on the blank die, and then lowered the surface of the die within the outline by a small amount, producing a shallow but sharply outlined depression. He then engraved the details of the design itself. When he had completed this work, he then cut away the metal for a short distance outside the outlined cutting edge, leaving a sharp and undulating ridge surrounding the design, and, surrounding the ridge, a small moat beyond which appeared the original surface of the die. In some cases, this surrounding area itself was lowered.

From the die a force was made in the usual way. The die was then inked, the ink of course, and inevitably, being applied also to the cutting edge. The inked die was then fitted into position on the press; and, with the force in position beneath (or, as the case may be, above) the die, the press was

---

[12]Incidentally, this stamp provides an interesting agglomeration of various printing methods: The basic stamp was produced by intaglio-printed line engraving, the word "Habilitado" was overprinted by relief printing and the surcharge was die-stamped.

Cameo stamping individual subjects. Dresden (German Local) 1887 Control 50p., 1888 Control 10m., Frankfurt (German Local) 1888 (June) 10th Anniversary of the Founding of the Frankfurt Philatelic Society 1p., and Magura (Hungarian Hotel Posts) 1903 2f. Each of these adhesive postage stamps was produced one at a time from a die that incorporated a hand-engraved cutting edge — so that when the die was inked, the ink was applied also to the cutting edge, and when the cameo stamping took place, the cutting edge not only marked the paper with ink, but also pierced the paper. For that reason, no multiples exist.

operated upon a strip or piece of paper already gummed.

This had the effect not only of cameo stamping the stamp and ink marking the paper in contact with the cutting edge, but also of causing the cutting edge to pierce the paper. The amount of this piercing was so adjusted by pressure that, when the strip or piece of paper was removed, only the slightest shake was required to loosen the stamp which, thereupon, fell free, bearing its design surrounded by a colored edging reflecting the shape of the cutting edge.[13]

This type of production has been largely used for adhesive labels, and in its modern form is effected by running a long strip of paper through counter-revolving small cylinders, one comprising the die or dies, the other the force or forces.

---

[13]Although such stamps are, generally, referred to as being rouletted in color, it is clear from the description of their method of production that the "rouletting" bears no relation to that process as usually understood by philatelists.

404

Cameo stamping individual subjects. Czechoslovakia 1918 (October) Scout Stamps 20h. This stamp was produced, one at a time, from a die that incorporated a hand-engraved cutting edge — so that when the die was inked, the ink was applied also to the cutting edge, and when the cameo stamping took place, the cutting edge not only marked the paper with ink but also pierced the paper. For that reason, no multiples exist.

Strip Production

The production of embossed designs upon a long strip or coil of paper in single-stamp width by means of rotating cylinders is not a new idea. Indeed, it formed the basis of the entry of Benjamin Cheverton in the competition held by the Lords of the Treasury in Great Britain in 1839 for suggestions on how the stamps forming part of Rowland Hill's proposals for uniform penny postage could best be brought into use. Benjamin Cheverton won a prize of £100, but his suggestion was discarded later, and no adhesive postage stamps ever were produced on his machine.

However, there have been several "embossed" issues produced upon long strips of paper just stamp width. These issues include, for example, Peru 1862 1d. and 1873 (Mar. 1) Llamitas 2c., which were manufactured on a machine known as *Lecoq* and imported into Lima from Paris.

This was an ingenious machine that used two sets of male and female dies; either or both of the female dies could be inked. The paper, gummed and in a strip or coil 23 to 24 mm wide, was fed into the machine and was then pierced by two prongs that regulated the paper's forward movement. The paper was led between the first pair of dies which, for the 1862 issue, comprised the male and female in steel of the frame. When these had closed, and printed and embossed the frame, they opened, permitting the paper to be moved forward the necessary distance by the prongs, and to be centered beneath the next pair of dies, which embossed the central arms in colorless relief. Actually, the two pairs of dies operated simultaneously on different parts of the paper, which was advanced about 24 mm at a time; so that, as the two pairs of dies opened to permit the paper to travel forward, it bore a complete stamp and, adjoining, an embossed frame — in addition to any completed stamps that had already been extruded. Because of the necessity of keeping the machine in continuous operation during a run, the end of one strip or coil of paper was pasted on to the next — with the consequence that joined paper varieties[14] are frequently encountered.

The pair of dies for the frames of these stamps were square; and, it seems, no provision was made during the manufacture of the machine or the dies to ensure that they could not be inserted the wrong way 'round. As a consequence the inevitable occurred, and gave rise to a variety that has been listed in the standard catalogues as "arms sideways"; in fact it was the dies of the frame that were inserted one-quarter turn wrongly, and this is proved by an examination of any pair of the variety with any pair of the normal stamps. The stamps were printed in horizontal strips, and a pair of the variety exhibits the frames sideways, one-quarter turn counter-clockwise, when the shields or arms are upright. The variety should, therefore, be listed as "frame sideways."

Incidentally, on this machine was produced what has some reasonable claim to be called the first issue of commemorative adhesive postage stamps — namely, Peru 1871 (April) Trencito 5c. The year 1871 was the twentieth anniversary of the establishment of the first railway in Peru — indeed, in South America — the so-called "English" line (as distinct from the "Central" line), which linked Lima, Callao and Chorillos. The names of these three towns and the little train (which gives the stamp the name Trencito, Peruvian for "little train") appear in the design, together with the arms and the value 5c. — a concessionary postal rate introduced in April 1871 to underline the merit of the rapidly expanding rail service between the principal cities and the interior. The 5c. rate was available between any points served by the railways, and was not limited to the three named towns. In the remainder of the country, the rate was 10c.

Cameo Stamping for Sheets

The cameo stamping of individual subjects on a sheet of paper is a method of production exemplified by two groups of issues: (a) Great Britain 1847 (Sep. 11) 1s., 1848 (Nov. 6) 10d., and 1854 (Mar. 1) 6d.; and (b) all the "embossed" adhesive postage stamps of Portugal and Portuguese Colonies issued between 1853 and 1886 and later.

Indeed, all these issues were produced on similar machines supplied by Dryden Brothers of Lambeth, London, the machines used in Portugal being provided with an attachment (lacking in the machines used in Great Britain) that enabled the spacing between subjects to be regulated with comparative ease and accuracy.

In essence, the production of the dies by which the cameo stamping was effected was similar in both these groups of issues; but, of course, there were variations in detail. For the stamps of Great Britain, the original engraving comprised only the head (and neck) with the crown and bun of hair. This was cut in recess and in reverse — that is, the head faced to the right of the metal — on a small, soft steel octagonal block that was hardened, and formed the equivalent of the master die. From this hardened original master die, a

---

[14]See "Joined Paper," in the alphabetical list to the chapter entitled "Paper."

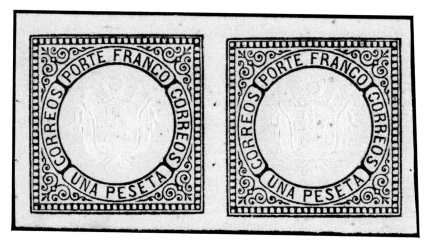

Cameo stamping. Strip production at two operations. Peru 1863 1 peseta, shown in a proof pair. These stamps were produced on gummed strips or coils of paper on a "Lecoq" machine that used two pairs of steel dies. The first pair, of which the female die was automatically inked, was employed for the frame; the second pair, uninked, was employed for the center, which was embossed in colorless relief. [In the issue of 1868 (July) 1d., the female die of the second pair also was automatically inked, and the center appears in colorless relief on a colored ground.] The movement of the strip of paper in the machine was effected by prongs that pierced two holes either side of each stamp; the two pairs of holes can be seen in the vertical margins of the stamps.

punch or primary hob die was made in soft steel; on this, the design was in relief, and the head faced to the left of the metal. The primary hob die was then hardened and used for the production of three soft steel copies of the original; these copies, later, formed the equivalent of supplementary-master dies.

Upon each of these copies, certain details were added by engraving in recess: the pendant curl, the uncolored lines, the engine-turning and, in the case of the 6d. value, the emblems. Each supplementary-master die was then hardened and, from each, a soft hob die was made. On these hob dies, the details appeared in relief. And the design read normally, the head facing to the left of the metal. Then the engraver added (by eliminating the relevant parts of the reliefs, so that the added lines represented the original surface of the hob die) the words of value and "postage," reading normally from left-to-right.[15] These hob dies were then hardened and used in the production of the working dies or printing dies which, before in their turn being hardened, had die numbers engraved or "incused" upon them.

The working dies were used in the machines for producing the stamps. In use in the machine, of course, each die required a counterpart or force, which pushed the paper into the recessed portions of the die, thus embossing the paper.

---

[15]Compare the 6d. and 10d. value illustrated earlier in this chapter.

The precise form of these counterparts and details of the machines in operation for the Portuguese stamps have been recorded[16] by philatelists from their personal observations at the mint in Lisbon. Each machine comprised an arrangement that caused a plunger holding the female dies to move up and down. The plunger in essence was a bar provided with a screw thread and held vertically in a threaded collar fixed to the frame of the machine; turning the bar resulted in its moving up and down. Originally it was operated by hand, but later it was operated by steam power. When the die was at the top of its travel, an inking roller passed over the face of the die, depositing ink on the non-recessed portions only. The plunger then descended toward the paper. The paper lay in a tray that could be moved into different positions by two hand levers, each movement sideways or upright being controlled by one of two simple arrangements of a slotted brass plate working over a stationary pin.

The force card was in the tray, and bore separate relief images comprising the forces. With the earlier issues, there were forty-eight relief forces, and with the later issues there were fifty-six.

The sequence of operations was: the operator placed a sheet of paper over the force card in the tray while the die was being raised and inked; the die descended and cameo-stamped the first subject; while the die was then ascending, the operator moved the tray so that, upon the next descent of the die, the paper was cameo-stamped in a different position and by the next appropriate force subject. These operations were repeated until the sheet bore the required number of subjects.

During the next ascent of the die, the operator moved the sheet and replaced it with a new one. If he should fail, as he sometimes did, to replace the sheet, and the die descended upon the paper again, the result was that, in that position, a double impression occurred — as would be the case if the operator failed to move the tray between impressions.[17] If, by inadvertence, two sheets were inserted in the tray at once, the result would be that the top sheet would receive a normally inked impression, but in slightly less relief than normal, while the lower sheet would receive an albino impression.[18] If the sheet bearing the albino impressions were then to be placed in the machine and impressed normally, the result would be the variety termed "double embossing."

The Gambia 'Cameos'

The exact method of making the dies and plates used for producing the issues philatelically termed the Gambia "Cameos" is not known, and the surviving records of the printers, Thomas De La Rue & Company Ltd., are equivocal.[19] (While the stamps are termed "cameos," from the cameo-like

---

[16]See *The Dies of the Postage Stamps of Portugal* (etc.) by R.B. Yardley (1907), Pages 4-5.

[17]See "Double Impression (2)" in the alphabetical list to the chapter entitled "Printing Problems and Varieties."

[18]See "Albino" in the alphabetical list to the chapter entitled "Printing Problems and Varieties."

[19]See *The De La Rue History of British & Foreign Postage Stamps 1855 to 1901* by John Easton (1958), Page 280.

Embossing. Embossed flaw and embossed printing flaw. Gambia 1880 (and 1887) Cameo ½d., stamp No. 6 — enlargements of portions of three states. (1) The first state: printing normal and embossing normal. (The uncolored projections to the left of the "L" and the "F" are not on the stamps, being caused by minute photographic imperfections.) (2) The second state: "embossing flaw" — printing normal but embossing abnormal. The embossing includes a relief in part of the colored portion of the design, the spur-like projection left of the horizontal stroke of the "L." (Because of the lighting, part of this spur seems uncolored; actually it is uniformly colored.) (3) The third state: "embossed printing flaw" — printing abnormal and embossing abnormal. The background, left of the horizontal stroke of the "L," contains an uncolored flaw because of an indentation on the printing plate. The area within the indentation, being below printing height, did not receive ink or did not deposit it upon the paper; the printing flaw is embossed, providing an uncolored relief where none was desired. (NOTE: For the photographs, the first and second states were lighted from the bottom, and the third state was lighted from the top of the stamp. This accounts for the seeming difference of overall appearance.)

Proof being otherwise available that the stamps were printed at one operation and embossed at another, this sequence of flaws proves that the same plate was used for both printing and embossing.

effect of the head within the center frame, they were not produced by cameo stamping.) The method must have been simple; certainly it was inexpensive compared with the process usually adopted by the firm in 1868.

For the engraving of a die with the use of an existing head to be employed for relief-printed stamps, the firm charged £50, and the charge for an electrotype relief-printing plate of 120 subjects amounted to £50.[20] Two dies and plates, therefore, usually cost £200. The dies and plates for Gambia 1869 Cameo 4d. and 6d. cost a total of £10 — that is, £5 for each value. Even making full allowance for the firm's almost derisory views of the printing-embossing process for postage stamps,[21] and for the facts that the design was

---

[20]See *The De La Rue History of British & Foreign Postage Stamps 1855 to 1901* by John Easton (1958), Page 269.

[21]See *The De La Rue History of British & Foreign Postage Stamps 1855 to 1901* by John Easton (1958), Page 278, where the firm, answering a letter of inquiry about cost based on samples of Heligoland stamps, stated: "The four specimens of printed paper used as Postage Stamps in Heligoland are made in very simple fashion . . . but we think it only right to protest against their being considered stamps in any but a conventional sense for they offer none of the securities which, in all countries are considered indispensable for the protection of the Revenue."

simple and that each plate comprised merely fifteen subjects, the disparity in costs is so great as to give rise to the suggestion that neither engraved steel dies nor the firm's normal method of multiplication by means of struck lead moulds[22] was employed for the Gambia Cameos.

Varieties that occur with these stamps make two deductions reasonably certain. First is that the embossing was carried out on sheets that had previously been printed. This follows from the fact that stamps are to be found in which the embossing and the uncolored portions of the design are out of register — that is, "embossing misplaced" varieties. Such a happening could not occur with cameo stamping in which the printing and embossing are effected simultaneously. Second, the plate used for the printing with a normal make-ready was used also for the embossing with a force, and the plate comprised a comparatively soft material. This follows from the sequence of flaws affecting some subjects — for example, Gambia 1880 (and also 1887) Cameo ½d., stamp No. 6.

In the first state, the stamp is normal both as to printing and as to embossing. In the second state, the stamp is normal as to printing — that is to say, color appears where color was intended to appear — but the embossing is abnormal. There is, for example, in "Halfpenny," at the left juncture of the vertical and horizontal strokes of the "L," and encroaching upon the background, a colored relief. In other words, the second state exhibits an "embossed flaw" variety. Such a colored relief could be accounted for only by some damage to the plate after printing had taken place and before embossing occurred. The damage took the form of an indentation on the printing surface; both the indentation on the plate and the corresponding protuberance on the force were present at the time when the embossing occurred — and the likelihood is that the indentation was present when the force was made.

In the third state, the stamp is abnormal both as to printing and as to embossing — that is to say, color does not appear where it should appear (at the location of the flaw), and a relief appears in the flaw. In other words, the third state exhibits the variety "embossed printing flaw"; this follows from the force having reproduced the protuberance caused by the indentation on the plate. The cause of the flaw — that is, the cause of the indentation upon the plate — must remain uncertain; but (unless the flaw was caused by some entirely foreign substance — which is unlikely because there are numerous such flaws on other stamps and values) its occurrence gives rise to speculation about the actual substance used for the force — or forces, if, as seems likely, a new force was made for each series of embossings. Substances commonly used, apart from force card and leather, were hard wax, plaster and cement. An extraneous fragment of any of these could cause such an indentation, but only if the printing plate were comparatively soft.

---

[22]See "Moulds for Electrotyping" in the chapter entitled "Relief Printing."
[23]See "The Roller Die" in the chapter entitled "Intaglio Printing — I: Line Engraving."

410

German Procedure

Embossing has long been a feature of issues emanating from Germany. Among the embossed stamps produced during the period since World War II may be mentioned: 1953 (May 9) Prisoners of War 10p.; 1954 (Jun. 1) St. Boniface 1200th Anniversary 20p.; 1955 (May 9) Schiller 40p.; 1955 (Oct. 24) United Nations Day 10p.; 1957 (Sep. 16) United Europe 10p. and 40p; 1969 (Sep. 4) German Philatelic Federation Congress and Exhibition, Garmisch-Partenkirchen 30pf., and (West Berlin) 1982 (Apr. 15) Berlin Philharmonic Orchestra Centenary 60pf. All these stamps were produced in two series of operations — the frames in one and the embossed centers in another.

So far as concerns the embossing, this is effected on a letterpress machine. A plaster relief is made of the design, approximately six times original size. This plaster relief serves as the basis of the finished master die, which the engraver cuts on steel. The master die is hardened, and used in a transfer press to produce a roller die in the usual manner.[23] This roller die then serves for transferring to the steel embossing dies (working dies) used in the actual embossing. The forces (termed "patrices") are made from matured ox leather, approximately 1.6 mm thick.

Stamped Envelopes

As has already been stated, by far the greatest use of embossing procedures, so far as stamps are concerned, has been in connection with stationery, especially envelopes — although embossed postcards and wrappers are by no means unknown. However, this review is confined to stamped envelopes.

Stamped envelope production may be summarized as comprising three main stages. They are:

1. The design.
2. Die production.
3. Producing blanks and finishing the envelopes.

Philatelically, perhaps, the greatest basic interest lies in the production of the dies. Procedures may be very complex and, as in the case of almost every printing process, are capable of a wide range of variations. The steps involved, particularly in the early stages of production, can rarely be deduced in their entirety from the finished products. For that reason I instance, if in only little more than outline, stamped envelope production as it obtained in Great Britain until recently and in the United States.

British Envelope Die Production

In Great Britain, production of a new design for envelope embossing dies, after the design was approved, was undertaken by the Royal Mint in London. One method of production was used, and comprised six stages; but, as a preliminary stage, a plaster relief of, usually, the head only was prepared by an artist. This plaster relief was, ideally, six times linear the size of the head on the finished die. The subsequent stages may be listed as:

1. Making a plaster mould (in recess).
2. Growing an electrotype model (in relief).
3. Cutting a reduction punch (in relief).
4. Making a matrix (in recess).
5. Making a working punch (in relief).
6. Making working dies (in recess).

Little need be written here about Stages 1 and 2. Except for the large size of the subject involved, the processes were substantially identical with those referred to in other chapters.[24] The artist's plaster relief was impregnated with wax, and a circular mould was made. The mould was graphited and suspended first in a nickel electrodepositing bath where nickel was grown to the depth of about 0.005 of an inch, and then suspended in a copper electrodepositing bath where the nickel was backed to the depth of about three-thirty-seconds of an inch of copper. The compound electrotype was then removed and comprised the model.

Reduction Punch

The cutting of the reduction punch (which is the term used in the Royal Mint for the equivalent of the "primary hob"[25]) is effected on a machine that produces wonderfully fine work and is known as the "Reducing Machine." There are several of these machines in the Royal Mint, where they have been in operation for very many years, having been made by J.L. Janvier and L. Berchot of Paris.

In order that the model may be fitted in position on the machine, the model is first mounted in a bed of wax on a metal support about the size of a gramophone or large compact disc turntable. This metal support, together with the superimposed wax and model, is then fitted at one end of the machine that bears a tracing point.

The machine is a complex assembly of engineering work, but the principle upon which it operates is, essentially, simple. It is that, if a bar is pivoted, large movements far away from the pivot are represented by smaller movements near to the pivot; and the nearer the approach to the pivot, the smaller the corresponding movements.[26]

The tracing point in the machine is near one extremity of a pivoted bar and mounted on it; near the pivot, and also mounted on the bar, is a cutting tool. Consequently, every movement of the tracing point is transmitted to the cutting tool by the bar; and the proportionate movements of the cutting

---

[24]See "Multiplication of the Design Galvanically" in the chapter entitled "Intaglio Printing — I: Line Engraving," and "Electrotyping" in the chapter entitled "Relief Printing."
[25]See "The Hob Die" and the illustration of Stage 2 on the accompanying diagram and chart earlier in this chapter. From the outline of the process referred to in this chapter, it will be appreciated that, in the case of Great Britain's envelopes, no hand-engraved master die (Stage 1) ever exists. In other instances, a hand-engraved master die is made, the reducing machine is not used, and no reduction punch is made.
[26]This principle can be easily demonstrated by, for example, pressing the point of a sharpened pencil on to a sheet of paper, and then moving the free end of the pencil. A movement of a few degrees will cause the unsharpened end to travel through an inch or so while the part of the pencil near the point moves only a millimeter or so.

412

tool and the tracing point have been calculated, depending upon the distance between these two and the position of the pivot. Therefore, if the tracing point is made to cover all the area and reliefs of the model, the cutting tool will reproduce the model in reduced size; it does this on a circular blank of soft steel, 1⅝ inches in diameter and 1 inch thick, mounted appropriately in the machine.

The method adopted in the machine for thus covering the model is to revolve the model (as on a gramophone turntable, but vertically), to set the tracing point in the center of the model, and to cause the tracing point to travel downward along the radius of the circle. When the tracing point has reached the end of the radius — that is, at the circumference of circular model — every part of the design and reliefs of the model have been covered. In order that the cutting tool should similarly cover the area of the blank and impart similar reliefs to it, the blank is made to revolve at exactly the same rate as the model. In fact, the bar is pivoted in such a manner as to enable the ratio of the in-out movements to be adjusted independently of the other movements, with the consequence that the proportionate amount of relief in the reduction punch can be increased.

In practice, two complete coverages of the model are made. On the blank the first coverage produces a roughing cut, and the second a finishing cut. These operations are lengthy, and about seventy-two hours are needed to set up the machine and cut a reduction punch. After it has been cut, the reduction punch is hardened. It comprises the master (head) die for use with all duties incorporating that head; it is, of course, in relief and is the equivalent of a primary hob.

The Matrix

"Matrix" is the term used in the Royal Mint in reference to what, at first, is merely a soft steel counterpart[27] of the reduction punch, and later becomes the sub-master die.[28] The matrix is in recess, and is made in two stages: first by striking; second by hand-engraving.

Striking is effected in a massive press[29] capable of imparting pressure on the order of 200 tons. To prevent possible injury to operators caused by flying fragments of metal that could result from a shattered hardened die — always a possibility when such high pressures are involved — every hardened die is surrounded by an iron ring that would contain the shattered pieces.

The operator takes the reduction punch and places it in the bed of the press, then manually holds a soft steel blank in position in contact with the punch;

---

[27]That is, Stage 3, the sub-master die (blank) — see the diagrams and chart earlier in this chapter.

[28]Stage 4. Seemingly it is more logical to term a female die "matrix" rather than to term it "master."

[29]The press is termed a friction press. The power is derived from two great flywheels that are supported vertically; they can be closed on to another flywheel, supported horizontally and with strips of leather around its circumference. When the vertical flywheels converge upon the horizontal flywheel, they drive it by friction; it operates a screw-threaded bar (working in a collar) that is driven downward with great force.

he then operates the press which, for postage dies, applies the heavy pressure comparatively gently. After sufficient depth has been obtained — the operation is termed "hobbing in" — the matrix is worked upon by hand, appropriate words, symbols and designs being added, of course in recess, around the head. The engraver cuts away the metal to the required depth, sometimes after having incused the letters and figures by use of appropriate punches and a hammer. The recesses he engraves produce uncolored reliefs on the eventual stamps.

When the design has reached the required stage of completeness on the matrix, it is machined to the necessary size, 1⅝ inches by 1 inch, and a proof is taken from it for approval by the postal authorities; afterward the matrix is hardened. After being hardened, the matrix is surrounded by an iron ring, as the reduction punch was earlier and for the same reason.

The Working Punch

"Working punch" is the term used in the Royal Mint to designate the hardened steel counterpart[30] of the matrix. The working punch is made by direct pressure on a soft steel blank in the friction press in the same manner as the matrix.

In fact, as a matter of precaution, usually two working punches are made, one as a reserve; usually, however, one suffices for all the requirements. In the normal course of events, no alteration is made to the design of the working punch, working being limited to clearing up the design. The working punch is machined to the necessary size, again 1⅝ inches by 1 inch, and is then hardened and surrounded by an iron ring.

Occasionally a working punch is used for a particular purpose, and some reliefs are removed from it. Such a purpose would be the production of a new value identical in design with an earlier stamp except for the figures of value. An instance of a requirement of this nature is provided, for example, by the 1s.9d. postage and registration rate of Great Britain 1961. In this instance, the figures of value "⅓" were removed from one of the working punches by use of a minute grindstone to leave an unraised portion of the design; for that purpose no annealing was necessary. The working punch then became the primary hob (Stage 2) of the new stamp.[31] From the primary hob, a soft steel matrix (sub-master die, Stage 3) is obtained in the usual manner; this has, of course, a blank in the place where the figures are to go. In this space, the engraver incuses the required figures. The completed new matrix is then machined to size, hardened (Stage 4), ringed and used to produce the working punch (Stage 5) for the new 1s.9d. value.

---

[30]That is, Stage 5, the hob die. See the diagram and chart earlier in this chapter.
[31]On the die (primary hob), a faint outline of the erased figures is often discernible.
[32]It corresponds to a plate number or cylinder number — see "Cylinder Number" and "Plate Numbers" in the alphabetical list to the chapter entitled "From Design to Issued Sheets." There are four different types of die markings: a number by itself — on dies for use at Somerset House; a number followed by a full stop — for use at Wolverton; the letter "M" followed by a number — for use at Manchester; and the letter "E" followed by a number — for use at Edinburgh.

Embossing. The friction press. Pressure on the order of 200 tons is imparted by this massive press. Two great flywheels operate another flywheel by friction (all out of the picture at the top), which turns the screw-threaded bar, in the center, driving it downward. The operator is pictured positioning a blank above a working punch (hob die), to make a working die. He holds the blank in position during the actual striking. The working punch is surrounded by an iron ring to prevent injury to the operator caused by flying fragments if the hardened steel of the working punch should shatter — always a possibility with the use of such high pressures. Should the punch shatter, the ring contains the fragments and prevents them flying.

The working die — that is, the printing die — which is in recess, is made by direct pressure on a soft steel blank in the friction press, in the same manner as the matrix and working punch are made.

The Working Die

As the last stage before the working die is hardened, a number or prefix and number are incused on the truncation of the bust. This serves to identify the working die and the stamps printed from it.[32]

Embossing. British envelope dies. Top row: the 3d. value. Bottom row: the 1s.3d. value. At left: the reduction punch (primary hob) cut on the reducing machine, and subsequently machined to size. Center: the matrix (completed sub-master die) made by direct pressure from the reduction punch, then hand-engraved, and subsequently machined to size. At right: the working punch (completed hob die) made by direct pressure from the matrix, and subsequently machined to size. Each die is of hardened steel, measures 1⅝ inches by 1 inch, and is surrounded by an iron ring. Each die bears, on the bevel so as not to reproduce, details of the duty and the date.

Embossing. British envelope dies. The working die. The engraver finally clearing up the working die before incusing the die number on the truncation of the neck. Resting on a raised support, the working die has been fitted into its shank for use in the press; the engraver is holding the shank between the thumb and forefinger of his left hand, and the tops of other shanks can be seen in the stand by his right hand.

Embossing. British envelopes. Working dies, forces and proofs. The picture shows two working dies (without the shanks into which the dies are fitted for use in the press). Being held in the hands are the working die and force for the 3d. value. On the truncation of the neck on each force, the light patch in the picture represents a thickness of paper specially added to provide additional local pressure and so emphasize the die numbers on the proofs. The numbers written on the sheet beneath the 1s.3d. proofs identify the working dies for use at Wolverton. On the dies themselves, and on the proofs, these numbers appear followed by a full stop for identification — that is, without the prefix "W."

The working die, which, like the previous dies in the series, measures 1⅝ inches by 1 inch, is fitted into a special shank for use in the press.

The force is made of leather. The working die is struck on to a rectangular piece of leather, which takes up the design. Then, outside the design, the surface of the leather is removed to a slight depth.

British Production

In Great Britain, envelopes are produced at two or four operations, depending upon the type of envelope. There are two main types: the plain embossed envelope and the registered envelope. Both types are available in different sizes.

Envelopes are not printed in the sheet. Each envelope is printed separately, and production involves two main stages:
1. Producing the shapes.
2. Producing the finished envelopes.

British Post Office embossed stamped envelopes. At left, the 3d. value, with the working die. At right, the 1s.3d. registration and postage, with the working die.

Shapes

The envelope shapes are cut by shaped knives or cutting dies from a stack of paper. The operator places an appropriate number of sheets on the bed of a special press — a die cutting press. He then positions the knife near one

British commercial embossed stamped envelopes. Positioning the knife to make a further cut. Previously cut shapes are stacked on the table at right.

British registered envelopes. Cutting the shapes. The operator is seen with a stack of shapes he has removed from the die (knife) visible beyond the shapes on the table at his left. Behind him is a pile of previously cut shapes. After he has disposed of the shapes in his hands he will take the knife, lay it on the stack of sheets just beyond the two cuts already made, move the sheets and superimposed knife under the press (die cutting press) and apply pressure that drives the knife through all the sheets. He will then withdraw the sheets, remove the shapes from the knife and repeat the operations.

edge of the sheets, moves them into position and applies pressure that drives the knife right through the stack of sheets. He then releases the pressure, removes the cut shapes from the knife, repositions it, and repeats the operations until he has exhausted the paper. He then begins again.

Envelopes

After the shapes have been cut, their subsequent treatment varies. Each registered envelope is first put through a machine that gums the sealing flap, and then the letterpress inscriptions are relief-printed. After this, another machine applies gum for the envelope itself, embosses the stamp and folds the envelope. The shapes for ordinary envelopes are put through a machine that applies the gum, embosses the stamp and folds the envelope.

U.S. Envelope Die Production

In the United States, die production for envelope embossing dies is undertaken by the Bureau of Engraving and Printing.[33] The working dies are re-

---

[33]Also at the U.S. Mint in Philadelphia.

British registered envelopes. After the sealing flaps on the shapes have been gummed in one machine and the letterpress applied in another, the machine in this picture applies the envelope gum, prints and embosses the stamps and folds the envelopes, delivering them on the endless band.

quired in two states: flat and curved. They are produced by two main processes: the "transfer roll" process; and the "hub" process. By an additional step in these processes, curved dies are produced, but by an ingenious adaptation of the "hub" process, curved dies are made without the necessity for subsequent bending.

Transfer Roll Process

The transfer roll process is an adaptation of the Perkins Die and Mill process, to which reference has been made earlier.[34] However, as there are variations specially adapted to the production of embossing dies, details are set out provided by the U.S. Bureau of Engraving and Printing.

Master Embossing Die

To produce the master embossing die for making transfer rolls, the die sinker (as the engraver is termed) first prepares a tracing by outlining each

---

[34]See "Multiplication of the Design Mechanically" in the alphabetical list to the chapter entitled "Intaglio Printing — I: Line Engraving."

Embossing. U.S. envelope dies. The transfer roll process. The transfer press. The operator is pictured examining the state of progress of transfer to the roll of a design from the flat master embossing die. The hardened master emboss-ing die, with the design in recess, is on the bed of the transfer press, and the soft transfer roll is being rolled back and forth under pressure applied through compound leverage. The steel of the transfer roll is being forced into the recesses of the master embossing die, and the rolling operations are repeated as many times as are necessary to obtain perfect reproduction in relief. Note the spare transfer rolls that lie along the top arm of the press. (The plate of the press bears the inscription "W.H. CHAPMAN. NEWARK, N.J. U.S.A.")

element of the design with a steel point in a thin sheet of transparent film. This tracing is prepared so that the design reads normally — from left-to-right. This enables the engraver to transfer the design to the steel by rolling over the tracing a specially prepared wax cylinder of sufficient consistency to coat its surface without entering the scribed lines. The waxed surface is then applied to the flat soft steel die and burnished down sufficiently to apply the wax to the surface of the metal. When the tracing is peeled off, the design is revealed in reverse by bare metal corresponding exactly to the surface scratched away from the film. A weak acid is then washed over the die to

Embossing. U.S. envelope dies. The transfer roll process. U.S. stamped envelopes 1960 (Jul. 19) Pony Express 4c. The three dies: (1) the master embossing die, hand-engraved with the design in recess and reversed; (2) the transfer roll, with the design in relief and reading normally; (3) the printing die (curved) with the design in recess and reversed.

stain the unprotected areas of the metal. The wax is then removed, and the die is ready for the next step.

Using the "stain" as a key, the engraver cuts the lettering and border (in reverse) into the die to the desired depth with the aid of gravers. These areas are generally of equal depth, but the portrait or vignette presents the greater problem of interpretation from a two-dimensional picture into three-dimensional depth to create the proper relief for the embossing process. This requires additional tracings for a series of arbitrary depths as the engraver cuts away the metal in successive layers to reach the greatest depth. During all the cutting processes, he is enabled to check his progress in relief by forcing modeling wax into the work; this wax, upon removal, gives an exact relief moulding of the state of the die. This further enables him to shape the finer transitions of planes and features that raise the result from the level of a mere method to that of an art. When the engraving is finished, guiding lines and other markings that are no longer needed are removed, and the die is ready for hardening. The hardening is effected by heating the die in cyanide of sodium, then quickly dipping it into brine.

Transfer Roll

To make the transfer roll, the flat die is placed on the bed of a transfer press, and a soft steel cylinder or roll is placed over the engraving on the flat die. Pressure is then applied through compound leverage, and the roll is rolled back and forth slowly, forcing the soft steel roll into the hard steel die. This

Embossing. U.S. envelope dies. The hub process. U.S. stamped envelopes Airmail 8c. The three dies: (4) the master embossing die (cylindrical, with flat surface), with the design in recess and reversed; (5) the hub die (cylindrical, with flat surface), with the design in relief and reading normally; (6) the printing die (angular and flat) with the design in recess and reversed.

operation is repeated until a perfect reproduction in relief is obtained. On this reproduction, the design reads normally from left-to-right. The roll is hardened by the same process used for the master embossing die.

Printing Dies

The printing dies are transferred on a strip of soft steel, ⅝ inch thick by 1½ inches wide, in sequence, allowing about ½ inch between subjects. The soft tool steel is placed on the bed of a transfer press, and the hard transfer roll, bearing the design in relief, is placed in its proper position on the strip of steel. Pressure is then applied to the roll, and it is rolled back and forth, imbedding the design into the soft steel strip. The process of rolling is repeated as many times as required to make a perfect reproduction of the original (the master embossing die). After completion of transferring, each subject is separated by sawing the strip of steel about ⅛ inch longer than the finished size.

Curving by Bending

The printing die is provided with a curve by bending the die. It is put face down on a smooth, finished, hardened curving block with the proper curve. A corresponding curved block is placed on the back. Pressure — hydraulic pressure — is applied to the blocks with the printing die between them; this bends the die, and forces it to take the curve of the blocks.

After this has been done, if the curving and bending process has caused any damage or distortion to the design on the printing die, the die is "restored" by hand-engraving.

The printing die is then placed on a router machine, and the bottom side and edges are smoothed and given a bevel to the proper size. The printing die is then hardened by the same process used for the master embossing die.

Hub Process

The hub (or hob) process for the production of flat dies has already been outlined earlier in this chapter.[35] Flat printing dies can be bent and curved in a manner similar to that described for dies produced by the transfer roll process. Therefore, only a brief description, from details provided by the U.S. Bureau of Engraving and Printing, is given of the production by the hub process of curved dies without bending.

The master embossing die is engraved on a properly curved piece of thick soft tool steel, following the same process as for engraving the master embossing die for making a transfer roll. The top, bottom, sides (or oval) are machined to the proper size and depth. The die is then hardened by the usual treatment of cyanide of sodium and brine.

The curved master embossing die is then forced into contact, by hydraulic pressure, with another piece of soft tool steel (the hub die blank) to make the hub die. The hub die is then machine finished and hardened in the usual manner.

For the printing dies, a piece of soft tool steel is placed over the engraving on the hub die and is forced by hydraulic pressure into the hub die to make an impression to equal the quality and depth of the matter embossing die. The printing die is then machined to size and hardened in the usual manner.

U.S. Envelope Production

United States stamped envelopes are produced by a contractor — International Envelope Corp., Dayton, Ohio. These envelopes are produced in two, three or four operations, depending upon the type of envelope and the machines used. There are two main types: the plain embossed envelope; and the window envelope. There are three different types of processes: the "Harris"; the "Huckins"; and the "OC" (O'Connell) (Hartford); and two auxiliary machines: the envelope-folding machine — plunger type; and the "punch press" for cutting windows.

Envelopes are produced from blanks — not sheets. However, both sheet and web printing have been used;[36] for example, during 1907 and 1909, envelope stamps were embossed on a Miehle flat bed relief-printing press using a sheet of paper thirty-four inches wide by twenty-eight inches deep. Subsequently the sheets were cut, but the mounds resulting from the stamps

---

[35]See "Various Types of Dies" earlier in this chapter.
[36]See, for example, "U.S. Envelope Stamps" by T.D. Perry and the references there given. *The American Philatelist*, Vol. 65, Pages 247-59 (January 1955).

Embossing. U.S. stamped envelopes. The "OC" (O'Connell) (Hartford) press that gums, prints, embosses and folds envelopes at the rate of 54,000 per eight-hour shift.

Embossing. U.S. stamped envelopes. The Huckins presses. These presses print and emboss the stamp and print the return address on the envelope blank. Each machine produces 100,000 prints per eight-hour shift. Printed blanks are seen stacked on skids by the operators, unprinted blanks are on skids beyond the machines. In the background, at the upper left of the picture, two paper cutters can be seen at work.

U.S. stamped envelopes. Airmail 6c. The machine (plunger type) that gums and folds the envelopes at the rate of 52,000 per eight-hour shift.

in the sheets caused difficulties in obtaining proper cutting register, and the process was abandoned. The details that follow were supplied by the U.S. Post Office Department in 1960.

Envelopes are furnished in three sizes: Nos. 6¾, 7 and 10, using one grade of paper. The paper suppliers furnish the paper on skids for ease of handling. Details are as follows: Size No. 6¾ — sheet size, 27⅛ inches by 29⅛ inches; reams per skid, twenty-seven; number of die cuts per sheet, twelve. Size No. 7 — sheet size, 17¾ inches by 32⅝ inches; reams per skid, fifty-five; number of die cuts per sheet, six. Size No. 10 — sheet size, 19 inches by 33½ inches; reams per skid, fifty-five; number of die cuts per sheet, six.

The skids of paper are placed by each cutting machine; and the paper cutter, using the appropriate cutting die (knife), cuts one ream of paper at a time in a die-cutting press. The blanks are then placed on another skid, which is spotted by the presses for embossing and folding.

The contractor has three types of presses: O'Connell (Hartford), Harris and Huckins. The Harris and Huckins are rotary presses,[37] which emboss the stamp and print the return address only. The flat blanks are then given to a folder machine that puts the seal on, folds the envelope and counts the finished envelopes in groups of twenty-five. The O'Connell (Hartford) is a flat-bed machine[38] that embosses and prints, seals, folds and counts the envelopes in groups of twenty-five at one operation.[39] Production figures for an eight-hour shift for each machine are as follows: O'Connell (Hartford), 54,000; Harris and Huckins, 100,000; folder, regular, 52,000; folder, window, 36,000. The contractor also has one new folding machine that can fold a maximum of 900 envelopes a minute; the normal running speed of this machine is between 700 and 750 a minute.

---

[37]The Harris has a printing cylinder eight inches in diameter, and uses printing dies about ¼ inch thick. The Huckins, using similar dies, has a printing cylinder six inches in diameter.
[38]The O'Connell uses flat printing dies type high.
[39]All of these machines use leather or material forces.

U.S. stamped envelopes. The punch press that cuts windows in embossed envelope blanks. The unpunched but embossed blanks are at the left; the punched blanks are on a skid at the right of the operator.

The manufacture of window envelopes has one additional step. After stamps have been embossed on the flat blanks, they are taken to a punch press, which cuts out the aperture for the window. The folding machine then performs the additional step of affixing the glassine to the aperture while the folding process is in operation.

Varieties and Terms in Embossing

The alphabetical list that follows includes some of the terms and varieties appropriate to stamps produced by the various processes that the philatelist generically refers to by the term "embossing." As with the alphabetical lists to the previous chapters relating to other specific printing methods, the following list does not and is not in the main intended to incorporate those varieties that, although encountered in "embossed" stamps, occur also in other processes — being varieties of printing generally rather than of "embossing." However, in a few cases, special references have been made to other general or special varieties with the object of enabling a comparison to be drawn so that they may be seen in perspective.

Blank. In reference to envelope production, the term "blank" means the individual piece of paper cut from the sheet by the knife — see "Die (3)." Often, where the production involves several operations after the cutting of the blanks,

427

the term "blank" is used to identify this piece of paper at every stage before the envelope is finished. "Shape" is often used synonymously with "blank."

Cameo Stamping. The simultaneous raising of uncolored reliefs on a colored ground and application of color to the ground; the embossing process equivalent to relief printing, the color being applied to the non-recessed portions of the embossing die. See "Embossing Die."

Counter. An abbreviation of "counterpart." See "Counterpart (2)."

Counterpart. (1) This term has the meaning, philatelically, of "exact opposite" — in contrast to its general meaning, often, of "exact copy." In reference to die production, a counterpart is the complement of the die, so that the die and counterpart fitted together form a solid mass; thus, the counterpart of the master die is the hob, and, subsequently, the counterpart of the hob is the working die. (2) Also "counterpart" has a special application in designating the force (the counterpart of the embossing die), especially when metal is used to force the paper into the recesses of the embossing die. See "Embossing Die"; "Male Die." Compare "Force."

Cutting Press — see "Die-Cutting Press."

Die. (1) See "Die (1)" in the alphabetical list to the chapter entitled "Printing Problems and Varieties." (2) Occasionally, in connection with the embossing processes, the term "die" is used to designate an assemblage of female embossing dies, in the sense of (and see) "Embossing Plate." (3) In reference to stamped stationery, the term "die" signifies also the specially shaped knife that, used in conjunction with the die-cutting press, cuts the blanks from the stack of paper. See "Blank"; "Die-Cutting Press."

Die-Cut Stamps. This term, used in reference to certain cameo-stamped issues, denotes that each stamp was individually severed from the surrounding paper at the time the impression was made. The severance from the paper is effected by a cutting edge incorporated in the die by the engraver — either by lowering the surface of the die surrounding the cutting edge, or by raising the cutting edge in the form of a deliberate burr. Of such stamps, no multiples are known. Because the cutting edges are usually denticulated rather than straight, the stamps have the appearance of having been rouletted in color, because the cutting edge was inked with the surface of the die and the ink was deposited on the paper. Instances of such stamps are provided, for example, by Czechoslovakia 1918 (October) Scout Stamps 10h. and 20h.

Die-Cutting Press. A special machine for applying pressure that drives the knife through the stack of sheets and so produces the envelope blanks; in the press, two parallel flat surfaces converge. See "Blank"; "Die (3)."

Die Plain. This term is used to designate embossing without the use of color at the time when reliefs are raised — emphasizing the absence of color in or on the embossing die. See "Embossing (1)."

Die-Reducing Machine. A machine that, from an electrotype model in relief, produces a relief steel die in a smaller size, the degree of reduction being, usually, about six-to-one. The machine has a tracing point that is made to cover the whole area and all the reliefs of the model. This tracing point is mounted on a pivoted bar; near the pivot on the bar, a cutting tool is mounted in contact with a die blank; the cutting tool reproduces all the movements of the tracing point and thus cuts the design on a reduced scale on the die. See "Model"; "Reduction Punch."

Embossing. Double embossing. Gambia 1880 (June) Cameo 1d. and enlargements of parts of the design exhibiting the inconstant variety "double embossing" because the sheet of paper was twice fed between the embossing plate and force. The properly registered embossing comprises the uncolored portions of the design, and is in normal relief. The out-of-register embossing can be traced throughout the design, but the relief, as is usual, is comparatively shallow, and only parts of the duplication are visible in the photograph. Especially noticeable is the out-of-register lettering which, above "GAMBIA" infringes the stamp margin, and above "ONE PENNY" infringes the framelines.

Die Sinker. This term is used to designate an engraver of dies for stamping and embossing.

Die Stamping. (1) Sometimes used to designate "embossing" — see "Embossing (1)." (2) More often used to designate the raising of colored reliefs on an uncolored ground by means of a recessed die and relief force in a stamping press. The embossing process equivalent to intaglio printing line engraving, the ink being applied to the whole area of the die, being wiped off the non-printing (non-recessed) surface and being permitted to remain only in the recesses — see "Relief Stamping"; "Stamping Press." Instances of stamps bearing die-stamped overprints are Czechoslovakia 1925 International Olympic Congress on Fifth Anniversary of Republic 50h., 100h. and 200h.

Double Embossing. This term designates, literally, duplication of uncolored reliefs only, caused by subjecting the paper to two embossing processes when it, properly, should have been subjected to only one embossing process. The variety "double embossing" rarely occurs in stamps embossed without the use of color at the time the reliefs are raised. With issues involving the use of color at the time the reliefs are raised, the term "double embossing" is used in contrast to double impression and double strike to emphasize that only the reliefs (not the colored portions) are double — see "Double Impression"; "Double Strike." The most usual cause of double embossing is that a piece of paper with an albino impression (because two sheets were fed into the press at once — only rarely because of an inking failure) is fed into the press again and properly impressed.

429

Double embossing can occur on stamps produced from a single-subject or from a multiple-subject embossing plate. The variety is inconstant.

Double Impression. See "Double Impression (2)" and "Double Print (2)" in the alphabetical list to the chapter entitled "Printing Problems and Varieties." In reference to stamps produced by embossing processes, the term "double impression" is used to designate an inconstant variety that has had two lots of ink and two embossings because the press operated fully twice on the same piece of paper. The most usual cause of such a variety is that the operator omitted to move or remove the paper before the press operated again. In this sense, the term "double impression" is used in contrast to double embossing and double strike — see "Double Embossing"; "Double Strike."

Double Strike. See "Double Strike" in the alphabetical list to the chapter entitled "Relief Printing." In reference to the embossing processes, the term "double strike" is limited in use to designate a constant variety exhibiting colored and uncolored duplication in the design because of duplications appearing in the subject on the embossing plate. Such varieties are not frequently met with. A remarkable instance of a true double strike, one inverted, occurs in Switzerland, for example, 1881-82 Sitting Helvetia 5c, pane 1, stamp No. 28, where the complete outlines of the inverted design can be traced, the duplication appearing strongest in the name and value tablets.

Embossed Flaw. In reference to stamps produced by the embossing processes, the term "embossed flaw" is used to designate a variety exhibiting an unusual relief in a colored portion of the design — that is, in a portion that should exhibit an absence of relief. The term is used in contrast to (a) an embossed printing flaw — see "Embossed Printing Flaw"; (b) a printing flaw resulting in only the unusual absence of color from part of the design — see "Printing Flaw"; (c) an impressed printing flaw — see "Impressed Printing Flaw"; and (d) misplaced embossing — see "Embossing Misplaced." A true embossed flaw occurs during the embossing process, and can occur only when the force bears some excrescence and the female die or embossing plate is composed of some comparatively soft material. Embossed flaws must be constant for the state of the embossing plate in which they occur. Embossed flaws must, of course, be distinguished from inconstant flaws (affecting a stamp's collectible condition) resulting from post-production damage to a stamp — see "Flaw C" in the alphabetical list to the chapter entitled "Printing Problems and Varieties." Many embossed flaws occur, for example, in Gambia 1880 (and 1887) Cameo ½d., including stamp No. 6, second state.

Embossed Printing Flaw. In reference to stamps produced by the embossing processes, the term "embossed printing flaw" is used to designate a variety exhibiting an unusual uncolored relief — that is to say, both printing and embossing are abnormal in that the printing has left an uncolored flaw and the embossing has produced a relief extraneous to the design. Compare "Embossed Flaw"; "Embossing Misplaced"; "Impressed Printing Flaw"; "Printing Flaw."

Embossing. (1) Strictly, the raising of reliefs without the use of color at the time the reliefs are raised. The term "plain stamping" is sometimes used synonymously with "embossing." See "Die Plain." (2) Loosely, in philatelic use, the term "embossing" is employed generically in reference to any or all of the processes involving distortion of the paper by a die and force.

Embossing Die. Usually the term "embossing die" is used to designate the female working die — see "Die (2)." Sometimes "embossing die" is used in reference to any of the female dies that come into existence during the making

Embossing. Double strike. Switzerland 1881-82 Sitting Helvetia 5c., pane 1, stamp No. 28, exhibiting the variety "double strike" — one inverted — caused by duplications occurring in the subject on the embossing plate that was used also for printing. This remarkable variety resulted from two impressions being made by the punch or its equivalent from which the female embossing subject was produced, one normal and one inverted. Apart from the duplications in the frame, the most clearly noted (inverted) features are the oval of the shield, the outline of the skirt, the spear and the forearm.

of a series of dies for use with the embossing processes. Occasionally, and inaccurately, "embossing die" has been used to designate the male die, counterpart or force.

Embossing Double — see "Double Embossing."

Embossing Misplaced. (1) In reference to stamps produced by the embossing processes, the term "embossing misplaced" is used to designate an inconstant variety exhibiting lack of register between the printing and the embossing — that is to say, parts of the uncolored portions of the design are not in relief, and parts of the colored portions are in relief. In this sense, use of the term is necessarily limited to stamps printed at one and embossed at a subsequent operation from one plate used for both operations. Such a variety is to be distinguished from, although it is sometimes mistaken for (and see) "Double Embossing"; "Double Impression." Sometimes the terms "Embossing Shift," "Registration Flaw" and "Shifted Embossing" are used as synonyms for "embossing misplaced." See "Registration" in the alphabetical list to the chapter entitled "Printing Problems and Varieties." Instances of embossing misplaced are to be found, for example, in Gambia 1887 Cameo ½d., and in Switzerland 1862-78 Sitting Helvetia 2c. (2) In another sense, "embossing misplaced" means no more than center misplaced — see "Center Misplaced" in the alphabetical list to the chapter entitled "Printing Problems and Varieties."

Embossing Plate. An aggregation of female printing dies, whether separate subjects or on a continuous surface.

Embossing-Printing Process — see "Printing-Embossing Process."

Embossing-Printing Register — see "Embossing Misplaced."

Female Die. In reference to the embossing processes, the term "female die" is used to designate the recessed working die; also, occasionally, any recessed die.

Force. The counterpart of the female working die. The term "force" is used particularly when the counterpart comprises card, leather or some other resilient material. Compare "Counterpart."

Force Card. A special type of cardboard comprising thin layers that can be easily cut away for use in making forces. See "Force."

Hob (Hub). The relief die from which the working dies are made. Sometimes the term "Working Punch" is used as a synonym for "hob" or "hub." Sometimes, if a series is to be made all of the same design except for one feature (for example, figures of value), a hob die (termed a "Primary Hob") is made from the original engraving (the master embossing die). The relief figures are ground off the primary hob, which is then used to make several undenominated female dies, termed "sub-master dies"; upon these sub-master dies new figures of value are engraved in recess, and from each sub-master die a hob die is made from which the respective working dies are produced.

Hob Primary — see "Hob."

Hub — see "Hob."

Impressed Printing Flaw. In reference to stamps produced by the embossing processes, the term "impressed printing flaw" is used to designate a constant variety exhibiting absence of color in a part of the design where color should be present — resulting from the lowering of part of the surface of the female working die that should have received ink but did not, because of being below inking level. In such cases, the relevant portion of the stamp exhibits what is in fact an albino, but, of course, not in relief. In such cases, the force, being resilient, compensates for the indentation in the female die and the paper is distorted, but to a lesser extent than usual. In the embossing processes, impressed printing flaws are to be distinguished from printing flaws, which are inconstant — see "Printing Flaw." Compare "Embossed Printing Flaw."

Impression Double — see "Double Impression."

Knife — see "Die (3)."

Lever Press. A simple instrument used for embossing paper between male and female dies, the pressure being applied (by hand) to a pivoted lever that drives the female die down on to the male die. One type of stamping press — see "Stamping Press."

Male Die. In reference to the embossing processes, the term "male die" is used to designate the relief counterpart of the working die, particularly when the male die is metal. See "Counterpart"; compare "Force." Occasionally the term "male die" is used in reference to any relief die.

Master (Embossing) Die. In reference to the embossing processes, the terms "master die" and "master embossing die" are frequently used to designate the original engraving in recess. It is curious that this, a female die, should be termed "master."

Matrix. See "Matrix" in the alphabetical list to the chapter entitled "Printing Problems and Varieties." At the Royal Mint in London, the term "matrix" is used to designate the sub-master die — see "Hob." Compare "Patrix."

Misplaced Embossing — see "Embossing Misplaced."

Model. In reference to embossing processes, the term "model" is used to designate an electrotype copy of a plaster relief of the design or a feature for use in making the reduction punch through the medium of the die-reducing machine. The plaster relief is made by the artist. From this, a mould is made and used to grow the electrotype, which is nickel backed with copper. See "Die-Reducing Machine"; "Reduction Punch." Compare "Model" in the alphabetical list to the chapter entitled "Intaglio Printing — II: Gravure."

Embossing. Impressed printing flaw. Portugal 1866-67 5r. exhibiting an impressed printing flaw in part of the "A" of "PORTUGAL," the left diagonal being albino instead of colored, because the surface of the die has become lowered and therefore was not inked. That the flaw is constant (for that state of the die) is proved in the picture: It occurs on the four stamps.

Patrix. A synonym for a male die used for producing a female die by pressure. The term "Punch" is used synonymously, particularly, with "patrix." Compare "Matrix."

Plain Die — see "Die Plain."

Plain Stamping — see "Embossing."

Primary Hob — see "Hob."

Printing Die. In reference to the embossing processes in which color is used at the time the reliefs are raised, the term "printing die" is used to designate the female die that is inked either on the non-recesses or in the recesses. Often the term "Working Die" is used as a synonym for "printing die," but "working die" embraces dies used for embossing that comprises the raising of reliefs without the use of color at the time the reliefs are raised.

Printing-Embossing Process. This term is used in two senses: (1) to designate two separate operations — that is, printing followed by embossing with the use of the same plate; and (2) to embrace both cameo stamping and relief stamping in contrast to plain embossing — see "Cameo Stamping"; "Relief Stamping."

Printing-Embossing Register — see "Embossing Misplaced."

Printing Flaw. In reference to the embossing processes, the term "printing flaw" is used to designate an inconstant variety exhibiting absence of color in a part of the design where color should be present (uncolored flaw), or presence of color in a part of the design that should be uncolored (colored flaw). The term "printing flaw" is used in contrast to (and see) "Embossed Flaw," "Embossed Printing Flaw," "Embossing Misplaced" and "Impressed Printing Flaw."

Printing Shift. A misnomer in reference to stamps produced by embossing processes. See "Embossing Misplaced."

Punch. See "Punch" in the alphabetical list to the chapter entitled "Printing Problems and Varieties." A synonym usually for "patrix," but sometimes also for "matrix" — see "Matrix"; "Patrix."

Reducing Machine — see "Die-Reducing Machine."

Embossing. Printing flaw. Portugal 1856-58 Curly Hair 25r. exhibiting a typical inconstant printing flaw, the "I" of "REIS" being entirely uncolored because some ink-repellant substance prevented that letter from being inked on the female working die. The same substance also affected other portions of the design — and the enlargement of part of the design shows the "S" of "REIS" with ink in only a comparatively small portion of that letter as surrounded by relief; such inking failure affected other parts of the inscription.

Reduction Punch. A relief die cut on a die-reducing machine and used in the preparation of a matrix or sub-master die. Usually the reduction punch comprises only a feature of the design, further features being engraved on the matrix. See "Die-Reducing Machine"; "Matrix."

Registration Flaw — see "Embossing Misplaced."

Relief Stamping. The raising of colored reliefs as in die stamping — see "Die Stamping (2)."

Screw Press. An instrument for use in embossing paper between male and female dies or between a female die and counterpart with or without the use of color, the pressure being applied (by hand or mechanically) by the turning of a screw-threaded bar operating in a collar fixed to the frame of the press, thus forcing the end of the bar downward. One type of stamping press — see "Stamping Press."

Shape — see "Blank."

Shifted Embossing — see "Embossing Misplaced."

Shifted Printing. A misnomer in reference to stamps produced by embossing processes. See "Embossing Misplaced."

Stamping Press. A machine that prints or embosses or both prints and embosses by a sharp blow. See also "Lever Press"; "Screw Press."

Sub-Master Die — see "Hob."

Working Die — see "Printing Die."

Working Punch — see "Hob."

12. Relief Printing

RELIEF PRINTING IS PRINTING from the non-recessed or "relief" surface of the printing base, so that the design on the paper represents those portions of the printing base that are not sunk below that surface. Relief printing is the antithesis of intaglio printing, and differs from both intaglio and planographic printing in this: that in intaglio and in planographic printing, at the moment of printing, the paper is pressed into contact with the un-inked surface of the printing base as well as with the inked surface; but in relief printing, the paper is pressed into contact only with the inked printing surface. In relief printing, as with planographic printing, the intensity of the design printed on the paper is in direct proportion to the size of each area of color, and the depth of the film of ink does not, or should not, vary.

Terms used in relation to this form of printing include: En épargne, letterpress and relief; in philatelic circles, also used are the terms "surface printing," "typographic printing," "typographed," and "typography" — usually abbreviated to "typo." The term "surface printing" in this connection is, strictly, a misnomer, as the word "surface" here relates solely to the non-recessed or "relief" surface comprising the printing areas; to the printer, the term "surface printing" denotes planographic printing in which both the printing and the non-printing areas are on the one surface. Outside exclusively philatelic circles, the term "typography" bears the meaning of "the arrangement and display of type." The use of the term "typography" by philatelists to designate "relief printing" provides merely one instance of the philatelist and the printer being incomprehensible to one another by using the same words but talking a different language. The term most widely used by printers to identify this method of printing is "letterpress"; but this term has acquired little philatelic usage, perhaps because of the ill-founded objection that, often, the lettering forms only a small portion of the design of a stamp printed by this method.

The principle of relief printing is the simplest of all the methods: A surface to which ink can adhere, when inked and pressed into contact with paper, will yield an impression. A relief-printing design on the printing base consists of "ups" (which are series of lines or patches varying in area) representing the original surface,[1] separated by "downs" (which are spaces varying in size) representing areas removed from the original surface. If the printing base is, or were to be, laid out flat, the "ups" are (and must be) all at the

---

[1]This concept is somewhat artificial in connection with printing from typeset printing bases unless it is related in time to the originals of the individual components of the design.

435

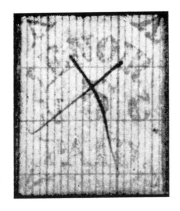

Relief printing. Xylography. U.S. (Confederate States) Lenoir, North Carolina, 1861 5c. The printing base for this stamp was a woodblock bearing a single subject hand-engraved. Printing was by hand-stamping.

same level; on the other hand, the "downs" may be at varying levels, so long as they are below the "ups." Ink is applied, by roller or otherwise, to the "ups"; no ink is, or should be, applied to the "downs."

Paper is pressed into contact with the "ups," with the result that the series of lines and patches press the ink on to the paper; and, moreover, press into its substance, while the pressure also results in the paper being forced to a slight extent into the spaces above the "downs." The paper does not, or should not, come into contact with the "downs," or any part of them. A relief-printed design on paper consists of series of ink marks corresponding with the lines and patches of the "ups," and of unprinted paper corresponding with the areas of the "downs." The film of ink on the paper should be of even thickness throughout all printed areas of the design; however, because of the squeezing or squashing imparted by pressure in the press, the depth of ink may vary within the area of even the thinnest printed line — see "Relief Printing" and the accompanying illustration in the chapter entitled "Printing Characteristics."

Perhaps more different processes have been used to make printing bases for relief printing than for any other method of printing. The relief printing of stamps has been carried out directly from printing bases engraved or cut by hand, from printing bases produced only after many processes subsequent to the original engraving, and from printing bases during the manufacture of which hand-engraving has played no part.

Xylography

Historically, the earliest form of relief printing was from woodblocks[2] engraved by hand; this process is termed "xylography," from the two Greek words *xylos* (wood) and *graphein* (to write). Upon the end grain of a block of fine-grained wood made regular and smooth, the xylographer operates with wood-cutting tools; and, of course, cuts away the "downs" while leaving the "ups" at the original surface. The hand-engraving upon wood of

---

[2] See "Woodblock" etc., in the alphabetical list to the chapter entitled "Printing Characteristics."

Relief printing. Xylography. Multiplication of design by hand. Victoria 1854-58 2s. The printing base for this stamp comprised fifty woodblocks, each separately engraved by hand, assembled and fixed for printing, which was effected in a press.

a single design, and its subsequent inking and hand-stamping upon paper, is the crudest form of relief printing from a xylograph. This primitive process has been used to produce postage stamps. Instances are to be found, for example, in the United States, including U.S. (Confederate States) Postmasters' Provisionals, Grove Hill, Alabama, 1861 5c. and Lenoir, North Carolina, 1861 5c.

Direct Hand-Engraving

Numerous other adhesive postage stamps have, from time to time, been hand-stamped or printed from hand-engraved dies of wood, ivory, rubber,

(text continues on Page 440)

Relief printing. Direct hand-engraving. Aleppo (Syria) 1918 (November) (no value expressed). The adhesive stamp was produced by hand-stamping.

437

Relief Printing: Direct Hand-Engraving

Relief printing. Direct hand-engraving (metal). Drammen (Norway) 1871-76 Hagen 2sk. This stamp was printed by hand-stamping.

Relief printing. Direct hand-engraving. Bermuda (Postmasters') 1848-54 Perot 1d. This stamp was printed by hand-stamping; the value and signature were added in manuscript.

Relief printing. Direct hand-engraving (rubber). New Republic (South Africa) 1866 1d. This stamp was printed by hand-stamping, the date being added at a separate operation.

Relief printing. Direct hand-engraving. Ruhleben (British Prisoners' Camp) (Germany) 1915 (Jul. 18) ½d. on ⅓d. This stamp was printed by hand-stamping.

Relief printing. Direct hand-engraving (copper). U.S. Locals, Bicycle Mail (Fresno-San Francisco) 1894 25c. The printing base for this stamp was a copper block bearing a single subject hand-engraved. Printing was effected in a press.

Relief printing. Xylography. Direct hand-engraving. U.S. Postmasters' Provisional, Millbury, Massachusetts, 1846 5c. The printing base for this stamp was a woodblock bearing a single subject hand-engraved. Printing was effected in a press.

Relief printing. Direct hand-engraving. Wei-Hai-Wei (Great Britain, Chinese Treaty Ports) 1898 (December) 2c. The design of this stamp was printed by hand-stamping; the figure and letters were added in manuscript.

Relief printing. Direct hand-engraving (brass). U.S. Postmasters' Provisional, New Haven, Connecticut, 1845 5c. The printing base for this stamp was a brass block bearing a single subject hand-engraved.

Relief printing. Hand-stamped overprint. Ukraine 1918 1k. This provisional stamp was produced by hand-stamping the device (a trident) on Russia 1909-12 1k.

Relief printing. Hand-stamped surcharge. Randers (Denmark) 1887 (April) 2c. This stamp was produced by hand-stamping the figure "2" on 1885 5c.

stone, brass, copper and other metal. Among such issues are, for example, Afghanistan 1880-90 1a. (stone or metal); Aleppo (Syria) 1918 (November) (no value expressed) (wood or metal); Bermuda (Postmasters') 1848-54 Perot 1d. (metal); Drammen (Norway) 1871-76 Hagen 2sk. (metal); New Republic (South Africa) 1866 1d. (rubber, with date hand-stamped separately); Ruhleben (British Prisoners Camp) (Germany) 1915 (Jul. 18) ½d. on ⅓d. (wood or metal); Shanghai 1865 1c. (ivory or wood center); U.S. locals, Bicycle Mail (Fresno-San Francisco) 1894 25c. (copper); U.S. Postmasters' Provisionals, Millbury, Massachusetts, 1846 5c. (wood) and New Haven, Connecticut, 1845 5c. (brass); and Wei-Hai-Wei (Great Britain, Chinese Treaty Ports) 1898 (December) 2c. (metal).

Further, on many occasions, an overprint or surcharge has been applied to a basic stamp by hand-stamping it with a device — a word, initials or a figure of value hand-engraved on wood, rubber or metal. Two examples, chosen at random, will suffice to represent this large class of provisional postage stamps produced by this crude form of relief printing: overprint — Ukraine 1918 1k., bearing a trident hand-stamped on Russia 1909-12 1k.; surcharge — Randers (Denmark) 1887 (April) 2c., bearing the figure "2" hand-stamped on 1886 5c.

Multiplication of Design by Hand

The crudest method of multiplying a design for relief printing is separately to engrave each subject by hand. Of course, because handwork repetition can never attain perfect identity, each separately engraved subject will differ from every other such subject.

At least two variations in procedure are available: to cut repetitions of the subject on one piece of material sufficiently large to bear the required number of subjects; and to cut each subject on different small pieces of material, each of an area sufficient to bear only one subject.

440

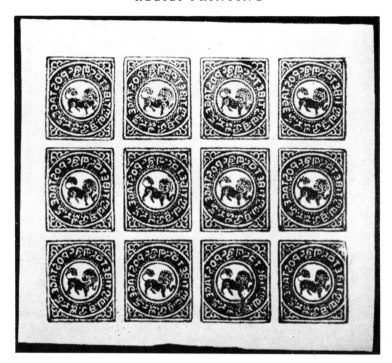

Relief printing. Xylography. Multiplication of design by hand. Tibet 1912 ⅓t.
This sheet of stamps was printed from a single woodblock bearing twelve subjects, each separately engraved by hand.

Such variations in procedure have been used to produce postage stamps.
As examples:

Tibet 1912 ⅔t. was printed from a single woodblock on which were twelve
subjects, each separately engraved by hand.

Victoria 1854-58 2s. was printed from a printing base comprising fifty hand-
engravings, each executed on small pieces of wood subsequently assembled
and fixed for printing.

Tibet 1933 ½t. was printed from a printing base comprising twelve subjects, each separately hand-engraved on a brass block; the twelve blocks were
tied together to form the printing base.

These crude methods of multiplying designs for relief printing have been
used only on rare occasions, and when more advanced methods were not
available. By far the most frequently used methods of preparing a printing
base for relief printing have been to multiply the design with the assistance
of mechanical or other means, which are referred to later in this chapter.

Typewriting

Typewriting, on rare occasions, has been used to produce postage stamps.
Use of the typewriter, with or without "carbon paper," results in every stamp
being entirely different from every other stamp, even in those few cases in

Relief printing. Typewriting. Long Island (Aegean Sea) 1916 (May 7-26) ½d.

Relief printing. Typewritten surcharge. Tonga 1896 (May) ½d.

Relief printing. Typewritten overprint. Tibet 1903-1904 ½a. This stamp, with the typewritten overprint "Tibet," formed part of the first (unofficial) issue made in that country and used by members of Col. F.E. Younghusband's Tibet Frontier Commission. The commission lasted from July to December 1903, but the stamps are known used also in 1904. The stamp illustrated is canceled "Kamba Jong OC 3 03."

which no typing errors occurred. The first recorded issue of typewritten stamps is Uganda 1895 Cowries 5(c) to 60(c). Another typewritten issue of postage stamps was made by the British armed forces in the Aegean Sea, for Long Island 1916 (May 7-26) ½d., 1d., 2d., 2½d. and 1s.[3]

A typewriter was pressed into service to surcharge "Half-Penny" on a provisional stamp, and so to make the further provisional issue of Tonga 1896 (May) ½d.

Further, a typewriter — or, rather, two typewriters — were used to overprint "Tibet" on India 1882-87 ½a. and 1899 3p., and so create the first (unofficial) issue of Tibet 1903-1904 3p. and ½a., for the use of members of Col. F.E. Younghusband's Tibet Frontier Commission, July to December 1903. Almost a half century later, typewriters were used to produce some of the provisional overprints, authorized locally, of "Pakistan" on stamps of India, for the issue of Pakistan 1947-49 3p.

Typesetting

The form of relief printing most widely practiced throughout the world is printing from printers' type and ornaments; and, from the very early days of stamps until the most recent, this form of relief printing has been used on many hundreds of occasions to produce postage stamps as well as surcharges and overprints — as examples, U.S. Postmasters' Provisionals, Alex-

---

[3]*Scott's Standard Postage Stamp Catalogue* does not list these stamps, but they are listed in *Stanley Gibbons Priced Postage Stamp Catalogue*, Part 1, as Long Island Nos. 4 to 26.

Relief printing. Typesetting. U.S. Postmasters' Provisional, Alexandria, Virginia, 1846 5c. An instance of the early use, for a stamp, of printers' type and ornaments to make the design.

Relief printing. Typesetting. Upper
Columbia Co. (Canada) 1898 (Jul. 27)
5c. A stamp printed from printers' type
and ornaments.

andria, Virginia, 1846 5c. and Seychelles 1957 5c. on 1954 45c.

In its most direct form, typesetting involves the assemblage of individual
pieces of type and printers' rules and ornaments in a small holder, termed
a "composing stick," and the subsequent arrangement and securing of the
assemblages in a large holder, termed a "chase," from which, when it is
placed in the press, printing takes place.

Numerous postage stamps have been thus printed directly from
assemblages of types and rules and ornaments. Examples chosen at random
are: British Guiana 1882 1c. and 2c.; Carupano (Venezuela) 1902 5c. to 1b.;
Madagascar 1891 (Jun. 24) 5c. to 5f.; Upper Columbia Co. (Canada) 1898 (Jul.
27) 5c.; and Zanzibar 1931 Postage Due 1c. to 75c.

Sizes and Styles of Type

Numerous different sizes and more than 15,000 different styles, or "faces,"
of type have been used throughout the world.

Even in the restricted field of the Roman alphabet and Arabic numerals,
much artistic and technical learning is involved in naming the sizes and faces
of types. In this restricted field, reference to size has been, to some extent,
standardized by the adoption of a "point" system — the fewer the points,
the smaller the type — there being seventy-two points to the inch. However,
with regard to style names, the difficulties are very great, and type founders
sometimes use different names to refer to the same or similar styles, and the
same names in reference to different styles.

Study of the various styles of lettering and types used for postage stamps
more properly relates to the subjects considered in the chapter entitled
"Stamp Design." Philatelically speaking, the bulk of the learning involved
in naming the sizes and styles of types is unnecessary; and it is, as a general
rule, only when type from more than one font[4] is encountered on the same
value or in varying settings that it becomes necessary, philatelically, to
distinguish between types. Even in such cases, usually only the most elementary terms of distinction are necessary.

Philatelically, so far as size is concerned, no reference is usually necessary
to the "point" system, and the qualifications "large," "normal" and "small"
nearly always suffice when any question of differentiation arises.

---

[4]A "font" is a complete set of type of a particular face and size.

Relief printing. "Fancy" type. Cook Islands 1937 Coronation 1d. An example of "fancy" type used for the overprint.

More frequently, differentiation in styles or "faces" of type presents certain difficulties. It would be quite impossible in a work of this nature to deal with every face of type that has been used for postage stamps throughout the world, and with all the considerations that may be important in particular cases. Nor would it be practicable to do more than mention here in passing that many types have been used on stamps for alphabets and scripts of languages other than those for which the Roman alphabet and Arabic numerals are normal. The most that it is practical to attempt in this work is to set out, in general terms, some of the main considerations, and to indicate others.

Type may be regarded from various viewpoints, and may be divided into different and not necessarily exclusive classes, based upon considerations of, *inter alia*, form, character, style, breadth, weight and size of the letters or characters.

(a) Roman Type. "Roman" is the name given to type of which the letters appear upright — such as are used in the text of this work. (Roman *numerals* are, of course, numerals as used in Roman times — for example, I, IV, X — as contrasted with Arabic numerals — for example, 1, 4, 8 — which, incidentally, are of Indian origin.)

(b) Italic Type. "Italic" is the qualification given to type of which the letters (and figures) slope to the right.

This sentence is set in italic type.

Generally speaking, italic type has not been much employed for typeset stamps, overprints or surcharges. But instances of its use are to be found,

Relief printing. Italic type. Straits Settlements 1880-81 10c. on 1867-68 6c. A surcharge printed in italic type.

445

for example, in the surcharge of Straits Settlements 1880-81 10c. on 1867-68 6c., and of Zelaya (Nicaragua) 1911 5c. on (Nicaragua) 1905 1p.

(c) **"Fancy" Type.** This term is the most practical for use in describing type with unusual or extravagant flourishes or forms. Indeed, "fancy" or "ornamented" may be the only practical description in the absence of a specific name, the discovery of which may be the fruit of, perhaps, years of research. Many different "fancy" types have been used for postage stamps, including, for example, the overprint that created Cook Islands 1937 Coronation 1d. on New Zealand 1937 1d., Bolivia 1947 1.40b. on 1938 75c., and "V.R." overprints on Fiji 1874 and 1876.

(d) **Type with Serifs.** Serifs are the small thickenings or strokes that are made at the ends of the lines of letters so that those ends appear somewhat wider than the main body of the lines. The text of this work is set in type with serifs.

Very many instances occur of the use of type with serifs for postage stamps and overprints. Two examples, chosen at random, are: Fiji 1870 Times Express 1d., and Canal Zone 1939 ½c. bearing the overprint "Canal Zone" on U.S. 1938-43 ½c.

(e) **Sans-Serif or Non-Serif Type.** These terms refer to type in which the ends of the lines of the letters are of the same width as the main body of the lines.

This sentence is set in sans-serif letters.[5]

Again, very many instances occur of the use of sans-serif type for postage stamps and overprints; and again, two examples, chosen at random, are: Malta 1948 Self Government ¼d., and Mount Currie Express (South Africa) 1874 1d.

Sans-serif type often is used together with type with serifs, and instances of typeset stamps that combine both styles of type are to be found, for example, in Antioquia (Colombia) 1901 1c., and Pietersburg (Transvaal) 1901 1d.

(f) **Bold Face or Heavy, and Light Face Types.** Many types are cut in which letters of the same "point" size may be obtained with different thicknesses of the strokes or width of the individual lines. Type in which the lines are thick is termed "bold face" or "heavy"; type in which the lines are thin is termed "light face"; while the normal type between the extremes is, usually, undesignated by a particular term, or is called "medium face."

This sentence is set in bold face type.
This sentence is set in medium face type.
This sentence is set in light face type.

A bold face, sans-serif type is to be found, for example, in the surcharge of New Zealand 1922 2d. on 1919 ½d.

A light face sans-serif type is to be found, for example, in the surcharge of Costa Rica 1953 Air 5c. on 1947 45c.

---

[5]This style of type is designated "Gothic" in the United States, but is termed "Grotesque" in Great Britain, where "Gothic" designates the black-letter type such as that used for printing German — the style of type that is found, for example, on Württemberg 1851-52 1k.

Relief Printing: Some Typefaces Used

Relief printing. Bold face type. New Zealand 1922 2d. on ½d. An example of a surcharge printed in bold face type.

Relief printing. Mixed type. Antioquia (Colombia) 1901 1c. An example of a stamp printed from a mixture of serif and sans-serif type, and printers' rules and ornaments.

Relief printing. Type with serifs. Canal Zone 1939 ½c. An example of an overprint set in type with serifs.

Relief printing. "Fancy" type. Bolivia 1947 1.40b. on 1938 75c. An example of "fancy" type used for the surcharge.

Relief printing. Mixed type. Cauca (Colombia) 1902 20c. An example of a stamp printed from a mixture of bold face and light face type, and printers' rules and ornaments.

Relief printing. Sans-serif type. Mount
Currie Express (South Africa) 1874 1d.
An example of a stamp printed from
sans-serif type, and printers' rules and
ornaments.

An instance of a postage stamp typeset in a combination of bold face and
medium or light face type is to be seen, for example, in Cauca (Colombia)
1902 20c.

Among other considerations affecting typefaces are whether the individual
letters are deliberately made wider ("extended") or narrower ("condensed"),
and whether, in the individual letters, the contrast between the thick and
thin strokes — if there is any contrast — is great or little ("modern" and "old
style" or "antique").

Types have "family" names, and are named, usually, after the designers
who first cut them; but there are many modern copies of types first cut centuries ago. The positive identification of a typeface as used for a particular
stamp is a matter, often, of considerable difficulty. The problem may
sometimes be solved by careful comparison of the stamp with examples of
type appearing in the catalogues and proof sheets issued by type founders,
or by reference to published works that deal with various aspects of type.[6]

Composing Type by Hand

When assembling type by hand into a composing stick, the compositor,
as the operator is called, stands in front of "cases," which are large containers
divided into compartments of varying sizes. The "cases" hold, or should
hold, type of one font. Each compartment holds many separate pieces of type,
and each piece of type is an individual letter, symbol or space, termed "sort";
the definition of "sort" is "any single type character." Of course, each compartment should hold type of not only one font but also of one "sort";[7]
however, it is by no means unknown, when type is being distributed into
the compartments, for missorting to occur, particularly with letters such as
"p" and "d," and "b" and "q," and also with fonts that differ only slightly
from one another.

There are two "cases": the "upper case," containing capital letters
(CAPITAL LETTERS), small capital letters (SMALL CAPS) and certain symbols;
and the "lower case" containing ordinary small letters, punctuation marks,
hyphens, spaces and other symbols frequently used. Rules and ornaments
are kept in other cases or boxes.

---

[6]See, for example, *A Handbook of Printing Types . . . Used by Cowells*, Faber & Faber Ltd.
(1947), and *The Encyclopedia of Type Faces*, by W.T. Berry, A.F. Johnson and W.P. Jaspert,
Blandford Press Ltd. (1958).

[7]If a printer, because of unusually heavy demands upon certain letters or characters, has
none left in the appropriate compartments, he is said to be "out of sorts."

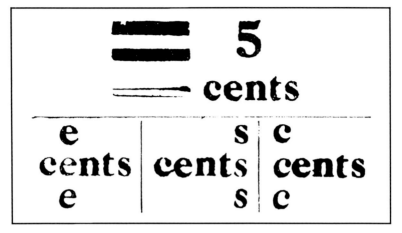

Relief printing. Typesetting faults. Seychelles 1957 5c. on 45c. The illustration shows the normal surcharge and part of the surcharges appearing on stamps Nos. 11, 23 and 26, together with samples of Roman and italic letters of the same type (Caslon Old Face heavy, 10 point). By error — or, possibly, because he was out of sorts — the compositor used the italic instead of the Roman "e," "s" and "c" on these stamps.

Relief printing. Typesetting faults. British Guiana 1898-99 2c. on 10c. The surcharge reads "TWO GENTS" because the compositor either made an error or was out of sorts and deliberately used "G" instead of "C."

The individual pieces of type are solid metal; they are, or should be, perfectly rectangular and identical in height[8] and depth, but the width varies according to the amount of space occupied by each letter or symbol.

The printing surface of each piece of type is known as the "face";[9] and on one of the rectangular sides of the body or shank of the piece of type is cut a nick. Nicks are always cut on the same side (called the "front" or "belly") of type, and they assist the compositor in determining that all the individual pieces of type are set the right way around in the stick.

Errors on the part of the compositor are not unknown; and sometimes he has been "out of sorts" and has deliberately used a letter inverted or a dif-

---

[8]The height of a piece of type is standard at 0.918 inch, known as "height to paper"; the spaces, which are not intended to print, are not as high.

[9]The term "face" is used also in the sense of "style."

Relief printing. Typeset design. Loose setting. Hawaii 1859-65 1c. (setting XIV), stamp No. 10 in two states. Because the setting was loose, the majority of the letters in "HAWAIIAN POSTAGE" failed to print, giving rise to these two varieties in sequence from the same position in the setting.

ferent letter to resemble another, or has "borrowed" a letter from a different font.

Many instances of varieties occasioned by faulty typesetting or by being out of sorts are to be found among stamps issued in all parts of the world. The following examples, chosen at random, will suffice to illustrate such errors and varieties: British Guiana 1898-99 2c. on 10c. reading "TWO GENTS"; Lithuania 1918 (Dec. 31) 20s. with inverted "h" used for "u" with accent under; Seychelles 1957 5c. on 1954 45c. with italic instead of roman "e," "s," "c" and "c," respectively, on stamps Nos. 11, 23, 26 and 42; Sonora (Mexico) 1913 10c. with an exclamation mark ("!") instead of the second "1" in 1913; and the many variations of overprint on Indian stamps comprising the early issues of Zanzibar, including for instance, Zanzibar 1895 (November) ½a. with inverted "q" for "b" in "Zanzibar," and the same basic stamp with the overprint reading "Zanzidar."

Repeated Hand-Setting

To obtain repetitions of a design by hand-setting, the compositor must assemble, or "compose," the design — whether merely of letters and spaces, or of letters, figures, other characters, ornaments, rules and spaces — over and over again as required. Each design, even the most simple, properly spaced, will comprise many separate pieces of type.

While he is setting each design and repetitions of the design, the compositor will "justify"; that is, he will insert spaces between the individual pieces of type and between each group of letters or figures so that each line occupies, overall, a pre-determined length. Later, when dealing with the repetitions of the design, he will justify those so that they are properly related to each other, and appear in regular rows and columns.

After the compositor has assembled the wording or designs, he must so tighten or clamp them that they are fixed together tightly in a solid mass to

Relief printing. Typeset design. Draw out. Hawaii 1859-65 2c. (setting III), stamp No. 4, variety " NTER." The piece of type bearing the letter "I" apparently was loose and was plucked from the setting by the ink roller. Consequently, the letter could not print.

Relief printing. Type-cast surcharge. Barbados 1947 1d. bearing the surcharge "ONE PENNY" printed from slugs cast in 12-point No. 3. Ludlow 6-LPHC type on a Ludlow type-casting machine.

form the printing base — or, perhaps, to form the original for copying by electrotyping or stereotyping. They are first laid on a flat surface, and then are fitted in a chase.

In the chase, the tight fixing of the type is effected by filling the spaces surrounding the justified designs — that is, the spaces between the inside edges of the chase and the outside edges of the groups of designs — with pieces of metal or wood known as "printers' furniture." If the pieces of type and type spaces do not by themselves fit tightly within the designs, pieces of thin cardboard or paper are inserted to make the type secure.

Sometimes, in spite of the precautions taken, type when printed from has worked loose, with the result that, when the ink roller was run over the face of the type, an individual piece of type was plucked from the setting, leaving a gap and, consequently, a missing letter or symbol in the print. Occasionally, several pieces of type, or even a whole word, may be removed in this manner. Such an occurrence is termed "draw out." Examples are to be found, for instance, in Hawaii 1859-65 2c (setting III) stamp No. 4, variety "NTER" showing the effects of a draw out of the "I" of "INTER." Similar causes account for Hawaii 1859-65 1c (setting XIV) stamp No. 10 showing first "HA   E" and later, "HA   " for "HAWAIIAN POSTAGE."

Type-Cast Overprints and Surcharges

Before I go on to discuss electrotyping and stereotyping from printers' type set in a chase, it will be convenient to mention here a method of type-casting in slugs that has been used in the production of some stamps.

A slug is a strip of solid type metal bearing a line of characters or letters on its upper edge, and is made by pouring or forcing molten type metal into

Relief Printing: Ludlow Type-Casting

Typical matrices of different type as used in a Ludlow type-casting machine.

Gathering matrices and inserting them in the composing or matrix stick.

A typical slug cast on a Ludlow typecasting machine in type of the same point size as that used for Barbados 1947 1d.

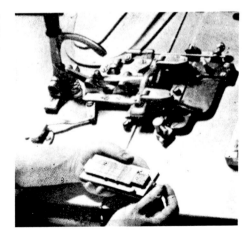

The matrix stick holds the matrices firmly when its adjustable screw is tightened. The stick, with the contained matrices, is then slid, face-downward, beneath the lock-down combination

The table top and delivery tray of the machine, with the matrix stick locked in position. The machine is set for repeat casting, and slugs are being delivered on the tray. The operator is holding a slug in his right hand.

an appropriately shaped container consisting of a steel stick and matrices made, usually, of brass.

Occasionally, repetitions of an overprint or surcharge have thus been produced individually on a type-casting machine; for example, Barbados 1947 1d. on 1941 2d. and 1943 2d. was produced by surcharging sheets of the basic stamps with repetitions of the words "ONE" and "PENNY" cast in slugs on a Ludlow type-casting machine in 12-point No. 3 Ludlow 6-LPHC Lining Plate Gothic heavy condensed type. After the necessary number of slugs was cast, they were assembled, clamped in a chase, and thus formed the printing base.

The principle upon which the Ludlow machine works is that brass matrices of the individual letters, separated by appropriate spaces, are gathered by hand into a special composing stick where they are clamped tight. This stick is then placed face-downward on the table of the machine, locked in place, and a lever is operated. This causes molten type metal to be forced, through a mouthpiece, into the collection of matrices, where the type metal solidifies. After a few seconds, the finished slug is delivered on a tray at the front of the machine. The machine can be set to repeat casting automatically at intervals of a few seconds until the requisite number of slugs has been delivered.

A slug consists of only a single line of letters or words. Consequently, if it is necessary, as it was in the case of Barbados 1947 1d., to print different words one above the other, a sufficient number of slugs must be cast from each of two different compositions. In the chase, these slugs are placed alternately one above the other, separated by blank slugs. Of course, as well as being arranged the one above the other, slugs can also be set side by side to cover the desired width of paper at one printing operation; and it was in this manner that the Barbados 1947 1d. was produced.

Somewhat similar in principle of operation is the Linotype machine, which casts slugs comprising a line of type; the matrices are selected mechanically by the operator depressing the appropriate keys, which are set out on a keyboard rather like that of a typewriter. Among stamps overprinted from Linotype slugs are, for example, Newfoundland 1919 (Jun. 9) Air, Alcock and Brown $1 on 1897 15c., and 1927 (May 18) Air, De Pinedo 60c.

Although many typeset stamps, overprints and surcharges have been printed direct from type or slugs, many others have been printed from plates made by the galvanic process of electrodeposition and by stereotype casting in moulds made from the type fixed in the chase. This has been the case, particularly, with duty plates used with a key-type design.

Electrotyping from Typesetting

Electrotyping from typeset chases has been employed, for example, by Thomas De La Rue & Company Ltd. for the key-types of the British Commonwealth. Methods of producing moulds, their composition and the eventual steps taken for producing a finished printing plate ready for the press have varied greatly and in detail throughout the world. It would be quite impossible to survey all the variations in procedure in a work such as this.

The preliminary step is the composition of the original typeset wording and figures, and their assembly and fixing in the chase. This original, of course, reads reversed — that is, from right-to-left. The other basic steps involved in producing an

Relief printing. Type-cast surcharge. Newfoundland 1919 (Jun. 9) Air, Alcock and Brown $1. The overprinting was carried out from slugs produced on a Linotype machine.

454

Relief printing. Electrotyping. Distorted electro. Leeward Islands 1902 1s., plate 2, pane 1, stamp No. 1, variety dropped "R." When the electrotype for the duty plate was made, the letter was squeezed, owing to the softness of the material, and resulted in the irregular alignment of "LEEWARD."

electrotype printing plate of type characters may be summarized as follows:

1. Making the mould or matrix, by sinking the original into and withdrawing it from a suitable material such as wax, gutta-percha or lead. The mould reads normally, from left-to-right.

2. In appropriate cases, covering the face of the mould with a coating such as graphite to provide a conductor of electricity.

3. Placing the treated mould in an electrodepositing bath, and growing a shell or skin of copper (or, perhaps, other metal) on the face of the mould. When the shell is removed, that face of it that was in contact with the mould presents an exact replica of the original, reading from right-to-left.

4. Filling the back of the copper shell with molten type metal; this process is termed "backing." When the backing of the shell is complete, the shell and backing together form the printing plate, which is subjected to finishing treatment and is ready for the press.

The material from which the mould is made is, necessarily, soft, and the shell of copper grown in the electrodepositing bath is very thin. Handling of the mould, the separation of the shell from the mould and the subsequent handling of the shell demand great care, because of their liability to damage. Philatelic varieties caused by damage to or distortion of a mould or shell are sometimes encountered. A well-known and prominent instance of distortion is to be found, for example, in Leeward Islands 1902 1s., plate 2, pane 1, stamp No. 1, where "LEEWARD" has a dropped "R," the letter having been "squeezed" owing to the softness of the material.

Stereotyping from Typesetting

As with electrotyping, so with stereotyping from typeset chases — it has been widely employed, and the methods used for the production of the printing plates have varied greatly and in detail throughout the world. Equally impossible would it be in a work such as this to survey all the variations in procedure.

The preliminary step is, of course, the preparation of the typeset chase. The other steps undertaken may be summarized as follows:

455

1. Making the mould or matrix by placing the type face-upward and pouring over it a mixture of plaster of paris and water, and removing it when set; or by covering the type with a flong,[10] beating the back with a brush to force the face into the interstices of the type, allowing or causing the flong to dry, and removing the resultant *papier-maché*.

2. Casting from the mould, by pouring into it molten type metal which, when it has solidified and has been removed from the mould, comprises the printing plate in its rough state ready for finishing.

Diagnosing the Method

Each of the foregoing methods of producing typeset or typecast stamps, overprints and surcharges, whether printed from type or slugs or from electros or stereos, has its individual characteristics, and a study of the product will, in some cases, enable the method of production to be determined with certainty. Of course, standards both of production of the printing base and of printing vary greatly, and allowance must be made for these variations when diagnosis is attempted.

Generally speaking, if the setting of the letters is not regular, especially if the letters appear battered and uneven, and if the paper is heavily and unevenly impressed, the indications are that the printing was from hand-set type.

Again, generally speaking, if the setting of the letters is very regular, their edges are clean-cut and the paper is evenly impressed, the indications are that the printing was from type-cast slugs.

The finest and most regular impressions with the sharpest line edges result from good electrotyping; and good stereotyping produces fine and regular results.

Multiplying the Design

As has been stated earlier in this chapter, by far the most frequently used methods of preparing a printing base for relief printing have been to multiply the design with the assistance of mechanical or other means. From time to time and throughout the world, many different such processes have been used in the production of relief-printed stamps, and it would be quite impossible in a work of this nature to deal in detail with all the processes and their many variations. The most that can be attempted is to survey in broad outline the general aspects, and to consider some of the details more closely.

Broadly speaking, all these processes of producing printing bases for relief-printed stamps may be classified according to the methods used to multiply the design. These methods fall into two broad divisions: when the design is multiplied from a die; and when the design is multiplied photographically.

When a die is produced, the design may be multiplied from it by a number of entirely different methods: that is, through the medium of moulds, or by

---

[10]"Flong" is the primary, damp stage of *papier-maché*, and consists of layers of paper in decreasing thicknesses, bonded together with an adhesive composition.

means of a transfer roll or a punch. When the design is multiplied through the medium of moulds, various processes have been used. They may be summarized as: electrotyping, stereotyping, polytyping and vulcanizing rubber. When the design is multiplied by photography, although various results may be attained, all the processes embody photomechanical etching similar to that used in photogravure and photolitho. Indeed, to some extent, many of the subjects dealt with later in this chapter have already been mentioned in relation to the production of some printing bases for line engraving, gravure and, generally, in the chapters entitled "Printing Problems and Varieties" and "Printing Characteristics."

In some cases, the printing bases have been produced as the result of combinations of photography and moulding — photomechanical etching being used in the earlier stages, and moulding for electros, stereos or rubber plates in the later stages of multiplication of the design.

Multiplication of Design from a Die

Multiplication of the design from a die through the medium of moulds may be considered conveniently in three stages: producing the die; producing the moulds; producing the printing bases.

Producing the Die

When moulds are to be used, the steps taken in the production of the die, and the nature of the die itself, depend upon the treatment it is to receive when the moulds are produced. In some processes, the die is subjected to considerable strain during the production of the moulds; to withstand the strain, the die is made of hardened steel. In other such processes, the strain to which the die is subjected is relatively slight, and an engraving on box-wood or, perhaps, copper or other comparatively soft material suffices.

An instance of the multiplication through the medium of moulds of a design from a hardened steel die is provided by the engraving made by J.F. Joubert de la Ferté for U.S. Confederate States, General Issues, 1862 Jefferson Davis

Relief printing. Hardened steel die. U.S. Confederate States, General Issues, 1862 Jefferson Davis 5c. The die was engraved on steel by J.F. Joubert de la Ferté. (Because of the lighting, the "ups" appear dark and the "downs" light in the picture.)

457

Relief printing. Composite die. Great Barrier Island (New Zealand) 1898 (Oct. 27) 1s. For this stamp, the die comprised several parts: The frame, the ornamentation, the bird and the wording in the upper scroll were photomechanically etched on zinc; the words "Special Post" and "One Shilling" were typeset; and the type and zinc were joined together into a compact whole by treatment with molten metal.

5c. An instance of the multiplication through the medium of moulds of a design engraved on a wooden die is provided, for example, by Victoria 1857-63 Emblems 1d. An instance of the multiplication through the medium of moulds of a design photomechanically etched on zinc, and mounted to form a die, is provided, for example, by Great Barrier Island (New Zealand) 1898 (Oct. 27) 1s.[11]

By far the most usual form of die (for relief-printed stamps of which the design has been multiplied through the medium of moulds) is an engraving upon steel. The majority of such dies comprise line engravings in which the metal that is not to print is cut away from the surface of the die, leaving the printing surface, so to speak, "in relief."

The simplest form of steel die for relief printing is one on which the complete design has been engraved *en épargne* and in reverse by one engraver. Such a die is, however, the exception rather than the rule. Several reasons account for this. For example, the engraving of a portrait is a highly specialized form or branch of an art or craft that is itself highly specialized, and a portrait engraver rarely does other work upon a stamp die. Also, it has been by no means unusual for work upon a stamp die to be done at two or more stages: that is, engraving *en épargne* upon one piece of steel; engraving in intaglio upon a counterpart of the *en épargne* engraving; and further engraving *en épargne* upon a counterpart of the intaglio counterpart. Further, while procedures and techniques vary from printer to printer, it is not unusual for a separate die to be engraved of a particular feature with the intention that

---

[11]Only the main features of the design were photomechanically etched; the words "Special Post" and "One Shilling" were typeset, the type and zinc being joined together (by treatment with molten metal) to form the die.

that feature shall appear in several different monochrome designs. These circumstances merit more detailed discussion.

Many series have been issued in which a feature of a design is common if not to all the stamps, then to several monochrome stamps in the series. For example, in Great Britain 1912-22 ½d. to 1s., one head was used for the ½d., 1½d., 2d., 3d. and 4d.; a different head for the 1d. and 2½d.; and a third head for the 5d. to 1s. values. Additionally, in that series, five different frame designs were used in combination with the different heads. And, of course, each of the fourteen different denominations bore different figures and words of value.

So far as concerns the heads, only one die of each design was engraved; such a die is termed an "original (head) die." From each original (head) die, by a process of transferring similar to that referred to in detail in the discussion of multiplication of the design in the chapter entitled "Intaglio Printing — I: Line Engraving" and also referred to later in this chapter, roller dies were made and used to reproduce the heads upon a total of five different dies, termed at that stage "subsidiary (head) dies." Upon each of these, a different frame was engraved, and these dies then became the "original (undenominated) dies" or "blank duty dies." By a similar process of transferring, a total of fourteen different undenominated dies was produced, and on each of these were engraved the appropriate figures and words of value, whereupon each die became the "original die" (or, as it is sometimes termed, the "duty die") of that value.[12]

Where work upon a die was done at two or more stages, and a counterpart was made of a partly engraved *en épargne* die, the counterpart was termed a "punch." The punch was made by striking the relief die into soft metal, in a coining press or similar apparatus. Upon the unhardened punch thus made the engraver operated, and the engraving of a punch involves, of course, that a print direct from the engraved metal appears as a tonally negative mirror print of the design.

In such engraving, unlike the more usual *en épargne* engraving, the engraver cut away metal corresponding with areas and lines that were (in the eventual stamp) to be printed in color, and left untouched metal corresponding with areas and lines that were (in the eventual stamp) to appear uncolored. In other words, except that he cut the design so that any lettering read normally from left-to-right, he proceeded very much as though he were producing a die for a line-engraved recess-printed stamp. If the punch he engraved had been inked, wiped and polished in the manner[13] of a recessed die, a print from it would have yielded an intaglio, tonally positive mirror print of the design.

It has been stated that the reason for the adoption of this form of engrav-

---

[12]The foregoing account is a simplification of the steps actually undertaken, and illustrates some of the possibilities inherent in the process. For further and more detailed information on the issue see, for example, *The London Philatelist*, Vol. 31, Page 134 (June 1922) and *The Postage Stamps of Great Britain — Part Four*, by K.M. Beaumont and J.B.M. Stanton (1957).

[13]See "Printing from Flat Plates" in the chapter entitled "Intaglio Printing — I: Line Engraving."

Head A and Frame 1 —
½d. and 1½d.

Relief printing. Above and on opposite page, master dies; subsidiary dies or blank duty dies; and original dies or duty dies. Great Britain 1912-22 ½d. to 1s. Three different heads, five different frames and fourteen different denominations, all printed in monochrome. For this series, only three original head dies were engraved. These were then transferred to five separate subsidiary dies. Upon each subsidiary die a different frame was engraved, producing five original undenominated dies, or blank duty dies. Each of these was then multiplied the requisite number of times to produce fourteen undenominated dies. The appropriate figures and words of value were engraved on each die to produce the original die or duty die for that value.

ing was, perhaps, that, in the early days, the engravers found difficulty with white lettering.[14] After the engraving had proceeded to a stage at which the engraver was satisfied and any necessary modification had been made, the punch was hardened.

The punch then was used as a "die matrix" — that is, by striking the punch into soft metal, a counterpart of the punch was produced, and this counterpart comprised the die.[15] On this die the design appeared in relief and reversed, any lettering reading from right-to-left. Dependent upon the evolution of the design throughout the preliminary stages, at this stage the die would be undenominated, and would be termed a "blank duty die."

On the blank duty die the engraver finished the engraving and completed the design by inserting the words or figures of value to form the original die for the relevant stamp. At that stage of the engraving, he would cut en épargne — that is, he would cut away metal in areas to appear uncolored in the eventual stamp, and leave untouched metal in areas to be printed in color on the eventual stamp. This duty die would then be hardened for use in striking moulds. If more than one denomination in the same design were required, as many blank duty dies would be struck as were necessary, and upon each of them the engraver would cut the relevant words or figures of value.

In such a series of steps, when progress proofs[16] exist, they reveal the steps,

---

[14]See *The London Philatelist*, Vol. 65, Page 203 (November 1956).

[15]The early dies for Thomas De La Rue & Company were hardened and struck by the Royal Mint, and so were the punches. The procedure is referred to in *The De La Rue History of British & Foreign Postage Stamps 1855 to 1901* by John Easton (1958), for example, on Pages 180-81.

[16]Sometimes termed "progressives." See "Dies and Die Proofs" in the chapter entitled "From Design to Issued Sheets."

Head A and Frame 2 — 2d., 3d. and 4d.

Head B and Frame 3 — 1d. and 2½d.

Head C and Frame 4 — 5d., 6d., 7d. and 8d.

Head C and Frame 5 — 9d., 10d. and 1s.

461

because the proofs taken during some stages are reversed and tonally negative representations of the eventual design, and in other stages are normal and tonally positive prints. A series of six such proofs, in the collection belonging to H.M. Queen Elizabeth II, of India 1855 4a. was first illustrated in *The London Philatelist* for November 1956 (Vol. 65, Page 203), together with a letter from G.L. Newman, company archivist of Thomas De La Rue & Company Ltd.[17]

Quite apart from handwork engraving upon a die, background features such as closely spaced parallel lines may be added by machine, and assistance in engraving may be provided by the process of etching.

Because the making of a punch from an *en épargne* die involved translating the recesses representing non-printing areas of the die into relief areas on the punch, and some of those relief areas could, with comparative ease, be removed by filing or scraping from the soft punch without affecting other relief areas on it, this afforded an opportunity for an engraver to amend his work by adding color to the finished product — a process that otherwise presented very great difficulty.[18] The process adopted was to remove the unwanted reliefs from the punch, harden it, and then use it in the coining press to make a fresh die. On this fresh die, the area corresponding with that on the punch from which the reliefs were removed was the height of the original surface, and a print from that fresh die in that state would present that area as solid color. Upon the fresh die, the engraver could engrave new work as desired. This process was used freely by, among others, the engravers of De La Rue & Company, including J.F. Joubert de la Ferté, who more than once engraved a new diadem on the head used originally for Great Britain 1855 4d. This head later was used, with different diadems, for the stamps, among others, of Sierra Leone and Hong Kong.

The depth of engraving on dies varies considerably with different engravers and processes. Speaking generally, the "downs," or portions that are to appear uncolored on the stamp, are something less than one millimeter below the "ups," or portions that are to appear colored on the stamp.

Usually the master dies are carefully preserved and used only comparatively infrequently. In many cases, copies or reproductions termed "working dies" are used for the purpose of making the subsidiary dies and original dies or duty dies. There is, substantially, no limit to the number of removes from the original engraving that can be made through the media of punches or transfer rolls and subsidiary dies. A slight thickening of lines may occur, causing a perceptible coarsening of the work (the deterioration can be remarked by comparing a die proof with an issued stamp), but this is mainly because proofs are printed with greater care than are stamps.

As is implicit from what has been stated, in some cases in which stamps in a series differ from each other merely in words and figures of denomina-

---

[17]The only feature of the transition from negative to positive calling for special comment is that, in the last negative and first positive progressives, the lower part of the oval frame appears in color on both proofs. This fact can be accounted for by the cutting away of the metal within that part of the frame before the punch was hardened.

[18]It was sometimes effected by drilling the die, plugging it, and engraving the face of the plug.

Relief printing. Dies from altered punches. The upper picture shows a print from a die made from a punch that had had relief areas of metal cut away. The punch itself was originally made, in a coining press, from a fully engraved relief die — that is, a hardened die on which (in the area corresponding with the blank area within the blank surround) recesses had been cut to provide non-printing areas and to give the effect of hair and a diadem. On the soft punch, those non-printing areas were reliefs; the requisite reliefs (representing the hair and diadem) were filed or scraped away, leaving the remainder of the punch unaffected. The punch was then hardened, and a soft steel die was made from the punch in a coining press. From that die the print in the upper picture was made, the uncolored areas (representing what was once hair and diadem) being the natural surface (or "up") of the die. The engraver then worked on this soft die, cutting away the non-printing areas, giving a different shape to the hair and making a new diadem. After his work was finished, the die was hardened and a new punch was made.

Further background was added either at that or a later stage, and, eventually, a new die resulted, from which a print was made. This is shown in the lower picture.

tion, the duty die for each value comprises a single piece of steel with the design complete and including the denomination. All these dies are derived from an undenominated die or blank duty die, which itself may be the result of several building-up processes.

In other cases in which stamps in a series differ from each other merely in words and figures of denomination, no single duty die comes into existence. Instead, an undenominated die is engraved, and spaces are hollowed out of, or holes are cut through, the die, allowing for the insertion of closely fitting plugs. Each plug bears the necessary words or figures, and the plugs are fitted into and removed from the undenominated die as required. Well-known stamps providing instances of the use of such procedures are to be found in Australia 1913-48 Kangaroo ½d. to 1s.; indeed, all the Kangaroo stamps except the 2s. of 1945-48 stemmed from a single undenominated die with interchangeable plugs for the figures and letters of value.

Similarly, in the cases of many of the issues made during the reign of Queen Victoria in Great Britain, including, for example, Great Britain 1880-81 1d., in which different check letters appear in the corners of every differently posi-

Relief printing. Master die — key-type. A proof from the complete master die, without country inscription and undenominated, from which stemmed all the dies for the monochrome and bi-colored stamps of East Africa and Uganda Protectorates (Kenya, Uganda and Tanganyika) 1903-1907 ½a. to 8a. and 1907-1908 1c. to 75c.; British Central Africa (Nyasaland Protectorate) 1903-1907 1d. to 1s.; and Somaliland Protectorate 1904-1909 ½a. to 12a.

tioned stamp in the sheet, spaces were made in the dies so that plugs bearing the check letters could be inserted as required.

The instances mentioned do not and are not intended to exhaust the different techniques relative to dies employed from time to time and in different parts of the world in the production of relief-printed stamps where the design has been multiplied through the medium of a mould. The procedures are

Relief printing. Original (undenominated) die. British Central Africa (Nyasaland Protectorate) 1903-1907. A proof from the complete original (undenominated) die or blank duty die, from which stemmed the dies for the bi-colored stamps of British Central Africa 1903-1907 1d. to 1s.

Relief printing. Die with inter-changeable plugs. Australia 1913-48 Kangaroo stamps. For all these stamps except the 2s. of 1945-48, only one die was engraved, and this had spaces in-to which could be fitted and removed as required plugs bearing different figures and words of value.

capable of almost limitless variations in detail. In the cases of some issues, the detailed procedure has been established with reasonable certainty by students; in other cases, much remains to be established. Each issue must be studied by reference to the steps taken in its particular production, and these can be ascertained only by a consideration of all the facts relevant to the particular stamps. It is unsound to take any process or series of processes as used by any printer at any one time as standard, and to refer exclusively to it for the purpose of making purported certain deductions in relation to any other stamps produced by the same printer at a different time — much less other stamps produced by other printers at different times.

Whatever may be the detailed steps taken to arrive at the stage where the die is ready for use to multiply the designs, at that stage the die is negative and in relief, as was tabulated in "Dies and Die Proofs" in the chapter en-titled "From Design to Issued Sheets."

It is, of course, a characteristic, and a desired characteristic, of the processes of multiplying a design from a die that the copies should faithfully reproduce what appears on the die. A die, even a hardened steel die, is susceptible to damage. As a consequence, if the die, before or during use, suffers damage, the effects of the damage will be transmitted to every stamp that subsequently results from use of the damaged die.

Instances are known where, for example, the die has cracked, or part of the metal has broken, and the effects of the cracking or breaking are visible on the stamps. An example of such damage, caused by injury or inherent defect, is to be found, for instance, in New Zealand 1882 1d., where the die cracked or crumbled in more than one place during the course of time. One part of the damage reveals itself as a nick and uncolored break in the right outer frameline, about one-third of the way down from the northeast corner of the stamp. Another instance of stamps reflecting damage to the die is pro-vided, for example, by France 1876-1900 Peace and Commerce 1c. to 5f. in which case, after the undenominated die had been used, it cracked, and a re-engraving of part of the design resulted in the production of the two design types usually distinguished as "N under U" and "N under B" (having reference to the position of the imprint in relation to the word "Republique"); these are illustrated in the chapter entitled "Stamp Design."

Apart from being susceptible to damage, some relief dies have, during the course of time, been subjected to repair or retouching. The full extent of the possibilities of repair work on such dies has not had general philatelic recogni-

Relief printing. Die cracks. New Zealand 1882 1d., a block of four and an enlargement of part of the design of the so-called "Die 3," being, in fact, the last state
of the single die from which all the 1d. stamps in this design stemmed. The
frameline at the right, opposite the first "E" of "Revenue," has a nick and is
interrupted, resulting from a crack caused by damage or inherent defect. That
the flaw is not merely a plate flaw is proved by its repetition (so far as the picture is concerned) on all four stamps.

tion. As a consequence, instances are known where stamps stemming from
the one die before and after repair have been thought to be derived from
different dies, and have been referred to as "Die I," "Die II," etc. An example of such erroneous belief is provided, for instance, by the Australia 1913-48
Kangaroo stamps (mentioned where undenominated dies and plugs were
discussed); the existence of only one die, except for the 2s. of 1945-48, was
not accepted until after 1949.[19]

In some cases, the terms "Die I," "Die II," etc. are deliberately adopted
to refer to different states of the one die, as, for instance, in the case of New
Zealand 1882 1d., mentioned just above in the discussion of damage to a die.[20]

---

[19]See *Philately from Australia*, Vol. 1, Page 11 (March 1949), and compare *The Australian
Commonwealth Specialists' Catalogue* 17th ed. (1956) with the same work, 18th ed. (1957).
[20]See *The Postage Stamps of New Zealand*, Vol. 1 (1938), Page 113, and Vol. 2 (1950), Page 293.

Producing the Moulds

In surveying the methods of multiplying the design from a die, one may state that, broadly speaking, these methods are divisible into two classes: first, where the die itself is used directly in the processes of multiplication; and second where the die is used merely to produce some intermediate object, such as a punch or transfer roll, that then becomes the medium by which the operations of multiplication are effected. Whatever method of multiplication is adopted, the design on the die is, usually, negative and in relief; and in the next stage, the design is positive and in recess; so that the representations of the design are complementary to or are counterparts of each other. In other words, usually, on the die the design reads reversed, from right-to-left, with the printing surface in relief; and in the next stage, which is termed the "mould" or "matrix" stage, the design reads normally, from left-to-right, with what are eventually to be the printing areas in recess.

Thus, briefly to survey without attempting to exhaust the methods of multiplying the design from a die, one may state that the classes comprise: (1) multiplication directly and (2) multiplication indirectly from the die.

In multiplication directly from the die, the die is used to produce numerous impressions in a comparatively soft, cold or semi-fused substance, such as wax, lead or gutta-percha on the one hand, or plaster of paris or copper on the other hand; and these impressions, termed "moulds" or "matrices," are then used (dependent upon their characteristics) for electrotyping or stereotyping purposes. After subsequent treatment, the electrotypes or stereotypes are ready for use. These processes of electrotyping and stereotyping allow considerable flexibility in the methods of multiplication, which may be carried out in any manner used in transferring for lithography.[21] That is, the same number of moulds as there are to be stamps in the sheet may be made from the die; or the die may be used to make a conveniently small number of moulds, which are then grouped together and re-copied *en bloc* until sufficient groups have been produced to bear, when they are assembled, in aggregate the same number of subjects as there are to be stamps in the sheet. Thus, the printing bases produced comprise: (a) a collection of individual subjects clamped or affixed together, or (b) a collection of small groups of subjects clamped or affixed together, or (c) solid plates made by taking electrotype or stereotype copies of (a) or (b).

In multiplication indirectly from the die, the die is used to produce, on the one hand, a "punch" by direct pressure, or, on the other hand, a "transfer roll" by the die and mill process of rocking. A punch is (or, rather, has been) used to stamp individual copies of the design upon cold metal or semi-fused metal. After subsequent treatment, these pieces of stamped metal, termed *clichés*,[22] are clamped or fixed together, and comprise the printing bases; or

---

[21]By means of stones bearing increasingly multiplied subjects — see "Multiplying the Design by the Transferring Process" in the "Addendum" to Chapter 10, "Planographic Printing."

[22]Strictly, the term *cliché* refers exclusively to the result of stamping semi-fused metal. However, it has become widely associated, so far as philately is concerned, with a separate subject however produced; and, indeed, has been used, with scant justification, to describe an individual subject in a solid plate.

else the printing bases consist of electrotype or stereotype copies or re-copies of a group or groups of individual *clichés*. A transfer roll is used directly to lay down the requisite number of impressions on a soft steel or other metal plate; and this plate, or a copy of it made by electrotyping or stereotyping, is used for printing.

Moulds for Electrotyping

In multiplication directly from the die, many different methods have been used from time to time for the production of lead moulds in the preparation by electrotyping of printing bases for postage stamps. Of these methods, the process used by Thomas De La Rue & Company Ltd. resulted in the production of more different stamps than, perhaps, any other method. This process produced, substantially, identical impressions on many pieces of lead.

This identity was obtained, mainly, because of the ingenuity and excellent workmanship of the collar and plunger that control the lead and die during striking. The collar comprises a heavy steel cylinder with a rectangular shaft vertically through the center. The area of the rectangle is equal to the size of the stamp plus half the gutters between stamps. At one end of the cylinder, the body has been shaped to permit the die to rest so that the engraving faces into the rectangular shaft. The die is held firmly in place by a wedge-shaped and substantial piece of steel that slides into an appropriately shaped gap at the base of the collar.

The other end of the rectangular shaft is free. Into this end is put a piece of lead, previously cut to exact area and thickness. Along the shaft the lead is pushed until it comes into facial contact with the design on the die. Then a two-part plunger is inserted into the shaft and pushed home until one end comes into contact with the back of the piece of lead; the other end of the plunger projects from the collar.

The collar is fitted into a type of fly-press; and, with skill born of fine judgment and long experience, the operator causes the plunger to be struck by the press,[23] thus forcing the lead on to the die and causing the soft metal to take on a positive and recessed impression of the negative and relief design on the hard steel. The struck lead mould is removed,[24] another lead is inserted, and the operation of striking is repeated. These operations are carried out again and again until the requisite number of leads has been struck.[25]

Because the steel collar has been accurately made and a perfect fit ensured

---

[23]This was the old method. Hydraulic pressure long ago supplanted the fly-press.

[24]By removing the wedge-shaped piece of steel, thus releasing the die and allowing the struck lead to fall into the hand of the operator.

[25]It is usual for some printers, certainly for Thomas De La Rue & Company Ltd., to keep careful watch on the die, and to examine it after use for striking. Sharp edges of even hardened steel reliefs may become dulled by repeated striking, despite the use of lead, which is soft in comparison. Die proofs, inscribed "After Striking," reflect this attention — see "Dies and Die Proofs" in the chapter entitled "From Design to Issued Sheets." Such proofs are known with an indication of the number of leads struck from the die, probably because, for some reason or other, the die is suspect.

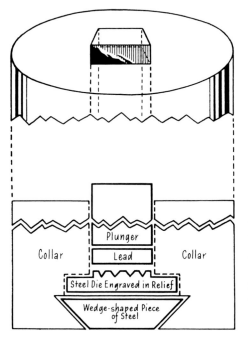

Lead mould striking. Diagrammatic representation of the collar and plunger used by Thomas De La Rue & Company Ltd. for controlling the die and lead during striking of moulds. A perspective representation of the upper part of the collar with the top of the plunger projecting from the aperture.

for the die and the plunger, and because the leads fit the space exactly and are of standard thickness, no lateral movement is possible, and substantial identity of moulds is obtained.

Under such ideal conditions, the only philatelic variety that could occur at this stage would be caused by the presence of impacted metal in the die; and this would give rise to the presence, on the eventual stamp, of color in what should have been an uncolored portion of the design.[26] Such a variety would occur on every different mould and its consequent stamps resulting from use of the die after the extraneous piece of metal became impacted and until it became dislodged or was removed. The variety would be the equivalent of a "colored roller flaw."[27]

Philatelists generally have not come to grips with the terminological problem set by this class of variety. A term that has been used in this regard is "sub-type"; but this, even when surrounded by quotation marks, is liable to cause confusion.[28] The term "impacted metal flaw" is available for use,

---

[26]The presence of excess color distinguishes such a variety from one caused by damage to the die, this being characterized by the unusual absence of color.

[27]See "Roller Flaw" in the alphabetical list to the chapter entitled "Intaglio Printing — I: Line Engraving."

[28]For the following reasons: The term "sub-type" is well-understood and widely used in reference to lithographically printed stamps — see "Type" in the alphabetical list to the chapter entitled "Planographic Printing." In the same sense, sub-types sometimes occur

(Footnote 28 continues)

graphically diagnostic and accurate — at least in cases in which the moulds are metal.

Impacted metal flaws are to be found, for example, in New Zealand 1882 (1891) 2d., pane 2, stamps Nos. 11, 13, 14 etc. (produced by the Government Printer of New Zealand),[29] and in Cook Islands 1893-1902 2½d., pane 2, stamps Nos. 2, 3, 4, 5 and 13.[30]

Striking Varieties

When the leads are not subject to ideal control before and during striking, other philatelic varieties can occur. Chief among these is the "double strike," which causes duplication of some of the lines of the resultant stamps.

"Double strike" is the effect caused by a "bouncing" of the die when struck upon the lead, so that the face of the die comes into non-coincident contact more than once with the stamped surface of the lead. This effect can result from the employment of a collar with an aperture slightly larger than the die, from the employment of a piece of lead of which the area measurement is somewhat smaller than that of the shaft in the collar, and, of course, also from striking without the use of a collar.

Double strikes are encountered on the stamps of many countries, and the areas of duplication and degrees of displacement vary greatly. As instances: Denmark, 1851-54 4 rbs., plate 1, stamp No. 55, where the doubling, slightly displaced, occurs at the top of the wreath and the top tablet of the stamp is deformed; France 1863-70 5f., pane 1, stamp No. 13, where the doubling,

---

in relief printing when the printing base comprises the aggregate of several individually identifiable *groups* of subjects and each group stems from a "master group" comprising individually identifiable *subjects;* in such a case, the flaws first occurring on each subject in the master group identify the "types," and the flaws first occurring on each copy of the master group identify the "sub-types." Such flaws — that is, the "type" flaws — can rightly be said to recur or repeat. They are in one class. In a completely different class is a flaw caused by metal inadvertently impacted in the die. Such a flaw, unless it is characteristic of an individual unit in a master group that has been multiplied, cannot truly be said to recur or repeat — although it can justifiably be stated that a similar (albeit different) flaw arising from similar causes occurs on several or many successively struck subjects.

[29]See *Philately from Australia,* Vol. 1, Pages 123, 128 (December 1949).

[30]See *The Australian Stamp Journal,* Vol. 36, Page 98 (September 1946).

[31]It might at first be thought that the only effect of the die entering the mould unevenly would be the creation of an uncolored or insufficiently heavily colored area over that part of the resultant stamp corresponding with those recesses of the mould that are comparatively shallow. When the reversal of this effect occurs, it is caused, subsequent to the striking, when the electrotype is straightened after backing. When the electrotype is straightened (printers term the process "slabbing") by hammering upon a suitable punch applied to the back of the plate with its face upon a hard level surface, the "ups" are brought to the same level; the "downs," therefore, are at different depths and, unless they are accentuated downward by the operator using a burin, sometimes there is insufficient difference between some of the "ups" and "downs" — so that what should be "downs" are inked and print, resulting in an absence of uncolored portions in part of the design.

[32]Similar effects can occur in casting stereotypes if the box is not kept hot. If the box is not kept at a sufficiently high temperature, the metal will solidify irregularly, causing distortion and other defects in the cast.

[33]See "Reglet Flaws" later in this chapter.

470

slightly displaced, occurs in the top third of the left "numeral" panel and affects the horizontal lines and part of the inner frame; Victoria 1864-69 Laureated 2d., setting 1, stamp No. 33 (Type C.9), where the doubling, substantially displaced, affects all the letters of the words "TWO PENCE."

Other varieties that can occur during striking include "partial strike." Partial strike is the effect caused by uneven distribution of the force applied when the die is struck; so that, instead of entering the mould to an even depth, the die enters at an angle. This may cause on the resultant stamps a marked or, perhaps, complete absence of any uncolored part of the design over the area where the die has failed to enter the mould to the correct depth.[31]

When the die is struck not into cold but into semi-fused metal, another class of variety of sometimes outstanding appearance can result, because of irregular solidifying of the metal. Unless the lead is pure, or reasonably so, and solidifies regularly, internal stresses are set up to which the still soft portions of the mould are subject, with the result that distortion of the design may occur in these portions.[32] Stamps exhibiting the effects of such stresses fall within the class termed "distortion varieties," and are called "internal distortion varieties" to distinguish them from "external distortion varieties," which are caused by the application of external force to the finished electrotype (or stereotype).[33] A prominent instance of an internal distortion variety

is to be found, for example, in Victoria 1864-69 Laureated 2d., setting 1, stamp No. 53 (Type B.14), where the distortion has caused the circular frame at the right to become indented, and has also, by the southeast spandrel, affected the right inner line of the rectangular frame, causing it to be discontinuous.

After the moulds have been struck, if no collar has been used, the next step in the process is to trim the leads — that is, to square them up

Relief printing. Double strike. Victoria 1864-69 Laureated 2d., setting 1, stamp No. 33 (Type C.9) and a photographic enlargement of part of the design exhibiting the variety "double strike." This stamp was printed from an electroplate grown on a lead mould made by striking the die upon the lead. Because the lead and die were not held in immovable contact during the striking, the die met the lead more than once in non-coincident contact, causing duplication in part of the mould, which the electrotype reproduced. Duplication is visible, particularly in the words "TWO PENCE."

Relief printing. Internal distortion. Victoria 1864-69 Laureated 2d., setting 1, stamp No. 53 (Type B.14), and a photographic enlargement of part of the design exhibiting the variety "internal distortion." When a die is struck into semi-fused metal, it may solidify irregularly and set up internal stresses that affect the unsolidified parts of the mould. When these parts solidify, the design is distorted; the distortion is reproduced by the electrotype, and appears on the resultant stamp.

— so that they may be joined together for the purpose of growing a shell. This trimming, if imperfectly guided, may result in part of the design being infringed, with the effect that the resultant stamps do not bear the whole of the design. A stamp bearing evidence of this trimming, usually in the form of the absence or attenuation of part or all of one frameline, is referred to as a "cut edge" variety.[34]

The process of electrotyping involves that the mould or matrix will be immersed in liquid. As a consequence, the material from which the mould is made must be, or must be capable of being made, impervious to the liquid, notwithstanding that the mould is partly protected by a coating that renders it a conductor of electricity. For these reasons, *papier-maché* is not usually used for moulds for electrotyping.

When moulds of gutta-percha, or wax, or similar material are produced,

---

[34]A "cut edge" variety can occur not only as the result of trimming a mould (in which case the trimming infringes what is a "down" of the mould), but also as the result of cutting apart the individual subjects comprising a single (but multiple-subject) electro or stereo (in which case the trimming infringes an "up" of the electro or stereo), and also in steel plates — see "Multiplication By Means of a Transfer Roll" later in this chapter.

the class of philatelic variety most likely to be encountered as the result of striking (which is a much less forceful process than when cold lead is used) is of the nature of an impacted metal flaw — but in such cases, the probability is that not metal but some other substance becomes impacted in the die.

Gutta-percha moulds were used, for example, by M. Anatole A. Hulot, who printed, among other issues, France 1853-60 1c. to 1f.

Wax moulds were used, for example, for France 1945-47 10c. to 15f.

Plastic moulds were used, for example, for France 1955 Marianne 6f., 12f. and 15f.

Moulds for Stereotyping

The process of stereotyping[35] involves that the moulds or matrices will be subjected to the heat of the molten metal cast in them. As a consequence, the material from which the moulds are made must be, substantially, impervious to heat.

Almost endless variations in techniques are encountered in the use of the materials available for moulds suitable for stereotype casting, and the following discussion refers to only an outline of the two main processes adopted in some cases — plaster of paris and *papier-maché*.

By one method when plaster is used in making a mould, a small wall is built around the object to be copied. Then the resulting open box, with the design or designs at the bottom, is filled with a thick mixture of plaster of paris and water. After a short interval, and before the mixture hardens, a roller or squeegee is run across the top of the filled box for the purpose of ensuring that the plaster is evenly distributed and of forcing out such air bubbles as may have formed. The plaster-filled box is then placed in a heated oven to dry.

In one variation of the plaster process, the mixture is not poured on to the object to be copied but upon a sheet of paper; the top of the mixture is then scraped with a straightedge, which imparts a level surface to the plaster and ensures that it is of a predetermined depth. When air has acted on the plaster for a sufficient time and the sheet of paper has absorbed the correct amount of water — matters entirely within the judgment of the moulder — the paper is lifted and placed face-downward on the object to be copied. They are then subjected to light pressure, and allowed to dry without heating.

After the plaster has dried, the original is separated from the mould, which is then prepared for casting.

Plaster moulds, when expertly and carefully prepared, result in substantial identity of designs. However, such expert care has not always obtained in their preparation.

One of the chief causes of philatelic varieties encountered as the result of moulding in plaster is the formation of air bubbles in the mixture. The air bubble, covered by a thin skin of plaster, bursts and leaves a depression in

---

[35]The process of stereotyping was invented in 1727 by William Ged of Edinburgh. The process of electrotyping was evolved between 1836 and 1839 as the result of independent experiments by Thomas De La Rue of London, Professor Jacobi of St. Petersburg and J. Spencer of Liverpool. Professor Jacobi is accredited as the inventor of the process.

the mould or matrix. If this depression coincides with what should be an "up" of the mould (that is, a "down" of the subsequent cast), the resultant stamp or stamps will exhibit color in what should have been an uncolored portion of the design.[36] Bubbles of this nature vary greatly in size, from a mere pinpoint to several millimeters in area.

Another cause of philatelic varieties encountered as the result of moulding in plaster is the tendency for plaster to shrink, thus giving rise to variations in size of the resultant stamps.[37]

One method of producing *papier-maché* moulds is by covering the design to be copied with freshly prepared wet flong that is forced into close contact with the "ups" and "downs" of the die.

There are many different methods of preparing flong; it is composed of layers of different thicknesses of paper stuck together with a special paste. The paper next to the design to be copied is, usually, a thin, tough, tissue paper, specially made for the purpose; the paper farthest away from the design consists, usually, of a backing sheet of brown paper.

The flong is laid on the object to be copied, and is beaten in and around the design with a long-handled and stiff-bristled brush. When the face of the flong has penetrated to the lowest of the "downs," the object to be copied and the covering of flong are heated so that the flong may dry out; when it is dry, it is *papier-maché*. It is separated from the object to be copied, and forms the mould which, after some preparation, is ready for the casting box.

In one variation of the *papier-maché* process, dry flong is used — it is ready prepared — and pressed on to the object to be copied by hydraulic pressure.

As in the case of plaster, so with *papier-maché* moulds, expert and careful preparation result in substantial identity of designs. *Papier-maché* is less apt to shrink than plaster, and less liable to exhibit the effects of air bubbles, caused by air trapped between the layers of paper.

However, care must be taken to avoid air becoming trapped between the object to be copied and the flong; if air should become so trapped it will, probably, give rise to doubling of the lines of the design on the mould or matrix,[38] which will be conveyed to the resultant stamps.

---

[36]If the depression in the mould occurs on a "down" of the mould, corresponding with an "up" of the subsequent cast, the resulting projection would be removed by cutting it away with a knife when the cast is prepared for printing. That this had occurred might be unnoticeable, or visible in the form of a mere thickening of a line of the design in a position corresponding with the air bubbles. For other causes of air bubbles, see later in this chapter, where "Casting" is discussed.

[37]This tendency of the plaster to shrink is not the only possible cause of size variation in stamps resulting from stereotype casts made from plaster moulds derived from a single die. Stereotype metal nearly always contains a proportion of antimony, of which one property is expansion on cooling — antimony being an exception to the general rule that metals contract on cooling. As a consequence, if stereo casts are made from different mixtures, the casts will vary in size, affecting the resultant stamps. Also, of course, size variation can occur because of the paper. See "Shrinkage" in the alphabetical list to the chapter entitled "Paper."

[38]Printers often use the term "mat," an abbreviation of "matrix," to designate both a flong and a mould.

474

Producing the Printing Bases

As has been stated earlier in this chapter, at the mould stage the design reads normally from left-to-right, with what are eventually to be the printing areas in recess, and the non-printing areas in relief. This obtains, of course, whether the printing base is to be produced by electrotyping or stereotyping, or as the result of a combination of these processes. At the next stage (the "shell" stage in the case of electrotyping, and the "cast" stage in the case of stereotyping), the design reads reversed, with the printing areas in relief and the non-printing areas in recess.

When this stage is reached, the actual printing surface has been attained — except, perhaps, that the face of the shell or case may be covered with a deposit of special metal to guard against undue wear or the chemical reaction caused by certain inks,[39] and with this further reservation, that the printing surface thus produced may never be printed from but may be merely the master from which the printing bases actually used for printing are obtained — by copying the master galvanically or by stereotyping.

Electrotyping

Before receiving the electrodeposited metal, the mould is prepared by coating its face with graphite that is then polished. This process requires care because, even in the case of metal moulds, the electro-metal will not be adequately deposited on uncovered portions of the mould. Of course, in the cases of moulds of wax and other non-conductors of electricity, no metal at all will be deposited on uncovered areas.

After the face of the mould has been covered with graphite, metal tabs or hooks, to form an electrical connection, are joined to the graphite on the mould, and the back and sides of the mould are protected, by varnish or wax, from receiving undesired deposit.

The graphited face of the mould is then treated by sprinkling iron filings on it and then pouring over it a solution of copper sulfate. This has the effect of depositing on the face of the mould a thin film of copper, and is termed "flashing." The object of flashing is to obtain a surface that will act as a better conductor of electricity than is graphite, and so enable a more even shell of metal to be electrodeposited. The metal "flashed" on to the mould varies according to the practice of the establishment concerned, and with different materials used for moulds; for example, when gutta-percha moulds are used, often the flashed metal is silver. Afterward, the prepared mould is carefully washed.

The prepared mould is then suspended in the depositing bath. This consists of a water-tight container, usually of wood and lined with lead, with

---

[39]This covering, or "facing," may be effected at one of two stages. The universally more usual method is to deposit the special metal on to the finished electrotype or cast — and this is the only method available to protect a stereotype. The other method, available only for electrotyping, is to deposit the special metal, as a preliminary operation, on to the mould, and then to deposit the "shell" proper.

Relief printing. Electrotyping. Queensland 1879-81 2d. Because the electrotyping bath was too small to accommodate a larger plate, only a block of four to a mould was grown at a time. The printing base consisted of 120 subjects, being thirty repetitions of a block of four.

Relief printing. Electrotyping. New Zealand 1899 Postage Due 1d. The plate for the printing of the frame of this stamp contained 120 subjects, comprising four repetitions of thirty subjects; only thirty subjects were grown at a time.

the top uncovered. Across the top of the bath is a conductor of electricity, in the form of a rod or cross-bar, connected to one pole of the supply of electricity. The electrical connection on the mould is brought into contact with this cross-bar, which leads to the "negative" pole, as the mould is suspended in the bath. Also across the top of the bath is another cross-bar, connected to the other, "positive" pole of the supply of electricity; and from this cross-bar is suspended a sheet of copper (electrically termed the "anode"), somewhat larger than the mould (electrically termed the "cathode").

The face of the mould is toward the copper sheet; they hang suspended in the bath, separated by a distance that varies in different establishments, with different circumstances, but that is usually no more than five inches.

Historically speaking, the capacity of different baths varies, and so does the strength of electric current available; but usually more than one mould and anode can be suspended at one time, each from a different cross-bar connected to the appropriate pole. Another variable factor, particularly in the earlier days of stamp production, is the size of the bath. In some establishments, the bath was always large enough to accommodate a mould or moulds of a size equivalent to a sheet of 100 or more stamps; in other establishments, the bath was too small to permit this, and the size of the mould had to be regulated according to the size of the bath.

These factors explain why some, particularly early, stamps were produced from electrotyped printing bases comprising repetitions of a comparatively small number of subjects.

For example, William Knight, the government engraver of Queensland, until after 1882 used to prepare his electrotypes in pairs or blocks of four, the bath being too small to accommodate a large plate. This did not mean that he necessarily grew only one shell at a time; he would grow at one operation as many pairs or blocks of four as could be fitted along the length of the bath and could be grown by the strength of the current available to him. For instance, Queensland 1879-81 2d. was printed from plates of 120, comprising thirty repetitions of a block of four subjects. Again, for instance, New Zealand 1899 Postage Due 1d. (frame) was printed from plates of 120 comprising four repetitions of thirty subjects (five across, six down). Printers such as Thomas De La Rue & Company Ltd., which produced so many electrotyped plates for stamps of the British Commonwealth and other countries, and Anatole A. Hulot, which supervised the production of many French and other stamps, did not meet with difficulties imposed by limitations of size; the depositing baths used by these printers were always large enough to accommodate moulds of sheet size. And the fact that these printers rarely grew shells in excess of about sixty-subject size was the result of prudence rather than necessity; if an electro were to be irretrievably damaged, it would have to be discarded. The discarding of a sixty-subject electro caused less loss than the discarding of an electro of 240 or 480 subjects.

The bath contains a solution of copper sulfate. The solution is termed the "electrolyte." Many different formulas have been used from time to time, varying with many factors, including, for example, the strength of current available.

After the mould and anode have been immersed in the solution and the electric current has been connected, an electro-chemical action and reaction take place, whereby copper is removed from the anode and solution, and is deposited as a shell upon the prepared face of the mould. All other factors being equal, the longer these processes are allowed to continue, the thicker will be the shell of copper deposited.

The shape of the copper deposited on the face of the mould is governed by the shape of the mould itself; therefore, that face of the shell is an exact counterpart of the face of the mould, and an exact copy of the die — or as exact a copy of the die as the mould will permit.[40] The back of the shell is not governed in the same way as is the face; it does not have the sharply confined outlines of the face, and is rough.

The desired thickness of the shell is a requirement that varies within wide limits. The thickest shells vary between about one-hundredth and one-twentieth of an inch.

Throughout this discussion of electrodeposition of the shell, reference has so far been made exclusively to copper as the metal concerned. By no means,

---

[40]When a shell or cast is faced by subsequently depositing protecting metal on its printing face, the result is that, very slightly, every printing area is broadened or thickened at the expense of the non-printing areas, which are narrowed. When the protective metal is deposited as a preliminary operation on to the mould, before the shell proper is deposited, such broadening of the printing areas and reduction of the non-printing areas does not occur, the protective metal being governed by the shape of the mould.

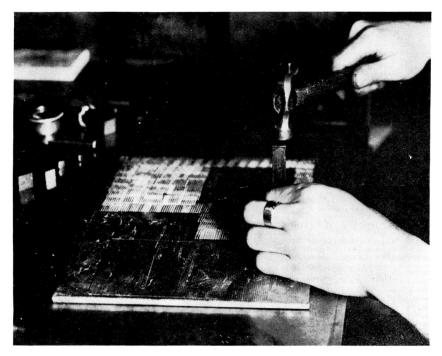

Relief printing. Slabbing. The process of bringing low "ups" to printing height, and ensuring that all reliefs are at the same height. The picture shows the printing plate face-downward on the slab, and part of the slabbing operation is completed.

so far as stamps are concerned, is copper the only metal that has formed the shell, and many metals have been used for facing.[41] When other metals are used, of course, the anode is not copper and the solution in the bath does not contain copper sulfate.

In the early days of electrotyping, and when the electric current was supplied from batteries, the growing of a shell to the desired thickness was a process occupying several days. Because of the time involved in growing a shell, any shell produced, even though it might be faulty, was intended to provide a printing surface. Faulty shells were not lightly discarded, and a metal worker would spend hours, if necessary, retouching a shell so that a passable printing surface might result. Such handwork inevitably left its mark to be reflected in the resultant stamps. With the use of dynamos to supply electricity, and by modern methods, satisfactory shell growing has been reduced to a matter of as many hours as days were previously necessary in some cases. However, even with the great saving of time in shell growing, the retouching instead of the discarding of a shell is not unknown.[42]

After the required thickness has been attained, the mould and adherent

---

[41]The subject of facing is discussed later in this chapter.
[42]See "Damage and Retouching" later in this chapter.

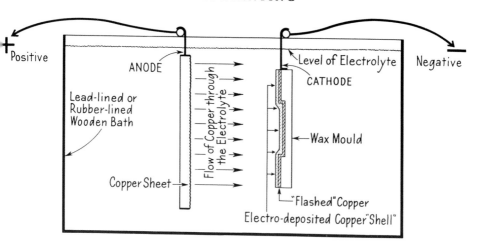

The electrodeposition of copper.

shell are removed from the depositing bath, and the next step is to separate the shell from the mould. This operation requires care, and the detailed steps undertaken depend on the nature of the mould. For example, in the case of a wax mould, use is made of hot water and a knife; the hot water is poured over the back of the mould, melting the wax beneath, and the knife is used to lever the mould gently away.

The shell separated from the mould is thin but tough; it is fragile, and useless as a printing medium. It must be strengthened, and this is effected by the process known as "backing." First the back of the shell is made chemically clean, and it is then "tinned" or "fluxed" by one of a number of methods. Tinning involves heating the shell and covering its back completely with a fine layer of solder or tin. After this has been done, molten metal is poured into the back; this metal is a mixture of lead, tin and antimony.[43] When the backing has solidified and cooled, it and the shell form an entity about three-eighths inch thick. This, in its rough state, is the printing plate.

Much work still must be done to the plate before it is fit to be used for printing. An essential condition of a satisfactory plate for flat-bed printing is that all the "ups" shall be at the same level, and that that level shall be parallel to the back of the plate. An electrotype plate, when backing is complete, does not fulfill that essential condition, which is brought about by the process of "slabbing" in the course of finishing the plate.

As a preliminary to slabbing, the back of the plate is skimmed in a machine that forces the plate to travel under a knife which, at predetermined height, moves backward and forward; this produces a certain degree of flatness as the excess backing metal is cut away. Slabbing itself calls for great skill and

---

[43] It is differently proportioned from and much softer than stereotype metal, which contains the same constituents. Backing metal does not attain maximum hardness until about forty-eight hours after pouring.

experience. The plate is placed face-downward on a perfectly flat surface, and the "slab-hand" (as he is called) operates upon the back of the plate with a variety of punches and hammers, working the face of the plate level. He applies a straightedge to the face of the plate, and where a "hollow" shows — that is, where the "ups" do not reach the required height — he marks the corresponding portion of the back of the plate, finding the location with the aid of a pair of long-armed calipers. Then, with an appropriate punch — depending upon the area and shape of the hollow — applied to the back, he hammers until the face is brought to the required level.

This process is highly skilled, and calls for specially nice judgment. Too heavy a blow will cause its force to travel through the thickness of the plate to the face and, instead of bringing the "ups" level with the flat surface, will bring them into too forceful contact with it, thus causing those lines or that area of the design to spread. Similarly, too large a punch will affect too large an area of the face. Any such occurrence will, of course, leave its mark visible upon the resultant stamps in the form of thickened lines of color, or in the absence or attenuation of uncolored areas. Diagnosis of the cause of such abnormalities is assisted by the fact that they occur in the earliest state of the plate.[44]

If lines of the design should be coarsened in this manner, they may be corrected by use of a burin to cut away the excess metal from the face of the plate. Such an operation, too, would leave traces inevitably associated with handwork and visible on the resultant stamps.

When all the "ups" have been brought level by this process, the back of the plate is planed again, until the plate is reduced to the thickness of, often, about one-sixth inch. The subsequent treatment of the plate, when it is to be used for flat-bed printing, has varied between two extremes, philatelically considered. Either it is cut up into single or multiple designs that are mounted on supports, or else the whole plate is mounted on a support. The support is of wood or metal, and the mounted plate is type-high. Philatelically considered, this subsequent treatment of electrotype plates has much in common with the treatment of stereotype casts, and it is convenient to defer a discussion of these considerations[45] until after a reference has been made to casting.

For rotary printing, the plate will be curved. Techniques of curving vary but, for example, in France the flat plate is encased in a special mould comprising a sheath of malleable metal, and is then passed through a bank of rollers that imparts a curve exactly corresponding with that of the printing cylinder.

Casting

Small purpose would be served here in discussing minutely all the details of the various methods of casting stereotypes. In its essentials, stereotyping comprises the filling of a mould with molten metal, allowing it to set, and separating the cast from the mould. Many of the subsidiary steps undertaken in these essentials have no philatelic significance, and are not reflected in the resultant stamps. Therefore, what follows consists of an outline of two variations of casting, sufficient merely to enable the philatelic considerations attendant upon it to be viewed against a background of the essential work involved.[46]

Casting in plaster moulds may be effected by dipping the moulds, suitably arranged on a tray or pan, into molten stereotype metal, and then withdrawing the tray and metal-filled moulds. After the metal has solidified and cooled, the cast is separated from the mould — sometimes by breaking it. The depth, or "height," of stereotypes made in this manner varies, and sometimes they are type-high, or slightly more than type-high, when separated from the mould. The back of the stereotype is planed, and any other necessary work is carried out on the cast to ensure that it is "squared up" and of the required depth.

Casting in *papier-maché* moulds has the advantage that the moulds do not break and usually are available for repeated casting, but it involves the use of a casting box. The casting box consists of a metal bed and back that can open independently but are pivoted so that the box can lie horizontally or be raised vertically. The distance between the bed and the back of the box is regulated by metal strips, termed "gauges," that determine the depth, or "height," of the cast when made. The bed, gauges and back form a "box" with an open end into which the molten metal is poured.

The mould is laid on the bed, the gauges are set, the back is closed, and the box is then raised to and clamped in the vertical position. Molten stereotype metal is poured into the open end of the box, and flows down into and fills the mould. After the metal has cooled, the bed is lowered, and the cast is removed from the mould, which is then ready to receive another cast after the box has been suitably positioned.

Special considerations apply to stereotype casting of plates for use in rotary presses. A flat master-plate is prepared, containing the requisite number of subjects spaced to allow for shrinkage caused by concave bending of the mould after it has been made from the master-plate. The mould is bent around the inside of a cylindrical casting box, which permits a cast approximating the required thickness to be made. The subjects appear on the convex surface of the cast, and the back of the cast is machined by a circular cutter to reduce the plate to the finished thickness required for fitting around the printing cylinder.

Stereotype metal consists of a mixture of lead, tin and antimony; the proportions of the metals vary according to the nature of the cast required.

Important considerations in casting are the heat of the metal in the melting pot from which the metal is poured into the box, and the heat of the box itself. If the metal should be too hot it will cause vaporization of the moisture inevitably present in the mould in spite of the drying to which it is subjected.[47]

---

[44]Slabbing, too, can account for an excessively colored partial strike; see Footnote 31 of this chapter.

[45]See "Mounted Electros and Stereos" later in this chapter.

[46]In essence, the production of moulded and vulcanized rubber printing bases is akin to stereotyping, and this, philatelically considered, unusual form of production is referred to later in this chapter.

[47]See "Moulds for Stereotyping" earlier in this chapter.

Relief printing. Stereotyping. Air hole flaw. Denmark 1851 (Apr. 29) 2 rbs., variety Pointed Foot (Type 2), and an enlargement of part of the design. The foot of the "2" appears almost disjoined from the body of the figure. The almost circular flaw caused by an air hole resulted from casting in a box insufficiently hot.

This liberation of gas under excessive heat may cause the face of the stereo to become porous, and result in a multiplicity of minute bubbles that will, unless inking obscures them, be reflected in the resultant stamps as a series of minute uncolored dots in areas that should be colored. Printers term such an effect "cokey face."

If the box itself is not sufficiently hot, the metal will solidify irregularly, and air holes may occur in the cast, resulting in comparatively large uncolored dots in areas that should be colored. A well-known instance of such an "air hole flaw" is to be found, for example, in Denmark 1851 2 rbs., plate 2, stamp No. 2 (Type 2), the so-called Pointed Foot or Broken Foot, where the left of the foot of the "2" appears almost disjoined from the body of that figure because of a nearly circular small uncolored flaw. In extreme cases of irregular solidification, the design itself may be distorted,[48] with consequent loss of detail in the subject or subjects affected. Printers term such an effect "chilled face."

---

[48]See Footnote 32 in this chapter.

Relief printing. Mounting mark. Jammu and Kashmir 1883-94 4a. and 8a. in black. The plate from which this sheet was printed was mounted on the wooden base by six wood screws that remained at printing height; as a consequence, the screwheads were inked and left impressions on the paper. The mounting marks affect parts of the designs of 4a. stamps Nos. 1 and 4, and 8a. stamps Nos. 5 and 8. (The stamps are imperforate; the uncolored dotted lines resembling perforation holes result from "downs" in the plate made by punching when the plate was engraved.)

Mounted Electros and Stereos

Stereotypes, usually, when cast, and electrotypes when backed and slabbed are too thin to be used flat in the press without some additional treatment to bring them up to type height. Such stereos and electros are, often, ap-

Relief printing. Mounting mark. Denmark 1852 (August) 2 rbs. (Type 9) and an enlargement of part of the design. Each of the ten ten-subject stereos was mounted on the wooden base with nails driven through non-printing areas of the design beneath the word "SKILLING." Parts of some of these nails were not sufficiently below printing height, and consequently made arc-shaped marks when the stamps were printed.

proximately one-sixth inch thick, and the treatment consists in mounting them upon a wooden or metal base.

The particular steps undertaken in any case depend largely upon the area of the electro or stereo to be mounted. Often rivets, nails or screws will be driven through the face of the metal — usually, of course, in non-printing areas of the design — to secure it to the mount. The rivets, nails or screws are, or should usually be, below printing height. Sometimes, for one reason or another, they are insufficiently driven home or have worked up during printing, with the result that they have received ink that has been transferred to the paper, giving rise on the stamp to a colored flaw in the shape of a full circle, or an arc, or a mere circular blob. Such flaws are termed "nail marks," or "mounting marks." They may occur not only on electros and stereos but also on photomechanically etched printing bases.[49]

Good instances of mounting marks, which immediately reveal their cause, are provided in later sheets from the plate used in printing Jammu and Kashmir 1883-94 4a. and 8a. (The subjects were all handcut.) At first the plate was affixed to the wooden mount by rivets, but after separation, probably more than once from the mount, the plate required more substantial securing. Six screws replaced the rivets, and the screwheads have left their imprint on the sheet, infringing the designs of stamps Nos. 1 and 4 of the 4a. and stamps Nos. 5 and 8 of the 8a.

Denmark 1851 2 rbs. was referred to as instancing a stereotyping air hole flaw. The same stamp provides many examples of a nail flaw. For each plate, the ten stereos, each of ten subjects, were secured to the mahogany mount with six nails driven through the non-printing area beneath the word SKILLING. Many of the sixty subjects thus treated in each plate produced colored arc-shaped flaws on the resultant stamps.

Some uncolored flaws occurring on some stamps — for example, some subjects of Denmark 1851 2 rbs. just mentioned — are caused by damage to the reliefs resulting from careless hammering-in of rivets.

Occasionally, electros and stereos are mounted on metal bases. Sometimes metal screws are used to effect such mounting; sometimes the two metal surfaces have been joined by treatment with suitable molten metal.

Relief-Printing Bases for Flat-Bed Printing

For use in a flat-bed press, the printing base (or "form" as the printers term it) must be rigid and, in effect, solid, whether it be in fact a single solid plate or merely a collection of individual items clamped together and held tight within the chase by means of printers' furniture.

For many stamps, the printing base has consisted of individual subjects clamped together — as many individual subjects as there are stamps in the sheet.[50] Several reasons may account for such an occurrence. The prime reason, in many cases, is the flexibility of the procedure both in the choice of sheet format eventually adopted, and also in permitting any damaged subject to be easily and economically replaced.

The fact that the printing base consists of individual subjects does not imply, necessarily, that the subjects resulted from a mould containing a single subject. Indeed, while single-subject moulds are by no means unknown philatelically, they are the exception rather than the rule in both electrotyping and stereotyping. Printers have, in many cases, been at pains to construct moulds each containing several or many subjects, only to cut up the resulting electros or stereos into individual subjects, each of a single design.

---

[49]Occasionally, mounting marks are encountered on some printings and not on others from the same plate. This occurrence does not necessarily mean that the plate has undergone treatment; the presence or absence of the flaw may be accounted for by, respectively, a heavy or light make-ready. See "Make-Ready" later in this chapter.

[50]In such cases, and there have been many, the use of the term "plate" is quite inapt to designate the printing base.

Relief printing. Stereotyping from a single matrix. Norway 1855 (Jan. 1) 4 sk. These stamps were printed from a plate arranged in four panes of fifty, comprising 200 mounted stereos cast from a single copper matrix struck from a steel die.

Relief printing. Stereotyping. Faulty casting. Norway 1855 (January) 4sk., variety Double Foot of Lion (above first I of SKILLING), pane D, stamp No. 40, and an enlargement of part of the design.

Relief printing. Electrotyping. Mould group. Regular repetition of "types." Prince Edward Island 1872 (Jan. 1) 3c. The printing base of these stamps comprised 100 subjects, being two groups of fifty subjects side by side. One group was made from five separate electros derived from a ten-subject mould, arranged as in the picture. The other group was a single electro copied from the group of five ten-subject electros. The ten "types" repeat regularly throughout the sheet.

Philatelically, the results of such procedures have several implications. Of these, the instances that follow provide examples; they do not pretend to be exhaustive.

The most simple case occurs where a single mould or matrix is used to produce all the casts or electros. For example, in Norway 1855 (Jan. 1) 4 sk., from a steel die a copper matrix was struck, and from this matrix more than 200 stereos were cast and arranged to make up the printing base of 200 subjects in four panes of fifty (ten across, five down). This procedure resulted in 200 "types" — or, rather, one "type" repeated 200 times in the sheet. The stamps may be "plated" because each stereo and its resultant stamp differed from every other; some stereos exhibit quite prominent casting flaws — such as the so-called "cracked stereo," pane D, stamp No. 16, and the "double foot of lion" (above the first I of SKILLING), pane D, stamp No. 40.

A much more complicated and, philatelically, more interesting form of procedure is instanced by that adopted, for example, for Prince Edward Island 1872 (Jan. 1) 1c. From a single die, ten moulds were made and arranged in a group of five across, two down. Such a group, when, as is usually the case, it contains individually identifiable subjects, is termed philatelically a "mould group." From the mould group, five electros were made, backed and formed into a plate of fifty (five across, ten down). Next, this plate of fifty was copied by making a single electro of fifty subjects; this was backed. The printing base contained 100 subjects (ten by ten), comprising the two plates of fifty side by side. As a consequence, the sheets contain ten "types" regularly repeated throughout; the first row of ten in the sheet comprises Types 1 to 5 regularly repeated twice, and the second row comprises Types 6 to 10 similarly repeated — and this arrangement is repeated down the sheet. The

487

Relief printing. Electrotyping. "Types" occurring haphazardly in sheet. Norway 1872 Shaded Posthorn 50 ö. The printing base of these stamps comprised 100 subjects classifiable into six "types" appearing haphazardly in the sheet. A mould group of six subjects was used in multiplying the design, but the electros were afterward cut into single subjects that were gathered haphazardly when the printing base was prepared.

types are, of course, distinguished by the primary flaws — the flaws arising from the mould group. It follows that each of the ten types is represented five times (twice repeated); that is to say, each type is represented by five "sub-types," which are duplicated in the full sheet.

The sub-types are distinguished by the secondary flaws — the flaws first occurring on each copy of the mould group. Additionally, the sub-types on one half of the sheet bear further flaws — the tertiary flaws, first occurring on the copy of the plate of fifty — that enable the sub-types to be further separated into "sub-sub-types" and "sub-types." It follows that every stamp on the sheet bears two sets of flaws, primary and secondary, that enable every stamp to be arranged according to type and sub-type, and fifty stamps in the sheet bear three sets of flaws, primary, secondary and tertiary, that enable each of these stamps to be assigned to its position in the mould group (type), to the position its particular mould group occupied in the pane (sub-type) and to the correct half of the sheet (sub-sub-type). By a process of elimination — that is, by the absence of the tertiary flaws — the other fifty stamps can be assigned to their correct half of the sheet.

When types repeat regularly, they clearly point to the employment of a mould group. However, a mould group may have been employed when there is no regularity in the arrangement of types in the sheet; and, conversely, a sheet may contain more than one apparent type when only single moulds were used.

For example: in Norway 1877 Shaded Posthorn 1 ö to 60 ö, for the early plates, from an undenominated die, into which plugs were fitted for the central numerals, sometimes six and sometimes twelve lead moulds were struck for each value. These were grouped and copied galvanically to make a small plate of, as the case may be, six or twelve subjects with a central numeral but with an undenominated center frame. Each small plate then had the appropriate denomination cut by hand into each center frame. From each small plate, a sufficient number of wax moulds was made, and upon them shells were grown. These shells were backed, the electros being separated, by cutting, into individual subjects that formed the printing bases of 100 subjects. As a consequence, each sheet contains six (or, as the case may be, twelve) types, but they do not repeat in any regular order, occurring in the sheet merely as chance directed the workman who gathered the separate electros for the printing base. Apart from the primary flaws that characterize the types, every stamp bears other flaws that enable the stamps to be ''plated'' — such flaws are termed, in this instance, ''secondary'' flaws (there being no recopying of an aggregation of mould groups to give rise to sub-sub-types). Flaws that occurred as the result of damage caused by extraneous force to the individual subjects are termed tertiary flaws or plate flaws.

When an appreciable number of types appears in a sheet, even though there is no regular order of repetition, the clear indication, philatelically, is that a mould group was employed in multiplying the design. The multiplication may, possibly, have been effected by repeated use of the one mould, or by making from the mould an electro or stereo and using this as a master-plate (being, in effect, the equivalent of a ''die'' — but a die with several subjects) from which several moulds were made and used for subsequent electrodeposition or casting. However, when only two or three apparent types occur in a sheet, the indication is that no mould group was used, but that the types resulted from one of the following causes: (a) either the die, after a number of moulds had been struck, or possibly a single mould, after a number of subjects had been made, suffered damage (and the damage characterizes the type resulting in subjects subsequently made); or (b) one mould having become unserviceable after repeated use, another mould was brought into use for later subjects.

Another form of procedure is instanced by that adopted in France about the turn of the century for the series of fifteen Peace and Commerce (''Type Sage'') stamps then in use. From an undenominated die, fifteen separate lead moulds were struck. Fifteen separate electros were made, and upon each of them was engraved by hand the appropriate figure of value. Each of these denominated electrotypes then was used as the die for the appropriate value. Each die was copied fifty times, the electros being two groups of twenty-five subjects each. These electros were used as masters to produce, via wax moulds, six plates of fifty subjects each, the printing plates comprising 300 subjects in two panes of 150.

Before I discuss printing bases produced by moulding and vulcanizing rubber,[51] and also multiplication indirectly from the die,[52] it will be convenient here to continue considering some of the philatelic varieties arising from the use and misuse of printing bases comprising electrotypes or stereotypes. These varieties include "reglet flaws," "external distortion flaws," the effects of damage and retouching, and "substituted subjects."

Reglet Flaws or Rising Spaces

Reglet flaws can occur only in cases in which the printing base consists of several or many separately mounted electros or stereos clamped together by pressure to make the form.[53]

"Reglet" is the printer's term for a strip of wooden furniture, or sometimes a strip of metal, for spacing; reglets — they are, sometimes, termed "spaces" — are used between the individually mounted electros or stereos to keep the subjects the required distance apart. Usually the reglets are below printing height, and should remain there throughout the printing, locked in position in the form by the pressure applied by printers' furniture and quoins.[54]

Ideally, a form properly locked up is as rigid as a solid plate. However, the rigidity depends upon many factors; among the most important of them are that each individually mounted electro or stereo has been truly "squared up" throughout its height, that the reglets are similarly true, that the chase is unwarped, that the furniture is properly arranged and that pressure is properly distributed. If anything short of rigidity occurs within the form, or it becomes sprung, movement within it will be imparted by the fact of printing and will cause the reglets to work upward until they arrive at printing height. This type of fault, well-known to all printers, is termed in the trade "rising spaces."

Even a minute degree of movement is sufficient to cause the reglet to rise. For example: a reglet might be about one-quarter inch below the printing surface; if the reglet moves no more than 0.0005 inch per impression, it will be at printing height by the time 500 or so sheets have been printed; this will result, on subsequent impressions, in the presence of unwanted color in the margin of the stamp. Such an area of color is termed a "reglet flaw."

An excellent example of a reglet flaw is to be found, for instance, in Victoria 1863-67 Laureated 4d. (Type B.7) where, in some printings, the reglet has fully worked up to printing height and has resulted in a line of color

---

[51]See "Multiplying the Design" and "Moulded and Vulcanized Rubber" elsewhere in this chapter.

[52]See "Producing the Moulds" earlier in this chapter.

[53]A "form" may be defined as "a complete printing unit after the components have been locked up in a chase." A "chase" may be defined as "a metal frame used for surrounding and securing type, blocks, and other material for printing." A form, in this sense, is a properly filled and locked up chase.

[54]A "quoin" is a wooden wedge or a metal device that can be made to expand sideways and so exert and maintain pressure.

Relief printing. Reglet flaw. Victoria 1863-67 Laureated 4d. (Type B.7). At the left, a stamp from an early printing; center and right, the same stamp from later printings, exhibiting vertically in the left margin the variety "reglet flaw." Because the form was not entirely rigid, the reglets, placed between the individual electrotypes to space them adequately, worked up to printing height during the course of printing. The reglet worked up unevenly, and not all of it had reached printing height when the stamp pictured at the center was printed. The stamp at right exhibits the reglet flaw throughout the left margin.

extending vertically upward throughout the left margin of the stamp.[55] Not all reglets are of the length or thickness of the example provided, and a reglet flaw may consist of no more than a comparatively thin line extending along only part of the side of the stamp.

Before damage generally is discussed, it is convenient here to consider, briefly, a particular form of damage in which there is, sometimes, a connection with reglet flaws. This damage results in varieties in the class termed "external distortion varieties," and the connection lies in the steps that have been taken to remedy the cause of the reglet flaw.

The fault of rising spaces may be rectified by several methods; most of them are time-consuming. One method of effecting an improvement while the form is on the press is to push the offending space down hard with a pointed instrument. The thought behind this practice is that it will have two effects: by pressing down the reglet, the flaw will be eliminated on subsequent impressions; and, by pressing into and expanding or spreading the substance of the reglet, the pressure in the form will be increased sufficiently to prevent the reglet rising again. Whatever views may have been held about the efficiency of this practice in effecting the desired results, there is no doubt that its adoption, without adequate care, caused damage to contiguous subjects — damage in the form of distortion to the frames. Consequently, these

---

[55]Reglet flaws of this nature must be distinguished from, although sometimes they resemble in appearance, Jubilee Lines that are to be found in the margins of panes or sheets of many relief-printed stamps of Great Britain and the British Commonwealth. Jubilee Lines resulted from devices deliberately introduced to protect the outer subjects of a printing base, and were intended to print. See "Jubilee Lines" in the alphabetical list to the chapter entitled "From Design to Issued Sheets."

subjects from subsequent printings exhibit flaws, and are termed "external distortion varieties."[56]

The stamp previously mentioned in connection with a reglet flaw — Victoria 1863-67 Laureated 4d. (Type B.7) — provides an instance, in later printings, of an "external distortion flaw," where the left frame, near the upper spandrel, is indented. A more prominent example of an external distortion flaw resulting from the same cause is provided, for instance, by Victoria 1863-67 Laureated 2d., Setting 1, stamp No. 82, and Setting 2, stamp No. 120 (Type H.4.), where the external force applied has resulted in a section of the left frameline being indented irregularly near the upper spandrel.

Damage and Retouching

Damage to subjects in printing bases composed of electros or stereos used for relief printing may take an endless variety of forms, and may result from many different causes. Perhaps the most usual cause is the application of external force, and one effect of such application in correcting a rising space has been referred to — the creation of an external distortion variety about the frame of the stamp affected.

As a class, external distortion varieties embrace all flaws resulting from the application of external force that damages a subject or subjects in such a printing base. Such varieties are, invariably, uncolored; almost invariably they are the result of accident. The damage causes the lowering below printing height of an area of what should be the printing surface, with the result that, within the area of damage, no part of the plate is inked or meets the paper, which, consequently, bears an uncolored area comprising the flaw.

Other uncolored varieties can result from accidental stress, such as that which results in the cracking of the printing surface of an electro or stereo.

As the causes and effects of damage to such subjects vary greatly, so do the steps and the effects of the steps taken to remedy damage. Usually, but not invariably, stamps printed from such subjects after repair exhibit colored flaws.

It would be quite impossible in a work of this nature to attempt to deal with the effects of every possible type of damage to electros and stereos resulting from the various causes; equally impossible would it be to deal with every form of repair that has, at one time or another, been adopted to remedy defects in printing bases used for relief printing. The most that it is practical to do is to instance some typical examples of the effects of damage and repair that are to be encountered on the stamps world-wide that have been relief-printed from electros and stereos.

From what has already been stated, it is clear that the varying possibilities of repair work of different kinds to printing bases for relief printing are very great indeed. Sometimes the steps undertaken in such repair have been established by students; in many other cases, the fact that repair has occurred has, perhaps, not been appreciated. Speaking generally, it is true to state that repairs to relief-printing bases are of comparatively rare occurrence; and,

---

[56]The qualification "external" distinguishes such varieties from "internal" distortion varieties caused by irregular cooling of metal. See "Striking Varieties" earlier in this chapter.

Relief printing. External distortion flaw. Victoria 1863-67 Laureated 2d. Setting 1, stamp No. 82, and setting 2, stamp No. 120 (Type H.4), and an enlargement of part of the design exhibiting a prominent external distortion flaw caused by the operator damaging the frame of the stamp when he pushed down a reglet that had worked up during printing.

certainly, some philatelic varieties that have been and are classed as repairs and retouches owe their origins to other causes. Perhaps the most frequent cause of such varieties is a variation in "make-ready,"[57] and the importance of make-ready in affecting the appearance of the printed stamp does not seem to be generally appreciated by philatelists.

When the cause of an effect upon relief-printed stamps is to be evaluated, that effect must be studied by reference to the composition of the printing base, the particular method by which it was produced and the particular process used for printing the stamps under examination. Methods, intermediate steps and practices vary almost infinitely from time to time, from person to person, from shop to shop, from printer to printer. Perhaps with no method of printing more than relief printing, it is unsound to refer exclusively to the practices of one printer at any one time for the purpose of establishing a standard, and by reference to that standard to purport to diagnose the cause of an effect exhibited by stamps produced even almost contemporaneously by the same printer.

An instance of damage resulting, doubtless, from the dropping on to the plate of a screwdriver or wrench is to be found in New Zealand 1882-97 1d., plate 7, pane 3, stamp No. 50, which shows, diagonally above the ear, an elongated oval uncolored flaw.

Another well-known instance of a variety arising initially from damage caused by a scratch from a sharp instrument is to be found, for example, in Jamaica 1860-63 1s., pane 1, row 2, stamp No. 2, variety "$" for "S" in SHILLING; and this variety occurred, of course in the same position on the sheet, on all issues up to and including 1905-11. In the same country, another instance of a flaw arising from external force of one kind or another is pro-

---

[57]See "Make-Ready" later in this chapter.

Relief printing. External distortion flaw. Victoria 1863-67 Laureated 4d. (Type B.7), and an enlargement of part of the design exhibiting the variety "external distortion flaw." This stamp is from a yet later printing of the same stamp pictured to illustrate "Reglet Flaw." The reglet was forcibly pushed down below printing height by the operator who, because he failed to exercise sufficient care, damaged the stamp contiguous to the reglet, causing the frame to become indented by the left upper spandrel.

vided by Jamaica 1903-1904 ½d., 1d., 2½d. and 5d., pane 1, row 4, stamp No. 2, variety SER. ET for SERVIET in the inscription in the scroll beneath the supporters to the shield.

An outstanding instance of a flaw resulting from accidental stress that

Relief printing. External distortion variety. Flaw caused by damage. New Zealand 1882-97 1d., plate 7, pane 3, stamp No. 50 exhibiting, diagonally above the ear, the variety "external distortion flaw" in the shape of an uncolored elongated oval caused by the dropping on to the plate of a tool such as a wrench or a screwdriver.

Relief printing. External distortion variety. Flaw caused by damage. Jamaica 1860-63 1s., pane 1, row 2, stamp No. 2 and an enlargement of part of the design exhibiting, in the oval frame, the variety "$" for "S" in SHILLING, being an "external distortion flaw" caused by a scratch from a sharp instrument.

caused the surface of the electro to crack completely is to be found in Victoria 1857-63 Emblems 1d., pane D, stamp No. 25. This "cracked electro" is to be found in two states. In the first state, the two parts of the electro are only slightly separated, and the design appears merely to have been pulled slightly apart. In the second state, the two parts of the electro are farther apart, and the lower of the two portions of the design appears pushed to the right, while other damage appears at the lower-left corner, probably because some effort was made to remedy the defect or to restrain the progressive deterioration of the electro; and colored marks appear, one to the left of the "O" and another above the "E" of ONE, where nails or rivets were driven through the surface to secure the copper to the backing or mount.

Usually, cracks in electros or stereos are far less prominent than the instance just quoted; and a cracked electro is, often, characterized by a fine uncolored line passing irregularly through part of the design. Many examples of such cracks are to be found, for instance, among the stamps of Great Britain. An example is provided by Great Britain 1887-92 Jubilee ½d., where,

Relief printing. External distortion variety caused by damage. Jamaica 1903-1904 5d., pane 1, row 4, stamp No. 2 and an enlargement of part of the design exhibiting, on the scroll, the variety SER. ET for SERVIET, being an "external distortion flaw" caused by the application of external force.

Relief printing. Electrotyping. Cracked electro. Victoria 1857-63 Emblems 1d., pane D, stamp No. 25, two states exhibiting the variety "cracked electro." In the stamp at the left, the crack, although passing horizontally throughout the design, only slightly separates the two parts. In the stamp at the right, the separation of the two parts of the design is greater, the frame near the lower-left corner is damaged, and two colored marks appear, one to the left of the "O" and one above the "E" of "ONE," resulting from the heads of nails or rivets driven through the surface to secure the copper to the backing or mount.

Relief printing. Electrotyping. Cracked electro. Great Britain 1887-92 Jubilee ½d. and an enlargement of part of the design exhibiting the variety "cracked electro." The crack affects the "A" of POSTAGE and can be traced throughout the upper part of the design to the top outer frame at the obtuse angle where it dips. Note that ink has accumulated in the crack, and has resulted in a slight excess of color at the left of the crack by the "A," at the center frame, and in the top inner frame. In the top outer frame, the excess ink is visible to the right of the crack, which is almost obscured by the accumulation.

Relief printing. Repair to damage. Retouching. Ireland 1929 Catholic Emancipation Centenary 2d., pane 2, stamp No. 180, and an enlargement of part of the design exhibiting ''retouch,'' together with an enlargement of part of a normal stamp for comparison. The subject on the plate was damaged by a workman. The damage affected part of the outer lines of the center frame, the horizontal lines of the background, the frame of the stamp and the Jubilee Line. Before the plate was printed from, the damage was repaired by a Dublin jeweler. The repair, or ''retouch,'' has resulted in a thickening of the relevant part of the outer lines of the center frame, irregularity in the horizontal lines of the background and a thickening of the framelines. The repaired Jubilee Line presents a mottled appearance and an irregular outer edge.

in some stamps, a crack is found passing through the whole subject.

Many cracks are limited to framelines only, and a stamp exhibiting such a variety is termed ''split frame'' or ''cracked frame.'' Instances of ''split frame'' are to be found, for example, in Great Britain 1887-92 Jubilee 3d.

An example of retouching or repair to damage caused by the application of external force is provided by Ireland 1929 Catholic Emancipation Centenary 2d., pane 2, stamp No. 180, where the repair is in the lower half of the stamp at the right above the corner square, and takes the form of a thickening of the outer lines of the center frame, an irregularity or attenuation of the horizontal lines and a thickening of the vertical framelines of the stamp. The plate was damaged by the dropping upon it of a tool by a workman, and the repair was effected by a Dublin jeweler hastily summoned because printing had to be carried out in a limited time.

Another example of a variety and a correction is to be found in Great Britain 1912-22 1½d., plate 12, stamp No. 180, state I and state II — respectively, the so-called error THREE HALFPENCF and the ''corrected E with long foot.'' On the stamp, the letters are colorless upon a colored tablet; therefore, on the plate they were represented by ''downs'' on a tablet comprising an area of ''ups.'' The printing plates for these stamps were electrotypes grown upon ozokerite (wax) moulds taken from a master-plate made by growing an elec-

Relief printing. Electrotyping. Split frame (cracked electro). Great Britain 1887-92 Jubilee 3d. and an enlargement of part of the design exhibiting, in the top frameline, the variety "split frame," being a "cracked electro" with the crack limited to the frameline. Note that this stamp was printed before the inclusion of Jubilee Lines in the sheets. The Jubilee Lines resulted from a suggestion made in January 1887 by Thomas De La Rue & Company Ltd. to the Board of Inland Revenue, that the lines would assist and improve the work. Permission to include them was given in February 1887.

trotype upon lead moulds struck from a hardened steel die. Either one master-plate had a defective subject (corresponding with stamp No. 180) resulting, probably, from a damaged lead mould, or else, for a short period of use, the master-plate had in that subject impacted in the foot of the "E" a piece of wax or other substance.

The effect of either of these alternatives was to make an "up" of what should have been a "down." As a result, four plates made from the master-plate bore, in that subject, and "F" instead of an "E" as the last letter in what should have been the word HALFPENCE. Each of these plates, one of which is numbered 12,[58] resulted in sheets containing the so-called "error" on stamp No. 180. After a time, the "error" (it was, of course, a plate flaw[59]) was noticed, and on some of the plates,[60] a correction was made by cutting away the appropriate part of the "up" to make a "down," thus providing the wanting foot of the "E." This cutting operation, performed doubtless with a burin, resulted in an over-long foot to the "E," which differs appreciably from the normal letter.

Other methods of retouching and repairing individual subjects include "added metal" and "repoussage," or "bump retouching."

Retouching by added metal, a crude method that yields only partially satisfactory results, involves flowing molten metal onto the face of the subject, and, when the added metal has hardened, engraving the affected portion of the design by handwork.

Repoussage is a development of slabbing,[61] the object being to provide a

---

[58]Philatelically, the plates were given arbitrary numbers. See *The Postage Stamps of Great Britain — Part Four* by K.M. Beaumont and J.B.M. Stanton (1957).

[59]See "Flaw AI(a)" in the alphabetical list to the chapter entitled "Printing Problems and Varieties."

[60]At least two: those numbered "12" and "29."

[61]See "Electrotyping" earlier in this chapter.

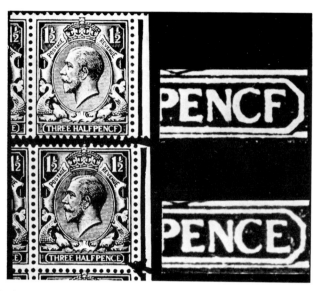

Relief printing. Repair. Recutting. Great Britain 1912-22 1½d., plate 12, stamp No. 180. Two states and enlargements of a portion of each state. Each printing plate for this issue was made by growing an electrotype on an ozokerite (wax) impression or mould taken from a master-plate. The printing plate numbered "12" was one of four on which the subject corresponding with stamp No. 180 bore the inscription THREE HALFPENCF instead of THREE HALFPENCE. Stamps of early printings from this plate exhibit the variety "F" for "E," the so-called "error." The flaw was noticed and corrected by hand, the foot of the "E" being supplied by cutting away the appropriate portion of the printing surface. This handwork resulted in an "E" with a foot appreciably longer than that of the normal "E" (exemplified by the letter following "P"). Stamps of later printings from this plate exhibit the recut or "corrected E with long foot." (In the picture of the lower stamp, a black arrowhead crosses the margin and Jubilee Line.)

flush surface at printing height so that the non-printing areas may be cut away. Whereas in slabbing proper, the object of the operation is carefully to avoid excess force that travels through the thickness of the plate to the face and brings it and the slab surface into too forceful contact, causing the line of the design to spread, in repoussage, the converse is the case; and specially heavy blows are applied to appropriate punches to drive the metal firmly into contact with the slab and so spread and produce a flat area ready to be operated upon by the retoucher's burin. The process of repoussage calls for great skill and care, the more especially so because the electrodeposited copper is fragile. Repoussage is sometimes effected after the backing of the plate has been partially drilled, rather in the manner of preparing a flat steel plate for fresh entry.[62]

---

[62]See "The Flat Plate" in the chapter entitled "Intaglio Printing — I: Line Engraving."

Relief Printing:
Substituted Subject, Different Settings
Tibet 1933 4t. The Sheet in Three States

These stamps were printed from brass blocks individually hand-engraved and secured together for printing by a cord or strip of leather. Because the subjects were hand-engraved, they differ from each other and are readily identifiable.

STATE I shows the sheet as first printed and containing twelve subjects. These are identified, in the usual manner, by assigning numbers to the stamps relative to the position each occupies in the sheet, beginning in the northwest corner with "1," continuing along the top row to "4"; "5" appears immediately below "1," and the last stamp in the sheet is numbered "12." (These "type" numbers are the same as the sheet-position only so long as the setting is not re-arranged).

Substituted Subject

If a subject should be severely damaged or unsatisfactory for any other reason — for example, if it were a subject comprising a different value — the steps taken to remedy the defect would depend upon the nature of the printing base. Whatever the steps taken, the effect is termed "substituted subject," or, more precisely as the occasion demands, "substituted electro" or "substituted stereo." Often the term "substituted *cliché*" is employed.

500

STATE II shows the sheet as printed later, containing only eleven subjects, with no subject at sheet-position "4." The missing "type" is Type 4 from the sheet in State I. The other eleven "types" all occur as in State I, with the addition of two sets of flaws: (a) those caused by damage, which are constant; and (b) those caused by printing, which are inconstant.

If the printing base contains as many separate electros or stereos as there are subjects in the sheet (whether grown or cast individually, or subsequently cut apart from a mould group) clamped together in a form or otherwise secured, the replacement of the defective subject is a comparatively simple matter, provided that a spare subject is available. All that is involved is the unlocking of the form, or loosening of the other method of securing the individual subjects, so that the defective subject may be lifted out and the replacement inserted in the vacant space. The form is then locked up again, or the subjects otherwise appropriately secured, and printing is resumed.

Often the fact that substitution of this nature has occurred can be deduced philatelically from the fact that the substituted subject bears design characteristics that differ from those of the subject that has been removed. Of course, if the original subject was severely damaged, and printings were made with the subject in that state, the substitution would be readily apparent by the absence of that damage from later printings. A more percipient eye is required to detect a substituted subject when the original subject has not suffered severe damage, or when no printings have been made in such a state.

STATE III shows the sheet as printed still later, containing twelve subjects. All eleven "types" of State II are present, and occupy sheet positions "1" to "11," but in different order — as examples, Type 1 appears at sheet-position "11" in State III, and Type 6 appears at sheet-position "4." These eleven subjects bear the damage flaws present in State II. Sheet position "12" is occupied by a new subject, substituted for the missing Type 4. This "substituted subject" comprises Type 13.

In practice, however, it is rarely the case that a single defective subject will be lifted out and replaced directly in this manner. Often, when the subjects are loosened they are removed for cleaning or some other operation; when they are re-assembled and secured again, in the chase or otherwise, the individual subjects occupy different positions in relation to one another, thus giving rise to different settings.[63]

An outstanding instance of substituted subject and different settings occurs in Tibet 1933 4t. In that case, the printing base consisted of twelve separate subjects, each individually engraved on brass and secured by a cord or strip of leather, to make a group four across, three down. Of course, being hand-engraved, every subject differs from every other, and is readily identifiable. As first printed and issued on May 1, 1933, the 4-trangka value ap-

---

[63]See "Setting" in the alphabetical list to the chapter entitled "Printing Problems and Varieties."

peared in sheets bearing the twelve subjects in an arrangement of types, numbered as follows:

1	2	3	4
5	6	7	8
9	10	11	12

Sheets of this value printed later bear no subject at all in position 4, and the subject at position 7 is irregularly set, canting somewhat counterclockwise. These sheets as printed contained only eleven subjects instead of twelve.[64] From this it is clear that type 4 either suffered severe damage and was deliberately omitted, or it was mislaid and was not available for these later printings. As a consequence, the cord or strip of leather passed normally around the outside of the three corner subjects which, on the printing base, comprised the northeast, southeast and southwest corners; but, at the northwest corner, the cord or strip, so to state, "cut the corner," because the subject was missing, and passed diagonally across the space that should have been occupied by the missing subject. (The cant on the subject at position 7 owed its origin, probably, to some cause other than the mere absence of the missing subject; in the ⅔t. value of the same series, the subject at position 7 is, likewise, canted counterclockwise.)

Some seventeen years after the sheets of the 4t. had first been printed with only eleven subjects, new printings were made in which the sheets bore, once more, twelve subjects. The missing subject had been replaced, or "substituted," by a new subject specially engraved for the purpose and differing widely from the other subjects in size as well as in design characteristics. The new printings revealed that the printing base was completely re-set, and the types (using the numbers assigned to them in the first setting) appeared as follows:

10	2	9	6
12	8	11	7
3	5	1	Substituted

Of course, such substitution need not affect only a single subject, either at one operation or at different operations carried out in the course of time. In such cases, however, what has occurred can be deduced philatelically only as the result of plating and plate study — the identification of every subject in each setting, combined with the absence in a later setting of a subject or subjects demonstrably present in an earlier setting, and the presence in a later setting of a subject or subjects demonstrably absent in an earlier setting. In the case of, for example, Victoria 1863-80 Laureated 4d., such philatelic deduction has revealed that no fewer than sixteen substituted subjects were employed; the stamps were printed from a form of 120 subjects in various settings, and during that time not less than 136 subjects were used.

If the printing base comprises separate subjects affixed to a wooden or metal mount, the replacement of a subject is a somewhat more complicated, but still essentially simple matter. The affected subject must be removed from the mount, and the replacement affixed in position to constitute the

---

[64]Some sheets sold contained twelve stamps, the full sheet being made up by pasting in the vacant space a stamp cut from another sheet.

Relief printing. Substituted subject. Poland 1924 (May 1), a block of nine exhibiting in the center the error of color 25g. in the sheet of 40g. (stamp No. 35 in one of the six "panes" of 100 comprising the printed sheet). This sheet was printed before the error was corrected by substituted subject.

substituted subject. The actual steps undertaken in removing the defective subject and in affixing the replacement in position depend, of course, upon the steps taken in the first place to affix the subjects to the mount. If they were affixed by rivets or screws, they must be removed and the replacement similarly affixed; if the subjects were soldered in place, the solder must be melted or otherwise loosened, and the replacement soldered in position.

Classic instances of substituted stereos are provided by Cape of Good Hope 1861 Woodblocks 1d. and 4d., where each printing base, which comprised twenty-four, sixty or sixty-four stereos affixed to wooden mounts, at one time contained one stereo of the wrong value. The 1d. stereo in the 4d. plate was subsequently removed and replaced by the substituted stereo — of the 4d., which was taken from the position it had erroneously occupied in the 1d. plate. Similarly, the then missing 4d. stereo was replaced by the corresponding 1d.

When the printing base comprises a solid plate, whether mounted or not, the substitution of a defective or otherwise unsatisfactory subject is a far more complex operation, and involves cutting the defective subject from the plate, and affixing the replacement in position with the use of suitably molten metal. These operations require great skill, both in the cutting out and in the affixing. Almost invariably they result in evidence from which, philatelically, the deduction can be made that the substitution has been effected. This evidence, apart from that of design characteristics when they are available, consists in variation of alignment.

When a printing base comprises an electro or stereo forming a solid plate, it is almost invariably the case that the greatest of care was taken in aligning the subjects with exact regularity in rows and columns, because of the importance of these requirements in connection with perforation of the sheets.

Relief printing. Substituted subject. Poland 1924 (May 1). Part of the plate of 40g. exhibiting in the center of the picture a substituted subject. When the plate was made, that position (corresponding to stamp No. 35 of one of the six "panes" of 100 comprising the plate) was occupied through error by a 25g. subject. This was cut from the plate, and the substituted subject, a 40g., was riveted and soldered in place. The picture clearly shows the holes surrounding the central subject where it is secured to the mount, and also the ridges caused by the setting of molten metal used to join the non-printing surfaces. Note the inexact alignment of the substituted subject.

Although, of course, such considerations were not, usually, absent when electros and stereos comprising single subjects were mounted to form a printing base, the regularity of alignment of single subjects is or tends to be less exact.

The positioning, in exact alignment, of a substituted subject in an otherwise solid plate is a matter of great difficulty, and perfection is rarely attained. Therefore, in connection with sheets printed from a printing base comprising an electro or stereo forming a solid plate, the fact that irregularity appears in alignment of the subjects is strongly indicative that a subject has been substituted; and this obtains quite irrespective of the fact that other indications may be provided by the absence or presence of design characteristics in the substituted subject on sheets that can be proved to have been printed, respectively, before and after the substitution.

However, the absence of such irregularity is not conclusive evidence that substitution has not occurred, and the factors of design characteristics, when they are available, are important, indeed primarily important, considerations.

A well-documented instance of substituted subject in regard to stamps produced by Thomas De La Rue & Company Ltd. is provided by Great Britain 1867-80 6d., plate 8, stamp No. 103.[65]

The plate for these stamps comprised a single electrotype grown upon an aggregation in a chase of lead moulds stamped from a die held in a collar.[66] Because of some mischance during the moulding and finishing of the plate, one of the subjects was faulty. The printers therefore made application to the Postage Department of the Board of Inland Revenue for permission to

---

[65]See *The De La Rue History of British & Foreign Postage Stamps 1855 to 1901* by John Easton (1958).
[66]See "Moulds for Electrotyping" earlier in this chapter.

repair the damage by cutting the defective subject from the plate and substituting a new subject. Because the steel die was kept under the control of the board, for security reasons, and because, of course, the printers had no spare ready-stamped leads, and would have to make one specially to effect the substitution, this involved a particular application to the board to release the die to the printers for this express purpose.

On December 2, 1867, Ormond Hill in the Postage Department of the Board of Inland Revenue wrote to the printers:

> The defective stamp piece may be cut out of the new 6d. Postage Plate and a new piece inserted as you suggest, on the understanding that if the plate fail in this place or in consequence of its being a patched plate before producing a fair average number of good impressions, the loss so arising shall be made good by your firm.
>
> I will instruct the offices to give out the die for the striking of an impression for this purpose.[67]

In due course, the lead was stamped, and upon it was grown an electrotype that was backed and used as the substituted subject in the plate; this was registered on January 23, 1868.

A more modern instance of a substituted subject, but for a different reason, is provided by Poland 1924 (May 1) 40g., stamp No. 35. In that case, the plate of the 40g. comprised six ''panes'' of 100 subjects each. The subject corresponding to stamp No. 35 in one of these ''panes'' consisted, by error, of a subject of the 25g. value. This was cut bodily from the plate, and a subject of the 40g. affixed in place. The actual printing plate, together with a sheet bearing the consequent error of color (the 25g. indigo instead of red-brown), was exhibited at the Vienna International Philatelic Exhibition (WIPA) in 1933; and photographs exist of the plate with the substituted subject, showing clearly how it was affixed in place by the use of molten metal. Sheets of the 40g. printed after the substitution had been effected exhibit irregularity of alignment of the substituted subject; indeed, this irregularity can be remarked in the photographs of the plate.

Such cutting out of the substance of the metal is not limited to a whole subject; and an instance where only part of a subject was cut out and replaced or substituted by another part is provided by Sweden 1876-78 20 ö, row 4, stamp No. 4, the ''Tretio Error,'' illustrated earlier in this work.[68] In that case, when it became necessary to substitute a defective subject in the printing base of the 20 ö, no 20 ö subject was available, and a makeshift was employed by providing a 30 ö. subject with a center comprising the figures ''20.''

Moulded and Vulcanized Rubber

Philatelically considered, the production of printing bases made of moulded and vulcanized rubber is a rarely employed process, although its use in print-

---

[67]This extract from Ormond Hill's letter is reproduced from *The De La Rue History of British & Foreign Postage Stamps 1855 to 1901* by John Easton (1958), Pages 32-33.

[68]See ''Error of Value'' in the alphabetical list to the chapter entitled ''Printing Problems and Varieties.''

Relief printing. Rubber plates. Austria 1945 (Jul. 3) Arms 5(pf.). Early printings of the 8(pf.) in this design were effected, in sheets of 100, from rubber plates made by the "Semperit" process.

ing is by no means infrequent. It has already been stated that, in essence, the production of such printing bases is akin to stereotyping.[69] Printers refer to the products as "rubber stereos," and the vulcanizing of rubber involves the application of heat.

Perhaps the best-known examples of stamps printed from such rubber plates are the early printings of Austria 1945 (Jul. 3) Arms, for example, 8 (pf.). Later printings of this value were effected from galvanic (electrodeposited) plates.

The first step in the production of the rubber plates for these stamps was the making of the equivalent of the "die." In this instance, the "die" for each of these values comprised not a single subject but ten subjects regularly spaced on a zinc plate; the zinc plate was, in fact, a "line block," photomechanically etched,[70] with the lines of each design in relief in zinc and reading from right-to-left. From this zinc "die," a matrix was made by placing the "die" in a special press, in which pressure is imparted by a system of leverage similar to a human knee and termed a "knee lever press."

When in the press the "die" was covered by a series of thin sheets of various

---

[69]See "Casting" earlier in this chapter.
[70]See "Photomechanical Etching" later in this chapter.

Relief printing. Rubber plates. China, Chung Chow Posts, 1948 (Dec. 27) $42. This stamp was printed, in sheets of 200, from rubber plates.

materials[71] that were pressed on to the "die" at a temperature of about 130° Centigrade, maintained for about fifteen minutes. The pressure and heat ensured that the face of the sheets of the various materials was forced on to the "ups" and into the "downs" of the designs, and the sheets themselves became fused into a solid mass, which hardened. After this hardening was complete, the matrix was removed from the "die." The matrix then bore the designs in recess and reading from left-to-right.

The next step in the operation was to remove the "die" from the press, and then to use the matrix for the purpose of obtaining the rubber printing plate. In the knee lever press, the matrix was covered by the rubber plate; and, again under pressure and maintained temperature, the rubber was forced into the recesses of the matrix and vulcanized. After the vulcanizing process was complete, the rubber plate comprised an exact copy of the "die," being a "mould group" of ten subjects.

The ten-subject plate was then affixed to a wooden or metal mount. These operations were repeated ten times, and the ten ten-subject mounted plates were locked into a form, and comprised the printing plate of 100 subjects.

It is characteristic of printings from these plates that there is a pronounced absence of "bite" and distortion of the paper when viewed at the back of the stamp;[72] as a consequence, except for the difference in size, they are very difficult to distinguish from the products of offset-lithography, the process by which, for example, the 30, 38 and 42 (pf.) values of this series were printed in sheets of fifty subjects.

Other stamps printed from rubber plates include China, Chung Chow Posts, 1948 (Dec. 27) Mao Portrait, $1 to $42 printed in sheets of 200 subjects by the New Honan (Hs'n Yu) Printing Company, Kaifeng.[73]

Multiplication of the design indirectly from the die involves the making of a counterpart of the die, and effecting the multiplication by use of this counterpart. As has been stated earlier in this chapter, such counterparts comprise punches or rollers, and these methods may be conveniently considered under two heads: multiplication by means of a punch; and multiplication by means of a transfer roll.

Multiplication by Means of a Punch

The process of multiplication of the design by means of a punch may be said to comprise four stages: the preliminary stage is the production of the die; the second stage is the production of the punch or punches; the third stage is the production of the individual subjects by use of the punch or punches; and the final stage is the mounting of the individual subjects to

---

[71]In the production of these Austrian stamps, the "Semperit" process was employed, and the sheets comprised one relief sheet, three or four pressing sheets, one body and one covering sheet.

[72]See "Relief Printing" in the chapter entitled "Printing Characteristics."

[73]These issues, among others of Central China, are not listed in *Scott's Standard Postage Stamp Catalogue*, or in *Stanley Gibbons Priced Postage Stamp Catalogue*.

Relief printing. Punch-struck plate (undenominated die). Greece 1875-80 1 l. All the stamps in the first type of Greece (except the 30 l. and the 60 l.) were printed from punch-struck plates.

(a) The steel die was engraved undenominated, then hardened.

(b) It was placed in a coining press together with a blank of soft steel. By direct pressure, the design on the die was impressed into the soft steel, which then became the "punch"; it was hardened.

(c) The undenominated punch was placed in the coining press together with a stamp-sized, 6 mm thick blank of copper. By direct pressure the design on the punch was impressed into the copper, forming an undenominated subject.

(d) A special small punch, bearing the figures of value, was then hand-struck twice on the subject, making it denominated.

Operations (c) and (d) were repeated on 150 separate subjects for each denomination. Variations, more or less minute, in alignment and strength of the figures of value occur and can be remarked from stamp to stamp. The individual denominated copper subjects were arranged upon and affixed to a copper mount 21.5 by 38 centimeters and formed the printing plate from which these stamps were printed.

form the printing base. Such a printing base has been termed a "die-struck plate"; more accurately it is termed a "punch-struck plate," for it comprises an aggregation of punch-struck subjects.

About the production of the die it is necessary to state only that it follows the usual pattern of producing any relief-printing die in steel. As many details of the design appear on the die as are required in light of the needs of production. If only a single value is to be produced in one design, all the relevant details will be incorporated in the design on the die. If several values, differing only in symbols of value, are to be produced, the die will be undenominated, and appropriate provision made for the incorporation of the symbols at a later stage of production.

The design is engraved on soft steel that is then hardened and comprises the die. The design on the die reads reversed, and the parts of the design to appear in color are represented by "ups," while the uncolored areas are represented by "downs."

The hardened steel die is placed in a coining press or fly-press,[74] and, by direct pressure or striking, an impression is made on a piece of soft steel that, after it has been hardened, is the punch. It follows that the punch is an exact counterpart of the die — that is, the design reads normally from left-to-right, and what are eventually to be the non-printing areas are represented by "ups," while what are eventually to be the printing areas are represented by "downs." Although one punch should be capable of producing as many subjects as are required, in practice several punches are made.

The punch is then used to produce the individual subjects in exactly the same manner as the die was used to make the punch. That is to say, the punch is placed in the coining press and is used to strike as many separate subjects as are required. For this purpose (and for each subject required), a piece of blank metal is introduced into the press beneath the die and is impressed by it.

Each subject is, of course, an exact counterpart of the punch and an exact copy of the die — or as exact a counterpart or copy as the process allows. In some cases, complete identity has been attained; in others, variations occur.

The essential differences between the "punch" used in "punch-struck" plate production, and the "punch" used in, for example, electrotyping may be stated as follows: In the process exemplified by that used by Thomas De La Rue & Company Ltd. (described earlier in this chapter), the punch represented a step in the production of the finished die, being a matrix for the die, and came into existence before the die was ready for use in multiplying the design. In "punch-struck" plate production, the punch represented a step in the process of multiplication of the design, being a matrix for the individual subjects, and came into existence only after the die was finished. The die-punch was, or may have been, used on only one occasion to fashion a single piece of steel; the subject-punch was, or may have been, used on many occasions to fashion many separate pieces of copper, bronze or other material.

After the subjects have thus been struck, any necessary additions are made to the design — additions such as symbols of value. These may be inserted on each subject by means of other appropriate punches.

When the designs are complete, the subjects are arranged on and affixed to a mount; they then comprise the printing plate.

Classic instances of stamps printed from punch-struck plates are provided by Greece 1861 (Oct. 1) 1, 2, 5, 10, 20, 40 and 80 l.;[75] and, curiously enough, nearly all the details of their production were accurately recorded, philatelically, as long ago as 1864 by Armand Martin under the pseudonym "Natalis Rondot," in Le Magazin Pittoresque (Vol. 32, Page 215).[76] He wrote:

The Greek stamp is one of the most beautiful postage stamps; it is rectangular, and 23mm. x 18.5mm. It was designed and engraved in relief (tailles de relief) on steel by M. Albert Barre, engraver-general of the Mint (1861).

The seven plates intended for printing were reproduced by the same artist; they are each composed of 150 stamps of copper; these were struck separately in the

Relief printing. Punch-struck plate (denominated die). France, essay by Albert Barre, 1859. The steel die was engraved denominated, then hardened. From it a single "punch" was made, and hardened. From the punch, 150 separate subjects were struck and mounted on a plate from which this essay was printed. This strip bears, in the margin at the foot, the inscription "Epreuves d'une planche obtenue á l'aide du balancier monétaire 1858-1859" (signed) "Albert Barre."

monetary fly-press, and between hardened steel matrices, then placed together and soldered on a plate of copper. This method of letterpress (*typographique*) engraving by cold striking (*percussion a froid*) is less an innovation than a reintroduction of the process applied, towards the end of the last century, to the multiplication of the plates of *assignats*.[77] These processes, of which the "knowhow" (*tradition*) had been lost, and which M. Barre had revived once before in the French essays of 1859,[78] furnished letterpress plates of a perfect identity, and of superior wearing properties to those of electro-chemical *clichés*.

Studies of the stamps have shown that they are not completely identical; and from this it has been deduced that more than one punch was used for striking the subjects.

---

[74]Or a "friction press." See the illustration, "Embossing. The friction press," in the chapter entitled "Embossing."

[75]The same plates were used for all issues up to 1886, when stamps in a different design appeared. The 30 l. and 60 l. in the same design, issued in 1876, were printed from plates produced by electrotyping.

[76]The article was one of a series entitled "Les Timbres-Poste de Tous Les Etats du Globe," which extended over five volumes of the magazine and was never completed. This series was one of the most important early philatelic works, and is still the authoritative source of some recorded facts. The only stamps for which "Natalis Rondot" provided detailed information with regard to production was this issue of Greece, and it is clear that the source of his information was the engraver, Albert Barre himself. Nevertheless, for decades the study of the production of the first issue of Greece was hindered by theories advanced by philatelists that these stamps were printed from electrotypes. The confusion caused by these theories has not yet been entirely eradicated.

[77]"Assignats" were paper money, in the nature of mortgage bonds on the national lands, issued by the French Revolutionary government. The plates for relief printing them were made by polytyping — that is, striking a recessed matrix or punch into semi-fluid metal. It is on record that Guillot, one of the polytypers, from a single engraving of the 400-livres assignats, polytyped 897 mother punches and 1,487 daughters.

[78]These essays are Ceres heads with the inscription "Essai — 1858."

Substantially throughout the sheet of each value there are variations in the positions of each individual figure, or pair of figures, of value; from this it is deduced that, because handwork inevitably can never repeat itself identically, the figures were added by means of a punch bearing the appropriate figure or figures, being struck twice to each subject; and that, when struck on the coining press, each subject was undenominated.

In 1933, the original plates for these stamps were found in the basement of the Government Printing Office at Athens. Each plate comprised a flat mount measuring 215 mm by 380 mm, on which were affixed 150 subjects, ten across, fifteen down. Each subject was approximately six mm thick. It was positioned on the mount by means of a projection at the back of the subject, which fitted into a hole in the mount. A sticky reddish substance filled the spaces between the subjects, and held them firmly to the mount.

An instance of a plate comprising punch-struck subjects in which the symbols of value were incorporated in the die, and, therefore, do not vary from subject to subject, is provided by that from which the Barre essay in the Ceres design and inscribed "Essai — 1858" was printed. The symbols of value in that case are "00," and they appear twice on each subject. There is in existence a part sheet inscribed, in the margin at the foot, in French, "Proofs of a plate obtained with the aid of the monetary fly-press 1858-1859" and signed by Albert Barre.

Multiplication by Means of a Transfer Roll

The process of multiplication of the design by means of a transfer roll involves essentially the same nine steps involved in the more usually encountered application of the Perkins Die and Mill process — that is, for intaglio printing line engraving.[79]

The use of this process for the production of relief-printing plates is unusual, but it was employed by Perkins Bacon & Company for some stamps of Australia and New Zealand — for example, Australia 1914 1d., and New Zealand 1909-12 ½d. and 1d., and also for issues of Germany, including, for example, Germany 1954 Heuss, 2(p.) to 25(p.).

For relief printing, the soft steel die is, of course, engraved in relief. After it has been hardened, it is placed in the bed of the transfer press, and the soft steel transfer roll is rocked over the die under pressure. As a result of the pressure, the metal of the roll on its periphery is distorted and forced into the areas corresponding with the non-printing parts of the design. When these non-printing areas have been completely taken up on the transfer roll, it is removed from the press.

The transfer roll now comprises an exact counterpart of the die, with what are eventually to be the non-printing areas in relief; what are eventually to be the printing areas are represented by the original surface of the periphery of the roll. Outside the design (and a narrow margin surrounding it) — that is to say, in the areas corresponding with the stamp gutters — the metal is

---

[79]See "Multiplication of the Design Mechanically" in the chapter entitled "Intaglio Printing — I: Line Engraving."

Relief printing. Die and mill process. Germany 1954 Heuss 10(pf.). The flat die engraved in relief, lower right, has been hardened and used in a transfer press to produce the roller (mill) bearing repetitions of the design. The roller is unhardened as yet, and the engraver is shown working over the design, clearing metal from unraised portions that will produce reliefs for the colored portions of the design as printed.

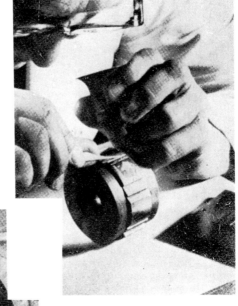

Relief printing. Die and mill process. Germany 1954 Heuss 10(pf.). After hardening, the roller in a transfer press has produced a small curved plate of ten subjects that has been mounted on a steel support. Another small curved plate of ten subjects is shown at the right of the illustration. The engraver is working over the plate, clearing away metal from what are intended to be unraised portions that will not print and will result in uncolored portions of the design.

not raised, although, of course, those are eventually to be non-printing areas.

If a series of stamps, differing only in denominational figures or inscription, is being prepared — as though in Australia 1914-23 ½d. to 4d. — only one flat master die will be engraved, and from this master die two roller dies will be taken up. One of these will be used for the appropriate denomination. From the other, the denominational symbols will be erased by removing the appropriate reliefs, leaving the periphery unrelieved over the corresponding area or areas, and that roller die will be used as the basis for other flat dies.

The roll is then hardened and used as required: if denominated, to roll in a plate; if undenominated, to roll in as many other undenominated flat dies as are needed. Each flat die will then be engraved with the requisite denominational symbols and, after hardening, will be the die from which stem the transfer roll and plate or plates of that denomination.

The rolling-in of the plate takes place in a manner almost identical with that for intaglio printing. The plate is marked out with guides for the siderographist, and entries on the plate are made by use of the transfer press.

Some of the difficulties that were encountered, and considerations that had to be borne in mind, were referred to by James Dunbar Heath, managing director of Perkins Bacon & Company, in a paper read by him to the Royal Philatelic Society, London, on February 6, 1913. He stated:[80]

. . . when you lay down separately 240 single stamps by the roller process, the metal, which after all is only as it were solidified liquid, expands by the pressure.

---

[80]*The London Philatelist*, Vol. 22, Pages 234-35 (September 1913).

Relief printing. Cut edge or frame cut. New Zealand 1909 1d. Dominion and an enlargement of part of the design exhibiting the variety "cut edge," together with an enlargement of part of a normal stamp for comparison. The cut edge appears near the northwest corner and has affected the ball of the floreate ornament and part of the circle bearing the engine-turning. (A minor infringement of part of the upper frameline of the stamp is visible above the "O" of DO-MINION.) These infringements were caused when clearing away unwanted metal from the gutters of the steel plate upon which the designs had been multiplied by the Perkins Die and Mill process.

Relief printing. Cut edge and compartment line. New Zealand 1909 1d. Dominion and an enlargement of part of the design exhibiting the varieties "cut edge" and "compartment line," together with an enlargement of part of a normal stamp for comparison. The cut edge appears at the right of the stamp near the center where, on the shield containing "1D," the upper right projection has been cut away. The compartment line appears above, opposite and below the shield (in the stamp margin), in the form of three or four dots of varying sizes and a dash of color. This stamp was relief-printed from a plate made by the Perkins Die and Mill process. The stamp gutters contained metal at printing height. This had to be removed to provide uncolored gutters. The cut edge resulted from careless use of the machine when the metal was removed from the gutters. The compartment line represents minute ridges of metal in the gutters, usually below printing height, but which attract ink and — when a soft make-ready or soft paper and heavy impression are used in printing — deposit the ink upon the paper.

You all know that you can beat out a plate of iron or other metal, making it thinner and larger. The same thing happens when, under a pressure of several tons, the roller is pressed on to the steel plate, and the metal displaced must go somewhere, and thus it happens that if you start at one end, the metal will have "crept" or expanded quite an appreciable length, perhaps one-sixteenth of an inch at the other end. If this were not allowed for in the calculations, the end of the row would not fit the comb perforation, as in that direction the head of the perforating machine is immovable and cannot be altered; that is, in the ordinary comb machines in general use. This stretch of metal, which takes place somewhat irregularly, according to the quality of steel, has to be allowed for by very nice calculations. . . . If great care is not taken, the block of stamps, which as marked out on the plate appears perfectly rectangular, may come out in the result with the sides curved instead of straight, causing of course endless trouble to the perforators.

Another trouble is the clearing out of the margins between the stamps. In recess printing the metal can be left as it is, as the printer will wipe it clean; but in surface printing the metal must be removed entirely, and grooves as deep as possible left, otherwise the spaces between the stamps will appear dirty, and bits of metal be left catching the ink from the inking roller. We have a special machine for cutting out these grooves, but even with this it is a tedious job, requiring great care, lest the edges of the stamps be damaged, for, remember, you cannot replace for surface printing any part damaged or cut away, like you can for recess printing, as the work stands up instead of being recessed. Yet another trouble may be mentioned. . . . Steel is rather a springy metal, and partly no doubt from the effect of pressure in rolling in the stamps, and partly from the effect of the hardening, the plates sometimes get bent and springy in the middle, so that there is a difficulty in fixing the plate quite flat on the printing machine; it is manifestly difficult or impossible to print from a block that springs up at every impression. We have by great care overcome to a great degree this tendency to springiness, and as the plates are screwed down by very small screws to the metal-mounting blocks to make the blocks what is called "type high," the holes being drilled between the stamps in suitable positions, there appears to be no difficulty from this cause in the printing.

The nature of the machine used by Perkins Bacon & Company for cutting away the gutters has not been disclosed; doubtless it bore an affinity to a routing machine as used by block-makers. When referring to the tedium involved and care demanded in clearing off all the metal between the subjects, J.D. Heath humorously implied[81] that Fisher, who was the transferrer responsible, could be regarded as having three new gray hairs on his head for every new plate laid down.

These difficulties of clearing the gutters led to the creation on these plates of two types of philatelic varieties — the "cut edge" or "frame cut," and the "compartment line."

The term "cut edge," or its synonym "frame cut," is almost self-explanatory, and the variety comprises an absence of color in part of the extremity of the design caused by an inadvertent cutting away of the corresponding relief while clearing the gutters.[82] Individual subjects may exhibit this variety in one or more parts of the same or different sides of the design; and the extent of individual infringements varies considerably from stamp to stamp exhibiting the variety. However, in regard to the individual subject, the variety is standard, and the "cut edge" occurs in the earliest as well as later printings from the subject affected. This characteristic assists in differentiating between such a variety and one of, perhaps, similar appearance caused by subsequent wear or damage to a subject.

Instances of "cut edge" abound, for example, in New Zealand 1909 1d. Dominion.

The term "compartment line," or "compartment lines," is a term of art, coined to describe a particular effect — the appearance of one or more lines, dashes or dots in color in one or more margins of stamps relief-printed from

---

[81]*The London Philatelist*, Vol. 22, Page 203 (September 1913).
[82]See also Footnote 34 in this chapter.

Relief printing. Compartment lines. Australia 1914-21 1d. exhibiting in the margins the variety "compartment lines." The variety comprises, in the top and right margins, an almost continuous irregular line of color, and, outside the southeast and southwest corners of the design, short angular colored marks. These compartment lines resulted from ridges, below normal printing height, that were inked and printed because the paper and make-ready were soft and the impression was heavy. The same subject printed upon hard paper, with hard make-ready and lighter impression, did not exhibit these compartment lines, although the ridges were always present and inked. The plate from which this stamp was printed was made by the Perkins Die and Mill process. After the designs had been rolled in, the stamp gutters were at printing height. They were reduced in height by machining, but ridges remained that attracted ink and sometimes deposited it on the paper.

plates made by the Perkins Die and Mill process, and resulting from a combination of causes: (1) the imperfect cutting away of metal from the gutters between subjects on the plate, leaving ridges in the gutters — ridges that are, in fact, below normal printing height; (2) the undesired but inevitable inking of the ridges of metal in those gutters; and (3) soft paper or soft make-ready[83] and weight of impression that result, during printing, in the paper being pressed not only on to the lines and areas of the subjects at printing

---

[83]See "Make-Ready" later in this chapter.

height but also somewhat into the spaces corresponding with the non-printing areas, so that the paper comes into (undesired) contact with the (unintentionally) inked ridges, and so picks up from them ink that is deposited in the stamp gutters on the printed sheet.

"Compartment lines" are not a factor of every subject. When they are a factor of a particular subject, they do not occur on every printing of that subject; their appearance or non-appearance depends upon the softness or hardness of paper or make-ready, and weight of impression. Consequently, the same subject (of which a "compartment line" is, or "compartment lines" are, a factor) may, in one printing, exhibit a line or lines complete, in another printing only part of a line or a dash or dot, and in yet a third printing no marginal color at all.

Instances of "compartment lines" abound, for example, in Australia 1914-21 1d.

In the case of the Australian stamps, an unusual method was resorted to for the purpose of repairing one of the 1d. plates that was damaged by rust. The plate affected was the lower left plate containing panes III and IV. Two subjects were affected by rust caused, it is said, by rats that, *inter alia*, disturbed the protective coating of vaseline when the plates were stored between October and December 1916. The subjects were pane IV, stamps Nos. 34 and 35. When the plate was printed from, it was found that the rust, or corrosion, had resulted in uncolored[84] areas of the design, on stamp No. 34 behind the King's neck and at the top right of the stamp, and on stamp No. 35 at the left by the kangaroo and wattle. Stamps exhibiting these varieties are very rare. To make the plate serviceable, a quite extraordinary procedure was adopted — extraordinary, that is, when dealing with a solid steel plate.

First, the two offending subjects were cut from the plate, leaving in it a gap of which the edges were finished carefully and measured accurately. Next a transfer roll was used to lay down two subjects on a small piece of soft steel. After this had been done, the small plate of two subjects was carefully reduced to the size of the gap. Then the small plate was frozen to reduce its bulk. Its bulk thus reduced, the small plate readily fitted into the gap in the large plate. When the temperature of the small plate reverted to normal, its size increased so that the small plate fitted tightly into the gap on the large plate, forming a continuous surface. Printings took place from the plate in its repaired state; of course, the substituted subjects[85] do not show the corrosion damage, and can be identified by distinctive design characteristics.

---

[84]Compare "Corrosion" in the alphabetical list to the chapter entitled "Intaglio Printing — I: Line Engraving." The corrosion is identical in both cases, resulting in pitting of the surface of the metal. In intaglio printing, it is the non-printing surface that is attacked, and therefore yields the presence of unusual color; in relief printing, it is the printing surface that is attacked, and therefore yields the unusual absence of color.

[85]In relation to these varieties and sheet positions, an instance of confusing misnomer occurs, and is calculated to mislead anyone not well-acquainted with the method by which these plates were made and the substitution effected. The term *cliché* is mis-used in regard to these subjects, and the states are termed "pre-substituted *cliché*" and "substituted *cliché*." Whatever may be said for or against the use of the term *cliché* as designating an individual subject in an electro or stereo, there can be no doubt that the employment of the word

A further interesting feature of this remarkable plate repair is that the steel used for the repair was unhardened, with the consequence that it wore rapidly in comparison with the remainder of the plate, giving rise to "worn impressions,"[86] one of the most prominent features of which is the absence of the cross on the crown. At a much later stage in the life of the plate — that is, in June 1928 — further substitution of these two subjects and a contiguous subject — stamp No. 40 — was made by the same method.

Multiplication by Means of a Pantograph

The process of multiplication of the design for relief printing by means of a pantograph involves the making of a large model engraving of the design on zinc. This is termed the "zinco," and is the equivalent of the "die."

After engraving, the "zinco" is used by the operator to trace over the outline with the stylus or tracing needle of the pantograph. This causes repetitions of the design, in stamp size, to be cut by diamond points into a plate that later serves as a mould upon which, galvanically, the shell for the printing plate is grown.

The principle of operation of the pantograph in producing a die has been discussed earlier in this work,[87] where an illustration appears of an operator at work at a modern pantograph with a single diamond cutting point.

The designs of Argentine Republic 1882 (Jul. 13) ½c., 1c. and 12c. were multiplied by means of the pantograph by Bradbury Wilkinson & Company. For these stamps, the pantograph used had not one but ten different cutting diamonds, appropriately spaced and all simultaneously controlled by a single stylus. When the operator traced out the design once, ten copies of the design were made on the plate.

The pantograph operated to cut a column of ten stamps vertically, not a row horizontally. Consequently, to complete a plate of 100 designs (ten by ten), the operator had to trace the design ten times, shifting the plate appropriately between each tracing.

Because it is fundamental that the hand cannot repeat itself identically, even in tracing the outlines of a "zinco," it follows that ten distinct "types" resulted

in reference to a subject on a plate made by the Perkins Die and Mill process is to do violence to the language — violence as great as the indiscriminate use of "re-entry" to designate every form of duplication encountered in intaglio-printed line-engraved stamps. And the likelihood of confusion, in this instance, is heightened by the fact that many Australian stamps in the same design were printed from electrotypes, in connection with which the use of the term cliché is common. As a consequence, in this case, use of the term "substituted cliché" is calculated to mislead all but the best informed into the belief that electrotyping was employed in the production of the 1d. plates.

[86]Unlike the case of "corrosion" (where the effect in intaglio printing line engraving is the opposite of the effect in relief printing), the case of "worn impression" produces similar effects in both modes of printing — the absence of color. In intaglio printing, this effect is caused by the wearing away, by the abrasive action of the wiping, of the non-printing areas with the result that the recesses become shallower and hold less ink; consequently, less color is transferred to and appears on the paper. In relief printing, the same effect results from the wearing away of the printing areas until they are below printing height, and consequently do not yield ink upon the paper.

[87]See "Dies and Die Proofs" in the chapter entitled "From Design to Issued Sheets."

from these ten separate tracings. Because the designs were cut in columns, it follows that a horizontal strip of ten stamps will contain one each of the ten "types." The most prominent of the "type" characteristics occurs in the 12c. value, where Type 4 is characterized by the absence of the serif from the foot of the "2." This was caused by the failure of the operator to trace out the appropriate line with the stylus, resulting in the absence of the line from all the designs in the fourth column. By a curious coincidence, an exactly similar fault characterizes Type 6 of the ½c.

Doubtless the model engraving for this series of designs was undenominated; the figures of value being applied to the undenominated designs by the use of separate models.

The diamond points were not intended to cut into the metal plates. The plates were covered by an acid resist, and the diamond points merely bared the metal beneath the resist. After the pantographic tracing operations were complete, the plate was etched until the metal was eaten away to a sufficient depth. Of course, where the resist had not been removed, the metal was unaffected.

After etching, the plate was cleaned. It comprised 100 copies of the design, in recess and reading normally from left-to-right. The plate then was used as a mould; upon it, by electrodeposition, was grown a shell of copper. This shell, stripped and backed, formed the printing plate of the relevant value, with the designs in relief and reading from right-to-left.

Multiplication of the Design Photographically

Multiplication of the design photographically, as a stage in the production of a relief-printing base, is effected only in connection with photomechanical etching. However, not all stamps printed from photomechanically etched printing bases have had their designs multiplied by photography.

When photography is associated with photomechanical etching in the production of a relief-printing base, many variations are possible in the steps taken to effect multiplication of the design. Broadly speaking, these variations may be grouped under three different methods. In two of the methods, the multiplication is, substantially, the equivalent of the processes adopted in photolithography;[88] and in the other method, the multiplication is the equivalent of the processes adopted after the production of a hand-engraved die. The philatelic significance of these methods and others is that they, and the process of photomechanical etching, inevitably result in minor variations between one subject and another at the different stages of production; and these variations, being reproduced at subsequent stages, enable the philatelist to determine (usually within reasonably narrow limits) the stages actually undertaken in production. These methods are as follows:

First, a large photographic glass plate may be produced upon which multiplications of the design appear, either because a single photograph is made of an assembly of representations of the design affixed in place by hand

---

[88]See "Summary of Manufacturing Differences" in the chapter entitled "Planographic Printing."

Relief printing. Halftone process. Thuringia (Germany, Russian Zone) 1945 (Oct. 1) 5(p.) and 12(p.), bearing designs printed from halftone blocks.

on a large card or sheet of paper, or because repeated exposures of a master-photograph have been made in a step-and-repeat camera. Examples of this method are to be found, for instance, in New Zealand 1925 (Nov. 17) Dunedin Exhibition ½d., 1d. and 4d., and in Union of South Africa 1929 (Aug. 21) Air 4d. and 1s., which are referred to later in this chapter;[89] and in Thuringia (Germany, Russian Zone) 1945 (Oct. 1) 3(p.)[90]

Second, a comparatively small photographic glass plate may be made bearing a master-photograph, and this may be multiplied directly on to a large printing base by means of a step-and-repeat printing down machine, or the master-photograph may be multiplied repeatedly to make several or numerous blocks.[91] Examples of this method are to be found, for instance, in Hohe Rinne (Hungary) Hotel Post, 1910 3(h.) and 5(h.), where four zincos[92] were made of each value and grouped to print 22,860 of the 3(h.) and 14,960 of the 5(h.) stamps in sheets of four; for the issue of 1923, the same blocks, re-set, were used to print 1,340 sheets of each value.

---

[89]See "Multiplying the Design" later in this chapter.

[90]The issues of Thuringia (Thuringen) are not listed in *Scott's Standard Postage Stamp Catalogue*, but they are listed in *Stanley Gibbons Priced Postage Stamp Catalogue*, Part 7, as Germany. III Allied Occupation E Russian Zone (f) Thuringia, numbers RF 1 to RF 10.

[91]"Block" in this sense means a "line" or "halftone" photomechanically etched on zinc or other metal relief-printing surface. See "Block" in the alphabetical list to the chapter entitled "Printing Problems and Varieties."

[92]"Zinco" is frequently used to designate "line" or "halftone" photomechanically etched zinc.

Third, from a master-photograph, a subject in relief may be produced by photomechanical etching, and that subject may then be multiplied by electrotyping or stereotyping. Examples of this method are to be found, for instance, in Austria 1945 (Jul. 3) Arms 5(g.), where a ten-subject zinco was used as a die copied by the Semperit process;[93] and Western Australia 1902 4d. where a zinco was produced from a master-photograph made from a photographic enlargement of the 1885 2½d. stamp with new lettering affixed in place.

Just as there have been exceptional cases in which intaglio-printed stamps have been printed direct from a single hand-engraving,[94] and similar cases with relief hand-engraving,[95] so cases occur in which, for stamps printed from printing bases produced with the aid of photomechanical etching, the printing bases themselves are made directly from the master-photograph. Such an instance occurs, for example, in Lake Lefroy (Western Australia) Cycle Mail 1897 (February) 6d., where a zinco was made and 1,000 stamps were printed in sheets of four subjects.

Photomechanical etching, or, as it is often termed, "photo-process engraving," may be defined as the art or practice of printing photographically an acid resist in the required design on a metal plate, and then etching the unprotected parts of the plate. By etching, the unprotected parts are eaten away below the original surface of the metal, and represent the non-printing areas; the protected parts of the plate remain at the original surface of the metal and are, therefore, in relief in comparison with the parts etched away. These relief parts represent the printing areas.

The basis of the acid resist is light-hardened bichromated albumen, fish glue or gelatine, and the photographic processes that precede the printing on to metal involve various steps. They are directed to the end of producing a suitable negative through which the light-sensitized surfacing on a zinc or other metal plate may be exposed to light.

The stages in the production of a photo-process engraved printing base may be divided, broadly, into two: the preliminary and photographic processes, and the etching and finishing processes. These stages may be considered, conveniently, under five headings: (1) producing the original; (2) producing a master-photograph; (3) multiplying the design; (4) applying the design to the metal printing surface; and (5) etching the plate.

There are two main classes of photo-process engraving, and they are: (a) the "line process," in which the subject is reproduced in monochrome "black and white" — or any one color ink upon whatever color the paper may be — with clearly solid lines or areas of color; and (b) the "halftone process," in which the subject is reproduced in monochrome, in fact in solid areas, but apparently in "light and shade" containing one color not only solid and entirely absent, but also seemingly in all the intermediate tints of the color, mixed with whatever color the paper may be.[96]

The halftone process is the more complex of the two, the complications arising because of the steps taken to represent light and shade — and these are dictated by the fact that, on a relief-printed subject, the thickness of the ink on the paper is, or should be, identical over all the design.

Relief printing. Line process. Hohe Rinne (Hungary) Hotel Post 1910 3(h.), used on a postcard together with Hungary 1913-16 Turul 5f. The Hohe Rinne stamp bears a design printed from a line block.

For a subject relief-printed in monochrome, all that is available is a printing surface that can produce solid lines or areas either fully colored or entirely uncolored; that is to say, a printing in black ink upon white paper produces only "black and white" — no shades of gray. Shades of gray, from the darkest to the lightest, can, in fact, be simulated optically by mixing the color of the paper and ink — that is, by varying within a given space the areas occupied by ink and paper. Within that space, the larger the aggregate areas covered by ink, the darker appears the shade of gray; the smaller the aggregate areas of ink, the lighter the shade of gray. But these effects depend upon such a blending of the colored and uncolored areas that the eye is deceived.

The artist can create this optical illusion by pen-and-ink hand-work, varying the size of the areas of solid color and the thickness of the lines and the spacing between them. The result is a drawing in "line," and the camera can faithfully copy the work. The drawing will be reproduced by the line process.

The optical illusion, carried to great lengths, can be created mechanically by use of the camera and the "halftone screen." The effect of the halftone

---

[93]See "Moulded and Vulcanized Rubber" earlier in this chapter.
[94]For example, Mauritius 1847 Post Office 1d. and 2d. — see "Direct Hand-Engraving" in the chapter entitled "Intaglio Printing — I: Line Engraving."
[95]For example, U.S. Locals Bicycle Mail (Fresno-San Francisco) 1894 25c. — see "Direct Hand-Engraving" earlier in this chapter.
[96]For more than one color, see "Color" later in this chapter.

screen and its effect in connection with printing characteristics have been discussed.[97] It is sufficient to state here that, if a continuous tone ("full tone") subject, such as a monochrome photograph, is photographed through a halftone screen, the screen splits up the subject into myriads of dots.[98] On a positive print in black on white paper of the screened photograph, the lightest tones of gray are represented by minute black dots surrounded by large areas of white; and, on tones progressively deeper, the black dots are progressively larger, while the surrounding white areas progressively decrease. In the black areas, the dots coalesce and no white at all is present. In fact, the distance between the center of one dot and its neighbor is constant over all the design; but, because of the varying areas of white, the dots in the light areas appear farther away from each other than do the dots in the darker areas.

Relief printing. Line process. Lake Lefroy (Western Australia) Cycle Mail 1897 (February) 6d., bearing a design printed from a zinco.

An excellent example of the difference in effect produced by the line process and the halftone process is provided by a comparison of two illustrations in the present work. Compare the *representation* of the enlarged halftone screen (in fact produced by the line process)[99] reproduced in Chapter 10, "Planographic Printing," with the *representation* of the enlarged photogravure screen (in fact produced by the halftone process) shown in Chapter 9, "Intaglio Printing — II: Gravure." The striking contrast between the black and white of the *representation* of the halftone screen, and the grayer overall nature of the *representation* of the photogravure screen pinpoints the differences of effect produced by two methods (line and halftone) of photo-process engraving for relief printing.

Amalgamation of the two main classes of photo-process engraving is possible, and the resulting printing base then bears what is termed "combination line and halftone work," which may be defined as line and halftone work

---

[97]See the discussion of the halftone screen and the process color separation method in "Relief Printing" in the chapter entitled "Printing Characteristics," and "Color Separation" in the alphabetical list of terms in the same chapter. For a further discussion of the halftone screen, see "Halftones" in the chapter entitled "Planographic Printing."

[98]The number of dots per square inch depends upon the fineness of the screen — that is, the number of lines per linear inch. With a 120-line screen, the number of dots per square inch is 14,400; with a 150-line screen, 22,500, and so on.

[99]See "Photographic Lithography" in the chapter entitled "Planographic Printing."

Relief printing. Combination line and halftone. Hohe Rinne (Hungary) Hotel Post 1924 (50b.) bearing a design printed from a combination line and halftone block. The portraits and vignette are halftones, and the remainder of the design is line.

combined and etched on one plate. Philatelically this combination is rarely encountered, but it occurs, for example, on Hohe Rinne (Hungary) Hotel Post 1924 50b. and 1h., where the portraits and vignette appear in halftone and the remainder of the design in line, the sheets containing ten subjects, five across, two down.

Producing the Original

The use of photomechanical etching avoids the necessity of employing the expensive skill of the metal hand-engraver; and, instead of an engraving, a line or tone drawing or a composite photograph of the design is employed. The nature of the original is dictated by the limitations of the processes.

If the line process is to be used, the original must be a line drawing, and can consist only of lines or other areas fully colored or entirely uncolored — no tones are possible except in the limited sense already mentioned.

If the halftone process, or the combination line and halftone process, is to be used, the original may contain not only lines and solid areas, but also tones of all intensities between solid color and complete absence of color. Specially prepared wash drawings or composite photographs may be used.[100]

---

[100]However, it is, technically, possible to produce a "line" copy of a "halftone." Such a procedure is known as a "dot for dot copy."

The normal practice is to employ a drawing or composite photograph much larger than stamp size, and to reduce the original photographically when making the master-photograph to be used in the multiplication. The special circumstances in which a stamp or an issue is produced will determine whether the original is denominated or undenominated.

Producing the Master-Photograph

The master-photograph is the photographic equivalent of the die, and may be the first photograph produced or may result from several steps intermediate between it and the original, depending upon the processes adopted in producing the printing base. When the design is to be multiplied by means of a step-and-repeat camera, the master-photograph bears, usually, a tonally positive image with the design reversed reading from right-to-left. In other circumstances, the master-photograph may comprise a normal photographic negative — that is, a tonally negative image with the design reversed reading from right-to-left.

A necessary incident of photo-process engraving is that the photographic plate through which the light-sensitized metal plate is exposed to light should be tonally negative, with the image, viewed from the emulsion side, reading normally from left-to-right (unlike the more usually encountered photographic negative, which is tonally negative when viewed from the emulsion side, and reads reversed from right-to-left).

The necessary reversal of the image can be effected at any of the photographic stages from the first photograph onward, and many variations are possible in the steps undertaken to attain the negative for ultimate use with the light-sensitized surfacing of the metal plate. It would serve small purpose here to survey all these variations; their philatelic significance is, usually, very slight and undetectable in the absence of one or more photographic proofs made during the intermediate steps in the process — and such proofs are rarely made.

Two main forms of the reversal procedure are common: (a) photographing with a prism or mirror in the camera, which automatically effects the reversal; and (b) producing a normal photographic plate, stripping the emulsion from the plate, turning the film of emulsion bodily over, and attaching it face-downward to the plate.

Multiplying the Design

In cases in which a step-and repeat camera is used, the multiplication of the design photographically is a more or less automatic process, with the camera or plate movements dictated by pre-determined spacing controlled mechanically or by hand.[101]

The reversed positive is the master-photograph, and is inserted in the carrier of the step-and-repeat camera. After the necessary exposures have been

---

[101]See ''Modern Influences in Printing'' in the chapter entitled ''Printing Problems and Varieties,'' ''The Diapositive or Multipositive'' and the accompanying illustration in the chapter entitled ''Line Engraving — II: Gravure,'' and ''Step-and-Repeat Camera'' in the alphabetical list to the same chapter.

Relief printing. Line process. New Zealand 1925 (Nov. 17) Dunedin Exhibition ½d. This stamp was printed from a line block made by use of a multinegative of sixty subjects, being a photograph of an arrangement of lithographed designs.

made, and the large photographic plate has been processed, the result is a multinegative on which the images are tonally negative and contain the necessary reversal of the designs.

Some of the more mechanical methods of multiplying the design are instanced, for example, by the steps taken for two issues to which reference has already been made:[102] New Zealand 1925 (Nov. 17) Dunedin Exhibition ½d., 1d. and 4d.; and Union of South Africa 1929 (Aug. 21) Air 4d. and 1s.

In the case of the New Zealand 1925 (Nov. 17) Dunedin Exhibition ½d., 1d. and 4d., the artist made one working drawing, three times stamp size, denominated "1d." This drawing was photographed on to a glass plate, and the image on the photographic glass plate was reduced to stamp size in the camera. The image was tonally negative, the wording reading from right-to-left.

This image was then photographically "printed" on to a special type of photographic transfer paper as used in lithography.[103] Such transfer paper has a coating of gelatine treated with potassium bichromate that hardens, or becomes insoluble in water, in proportion to the amount of light permitted to fall on the gelatine. "Printing" consisted of exposing the photographic transfer paper to light for a carefully calculated length of time through the photographic glass negative.

Immediately afterward, the gelatined surface of the paper was coated with greasy ink. Then the greased paper was moistened with water, or, as it is termed, "developed." This had the effect of dissolving away the gelatine unaffected by light, and that gelatine carried away its superimposed greasy ink. When development was complete, the paper bore, in almost impalpable relief, a stamp-sized copy of the working drawing comprising hardened or insoluble gelatine with a coating of greasy ink. This photographic transfer was tonally positive, reading from left-to-right. Four such transfers, spaced in a block of four, were then laid down on a lithographic stone in the usual way.[104]

On the stone, the subjects were tonally positive but reversed, reading from right-to-left. From the stone, fifteen lithographic prints in black were made

---

[102]See "Multiplication of Design Photographically" earlier in this chapter.

[103]Photographic transfer paper is referred to briefly under the heading "Photographic Lithography" in the chapter entitled "Planographic Printing." I have no record of planographically printed stamps produced by such means. It is the equivalent of the "carbon tissue" used in gravure printing — see "The 'Carbon Tissue' Print" in the chapter entitled "Intaglio Printing — II: Gravure."

[104]See "Transferring the Design" in the chapter entitled "Planographic Printing."

on smooth white paper. These prints were tonally positive and read normally from left-to-right. The fifteen blocks of four were mounted, appropriately spaced, on a white card, to make a sheet of sixty subjects. This sheet was then photographed, with the designs reversed by means of a prism in the camera, on to a large glass plate, which formed the multinegative to be used for the 1d. value, ready for printing down on to the zinc plate. On the multinegative, the designs were tonally negative but, viewed from the emulsion side, read normally from left-to-right.

After the multinegative for the 1d. value had been made, the card bearing the sixty subjects was altered in that previously prepared lithographic prints of ''½d.'' were pasted in place in the 120 value tablets. The altered sheet was then photographed to make the multinegative for the ½d. value. Later, the card bearing the sixty subjects was again altered; the 120 ''½d.'' symbols were removed and replaced by 120 ''4d.'' symbols. Again a multinegative was made, to serve for the 4d. value.

In the case of Union of South Africa 1929 (Aug. 21) Air 4d. and 1s., one undenominated working drawing was made, together with two drawings each of ''4d.'' and ''1/-.'' This drawing was then copied, and the denominations affixed in place in the value tablets. Each design was then photographed through a prism to produce a photographic negative that, viewed from the emulsion side, read normally from left-to-right. Each image was approximately twice stamp size. Each negative was then used to produce a line-block or zinco in the normal manner.[105]

On the blocks, the printing surface was in relief, and the design was reversed reading from right-to-left. These blocks were then inked and used to produce sixty prints of each in black ink upon white art paper. These prints were tonally positive, reading normally from left-to-right. For each value, the sixty prints were mounted, appropriately spaced, on white card to form a pane ten across, six down. Each card was then photographed, with the designs reversed by means of a prism in the camera, on to a large glass plate that formed the multinegative for use in connection with the respective value. The printing plate for each value bore 120 subjects in two panes of sixty, and comprised two sixty-subject line-blocks made from the one multinegative of the respective value.

Photomechanical Etching

As has already been indicated, the last steps in the preliminary and photographic processes result in the production of the reversed negative through which the light-sensitized surfacing of the metal plate is exposed to light.

This reversed negative, depending on the methods decided upon in production, bears an image or multiple images, and is ''line'' or ''halftone'' or ''combination line and halftone.'' The image, or every image, is stamp-size.

In practice many variations in detail are encountered in the various steps undertaken by different printers or blockmakers in the production of the

---

[105]See ''Photomechanical Etching'' below.

Relief printing. Line process. Union of South Africa 1929 (Aug. 21) Air 4d. This stamp was printed from a line block made by use of a multinegative of sixty subjects, being a photograph of an arrangement of designs themselves printed from a line block.

finished zinco or copper or other metal printing surface, and no useful purpose would be served here in discussing minutely these differences. Further, certain variations in procedure occur according to whether the subject is line or halftone or combination line and halftone. These differences have little philatelic importance, and the ultimate stages in photomechanical etching may be summarized as follows:

(1) Obtaining a metal plate with a light-sensitized surfacing.

(2) Placing the reversed negative and the metal plate in close contact in a printing frame.

(3) Exposing the light-sensitized surface to light through the reversed negative for a carefully calculated length of time.

(4) Placing the exposed metal plate under running water to dissolve away all the surfacing not affected by light.

(5) Heating the metal plate to cause the remaining surfacing to become tacky, and dusting it with a powder that reinforces acid-resisting qualities.

(6) Subjecting the plate to several baths containing acid, interspersing such bathing with further acid-resisting treatment to prevent the acid from "undercutting," or dissolving away sideways, the metal under the protected areas of the surface.

(7) Cleaning the fully etched plate, and perhaps routing out any substantial areas, such as stamp gutters and sheet margins that are to appear entirely uncolored, to minimize the risk of their catching ink from the press rollers and depositing it upon the paper; also, perhaps, hand-tooling the plate, to ensure that the subject or subjects reasonably accurately reproduce the original, and to clear away major imperfections resulting from faulty processing.

(8) Fixing the finished plate to a mount or support so that the surface is type-high.

What is of philatelic importance is that photomechanical etching, however carefully it is carried out in all its stages, does not, broadly speaking, produce results that fall within the more stringent requirements of identity of design usually demanded by the security departments of responsible governments. The process itself, as has already been stated, results inevitably in numerous minor imperfections in design; so that, in one or more particulars, one subject differs from another. These imperfections often enable the

Relief printing. Line process. Color separation. "Mass separation." Herm Island (Great Britain) 1959 (Jun. 1) 4 doubles, printed in two colors in sheets of thirty from copper line blocks by Harrison & Sons Ltd.

philatelist to determine each step actually undertaken in producing the printing base; further, they almost invariably are sufficiently pronounced to enable every subject to be characterized and assigned to the position it occupied in the sheet as printed — that is, to be plated.

Color

So far in this discussion of photo-process engraving, reference has been made exclusively to monochrome design. Printing from photo-process engraved blocks is not limited to the production of stamps in monochrome, and, if the designs are to be printed in more than one color, a separate reversed negative and block must be made for each color to be used. For "line" subjects, the separation of the color so that only the appropriate parts of each design appear on the appropriate printing bases is, substantially, the work of the artist producing the design, and is termed "mass separation" or "flat color."

Instances of the use of mass separation are to be found, for example, in Herm Island (Great Britain) 1959 (Jun. 1) 4 and 8 doubles and 1½d. to 1s.6d., each printed in two colors in sheets of thirty from copper plates by Harrison & Sons Ltd.

Three-Color Process

There is another color separation process[106] available for employment only in conjunction with the halftone screen. By use of this process, an effect of almost limitless multicolor can be obtained on stamps printed in fact in no more than three or four colors. The process is termed, variously, "process color," "process separation," "three-color process" or, if four printings are involved, "four-color process." With this procedure, a multicolored con-

---

[106]See "Color Separation" in the alphabetical list to the chapter entitled "Printing Characteristics."

Relief printing. Color separation. Process color and mass color. Russia 1940 All Union Agricultural Fair 30k. bearing a vignette comprising blue, yellow and red in process color, with a frame in green in mass color. No screen was used for the green. For the red, the halftone screen was set at a different angle from the angles used for the screens of yellow and blue.

tinuous tone original can be reproduced in halftone in multicolor.

The first use of process color for postage stamps occurs in Christmas Island (Pacific Ocean) Central Pacific Cocoanut Plantations Ltd. [1915 (?)] 5c., relief-printed in sheets of four.

The method depends upon the theories and science of color vision. While these are only incidentally of philatelic importance, their practice is becoming increasingly evident among the postal issues of the world, and a knowledge of some of the relevant considerations is necessary for an appreciation of how the brilliantly multicolored effects are obtained. The effects of the process are to be seen not only on relief-printed but also on planographically printed stamps; and basically the effects are obtained by identical means for both methods of printing.

Yellow, red (or "magenta") and blue (or "cyan") are primary colors, and theoretically all other colors can be made up by mixing two or more of the primary colors in different proportions. The three-color process does this by two steps: first, every area of the picture is split up into dots of different colors; second, those differently colored dots are printed at seemingly varying distances from each other and in different proportions upon white paper and thus present an optical illusion that an infinite variety of colors is employed.

The splitting up of the design into dots is effected by the halftone screen. The separation of the colors is effected by use of appropriate color filters in the camera, by use of which three separate halftone multinegatives are made.

The effect of the color filters is photographically to divide the colors of the original into the three primary colors, so that on the "yellow" plate appears every portion of the original that is yellow or has yellow in its composition. On the "red" (or "magenta") plate appears every portion that is red or has red in its composition; and on the "blue" (or "cyan") plate appears every portion that is blue or has blue in its composition. Each plate is named by the printing color, not by the color of the filter used when exposing the photographic plate to the original.

A useful example, sometimes given, to explain the functions of the color filters is that of a bright red poppy with a green leaf. If this is viewed through a green glass, the poppy appears black and the leaf very light. A photograph taken through such a filter and a resulting halftone plate printed in black ink upon white paper would show a black poppy with a leaf light gray except in the shadows. If the printing were in red ink, the poppy would be red and there would be hardly any red on the leaf except in the shadows.

If the same poppy and leaf are viewed through a red glass, the leaf appears almost black, and the poppy very light. A print in black ink upon white paper from a resulting halftone plate would show a light gray poppy with dark gray leaf. If the printing were in blue, there would be hardly any blue on the poppy, and a large amount of blue on the leaf.

In fact, neither the red of the poppy nor the green of the leaf is an entirely pure color. Both contain some yellow. Yellow appears dark when viewed through a violet glass. From a resulting halftone plate a print is made in yellow and has superimposed on it the prints from the red and blue plates. The result is an accurately colored representation of the red poppy and green leaf, or as accurate a representation as the colors of the inks will permit.

As the sensation of multicolor in the finished print depends upon the proximity to one another of dots of different colors, and to prevent the dots of all three colors falling upon the same spaces on the paper, the halftone screen is set at a different angle for each color. In fact, the lines of a halftone screen always cross at right-angles, and setting the screen at a different angle merely means that the screen itself, always parallel to the photographic plate in the camera, is rotated. Thus, for example, on the "yellow" plate, the dots appear in lines tilted at 75°; on the "red" plate, at 15°; and on the "blue" plate, at 45°. Sometimes, to obtain a better effect, a fourth printing is made in black or gray. In such cases, the dots of the "black" or "gray" plate appear in lines at an angle of 90°. This rotation of the screen imparts a "reseau" or "rose" effect to those areas of the design where the colors are evenly mixed — an effect that can be seen clearly under magnification, and one that can be described as a representation, in colored dots, of a Tudor rose.

Instances of relief-printed stamps incorporating four colors — of which three (blue, yellow and red) are process color and one (green) is mass color — and presenting a multicolor effect are provided by Russia 1940 All-Union Agricultural Fair 10k. to 60k., printed in various sheet formats including different designs se-tenant.

Printex

A form of line photo-process engraving used experimentally about 1912 and termed "Printex" came into philatelic prominence because of its employment in producing the plates used for printing the "Ideal Stamp" at the Jubilee International Stamp Exhibition held in London in that year. Further experiments were authorized in connection with Great Britain 1912-22 issue,[107] but none of the issued stamps was printed from Printex plates.

Other experiments were made in connection with Australia 1913-14[108] and

---

[107]See *The Postage Stamps of Great Britain — Part Four* by K.M. Beaumont and J.B.M. Stanton (1957), Appendix E, letter number 35.

[108]See *Commonwealth of Australia. The Line Engraved Issues of 1914, and the Essays, Die and Plate Proofs of the Georgian 1d.* by Major J. Dormer Legge T.D. (no date), Pages 86 and 87.

Relief printing. "Printex" process. The "Ideal Stamp" produced for the Jubilee International Stamp Exhibition, 1912, in London, and printed from plates made by the Printex process. The treatment of the portrait head is very unusual, and bears a striking similarity to the head used for Australia 1914 1d. The Australian stamp, however, was not printed from plates made by the Printex process.

1914-21 1d.; but, although the head adopted for that issue bears a clear resemblance to the head used for the "Ideal Stamp," the Australian issue was printed from plates made by Perkins, Bacon & Company, and not by the Printex process. A master-photograph on glass, positive and reversed, placed in a form of step-and-repeat printing machine produced a reversed multinegative; and a copper plate with a light-sensitized surface, after exposure to light through the multinegative and development, was etched by having mordant fluid forced into the non-printing areas of the designs.[109] The British patents for the photographic printing frames (24,487 and 27,264 of 1911) were registered in the joint names of Alfred Henry Motley, Clark Aubert Miller and Herbert Morris Pilkington.

Spitzertype

Of the many different forms of photo-process engraving or photomechanical etching, one in particular produces results that are difficult to reconcile with the effects usually associated with these processes. The exceptional process is termed "Spitzertype." Its philatelic employment has not been great, but it was used to produce Bulgaria 1907 (Aug. 28) 5s., 10s. and 25s. The process results in an irregular granular appearance of the print, and the granulation

---

[109]For relief printing. The process was adapted also for the production of intaglio line plates, in which case the printing areas were etched away.

Relief printing. "Spitzertype." Bulgaria 1907 (Aug. 28) 5s. printed from plates made by the Spitzertype process (German patents Nos. 161911 of December 10, 1901, and 194586 of February 3, 1905, registered in the name of Edmund Spitzer). This photomechanical etching process results in a granular formation on the printing base, and the print resembles the effect of a collotype or a print in grained gravure.

simulates a continuous tone effect. The basis of the process is the usual copper plate coated with a light-sensitive layer of bichromated gelatine or glue. This is exposed to light through a continuous tone negative, and is then immediately etched with solutions of iron perchloride in varying strengths. This results in the formation of granulation in the light-hardened resist. This granulation is irregular, and the print resulting from use of an inked copper printing base made by Spitzertype somewhat resembles the effect of a collotype or a print from a grained gravure printing base.

Protective Facings

Passing mention has been made[110] of coating as a protective facing for stereotypes and electrotypes. Two unconnected causes gave rise to the development of protective facings. First, in connection with copper electrotypes, was the chemical reaction that occurred when the copper came into contact with a constituent primarily in vermilion but also in ultramarine and certain other inks, including orange, olive and brown, resulting in amalgamation of the copper and decomposition of the ink. Second, in connection with all plates other than steel, was the comparatively rapid wear that occurred during printing when hand presses were superseded by power-driven machines.

Facing is effected by electrodeposition, and, in the case of electrotype plates, may be carried out as a preliminary operation on the mould before the copper shell itself is grown. Alternatively — and necessarily in the case of stereotype plates — facing may be carried out after the plate itself has been made.

The philatelic significance of such electrodeposition is twofold. First, unless the facing is perfectly done (as it invariably was in the larger printing houses), slight inequalities in thickness over the surface of a plate may give rise to vague, streaky, uncolored, constant flaws in the resultant stamps. Second, if the facing is carried out as a preliminary operation, the resultant plate will be an exact counterpart of the matrix or mould — or as exact a counterpart as the process admits — in regard to the size of each subject and the thickness of each individual line. However, if the electrodeposition is carried out after the plate has been made, the facing being added at a subsequent operation, this will have the effect of very slightly broadening or thickening every printing area at the expense of the non-printing areas, which are narrowed. As a result, a minute difference in size occurs between each subject on the faced plate and the corresponding subject on an unfaced plate. Further, repeated stripping of a facing and re-facing of the same plate may be carried out, with the result that minute differences between identically positioned subjects in different sheets of the same stamp may be occasioned by the facing process, and do not necessarily import that different plates were used.

Many different metals have been used for facing. Among the more usual in stamp printing are nickel, steel and, comparatively recently, chromium.

Silver was employed for some of the earliest facings on plates; it was used for Great Britain 1862 4d. printed in vermilion by De La Rue. When it became

---

[110]See "Producing the Printing Bases" and "Electrotyping" earlier in this chapter.

534

necessary to change the color of the 4d. stamp from carmine (rose) to scarlet (vermilion), the printers experienced great difficulty because of the reaction between the ink and the copper-deposited electrotype, and they carried out a number of trials to produce a fugitive ink imitating vermilion. But although they succeeded in imitating the pigment, the experiments failed because of lack of fugitiveness and stability. As the result of further experiments, it was found possible to deposit silver on the copper electrotype; and silver, being impervious to the action of the sulfide of mercury in vermilion, enabled satisfactory printing to be carried out.

When referring to this plate in a letter to Ormond Hill dated December 18, 1861, Warren De La Rue stated that the "present fourpenny plate is backed with copper."[111] In that same letter, he asked for permission, which was subsequently granted, to make another plate[112] "thick enough in silver to prevent the necessity for any copper backing." When the first of the two plates was invoiced, a charge of £6.5s. was made for twelve and one-half ounces of silver used in silvering; Warren De La Rue offered to allow £10 on the return of the second of the two plates for the silver, and this implies that twenty ounces of silver were used during the manufacture of this silver printing plate.

Steel facing of copper plates was patented in Great Britain in 1858 (Patent No. 667), and was used by J.F. Joubert de la Ferté[113] during that year, but the patent is registered in the name of Edmond Auguste Jacquin of Paris.

It is thought that Samuel Calvert, the printer of Victoria, Australia, was an early experimenter with methods of facing electrotypes, and it has been stated that his experiments were in progress as early as 1857.

A clear insight into the methods of producing and facing plates used in Spain during 1871 is provided by a letter dated July 21, 1871, and written from the Fabrica Nacional del Sello, Madrid, by W. Nichols to J.P. Bacon, and preserved in the records of Perkins, Bacon & Company.[114] W. Nichols had been employed by Perkins, Bacon & Company as a letterpress printer, and he may have owed his appointment in Madrid to the firm. He wrote: " . . . the Plates are Very Small the System Stereo from the head copper Face them and then Steel face them a great deal of trouble they say it is cheap but I very much doubt it."

The steel surfacing of plates for use in Great Britain became general about 1880, and the reasons are set out succinctly in a letter from De La Rue to the Director General of Stores for India, dated September 23, 1882:[115]

Upon the introduction of the system of printing Adhesive Stamps by machine, it became necessary for us to apply to the surface of the copper printing plates

[111]See *The De La Rue History of British and Foreign Postage Stamps 1855 to 1901* by John Easton (1958), Page 20.
[112]The "hair lines" plate.
[113]The engraver whose fine work is represented on so many stamps produced by De La Rue, including U.S. Confederate States, General Issues 1862 Jefferson Davis. The 5c. die is pictured earlier in this chapter.
[114]*Perkins, Bacon Records* by Percy de Worms (1953), Vol. II, Page 667.
[115]*The De La Rue History of British and Foreign Postage Stamps 1855 to 1901* by John Easton (1958), Pages 215-16.

a film of steel, as we could not have obtained good work from a plate with a copper surface. By reason of the peculiar nature of the steel surface, greater intensity in the color of the impression can be obtained than would be possible in printing from copper, and that too although a thinner layer of ink (this is a most important point) is actually laid on to steel-faced plates by the rollers than on to copper plates. In addition to the great superiority of the work which is obtained from steel-faced plates, there are several other advantages attending their employment, one being that they wear out much less quickly than ordinary plates, and that throughout their life they remain in the same condition. The lines do not thicken, as they do after an ordinary copper-plate has been in use for some time.

The reference in the letter to the fact that the lines do not thicken on steel-faced plates implies that, after the facing has become worn and before the wear has affected the copper itself, the remaining facing can be removed by a solution that dissolves steel while leaving copper unaffected. Upon the unaffected copper a fresh facing of steel can then be electrodeposited, and the plate be brought into use again. Such stripping and re-facing can be carried out many times to the same plate, which, in the absence of damage by physical force, will yield many thousands of satisfactory impressions.

The useful working life of a relief-printing plate depends upon many factors, including the printing pressure and the nature of the paper surface. Unlike an intaglio printing plate, a relief-printing plate is not subjected to the continuous abrasive action necessarily involved in wiping the surplus ink away from the non-printing areas.[116]

The printing pressure and wear on the plate is less on a hand-operated press than on a power-operated press. Although De La Rue, as late as 1889, printed all the stamps produced by the firm (except those for Great Britain and India) on hand presses, the average life of a plate was considered to be no more than about 70,000 impressions.[117] However, even as early as 1871, Warren De La Rue was writing to Ormond Hill stating that although the average number of impressions from each plate over the previous few years had been 70,000, the work began to deteriorate after about 35,000 impressions. The difficulties encountered by the printers in using worn plates are emphasized in the following extract from a letter[118] written by the printers on November 19, 1875, to the Crown Agents:

. . . when a plate became so worn as to be past its work, we were called upon to produce stamps under conditions which precluded good work and this moreover at a great cost to ourselves, seeing that the plate had to be cleaned after every six or seven impressions.

The enormous difference that steel facing made to the useful life of a plate is reflected in a table[119] prepared by De La Rue and dated September 24, 1883.

---

[116]See "Printing from Flat Plates" in the chapter entitled "Intaglio Printing — I: Line Engraving."

[117]There were, however, exceptions; and, quite remarkably in view of the softness of the metal, Warren De La Rue expected that the (first) silver-faced plate for Great Britain 1862 4d. would print 80,000 sheets.

[118]*The De La Rue History of British and Foreign Postage Stamps 1855 to 1901* by John Easton (1958), Page 310.

[119]*The De La Rue History of British and Foreign Postage Stamps 1855 to 1901* by John Easton (1958), Page 125.

In reference to two plates used for printing the then current ½d. stamp of Great Britain, the table shows that each plate had printed about 550,000 impressions, while two plates of the 2½d. stamps had each yielded 130,000 impressions.

The result of using a badly worn or dirty plate is to produce an excessively colored print. Plates upon which old ink has filled in parts of the non-printing (recessed) areas of the designs yield impressions showing spots or other areas of unusual color, and these are termed philatelically "crust flaws." A crust flaw usually remains constant or increases in size until the plate is cleaned. Stamps that bear conspicuous crust flaws include, for example, Greece 1862-67 (Athens printings) 1 l. red-brown, 20 l. dark blue on bluish paper and 80 l. dull pink. When such a plate is effectively cleaned by scrubbing with an appropriate solvent, such as lye, subsequent impressions do not bear crust flaws.

Make-Ready

Make-ready may be defined as the operation of making a form[120] ready to be printed. The operation is carried out by hand, on the press, and has as its object the production of as even and well-balanced an impression as possible, with the areas of solid color truly solid, the fine lines and dots clearly and cleanly printed and duly emphasized, and the uncolored areas of the design free from unwanted color.

Variations caused by make-ready are printing varieties, and the philatelic importance of knowledge of the causes and effects of such variations is that it is of assistance to the student in distinguishing between them and significant plate varieties. Further, such knowledge is important and of assistance when attempts are made to separate different printings — such as obtains, for example, in the classic instances of France 1853-61 and Greece 1861-62.

So that the operations and effects of make-ready may be more clearly envisaged, it will be convenient here to discuss briefly the main types of relief-printing presses and the forms used with them.

Relief-printing presses are of three main types: "platen," "cylinder" and "rotary."

Platen and cylinder presses have flat beds — that is, the printing base is flat, whether it comprises a mounted solid plate or many separate pieces of type metal, clichés or other subjects clamped together.

In a platen press, the pressure or impression is imparted by a flat surface (termed the "platen") and is applied at once to the whole of the area to be printed at one operation.

In a cylinder press, the pressure or impression is imparted by a cylinder (termed the "impression cylinder") and is applied only to an axial line on the paper that is in contact with the flat form. As the form moves under the cylinder, so the axial line of pressure moves in relation to the paper, until the whole area to be printed at one operation has been affected.

In a rotary press, not only is the pressure or impression imparted by a

---

[120]The term "form" is used synonymously with "printing base." See "Printing Base" in the alphabetical list to the chapter entitled "Printing Problems and Varieties."

cylinder (the "impression cylinder"), but the printing base itself is a cylinder[121] (termed the "printing cylinder"). As the cylinders of the rotary press rotate, the paper passes between them at the axial line of pressure, until the whole area to be printed at one operation has been affected.

In theory, the whole printing surface of every relief-printing flat form is level and parallel with its back or underside, and the bed of the press and its platen or cylinder are even and level. Manufacturers of printing plates and presses strive to obtain the results theoretically possible; however, practically, such perfection is never attained. Invariably, when a form is first put in the press and a proof pulled,[122] the result is that the print is uneven, in that different portions that should bear equal amounts of color in fact differ from each other — dark portions print too dark or too light, light portions print too dark or fail to print at all and, sometimes, areas that should be uncolored contain unwanted areas of color. These differences are caused by varying amounts of pressure over different parts of the paper at the moment of printing, as the result of, usually, minute variations in level or height of the bed, the form and, perhaps, the platen or impression cylinder. The function of make-ready is to compensate for these differences, and to prevent undue wear occurring in those portions that, before make-ready, print too dark.

The minuteness of the differences that will adversely affect the impression may be appreciated by the fact that printing height or "height to paper," 0.918 inch, is measured to three decimal places, so that the factor to be borne in mind by the printer who is "making-ready" is one-thousandth of an inch of thickness.

The operations involved in make-ready consist of locally varying the pressure. This is done by adding one or more thicknesses of paper corresponding with those portions that have printed too light, and similarly removing paper corresponding with those portions that have printed too dark. Until comparatively recent times, this could be done only by cutting or tearing out appropriately shaped pieces of paper; and upon the delicacy and skill of the individual workman depended the quality of the finished result. More recently — for the stamps of Great Britain, from about 1911 onward — a form of semi-mechanical overlay was introduced, relying for its result upon a process equivalent to etching specially treated paper bearing a mordant resistant print from the plate to be made ready.

The equalization of pressure that is the object of make-ready may be effected by making adjustments at three different levels to a flat printing form: beneath the support or mount — termed "underlay"; between the support or mount and the plate — termed "interlay," and between the platen or impression cylinder and the paper to be printed — termed "overlay." In the cases of underlay and interlay, the pressure is adjusted locally from beneath the printing surface, so that the printed side of the stamp paper is affected

---

[121]Confusion sometimes arises because of the use of the term "cylinder" in this connection. However, this confusion can be avoided by bearing in mind that, in relief printing, cylinder presses employ flat beds; and that, if printing is effected from a cylinder, the term applicable to designate the press is "rotary."

[122]The term "pulled" means "printed," and is a survival from the times when, on hand presses, the printer had to pull hard on a lever or a spoked wheel to impart the impression.

directly by the locally adjusted pressure. In the case of overlay, the pressure is adjusted locally from the impression side of the press, so that the printed side of the stamp paper is affected only indirectly, the locally adjusted pressure traveling through the thickness of the stamp paper. In other words, overlay affects the pressure of the paper onto the printing surface; underlay and interlay affect the pressure of the printing surface onto the paper.

In the cases of rotary presses, such as those used in the production of, for example, France 1923-26 Pasteur 15c., 20c., 45c. and 90c., only overlay is possible by way of make-ready.

Underlay and Interlay

Underlay is, substantially, no more than the leveling-up of the form on the bed of the press, so that the back of the form and the bed of the press are in close contact throughout the whole area. Underlay, of everyday and regular use in commercial printing, is encountered philatelically only in the comparatively unusual cases in which the form comprises many separate pieces of metal mounted singly on wooden or other supports. This is because stamp printing is security printing; and, speaking generally, manufacturers of printing bases for security printing take greater care to attain the theoretically attainable perfection of complete evenness than do manufacturers of printing bases used for ordinary commercial work.

Underlay comprises pasting one or more thicknesses of paper to the underside of the plate or subject support or mount, or to a part or parts of it, so that, within narrow limits, the printing plane of the plate or subject is at type height. This is judged by employing a gauge, something like a tuning fork or horseshoe, the prongs being 0.918 inch apart. The mounted plate or subject is passed between the prongs. If it is evenly at type height, the gauge will fit tightly on all sides; if one side or corner is below type height, the gauge will not fit tightly there, and one or more thicknesses of paper are pasted onto the underside at the appropriate place or places until the tightness of fit is equal on all sides. Sometimes micrometers are incorporated in the gauges.

Interlay is of rare occurrence in stamp printing. Interlay comprises the insertion of one or more thicknesses of paper, specially cut to shape, between the plate and its mount, and is limited in use, almost exclusively, to halftone process blocks.

Overlay

Overlay, of universal use in relief printing, is the most important part of make-ready, philatelically considered; and different overlays can give rise to widely differing results from the same printing base.

The paper on which stamps are printed does not come directly into contact with either the platen or the impression cylinder. Between the printing paper and the platen or the impression cylinder is an arrangement of parchment or other material and several sheets of paper known as "packing"; the number of sheets can be varied as occasion demands with individual printing bases, so that the appropriate overall pressure may be imparted in the

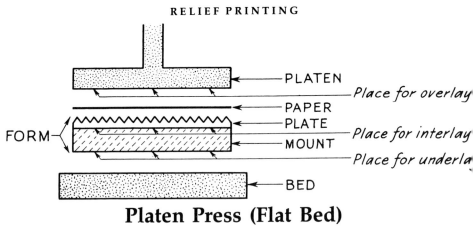

Platen Press (Flat Bed)

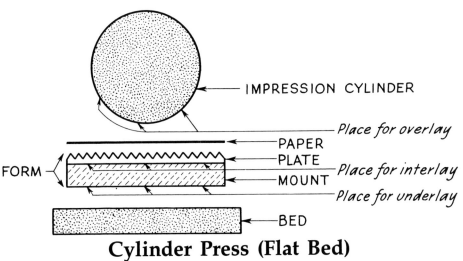

Cylinder Press (Flat Bed)

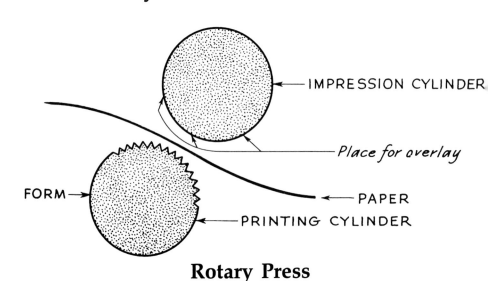

Rotary Press

press. Also, pressure can be regulated locally in any number of places by adding to or decreasing the thickness of the packing — by means of appropriately shaped pieces of paper pasted onto or cut away from it.

These local additions to or removals from the packing comprise one of the major factors of the overlay, philatelically considered, and are referred to by the French term *"découpage."*[123] The overlay itself comprises the whole arrangement of parchment or other material and the sheets and scraps of paper; considered as a whole, they are, occasionally, referred to as "the blanket." On the one hand, the hardness, and on the other hand, the softness or resilience of the blanket as a whole comprise another of the major factors of overlay, philatelically considered. These two factors, which can so greatly affect the appearance of stamps printed from the same plates and plate positions at different times, are referred to later in this chapter.

In platen hand presses and in some types of cylinder presses, the "blanket" is held in a tympan (an arrangement of hinged iron frames) upon which the paper to be printed is laid, and which is then swiveled or turned over so that the printing surface of the paper is in contact with the printing surface of the form. Behind the paper to be printed, and between it and the platen or the impression cylinder at the moment of printing, is the blanket comprising the overlay. In some cylinder and in rotary presses, the overlay is attached to the impression cylinder.

Découpage

Preparing the *découpage* for stamp printing is an undertaking requiring great skill and painstaking care because of the small size of each stamp and its individual features.

The form is placed in the press, carefully inked, and a proof impression is taken, the exact position occupied by the sheet of printing paper in relation to the packing sheets having been carefully marked and noted. This proof is then carefully examined. Inevitably, some of the areas that should be dark are insufficiently colored, because the impression at those parts has not been heavy enough. Also inevitably, some of the finer lines of the designs appear too dark and, perhaps, smudged, because of too much pressure in those areas; for the same reason, in some of the smaller uncolored areas, the ink has clogged on the paper.

Using this first proof sheet as a guide, the printer takes another proof sheet. From it, he cuts away all those areas that have printed too heavily. Then he pastes onto it, in careful register, pieces cut from yet another proof sheet corresponding with those areas that have printed too lightly. At this stage, his sheet of *découpage* is a patchwork and represents three levels: two thicknesses of paper corresponding with the too lightly printed areas on the first proof; one thickness corresponding with the properly printed areas; and the absence of paper corresponding with the too heavily printed areas and, perhaps, with the entirely uncolored portions of the designs.

---

[123]Sometimes used as a synonym for *découpage* is another French term, *"mise en train."* But this term has wider connotations and signifies all the operations involved in make-ready, including underlay, interlay and overlay.

Relief printing. Make-ready. Shifted *découpage.* Antigua 1921-29 2d. and an enlargement of the value tablet showing the variety "shifted *découpage,*" revealing itself as a partial doubling of the "2," the "d" and the right edge of the colored area of the value tablet. Because the *découpage* shifted, the cut- (or etched-) away portions of it corresponding with these elements of the design did not register during printing, and somewhat overlapped the colored background. As a consequence, there was, in those portions of the background, insufficient printing pressure — giving rise to the uncolored or undercolored areas that cause the "2," the "d," etc. to be partly doubled.

This *découpage* the printer then carefully affixes on the packing sheets in the position previously marked. Then, having made an adjustment to allow for the additional thickness of the *découpage* in the areas corresponding with the properly printed areas on the first proof, he pulls a fresh proof. This is examined with the same attentive care as was bestowed upon the first proof. If further local adjustments of pressure are required, the *découpage* is removed, and more pieces of paper are pasted to or removed from it until, perhaps, as many as or more than six different levels are represented, perhaps in paper of different thicknesses.

The *découpage* is complete when the form yields proofs of the desired quality of evenness and balance. The printer has then finished making the form ready for printing.

The painstaking care and attention to detail necessarily involved in proper *découpage* for postage stamps may be appreciated by considering, for instance, the first type (the Hermes Heads) of Greece. The printing plates consisted of 150 subjects, and the basic *découpage* for each of the subjects (each less than three-quarters of a square inch in area) comprised: maximum thickness for the dark areas surrounding the head to the pearls, and for the tablets comprising the frame of the design; medium thickness in the four spandrels, the helmet, and face and neck shading; and minimum thickness for the uncolored portions of the face and neck. See *"Découpage"* and the accompanying illustration in the alphabetical listing at the end of this chapter.

There is, clearly, room for differences of opinion about what constitutes the proper effect to be produced from any particular form, and no two printers will overlay the same form in exactly the same manner. As a result, stamps have been printed from the same form with different overlays and differ appreciably from one another.

The overlay sheets, being of material or paper, are less durable than the printing surface of the form. As a result, after the form has been at press for any length of time, the overlay becomes subject to wear before the form does, and ceases to yield entirely satisfactory results. The machine-minder is, or should be, attentive to the quality of the impressions, and when he notes signs of deterioration or breaking down of the overlay, he repairs or renews it.

Wear on the overlay or blanket takes the form of indentations in the shape of the design.[124]

It follows from what has been written that, for the overlay to have its proper effect, it is essential for the *découpage* to be in exact register with the form. Any deviation from exact register will result in, in exaggerated form, the very effect that overlay is intended to correct. It sometimes happens — particularly when a plate for one reason or another is removed from and returned to press — that exact register between the form and the *découpage* is not attained or maintained, and instances are known of stamps exhibiting areas in which the unusual lack or entire absence of color is pronounced. This occurs particularly in areas of what should be solid color adjoining areas that should be entirely uncolored — that is, in adjacent areas of maximum and minimum thickness of *découpage*. Examples of this occurrence are to be found, for instance, in Austria 1867 Newspaper Stamps (1k.) and Greece 1861-62 5 l. where, to one side or other of the head, appears an uncolored or undercolored contour of the features it adjoins. A more modern instance is to be found in some printings of Antigua 1921-29 2d. in the value tablet, where the shifting of the *découpage* resulted in an apparent partial doubling of the figure "2," the "d" and the right outline of the tablet. Such varieties are termed, variously, "*découpage* shift," "overlay shift," "shifted *découpage*" and "shifted overlay."

It has already been stated that it is common practice for the *découpage* not to come directly into contact with the back of the paper to be printed. The nature of the material inserted between the *découpage* and the back of the printed sheet or the platen or impression cylinder has an important bearing on the overall effect of the impression on the printed sheet. If the material is hard, make-ready and the actual printing call for the exercise of maximum printing skill to produce satisfactory results; and the resulting impression

---

[124]Sometimes the covering of the packing sheets is attached to the impression cylinder, enabling the *découpage* and the packing sheets themselves to be removed and replaced by others. If coverings bearing indentations are subsequently used for printing other stamps, the absence of adequate pressure in the indentations will give rise to vague shadowy uncolored or undercolored traces of the previous design on the subsequently printed design. Instances are known of such happenings in stamp printing — for example, the emergency inflation issues of Germany 1923 (September) 5,000 mark, in which some lightly printed stamps reveal traces of a different number with several digits.

Relief printing. Make-ready variations, hard and soft make-ready. "Fine print" and "coarse print." Austria 1867 Newspaper Stamp (1k.). Two examples of the stamp exhibiting effects of different make-ready. The stamp at the left, printed with a hard make-ready, exhibits the fine lines of the design with the uncolored areas clearly in evidence, typical of a "fine print." The stamp at the right, printed with a soft make-ready, exhibits excessive color almost throughout the design, with, for example, the detail at the back of the head and the wing at the top left of the helmet obscured, typical of a "coarse print."

is a fine, clear, clean print. If the material is soft or resilient, the demands made on the printer's skill are not so great, and the resulting impression presents a much coarser effect. Indeed, the degree of fineness of the impression will be directly proportionate to the degree of hardness of the material — and, incidentally, to the technical ability of the printer.

Many instances are known and recorded of stamps printed from the same plate existing in and referred to as "fine impression" and "coarse impression."[125] Outstanding instances of such variations are to be found, for example, in Austria 1867 Newspaper Stamps (1k.).

Mention has already been made of the variations of impression resulting from similar causes in the cases of mounting marks or nail marks,[126] and in connection with compartment lines, on Australia 1914-23 1d. and New Zealand 1909 1d.[127]

The importance attached by Thomas De La Rue & Company to proper make-ready is exemplified by instructions sent to the New Zealand government. The firm, delivering plates from which, later, New Zealand 1874 (Jan. 1) 1d. to 1s. were printed in the then colony, wrote, on April 28, 1873:[128]

In the same case will be found the overlay sheeters for each of the plates. These will, of course, have to be renewed from time to time, and we would advise that our system of preparing them should be adhered to. All the plates are properly underlaid, and should on no account be disturbed in any way, or unscrewed for mounting the plates. We find that it is necessary in order to get a proper impres-

544

sion of such fine work to use a parchment and satin tympan such as we have supplied with the Printing Press. The tympan will require about one to two quires of soft paper padding, and the pressure screws of the press must be so adjusted as to require a good swing of a strong man to pull over the impression. . . .

Further light on the procedure adopted by Thomas De La Rue & Company for make-ready, in the years before cylinder presses were in use, is provided by instructions that the printers sent to Tasmania together with a platen press and the plates from which Tasmania 1870-71 and later issues were printed in the colony. On March 10, 1870, the printers wrote:[129]

Having carefully underlaid his forme, he will do well to put half a quire of thin tissue paper inside his tympans before commencing his overlaying. The system adopted at Messrs. Thos. De La Rue's is as follows: — In the first place the plate is thoroughly levelled, the overlays being fastened to the inner tympan. When this is done the Pressman cuts out a sheet for the solids, that is to say, the rings and the more prominent parts of the engraving, which sheet or sheets are attached to the inner tympan by sewing. If they were put next to the forme the effect would be too sudden, and the overlays would not have their proper effect. . . .

'Jubilee Lines'

Many of the working difficulties encountered by stamp printers, and the steps taken to overcome such difficulties, leave no mark available for the philatelist to reason cause and effect. It is otherwise with other difficulties, and of these there are permanent reminders in the form of the "Jubilee Lines" and, later, the "pillars" resulting from the introduction by Thomas De La Rue & Company of devices to overcome the waste and cost occasioned to the printers by spoiled sheets of watermarked paper.[130]

As has already been mentioned,[131] "Jubilee Lines" first appeared on the issue for 1887; "pillars" first appeared on bi-colored stamps during the following year, and on monochrome stamps in 1900.

The exact nature of the early difficulties encountered by the printers has not been recorded; almost certainly these difficulties were associated with the new printing machines specially made for Great Britain 1887 Jubilee issue,

---

[125]See "Impression" in the alphabetical list to the chapter entitled "Printing Problems and Varieties."

[126]See "Mounted Electros" and "Stereos" and Footnote 49 earlier in this chapter.

[127]See "Multiplication By Means of a Transfer Roll" earlier in this chapter.

[128]*The De La Rue History of British and Foreign Postage Stamps 1855 to 1901* by John Easton (1958), Pages 702-703.

[129]*The De La Rue History of British and Foreign Postage Stamps 1855 to 1901* by John Easton (1958), Page 285.

[130]The printers were allowed ten per cent for spoilage, but it amounted in fact to about sixteen per cent before the introduction of the "Jubilee Lines" — see *The De La Rue History of British and Foreign Postage Stamps 1855 to 1901* by John Easton (1958), Page 144. The cost of the excess spoilage fell on the printers.

[131]Actually, "Jubilee Lines" first appeared in 1887, experimentally on a plate of the 1d. of 1881.

and comprised "slur" and, probably, "wipe,"[132] combined with injury to marginal subjects by the inking rollers.

There is no doubt that the plates were not printing as well as the printers desired, and this is evidenced by a letter written by Thomas De La Rue & Company to the Board of Inland Revenue on January 19, 1887.[133]

As we have already explained to you verbally, we believe that if lines were placed round the panes of Stamps as indicated on the enclosed dummy sheet it would assist and improve the work very much. If your Board acquiesce in this, we should like to try it experimentally on one forme of the 1d. Unified Stamps. Should the experiment answer our anticipation, we should desire to introduce the lines in all new Stamp-formes of every description.

The "Jubilee Lines" first appeared on Great Britain 1881 1d.,[134] plate 65 with control "G," first put to press in March 1887, the year of Queen Victoria's Jubilee. The experiment proved successful, and they were rapidly extended to all plates of Great Britain 1887, the so-called Jubilee issue, and the lines were termed, philatelically only, "Jubilee Lines."

That the main reason for the inclusion of "Jubilee Lines" was the improvement they effected in the actual printing is confirmed by the following extract from a letter concerning the stamps of India printed by Thomas De La Rue & Company. On April 26, 1887, the printers wrote:[135]

. . . we have for some time past placed lines round the panes of all new English Stamp printing plates. This addition to the plates has proved to be of so material an advantage that we are desirous of effecting the same modifications in all descriptions of the Indian Adhesive Stamp printing plates, as we renew them from time to time. We enclose a dummy sheet, in duplicate, of the ½ Anna Postage Stamps, upon which we have indicated the border lines, and it will be observed that those lines help to cover the plain margins of the sheets, and in that way help to render them useless to the possible forger, who would be glad to avail himself of a piece of the actual paper we use. This is a consideration which appears to us to be of some, although secondary, importance, the chief advantage of the lines being the tendency they have to improve the quality of the printing. . . .

As first incorporated around the panes of stamps in the sheet, the "Jubilee Lines" formed an unbroken line with rounded or angular corners. The unbroken relief giving rise to the so-called continuous "Jubilee Line" caused difficulty because of air trapped during printing, and resulted in fluttering and cockling of the paper, with consequent impairment of the impression. The difficulty was overcome by making the relief discontinuous, and this resulted in the so-called coextensive "Jubilee Line," substantially every line extending the width or height of the adjacent stamp.

---

[132]A "slur" has the appearance of a double impression, and is caused by movement between paper and form. "Wipe" is similar in appearance to slur, but is caused by the ink rollers; it is ink pushed to one side of the reliefs.

[133]*The De La Rue History of British and Foreign Postage Stamps 1855 to 1901* by John Easton (1958), Page 149.

[134]The "Unified" stamp, so called because it did duty for either postage or revenue. Previously there was a special stamp for postage and another for revenue.

[135]*The De La Rue History of British and Foreign Postage Stamps 1855 to 1901* by John Easton (1958), Page 227.

Other and allied difficulties in printing later gave rise to two thin parallel lines and one thick line spaced well away from the "Jubilee Lines" when Great Britain 1911-12 1d. was printed.

'Pillars'

The main reason[136] "pillars" were incorporated in the sheets clearly emerges from the request made by Thomas De La Rue & Company for permission to incorporate these devices. On January 12, 1888, the printers wrote:[137]

We experience certain difficulties in the production of 4d. and 9d. Unified Stamps, which we can only successfully overcome by inserting in the printing plates pieces to bear up the sheets as they are printed.

These two stamps, Great Britain 1887 Jubilee 4d. and 9d., were bi-colored, and the subjects were arranged in pane formation. As a consequence, comparatively large areas of paper were unsupported at the moment of printing, with the result that the paper tended to sag into the gutters and cause slur. This defect was largely remedied by the inclusion of the "pillars."

Printing from Relief-Printing Bases

Until quite recently, relief printing was by far the most common method of printing used in the commercial world. It also has had the greatest general and most widespread philatelic employment. Probably all stamp-issuing countries have, at one time or another, made use of relief printing for adhesive stamps or postal stationery. The earliest philatelic use of relief printing for government-issued postage stamps occurs in France 1849.[138]

As has been stated earlier in this chapter, the principle of relief printing is the simplest of all methods of printing — that is, that a surface to which ink can adhere, when inked and pressed into contact with paper, will yield an impression. The problems of the relief printer may be stated to be: to obtain the requisite printing form, to apply ink evenly to the reliefs only, and to deposit the ink satisfactorily and in such register as may be required upon the paper.

The different types of presses are very numerous; the different makes of presses are vastly more numerous. Yet, basically, all these presses fall into three main categories — "platen," "cylinder" and "rotary," and they and their principles of operation have already been briefly touched upon and illustrated.

No useful purpose would be served here in attempting to deal exhaustive-

---

[136]For other considerations, see "Printing Bases and Printed Sheets" in the chapter entitled "From Design to Issued Sheets," and "Pillars" in the alphabetical list to the same chapter.

[137]*The De La Rue History of British and Foreign Postage Stamps 1855 to 1901* by John Easton (1958), Pages 149-50.

[138]This statement omits from consideration all postal stationery, such as Great Britain 1840 Mulready, and, of course, U.S. Carriers, such as New York City Despatch 1846; Postmasters, such as Millbury 1846, and Locals, such as (D.O. Blood & Co.) Philadelphia Despatch Post 1842, or Hoyt's Letter Express 1844.

The Hand Press for Relief Printing

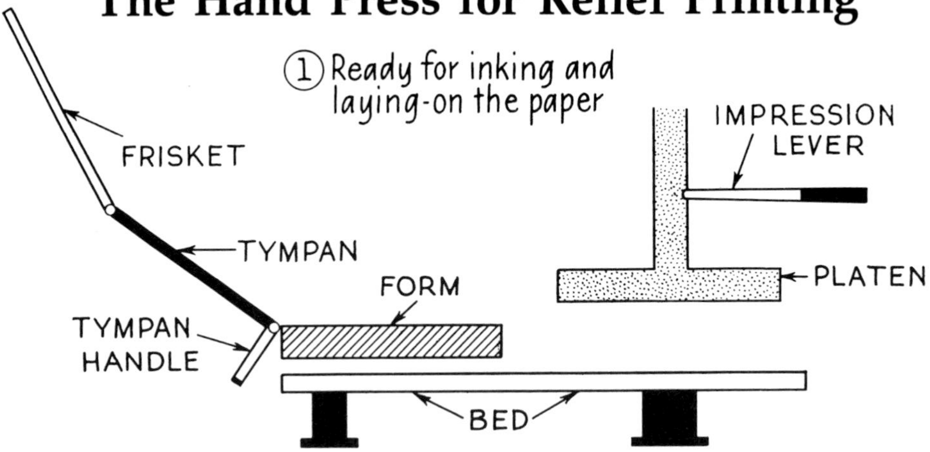

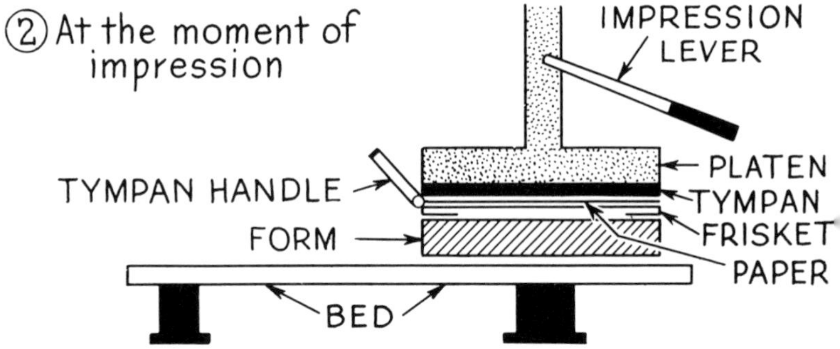

① Ready for inking and laying-on the paper

FRISKET

IMPRESSION LEVER

TYMPAN

FORM

PLATEN

TYMPAN HANDLE

BED

② At the moment of impression

IMPRESSION LEVER

TYMPAN HANDLE

FORM

PLATEN
TYMPAN
FRISKET
PAPER

BED

ly with, or even completely to survey, all the different makes or even types of presses that have been evolved to put the principle of relief printing into service. While, undoubtedly, a particular type or make of press will occasionally give rise to a particular blemish that causes difficulty in philatelic diagnosis — no less difficulty, sometimes, in diagnosis to the printer seeking to remedy the fault — such variations from the intended norm are merely inconstant flaws arising often from "slur" or "wipe."[139] Their philatelic diagnosis sometimes cannot be made with certainty by reference to a general standard, and can be accomplished, if at all, only by study of the particular methods of production and printing used for the particular stamps under consideration.

The simplest form of printing from a relief surface consists of impressing a handstamp first upon an ink pad and then upon paper. Postage stamps are security documents, usually strictly supervised at all stages of produc-

---

[139]See "Flaw A(2)," "Slurred Print," and "Stripped Color" in the alphabetical list to the chapter entitled "Printing Problems and Varieties." See also Footnote 132 earlier in this chapter.

tion; and, for obvious reasons, hand-stamping is difficult to control in respect to security, if for no other reason than the lack of identity of impression characteristic of such handwork. Nevertheless, hand-stamping has, over the years, been employed in the production of a, perhaps surprisingly, large number of issues not only of surcharges and other overprints, but of basic stamps also. Reference to several such stamps has already been made.[140] To these should be added what is probably the first adhesive hand-struck postage stamp issued anywhere in the world — U.S. Locals (D.O. Blood & Co.) Philadelphia Despatch Post (3c.), which was in use as an adhesive prepayer in December 1842.

Characteristics of issues so produced, apart from the lack of identity of impression between one subject and another resulting from variation in the amount of inking and weight of striking, are the irregularity of alignment of subjects in multiples, and similar variations from the vertical in individual subjects. As might well be expected, sideways and inverted subjects occur frequently.

Reference has previously been made also to stamps, overprints and surcharges produced by typewriting.[141]

Platen Presses

The simplest type of press used for the relief printing of stamps provided pressure from a platen that was operated by hand and moved vertically; the form rested on a bed, and could be moved by hand operation horizontally for the purpose of being inked, and then similarly returned to position under the platen. The ink was applied by hand from a previously charged roller. Such hand presses are encountered only very rarely today outside museums, but were used in the production of many relief-printed stamps, including, for example, France 1849.[142] Indeed, Thomas De La Rue & Company used hand presses exclusively for all the relief-printed stamps, except those of Great Britain and India, the printers produced until 1889[143] and even later.

The press and form having been prepared for printing by the necessary preliminary make-ready,[144] the operation of a hand press may be considered in two stages: The first stage comprises inking the form and laying on the paper; the second stage is the actual taking of the impression.

With the form on the bed of the press, the pressman or his assistant applies a film of ink to the reliefs, having charged his roller with ink from a coating on a separate inking slab or ink table. The pressman lays the sheet of paper on the tympan, folds the frisket over the paper and then swings the tympan over the form so that the printing surface of the paper, its margins

---

[140]See "Handstruck" in the alphabetical list to the chapter entitled "Printing Characteristics," and "Xylography" and "Direct Hand-Engraving" earlier in this chapter.

[141]See "Typewriting" earlier in this chapter.

[142]In fact, hand presses are still used in France for taking proofs — see *La Fabrication Des Timbres-Poste Francais* by R. Pouget (1954), Page 12.

[143]This is stated in a letter dated February 21, 1889, written by the printers to the Agent General in connection with the postage stamps of the Cape of Good Hope [*The De La Rue History of British and Foreign Postage Stamps 1855 to 1901* by John Easton (1958), Page 719].

[144]See "Make-Ready," "Underlay," "Overlay" and "Découpage" earlier in this chapter.

Relief printing. Hand inking. British Honduras 1866 (January) 1s. and 6d. se-
tenant with pane-gutter between. These stamps were printed from a form of
240 subjects arranged in four panes of sixty: two panes of the 1d. above one
each of the 6d. and 1s. The form was inked by hand-roller with a different color
for each value, and the three differently colored stamps were printed at one operation of the press.

masked by the frisket, is ready to be pressed into contact with the inked form.
This completes the first stage, and the operation can be followed by reference
to the accompanying sketches, which show also the first part of the second
stage.

The pressman next causes the form and its superimposed paper, frisket
and tympan to travel on the bed of the press until they are positioned under
the platen. He then operates a lever causing the platen to descend and press
the paper into contact with the inked reliefs, the pressure being judged with
skill born of long practice. The pressure must be just right for a perfect impression. If too much pressure is exerted, the impression will be blurred and
the paper heavily indented; if too little pressure is imparted, the print will
be incomplete and appear under-inked. This completes the second stage.

The pressman then raises the platen, returns the form to its earlier position, swings the tympan back, folds the frisket open and removes the printed
sheet. The press is then ready for the operation to begin again.

This method of inking by hand allows the printer great latitude in the manner in which he deals with particular problems, and enables him to cope simply with some tasks that would be beyond the more modern presses. An
outstanding instance of one such problem is provided by British Honduras
1866 (January) 1d., 6d. and 1s. Only 48,000 stamps were required;[145] the 1d.
in sheets of 120, and the two other values in sheets of sixty each. Thomas
De La Rue & Company divided the necessary number of press operations
by three, adopting the simple expedient of using a single form containing
240 subjects and comprising two panes side-by-side of sixty 1d. subjects (six
across, ten down) over two panes, again of sixty subjects each, but one pane

---

[145]In fact, 56,400 were supplied.

of 6d. subjects and the other of 1s. subjects. Instead of inking the whole form with one color, the pressman inked the 1d. subjects with blue ink, the 6d. subjects with rose and the 1s. subjects with green. Then he printed the form bearing three differently inked portions at one operation of the press. As a consequence, each printed sheet contained the three values in different colors *se-tenant* with pane gutters. No multiple is known of the three values in such a state, and it is possible, but unrecorded, that the printers separated the 1d. stamps from the others. However, the 6d. and 1s., being chronicled as new issues,[146] have, virtually ever since, been known *se-tenant* but separated by the pane gutter, and several such multiples exist.

A more complex form of printing press for relief printing, and substantially the first development from the hand press, is one in which the inking is carried out automatically. Such presses, of which there are many types, used to be operated by hand, or rather by foot and a treadle, so far as inking and impression are concerned. Later developments led to the press being power-assisted, although for many years the paper was fed by hand.

The presses were of two main types: the vertical-bed and the horizontal-bed. In the vertical-bed press, the bed, to which the form is attached, is substantially vertical and, unlike the hand press, does not allow movement of the form, which is held stationary. The platen and tympan form a unit that is hinged at the bottom to the bed, and, when open, lies almost horizontally in front of the pressman, so that the paper to be printed may be placed in position. In operation, the platen closes like a medieval drawbridge against the bed, so making the impression.

In some types of presses, the inking device is in the shape of a circular plate or table set above and at an angle to the bed, and is supplied with ink drawn by a roller from a fountain. When the table has an adequate supply of ink, other rollers run over it and then over the reliefs of the form, this operation being carried out automatically as the platen opens. In other types of presses, the circular table is replaced by a drum against which distributing rollers operate, transferring the ink to the inking rollers, which then run over the reliefs of the form.

In the horizontal-bed press, the form, on its travel to the platen, passed under a set of inking rollers that supplied ink to the reliefs, the tympan being incorporated with the platen. One development of this type of press — the Napier double-platen machine — was used largely in the production of stamps for New South Wales and the Netherlands. Actually, that machine was double-ended, with a single central platen. The platen operated on two different forms in turn, one from each end, the tympan for the appropriate form mechanically covering the form after it was inked and being similarly removed with the form after impression.

In all these, and in other and later presses, printing usually takes place from a continuous-surface plate or printing base — continuous-surface, that is, beneath the reliefs (although the continuity of surface might be provided merely by the sideways pressure exerted on pieces of type or separate sub-

---

[146]*The Stamp-Collector's Magazine*, Vol. 4, Page 88 (June 1866).

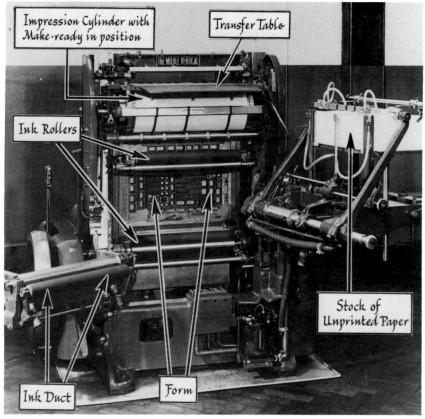

1. Relief printing. The Miehle Vertical. The press opens on the operating side.

jects in a chase). Except in such a rare instance as provided by the example of British Honduras, mentioned above, if more than a single color was to appear on the printed sheet, the second color meant that the paper had to be printed at two separate operations.

However, one form of printing enabled more than one color to be deposited on the paper at once, this being compound-plate printing, philatelically encountered, for instance, in regard to certain essays of Great Britain of 1839 known as the Charles Whiting or Beaufort House essays. Compound plates were of brass composition. Different parts of each design appeared on different plates, and usually two plates were involved. Each plate was separately inked with a different color. The plates were so constructed, perforated or pierced that they could be fitted perfectly together, and when they were fitted together, each design appeared as a composite whole. Consequently, when the paper was printed, it obtained an impression in two colors at one operation of the press.

(text continues on Page 556)

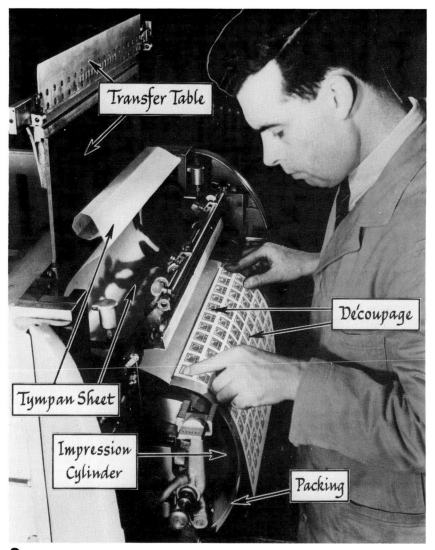

2. Relief printing. Make-ready on the Miehle Vertical. The operator is shown placing a sheet of *découpage* in position in the covering around the hollow impression cylinder. Of this covering, the outer sheet (sometimes termed the "tympan sheet") has been released, and is resting against the transfer table, which has been removed from its normal position and is held vertically. (When the press is in operation, the transfer table is nearly horizontal — see Illustration 3.) Between the *découpage* and the cylinder itself are several other sheets, termed packing. After the *découpage* has been positioned, it is covered by the tympan sheet; the tympan sheet, the *découpage* and the packing are then secured by tightening so as to make a close-fitting covering around the hollow impression cylinder.

Labels on image: Form · Feeder · Delivery · Stack of Paper for Printing · Transfer Table with Sheet of Unprinted Paper in position · Impression Cylinder with Make-ready in position · Ink Duct · 3

3. Relief printing. The Miehle Vertical. A cylinder press as used in the production of some relief-printed postage stamps. The picture shows student printers
undergoing training. In operation, pneumatic suckers on the feeder pick up a
sheet from the stack of unprinted paper and place the sheet on the transfer table,
where it is held in position, again by suction. As the impression cylinder moves
downward, the edge of the sheet is automatically transferred to the cylinder and
is held in position by grippers. In the picture, the cylinder is almost at the end
of its downward journey. The cylinder then begins to travel upward; the paper
is wrapped around the cylinder and pressed against the form, so receiving the
impression. When the paper has been printed, it is led to the delivery table at
the back (hidden in the picture by the metal side-guard). In operation, both the
impression cylinder and the form move up and down reciprocally, no printing
being carried out while the cylinder is on the downward journey. The press can
operate at speeds of up to 5,000 sheets per hour.

Relief printing. Rotary press. The Chambon rotary press as used in the production of relief-printed stamps for France and other countries. The whole press
can be seen at the upper part of the picture, and is capable of printing in four
colors "on the web." The various parts of the machine are: at extreme left (half-
hidden by the second ladder-like support, and below the table), the reel or web
of unprinted paper; next (above the table, and also half-hidden by the same support) the first wheel is part of the apparatus ensuring that the paper is fed properly into the press; the next four wheels are part of the four assemblies of printing and impression cylinders (each surmounted by different ink feeds) that print,
date and number the impressions; next (without a wheel) is the perforating apparatus, described as "oscillating," that while perforating the paper moves with
the web then disengages and returns to position to repeat the process; the next
wheel is part of an apparatus comprising two cylinders for ensuring that the
web remains at proper tension; next is a guillotine for severing the web into
sheets; and, at the extreme right is a delivery board upon which, by means of
an ingenious arrangement of geared wheels, counted sheets are delivered in
bundles.

→

Cylinder Presses

Cylinder presses also are of the two main types: the horizontal-bed and the vertical-bed.

In some types of cylinder press, the impression cylinder is hollow and incorporates the tympan, being covered by an arrangement of sheets of parchment or material and paper, including the *découpage*, all held securely in place stretched tightly around the cylinder by a square or slotted bar (termed "reel rod") that can be rotated and held in position by a ratchet. One end of the tympan sheet is secured to the cylinder; the other end is wound around or slotted through the reel rod.

In the horizontal-bed press, such as the Wharfedale type, the flat form travels in turn beneath the inking rollers and the impression cylinder, both of which rotate in fixed positions.

In the vertical-bed press, such as the Miehle Vertical, the inking rollers, the form and the impression cylinder move up and down reciprocally.

In these presses, which print on to sheets, the paper is fed automatically against the impression cylinder, and is held in place by grippers that open and shut automatically as required. After being printed, the paper is automatically led away to a delivery board or table.

Rotary Presses

In one sense, the most complex form of press for relief printing is the rotary press, developed originally to cope with the increasing demands for speed in newspaper production, and enabling printing to be carried out easily "on the web," which is to say on reels of paper of great length. In another sense, this form of press is very simple, and may be likened to the old-fashioned household mangle or wringer.

A country that has made extensive use of rotary presses for the relief printing of postage stamps is France. The first stamp of that country to be so printed was 1920-26 Sower 10c. green of March 4, 1922; after 1934, all French stamps relief-printed in France were printed on rotary presses. Another country that has widely used rotary presses for relief printing is, for example, Germany, among the issues so produced being, for instance, 1954 Heuss 10 (pf.).

In France, the printing cylinders are made by electrodeposition. In Germany, the printing cylinders of 400 subjects comprise forty segments, each bearing a mounted thin plate upon which, by the die and mill process, have been transferred ten subjects (five across, two down).

In rotary presses, make-ready overlay is applied directly to the impression cylinder. In France, these made-ready cylinders are preserved against future printing requirements.

Printing on rotary presses is entirely automatic once the paper has been threaded on to the press and the ink supply adjusted. There is no "bed"; the impression cylinder and printing cylinder press together against opposite sides of the paper, and the axial line of pressure is that at which printing takes place. As the cylinders rotate, the paper moves between them, and printing is continuous.

Relief printing. Rotary press. Germany 1954 Heuss 10(pf.). A picture of the printing cylinder, which is composed of forty segments, each comprising a mounted small curved plate of ten subjects. Also shown are ink rollers and the paper feed.

Usually such machines incorporate perforating and severing devices — compare, for example, the Swiss intaglio machine discussed in the chapter entitled "Intaglio Printing — I: Line Engraving."

Varieties and Terms in Relief Printing

The alphabetical list that follows includes some of the varieties and terms appropriate to relief-printed stamps. The list does not pretend to be exhaustive. It does not, in the main — and is not intended to — incorporate those terms and varieties which, although encountered in relief-printed stamps, occur also in other printing processes, being terms and varieties of printing generally rather than those occasioned by production from a specific kind of printing base. Those general printing varieties, or some of them, are to be found in the alphabetical list to the chapter entitled "Printing Problems and Varieties," and some of the terms relating to special printing processes are to be found in the alphabetical list to the chapter entitled "Printing Characteristics."

The majority of the varieties listed consist in either the presence or the absence of color where it should be, respectively, absent or present on the normal stamp. Where unwanted color is present, the variety is referred to as "colored flaw"; "uncolored flaw" signifies the absence of color that normally appears. Colored flaws result from many causes, some giving rise to constant varieties, others resulting in semi-constant or merely inconstant varieties.

Both these classes of flaw — colored and uncolored — can occur either as the result of happenings, during its manufacture or use, to the printing base, or as the result of happenings during printing. In diagnosing the cause of an abnormality, it is, therefore, not possible to draw any general rules based on either the presence or the absence of color — except to state that if the flaw stems from the printing base and is colored, it was caused by the presence of a relief that ought not to have been there; and if the flaw stems from the printing base and is uncolored, it was caused by the absence of a relief that ought to have been present.

Aciérage. The process of plating with steel by electrodeposition. The term "steel facing" is used synonymously with "*aciérage,*" which is derived from the French *acier* (steel). Patented in Great Britain in 1858 (No. 667) by E.A. Jacquin of Paris, the process of iron- or steel-facing copper plates was used by Joubert de la Ferté in London during that year, and has been employed widely for coating printing plates throughout the world. See "Coating."

Added Metal. Colored flaw. In the case of relief-printed stamps, the term "added metal" is used to designate a flaw caused as the result of remedying a defect in a subject by the addition of metal to the surface of the plate and subsequently cutting away by hand the non-printing areas within the space occupied by the added metal. Such repairs to the printing surface cause color to appear in what was previously, because of damage, an uncolored area, but the result is usually very crude. See "Retouch."

Air Hole Flaw. Uncolored flaw. In the cases of stamps relief-printed from stereotypes, the term "air hole flaw" is used to designate an uncolored flaw resulting from an air hole forming in irregularly cooling metal (sometimes caused by using an insufficiently heated casting box) and consequent absence or partial absence of a relief. For example, Denmark 1851 (Apr. 29) 2 rbs., variety Pointed Foot (Type 2), comprises an air hole flaw that has resulted in the foot of the "2" being almost disjoined from the body.

Anchor. In connection with some relief-printing plates, the term "anchor" is used sometimes to denote the individual rivets, nails or screws used to secure the plate or subject to its wooden or metal mount, the process of mounting being termed "anchoring." The anchors are sometimes located within the design, in a non-printing area, and sometimes outside the subject. Usually anchors are intended to be at non-printing height.

Anchor Mark. Colored flaw. In the case of relief-printed stamps, the term "anchor mark" is used to designate a colored flaw caused by the inking and printing of an anchor, either because it has become loose and worked up to printing height or because the impression was too heavy or the make-ready too soft — see "Anchor," "Overlay Varieties." The terms "mounting mark," "nail mark" and "rivet mark" are sometimes used as synonyms for "anchor mark." For example, in Denmark 1851 (Apr. 29) 2 rbs., there are many instances of anchor marks.

Backing. The process of filling the non-printing side of an electrodeposited shell of copper or other metal with molten type metal to form a printing plate. The plate, comprising the shell and backing, is (usually) subsequently mounted to bring it up to printing height. See "Mounting."

Blanket. In reference to relief printing, the term "blanket" is used sometimes to designate the whole arrangement of tympan material or impression cylinder covering, packing sheets and *découpage* that provides a resilient surface and locally adjusted pressure necessary to obtain a good and even impression. See *"Découpage."*

Block. In reference to relief printing, the term "block" is used generically to designate a woodcut, a wood engraving, a mounted electrotype or stereotype, and mounted line or halftone zinc or copper plate produced by photomechanical etching. Sometimes "cut" is used as a synonym for "block." See "Cut," "Halftone Block," "Line Block," "Wood Block." See also "Block" in the alphabetical list to the chapter entitled "From Design to Issued Sheets."

Bounce. This term is, occasionally, used to designate the cause of the variety termed "double strike." See "Double Strike."

Box — see "Case."

Case. In reference to letterpress, the term "case" is used to designate one of two wooden cases, each about 32½ inches long, 14½ inches wide and 1¼ inches deep, in which individual sorts and pieces of type all of the same font are held, and from which a compositor chooses appropriately when setting type by hand. Because of the relative positions they occupy, the cases are termed "upper case" and "lower case." They are divided into compartments termed "boxes." In the upper case, the boxes are of equal size, and each box contains one sort comprising either a CAPITAL or SMALL CAPITAL letter, or certain symbols; in the lower case, the boxes contain the non-capital letters and other sorts, and the sizes of the boxes vary according to the frequency of and employment of the various letters in the appropriate language in use. See "Face," "Font," "Lower Case," "Sorts," "Type," "Upper Case."

Cast. In reference to stereotyping, the term "cast" is used, sometimes, in reference to the stereotype reproduction.

Chase. In reference to relief printing, the term "chase" is used to designate a metal frame employed for surrounding and securing assemblages of type, blocks and other material for printing. The sideways pressure for securing the assemblages is exerted by means of "quoins," a quoin being a wooden wedge or a metal device that can be made to expand and retain the imparted expansion. Compare "Form."

Cliché. This term, in its original sense, refers exclusively to the result produced by stamping a unit in semi-fused metal by polytyping. By transference, the term *cliché* became adopted to designate a single subject produced as the result of casting in a mould by stereotyping, and also as the result of growing a shell by electrodeposition. Loosely, in philatelic use, *cliché* has been employed as designating also an individual subject in a solid plate — and such use, or misuse, of the term has often led to confusion. For such a general sense, the term "subject" is available — see "Subject" in the alphabetical lists to the chapters entitled "Printing Problems and Varieties" and "From Design to Issued Sheets."

Clog Flaw. Colored flaw. See "Crust Flaw."

Coating. In reference to printing plates, the term "coating" is used to designate a protective surface applied to a printing base comprising a solid unit. The term "facing" is often used synonymously with "coating" — see "Facing." Sometimes, however, the term "coating" is used to distinguish between a protective surface applied after the printing base is made, on the one hand, and, on the other hand, a protective facing grown in a shell as a preliminary operation. Coating results in prolonging the life of a printing base very considerably. The protective coating, when it begins to show signs of wear or for other reasons, can be stripped from the printing base (by dissolving it in a solvent that does not affect the printing base) and replaced by a fresh coating. This has the possible philatelic results that: (1) a stamp printed from one coating may differ appreciably from a stamp in the identical position printed from another coating, without there having been any repair or retouching to the subject; (2) a comparatively prominent flaw may be permitted to persist because stripping and re-coating are considered unjustified, and no repair could be effected without stripping; and (3) slight inequalities in the thickness of a coating may give rise to constant, vague, uncolored or under-colored areas over the sheet of stamps.

Collar. In reference to the making of lead moulds for use in electrotyping, the term "collar" is employed to designate a heavy steel cylinder with a rectangular shaft vertically through the center, the relief die being held in position at the base of the shaft by a wedge, and the piece of lead being forced into contact with the die by means of a plunger operating in and projecting beyond the top of the shaft and struck by a mechanically operated hammer. The collar was used by Thomas De La Rue & Company Ltd. for the majority of the relief-printed stamps produced by the printers. See "Lead (2) (c)."

Compartment Lines. Colored flaw. This term is used to designate lines, dashes or dots in the color of the stamp appearing inconstantly but in constant positions in gutters or margins of stamps relief-printed from steel plates made by the Perkins Die and Mill process and resulting from a combination of causes: (1) the imperfect cutting away of metal in the gutters (which, because of the process employed, are necessarily left at printing height during rolling-in) between subjects on the plate, leaving ridges in the gutters — ridges that are, in fact, below normal printing height; (2) the undesired but inevitable inking of these ridges; and (3) soft paper, soft make-ready and weight of impression that result, during printing, in the paper being pressed not only on to the subjects' lines and areas at printing height, but also somewhat into the spaces corresponding with the non-printing areas, so that the paper comes into (undesired) contact with the (unintentionally) inked ridges and so picks up from them ink that is deposited in the stamp gutters on the printed sheet. Compartment lines are not a factor of every subject, and are inconstant in that their appearance or non-appearance with a particular subject of which they are a factor depends upon, respectively, the softness or hardness of paper and heaviness or lightness of impression. See "Overlay Varieties." "Compartment lines" as such appear only on prints from plates made by the Perkins Die and Mill process — for example, Australia 1914 1d. and New Zealand 1909 "Dominion" 1d. — and are not to be confused with, for example, lines sometimes found surrounding subjects printed by lithography (which are guide lines marked on the stone, forming rectangles for the easy placing of transfers), or short intersecting lines or dots having similar objects — see "Guide Dot," "Guide Line" in the alphabetical list to the chapter entitled "Intaglio Printing — I: Line Engraving."

Composing Stick. An implement, rather like a small, oblong box open at the top and one side and with one end that can be adjusted so as to make the box narrower or wider, into which a compositor setting type by hand places, sort by sort, the individual pieces of type he selects from the cases. See "Case," "Sort."

Composite Die. In connection with relief printing, the term "composite die" is used sometimes in reference to a die comprising two separate elements: (1) the main features of the design that remain constant throughout; and (2) a subsidiary feature that varies — for example, the sheet position of the subject, the plate number when that appears on the subject, or the denomination. In that portion of the die bearing the main features of the design, provision is made, in the form of a specially shaped recess, for the reception of similarly shaped pieces of metal (termed "plugs" — see "Plug") bearing the subsidiary features; and different plugs can be inserted and removed as required. Sometimes the term "plugged die" is used as a synonym for "composite die." In the cases of some designs, more than one feature varies; in such cases, that portion of the die bearing the main features of the design has provision for the reception of more than one plug at a time — of course, in different positions. For example: in the case of Australia 1913-48 Kangaroo stamps, the variable features comprised the figure and words of value, and all the values (except 1945-48 2s.) resulted from a composite die comprising a single undenominated element bearing the main features of the design and plugs upon which appeared the figures or words of value. In the cases of these stamps, no single denominated duty die existed. Further, in the case, for example, of Great Britain 1873-79 3d., the variable features comprised the four corner letters (which varied with every sheet position) and the two plate numbers (which varied with every plate); in the case of this stamp, that portion of the die bearing the main features of the design was denominated. Distinguish "Duty Die."

Compound Plates. In reference to relief printing, the term "compound plates" is used to designate a set of, usually, two plates, on each of which a part only of each design appeared. The plates were so constructed, perforated or pierced that, after being separately inked, they could be fitted together, and the complete design, as a compound whole, was printed in two colors at one operation. The plates are sometimes termed "Congreve plates," the process having been developed before 1820 by Sir William Congreve; it was used for a wide range of revenue stamps printed at Somerset House. The process was employed also for the essays known as Charles Whiting and Beaufort House, produced in Great Britain in 1839.

Congreve Plates — see "Compound Plates."

Cracked Electro. Uncolored flaw. This term, encountered usually in connection with relief-printed stamps, is used to designate a stamp exhibiting an uncolored flaw as the result of fracturing of the electrodeposited shell which, backed and mounted, forms the printing base of the subject affected. Such flaws often take the form of a fine, uncolored line passing irregularly through the colored part of the design. They are, sometimes, helpful in determining whether the printing base was a continuous surface, or a form comprising separate subjects, because, in the latter case, the same crack can never affect more than a single subject. If several contiguous subjects are affected by the same crack, they must have formed part of a continuous surface. An outstanding instance of "cracked electro" is to be found in Victoria 1857-63 Emblems 1d., pane D, stamp No. 25, where the crack separates the lower part of the design from the top part.

Crust Flaw. Colored flaw. In reference to relief-printed stamps, the term "crust flaw" is used to designate a flaw comprising an area of color caused by encrusted ink accumulating in non-printing areas of the subject until this encrustation has built up to printing height, with the result that the ink crust itself becomes inked and deposits color in what should be an uncolored area of the design. A crust having formed at printing height, the crust flaw appears in each subsequent print, often increasing in area, until the printing base is cleaned. Crust flaws are, therefore, semi-constant, and may be philatelically important in enabling the sequence of printings and shade variations to be established. Sometimes the terms "clog flaw" and "ink clog" are used as synonyms for "crust flaw." Crust flaws

561

are to be found, for instance, on Greece 1862-67 (Athens printings) 1 l. red-brown; and a particularly prominent example occurs on Victoria 1857-63 Emblems 4d., settings V and VI, variety No. 43, having the appearance of a shadowed triangle extending over the right side of the stamp, the apex being at the northeast corner and the base extending about one-quarter the width of the bottom frameline.

Cut. In reference to relief printing, the term "cut" is used, loosely, as synonymous with "block" — see "Block." "Cut" also connotes "any printed illustration," and, in this sense, is an historical survival from the times when the only forms of illustrations available were woodcuts.

Cut Edge. Uncolored flaw. In reference to relief-printed stamps, the term "cut edge" is used to designate a variety exhibiting absence of color in one extremity or more of the design, because the corresponding portion or portions of the reliefs on the relative subject were cut, gouged or trimmed away during the processes of manufacture or finishing the subject or the plate of which the subject formed a part. The flaw is constant, and is the equivalent of a clipped transfer — see "Clipped Transfer" in the alphabetical list to the chapter entitled "Planographic Printing." Sometimes the term "frame cut" is used as a synonym for "cut edge." Many examples of cut edge varieties are to be found, for instance, in New Zealand 1909 Dominion 1d. and Bulgaria 1907 (Aug. 28) 5s.

Date Cuts. In reference to the postage stamps of Great Britain 1911-12 relief-printed at Somerset House, the term "date cuts" is used to designate certain uncolored markings in the "Jubilee Lines" appearing below stamps Nos. 11 and 12 in the bottom row (as the result of cuts or punches made in the reliefs by the printers), and indicating that the stamps were printed in, respectively, 1911 and 1912. Similar markings appear on many sheets. But the "date cuts" signify dates only in respect of certain printings of values from 1½d. to £1 made at Somerset House.

Découpage. Overlay. Romania 1876-78 25b. *Découpage* for merely a single subject in a plate of 300 — two panes of 150. Represented is a base sheet printed in blue, visible only in the spandrels, the face and neck and a small oval in front of the ear. Over the base sheet has been pasted a print in orange, from which has been cut the spandrels and the face but excluding the moustache, beard and hair and a small oval in front of the ear. Over that has been pasted yet another print, again in blue, consisting of only the central circle including the "pearls," but from it have been excised the face and neck including the moustache, beard and hair. For the other 299 subjects, different *découpages* were made, which, in aggregate, formed the overlay for the sheet. The overlay

would last for only one printing and, perhaps, not even for the whole printing if the *découpage* broke down or shifted or a general alteration had to be made.

Découpage. In relation to relief printing, the term *découpage*, being French for "cutting out," is used to designate that part of make-ready overlay that is concerned with local adjustments of pressure to compensate for slight inequalities in height of the printing surface of the individual reliefs on the printing base, and to ensure a proper impression over the sheet as a whole. *Découpage* comprises a specially printed sheet from which have been cut out portions of the designs where the pressure was initially excessive, and on to which have been pasted portions of the designs (cut from another sheet) where the pressure was initially insufficient. During a printing run, the *découpage* is, or should be, exactly registered so that it in fact compensates for the inequalities it is intended to correct. See "Overlay," "Overlay Varieties."

Découpage **Shift.** Uncolored flaw. In reference to relief-printed stamps, the term "*découpage* shift" is used to designate a variety exhibiting absence or reduction of color in part or parts of the design because printing pressure at the relevant portion or portions was insufficient owing to the fact that the *découpage* shifted from register, and thus actually accentuated the very effect it was intended to correct — see "*Découpage.*" The variety will persist (perhaps in decreasingly prominent form) until its cause is remedied; it is, however, a semi-constant printing variety. The terms "overlay shift," "shifted *découpage*" and "shifted overlay" are used as synonyms for "*découpage* shift." The effect presented by a *découpage* shift is, for example, a shadowy outline to one side of a head, as obtains, for instance, in some printings of Greece 1861-62 5 l., or an apparent duplication of an uncolored numeral on a colored tablet, as in some printings of Antigua 1921-29 2d. See "Overlay Varieties."

Deep Edge. Colored flaw. In reference to relief-printed stamps, the term "deep edge" is used to designate a variety exhibiting excessive color along one edge or adjacent edges of the design, resulting from the fact that the subject from which the stamp was printed was positioned at one side or corner of a pane or the plate and, therefore, at the edge or edges affected, was subjected to action of the inking roller known as "dwelling," causing pronounced wear and ink accumulation. As a result, the edge or edges appear more heavily inked than the remainder of the design, and details of the design within the deep edge are obscured. The flaw is progressive, and difficult to distinguish from some examples of "partial strike." See "Partial Strike."

Die Composite — see "Composite Die."

Die Flaw — see "Impacted Metal Flaw." Other flaws in line-engraved dies used in the production of relief-printing plates comprise, mainly, cracked relief lines caused by crystalline or other weaknesses of, or damage to, the metal or other material of the die and result in uncolored flaws — for example, the cracked frame at the right of New Zealand 1882 1d., the so-called "Die 3."

Die, Plugged — see "Composite Die."

Die-Struck — see "Punch-Struck."

Distortion Varieties. In reference to relief-printed stamps, the term "distortion varieties" is used in connection with abnormal twisting or contortion of lines or areas in the design. The design is flawed in that it is abnormal, but the abnormality consists in the distortion, not in the presence or absence of color. These varieties are constant and have been classified, philatelically, under two headings: (1) "Internal" Distortion Varieties, where the distortion results from some fault in the manufacture of the subject such as (a) unequal cooling of semi-fused metal, giving rise to, for example, the twisted inner frames in the southeast quarter of Victoria 1864-69 Laureated 2d., setting 1, stamp No. 53 (Type B.14), or (b) squeezing owing to the softness of the material, giving rise to, for example, the so-called ''dropped 'R' '' in the name tablet of Leeward Islands 1902 1s., plate 2, pane 1, stamp No. 1; and (2) ''External'' Distortion Varieties, where the distortion results from the application of physical force after the subject has been manufactured — for instance, the careless pushing down of a protuberant reglet, giving rise to the distorted outer frame in the upper part of the left side of Victoria 1863-67 Laureated 2d., setting 1, stamp No. 82 (Type H.4). See ''Reglet Flaw.''

Double Strike. Colored flaw. In reference to stamps relief-printed from electrotypes or stereotypes, the term ''double strike'' is used, philatelically, to designate a stamp bearing duplication in part or all of the design because the duplications appeared on the printing base, the mould having been impressed more than once non-coincidentally by the die. This may occur either because of bounce and lateral movement permitted by the shaft in the collar being larger than the lead, or striking without use of a collar, or because the mould was intentionally struck twice, the non-coincidence being unintentional. The variety is constant. An outstanding instance of double strike is to be found in Victoria 1864-69 Laureated 2d., setting 1, stamp No. 33 (Type C.9); another instance is to be found, for example, in Denmark 1851-54 4 rbs., plate 1, stamp No. 55.

Down. A convenient term signifying a non-printing area of a relief-printing base, and thus any non-printing area within any subject. Compare ''Up.''

Draw Out. Uncolored flaw. A printers' term designating the fact of a piece of type being plucked from the form by the action of the inking roller. For draw out to occur, the type within the subject affected must, for one reason or another, have been insufficiently compressed sideways to withstand the pull exerted by the sticky ink roller. A print made after draw out reveals an absence of part of the design — for example, Hawaii 1859-65 2c., setting 3, stamp No. 4, variety '' NTER,'' the ''I'' having been plucked out of the form.

Dropped Lead — see ''Reglet Flaw,'' ''Space.''

Duty Die. This term is used in reference to a subsidiary die, made from a master die that bears either no (country) name — if provision is made in the master die for subsequent incorporation of a name — or no figures or other symbols of denomination. Usually a duty die bears a name, and may be a ''blank duty die,'' when undenominated, or the duty die of a particular value when denominated. The term ''duty die'' is employed, usually, only in reference to one of a series of dies differently denominated. Compare ''Duty Plate.'' The term ''duty die'' is not limited in use to key-type designs — see ''Key-Type'' in the alphabetical list to the chapter entitled ''Watermarks.'' Distinguish ''Composite Die.''

Duty Plate. This term is used in reference to that one of a pair of printing plates that prints the value or (country) name, or both, on key-type stamps — see ''Key-Type'' in the alphabetical list to the chapter entitled ''Watermarks.'' Sometimes printers use the term ''overprint plate'' to designate the duty plate.

Dwelling — see ''Deep Edge.''

External Distortion — see ''Distortion Varieties.''

Face. This term is used, strictly, to designate the end or surface of a piece of type upon which appears the letter or symbol to be printed, and from which the impression is made. Also, ''face'' is used generally and loosely in the sense of designating lettering of a particular style. In addition, qualified by such terms as "light," "medium" and "bold," the term "face" indicates the thickness of the strokes comprising each letter or character of a particular style of lettering. See "Fount," "Type." Occasionally "face" is used in a completely different sense, and as an abbreviation for "facing" — see "Facing." These senses of the term must, of course, be distinguished from "face" as an abbreviation of "face value," being the value expressed in figures or words on the face of the stamp.

Faced Plates. This term is used to designate printing plates protected by "facing." See "Facing."

Facing. In reference to printing bases, the term "facing" is used to designate the actual printing surface when that differs from the principal shell, cast, plate or cylinder. See "Cast," "Shell." Facing is applied by electrodeposition. When the subjects themselves are electrodeposited, facing may be carried out as a preliminary operation in the mould before the principal shell is grown. In other cases, facing is carried out after the principal shell has been grown, or the cases or the plate or cylinder made. Many different metals have been used for facing: Great Britain 1862 4d. was printed in vermilion from a silver-faced plate; South Australia 1894 2½d. and 5d. were printed from nickel-faced plates; among very many others, India 1882-88 ½a. was printed from steel-faced plates. See "Aciérage," "Coating."

Flaw. See "Flaw" in the alphabetical list to the chapter entitled "Printing Problems and Varieties." In relief printing, sometimes, flaws of the same character occur, *mutatis mutandis*, as occur in planographic printing, and for somewhat similar reasons — see "Primary Flaw" in the alphabetical list to the chapter entitled "Planographic Printing." See also "Mould Group." If an arrangement of small plates made from a mould group is copied, not only "types" but also "sub-types" and "sub-sub-types" will occur — as in, for example, Prince Edward Island 1872 (Jan. 1) 3c. See "Die Flaw," "Impacted Metal Flaw," "Mould Flaw," "Sub-Type."

Flong. The primary stage of *papier maché*, comprising a moistened aggregation of sheets having on its face thin, fine paper backed by thicker, coarse paper. The flong is placed over the die or object to be copied and beaten or pressed from the back, then dried. The resultant counterpart of the die or object to be copied is a *papier maché* mould, used for casting stereotypes. See "Mat."

Form. In reference to printing generally, the term "form" is often used generically by printers in the sense of denoting the assemblage, plate or cylinder from which printing is actually effected; that is to say, "form" is used by printers in the sense that, philatelically, "printing base" is used — see "Printing Base" in the alphabetical list to the chapter entitled "Printing Problems and Varieties." In reference to relief printing, the term "form" is used to designate a complete printing unit after the components have been locked up in a chase — see "Chase."

Font. In reference to letterpress, the term "font" is used, strictly, to designate a complete set of type of a particular style and size as supplied by a type founder. Sometimes "font" is used synonymously with "face," generally and loosely in the sense of designating lettering of a particular style — see "Face," "Type."

Frame Cut. Uncolored flaw. See "Cut Edge."

Friar. A printers' term designating a light or imperfectly inked patch on a sheet of printed matter. Compare "Monk."

Frisket. A thin iron frame hinged to the tympan (or positioned between the printing surface and the platen) provided with tapes or paper strips to keep the sheet of paper in position while being printed, and providing protection for the margins (and, sometimes, other portions of the sheet) that are not to be printed. Maladjustment of this protection may give rise to a partial albino impression — see "Albino" in the alphabetical list to the chapter entitled "Printing Problems and Varieties."

Group — see "Mould Group."

Halftone Block. A result of photomechanical etching (sometimes termed photo-engraving) whereby a printing surface, mounted type-high, for relief printing is made by etching a zinc or copper plate after dissolving from its surface such portions of a light-sensitized mordant resist (bichromated albumen or fish glue) as remain unhardened after exposure, through a halftone screen in a camera, to light reflected from a continuous tone original. The halftone screen, comprising a grid of opaque lines crossing at right angles, has the effect of breaking up the continuous tones of the original into dots, so that all the gradations of tone values in the original are reproduced on the printing surface by variations in the formation of dots of geometrical arrangement. Halftone screens are referred to by the number of lines occurring in a linear inch — for example, a 175-line screen produces 30,625 dots per square inch. The first use of a halftone block in a general issue occurred in Uruguay 1908 (Aug. 23) Declaration of Independence 1c., 2c. and 5c., for the centers. Compare "Line Block." See "Cut."

Impacted Metal Flaw. Colored or uncolored flaw. In reference to stamps relief-printed from a printing base made through the media of die or master-plate, mould and shell or case, the term "impacted metal flaw" is used, generically, to designate a variety occasioned by a piece of metal or other substance becoming lodged in a recess of the die or master-plate while the mould was, or several moulds were, being struck (colored flaw), or of the mould while the shell was being grown or the stereotype cast (uncolored flaw). Impacted metal flaws are to be found, for instance, in Cook Islands 1893-1902 2½d., pane 2, stamps Nos. 2, 3, 4, 5, and 13.

Ink Clog. Colored flaw. See "Crust Flaw."

Ink Squash, Ink Squeeze. These terms, in reference to relief printing, are used to designate the effect of the edge of a line or area being more intensely colored than its other portions. This characteristic is almost unfailingly present in some portion of the design, but the eye may require the aid of a fairly powerful magnifying glass (X10) to observe the effect. It is caused by a combination of circumstances: (1) the printing pressure tends to cause the ink to flow toward the edges of a line or area; (2) the inking roller is flexible, and, when it meets the relief, compresses somewhat and tends to leave some ink on the vertical sides of the minute wall of metal (comprising the relief) of which the printing surface is the top. Consequently, when this printing surface meets the paper under pressure, the paper picks up this additional ink from the sides of the wall (just over the edge of the top), causing excess color to appear along the edges of the line or area.

Interlay — see "Make-Ready."

Internal Distortion — see "Distortion Varieties."

Key Plate. This term is used in reference to that one of a pair of printing plates that prints those parts of a key-type design that are common to several values or countries — see "Key-Type" in the alphabetical list to the chapter entitled "Stamp Design." See "Duty Plate."

Lead. In reference to relief printing, the term "lead" is used in two main senses.

(1) In connection with typesetting, (a) to designate a strip of metal inserted between lines of type for separating the lines of characters farther from each other than would be the case if the type bodies were juxtaposed. In many cases of typeset overprints, their registration on the stamps in the sheet has been obtained by the use of leads. A lead is usually below type height, but many cases have been recorded of leads having worked up during printing and causing printed marks to appear on one or more stamps in the sheets; (b) to designate a strip of wood or metal, usually below type height, used for separating individual electros, stereos or other blocks. In this sense, the terms "reglet" and "spacer" are used synonymously with "lead" — compare "Rule"; see "Reglet Flaw"; also see "Dropped Lead." (2) In connection with electrotyping, (c) to designate a small parallelepiped of metal upon which, usually in a collar, is stamped an impression of the die and which forms the mould of an individual subject; see "Collar"; (d) to designate a sheet of metal used as a mould for a whole plate or numerous subjects.

Letterpress-Printed. The result of printing from an assemblage of printers' type assembled for use on, usually, one occasion only and distributed after that use. Contrast with "Plate-Printed." In this sense, a synonym for "typeset" — see "Typeset" in the alphabetical list to the chapter entitled "Printing Characteristics."

Letterpress Printing. The printer's term for relief printing.

Line Block. A result of photomechanical etching (sometimes termed photo-engraving) whereby a printing surface, mounted type high for relief printing, is made by etching a zinc or copper plate after dissolving from its surface such portions of a light-sensitized mordant resist (bichromated albumen or fish glue) as remain unhardened after exposure to light reflected from an original drawing comprising monochrome color or its absence — compare "Halftone Block." An original for "line" reproduction must comprise only color or absence of color, as opposed to an original for "halftone" reproduction, which may comprise many gradations of tone. (A print from a halftone block may be used as an original for a line block.) Among the earliest uses of line blocks for printing local postage stamps are Lake Lefroy (Western Australia) Cycle Mail 1897 (February) 6d. This sense of the term "line block" is, of course, entirely separate from its use as an abbreviation for "guide line block" — see "Block" in the alphabetical list to the chapter entitled "From Design to Issued Sheets."

Lower Case. In reference to each individual letter of the alphabet, the term "lower case" indicates that the letter is not a capital letter; and the term signifies that the sort comprising that letter is to be found in the lower of the two cases from which type is set by hand — see "Case," "Sort," "Upper Case." Although much typesetting has long been effected mechanically and hand-work is limited to operating a keyboard resembling that of a typewriter, the term "lower case" has remained in use to designate non-capital letters.

Make-Ready. The operation of making a form ready to be printed. Also, the sheet or sheets used to effect the operation. In relief printing, make-ready comprises three possible elements: (1) underlay, which is leveling up the form on the bed of the press so that it and the back of the form are in close contact throughout; (2) interlay, which is the insertion of packing between the plate and its mount, and (3) overlay, which is positioned between the platen or impression cylinder and the back of the paper to be printed, and which comprises two elements: (a) *découpage* — see "*Découpage,*" and (b) packing sheets — see "Blanket."

Master Group — see ''Mould Group.''

Master-Plate. In reference to electrotyping, the term ''master-plate'' is used to designate a completed printing surface bearing multiple subjects (sometimes undenominated) that is employed as a multiple-subject ''die'' from which moulds are made and used for growing the shells that form the printing plates (to which denominations are added, if necessary, sometimes by means of a pantograph). Compare ''Mould Group.'' The main difference between a master-plate and a mould group is that the master-plate is, usually, the size of a sheet of stamps, whereas a mould group, usually, contains fewer subjects. A master-plate is not, usually, employed for printing.

Mat, Mats. Commonly employed abbreviations for ''matrix'' and ''matrices,'' particularly in connection with *papier maché* or composition moulds used for stereotype cases — see ''Mould.''

Matrix — see ''Mould.''

Mechanical Overlay — see ''Overlay.''

Metal Added — see ''Added Metal.''

Mise en Train. A French term signifying ''make-ready'' — see ''Make-Ready.'' Sometimes used as though synonymous with *découpage* — see ''Découpage.''

Monk. A printers' term designating a heavy or overinked patch on a sheet of printed matter; a dirty patch. Compare ''Friar.''

Mould. In reference to electrotyping and stereotyping, the term ''mould'' is used to designate the counterpart of the die or master-plate made in lead, *papier maché*, plaster of paris, wax or other substance in which is grown the electrodeposited shell or is cast the stereotype metal. Often the term ''matrix'' is used as a synonym for ''mould.'' The term ''matrix'' is used, often, to designate a piece of copper or brass having on it a letter stamped in recess by a punch, from which type is cast. See ''Mat.''

Mould Flaw. In relief printing, a flaw originating at the mould stage and comprising either (1) impacted metal, giving rise to an uncolored flaw — see ''Impacted Metal Flaw'' — and being the equivalent of damage to a recess in the mould; or (2) damage to the relief(s) of the mould, giving rise (if the damage is sufficiently pronounced and reaches the depth in the mould equivalent to printing height on the resultant cast or shell) to a colored flaw. Mould flaws are difficult to diagnose with certainty.

Mould Group. In reference to relief printing, the term ''mould group'' is used to designate an arrangement of ''types'' resulting from the use of a single-subject die to make a few moulds that were grouped together to form a multiple-subject mould from which a small plate was made, the small plate serving in turn as a multiple-subject ''die'' from which further multiple-subject moulds were made, these in their turn being used to provide the required number of copies of the small plate. These copies, either whole or cut up into single subjects, constitute the printing base — see ''Flaw,'' ''Mould.'' The use of a mould group in relief printing is the equivalent of the use of a transfer stone in planographic printing — see ''Transfer Stone'' in the alphabetical list to the chapter entitled ''Planographic Printing.'' The use of a mould group inevitably gives rise to ''types'' of which the characteristics are more or less prominent according to the technical skill of the manufacturers. Whether these ''types'' recur or repeat regularly, or appear haphazardly in the sheet of stamps, depends upon whether the electrotype or stereotype copies of the mould group are, respectively, used whole or cut up into single subjects. New Zealand 1899 Postage Due 1d. provides, in the frames, an instance of the use of a mould group and regular appearance of "types" in the sheet; Norway 1872 Shaded Posthorn 50 ö. provides an instance of the use of a mould group and haphazard appearance of "types" in the sheet. Sometimes the first group of moulds (made direct from the single-subject die) is termed the "master-group"; and sometimes that same term is applied to the small plate that forms the multiple-subject die. Compare "Master-Plate"; see "Primary Flaw," "Secondary Flaw."

Mounting. The process of fastening a printing plate or subject to a wooden or metal support, usually for the purpose of bringing the plate or subject up to type height, 0.918 inch. See "Anchor," "Block." Sometimes mounting is effected by the use of adhesives or molten metal.

Mounting Mark — see "Anchor Mark."

Nail Mark — see "Anchor Mark."

Nick. A notch on one side of the body of a piece of type, placed there as an aid to compositors.

Overlay. That part of make-ready positioned between the platen or impression cylinder and the back of the paper to be printed, comprising a method of increasing pressure on solids and darker tones of the printing plate, and decreasing pressure on lighter tones or "highlights" during actual printing. See "Make-Ready." The term "mechanical overlay" is applied to a method of obtaining *découpage* by printing on to specially treated paper in special ink and then etching away the non-printed areas of the paper — see "*Découpage.*"

Overlay Varieties. This term is used, philatelically, in reference to variations in appearance of stamps printed from the same printing base but with different overlays or because an overlay has shifted. Different overlays can profoundly affect the appearance of the resultant stamps, a soft-paper overlay producing a seemingly overinked and coarse impression, and a hard-paper overlay producing a seemingly underinked and fine impression. Classic instances of such overlay varieties are provided by, for example, Greece 1861 (November) – 1862 First Athens Print 5 1. and 1870 Special Print 5 1. See also "Anchor Mark," "Compartment Lines," "*Découpage* Shift."

Overprint Plate — see "Duty Plate."

Ozokerite — see "Wax Mould."

Papier Maché — see "Flong."

Partial Strike. Colored flaw. In reference to stamps relief-printed from printing bases resulting from the use of moulds struck from a die without the use of a collar — see "Collar" — the term "partial strike" is used to designate a variety exhibiting lack of uncolored portions in part of the design caused by the die entering the mould to an uneven depth because it was struck at an angle. The immediate result of such uneven striking is that, on the electro or stereo made from that mould, some "ups" are lower than others, and within the area of the low "ups" there is marked lack of difference in height between the "ups" and the "downs." A print from the subject at that stage would produce an only partly colored design and provide a variety exhibiting an uncolored flaw. See "Down,"

"Up." The reversal of this effect is caused by slabbing, and the lack of difference in height between "ups" and "downs" accounts for the absence of uncolored portions, the "downs" or some of them being inked and printing. See "Slabbing." Compare "Deep Edge."

Photoengraving — see "Photomechanical Etching."

Photomechanical Etching — see "Halftone Block," "Line Block."

Photo-Process Engraving — see "Photomechanical Etching."

Plate-Printed. The result of printing from subjects forming part of, or mounted on, a continuous surface prepared for use on more than one occasion. Contrasted with "Letterpress-Printed."

Plug. In reference to stamps relief-printed from plates or cylinders resulting from the use of moulds that are counterparts of a composite die, the term "plug" is used to designate a piece of metal, bearing a subsidiary feature of the design, that fits into a specially provided and specially shaped recess made in that portion of the die bearing the main features of the design. See "Composite Die"; distinguish "Plug Retouch."

Plugged Die — see "Composite Die."

Plug Retouch. This term is used as designating the result of piercing a die or printing surface at a faulty area, inserting a flush-surfaced piece of metal in the hole so made and, on the flush surface, re-engraving the missing portion of the design. Distinguish "Plug," "Plugged Die."

Primary Flaw. Colored or uncolored flaw. In reference to relief-printed stamps, and when appropriate (which is rarely), the term "primary flaw" is used to designate a flaw arising during the making of a mould group — see "Mould Group." Primary flaws characterize each subject of the mould group, and repeat at every subsequent multiplication from it. Primary flaws identify the "types." Compare "Primary Flaws" in the alphabetical list to the chapter entitled "Planographic Printing."

Process Engraving. An abbreviation of the term "photo-process engraving." See "Photomechanical Etching."

Punch. A tool employed for applying, by direct pressure as distinct from rocking, part of a design to a piece of metal prepared to receive it. For relief printing, mainly two types of punch have been used: (1) for use as a step in producing two or more dies, the punch being a counterpart of that part of the design common to both dies — a "die matrix" specially made for use during die manufacture and coming into existence before any die is completed. For example, for India 1856-64 ½a., 1a., 2a., 4a. and 8a., five blank duty dies were produced with the aid of a punch, these dies being denominated later; (2) for use as a step in multiplying the design after the die has been completed, the punch being a counterpart of the die — a "subject matrix." For example, for Greece 1861 (Oct. 1) 1 l., 2 l., 5 l., 10 l., 20 l., 40 l. and 80 l., each plate contained 150 subjects, and the 150 subjects were all produced with the aid of a single undenominated punch. They were denominated later by means of another type of punch, a "number punch" or "letter punch," such as was used also, for example, for Great Britain 1867-73 1s., plates 4 to 7, for punching the uncolored corner letters and plate numbers. See also "Punch" in the alphabetical list to the chapter entitled "Printing Problems and Varieties."

Punch-Struck. This term, used in reference to relief-printing plates, signifies that the subjects were produced by means of a subject punch — see "Punch (2)." Sometimes the term "die-struck" is used in this connection, but such employment is confusing.

Quad. An abbreviation of "quadrat," the printers' term for the larger spaces, comprising a small block of metal, less than type height. See "Space."

Quoin — see "Chase."

Reglet. A printers' term for a strip of wooden or metal furniture used for spacing. "Reglet" is used synonymously with one of the senses of "lead." See "Lead (1) (b)"; compare "Rule."

Reglet Flaw. Colored flaw. In reference to stamps printed from a form comprising separate subjects spaced apart by reglets or spacers, the term "reglet flaw" is used to designate a line appearing in color in the margin of the stamp and caused by the reglet working up to printing height, being inked, and depositing ink on the paper. Reglets are not usually intended to print, being below type height; consequently, when a reglet flaw occurs, it does so after the form has been at press for some time. As a result, identically positioned stamps from the same printing may be found without and with a reglet flaw, and sometimes with a flaw that progressively increases in length — for instance, Victoria 1863-67 Laureated 4d. (Type B.7) can be found in various states from entire absence of reglet flaw to a complete reglet flaw throughout the left margin. See "Distortion Varieties." Reglet flaws must, of course, be distinguished from "Jubilee Lines," which are intended to print — see "Jubilee Line" in the alphabetical list to the chapter entitled "From Design to Printed Sheets." Sometimes the term "reglet flaw" is used to designate a dropped lead in cases of typeset designs where a space between individual pieces of type has worked up type-high and printed. See "Space."

Relief. In reference to relief-printing bases, the term "relief" is sometimes used as a synonym for "subject," and often as a synonym for "up." See "Up"; see also "Subject" in the alphabetical list to the chapter entitled "Printing Problems and Varieties."

Répoussage. A method of remedying a plate defect comprising an absence of relief, whereby the surface of the plate is, at the relevant position, raised as a mass to printing height, and the non-printing areas are then cut away by hand. *Répoussage* is a development of slabbing — see "Slabbing" — and is the equivalent in relief printing from electrotypes and stereotypes of the method sometimes adopted in recess printing of making flush the surface of the plate for the purpose of fresh entry — see "Fresh Entry" in the alphabetical list to the chapter entitled "Intaglio Printing — I: Line Engraving." That is, sometimes the back of the plate is drilled to a certain depth and a punch inserted and hammered, the drilling removing some of the metal, thus making it easier to make the surface of the plate flush.

Resetting. See "Setting" in the alphabetical list to the chapter entitled "Printing Problems and Varieties." (1) In reference to any typeset design, the term "resetting" is used to denote that the individual pieces of the design have been taken apart and put together again differently. In this sense, "reset" or "resetting" is used in the same sense as "Recut," "Redrawn," "Re-Engraved" and "Retouched" in connection with an engraved die or its equivalent, and has reference to the design of the stamps — see "Recut" etc. in the alphabetical list to the chapter entitled "Printing Problems and Varieties." (2) In reference to stamps relief-printed from forms comprising separate subjects or an aggregation of small groups of subjects, the term "resetting" is used to denote that the form was taken apart and reassembled differently. See "Form." In this sense of the term "reset" or "resetting," there is no implication that the designs of stamps printed subsequent to resetting differ from those printed before resetting. Resetting of this nature may take place for a variety of reasons — for example, that the form requires cleaning because of crusts (see "Crust Flaw"), or that differently shaped paper or a different press is to be used.

Retouch. In the case of relief-printed stamps, retouching in the sense of repair or improvement to a subject on the printing base is a comparatively rare occurrence, and is encountered far less frequently than, for instance, such repairs to intaglio printing bases. Although mainly encountered on stamps printed from electrotypes in the days when the growing of a shell occupied many hours, retouching can be observed in some modern issues. The result of retouching is, usually, to provide a slight excess of color, as in the case of Ireland 1929 Catholic Emancipation Centenary 2d., pane 2, stamp No. 180, where the remedying of damage has caused thickened lines to appear in the design above the southeast corner square. An example of retouching that has resulted in the absence of part of the design is to be found, for instance, in Great Britain 1902-10 and 1911-12 2d., the so-called distorted value tablet; and an instance of a retouch resulting in the absence of color previously accidentally present is provided by Great Britain 1912-22 1½d., plate 12, stamp No. 180, with the variety corrected "E" with long foot, the originally missing foot to the last letter of "THREE HALFPENCE" being provided by manually cutting away on the plate the excessive relief. See also "Added Metal," "*Répoussage.*" In reference to photo-process engraving, the term "retouching" is used to designate corrective treatment of original, or photographic positive or negative, by means of brush, pencil, pen or other implement. Compare "Retouch" in the alphabetical list to the chapter entitled "Intaglio Printing — II: Gravure."

Rising Space — see "Space."

Rivet Mark — see "Anchor Mark."

Rule. A printer's term for a thin strip of metal, usually brass, used for printing lines. The distinction between rules and leads, reglets or spaces is that rules are intended to print, being of type height, while the others are not. Rules of different kinds have been used in many typeset stamps, overprints and surcharges, including, as examples, Fiji 1871 Times Express 1d. for the frame, and Seychelles 1957 5c. on 45c. for the bars cancelling the figures and words of value on the basic stamp.

Secondary Flaw. Colored or uncolored flaw. In reference to relief-printed stamps, and when appropriate (which is rarely), the term "secondary flaw" is used to designate a flaw first arising when a mould group is copied — see "Mould Group." Different secondary flaws characterize every copy made from the mould group, and aggregate with the primary flaws characterizing each subject of the mould group itself — see "Primary Flaw." Secondary flaws characterize the "sub-types" — see "Sub-Type."

Setting. This term designates a particular arrangement, and is used in two senses: (1) in reference to the arrangement of the separate pieces of type or other components of a subject; (2) in reference to the arrangement of separate subjects in a chase or on a plate or cylinder. See "Setting" in the alphabetical list to the chapter entitled "Printing Problems and Varieties."

Shell. The shaped metallic result of electrodeposition in a mould. Sometimes two different metals are electrodeposited in the same mould, one behind the other, the first metal deposited having better wearing properties but being, usually, a much thinner deposit than the second. In such cases, the first deposit is referred to as the "facing," and the second deposit is called the "principal shell." See "Facing."

Shifted Overlay — see "*Découpage* Shift."

Slabbing. The operation of leveling the printing face of an electrotype or stereotype plate to ensure that all reliefs are at the same height. Slabbing is effected by placing the plate face-downward on a level surface (termed the "slab") and striking the back of the plate with a hammer and special punches shaped to bring only the required "up" or "ups" into contact with the slab. As a preliminary to hammering, the slab-hand applies a straightedge to the face of the plate, and where any depression shows, he marks the back, locating the position by means of long-armed calipers. Slabbing can give rise to varieties exhibiting excessive color, if hammering is carried out too forcefully. See also "Partial Strike." Compare "*Répoussage*."

Slug. A printer's term designating, according to context: (a) a type-high bar produced by a linotype or other casting machine, and bearing on its face characters or symbols ready for use in printing; or (2) a specially cast bar, below type height, for use as a reglet or spacer.

Sort. A printer's term designating a piece of metal comprising one or other of the letters or characters in a particular font of type. Usually the plural, "sorts," is used — as in the sense of "all the sorts of the letter 'e' in the lower case of the font."

Space. A printer's term for a piece of type metal that causes an (unprinted) interval to appear between printed words, letters or other characters. A space is, usually, below type height, but sometimes works up during printing and makes a mark on the paper. This fault is termed, by printers, "rising spaces." Sometimes the mark is referred to as "dropped lead," and sometimes, philatelically, the term "reglet flaw" is used. See "Reglet Flaw." See also "Quad."

Spacer. An uneasy synonym for lead, reglet or space. See "Lead," "Reglet" and "Space."

Squash, Squeeze — see "Ink Squash."

Steel Facing — see "*Aciérage*."

Stick — see "Composing Stick."

Striking. The process of forcing the die into contact with plastic material to form a mould.

Striking Varieties. This term is used generically to denote variations from the intended norm occurring on the resultant stamps consequent upon some abnormality arising during the process of forcing the die into contact with the plastic material forming the mould. See "Double Strike," "Impacted Metal Flaw," "Internal Distortion Variety," "Mould Flaw," "Partial Strike," "Sub-Type."

Substituted *Cliché*. In reference to relief-printed stamps, the term substituted *cliché* is widely used, often generically, to designate the effect of removing from a printing base a damaged or otherwise unsatisfactory subject and replacing it by an unobjectionable subject. In cases of separate subjects, removal and replacement involve merely loosening and resecuring the chase; in cases of solid plates, excision and affixing in place by use of molten metal are involved, as also sometimes are stripping and re-facing. Philatelic deduction of such substitution will depend upon the presence or absence, in the substituted subject, of flaws previously absent or present, respectively, in the subjects of the form or plate — that is to say, a hitherto unaccounted-for subject has appeared in the sheet, or a subject hitherto identifiable by constant flaws has disappeared from the sheet. In a solid plate, substitution is usually characterized by uneven alignment.

Sub-Type. In reference to relief-printed stamps, the term "sub-type" has been used in two different senses: (1) to designate a stamp exhibiting secondary flaws in addition to primary flaws — see "Primary Flaw," "Secondary Flaw"; (2) to designate what are, in fact, different but similar varieties of several moulds, being the equivalent of the colored roller flaw encountered in intaglio printing — see "Roller Flaw" in the alphabetical list to the chapter entitled "Intaglio Printing — I: Line-Engraving." See "Flaw," "Impacted Metal Flaw."

Tertiary Flaw. Colored or uncolored flaw. In reference to relief-printed stamps, and when appropriate (which is very rarely), the term "tertiary flaw" is used to designate a flaw first arising when a copy is made of a collection of subjects comprising repetitions of a mould group — see "Mould Group." The tertiary flaws serve to distinguish each subject on the continuous surface that is the copy from the corresponding subject that appears in the collection of subjects. The tertiary flaws aggregate with the primary flaws and secondary flaws — see "Primary Flaw," "Secondary Flaw." Tertiary flaws characterize the "sub-sub-types." An instance of relief-printed stamps bearing tertiary flaws is provided by Prince Edward Island 1872 (Jan. 1) 1c., the left half of the sheet of 100 subjects being five copies of a mould group of ten, and the right half of the sheet being a continuous-surface copy of the left half.

Tympan. An appliance in a printing press comprising a (double) frame positioned between the platen or impression cylinder and the back of the paper to be printed, and covered with parchment or satin, enclosing or bearing the *découpage* and packing sheets — see "Make-Ready."

Type. In reference to letterpress printing, "type" means the aggregate of individual letters, numbers and other symbols that comprise all fonts. Generally speaking, types are distinguished by the breadth, character, form, size, style and apparent weight of the letters and symbols. Different type founders give different names to apparently similar types, and the same names to apparently dissimilar types. The size of type — the vertical thickness of the body — is designated by a "points" system, there being seventy-two points to one inch. For letterpress printing, sizes are graduated by points up to twelve point, and those above eighteen point are multiples of six point. See also "Type" in the alphabetical list to the chapter entitled "Stamp Design." These senses of the term "type" must, of course, be clearly distinguished from its other philatelic meanings — see "Type" in the alphabetical list to the chapter entitled "Printing Problems and Varieties," and in the alphabetical list to the chapter entitled "Planographic Printing." In this last sense, "types" occur in relief printing when mould groups are used — see "Mould Group," "Primary Flaw."

Underlay — see "Make-Ready."

Up. A convenient term signifying a printing area of a relief-printing plate, and thus any printing area of any subject. Compare "Down." A synonym for a "relief."

Upper Case. In reference to each individual letter of the alphabet, the term "upper case" indicates that the letter is a capital letter; and the term signifies that the sort comprising that letter is to be found in the upper of the two cases from which type is set by hand — see "Case," "Lower Case," "Sort." Although typesetting has long been effected mechanically and hand-work is limited to operating a keyboard resembling that of a typewriter, the term "upper case" has remained in use to designate capital letters.

Wax Mould. This term is used, strictly, to designate an electrotyping mould made of wax. At one time, beeswax was an important constituent of such moulds, but this has largely been superseded by patent compositions, among which Ozokerite provides an early example.

Woodblock — see "Woodblock" in the alphabetical list to the chapter entitled "Printing Characteristics."

Zinco. This term is used in three different senses: (1) as referring, generically, to "line" or "halftone" photomechanically etched zinc as opposed to copper — see "Halftone Block," "Line Block"; (2) as referring to the hand-engraved plate of zinc bearing a design many times stamp size, used for the model in a pantograph; (3) as an abbreviation for "zincography" — that is, printing from zinc plates.

The German firm of Gebrüder Senf, publishers of the *Illustriertes Brief-marken Journal* and the *Senf Katalog*, produced this card to show how the printing method used affects the appearance of an 1845 New York Post Office design inscribed "SPECIMEN," printed by lithography (*Steindruck*), copper-plate printing (*Kupferdruck*), and letterpress print-ing (*Buchdruck*). (The inscriptions in small letters beneath those key words are confusing and best ignored.) Of course, the characteristic print-ing differences, appreciable on examination of the card itself, are large-ly lost in reproduction.

13. Inks and Color

PHILATELICALLY CONSIDERED, inks are of importance from two entirely different aspects.

First the subject of printing inks is philatelically important because they are the means whereby the printer visibly records the work that has been put into the production of the stamp design; as such, the inks enable the philatelist to classify the stamps by reference to color standards and variations from them.[1]

Second, the subject of printing inks is philatelically important because some printing inks and some constituents of them react when treated with substances such as water or benzine — substances that the philatelist commonly uses in the separation of stamps from adherent paper and in the perception of watermarks.

From the point of view of the issuing authority, too, the subject of printing inks is of importance from two aspects, similar to but approached differently from those of the philatelist. First, the various colors of inks enable one denomination to be distinguished from another, even though one stamp design varies only slightly from another. Second, because some printing inks and constituents react when treated with certain substances, this property is employed deliberately as a safeguard against the cleaning and re-use of a canceled stamp and the consequent loss to the revenue.

Both of these aspects have always been considered important, but, from time to time and in different countries, greater emphasis has been laid on the importance of one rather than the other of them. More recently, stamp-issuing authorities have brought other considerations to bear upon what is, virtually, the subject of printing inks, and have demanded that they be capable of activating machines that automatically face, sort and, perhaps, cancel the mail. They are referred to later in this chapter under the heading "Graphite and Phosphor."

---

[1]One may disregard, for the purpose of the generality of this statement, the fact that, in the production of a few issues, no printing ink at all has been used — issues such as Natal 1857-58 1d. to 1s. (embossed on plain, colored paper); Fujeira 1969 President Eisenhower Memorial Issue Airmail 5r. (embossed on gold leaf bonded to paper; not listed in Scott, but mentioned in Stanley Gibbons Part 19, Fujeira "Appendix"); Mafeking (Cape of Good Hope) 1900 1d. and 3d. (ferroprussiate photographic prints); Chile 1919 Semi-Official Air 5p. Figueroa (silver-nitrate photographic print); and others, including, for example, Uganda 1895 Cowries 5(c) to 60(c) (typewritten).

From the point of view of the printer, the essential qualities of printing inks used for stamp production are that they should not damage the printing base, should be suitable for the paper, should be fast to light and heat and should be consistent in color.

Reduced to simple terms, the problem of the printer is to determine what method should be adopted to transfer to appropriate places on the paper sufficient portions of a heap or pile of a dry substance that is color. This problem is solved usually by grinding the color finely, and suspending or dissolving it in a suitable liquid; the colored liquid is then appropriately spread on the previously prepared printing base and transferred to the paper by pressure. Exceptions to this solution to the problem exist in two fields, foil blocking and thermography, which are discussed later in this chapter under those headings.

Pigment and Medium

Printing ink comprises, therefore, two main constituents: the "pigment" — that is, a dry substance that is the coloring matter; and the "medium," "varnish" or "vehicle" — that is, the liquid that holds the coloring matter. Each different printing method has a differently constructed printing base, and the particular method adopted for making the color[2] liquid is determined by the chemistry and physics of the particular printing method to be used. Broadly speaking, so far as stamps are concerned, the composition of printing ink falls into one of two classes. For intaglio printing line engraving, lithography, offset lithography and relief printing, the pigment is used with a medium comprising, essentially, linseed oil more or less thickened by heat. For rotary photogravure printing, the pigment is used with a medium that is, for dark shades, a solution of asphaltum, and, for lighter inks, pale resins in a volatile solvent such as xylol. But in some photogravure inks, the medium used is water.

However, although, generally speaking, the pigments may be used with any method of printing, the medium will vary with each different method. That is to say that, although, generally speaking, printing inks are stiff and heat is used to make them more easily worked on the printing bases, they are given different characteristics to meet different requirements. For example, an ink used for lithography must be greasy and must not dissolve or disperse in water, otherwise a satisfactory result could not be obtained because of the damping rollers.[3] On the other hand, an ink used for cameo stamping must resist any tendency to splatter when it is subjected to the impact at the moment of impression;[4] and an ink used for rotary photogravure printing

---

[2] It is interesting to note that, among printers, "color" has long been synonymous with "ink." This appears clearly from the answer of Henry Hensman, engineer to the Bank of England, when he gave evidence on April 27, 1852: "*Mr. C. Lewis . . . 1905.* Is there any ink in it? — Yes, colour is used; the technical name among printers is colour, not ink. . . ." *Report from the Select Committee on Postage Label Stamps* (1852), Page 183.

[3] See "Printing from Lithographic Printing Bases" in the chapter entitled "Planographic Printing."

[4] See "Cameo Stamping for Sheets" in the chapter entitled "Embossing."

must be highly fluid to enable it to fill the minute cells and to be wiped by the doctor blade from the non-printing surface of the rapidly revolving cylinder.[5]

Other constituents of printing inks include compounds that accelerate or delay drying and that provide a gloss or matte appearance to the print. Inks dry by filtration into the paper and evaporation of the solvent, by gelation, or by oxidation of the exposed surface, which forms a hard skin.

Passing reference has already been made to the grinding of pigments so that to them may be added the liquid that enables the printer to spread them as required upon the printing base. From the point of view of the printer, it is important that all pigments used for inks be soft; otherwise, however finely they are divided, they will abrade and ultimately spoil the surface of the printing base. No purpose would be served here in examining minutely the physics of dividing the pigment into sufficiently small particles to serve the particular purpose required.

However, one aspect of pigment division gives rise to a particular and striking — but philatelically unimportant — variety, and merits a little consideration.

Pigments are divided into minute particles, but, when they are to be used for intaglio printing line engraving, there is a limit of smallness that should not be exceeded. This limit is the size of the grain of the non-printing areas of the plate or cylinder. If the pigment is divided too finely, particles of it lodge in the grain of the highly polished plate or cylinder, and are not wiped off when the non-printing areas are wiped clear of ink and polished.[6] The consequence is that these minute particles are subsequently deposited on the paper in what should be uncolored areas of the design and in the gutters, giving rise to the variety "pseudo-colored paper."[7] Such a variety is more likely to occur when a plate or cylinder is first put to press than when it has been in use previously for any length of time.

The philatelist is interested only to a very limited extent in the highly involved chemistry of inkmaking and the problems encountered by ink manufacturers. He is concerned, almost exclusively, with the result and the naturally visible variations from a standard in color, and almost never seeks to discover the cause of those variations. Only when, as occasionally happens, some circumstance gives rise to a startling result does the philatelist seem to appreciate that there is more to ink than the color that meets the eye — a circumstance such as when the examination of some stamps by ultraviolet rays, perhaps because of suspected added margins, reveals a striking golden or flame-colored glow of fluorescence to the observer; or when the placing of a stamp in carbon tetrachloride, perhaps to discharge some grease, results in the removal from the fluid of a stamp of a completely different color.

---

[5]See "Printing from Gravure Printing Bases" in the chapter entitled "Intaglio Printing — II: Gravure."

[6]See "Printing from Flat Plates" in the chapter entitled "Intaglio Printing — I: Line Engraving."

[7]See "Pseudo-Colored Paper" in the alphabetical list to the chapter entitled "Paper."

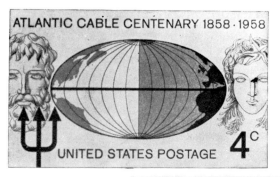

Water-soluble. U.S. 1958 Atlantic Cable Centenary 4c. and 1954-60 Regular 4c. (Lincoln). Two U.S. stamps that are affected by immersion in water because the ink has a water-soluble constituent. Prolonged soaking of the Lincoln stamp causes the color to permeate the paper and show through clearly on the back; on inspection under ultraviolet rays, a mint stamp appears dull, but a stamp that has been subjected to soaking fluoresces brilliantly. Such stamps, used, should be floated free from adherent paper.

It would, therefore, be out of place here to deal in any great detail with the chemical composition of printing inks generally used for stamps. However, it will be useful to devote some space to a brief consideration of certain phenomena.

Phenomena

Many inks used by stamp printers in the earlier days included Flake White as a constituent. Owing to a chemical reaction between the lead in this constituent and certain pigments, notably blue, green, red and yellow, sulfuretting occurred when the stamps were, over the years, exposed to the atmosphere. As a consequence, a stamp that once was a pleasing shade of, say, blue (as in Great Britain 1841 2d.), or green (as in New South Wales 1856 3d.), or red (as in Great Britain 1858-64 1d.), became a dirty, indeterminate color, predominantly black. Fortunately, no irreparable harm is caused by such sulfuretting (sometimes mistermed ''oxidation''), and the ink may be restored to its original color by treatment with peroxide of hydrogen and water — by soaking or, if original gum has to be preserved, by painting the face of the stamp alternately with peroxide and water.

580

Not only the atmosphere but also sea water results in some stamps losing their colors in this way, and early philatelic confusion was caused in Europe when some issues of Victoria and New Zealand arrived, the 1d. a dirty black, the 2d. a very dark blue and the 1s. nearly black — instead of, respectively, vermilion, blue and green — as a result of their sea water bath following upon the wreck of the *Colombo*.[8] Even before this occurrence, it was widely known among collectors that certain chemicals could effect a color change in stamps — and, indeed, gave rise to the term "chemical" as designating a fraudulently made color changeling.

Benzine or petroleum will sometimes affect some inks by dissolving part of one or more of the constituents. Often such treatment will visibly affect the stamp to a large extent by suffusing the paper with color that has run; but sometimes the visual change is slight, and it is only when the stamp is examined by ultraviolet rays that a dramatic effect is observed. The stamp that has been immersed in benzine or petroleum fluoresces brightly, while an untreated example of the same stamp does not fluoresce to anything like the same extent. It is important to bear this fact in mind, because some philatelists have wrongly accepted as axiomatic that marked difference in fluorescence inevitably points to the use of inks of different compositions, and, therefore, is incontrovertible evidence of a new or different printing.

Carbon tetrachloride[9] is sometimes used as an alternative to benzine or petroleum for watermark detection, or to remove a grease spot from a stamp, because of the property this chemical has of leaving the gum undisturbed. However, carbon tetrachloride can affect certain inks. It is well-known, for instance, that if Germany 1928-32 50p. brown is soaked in this chemical, an olive-green stamp will emerge. By no means is this the only stamp or this the only color that is affected.

Perhaps the collector feels the greatest sense of frustration in the realization that not even plain water can be used on every stamp without possibly deleterious consequence to the printing ink. Fortunately, only a small minority of printing inks used for stamps are water soluble or contain water-soluble constituents, but they have been used for different printing processes. To such inks especially the appellation "fugitive" has been applied. For example, the relief-printed issues of Germany 1922 (April) Munich Industrial Fair 1¼m. to 20m. are highly susceptible to water, and the colors will run upon the application of very little moisture; also, Great Britain 1900 ½d. blue-green when soaked in water may emerge from the bath as bright blue.[10] Further, certain photogravure issues, such as Netherlands Indies 1933-40 1c. to 5g.,

---

[8] This occurrence led to the coining of the now rarely encountered philatelic term "Colombo" as designating a fortuitous or fraudulent color changeling.

[9] The fumes of carbon tetrachloride may seriously affect health. See the discussion, "The Detection of Watermarks," in the chapter entitled "Watermarks."

[10] The technical explanation for this is provided in *The De La Rue History of British and Foreign Postage Stamps, 1855 to 1901* by John Easton (1958), Page 155: "The . . . colour . . . is composed of a mixture of Prussian Blue and yellow pigment consisting of impure Chromate of Zinc. The yellow colouring matter is of such a nature as to be in part fairly soluble in cold, and more freely in warm, water."

being printed in ink of which the medium was water, will lose their designs if water is applied to them.

Not even intaglio printing line engraving is entirely free from the threat of water as a solvent for some constituents. For example, the appearance of Ethiopia 1947 (Apr. 18) National Postal Service Jubilee 70c. will suffer if water is allowed to come into contact with the ink; and with U.S. 1954-60 Regular 4c. Lincoln and 1958 Atlantic Cable Centenary 4c., soaking in water will cause the color to run and the stamps to fluoresce brightly under ultraviolet rays. The instances referred to are chosen as representative only and, of course, do not pretend to be anything more than random examples of stamps printed in inks that are wholly or partly soluble in water.

In some cases, not only is the ink liable to be affected by water, but also some of the color may rub off against dry surfaces — such as the back of an opposite album page. This is especially so in the case of aniline inks. All of the aniline inks, or, rather, dyes stem from a discovery in 1856 by Dr. William Perkin. Then a chemistry student, Perkin, during his Easter holidays, was attempting unsuccessfully to synthesize quinine. Instead, he discovered that mauve could be made from aniline, a coal-tar derivative that, when pure, is colorless.[11] The brilliant colors, particularly in the red color range, that resulted from this and subsequent discoveries have been used in inks for some stamps, and these often are characterized by the color suffusing the stamp paper and showing through to the back. When such stamps are inspected by ultraviolet rays, the inks fluoresce a brilliant golden color.

The water solubility of these ingredients was, in general, not desired by the issuing authority, because of the liability of the stamp color to be affected when the stamp was moistened for the purpose of affixing it to a letter or other document. However, the fact that the authorities did require inks to be fugitive in reagents that could clean off postal and pen cancellations led, especially, to De La Rue & Company in Great Britain placing greater emphasis upon the desirability of stamps being printed in that firm's "doubly fugitive inks." There can be no doubt that this sustained pressure led, ultimately, to the issue of what has been described as "the most commonplace series of postage stamps that had yet been seen in stamps produced in the British Empire"[12] — that is, Great Britain 1883 (Aug. 1)–1884 (Apr. 1) ½d. to 1s. — an issue that may be regarded as the awful result of the apotheosis of the doubly fugitive ink cult.

Other water-sensitive colors are to be found, for example, in Jammu (India) 1867-77 and Poonch (India) 1876-88, all of which were printed or hand-stamped in water colors.

The fastness of stamp printing inks to light is only relative. The bleaching qualities of strong sunlight are well-known, as is the fact that prolonged exposure to bright natural light will, in time, adversely affect even the best papers and inks. Some stamp colors are especially susceptible to alteration

---

[11]The mauvine that he made was the first synthetic dyestuff, and later was used for coloring Great Britain 1881 1d.

[12]*The De La Rue History of British and Foreign Postage Stamps, 1855 to 1901* by John Easton (1958), Page 120.

by light. Broadly speaking, they are the mauve-violet group, of which Nova Scotia 1851 1s. cold violet (dull violet) is, perhaps, the most liable to damage by this means.

Further, not all colors are stable in heat; for example, if some gravure stamps, such as, say, Great Britain 1934-36, are subjected to prolonged heat, they will vary considerably in color. For instance, if Great Britain 1934-36 2½d. ultramarine is so treated, it may take on a greenish tinge approaching Prussian blue.

Foil Blocking

No pigment as such is used in foil blocking, which has been applied to parts of stamps in comparatively recent years — for example, Great Britain 1966 (Oct. 14) 900th Anniversary of the Battle of Hastings, 6d. and 1s.3d., in which the Queen's head was "gold" blocked; Great Britain 1966 (Dec. 1) Christmas 3d. and 1s.6d., in which the head was not only "gold" blocked but embossed; and Gambia 1966 (Jun. 24) 150th Anniversary of the Founding of Bathurst 1d. to 1s.6d., in which the central shield was "silver" blocked. No actual gold or silver was used for those issues, the foil ribbon of 50-gauge Melinex S polyester film being coated with layers of colored lacquer, aluminum deposited under vacuum, and adhesive.

In such cases, the "gold" or "silver" is transferred from the foil ribbon by pressure and heat applied electrically to the embossing brass, in precisely the same way as gold or silver lettering is applied to book covers by machine. Polyester film, the only material that can be used for the process, withstands high temperature and pressure without curling or tearing, and is unaffected by moisture and gases. The machine used by Harrison & Sons Ltd. was a Heidelberg blocking press that, instead of having lettering for the impression, had repetitions of the Queen's head or the shield, and these were transferred to each sheet, the sheets being fed to the press from batches of some 3,000.

Special precautions were taken to ensure that the foil of the heads and shields adhered to the stamp paper.

Foil blocking. Great Britain 1966 (Dec. 1) Christmas 3d. with the Queen's head "gold"-blocked from foil ribbon by use of heat and pressure and embossed.

The pressure involved in the process can be clearly appreciated by turning the stamp over; the outline of the head or shield can be clearly seen standing proud from the back, toward the viewer, presenting in classic form the characteristic of relief printing (see "Relief Printing" in the chapter entitled "Printing Characteristics").

Foil blocking must, of course, be distinguished from printing with metallic inks containing gold or silver or metals giving that appearance, illustrated, by way of random examples, so far as chromolithography is concerned, by Peru 1951 (December) Air San Marcos University Foundation 5s., and, so far as photogravure is concerned, by Spain 1962 (Mar. 24) Stamp Day and Zarbaran Commemoration 25c. to 10p.

Thermography

Thermography, from the Greek *thermos* "hot," and *graphein* "to write," falls for consideration under "Inks and Color" rather than any other branch of stamp production because thermography is not a process of printing, but a technique that is used in combination with printing for the purpose of obtaining a pattern in relief. As the derivation of the name of the technique suggests, the effect is obtained by heat. Indeed, thermography has sometimes been referred to as "heat raising" or, derisively in earlier days, as "fried printing."

By the technique of thermography, the subjects are printed by the conventional methods of planographic printing, relief printing or gravure, then a fine dust or resinous powder, or "compound," is applied to the wet ink by machine. Finally, heat is applied to the printed and dusted paper for the purpose of fusing the compound with the ink and raising those parts of the subjects to which the compound has adhered. The technique is recorded as having been used as long ago as 1903 in New England, and has been increasingly widely used in the production of greeting cards, letter headings and other commercial subjects. Its first philatelic application was by Ajans Turk of Ankara, on Turkey 1966 (May 15) Osman Faience Art 60k.

Those stamps were printed by photolithography in blue, green, brown and red with fast-drying colors in the usual way. The designs then were completed by a black printing to which, while the ink was still wet, the fine resinous compound was machine-applied by dusting it over the face of the printed sheet. The surplus compound was removed by suction and vibration or flicking, leaving the compound adhering only to the black-printed portions of the design. The paper, on a conveyor belt, then was subjected to heat that raised the compound on those parts of the design to which the compound dust had adhered.

If the stamps are examined under an adequate degree of magnification, slight raggedness of the heat-raised portions of some edges may be seen, where the fused compound has flowed beyond the boundaries of the black-inked portions of the design. In these ragged edges, the heat-raised portions appear clear, however, indicating that the compound used was in the broad category termed "neutral," so as to provide glossy relief in the color of the original ink.

More recent examples of stamps with designs raised thermographically by "neutral" compound are to be found in New Caledonia and Dependencies 1985 (Feb. 17) Shells 55f. and 72f., where both the shells, printed in color, and the main inscriptions, printed in black, are shiny and raised.

The other broad category of thermographic compounds is termed "pigmented." These are usually metallic, silver, copper — or gold, such as was used for the arch over the head on Turkey 1966 (Sep. 6) 400th Anniversary of the Death of Sultan Suleiman, 130 k.

A variety of the neutral compound provides a non-glossy rise.

Occasionally small irrelevant spots or areas of raised color may be observed on the stamps, indicating that particles of the compound dust were not, as they should have been, removed from the sheet when subjected to suction and vibration or flicking. Technically this is termed "spotting," and if it occurs to any substantial extent, its cause is, often, faulty adjustment of the machine. Another visible effect is small burst bubbles; the cause, usually, is that the paper was too moist and caused vapor to escape from the paper during heating.

Thermography. New Caledonia and Dependencies 1985 (Feb. 27) Shells 72f. The shell design, photographed with a halftone screen, was printed in red, yellow, blue, and black; the inscriptions, unscreened, were printed in black — all by lithography. The neutral compound was dusted over the design and the inscriptions while the ink was still wet.

Thermography. Turkey 1966 (May 15) Osman Faience Art 60k. printed by photolithography in blue, green, brown, red and black, with a neutral thermographic compound applied to the black and raised by heat. All the black portions of the design appear to stand up from the paper.

Philatelically, the most remarkable characteristic enabling a thermographically produced stamp to be distinguished from a stamp or overprint printed, or part-printed, by intaglio printing line engraving (see "Intaglio Printing in the chapter entitled "Printing Characteristics") or die stamping (see "Die Stamping" in the chapter entitled "Embossing") is the fact that the back of the thermographic stamp is entirely flat in the portions of the design that are raised on the face. This occurs because there are, in the thermographic technique, no recesses in the design on the printing base, and consequently no forcing of the paper under pressure into such recesses as are present when stamps are printed by those other processes. However, if the thermographic stamps are produced from relief-printing bases, there may be present the characteristic impression and the proudness of the paper in the lines of the design when viewed from the back (see "Relief Printing" in the chapter entitled "Printing Characteristics").

Graphite and Phosphor

Brief reference has already been made to the comparatively recent requirements of some stamp-issuing authorities that certain inks be capable of activating machines that automatically face and, to some extent, sort the mail. Many experiments have been carried out in this connection, to enable automation to replace, to a greater or less degree, some operations considered to be humdrum and unrewarding from the point of view of the postal worker. As these experiments have had, and are increasingly having effects upon the postage stamps of the world in regard to the inks used in production, it is appropriate here to devote some slight consideration to them.

In England, the first philatelic effects of these experiments made their appearance on Nov. 19, 1957, when stamps were issued bearing a line or lines in black as an endorsement. This was the result of preliminary efforts to solve some of the problems of the sorting office. The postal authorities explained that mechanization would have to cover the main jobs in the sorting office — that is, *segregation* of packets from letters, and separate treatment of each; *separation* of "long" from "short" letters (envelopes, etc.) for more efficient handling; *facing* of all letters with the stamp in the same position so that cancellation might be effected by machine, and, at the same time, removing the "deferred rate letters"[13] from the "ordinary rate letters"[14] for separate treatment; and *sorting* of all items of mail into appropriate receptacles for onward transmission in bulk to the post town or forwarding center. The philatelic effects of mechanization are linked with the machines that face the letters and remove the deferred rate mail.

The letters are fed at random into the complex piece of engineering that is the facing machine,[15] where they pass between several devices termed

---

[13]That is, accounts, printed papers, etc.
[14]That is, normal private letters, etc.
[15]Called, in Great Britain, "ALF," for the initials of "automatic letter facing (machine)." In other countries, such machines are referred to, often, by local names, usually represented by a mnemonic of initials or combination of parts of words.

Graphite and phosphor lines. Left: Great Britain 1957 (Nov. 19) 2d. and 3d. (photographed from back) showing, respectively, one and two lines of graphite. Right: Great Britain 1959 (Nov. 18) 2d. and 2½d. (photographed under ultraviolet rays) exhibiting, on the 2d., one line at the left, and, on the 2½d., a line on both sides of fluorescence caused by the presence of phosphor lines. These lines were printed on the stamps so that they could activate an automatic letter facing machine that also separates deferred rate letters (2d.) from normal rate letters. Except under ultraviolet rays, these phosphor lines are almost invisible. Because of the conditions under which they were photographed, the stamps seem to be badly printed, with lighter bars at the sides.

"scanners" that search for the stamp. When it is found, the letter is diverted to a part of the machine that collects only those letters that face the same way — that is to say, the machine arranges the letters in separate piles according to the corner in which the stamp is found. The scanners do more than this: They remove the "deferred rate letters" from the "ordinary rate letters," that is, the second class from the first class. Also, a special channel is incorporated in the machine for picking out letters with no stamp at all. All letters are then passed through a stamp cancelling unit.

The method of operating the scanners has varied. The earliest experiments in Great Britain were based on color recognition using visible light, and left no philatelic souvenir. The next experiments, which led to a public trial of the machine, were based on high-voltage electrical discharges, and the letters signaled to the machine how they were prepaid and where the stamps were by means of electrical conductors incorporated in each stamp.

The electrical conductor comprised one or more vertical lines of graphite one-thirty-second-inch wide printed on the back of the stamp. On the 2d. stamps, used mainly for deferred rate mail, only one line was printed; on other values, two lines appeared, three quarters of an inch apart. This graphite was applied to the stamp paper before it was gummed and before the stamps were printed by a special photogravure printing machine adapted to take the special graphited ink that had been evolved as a result of considerable experiments. The ink comprised deflocculated Acheson's graphite[16] (of which the proprietary name, "Dag," comprises the initials and indicates the makers, Acheson Colloids Ltd.) suspended in fluid. At first the fluid used in ex-

---

[16]"Deflocculated" means "separated into very fine particles." When inks dry, the particles of pigment flocculate, or join together.

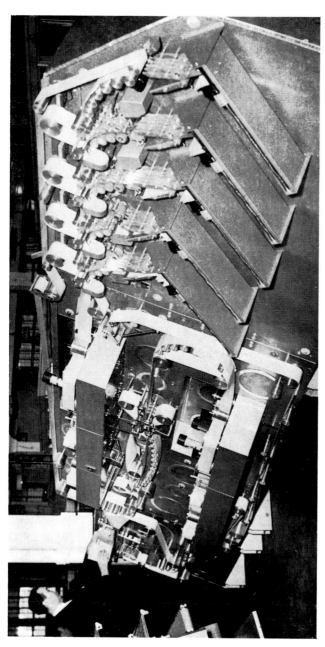

ALF. The automatic letter facing machine. This complex and ingenious machine receives letters and rearranges them in a stack with the stamps all facing the same way, and all in the same corner of the stack; makes a separate stack of deferred rate letters (and unstamped ones); and cancels the stamps.

The machine does its job by searching for the stamps on the letters as they pass through it at the rate of more than 300 each minute, rearranging the envelopes as necessary and stacking them in orderly piles. If no stamp is found in one corner of the envelope, the machine goes on searching until the stamp is located. A letter with a second-class stamp is automatically separated from the others and directed to a special pile. If there is no stamp, the letter is directed to another special pile.

The machine used to act (November 1957-November 1959) on high-voltage electric signals from graphite-lined stamps. Afterward it began to act on signals to a photoelectric cell from the fluorescence of phosphor-lined stamps.

Graphite Line Production

The printing unit, a specially adapted rotary photogravure machine, showing at upper left the graphite web of paper. In the foreground is the ink pump. The ink is a carrier fluid with "Dag" (deflocculated Acheson's graphite).

periments was naphtha — hence the term "Naphthadag." Although that term has been employed in connection with stamps bearing the graphite lines, in fact naphtha was not used as a carrier liquid for any of the issued stamps, other solvents having been substituted.

Later experiments reverted to the idea of light recognition, but, instead of visible light being used, phosphorescence by means of ultraviolet rays was employed. To cause the stamps to phosphoresce, they were provided with lines of phosphor printed by use of a colorless ink on a relief-printing machine after the stamps themselves were printed.

Rereeling the paper after the graphite lines have been printed. Drying is assisted by infrared rays. Afterward the paper is gummed.

Unlike the graphite lines, the phosphor lines appear as an overprint on the face of the stamp; they are, substantially, invisible except under certain conditions. If the stamps are held obliquely to normal light, the line or lines appear as a sheen on the paper. However, if the stamps are subjected to the "light" of ultraviolet rays of certain wavelengths, the lines fluoresce. The phosphor lines are much wider than the graphite lines were; only one line appears on the deferred or second-class value, and two lines on the other values.

In the automatic letter facing machine, the scanners are activated because the letters are subjected to ultraviolet rays that cause the stamps to luminesce while being exposed, and phosphoresce, or continue glowing, after exposure, thus enabling the letters to signal to the machine via a photoelectric cell how they are prepaid.[17] Different printing methods, relief printing and photogravure, have been used to apply phosphor lines in Great Britain.

Checking the electrical conductivity of the graphite lines with an Avometer. The graphite line had to be unbroken, otherwise it would not properly operate the automatic letter facing machine.

In North America, the first sale of phosphor-lined stamps, termed "luminescent"[18] or "tagged," was made in Winnipeg on Jan. 13, 1962, with Canada 1962-64 1c., 2c., 3c., and 5c. In the United States, the first experimental

[17]Although stamps have been issued bearing both graphite lines and phosphor lines, only the phosphor lines activate the automatic letter facing machine. The phosphor lines were added to stocks of graphite-lined stamps to avoid waste; when these stocks had been suitably overprinted, and graphite-line production ceased, only phosphor-lined stamps were used in the public trials — which, incidentally, were confined to the Southampton area. However, the production of normal stamps continued unchecked.

[18]"Luminescent" is an overall term meaning "glowing when excited by ultraviolet rays." It does not distinguish between materials that are "fluorescent" — that is, that glow only while being excited — and those that are phosphorescent — that is, that glow not only while being excited, but for a short time thereafter.

The printed and graphite-lined stamps (photographed from the back, with strong light shining through the paper) showing the relationship between the lines and the stamps.

"luminescent tagging," an overall coating of inorganic phosphors, occurred on stamps issued Aug. 1, 1963, at Dayton, Ohio, U.S. 1962-63 Air 8c.; on Nov. 2, 1963, at Washington, D.C., the 1963 Christmas 5c. and 1958-64 Regular 4c., similarly tagged, were put on sale. In Australia, tagged stamps with "helecon," a commercial name for a certain type of zinc sulfide, either incorporated in the printing ink or included in the surface coating of the paper, have been issued since 1963; the first such stamp to be issued there was Australia 1959-64 Regular 11d. Other countries, including West Germany [for example, 1962 (May 10) Second Millenary of Mainz 20p.] and Switzerland [for example, 1964 (Jun. 1) Pro Patria 5c. + 5c. to 30c. + 10c.] have made similar issues. The German tagged stamps, called "lumogen," are identifiable by a yellowish overprint to the paper. Swiss tagged stamps on granite paper are identifiable by violet fibers, clearly visible from the back of the stamp under magnification.

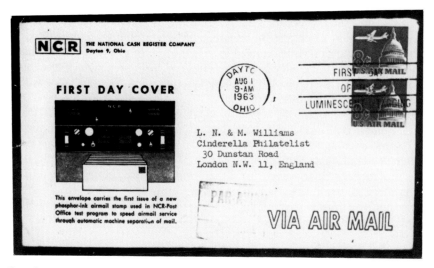

Luminescent tagging. U.S. 1962-63 Air 8c. tagged with an overall coating of inorganic phosphor. A cover sent on the first day of experimental use of tagged stamps in the United States, at Dayton, Ohio, on Aug. 1, 1963.

Tagged stamps that do not have phosphor lines, but that include the luminescing material in the printing ink or colorless on the paper without other characteristics, are difficult, if not impossible, to identify without the use of an ultraviolet ray lamp capable of emitting rays of the particular wavelengths necessary to activate the luminescing material used. The two main groups are 2,537 angstrom units, and 3,550 to 3,650 angstrom units, but variations occur in different countries.

Color Nomenclature

The references earlier in this chapter to color standards and variations from them should not be understood as implying the existence of any universally recognized philatelic standard of color nomenclature — for none exists, and in no other field is philately more inexact.

Color nomenclature, a difficult subject in any sphere, and a universal source of trouble wherever accuracy is important, is nowhere more confused than among collectors and students. The problem stems from many sources, and is complicated by the fact that color is a mixture of light of different wavelengths, and that few people, even with good color vision, are sufficiently trained to perceive, let alone name, more than a small proportion of the possible variations and blendings of color.

From time to time, various philatelic color charts and guides have been published; but none of them does more than merely indicate some of the colors that may have been used in stamp production. No such chart or guide is accepted universally as a standard. Inevitably, all of them suffer from the defect that they can be no more than a particular ink upon a particular paper — and, therefore, they can make no, or only inadequate, provision for the seeming variation that occurs when the same ink is printed on different paper. Further, there is, of course, no means of ensuring that the colors used on the charts have, in fact, been used in postage stamp printing. These charts are, however, useful in indicating the names that have been given to the colors that appear, and, therefore, in indicating to some extent the color range within which those color names occur.

Small purpose would be served in examining the problems of color and color nomenclature at length. It will be sufficient merely to indicate how color occurs, pausing long enough to state that color perception involves three interrelated but separate types of processes. The first is entirely physical, being the radiation of light waves from the source of the color; the second is physiological, being the reaction of the eye and other nerve centers to the light; and the third is psychological, being the mental interpretation within the brain of the physiological activity resulting from the radiation of the light waves.

It is elementary to state that "white" light comprises all colors, and that a "white" object reflects all the colors of "white" light and absorbs none, while a black object absorbs all the colors and reflects no color. An object that is neither black nor white absorbs some of the white light shining upon it and reflects the remainder, which comprises the color of the object.

But the exact processes by which the eye sees color are subject to debate. While it is known that some people are color blind to a greater or less extent, it is also, in fact, impossible to measure color vision by anything other than the very coarsest standards when set against the vast number of possible differences in color. It is, therefore, quite impossible to know whether any two people see color in exactly the same way. Furthermore there is ample room for disagreement about the name to be given to any particular combinations of the primary pigments — blue, yellow and red — and it would be quite impossible to describe accurately in words every one of the infinite permutations of colors, hues, shades and tints, even within so comparatively a circumscribed area as that of philately.

Moreover, under different lighting conditions, colors appear differently, as they do against different backgrounds. And if any person desires to attain reasonably consistent results in his or her own color evaluation, it is essential that he or she work in conditions that are standard — but not necessarily ideal. That is to say, variations caused by variations in lighting and background and, indeed, health, must, so far as possible, be eliminated.

Philatelically speaking, in the majority of cases, only the coarsest of distinctions by color names are possible or needed — and these distinctions usually give rise to a philatelic problem only when a stamp has been in issue for a considerable length of time, so that several or numerous separate printings have been made over the years. In such cases, it almost invariably happens that some printings were, or, perhaps, one printing was, smaller — much smaller — than the others, with the consequence that stamps from the smaller printings or printing are much rarer than those from the others.

Almost invariably, before the compounding and mixing of inks approached the almost exact science that it now is, a new printing involved a variation

Shade picture. This picture represents shades from white through the grays to black. Except in the black and white sections, optical illusion is at work. Only black ink upon white paper was used, but the eye mixes the black and white to produce all the gray gradations. This illustrates one of the difficulties in the way of precision in color nomenclature of stamps. Is the philatelist to name the color of the ink? If so, every part of the shade picture would be termed "black" (on white). Or is the philatelist to aim at recording what seems to appear? If so, the gradations of the shade picture would be termed "very dark gray," "dark gray," "gray," "pale gray," etc.

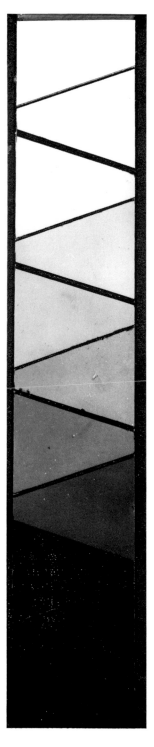

within the color ranges; and, because the student classified the stamps by his individually named color variations, difficulties came to be encountered when other collectors sought to identify among their own stamps those in the shade that the student had termed "rare."

This is a problem within a small compass and, narrowly viewed, is not incapable of rationalization. For if the issue has been printed in a range of shades of blue, and occasionally a stamp is encountered in a shade that is strikingly different from usual, it matters not greatly if the usually encountered stamps are termed, say, "dull blue," and the strikingly different shade is termed, say, "Prussian blue." The existence of the distinctive shade has been recorded and its identification made possible by the nomenclature.

The real difficulty to collectors generally arises when a completely different issue, perhaps from a different country, is printed in a blue color that is termed "Prussian blue." Now the person who names this color has forgotten, if he ever knew, about the existence of the distinctive shade of the first issue, and the normal color range of the one issue bears little or no resemblance to the distinctive shade of the other. So long as the two issues are viewed in isolation, no difficulty arises. But as soon as comparisons are attempted, the collector begins to become confused, the more particularly so when he attempts to identify the rare "Prussian blue" of the one issue by matching it against the readily available "Prussian blue" of the other issue.

These simple illustrations indicate how problems occur. Multiply the examples many hundreds of times, and the real difficulties in the way of philatelic color-standard rationalization begin to appear — difficulties that have been appreciated by philatelists from the earliest days of collecting.[19] Confusion has been rendered worse confounded by a century or so of haphazard color nomenclature, and no solution to the problem can be found while the human element continues to be employed both in viewing and in naming colors.

There are in existence certain costly instruments, some of which use color-matching fields of vision, others of which use the spectrum, that are capable of creating a numerical color standard and could be adopted for philatelic use. But the sheer magnitude of the task of processing all issues is sufficient to render even its beginning unlikely. And, if the standard were established even in regard to certain issues or countries only, there would remain the continuing problem of how to measure individual stamps against that standard — that is, how to relate the standard to the everyday needs of collectors.

One of the other difficulties of color nomenclature is that the philatelist tends to describe the impression that the design as a whole makes upon his eye and his knowledge of colors. In other words, what is described is, as often as not, not the color of the pigment upon the paper, but the color of the paper and pigment together.

To understand this and the problem it creates, look at the shade picture that accompanies this part of the text. Every shade from white through the grays to black is represented. Yet examination of the picture under magnification provides conclusive proof (if such confirmation is deemed necessary) that only black ink was placed upon white paper. In the case of stamps, can it be doubted that the lighter shades would be termed "gray"? Logically, of course, they should be termed "black" (on *white*) — and this, irrationally enough, causes difficulty to collectors who do not fully appreciate the problem.

A familiar instance of just such an occurrence is to be found in two issues: Great Britain 1937-39 ½d. to 3d. and 1941-42 ½d. to 3d. For both of these issues, identical pigments were used. The sole difference between the stamps is that, in the earlier issue, more color appears in the background than appears in the background of the later issue; the amount of color in the heads is the same in both issues.[20] The variations in shades or tints between the two issues as listed in the catalogues is an outstanding instance of the difficulties experienced by philatelists in confining color nomenclature to a description of

---

[19]See, for example, *Standard Guide to Postage Stamp Collecting* by Bellars and Davie (1864), Page ix: "There is too little notice taken of variations in colour by most collectors."

[20]The lighter effect was obtained by making new cylinders having shallower cells in the relevant portions of the design, thus reducing the amount of ink appearing there on the paper. See "Intaglio Printing — II: Gravure." Nevertheless, and in spite of the identity of the pigments, the stamps are listed in *Stanley Gibbons' Postage Stamp Catalogue*, Part I, as, respectively: green, pale green; scarlet, pale scarlet; red-brown, pale red-brown; orange, pale orange; ultramarine, light ultramarine; violet, pale violet; and in *Scott's Standard Postage Stamp Catalogue*, Volume 1, as, respectively: deep green, green; scarlet, vermilion; red-brown, light red-brown; orange, light orange; bright ultramarine, ultramarine; dark purple, violet.

the pigment itself, as opposed to a description of the appearance of pigment and paper together.

Further, the eye is easily deceived by small areas of color in close proximity, and this deception is the basis of "multicolor" reproductions when only three (or, perhaps, four) colors have been used in printing. Reference has previously been made to this process-color-separation method of printing,[21] and it is today more frequently used for postage stamps. However, an instance of misnomer in this connection is referred to for the purpose of illustrating the general problems of nomenclature.

The instance alluded to is that of the private local issues of the Central Pacific Cocoanut Plantations Ltd. for Christmas Island (Pacific Ocean) 1915 (?) to 1934 5c. and 10c. Over the years, several printings were made. All the stamps were printed from one set of process-color-separation plates, of which there were three[22] only — one for the "yellow" printing, one for the "red" printing, and one for the "blue" printing. When examined under a reasonably high-powered lens, each of these stamps quite clearly reveals that only those three, and no more than three, separate colors were used in the printing. Yet when viewed at arm's length or nearer, each stamp seems to contain all of the colors of the reasonably vivid setting or rising sun that is the background of the design.

In the standard work on these issues,[23] the colors are described, for the first issue, as blue, orange, red, green and black. It is, of course, true to state that each separate printing involved essentially different colors; so that, for example, the "blue" of the first printing (a dark, opaque color with plenty of black in its composition) is widely different from the "blue" of the final printing (a pale, translucent color with plenty of green in its composition). Similarly, differences occur with the reds and, to some extent, with the yellows. Further, the colors of the individual printings are not unvarying, so that it may be said, for example, of the "blue" of the first printing, as of the "blue" of each of the subsequent printings, that it has a considerable color range.

With five colors listed when three were used, the problem is pinpointed. Is the philatelist to be logical and aim at evaluation of the colors actually used, or is he to be subjective and aim to record what seems to appear?

Philatelic Sunshine

Speaking generally, the philatelist is interested in a variation in the normal color range only when that variation is significant, as indicating a new printing or a different ink. Variations within the color range often occur because of philatelically insignificant happenings — insignificant, that is, ex-

---

[21]See "Relief Printing" in the chapter entitled "Printing Characteristics," and "Color Separation" in the alphabetical list to the same chapter.

[22]In fact, a fourth plate was used for some printings, but this bore only the words of value, after the figures of value had been removed from the corner squares of the designs.

[23]*Christmas Island and Its Postal History* by The Pacific Islands Circle of the Royal Sydney Philatelic Club (1953), Page 13. Variations are given in respect of different issues elsewhere in the work.

cept as instances of what can occur. Shades or tints can result within a single printing from numerous possible causes — for example, inconsistency of the ink, instability of temperature or humidity control, uneven control of ink flow or uneven pressure on parts of the printing base — all of which can result in color of differing intensity, or shade or tint of color within the compass of a single sheet. Further, climatic and atmospheric conditions can affect both the ink and the paper of a stamp after manufacture, and sometimes the gum has an effect upon one or the other of these.

If no color chart can adequately deal with the sunshine of philately, how much less adequate must words be? For it is impossible to describe a color except by reference to other colors or colored objects. Nevertheless, it is possible to give some verbal indication of an arrangement of colors, combinations and nomenclature that are used by the philatelists who compile the standard catalogues. However, these authorities are not unanimous, and what follows should be regarded as no more than one person's view on the particular classifications.

The primary pigments are yellow, blue and red, from which all others are compounded by blending two or more of the primaries in varying proportions. The range of colors may be considered as on a clock face. With yellow at 12 o'clock, and the hands turning clockwise, the other colors are: 1, yellow-green; 2, green; 3, green-blue; 4, blue; 5, blue-violet; 6, violet; 7, purple; 8, crimson-red; 9, red; 10, red-orange; and 11, orange.

Although these colors are identified by name at the various hours, no sharp dividing lines occur between one color and the next, but one color gradually merges into the other as more and more of the pigment appropriate to the approaching hour becomes mixed with the steadily decreasing pigment of the hour that is past. Where a hyphenated color name occurs, it signifies that qualification comes before the hyphen, the main color afterward. Therefore, for example, yellow-green means green with a yellowish tinge.

One of the most difficult exercises in color evaluation is to determine which, in certain color combinations, are the predominant colors.

The minutes after 12 o'clock reveal lemon yellow and greenish yellow. But, because colors are compounded of three primary pigments, all will not fit into one clock-face circumference, and it is necessary here, before passing too many minutes onward to blue, to examine another group of colors in which browns and grays appear — for example, sage green, olive green and brown olive. On the clock face again we find emerald, blue-green, turquoise green, turquoise blue and Prussian blue. Among the blues are cobalt and ultramarine, both of which terms have been used widely to describe colors covering a substantial range of shades and combinations with and without additions of red.

The darkest shade in the blue section is indigo, which includes a distinct tinge of black; and when some red appears in the composition, the time is about 5:30 and the color is indigo violet. Lilac and mauve are used in relation to the paler tints of purple as the hour moves on toward the red groups and the blue diminishes; on this portion of the clock face are such colors and combinations as claret, crimson lake, crimson, carmine and carmine red.

Beyond 9 o'clock, scarlet appears, then vermilion and orange vermilion. Within this range is another group of colors, the brown and gray group: bistre, yellow-brown, chocolate, red-brown and chestnut. On the clock face again, we find chrome very near 12 o'clock.

Terms Relative to Inks and Color

The alphabetical list that follows does not pretend to deal with particular colors. Color nomenclature in philately — indeed, in general — is too inexact for any attempt to be made at describing any color; and it would be pointless to select for mention any particular color names that have been given to stamps of widely differing color ranges. The terms included in this alphabetical list are, therefore, those that the philatelist uses and encounters in reference to the subject generally and to those activities that may affect the color of stamps.

Aniline. An aromatic, colorless, oily and volatile fluid, slightly soluble in water but readily dissolved in alcohol or ether. Aniline, derived from coal tar, is of great importance as a source of dyes.

Aniline Color. This term is used, philatelically, in two senses: (1) as designating a water-soluble dye in the red color range, usually qualified "scarlet," that suffuses the paper and shows through the back to a marked degree, and that, when inspected by ultraviolet rays, fluoresces brilliantly with a golden or flame color — for example, Great Britain 1912 1d. aniline scarlet; (2) as designating any dye that suffuses the paper and exhibits marked fluorescence when inspected by ultraviolet rays. Compare "Water-Soluble."

Benzine. An inflammable, volatile fluid, petroleum ether, prepared from natural petroleum and used as a solvent. For many years used safely by philatelists for rendering stamp paper more transparent and thus enabling watermarks to be more easily perceived (with the stamp placed face-down on a black surface), and for detecting repairs to stamps, benzine has become less and less safe to use without fear of damaging stamps because of the increasing use of printing inks containing benzine-soluble constituents. Compare "Carbon Tetrachloride."

Bi-Colored. See "Bi-Colored" in the alphabetical list of terms in the chapter entitled "Printing Problems and Varieties." When an attempt is made to evaluate the colors on a bi-colored stamp, one color should be examined at a time, the other color being masked, and narrow concentration should be focused upon an area of solid color. See "Color (1)."

Bleaching. Destroying color, often by oxidation. Many stamps have, in this sense, been bleached, often unintentionally, by excessive exposure to light, or by repeated immersion in benzine, carbon tetrachloride, peroxide of hydrogen or, in some instances, even water.

Carbon Tetrachloride. A nonflammable, volatile fluid that has the property of rendering paper temporarily transparent and of not affecting gum. The fumes are toxic, and should not be inhaled. It is used by some philatelists as a substitute for benzine, and for similar purposes; also as a grease solvent. Many printing inks contain constituents soluble in carbon tetrachloride, and its use may adversely affect stamps. Compare "Benzine." See "Bleaching," "Changeling."

Changeling. In reference to color, this term is used to designate a stamp of which the color has undergone a permanent change to another color range since printing, because one constituent or more of the ink has been dissolved, either fortuitously or otherwise. Such color changelings occur either by exposure to light or because the stamp has been placed in a liquid or subjected to certain fumes or heat. For example, Great Britain 1900 ½d. printed in blue-green becomes bright blue when soaked in water; and Germany 1928-32 50(p.) brown becomes olive green when soaked in carbon tetrachloride. See "Fugitive Color."

Chemical. This term is, occasionally, encountered as a synonym for "color changeling," and its use in this sense dates back to the early days of philately. See, for example, *The Philatelist*, Vol. i, Page 17 (January 1867): A.L. Fenton: "The 12½ cents Canada, and the 10 cents, old issue, United States *blue* are possibly 'chemicals.' . . ."

Cleaned. This term is used to designate a stamp that has had a marking removed. The marking may have been of any kind — postal, fiscal or mere blemish — and the removal may have been effected by chemical or other means. Often cleaning is apparent on close visual examination because of a slight color change or disturbance of the ink of the design or the paper. Usually the fact of cleaning can be detected when the stamp is examined by means of ultraviolet rays. The object of cleaning is, usually, fraudulently to improve the apparent condition of a stamp by use of means considered unethical. However, the line between the ethical and the unethical is narrow and hard to draw. It is not considered unethical to improve the appearance of a stamp by, for example, discharging gum or dirt in boiling water, by discharging grease in benzine or carbon tetrachloride, or by restoring color in sulfuretted stamps with the use of peroxide of hydrogen and water.

Climatic. This term is used, occasionally, in two senses: (1) to designate a stamp of which the color or paper is especially liable to undergo permanent changes on exposure to air, damp or light; (2) to designate a stamp of which the color has, in fact, undergone a change of color because of exposure to air, but which can be restored by treatment with peroxide of hydrogen and water. See "Sulfuretted."

Colombo. This term was used as a synonym for "color changeling," stemming from the fact that stamps on mail from the *Colombo*, which was wrecked, were much changed in color because of sulfuretting. See, for example, *The Stamp Collector's Magazine*, Vol. i, Page 75 (May 1864): "these comprise . . . colombos, that is to say purposely or accidentally changed in colour."

Color. (1) Rays of visible light. When an attempt is made to evaluate the color of a monochrome stamp, narrow concentration should be focused on an area of solid color; under different lighting conditions, colors seem to change, and, if consistent results are desired, color evaluation should invariably be carried out in conditions that are standard, including the same aspect of light and the same background; see "Color Range," "Shade," "Tint." (2) Printer's ink. See "Printer's Ink."

Color Changeling — see "Changeling."

Color Proof. A trial impression of a completed stamp design made for the purpose of ensuring that the color matches a color selected from color trials. Compare "Color Trial."

Color Range. This term is used, philatelically, to denote the variation, within ill-defined limits, in shade or tint of color usually encountered on different examples of the same stamp. Because numerous factors can affect the intensity of color on a particular sheet or stamp — for example, heavier pressure will cause more intense color, and even a slight interruption in the ink feed will cause less intense color — variations of color within these ill-defined limits are, usually, unimportant and philatelically insignificant. However, when these ill-defined limits are exceeded, the particular example is said to be "outside the normal color range," and this is, usually, philatelically significant in indicating a different printing or different ink.

Color Trial. A proof impression of a stamp design made for the purpose of selecting an appropriate color or combination of colors in which the issue is to be printed. Compare "Color Proof"; compare also "Trial Color Proofs" in the section on "Plate Proofs, Color Trials, Color Proofs" in the chapter entitled "From Design to Issued Sheets."

Compound (Thermographic) — see "Thermography."

Crust Flaw — see "Crust Flaw" in the alphabetical list to the chapter entitled "Relief Printing."

De-Oxidized — see "Sulfuretted."

Dusting — see "Thermography."

Dye — see "Pigment."

Fast Color. This term is used, philatelically, to designate the ink of a stamp that can be soaked in water, benzine, carbon tetrachloride or petroleum without the color running. Neither will the color of such an ink be adversely affected by reasonably prolonged exposure to bright light. Compare "Fugitive Color."

Fluorescence. The differently colored glowing effect produced by subjecting certain inks to ultraviolet rays; a luminosity produced because of excitation by ultraviolet rays, but limited to the period of exposure. The fluorescence disappears immediately the ultraviolet rays cease to operate. Contrast "Phosphorescence"; see "Luminescence."

Fluorescent Paper. Paper with a coating of, or containing, material that causes the paper to fluoresce when excited by ultraviolet light. Fluorescent paper has no significant afterglow. The abbreviation "FCP" is used to indicate that the paper has been coated with a fluorescent agent — literally, "fluorescent-coated paper."

Foil. As applied to color, this term is used philatelically to designate (1) metal rolled into a thin sheet and bonded to paper to form a laminate that bears the stamp design applied by a conventional printing method, as in Hungary 1955 (Oct. 5) Air, Light Metal Industries International Congress Budapest 5f. (see "Aluminum Foil" in the alphabetical list to the chapter entitled "Paper") and Tonga 1963 (Jul. 15) First Polynesian Gold Coinage Commemoration 1d. to 2s. 9d.; or (2) metal dust or thin sheets bonded to part of the face of the stamp, as in Great Britain 1966 (Dec. 1) Christmas 3d. "gold" foil, and Gambia 1966 (Jun. 24) 150th Anniversary of the Foundation of Bathurst 1d. "silver" foil.

Fried Printing — see "Thermography."

Fugitive Color. This term is used, philatelically, to designate the ink of a stamp that cannot be in contact with water, benzine, carbon tetrachloride or petroleum without the color running, and of which the color will be adversely affected by even short exposure to bright light. There is no complete list available of stamps printed in fugitive colors, but the standard catalogues have cautionary notes on some of the issues — for example, Netherlands Indies (Dutch Indies) 1912-15. Benzine and carbon tetrachloride should not be used on photogravure issues. Compare "Fast Color." See "Carbon Tetrachloride."

Graphite-Lined. This term is used to designate a stamp that bears on the back one or two printed lines of colloidal graphite; the first issue was Great Britain 1957 (Nov. 19) ½d. to 3d., on sale in the Southampton area. The graphite acted as an electrical conductor for a high-voltage discharge, and so signaled to a scanner the rate prepaid by the letter bearing the stamp and also the position of the stamp. The scanner was an element in a complex automatic letter facing machine ("ALF") that also sorted normal rate from deferred rate letters. Compare "Phosphor Lined." See "Naphthadag."

Hand-Painted. This term is used to designate any stamp upon which coloring has been applied by hand. Instances are to be found, for example, in Tikhvin (Russian Zemstvo) 1878, where the centers were hand-painted.

Heat Raising — see "Thermography."

Helecon. The commercial name for a substance in the zinc sulfide group that becomes luminescent on excitation by ultraviolet rays. It is used for tagging stamps, and was so used, for example, first for Australia 1959-64 Regular 11d. See "Luminescence"; "Phosphor Coated"; "Tagged Stamps."

Hydrogen Peroxide — see "Peroxide of Hydrogen."

Ink — see "Printer's Ink."

Luminescence. The emission of light otherwise than as a result of incandescence, caused by the absorption of ultraviolet rays and the emission of visible rays. The term is descriptive only of the emission of light, and does not differentiate between light that appears only during actual exposure to ultraviolet rays and afterglow. See "Fluorescence"; "Phosphorescence."

Luminescent Paper. This is paper with a coating of, or containing, material that causes the paper to fluoresce or phosphoresce when excited by ultraviolet light. The term "luminescent" embraces both types of reaction and does not distinguish between them.

Luminescent Tagging. This term is used loosely to mean the application to a postage stamp by means of overprinting, in lines or overall, or by incorporation in the printing ink or paper coating, of a substance that phosphoresces when subjected to ultraviolet light, for the purpose of activating machines that face, segregate and, sometimes, cancel the mail. See "Luminescence"; "Phosphor-Lined"; "Phosphorescence."

Lumogen. The German term used to designate luminescent paper coating and inks. See "Luminescence."

Medium. The viscous fluid with which the pigment or pigments are combined to produce printer's ink. For stamp printing other than photogravure, the most commonly used medium is heated linseed oil; for photogravure printing, xylol has been used as a medium, and so, occasionally, has water. See "Pigment," "Printer's Ink."

Monochrome — see "Monochrome" in the alphabetical list to the chapter entitled "Printing Problems and Varieties."

Multicolored — see "Multicolored" in the alphabetical list to the chapter entitled "Printing Problems and Varieties." When an attempt is made to evaluate the colors in a multicolored stamp, one color should be examined at a time (the other colors being masked), and narrow concentration should be focused upon an area of solid color. See "Color (1)."

Naphthadag. Deflocculated Acheson's graphite ("Dag") carried in naphtha. This name was misapplied to the ink used for printing graphite lines on the first stamps issued with them — see "Graphite-Lined." In fact, "Naphthadag" was used only experimentally, and not for any of the issued stamps, other solvents having replaced naphtha as the medium. "Dag" is the registered trademark of Acheson Colloids Ltd.

Neutral Compound — see "Thermography."

Oxidized. This term is used sometimes as a misnomer for "sulfuretted." See "Sulfuretted."

Peroxide of Hydrogen. H_2O_2 used in solution to liberate oxygen and so restore the original color to stamps printed in inks that have become sulfuretted. Peroxide of hydrogen in a solution of about five volumes may, with reasonable safety, be employed for this purpose by immersing the stamp in the solution or by applying the solution alternately with water to the face of the stamp, except when coated paper or fugitive color has been used in the production of the stamp. See "Fugitive Color," "Sulfuretted."

Phosphor-Coated. This term is used to designate an adhesive postage stamp, or a postage stamp on postal stationery, over the whole surface of which a phosphor coating has been applied; contrast "Phosphor-Lined." The first phosphor-coated stamp of the United States, issued at Dayton, Ohio, on Aug. 1, 1963, was U.S. 1962-63 Air 8c. Unlike phosphor lines, phosphor coating is virtually invisible even when the stamp is held obliquely to the light, but phosphor coating luminesces on and after excitation by ultraviolet rays. See "Luminescence."

Phosphorescence. Philatelically, the luminosity produced because of excitation by ultraviolet rays, and enduring not only while the ray source is acting but continuing, for however short a time, after it has ceased to act. Contrast "Fluorescence"; see "Luminescence."

Phosphorescent Paper. Paper with a coating of, or containing, material that causes the paper to phosphoresce when excited by ultraviolet light. Phosphorescent paper has a significant afterglow. The abbreviation "PCP" is used to indicate that the paper has been coated with a phosphorescent agent — literally, "phosphorescent-coated paper." "AOP" is an abbreviation meaning that the paper has a coating of phosphorescent material covering the entire surface. A distinction sometimes drawn is to refer to "phosphor bands" (or "bars" or "lines") when the coating is limited to a band or bands printed on the paper, as opposed to all over phosphor. Two distinct types of phosphorescent material have been used: organic resins, used, for example, for British stamps, including 1977 (Jan. 12) Racket Sports 8½p. to 13p.; and inorganic metallic compounds, used, for instance, for U.S. 1978 (Jun. 26) Photography 15 cents. Different formulations of phosphor result in different colors of visible light.

Phosphor-Lined. This term is used to designate a stamp that bears on the face either one or two printed lines of phosphor. The first issue was Great Britain 1959 (Nov. 18) ½d. to 4½d. on sale in the Southampton area. The phosphor is almost invisible in ordinary light unless the stamp is held obliquely, but luminesces under ultraviolet rays. The phosphor, after excitation by ultraviolet rays, signals to a photoelectric scanner the rate prepaid for the letter bearing the stamp and also the position of the stamp — the scanner being an element in a complex automatic letter facing machine ("ALF") that also sorts normal rate from deferred rate letters. The first phosphor-lined stamps also were graphite-lined, but the machine had ceased to operate by using the graphite. See "Graphite-Lined," "Luminescence."

Pigment. The dry coloring matter or dye that is combined with the medium to produce printer's ink. Pigments are either organic or inorganic, and naturally or chemically obtained. Most pigments used for stamps are insoluble in water. See "Medium," "Printer's Ink."

Pigmented Compound — see "Thermography."

Printer's Ink. A combination of pigment or pigments and a medium. Most printer's inks are stiff, and sometimes heat is used to make them more easily worked. Inks used in photogravure printing are much more fluid. Sometimes "printer's ink" is technically termed "color." See "Medium," "Pigment."

Quartz Lamp. An instrument used for producing ultraviolet rays. A particular type of ultraviolet lamp. See "Ultraviolet Lamp."

Resinous Powder — see "Thermography."

Set-Off — see "Set-Off" in the alphabetical list to the chapter entitled "Printing Problems and Varieties."

Shade. (1) A gradation in depth of tone, as opposed to a difference in color. (2) Sometimes, a darker tone (because of the inclusion of more "black") as opposed to a tint. See "Tint."

Spotting — see "Thermography."

Sulfuretted. Combined chemically with sulfur. In stamps, sulfuretting occurs if lead used in one of the constituents of the printer's ink becomes changed, in the course of time, to lead sulfide by action of the atmosphere; this causes the original color, usually blue, green, red or yellow, to become brown or black. The term "oxidized" is sometimes used as a misnomer for "sulfuretted." See "Peroxide of Hydrogen."

Tagged Stamp. A stamp that, at some stage of production, has had incorporated into its paper or ink, or has had printed upon it, a substance that enables the mail to be automatically faced and segregated by machine. See "Luminescent Tagging."

Tagging — see "Luminescent Tagging."

Thermographic Compound — see "Thermography."

Thermography. A term employed to designate a technique by which raised lines or areas are produced on paper by the application of heat to resinous powder dusted on to designs printed by conventional methods. Thermography is characterized by reliefs on the face of the stamp, and the complete absence, at the back of the stamp, of indentations in the shapes of the reliefs. The terms "fried printing" (derisively) and "heat raising" have been used in reference to the technique. The resinous powder, termed "thermographic compound," is either "neutral" — that is, substantially colorless — or "pigmented" — that is, usually, metallic (gold, silver or copper) — and results in shiny raised lines or areas, but a variation produces matte results. The sheet, bearing lines or areas on which the ink has not dried, is dusted with the compound, the surplus compound is removed by suction and vibration or flicking, and the sheet is then subjected to heat for a few seconds, which causes the compound to fuse with the ink and raises the lines or areas apparently in the color of the ink. Any surplus compound not entirely removed will adhere to the paper when heated, producing fortuitous raised dots or other small areas of color, the effect being termed "spotting." Philatelically, the first use of thermography was on Turkey 1966 (May 15) Osman Faience Art 60k., on which the black portions of the design and inscriptions appear in relief; the first use of a metallic compound on a postage stamp was on Turkey 1966 (Sep. 6) 400th Anniversary of the Death of Sultan Suleiman 130k., on which the arch above the portrait appears in gold relief. Thermography was used also, for example, for part of the design of New Caledonia and Dependencies 1985 (Feb. 27) Shells 55f.

Tint. This term is, sometimes, used in philately to designate a lighter tone (because of the inclusion of more "white") as opposed to a shade. See "Shade (2)."

Ultraviolet Lamp. A term employed to designate an instrument used for producing nonvisible rays beyond violet in the spectrum. Unless special filters are used, visible rays in the violet range are emitted. The appearance of a stamp being inspected by ultraviolet rays often differs very considerably from that of the same stamp inspected by normal light. Colors appear more intense or change completely; some inks appear to glow — see "Fluorescence." Apparently similar materials of different composition, such as two pieces of paper, react differently under ultraviolet rays, and the ultraviolet lamp is used in the detection of repaired and cleaned stamps. See "Cleaned."

Varnish. A synonym for "medium." See "Medium."

Vehicle. A synonym for "medium." See "Medium."

Water-Soluble. A term occasionally used generically as designating an ink of which all or part of the color runs when in contact with water, and embracing aniline colors as well as those in inks of which the medium was water. See "Aniline Color"; "Fugitive Color"; "Medium"; "Pigment." Compare "Fast Color."

Gum. Drying gummed sheets in stacks of trays. An old photograph (c. 1914) showing how each gummed sheet of stamps was placed in a specially constructed wooden tray for drying at the works of Perkins, Bacon & Company.

14. Gum

THE TERM "GUM" in philatelic usage is a generic term employed to designate the substance applied to the back of a stamp so that it may adhere and justify its being called an "adhesive" — although, curiously enough, many adhesive postage stamps have been issued without gum. Nearly always, only the term "gum" is used, irrespective of the origin of the substance, and it embraces both animal and vegetable matter. The use of other generic terms, such as "cement," "glue," "mucilage" and "paste," is rarely encountered in philately. But, of course, sometimes references are found to specific types of "gum" such as "dextrine" or "British gum," "gum arabic" and "gum senegal."

Gum, from the point of view of the philatelist, forms one of the constituent parts of the mint examples of most issues of adhesive stamps, and the philatelic significance of gum may be considered from two aspects: first, as forming part of the production processes employed for the stamp and, therefore, producing effects resulting from the use of gum; second, as affecting the collectible condition of the stamp.

From the point of view of the student, it may be stated that the presence or absence of a stamp's gum is important only so far as it adds to the sum of knowledge about the stamp — that is, when the use or non-use of gum in production provides assistance in expertization, or when gum provides criteria by reference to which one issue or printing may be differentiated from a similar but different issue or printing, as in the cases of, for example, Belgium 1936-51 Leopold, the franc values; Great Britain 1924-26 and 1934-35 low values; Portugal 1923-26 and 1930-31 Ceres (with imprint); and Ryukyu Islands 1948 5s. to 1y.

Consideration of the question of how far, from the collector's point of view, the presence or absence of gum affects the desirability of a particular unused stamp issued gummed is more properly related to discussion generally of collecting techniques and "condition."

Here it is sufficient to state that, in the cases of some issues, two conflicting interests arise. In so far as many collectors desire to represent an issue as sold to the public, they find it necessary — if the item collected is to be accurately representative without alteration — to have the stamp bearing the original gum, if the stamp was so sold. That interest is considered by many collectors to be of great importance, and results in emphasis being placed upon "original gum." The conflict of interests arises in cases in which time and atmosphere have so worked upon the gum that it has cracked in such a manner as to affect the paper itself.[1] This process being progressive, the collector is faced with the alternative of retaining the stamp, representative and without alteration, in the knowledge that eventually irreparable damage will be caused to the paper in that it will separate into fragments or, at least, be permanently creased; or of removing or, perhaps, moistening and so altering the gum to preserve the paper and printing.

In the heart searching that follows the realization of this dilemma in the case of a rare and valuable stamp, the owner may well think that selection of the most important leg of a three-legged stool is an impossibility. However, the facts remain that a shooting stick has only one leg, and, at some stage of production of the stamp, the paper bore no gum. At that stage, the paper may also have borne no printing, because this may have been effected subsequent to gumming.[2]

The emphasis that has been laid upon the desirability of "original gum" on a mint stamp, and the consequent premium commanded by some of the older issues with gum, have led, almost inevitably, to the demand being catered to by the unscrupulous application of gum to stamps without it. As a result, the philatelist has found it necessary to acquire knowledge of the characteristics of the gum actually used during the production of particular issues, and of certain other characteristics and results, generally, of gumming.

As an obvious corollary, knowledge is necessary of which stamps were issued ungummed. For instance, the collector who buys a mint example of India 1854 4a. at an enhanced price "because it has full original gum" reveals his lack of knowledge that that stamp was issued without gum — as, indeed, does the collector who refuses to buy what is, in fact, a very moderately priced copy of that stamp, the refusal being based on the objection that the stamp was merely "unused without gum." Similarly, instances have been recorded of refusals to accept as collectible because of lack of gum U.S. 1934 (Feb. 10) National Stamp Exhibition souvenir sheet 3c. If that souvenir sheet, or any imperforate single from it, did have gum, the gum would have been applied by a faker.

From "original gum" to "full original gum" and the concomitant "unmounted mint" or "unhinged" are steps that have led to an unreasoned fad, providing a parallel with "fly mark," "flyspeck," and "dotty" collecting.[3] Some of the older issues are less readily available "with original gum," a fortiori "with full original gum," than they are unused or "passant pour neuf."

---

[1]Well-known instances of such occurrences are to be found, for example, in Great Britain 1858-64 Letters in All Four Corners 1d., the so-called "Plate Number Penny"; and Hungary 1871 (May 1) 2k. to 25k. Germany Semi-Postal 1935 Ostropa souvenir sheet [3 to 25(p.)], and Air 1936 50(p.) and 75(p.), bore on their backs the agent of their own destruction in the sulfuric acid content of the gum used. This, unless removed, destroyed the paper.

[2]The gum of most stamps can be removed by soaking the stamp in cold water and, if necessary, moving a fingertip lightly across the stamp under water. Very thickly gummed stamps, such as, for example, the early issues of Austria, will require prolonged soaking — perhaps as much as twenty-four hours — before the gum is sufficiently soft to remove; after such soaking the gum may be scraped away with a blade or the edge of a pair of tweezers (tongs). Techniques for removing adherent paper from stamps are dealt with in most general discussions of collecting techniques.

[3]See the introductory pages to the chapter entitled "Printing Problems and Varieties."

Ungummed. India 1854 1a. A mint block without gum — but the "faddist" collector who would refuse to accept this block solely because of its lack of gum would reveal his lack of knowledge about the circumstances of issue. These stamps never had "original gum."

Because of this comparative rarity, some collectors, desiring to represent a stamp unaltered as issued, pay the premium usually attendant upon rarity. Indeed, because some issues are known today only by reason of the fact that they were preserved by early collectors — and in singles, at that — such issues are unknown "unhinged" or "unmounted mint." Other early issues exist in multiples, and instances are known where the "unmounted mint" collector has been catered to by severing a multiple and removing from it the stamps that have been hinged in order to leave a smaller multiple or a single that qualifies for the appellation "unmounted mint" — to be sold, of course, at a hugely inflated price.

Incidentally, the buyers of such items are then faced with the problem of how to display their acquisitions while preserving their costly gum. This problem has been solved by special transparent mounts that obviate the need to use hinges. And some collectors have gone so far as to have hermetically sealed, transparent containers made for such items in an attempt to arrest the havoc wrought by age and atmosphere. As in the case of "dotty" collecting, so in the case of "full original gum": Others uncritically followed the seeming lead without adequate reason, and, in the cases of readily available modern issues, began to collect "unmounted mint," placing a quite unwarranted emphasis on having an unhinged stamp, to such an extent as, quite without justification, to regard a hinged stamp as something to be avoided and almost valueless. This pernickerty fad will, doubtless, prove to be no more than a passing craze. Being immoderate, it will, as all immoderate crazes do, give way to moderation. The craze has given rise to the derisory appellation "unhinged collector," echoing and reminiscent of the much earlier "timbromania."[4]

---

[4] See "Philately and Stamp Collecting" in the chapter entitled "Aims of Collecting."

Ungummed

Passing reference has been made earlier in this chapter to the necessity of the philatelist having knowledge of stamps issued without gum. No complete list has been published of such "adhesive" postage stamps. Often the general catalogues contain notes in reference to individual issues, but in none of the catalogues are these references comprehensive. An obvious reason for the issue of ungummed stamps has been that the climate in the country of issue is moist and humid so that gummed sheets would tend to stick together.

One such instance occurred in Gold Coast in 1883-84. In January 1883, Charles Pike took custody of the stamps in Accra from Frederick Evans, and the Audit Board that supervised the transfer discovered that the balance of stamps shown in the books amounted to a total of £1841.10s. made up of sheets of sixty stamps as follows: ½d., eighty; 1d., 120; 2d., 1,076; 4d., 1,004; and 6d., 173. However, the board could not verify the figures by counting the sheets because it "found that from their having been affected by damp and thus gummed together, the damage resulting from the process of separating them was such as to render it desirable to suspend the operation pending further instructions." The governor suggested that "the difficulty may be met by putting the packet of stamps in water and separating them so soon as the Gum has softened," and asked whether Evans had any objection to Pike's doing this, "the vessel of water in which the stamps are placed to soften being locked in the strong room."

Eventually, on January 31, 1883, Pike agreed to take over the stamps in the mass, Evans having assured him that they were correct.[5] At some later time, authority was given to separate the sheets, by steaming them apart,[6] during the stamp famine that occurred in the course of that year, and on May 5, 1883, E. Jose da Costa, postmaster at Cape Coast, returned a quantity of stamps to Accra stating that they had been sent to him defaced or otherwise unfit for use.[7]

On July 7, R. Cole, postmaster at Accra, wrote saying that the stamps returned from Cape Coast "as 'defaced or otherwise unfit for use' are the same as those now in use at Accra, and the Treasurer has not better ones in stock to give in exchange. With a little trouble in regumming some of them, they could be used by the Postmaster at Cape Coast." The stamps were returned in October for use in Cape Coast.

The stamp famine increased; and the difficulties caused by the solid mass of sheets were remembered when, on February 23, 1884, Frederick Evans, then Acting Colonial Secretary, forwarded to the Crown Agents a requisition for three months' supply of stamps.[8] To the covering letter he added a postscript: "H(is) E(xcellency) the Governor desires me to ask that the

---

[5]Gold Coast — Colonial Secretary's Minute Papers, 66/1883.
[6]Minute Papers 353/1844.
[7]Minute Papers 566/1883. The details were: eighteen sheets 1d. stamps ungummed at 5s. ea. £4.10.0; fourteen sheets 1d. stamps defaced at 5s. ea £3.10.0; forty-three sheets 2d. stamps ungummed at 10s. ea £21.10.0. A total of £29.10.0.
[8]The amounts requisitioned were: ½d., 200 sheets; 1d., 200 sheets; 2d., 100 sheets; 4d., 100 sheets.

Ungummed. Italy 1944 50c.; Poland 1919 Cracow 25h.; Sonora (Mexico) 1914 (October) 1c. Three issues made during various emergencies, and never provided with "original gum."

stamps may be supplied without being gummed at the back, as those now in store have in consequence of the dampness of the climate become 'stuck together' and a number of sheets have been wasted." When answering that letter, the Crown Agents, on April 28, 1884, stated:

As regards the difficulty experienced through the Stamps now in store at the Gold Coast having stuck together, I enclose a copy of a report on the subject by Messrs. De La Rue, and have to inform you that having further enquired into the matter we have thought it best to send out only half the quantity comprised in the present requisition ungummed, in accordance with the request of the Colonial Government, and the remainder gummed and interleaved with paper suitable for the purpose which can be accomplished at the small additional cost of 1d. per thousand. This will give the Colonial Postmaster an opportunity of testing the two methods of preparation, and enable the Government to form an opinion as to which of them it will be desirable to adopt in future. . . .

The report from De La Rue, dated April 9, stated that the firm could, of course, supply the stamps ungummed, that in the Gold Coast the stuck-together stamps must have been stored in some improper manner either in a damp place[9] or under heavy pressure. "We have never had," the report continued, "a similar complaint before, although we supply stamps to every part of the world. The gum which we use is specially devised to resist the action of a humid atmosphere." The stamps arrived in Accra on June 19, and on June 25 a newly appointed Governor minuted: "The omission of gum from the Stamps will prove an abominable nuisance." The next requisition was for all sheets to be interleaved.

Other stamps issued ungummed because of the climate include, for example, Curacao 1873 2½c. to 2.50g., and Surinam 1873-88 1c. to 2.50g.

The most usual reason for an ungummed issue of adhesive postage stamps is an emergency or otherwise primitive resources of production.

Among the not inconsiderable number of stamps issued ungummed, India 1854 has already been mentioned. Others, by way of examples only, include: China 1944 (Dec. 25) 50th Anniversary of Kuomintang $2 to $20; Cuba 1942 Democracy in America 1c. to 13c. imperforate; Japan 1923 ½s. to 20s. and

---

[9]Anyone who has experienced the "Coast" knows full well that it is a damp place!

1942-45 10s. gray; Latvia 1919 (Jul. 3) Rising Sun 10k.; Nicaragua 1932 (Dec. 17) Rivas Railway 1c. to 15c.; Palestine 1918 (Feb. 10) 1p.; Poland 1919 Cracow 2h. to 1k.; St. Lucia Postage Due 1931 1d. and 2d.; Samos (Greece) 1912 (November) 5 l. to 25 l.; Sonora (Mexico) 1913 (May 25) 1c. to 10c.; Tibet 1912 ⅛t. to 1s.; Uganda 1895 Cowries 5(c.) to 60(c.); U.S. Postage 1933 (Aug. 25) American Philatelic Society Issue 1c. and 3c., being the souvenir sheets (one of "Farley's Follies") of 1933 (May 25) Chicago World Exhibition 1c. and 3c.; U.S. Locals Penny Express Company 1866 5c.; and Zanzibar 1930-33 Postage Due 1c. to 75c.

Gumming After or Before Printing

The stage of production at which the gum is applied to the paper depends on the facilities available to the printer and the method of printing used. No universal practice obtains or has ever obtained in stamp production. Only in dry printing[10] was printing upon ready-gummed paper a possibility until research and development made practical wet printing upon ready-gummed paper.

For example, during the early years of stamp production, and before the introduction of perforation or other means of easy separation as a stage in the processes, the steps in production were: (1) paper; (2) print; and (3) gum. The paper was dampened for recess printing and, consequently, expanded and then contracted on drying after printing.[11] The fact that the printed paper again expanded as a result of dampening with the gum solution, and then again contracted — but differently — when the gum dried, was entirely without importance.

Even after the introduction of separation, which made the uniformity of one sheet with another a necessity if separation were to be carried out efficiently and simply, the most usual sequence of steps in production was: (1) paper; (2) print; (3) gum; and (4) separation. During experiments with perforation, it was appreciated that gummed paper, being more brittle, was better than ungummed paper for perforating. But great difficulties were experienced because of the irregularity of the sheets resulting from dampened and, therefore, inevitably ungummed paper that had been recess printed. So keenly was this difficulty felt that the inventor of stamp perforations instigated experiments that resulted in the "Prince Consort Essay,"[12] with the object of printing upon dry, ready-gummed paper and so avoiding any shrinkage attendant on gumming and printing on dampened paper.

Until 1872 in England, De La Rue printed on ungummed paper, but, by February of that year, the firm had succeeded in refining its gum sufficiently to enable relief printing to be carried out on gummed sheets without damaging the printing bases with impurities in the gum. The firm claimed that printing on gummed paper would result in the stamps being "extremely fugitive"

---

[10]See "Wet Printing and Dry Printing" in the discussion of "Modern Influences in Printing" in the chapter entitled "Printing Problems and Varieties."

[11]See "Shrinkage" in the alphabetical list to the chapter entitled "Paper."

[12]Illustrated and discussed in the section "Essays" in the chapter entitled "From Design to Issued Sheets."

— that is, that attempts to defraud the revenue would be frustrated because the design would be lost if attempts were made to remove the cancellation for the purpose of re-using the stamps — and that the colors would retain their bloom. Also, the printers pointed out the advantages so far as perforating was concerned. They were given authority by India to print on gummed paper, but in August 1872 the British Post Office requested that the higher values supplied by the printers should be printed on paper gummed after printing.

In the United States, from the outset, printing was carried out on un-gummed paper; and the great majority of U.S. stamps have been line-engraved and recess-printed on dampened paper. It was not until com-paratively recently that printing has been effected on paper already gum-med — termed "pregummed paper."

In Canada, all of the issues up to, for example, 1923, when the American Bank Note Company in Ottawa became the Canadian Bank Note Company, were printed on paper that was gummed after printing.

Throughout the world nowadays, most stamps are printed on paper that has already been gummed; and this is so irrespective of the method of print-ing, even when wet printing is employed. In appropriate cases, moisture is applied only to the printing side of the paper, and the amount of moisture is carefully controlled so that it does not penetrate the paper sufficiently to affect the gum.[13] When the sheets are stacked after printing, the moisture remaining on the face of one sheet is prevented from reaching the gum on the back of the next sheet above in the pile by a sheet of waxed or otherwise treated tissue that is intercalated between the printed sheets. This problem of moisture and gum does not, of course, arise in the case of dry printing — and the development of non-off-setting inks has, in large measure, resulted in the elimination of intercalation when dry printing is used.

Therefore, today, the most usual sequence of steps in production is: (1) paper; (2) gum; (3) print; and (4) separation.

Printed on the Gummed Side

A certain type of error can occur only if stamps are printed on paper that is already gummed. The error is termed "printed on the gummed side" or "printed on the gum."

The cause is obvious. The sheet of paper was inserted into the press with the wrong face upward so that the ink from the printing base was deposited only on the gummed surface of the paper. Instances of such occurrences are to be encountered, for example, in Great Britain 1881 (Dec. 12) 1d. 16 dots; 1887 Jubilee 1d. and 2½d.; 1924 (April)–1926 1½d. and 4d.; and 1934-36 1d; and Union of South Africa 1913 (Sep. 1)–1921 ½d. Such errors are, of course, inconstant.

It is to be observed that, if the error were to be washed, the design would disappear with the dissolving of the gum. And it is interesting to note that,

---

[13]See, for example, "Color Printing from a Single Cylinder" in the chapter entitled "In-taglio Printing — I: Line Engraving."

if the paper had not been gummed, the same cause would have resulted merely (in the case of watermarked paper) in the variety "reversed watermark."[14]

In the case of some issues, printing was deliberately effected on the side of the paper that was subsequently gummed, the intention being that, once affixed to the mail or other document, the stamp could not be removed without destroying the design, which showed through the transparent paper.[15]

A device adopted to prevent the occurrence of the error was used as long ago as 1854 for the later printings of Great Britain 1854 6d. (embossed), which were made on pregummed paper. To differentiate between the printing side and the gummed side of the paper, the authorities tinted the gum green. The idea, although basically sound, was not entirely novel and did not find general acceptance, instances of deliberately tinted gum being comparatively rare in stamp production. A few are referred to later in this chapter.

A variety somewhat similar to "printed on the gummed side" occurs occasionally on stamps that are printed on the printing side of pregummed paper. Even though great care is exercised when the paper is gummed, it occasionally happens that some gum is splashed on to the printing side, resulting in spots and streaks of various sizes. Of course, the paper is examined after gumming, and any obviously faulty sheets are rejected. However, sometimes, some less obviously splashed or streaked sheets are overlooked, with the consequence that when the stamps are printed, parts of the designs are printed on these streaks or splashes of gum and the remainder are printed normally on the paper. Such varieties appear substantially normal unless examined very closely; but if the stamps are washed, those parts of the design (and cancellation, if any) applied to the gum spots or streaks disappear with the dissolving of the gum.

Such varieties are, of course, inconstant; they have been termed "gum flaws," "gum streaks" and "gum spots." They are, in effect, partial albino impressions,[16] caused by the presence not of extraneous paper but of extraneous gum. Instances of such varieties are to be encountered, for example, in Union of South Africa 1913 (Sep. 1)–1921 1d.

"Gum flaws" causing partial albino impressions are not limited to basic stamps, and instances are known of their occurrence on surcharges and overprints. For example, in the case of Sarawak 1892 (May 23) 1c. on 1871 (Jan. 1) 3c., before the surcharging was carried out, some of the gum on the backs of some of the sheets had become transferred to the printed sides of others because the gum had been softened by the humid climate. When the sur-

---

[14]See the discussion of "Watermark Varieties" in the chapter entitled "Watermarks."
[15]See the illustrations and instances quoted in "Goldbeaters Skin" in the alphabetical list to the chapter entitled "Paper."
[16]See "Albino" in the alphabetical list to the chapter entitled "Printing Problems and Varieties."
[17]Another indication of regumming is this: In the case of an imperforate stamp bearing original gum, it is carried evenly — as evenly as the original gumming method permits — to the very edges of the stamp. But in the case of a regummed stamp, the gum nearly always tends to fall away, or lose thickness, at the edges.
[18]See *The De La Rue History of British and Foreign Postage Stamps 1855 to 1901*, by John Easton (1958), Pages 482, 487, 801-802.

Gum flaws. Union of South Africa 1913 (Sep. 1)–1921 1d., showing the effect of "gum flaws" (or "gum streaks" or "gum spots"). The sheets of paper were gummed before printing; occasionally, small amounts of gum were splashed on or otherwise transferred to the printing side of some of the sheets. When these sheets were printed, the printing ink was prevented from reaching the paper, but was printed on these small amounts of gum, so that the designs appeared complete. Later, the postmarking ink similarly lay over the gum. If such stamps were washed, the gum would dissolve, carrying away with it the postmarking and printing ink, and leaving, where the gum had been on the face of the stamp, vertical streaks or spots of uncolored paper, with the remainder of the design and postmark unaffected.

charging was effected, some printing occurred on patches of this transferred gum, with the consequence that washed stamps may be found with surcharges partly or wholly albino.

Gumming Before or After Perforating

Sheets almost always are provided with means of easy separation after they have been gummed, and this fact affords what is, often, a useful test in expertizing a perforated stamp when regumming is suspected. In the usual case of a stamp with original gum, the thickness of the paper within the perforation holes (or within the denticulations, if a single stamp is being examined) and, particularly, the edges of the teeth will be free of gum — and this can be observed when examining the "wall" presented by the edge of the stamp under an adequate degree of magnification. Regumming will, almost inevitably, result in excess gum appearing on the "wall." So far as the paper within the perforation holes is concerned, this test is not invariably infallible; for, if the stamps have been perforated under adverse conditions, original gum may exist on the "wall," having been carried there by the perforating pins.[17]

Instances are on record in which stamps have been gummed after perforating, usually because the coating of gum applied before perforation has become defective or was considered insufficient. Of course, this procedure is usually unsatisfactory, because the subsequent gum tends to fill the perforation holes, escape on to the face of the stamps, and render separation more difficult. Two instances of this occurrence may be mentioned by way of examples.

The first, which is well-documented,[18] occurred in regard to Egypt 1884 (Dec. 15) 10 par., 20 par. and 5 pias., printed by De La Rue. During the years 1886 to 1888, the printers received a number of complaints from various parts of the world about their gum and gumming but had stoutly defended both the system and the gum — although, after April 1887 and to placate the Crown Agents, they applied a slightly thicker layer of gum to all sheets. In 1887, the Egyptian government returned seven cases of stamps to De La Rue, claiming that the stamps were insufficiently gummed and requesting that they be regummed at the printers' expense. In the correspondence and investigation that followed the return of the stamps, De La Rue discovered that the stamps bore an adequate amount of gum, but that its adhesiveness had been partly or wholly destroyed by a process of fermentation that had occurred because, when the stamps had arrived in Egypt, they had been taken out of their airtight containers and allowed to stand in a damp place "for a day or two" and then put again into airtight containers. The sheets were sticking together.

Although at first the printers had stated that it was impossible to regum sheets that had been perforated, they later wrote: "it is impossible to regum the sheets by our machines. We are glad to add, however, that we have hit upon a plan by which we can apply an extra layer of gum by hand, and although it will be a tedious operation, we are willing upon the present occasion to undertake it for you free of charge. We enclose a specimen sheet, showing what we can do in this direction. We ourselves consider it quite satisfactory, the only objection being that it slightly increases the difficulty of separating the Stamps, as the gum of necessity flows somewhat into the perforations. . . . In separating the sheets which are stuck together we cannot, we fear, avoid injuring some of them. We will pack the damaged sheets separately, labelling them as waste." These stamps arrived in Egypt at the same time as the first consignment of Egypt 1888 (Jan. 1), which was shipped on November 18, 1887.

The second instance occurred in connection with Greece 1901 (July)–1902, printed by Perkins, Bacon & Company. No sooner had the stamps been issued than the printers received complaints that the gumming was inadequate and the stamps failed to adhere to correspondence. The printers, who had gummed the paper but had not been responsible for ordering it to be manufactured, immediately submitted the problem to an expert. He reported: "Nothing but pure gum arabic has been used (not perishable in any way) and the quality is as good and the coating certainly as thick as on the English stamps. It is considered, however, that for two reasons the gum should have been thicker. First the paper used is considerably thicker and more stubborn than the English stamp paper. Secondly, the stationery used in Greece is evidently such that it is not so suitable. . . ." As a consequence of this report, the printers immediately added a further layer of gum to all the gummed sheets on hand. Later, the printers were supplied with thinner paper.

The gum on stamps that has been applied one layer after another is, sometimes, termed "layered gum"; or, if only two layers are used, "double gum" — as, for example, in the case of some instances of Great Britain 1911 (King Edward VII) 1d. and 2½d.

Seasonal Gums

The balance between a layer of gum adequate to serve the purpose of enabling the stamps to adhere, and a layer so thick as to give rise to other troubles, is a fine one and difficult, at times, to achieve. By hand or by machine, either at one operation or at successive operations, a very thick layer or an aggregate of thick layers of gum can be applied. The thickness of the layer or layers themselves, and the gum itself, are not the only factors affecting its adhesiveness or practicability.

Attempts made to stick a stamp to a rough or unsized paper, such as blotting paper, will soon reveal that much more effort is required to obtain adhesion than to smooth paper or well-sized paper.

If the layer or aggregate of layers of gum is too thick, it will become brittle in dry weather, losing flexibility and being liable to crack, while in damp weather it absorbs moisture and causes the sheets to stick together.

Some gums are more easily affected by damp than are others; for example, dextrine is more hygroscopic than is gum arabic.

In some countries, where extremes of temperature and humidity are encountered, different mixtures of gum have been employed for different seasons of the year. The gum, tempered with, for example, gelatine is calculated the better to withstand the atmospheric conditions prevailing. For example, in the United States, the Bureau of Engraving and Printing, with the packets of stamps, distributed circulars, of which the following is an example:

SUMMER GUM

To the Postmaster.

The stamps in this package are prepared with "hard" gum, and intended for use in the summer or humid season when there is much moisture in the atmosphere. This is necessary to prevent, as far as possible, the premature sticking together of the stamps, or the sticking to the paraffin paper when in book form. Notwithstanding the hardness of the gum, it may be affected by excessive moisture, and postmasters should therefore exercise the greatest care to keep the stamps in as dry a place as possible, and to dispose of them to the public before the dry, cold season sets in, when the effect of this hard gum is to cause the stamps to curl, break and crack.

Stamps for winter use are prepared with a softer gum suited to that season.

Edwin C. Madden,
Third Assistant Postmaster-General.

[He held office from July 1, 1899, to March 21, 1907.]

Hand-Gumming

All the early stamps issued with gum were gummed by hand — and many later issues have been hand-gummed. That is, after the stamps were printed, the backs of the sheets were covered with a solution of gum applied by means of a brush, rather after the manner of a paper-hanger or painter at work;

or, in later times, by means of a cloth-covered roller dipped in the solution and then rolled over the paper.

This form of gumming is termed "hand-gumming"; and, sometimes, brush-applied gum is referred to as "painted gum," while the term "rolled gum" or "hand-rolled gum" is used in reference to gum applied by a hand-operated roller.

For example, when Perkins, Bacon & Company was asked on behalf of New South Wales in 1849 for details of gumming procedure, the printers stated that the gum solution comprised three pounds of gum arabic dissolved in five pounds of water and strained twice, and the gum was applied to the sheets with a "No. 2 painters brush." They had, of course (but much against their will), been gumming the British stamps since about the middle of April 1840, and, when New South Wales asked for information, had had nine years' experience.

Perkins, Bacon & Company's early gum had been supplied by John Rawsthorne of Manchester; and, although it was half the price and was claimed to be purer and stronger than gum senegal or other foreign gums, the printers discovered early on that gumming was no easy task. Indeed, on April 22, 1840, they wrote: "we have now been five days occupied in gumming the stamps and the difficulties we have met with are beyond description."

Having had no experience to draw upon, they discovered, empirically, the correct thickness of the layer to apply; but this could be only an approximation because of the handwork involved. If the gum were applied too thinly, the stamps failed to adhere, and too thick a layer led to other difficulties. The drying sheets buckled and curled up tightly, and the gum separated, leaving ungummed patches on the sheets.

After trying several methods of supporting the sheets during gumming, Perkins, Bacon & Company found that the best results were obtained by placing the sheet upon a block slightly smaller than the sheet. This ensured that the edges of the sheet were almost free of gum, and enabled the wet sheets to be handled. (Later in the twentieth century, Perkins, Bacon used a traveling band to carry the sheets, but continued to hand-gum them.) The gum was applied hot; and, later, the sheets were placed in stacked wooden trays to dry. Afterward the sheets were pressed to flatten them. Often half a dozen or so were taken at a time and rolled together tightly first one way and then the other to counteract the tendency to curl.[19]

Perkins, Bacon & Company and De La Rue, which also hand-gummed sheets until 1880, used good quality brushes with closely packed bristles. As a result, although the layer tended to be uneven, it was the exception rather

---

[19]Incidentally, this sometimes caused the gum to fracture, but the significance of thus leaving room for expansion and contraction and, therefore, minimizing curling, was not appreciated by the printers. Not until many years later was this principle successfully exploited by Samuel Jones & Company.

[20]A streaked effect is not, however, limited exclusively to hand-gumming; somewhat similar effects are to be encountered on some machine-gummed issues. Further, the term "streaked gum" is to be distinguished from the term "gum streak," which was referred to earlier in this chapter under the heading "Printed on the Gummed Side."

Gum. Economy gum (*Spaargummi*). Finsterwalde (Germany, Local Issues) 1946 (Feb. 16) 60 + 40p., and the back of the stamp exhibiting economy gum. Applied by a specially shaped roller, the gum is interrupted by circular patches on which no gum appears. This gumming was effected at one operation.

than the rule for brush marks to be visible. In instances of other stamps, however, brush marks are clearly visible; and, sometimes, bristles or hairs from the brushes may be encountered at the backs of the stamps. Such brush marks have given rise to the philatelic terms "streaked gum" and "streaky gum."[20] Sometimes differentiation is made between "horizontal gum," in which the streaks appear from side to side in relation to the stamp design, and "vertical gum," in which the streaks appear upright in relation to the design.

The early difficulties that Perkins, Bacon & Company had experienced were

Gum. Economy gum. (*Spaargummi*). Plauen (Germany, Local Issues) 1945 12 + 8p., and the back of the stamp exhibiting economy gum. Applied by a specially shaped roller, the gum is interrupted by overlapping circular patches in parts of which no gum appears. The circles are somewhat indistinct because the gumming was effected at two operations, deliberately out of register with one another. Consequently the pattern is twice repeated.

Gum. Ridged gum. U.S. 1947 (Apr. 10) Joseph Pulitzer 3c., the back of the stamp and a photographic enlargement exhibiting prominently the variety ridged gum. The gumming, incorporating in the gum fountain the use of a "Monel" metal roller with a finely threaded surface, results in streams of gum upon the paper. These streams sometimes coalesce into a continuous smooth surface, but, in the instance pictured, they did not coalesce completely before the gum dried, and resulted in the variety ridged gum, somewhat resembling ribbing in the paper. The disturbance near the top of the gum resulted from the removal of an excessively moistened hinge.

re-experienced in the United States. So troublesome, indeed, were the gum and gumming that a representative was sent to Perkins, Bacon & Company to investigate. What happened is reported in the words of Joshua Butters Bacon: "within five months the contractors for the United States' postage came over here on purpose to get our gum; they said they had had all the difficulties it was possible to conceive and they could find none that would answer but ours; they got a letter to the very man who supplies us, and then employed him."[21] Perkins, Bacon and Company obtained its gum from a Mr. Gentile at 38 Walbrook, London.

The National Bank Note Company and the Continental Bank Note Company used dextrine, and the American Bank Note Company's formula of ingredients for stamp "paste" in 1893 was: two parts dextrine, one part acetic acid, five parts water and one part alcohol. The sheets were held in an iron

---

[21]*Report from the Select Committee on Postage Label Stamps* (1852), Page 165, question 1722. Perkins, Bacon & Company was then using a mixture of dextrine (potato starch and wheat starch) and gum.

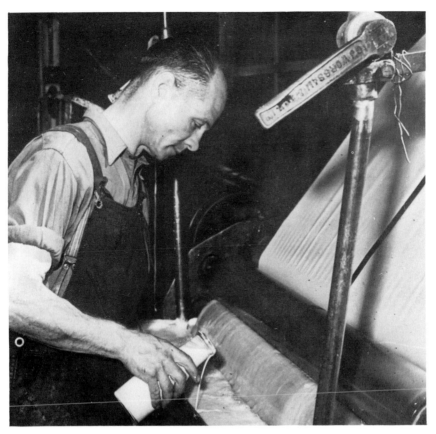

Gum. Machine-gumming. Adding milk to the solution of gum arabic to reduce frothing and crusting-over during working in a machine that was gumming two webs of paper passing through side by side at the works of Harrison & Sons Ltd. For many years, the milkman visited the works, but this interesting, domestic facet of modern stamp production has long been rendered obsolete by chemical research.

frame, or tympan, and the backs were coated with a large brush by "a dextrous young woman [who] can easily gum 30 or 40 sheets per minute." The tympan prevented the gum from reaching the edges of the sheets; and the sheets, held on wire frames, were dried in a heated drying room.

Machine-Gumming

In Britain, in 1880, De La Rue introduced gumming by machine; having filtered the gum solution, the printers fed it into the duct of a cylinder press,[22] and applied a coating of gum to the paper. The use of this type of machine has led to the application of the term "printed gum" in reference to such

---

[22]See the picture and the discussion, "Cylinder Presses," in the chapter entitled "Relief Printing."

Gum. Gum breaker. A general view of the "upright" gum-breaking machines (or gum-fracturing machines) in the works of Harrison & Sons Ltd. The gummed paper, led from the reel, was drawn over the diagonal knives in succession; this had the effect of breaking the gum layer into minute square- or diamond-shaped fragments. The paper was then re-wound in a reel. The operator is standing between the two reels that comprise this particular length of paper. Another gum-breaking machine, not in operation, is visible at the right.

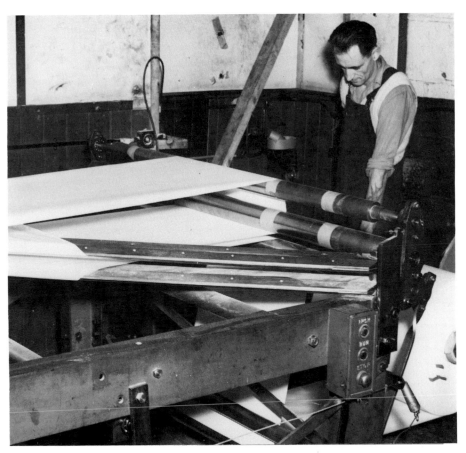

Gum. Gum breaker. A view of one end of a "horizontal" gum-breaking machine in the works of Harrison & Sons Ltd. The principle upon which this machine works is the same as that of the "upright" machine, but in the horizontal machine, the knives are parallel instead of at an angle to one another, the direction of the travel of the paper being reversed during its passage over the knives.

machine-applied gum, and to distinguish it from "painted gum." Sometimes the term "machine-rolled gum" is used to distinguish painted gum from "hand-rolled gum." The press was so adjusted that the gum was not printed to the very edges of the sheets, enabling them to be handled while still wet.

In New South Wales, in 1890, the sheets were machine-gummed on a cylinder press that delivered them face-upward on a rotating cloth from which they were taken and hung in a gas-heated drying cupboard.

The application of machine-rolled gum results in an even coating, and machine-gumming is, as a general rule, much more regular than hand-gumming. Some machines are capable of very fine adjustment, enabling the thickness of the layer of gum to be regulated within limits as narrow as between 0.0007 inch to 0.0009 inch.

Machine-gumming by means of rollers enables special results to be ob-

Gum. Ribbed gum. Germany 1921 (May) 10(p.), the back of the stamp and a photographic enlargement exhibiting vertical ribbed gum (or rippled gum) — the narrow vertical wavy lines — that resulted from the use of patterned rollers in a gum-breaking machine used for counteracting paper curl. The term used by the Germans for this type of gum is *geriffelter gummi*. The dark, irregular patches appearing on the back of the stamp and the enlargement are parts of the lozenge watermark.

tained. For example, during the period immediately after World War II in Germany, as a means of economizing on gum, and by the use of specially shaped rollers, gum was applied only to portions of the sheets; areas, usually circular in shape, were left without any gum at all. Such gumming has been termed "economy gum," "sparse gumming" or, in German, *"spaargummi,"* and is to be found, by way of examples only, on Thuringia (Germany, Russian Zone) 1945 (Oct. 1) 3(p.) to 30(p.); Finsterwalde (Germany, Local Issues) 1946 (Feb. 16) 60+40p.; and Plauen (Germany, Local Issues) 1945 12+8p. As a further example of special effects, the design printed on the back

Gum. Grilled gum. Switzerland 1934 5(c.), the back of the stamp and a photographic enlargement exhibiting grilled gum that resulted from the use of patterned rollers in a gum-breaking machine used for counteracting paper curl. This pattern is quite distinct from that of ribbed gum — compare the picture of Germany 1921 (May) 10(p.) — but, confusingly, both are referred to by the Germans as *geriffelter gummi*.

of Czechoslovakia 1923 Fifth Anniversary Commemorative has already been mentioned.[23]

At the Bureau of Engraving and Printing in Washington, D.C., the gumming machines during the early part of the present century were massive pieces of apparatus. Printed sheets were fed in, caught by metal fingers on an endless chain, drawn between two rollers of which the upper applied the gum, and were then carried slowly through a hot box about eighty feet long, from which they emerged dry, to be stacked originally by hand, but later automatically, ready for hydraulic pressure to flatten them. Then, until about

---

[23]See ''Pseudo-Watermarks'' in the discussion of ''Watermark Varieties'' in the chapter entitled ''Watermarks.''

1957, the gumming of flat-bed[24] printed postage stamps was accomplished on a flat-bed gumming machine where the sheets were fed into the grippers that carried them under a "Monel" metal roller that applied the gum. The gummed sheets were then rolled, and the gum broken so that the sheets would lie flat.[25]

"Monel" is a trade name designating a particular nickel alloy containing a large percentage of copper; it is especially resistant to corrosion. The surface of this "Monel" metal roller was provided with a fine thread on a lathe, for the purpose of controlling the proper amount of gum. This thread on the gum fountain roller resulted in fine streams of gum on the paper. When the paper was led away to be dried, the streams sometimes coalesced completely; more often, the streams did not coalesce completely before drying, resulting in the gum having a more or less ridged appearance, somewhat similar to uneven ribbing of the paper. This effect is termed "ridged gum" or, sometimes, "striped gum." Among the issues from which stamps can be found bearing this ridged gum, for example, may be mentioned U.S. 1946 (Feb. 26) Merchant Marine 3c.

In Great Britain, for the low-value stamps that were rotary-printed, after the paper was delivered from the mills to the printers, it was gummed on a machine in which a roller revolved in the gum trough. From this roller the gum was transferred to another roller, and from that to the web of paper. The gum used was gum arabic, which, agitated in solution, tended to froth and crust over during the gumming operations. For many years, Harrison & Sons Ltd. used to add fresh milk to the gum solution in the trough to prevent frothing; however, research overcame the difficulty, and less homely methods superseded the milk bottle. Since 1968, most British issues have been printed on paper with polyvinyl alcohol (PVA) as the adhesive.

In countries where machine-gumming superseded hand-gumming, the differences in appearance and regularity of application are useful in distinguishing one printing from another. An instance of this is to be found, for example, in Canada 1870-93, where the date and, indeed, place of printing can often be determined by determining whether the stamps were hand-gummed or machine-gummed.

Counteracting Paper Curl

The tendency of gummed paper to curl is known only too well to any collector who has ever left mint stamps exposed to air.

This propensity has always been a source of difficulty to stamp manufacturers. Indeed, it may be said to have been a great, if not the greatest, problem of production and handling.

Mention has already been made earlier in this chapter of the tight rolling by hand, first in one direction and then in another, of six or more dried,

---

[24]See "Flat-Bed Printing" in the alphabetical list to the chapter entitled "Printing Characteristics."

[25]In fact, from about 1954, pregummed paper has been used for flat-bed printed stamps in the United States.

Gum. Counteracting paper curl. U.S. 1956 (Jan. 10) Wilson 7c., rotary press printed and electric eye perforated, a plate number block of four and the back (photographed by oblique lighting) exhibiting slightly diagonal ridges resulting from the roller that, in the electric eye perforating machine, presses on the printed side of the paper and counteracts curling of the gummed paper.

gummed sheets at a time, and the subsequent flattening of sheets by pressure, that was sometimes hydraulic, to overcome the difficulty. These methods somewhat ameliorated the difficulty, but provided no cure. From time to time other methods were tried.

The Imperial Printing Works of Russia, from the outset of its issues in 1858, adopted the plan of coating the printing surface of the sheets with a solution of chalky size, and varied the manner of application. One of the objects of so doing was as a precaution against loss to the revenue from cleaning and re-use of the stamps;[26] but the primary objective was to counteract the tendency of a gummed sheet to curl — the idea behind the practice being that the atmosphere would act evenly on both sides of the paper, and, the stresses being equal, it would lie flat. Issues so treated, for example, include Russia 1883-88 1k. to 70k., and 1917-18 Severing the Chain 35k. to 70k.

More usually, however, the tendency to curl has been combated by treating the gum after it has been applied to the paper — subjecting it to a strain that fractures the gum film into minute fragments with even more minute air spaces between them, thus allowing for expansion and contraction of the individual fragments without the paper being affected. The principle is the same as that adopted for railway lines, to prevent their distortion in hot weather.

The machines that effect these results are termed "gum breakers," or "gum-fracturing machines," and two principal methods have been employed, of which, undoubtedly, the widest used in stamp production results in what is termed "non-curling gummed paper," developed and patented by Samuel Jones & Company. In this method, the paper, after it has been gummed, is drawn quickly and at acute angles over two knives in succession set across both diagonals of the width of the paper. The result of this is to split the

---

[26]See "Chalk" in the alphabetical list to the chapter entitled "Paper."

Gum. Dark brown gum. Schatzk (Russian Zemstvo) 1888 (Jun. 10) 3k., and the back of the stamp exhibiting dark brown gum. The very light patches at the back of the stamp are small pieces of paper adhering to the gum.

Streaked gum. These stamps were hand-gummed, and this stamp exhibits vertical brush marks, thus illustrating (vertical) streaky gum.

Gum stain. The gum has stained the paper, and the stains appear as irregular patches extending over most of the face of the stamp, thus illustrating the condition gum stained.

gum into minute squares or diamonds. This method was used, for example after World War II with two different models of machines, by Harrison & Sons Ltd. Instances of issues produced with the assistance of these gum breakers include Great Britain 1951 (May 3) Festival of Britain 2½d. and 4d., and New Zealand 1958 (Nov. 3) Centenary of Hawke's Bay Province 2d., 3d. and 8d.

The other method involves the use of rollers. Plain rollers have a limited effect in counteracting paper curl, but patterned rollers produce a better result. For example, the German State Printing Works, about 1921, introduced a new gum-breaking machine that resulted in the gum being impressed with a pattern of close, wavy lines that has been termed "rippled gum," or "ribbed gum," or, as the Germans themselves term it, "geriffelter gummi." Issues bearing rippled gum include, for example, Germany 1921 5p. to 50p., and most other German issues until 1945.

As in the case of "streaked gum," so in the case of rippled gum, sometimes differentiation is made between "vertical gum" and "horizontal gum" according to the way in which the ripples of gum appear in relation to the stamp design. The pressure used, sometimes, is sufficient to affect the paper itself, and stamps from which the gum has been removed have the appearance of being on ribbed paper.[27]

As a further example: From about 1932, Courvoisier produced Swiss stamps with the assistance of a gum-breaking machine that resulted in the gum being impressed with an all-over, close pattern of squares, reminiscent somewhat of certain grills used for U.S. 1867, and giving rise to the term "grilled gum" — although it also, and confusingly, is termed "*geriffelter gummi.*" Issues bearing grilled gum include, for instance, Switzerland 1936-42 3c. to 40c., and Liechtenstein 1937 Labor Issue 10r. to 50r.

On United States issues rotary-press printed on the web, a series of slightly diagonal ridges — about one-eighth inch wide and about one-quarter inch apart — result from the use of a roller that bears upon the printed side of the paper during its passage from the reel to the perforating wheels of the electric eye perforators. As a specific example, they are to be found on 1956 (Sep. 22) Nassau Hall 3c.

Tinted and Colored Gums

Passing mention has already been made in this chapter of the practice, adopted in connection with Great Britain 1854 6d. (embossed), of tinting the gum green to create a distinction between the gummed and ungummed sides of the paper.

Another instance of green-tinted gum occurs in the case of Switzerland 1924 50th Anniversary of UPU 20r., but the reason for the adoption of the colored gum in this instance is not clear — that is, other than experiments by the contractors, who used yellow and white gum as well.

The first issue with deliberately colored gum was Hanover 1850 1g., which had red gum. While the ability to distinguish the colored, gummed side from the uncolored, printing side of the paper may have been a factor in the decision to add color to the gum, another factor is said to have been that, if the stamp were applied to a letter but became detached (because of lack of adhesiveness or otherwise), the gum would leave a colored patch on the letter and so prevent its being dealt with as unpaid mail. On subsequent issues, Hanover continued to use its red gum, but on later issues it became rose, and on the last issue in 1864-65, the gum was white.

Except in the rare cases of deliberately tinted gum (as opposed to discolored gum), gum color varies for two reasons: the original constituents; and the effects of age, atmosphere and temperature. Dextrine, for example, is a variation of starch from one source or another[28] heated in solution either alone or in combination with acid or other chemicals. Its color depends upon the temperature to which the solution is heated — from almost colorless, or "white" through various shades of yellow to dark brown. Similarly, acacia gum, which is obtained from the plant, shrub or tree in different countries or places that give rise to the names "gum arabic," "gum senegal" and so

---

[27]See "Ribbed Paper" in the alphabetical list to the chapter entitled "Paper."
[28]For instance: corn starch, milo starch, tapioca starch, wheat starch.

on, varies somewhat in color according to its purity and country of origin. Animal glue also varies somewhat in color.

The gum used for stamps has varied enormously in composition, from "pure" gum arabic and "pure" dextrine to combinations of gum, dextrine and animal glue in different proportions and with and without additions of other substances. No purpose would be served here in attempting to set out those variations. See also "Polyvinyl Alcohol," Page 640.

The philatelist is little concerned with the actual gum formula except to the extent that, if one formula produces results demonstrably different from those produced by another formula, and those results assist in separating one issue from another, the characteristics will be noted and used for that purpose. On the other hand, chemical analysis of the gum may be used not only for that purpose but also for expertization in a case of suspected regumming or, indeed, of suspected application to a cover of a stamp that does not belong.

One of the difficulties associated with such tests is the obtaining of a sufficiently representative quantity of gum from the suspect item. However, one test that has been used successfully in gum analysis is chromatography, and the particular application of it employed in regard to stamps is known as "paper partition chromatography," discovered by A.J.P. Martin and R.L. Synge, who were awarded the Nobel Prize in 1952 for their discovery. The method depends upon the fact that the solubility of different substances differs in water (or a special solvent), and if the solution is made to travel along filter paper by capillary action, the different substances are carried different distances along the paper.[29]

Some very dark brown gums are encountered in philately. Among the darkest are, for example, Danish West Indies 1855 3c., of which the consignment sent from Denmark to Saint Thomas was affected by damp. On arrival, some of the sheets were gummed by a chemist named Beuzon of Saint Croix; his gum is distinguished by its dark brown color. Incidentally, other sheets were gummed in 1860 by another local chemist, called Rüse, and they are distinguished by the yellow color of his gum. The original "white" gum, applied in Denmark, is very rare. Other stamps with dark brown gum are, for example, Schatzk (Russian Zemstvo) 1888 (Jun. 10) 3k.

A greyish gum was used for Serbia 1869-80 10p. to 50p., printed during 1879 and 1880 at Belgrade. Some stamps of this issue were gummed with a mixture that included glycerine (added for the purpose of making the gum less brittle), which permeated the paper, causing it to appear more or less transparent, different from the stamps of the Vienna printings of 1869 that were made on thin, strong and slightly transparent paper.

Gum Staining

A not unusual occurrence is for the gum, especially the darker gums, to affect the color of the paper itself, either throughout or in patches, giving

---

[29]See *Maple Leaves* (journal of the Canadian Philatelic Society of Great Britain), Vol. 5, Pages 74-75, April 1954, "Paper Partition Chromatography," by J.S. Cannell.

Gum. Invisible gum. Venezuela 1959 8th Central American and Caribbean Games 50c., and the Airmail 50c. in the same series. The gum on the backs of these stamps is entirely invisible. The paper appears to be ungummed, and the gum is undetectable by visual inspection. When moistened and then dried, the gum is visible if the back of the stamp is held obliquely to the light, but appears matte.

rise to the term "gum-stained" in relation to the stamp. The stamps of the Danish West Indies 1855 and Schatzk (Russian Zemstvo) 1888 have already been mentioned in connection with dark brown gum; many of them are to be found gum-stained. As a further example chosen at random, in Portuguese India 1873 10r. to 900r. the paper was originally slightly bluish, but has been stained yellow by the gum in the majority of stamps.

Gum Textures

The texture of the gum presented to view depends upon many circumstances that are, philatelically speaking, usually only of academic importance. For example, during the period 1886 to 1888, when De La Rue was encountering complaints about its gum and gumming, the printers wrote that "under certain atmospheric conditions the gum dries on the sheets after application by us somewhat dull . . . but this does not in any way militate against its adhesive properties." Again, "we are led to believe that the complaints must have arisen through the gum having dried up with a dull appearance, and, as we explained to you, this is due to atmospheric causes entirely beyond our control.[30] As we believe we convinced you yesterday, a sheet of paper which has dried up dull in this way, although it has the appearance of having very little gum upon it, may have such an ample supply

---

[30]In those days, air conditioning (temperature and humidity control) played no part in the practice of stamp printers.

that . . . an attempt to raise the Stamps will result in the splitting of the paper. . . .''[31]

Broadly speaking, gum textures may be divided into two main groups — smooth and rough. The issues quoted as representative are no more than examples chosen at random.

Smooth gum can be divided into two classes — shiny and matte — and each of these classes can be further divided.

Shiny gum is represented by many degrees of shine that vary from moderate to glossy. Moderate shine is represented by the gum on Norway 1954 (Apr. 30) Railway Centenary 20ö to 55ö; while glossy shine appears on Portuguese India 1959 (Dec. 1) 5c. to 50e. Usually, if a stamp has gum with a highly glazed surface, two possibilities may account for it: first, that the stamp, originally provided with a thick layer of gum, has been carefully floated from adherent paper; or, second, that it has been stuck to or kept too long in a plastic mount.

Matte or dull gum can be more or less sharply divided into two sub-classes: visible and invisible. Matte or dull gum, clearly present, appears on Argentine Republic 1951 Five Year Plan 5c. to 40c. Almost invisible gum is to be found on Brazil 1939 (Dec. 20) Pro Juventude 100 + 100r. to 1,200 + 400r., and on some of the later World War II issues in Europe. For instance, it is present on Finland 1945 Sports Fund 1m. + 50p. to 7m. + 3m.50.

However, gum that is entirely invisible and defies normal visual perception unless wetted and allowed to dry is to be found on Venezuela 1959 Eighth Central American and Caribbean Games 5c. to 50c. Similarly invisible gum is found on the reverse, on the microprinted foil laminate used for Tonga 1963 (Jul. 15) First Polynesian Gold Coinage Commemoration, Regular 1d. to 2s., Air 10d. to 2s.9d. and Official Air 15s., and on many contemporary issues on which polyvinyl acetate was used as an adhesive.

Rough gum can be divided, broadly, into five different classes:

1. Crazed or crackly gum, which can exist irrespective of the original method of application, and which is to be found on many issues, including Suez Canal Company 1868 (July) 1c. to 40c.

2. Spotted gum, which comprises gum showing the effect of many dried small air bubbles. This, again, is found on many issues, but is an especially inconstant factor, depending upon fortuitous circumstances of application, and is found, frequently, in conjunction with crazed gum. It is to be found, for instance, on some examples of Honduras 1865 2r., particularly the green stamp.

3. Streaked gum, which comprises gum showing the effect of its application by brush.

4. Ridged gum, which is an effect peculiar to the gumming of stamps by machine where fine streams of gum do not entirely coalesce before drying — to be found on many U.S. stamps issued after 1922, including 1947 (Apr. 10) Joseph Pulitzer 3c.

5. Ribbed or rippled gum, in which the evenness of the gum has been

---

[31]*The De La Rue History of British and Foreign Postage Stamps 1855 to 1901*, by John Easton (1958), Pages 480, 481.

deliberately broken by treatment with rollers to counteract curling, and has resulted in a ribbed or rippled effect, sometimes imparted also to the paper. It is to be found on many issues printed by the German State Printing Works, including 1925 (May 30) Munich Exhibition 5p. and 10p. In this class, also, is "grilled" gum found on many stamps of Switzerland and Liechtenstein issued after 1932. Also in this class are the rotary-press printed issues of the United States bearing slightly diagonal marks in the paper resulting from the roller that is made to press upon the printed side of the paper after the web is unrolled and as it is fed into the perforating machine.

A philatelically unprecedented form of "gum" was incorporated in the production of Sierra Leone 1964 (Feb. 10) World's Fair New York, Regular 1d. to 5s. and Air 7d. to 11s. produced by the Walsall Lithographic Company. These (incidentally, the first "free form" stamps) and other such issues are referred to as "self-adhesive" in that it is unnecessary to apply moisture to cause them to stick. One side of the paper is coated with a pressure-sensitive material that remains permanently activated, the coating being applied by the paper-makers, Samuel Jones & Company Ltd. To enable it to be handled not only during stamp production but also afterward, the coated side of the paper is covered by a colored base sheet, and to enable the stamp to be easily separated from the base sheet it is coated with silicone release lacquer. The technique has had increasingly wide commercial application for small labels used as price tags and for other nonpermanent identification purposes. When the stamp is peeled from the base sheet paper, the pressure-sensitive side of the stamp will adhere to the envelope or whatever it is put into contact with under light pressure. The collection of used stamps is not an impossibility, despite the permanent activation of the adhesive. The adhesive can be removed by the use of benzine or lighter fuel, but care is advisable, with some stamps, to avoid contact with the ink.

In the United States, an experimental self-adhesive issue was made for 1974 (Nov. 15) Christmas Peace on Earth precanceled 10c. The imperforate stamps adhered to backing paper that was rouletted, and the stamps themselves had crossed slits through the central part of the design, a dove appearing on the weather vane at the top of Mount Vernon.[32] The experiment was not repeated.[33]

Experiments were carried out in 1985 by Walsall Security Printers under the direction of the Post Office of the Government of Tonga for the issue of self-adhesive stamps in perforated sheets as distinct from die-cut stamps on backing paper that was perforated. The first such stamps issued were Tonga 1985 (May 28) Marine Life 9s. The experiments failed because of what were described as "unsurmountable production difficulties" — in fact, critical temperature controls. The paper had to be refrigerated before perforating because, otherwise, the adhesive clogged the perforator, which had to be stopped and cleaned frequently.

---

[32]For a detailed description of the steps involved in the production process, see "Self-stick stamp experiment a failure" by George Amick in *Linn's Stamp News*, Vol. 56, Issue 2873 (Nov. 28, 1983), Page 20.

[33]Until U.S. 1989 (Nov. 10) 25c. self-adhesive, die-cut "EXTRAordinary Stamps."

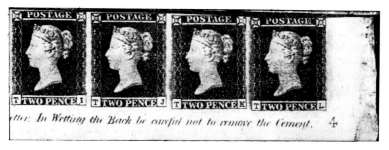

Gum. Cement. Great Britain 1841 2d. plate 4, a marginal strip bearing part of the inscription. The complete text is: "PRICE 2d. Per Label. 2s/- Per Row of 12. £2. Per Sheet. Place the Labels ABOVE the Address and towards the RIGHT HAND SIDE of the Letter. In Wetting the Back be careful not to remove the Cement."

Varieties and Terms of Gum

Acacia Gum. Gum obtained from the acacia plant, shrub or tree, being "tears" that form after the bark is stripped. Such gum is often named after the district in which the gum is collected — for example, "gum arabic," "gum senegal," "gum syriac." See "Colored Gum."

Arabic Gum — see "Acacia Gum."

British Gum — see "Dextrine."

Broken Gum. This term is used to designate the appearance presented by innumerable minute particles roughly similar in size and shape — squares or diamonds — caused by passing gummed paper through a gum-fracturing machine to counteract paper curl. Contrast "Cracked Gum." See "Gum Breaker." Fractured gum is used as a synonym for broken gum.

Cement. A synonym for gum. The term cement was employed officially in reference to the gum used for the first adhesive postage stamps — Great Britain 1840 1d. and 2d.; and each sheet bore a marginal inscription reading: "In wetting the back be careful not to remove the cement."

Colored Gum. This term is used, philatelically, to designate gum that has been deliberately tinted with color, as opposed to gum that has discolored because of age or atmospheric conditions, or is colored because of the nature of the adhesive matter used. The use of colored gums for stamps used to be comparatively rare; red- and rose-colored gum was used for Hanover 1850, 1851-55 and later issues; green-colored gum was used for Great Britain 1854 6d. (embossed), the later printings, and Switzerland 1924 50th Anniversary of UPU 20r., some copies; and yellow gum is to be found on many issues — including, for example, Danish West Indies 1855 (1860) 3c. ("Rüse" gum) — but this is, usually, the color of the adhesive matter used. Few gums are, naturally, colorless. Acacia gum varies from almost white to amber; dextrine powder varies from pale yellow to dark brown; animal or fish glue is more or less brown. These colors are strengthened or reduced by constituents in the gum formula used for particular issues. In Britain, after polyvinyl alcohol was adopted in place of gum arabic in 1968, at first yellowish, and later pale bluish-green coloring matter was added to make the adhesive visible.

Cracked Gum. This term is used to designate the appearance presented by numerous small particles differing widely in size and shape, caused by haphazard fracture of the gum layer by hand-rolling the sheets, or by age and atmospheric conditions. Contrast "Broken Gum." The terms crackly gum and crazed gum are used as synonyms for cracked gum. All old stamps with thick layers of hand-applied gum have cracked gum — for example, Great Britain 1858-64 1d.

Crackly Gum — see "Cracked Gum."

Crazed Gum — see "Cracked Gum."

Dextrine. A water-soluble, gummy substance into which starch is converted when heated to a high temperature. "Dextrine" was so named because it, unlike other substances, turns the plane of polarization to the right (*dexter*). Dextrine is obtained from many sources, including maize, milo, potato, tapioca, and wheat, and was commercially named British Gum and Leiocome, and is sometimes termed starch gum. See "Colored Gum."

Discolored Gum. This term is applied to an adhesive substance that has, since it was applied to the paper, undergone a change of color, usually to a darker shade. Most gums discolor upon exposure to hot or humid atmosphere. See "Colored Gum."

Double Gum. This term is used to designate two separate layers of adhesive applied to the back of a stamp. Usually, double gumming has been resorted to

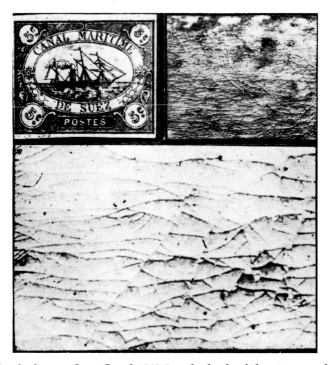

Gum. Cracked gum. Suez Canal 1868 5c., the back of the stamp and a photographic enlargement exhibiting cracked gum, being numerous small particles differing widely in size and shape and caused by haphazard fracture of the gum layer by hand-rolling the sheets (and by age combined with atmospheric conditions). Such treatment caused widely differing effects. Compare this illustration with that of Great Britain 1858-64 1d.

Gum flaw. Surcharge partly albino. Sarawak 1892 (May 23) ONE CENT on 3c. On this block of six from the top of the sheet, the surcharge is complete on only the two left-hand stamps. On the other stamps, the surcharge is partly albino because it was printed on top of gum spots and patches that were dissolved away, carrying the surcharging ink with them, when the block was soaked.

because the first layer proved insufficiently adhesive; instances of double gumming are encountered on some examples of Egypt 1884 (Dec. 15) 10 par., 20 par. and 5 pi.; Greece 1901 (July)–1902; and Great Britain 1911 (King Edward VII) 1d. and 2½d. See "Layered Gum."

Dull Gum. The qualification "dull" or "matte" is applied to gum when it does not shine, as contrasted with "shiny gum." See "Shiny Gum." Dull gum is divisible into two classes: clearly visible gum and invisible gum. See "Invisible Gum."

Economy Gum. This term is used to designate a layer of adhesive applied by roller so cut out that the gum reaches only portions of the paper, the intention being to conserve gum supplies — or to designate a very thin layer of gum applied with the same intention (sometimes termed "sparse gum"), as in the case, for example, of China 1902-1903 ½c. to $5. Economy gum applied so as to leave circular ungummed areas is to be found, for example, on Finsterwalde (Germany, Local Issues) 1946 (Feb. 16) 60+40p.

Fractured Gum — see "Broken Gum."

Geriffelter Gummi — see "Ribbed Gum"; see also "Grilled Gum."

Glazed Gum. This term is used to designate a layer of adhesive matter that has a glassy shine, as contrasted with glossy gum. See "Glossy Gum." Glazed gum is not natural, and occurs sometimes when a stamp with shiny gum is kept too long in or stuck to a plastic mount, or when a stamp with a thick layer of shiny gum, having become attached to paper, has been carefully floated from it and dried in contact with shiny plastic.

Glossy Gum. This term is used to designate a layer of adhesive matter that has a hard, shiny surface, to be found, for example, on Portuguese India 1959 (Dec. 1) 5c. to 50e. Contrast "Glazed Gum." See "Shiny Gum."

Glue. Strictly, gelatin obtained from animal or fish sources. The use of the term and the substance in connection with stamps is rare. See "Gum."

Grilled Gum. This term is used to designate the appearance presented by minute square or oblong indentations in the layer of adhesive matter (sometimes affecting the paper of the stamp) caused by passing the gummed paper through a machine that has a patterned roller to counteract paper curl. See "Paper Curl." Grilled gum is to be found, for example, on many stamps of Switzerland and Liechtenstein issued after 1932, including Switzerland 1936-42 3c. to 40c., and Liechtenstein 1937 Labor Issue 10r. to 50r. The term grilled gum derives from grilled paper. See "Grill" in the alphabetical list to the chapter entitled "Paper." Contrast "Ribbed Gum."

Gum. A generic term, used philatelically, in reference to adhesive substances employed for stamps. The term gum is used irrespective of the origin and the purity or combinations of the substances used in the gum solution. See "Acacia Gum," "Dextrine," "Glue," "Paste."

Gum Arabic — see "Acacia Gum."

Gum Blister. The result of a condition that sometimes occurs if the layer of adhesive is dried by excessive heat. The gum blisters, and leaves patches of ungummed paper.

Gum Breaker. A machine through which the gummed paper is passed, being drawn sharply over knives, set at an angle, that fracture the layer of adhesive matter into innumerable minute particles roughly similar in size and shape — squares or diamonds — with the object of counteracting paper curl. See "Paper Curl."

Gum Crease. This term is used to designate a defect in the collectible condition of a stamp, caused by the paper fibers being fractured or sharply bent as a result of the paper buckling or folding during the application of the gum, or because the gum has cracked severely after gumming, usually owing to age and atmospheric conditions. See "Cracked Gum."

Gum Damage. The adverse effect upon the collectible condition of a stamp resulting from the application of gum, whether because of creasing, cracking, chemical reaction or staining. Because of its imprecision, the term gum damage is rarely employed. See "Gum Crease"; "Gum Stain." Examples of chemical reaction between gum and paper, resulting from sulfuric acid, are to be found in Germany Air 1936 50p. and 75p., in which the paper has perished unless the gum has been removed.

Gum Flaw. This term is used to designate a variety exhibiting a partial albino impression resulting from printing on paper that has been unintentionally splashed or streaked with gum. Because the printing ink could not reach the surface of the paper beneath the splashes or streaks of gum, the design (and postmark, if any) bears uncolored patches, the ink being carried away when the stamp was washed or soaked for the purpose of removing adherent paper. The variety is inconstant, is liable to occur on any stamps printed on pre-gummed paper, and can occur, also, in the cases of overprints and surcharges. Instances are to be found, for example, in Union of South Africa 1913 (Sep. 1)–1921 1d. (basic stamp) and Sarawak 1892 (May 23) 1c. on 1871 (Jan. 1) 3c. (surcharge). The terms gum spot and gum streak are used, sometimes more graphically, to designate gum flaws. Compare "Printed on the Gum."

Gummed on the Printed Side. This term is used to designate a rare class of stamps printed in reverse on resinized paper through which the design shows, the printed side of the paper then being gummed over the design, the intention being that, once affixed, the stamp cannot be removed without destroying the design. See "Goldbeater's Skin" in the alphabetical list to the chapter entitled "Paper." Compare "Printed on the Gum."

Gum Senegal — see "Acacia Gum."

Gum Spot — see "Gum Flaw"; contrast "Spotted Gum."

Gum Stain. Discoloration, usually in irregular patches, upon the face of a stamp caused by the gum permeating the paper. Gum stains result, usually, from gums that, either originally or by reason of age and atmospheric conditions, are dark.

Gum Streak — see "Gum Flaw"; contrast "Streaky Gum."

Gum Watermark — see "Pseudo-Watermarks" in the chapter entitled "Watermarks." An appearance of double or ghost watermarks associated with gum sometimes occurs when gummed paper is plate-glazed. Plate glazing involves milling the sheets between polished metal plates in a powerful press. The sheets, face outward with a plain sheet of paper interleaved between the gummed surfaces, are placed between the metal plates and subjected to great pressure. This, apart from creating a glaze on the printed surface, results in the watermarks being imparted, as slight protuberances, to the interleaving paper; and when this interleaving paper is subsequently used for other sheets, the pressure results in false watermarks being imparted to them additional to the true watermarks. A somewhat similar effect may be encountered if no interleaving paper is used. Instances of such occurrences are encountered occasionally, for example, in Great Britain 1912-22 ½d. to 1s., and Egypt 1879 1pi. on mint examples. The gum watermark (or phantom watermark, or ghost watermark) disappears when the gum is washed off.

Hand-Gummed. Gummed manually by use of a brush or roller. Brush-applied gum is sometimes termed painted gum; the term hand-rolled gum is sometimes used to distinguish handwork from gum applied by machine. Sometimes brush work results in visible brush marks — that is, sometimes, brush work results in "streaky gum," comprising streaks of, usually, irregular widths. Contrast "Ridged Gum." Until about 1880, all stamps were hand-gummed. Compare "Machine-Gummed"; see "Horizontal Gum," "Vertical Gum."

Hand-Rolled Gum — see "Hand-Gummed."

Hard Gum — see "Seasonal Gum."

Horizontal Gum. This term is used to designate the appearance presented when a pattern, regular or irregular, is visible in the layer of adhesive matter, and the main direction of the pattern runs from side to side in relation to the stamp design.

Gum. Cracked gum. Great Britain 1858–64 1d. (the "Plate Number Penny") plate 222, the back of the stamp and a photographic enlargement exhibiting cracked gum, being numerous small particles differing widely in size and shape and caused by haphazard fracture of the gum layer by hand-rolling the sheets (and by age combined with atmospheric conditions). Such treatment caused widely differing effects. Compare this illustration with that of Suez Canal 1868 5c.

Streaky gum, resulting from brush application, and ribbed gum are often qualified as "horizontal." Contrast "Vertical Gum."

Invisible Gum. This term is used to designate adhesive matter that cannot be detected by visual inspection, as occurring, for example, on Venezuela 1959 Eighth Central American and Caribbean Games 5c. to 50c. Other instances of gum that is visible only under close examination occur, as examples, on Brazil 1939 (Dec. 20) Pro Juventute 100+100r. to 1,200+400r. and Finland 1945 Sports Fund 1m.+50p. to 7m.+3m.50.

Layered Gum. Gum that has been applied one layer after another at separate operations until an adequate thickness has been built up. Layered gum is encountered only on stamps printed on thick paper. Compare "Double Gum."

Leiocome — see "Dextrine."

Machine-Gummed. Gummed by use of a machine that consists, usually, of a trough of adhesive matter in which a roller revolves in contact with another roller that receives the gum and transfers it to paper pressed into contact by yet a third roller. By careful adjustment of the various pressures, the thickness of the gum on the paper can be controlled to within very fine limits. Such gum is sometimes termed printed gum to distinguish it from painted gum. Compare "Hand-Gummed."

Machine-Rolled Gum. This term is occasionally used to designate a layer of adhesive matter applied by a machine using rollers, to distinguish machine work from handwork. Compare "Hand-Gummed."

Matte Gum — see "Dull Gum."

O.G., Original Gum. This term is used, philatelically, to designate the layer of adhesive matter placed on the paper before the stamp was issued, and to distinguish such gum from adhesive matter subsequently (and, usually, fraudulently) applied to simulate the original gum. See "Regummed." Some stamps were issued ungummed, and such issues cannot bear original gum. See "Ungummed," "Without Gum."

PVA — see "Polyvinyl Alcohol."

Painted Gum — see "Hand-Gummed."

Paper Curl. The result of stresses placed on paper by coating one side of it with a layer of adhesive matter, which causes the sheet of gummed paper, especially in certain conditions of dry heat and atmosphere, to roll itself up into a cylinder. This tendency to curl is a great problem in stamp production, particularly when printing is effected on pregummed paper. Paper curl can be counteracted in various ways: by coating both sides, so that the stresses are equal or nearly so, as in the case, for instance, of Russia 1883-88 1k. to 70k.; or by fracturing the gum by hand-rolling the sheets in different directions; by fracturing the gum by machine — see "Gum Breaker"; by impressing the gummed side of the paper with a pattern, as in the cases of grilled gum and ribbed gum — see "Grilled Gum," "Ribbed Gum"; and by pressing on the printed side of the paper with a roller imparting slightly diagonal impressions, as in the case of those incorporated in the electric eye perforator used for many U.S. issues including, for example, 1956 (Jan. 10) Wilson 7c.

Passant pour Neuf. This term, French for "reputedly brand new" or "reputedly mint," is used to designate a stamp that has been attached to mail, has missed cancellation, and has been removed, thus losing its original gum (if any).

Paste. This term has been applied to the adhesive matter used for early stamps of the United States, the formula being: two parts dextrine, one part acetic acid, five parts water, one part alcohol. Dissolve two parts dextrine in five parts water and one part acetic acid, try the acid by heat, and then add one part of ninety percent alcohol. Philatelic use of the term paste is, however, rare; the term almost universally employed is gum. See "Gum."

Patterned Gum. A generic term used in reference to a layer of adhesive matter exhibiting evidence that it has been treated deliberately, by roller or otherwise, and bearing a design comprising indentations or a picture. See "Economy Gum," "Grilled Gum," "Gum Watermark," "Ribbed Gum."

Polyvinyl Alcohol. An adhesive substance used in place of gum arabic and other adhesives for postage stamps. Philatelic usage is to employ the abbreviation PVA for the adhesive. A less equivocal abbreviation is PVAl, to distinguish the substance from polyvinyl acetate (PVAc), which has been used as an adhesive for stationery. An alternative acronym is PVOH. PVA is, usually, matte and all but invisible, unlike gum arabic, which is usually shiny and clearly visible when used. Also, unlike gum arabic, PVA does not cause the paper to curl and does not need to be fractured. In Britain from 1973 onward, PVA adhesive has had dextrine added and has been referred to as PVAD. Also, coloring matter has been added to make the adhesive visible.

Pregummed Paper. Paper that bears gum applied before the stamp design is printed. For many years, only embossing and relief printing were effected on pregummed paper. Today, most stamps are printed on it.

Printed Gum — see "Machine-Gummed"; distinguish "Gum Watermark."

Printed on the Gum. This term is used to designate an error that occurs when a sheet of pregummed paper receives a print on the wrong surface, so that the design lies on the gum instead of on the paper itself. If the stamp were to be washed, the design would disappear with the dissolving gum. Instances of printed on the gum occur, for example, in Great Britain 1887 Jubilee 1d. Sometimes the term "printed on the gummed side" is used in reference to the error "printed on the gum." However, "printed on the gummed side" is somewhat equivocal in meaning, being capable of embracing "gummed on the printed side." See "Gummed on the Printed Side." See also "Gum Flaw."

Regummed. This term is used, philatelically, to designate a stamp from which all or part of the original gum has been removed, and to which a fresh layer of or some new adhesive matter has been applied — usually fraudulently, to simulate the original gum. See "Original Gum." Sometimes regumming can be detected because of incorrect texture or color, or because the gum tends to fall away from, or "flag" at the edges, or because it appears on the thickness of paper within the perforation holes or at the edges of the teeth. From the point of view of a stamp manufacturer, regumming involves adding a further layer of gum, as in (and see) "Double Gum" and "Layered Gum."

Ribbed Gum. This term is used to designate a layer of adhesive matter of which the evenness has been deliberately broken into closely set, narrow, parallel strips, with minutely undulating edges, by treatment with rollers for the purpose of counteracting paper curl. The term rippled gum is used as a synonym for ribbed gum. Instances are to be found, for example, on some copies of Germany 1947 (Sep. 2) Leipzig Fair 12p. and 75p. Contrast "Grilled Gum."

Ridged Gum. This term is used to designate a layer of adhesive matter that appears uneven in regular parallel stripes resulting from the use of a finely threaded "Monel" metal roller in the gum fountain so that the gum reached the paper in fine streams that did not coalesce entirely before drying. In the case of yellowish gum, the tint appears more pronounced and the gum more opaque in the humps of the ridges. Sometimes the term striped gum is used as a synonym for ridged gum. Instances are to be found on many U.S. stamps, including, for instance, 1948 (Nov. 19) Gettysburg Address 3c. Contrast "Streaked Gum."

Riffled Gum. A synonym for "rippled gum." See "Ribbed Gum."

Rippled Gum — see "Ribbed Gum."

Rolled Gum. Gum applied by hand- or machine-roller. See "Machine-Rolled Gum."

Seasonal Gum. Gum of which the formula contains ingredients calculated to make the gum particularly resistant to the weather and atmospheric conditions obtaining when the stamps are intended to be sold. Gum for use in summer months, termed "hard gum," causes the sheets to curl, break and crack in cold weather; "soft gum" resists the cold better, but is affected by moisture. For example, in the United States, the Bureau of Engraving and Printing distributed circulars giving instructions about the particular "seasonal gum" in the accompanying packet of stamps.

Self-Adhesive. This term is used to designate pressure-sensitive material, permanently activated, and coated to paper so that no moistening is required to enable the stamp to adhere. To avoid premature and unwanted adhesion, the back of the stamp paper is protected by a colored base sheet coated with silicone release lacquer, and the stamp is easily peeled away for use. The first self-adhesive stamps were Sierra Leone 1964 (Feb. 10) World's Fair New York, Regular 1d. to 5s. and Air 7d. to 11s.

Senegal Gum — see "Acacia Gum."

Shiny Gum. The qualification "shiny" is applied to gum when contrasted with "matte" or "dull" gum. Many degrees of shine can be found on different issues. See "Dull Gum," "Glossy Gum."

Soft Gum — see "Seasonal Gum."

Spaargummi — see "Economy Gum."

Spotted Gum. This term is used to designate a layer of adhesive matter with a rough, pitted surface resulting from dried air bubbles caused by frothing of the gum solution during application. It occurs in both hand- and machine-gumming, and is a particularly inconstant feature. Instances are to be found, for example, on some copies of Honduras 1865 2r.

Starch Gum — see "Dextrine."

Streaked Gum, Streaky Gum — see "Hand-Gummed"; contrast "Ridged Gum."

Striped Gum — see "Ridged Gum."

Tinted Gum — see "Colored Gum," "Discolored Gum."

Ungummed. This term is used, philatelically, to designate an issue made without gum by reason of climate, primitive resources of production, or emergency conditions. Many stamps have been so issued, and the general catalogues often make reference to the absence of gum in the headings to the issues concerned, but these references are not comprehensive. See "Without Gum."

Vertical Gum. This term is used to designate the appearance presented when a pattern, regular or irregular, is visible in the layer of adhesive matter, and the main direction of the pattern is upright in relation to the stamp design. Ribbed gum is frequently, streaky gum is less often, qualified as vertical. Contrast "Horizontal Gum."

Without Gum. This term is sometimes used to designate a stamp that was issued with original gum but has lost it — that is, "without gum" is used in contradistinction to the term ungummed. See "Ungummed." Sometimes "without gum" is used as a synonym for ungummed. The two uses of the term often create confusion, unless the meaning can be ascertained from the context.

15. Separation

PHILATELICALLY CONSIDERED, "separation" (or its plural form, "separations") is a generic term for the different methods of rendering a stamp or part of a stamp easily detachable as a unit from contiguous paper or stamps. These methods are known philatelically as perforation and rouletting.

Philatelically considered, "perforation" comprises the effect of the actual or intended removal from the sheet of many small, usually circular, pieces of paper; "rouletting" comprises the effect of actually piercing through the sheet, thus cutting or disturbing but not removing any part of the paper. It is worth emphasizing that philatelic usage limits the meaning of the unqualified terms "perforation" and "rouletting" to these *effects*, and does not take into account at all the method by which the effect is produced. That is to say, from the point of view of philatelic classification, separation may be divided into two broad and exclusive classes — perforation and rouletting — irrespective of the fact that each effect can be produced by different methods of application.

From the point of view of production, separation may be divided into two broad and exclusive classes that bear no relation to the effect produced. These classes are "stroke" or "flat bed," and "rotary." As these terms imply, stroke separation is effected by a blow or pressure upon the paper held on a flat support, while rotary separation is effected by passing the paper between rotating wheels or cylinders.

Philatelic interest in separation lies in the fact that, apart from being one of the processes used in the production of many stamps, it has resulted in the evolution of standards of classification by reference to which two otherwise similar stamps may be distinguished from one another. In the case of a significant variation, these standards may enable one printing or issue to be distinguished from another. That is to say, in many cases variations occur that are unimportant, except as instances of what can occur. In other cases, similar variations may reveal the use of a new method of production.

Before I go on to deal in greater detail with the various separations and variations, I believe it may be helpful to summarize the several different classes of standards that have evolved philatelically for the purpose of classifying stamps issued normally with or without separation. These classes may be summarized and grouped as follows:

First: *without separation*, termed "imperforate"; and *with separation*, termed "perforated" or "rouletted." The latter are subdivided, sometimes, into "of-

643

ficial" or "private," depending on whether the separations formed part of the plan of issue or were applied, after issue, by users of the stamps.

Second: *measurement*. The universal standard of measurement is the number of holes or cuts occurring within the length of two centimeters; with a subdivision when the number varies on contiguous or opposite sides, termed "compound," and a further subdivision when the number varies along the length of the same line of holes or cuts, termed "irregular" or "roughly" followed by a number.

In the vast majority of cases, measurement as such plays no part in reference to perforation. The only measurement involved was fixed in 1866 when the standard was adopted — namely, two centimeters. Thus, philatelic references are to the number of holes (or slits) in a length of two centimeters. That number is easily ascertained by use of an instrument called a "gauge." This avoids the need to perform any original measurement. The correct term for the operation of ascertaining the number by means of this instrument is "gauging." However, almost universally, the term used — albeit incorrectly — is "measuring."

In connection with perforation, the rare occasions when any implicit reference to measurement as such is made is when differences in the size of individual holes occur. On these rare occasions, the holes made by different perforating machines are contrasted — for example, by "large" and "small" — without any specific reference being made to the actual measurement of the relevant individual holes.

Third: *perforation*. This group contains five main standards:

(a) a standard based on the form of application — that is, (i) when applied to one side or two opposite sides of the stamp at a time, termed "line perforation," (ii) when applied to three sides of at least one row of stamps at a time, termed "comb perforation," with subdivisions, sometimes, into "vertical" (upright and inverted) and "horizontal" or "sideways" (left-to-right and right-to-left) and "reversed" (if the stamp design is face down when perforations are applied from the back of the sheet), depending upon the way the sheet was fed into the machine, and (iii) when applied to a whole pane or sheet at a time, termed "harrow perforation."

(b) a standard based on the comparative sizes of the pieces of paper removed, termed "large holes," "small holes," "large pins," "small pins," or "fine," "coarse," etc.

(c) a standard based on the shape of the paper removed, termed "round," "oval," "square," etc.

(d) a standard based on the appearance of the individual holes, termed "clean cut," "rough," etc.

(e) a standard based on the method of application, termed "stroke" or "flatbed" or "guillotine" and "rotary."

Fourth: *rouletting*. A single standard based on the shapes of the cuts in the paper, and comprising a list of terms arbitrarily chosen as being descriptive of the shapes.

Fifth: a class based on variations from the norm represented by the four classes of standards described above. That is to say, all of the standards described above may be regarded, generically, as *varieties of separation;* all were intentionally applied, and whether any particular variety of separation is usual or unusual on a particular issue or sheet depends upon the circumstances of production. The fifth class may be termed, generically, *varieties of separating.* All are unintentional, and owe their existence to the hazards of production that lead to abnormalities and freaks.

Varieties of separating include stamps imperforate between; with double or more separation; with separations unintentionally running through the designs; with indentations in, instead of pieces removed from, the paper and so on. Varieties of separating are likely to occur irrespective of the method actually adopted to effect the intended result. They occur only because different methods exist for effecting different results, and may be likened to the effects resulting from the use of different methods of printing.

Denticulated

In regard to separation, philatelic English usage suffers from a surprising lacuna that exists, so far as I am aware, in no other language.

Perforation comprises the making of small holes that in fact or in intention are in rows and usually surround and separate stamps in a sheet; and a sheet with such holes is properly and logically referred to as "perforated." Incidentally, those parts of the paper separating the holes from one another in the same line are, sometimes, termed "bridges," the arrangement being hole, bridge, hole, bridge and so on. When a single stamp is detached completely from the sheet, the stamp ceases to be surrounded by these holes, and, therefore, logically cannot be said to be perforated.

The early collectors and writers in the philatelic press were well-aware of the distinction. In *The Stamp-Collector's Magazine,* Vol. 2, Page 184 (December 1864), the following appears: "The impression is blue on white, and it is perforated, or, as the French, with much better reason, render it, *dentilated.*" Two years later, Adelaide Lucy Fenton, writing in *The Philatelist,* Vol. 1, Page 3 (December 1866), asked: "Is perforated or denticulated the correct word? . . . When together, stamps are certainly perforated, not denticulated. When separate, denticulated, decidedly not perforated. Therefore, a word is still needed which shall comprehend the aggregate and separate state."

Writing much more than a century later, I am constrained to accept that no such word has been coined to fill the gap, and a stamp bearing evidence of having come from a perforated sheet is referred to as "perforated" — this, in spite of the added difficulty, almost unknown to those early writers,[1] caused by the existence and collection of stamps that are, indeed perforated — with initials and devices. To designate such stamps, uneasy terms have been pressed into use — terms such as "perfins," "punch perforated," "punctured" and "spifs."

---

[1]The official stamps of Western Australia were an exception, and, writing about them in *The Stamp-Collectors' Magazine* for April 1867 (Vol. 5, Page 62), Overy Taylor stated: "The official puncture in the centre . . . is found in all varieties. . . . The plan of perforating stamps intended for official correspondence is a unique one. . . ."

In the early philatelic press, efforts were made to introduce a term for the singular state, and words such as "dentilated," "dents," and "notch-framed," among others, can be found.

The illogicality of the use of the term "perforated" to describe a single stamp from a perforated sheet is emphasized when reference is made, as is often the case, particularly in connection with a stamp's condition, in England to "the teeth of the perforation," and in the United States to "the perforation nibs," as designating the broken bridges — those portions of paper protruding beyond the bases of the semicircular indentations that result from the perforation.

Philately has an extensive jargon, and words frequently are coined and adopted in the interests of precision. If for no other reason, it is, therefore, surprising that neither "dentilated" (having teeth) nor "denticulated" (having a series of small teeth) has or has had any wide and general acceptance for use to designate a single stamp from a perforated or rouletted sheet.

Stroke and Rotary

Passing mention has already been made in this chapter to the two different principles of applying separations — stroke and rotary. These principles were evolved mechanically for stamps within a few years of each other during the mid-nineteenth century. In Britain, the stroke process was patented by Henry Archer in 1848, and William Bemrose and Henry Howe Bemrose secured a patent for the rotary process in 1854. These principles of separation have been in continuous use for stamps, and have not altered fundamentally to the present day. Since perforation was adopted officially in England in 1854, the Archer principle until recently had always been used for the postage stamps of Great Britain. Similarly, in the United States, since 1857 postage stamps have always been perforated by use of the Bemrose principle.

A consideration of the patent specifications[2] in some detail clearly reveals the different principles. These specifications, in common with all similar documents, comprise text that makes reference to accompanying drawings that are numbered and lettered. In these pages, those drawings are reproduced, as also is the text, from which the formal parts have been omitted.

Archer

Henry Archer, an impractical Irishman with what seems to have amounted to almost a genius for alienating the sympathies of those with whom he worked or came into contact, somehow hit upon the idea of separations.

Separation was, in some ways, a curious omission from Rowland Hill's plan for postage stamps. The explanation possibly lies in his not having expected the enormous demand that occurred for them. The omission must have resulted in the destruction or mutilation of countless desks and table tops subjected to the rigors of sharp-bladed knives guided painstakingly along

---

[2]Photocopies of them are obtainable from the Patent Office, Southampton Buildings, Chancery Lane, London, W.C. 2.

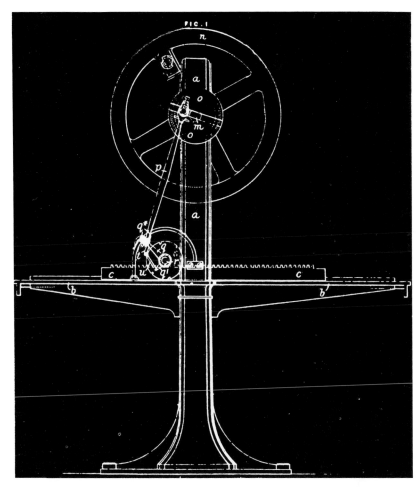

Separation. Archer patent, Figure 1. A side view of the machine showing the rack and pinion by which the frame c was moved mechanically after each descent of the pins, thus enabling the rows of stamps to be perforated one after another. This arrangement was subsequently re-designed several times before the results were satisfactory.

straight edges when stamps were cut from imperforate sheets during the four-teen years preceding the official introduction of perforation. Of course, scissors frequently were used, and stamps also were torn from sheets of which the paper had been weakened by sharp creasing. Not infrequently, the sellers of stamps cut them into singles and left them in boxes for the convenience of buyers.

Because he had not included the suggestion for separation in his plan for penny postage, Rowland Hill was lukewarm about the convenience. While not actively or overtly obstructing it, he did little to assist in its being brought into use. When giving evidence before the Select Committee on Postage Label

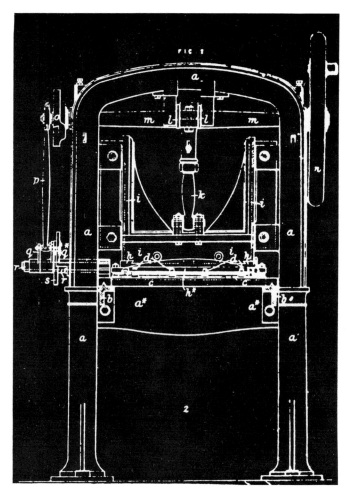

Separation. Archer patent, Figure 2. A front view of the machine (hand-operated). The machine was not, in fact, operated by hand.

Stamps — set up to investigate Archer's claims — Rowland Hill stated:[3] "I do not speak strongly upon the matter; my opinion is that it would be useful and acceptable to the public to a certain extent."

Rowland Hill, according to a long-term employee in the office of the Secretary to the Post Office, never believed any postal suggestion to be useful unless it was found in "my pamphlet," as he described *Post Office Reform; Its Importance and Practicability*. Thomas Peacock, who became Principal of the Stamping Department, noted that "The Hills were most ungenerous colleagues." Acceptable to a certain extent!

Archer's first experiments were carried out with small blades that cut slits

---

[3]*Report from the Select Committee on Postage Label Stamps* (1852), Pages 93-94, question 982.

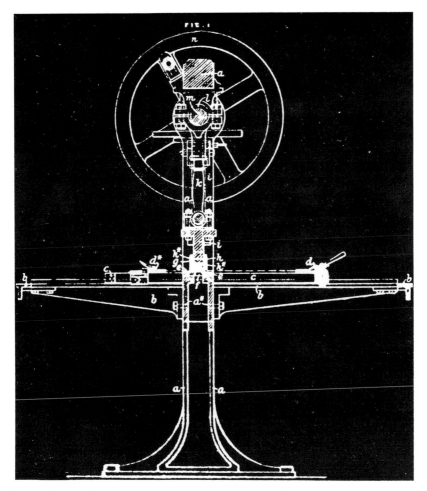

Separation. Archer patent, Figure 3 (incorrectly headed in the printed specification "Fig. 1."). A sectional view sideways through the center of the machine exhibiting the arrangement of clips for holding the sheets flat. This arrangement did not operate successfully, and was later replaced by a tympan.

in the paper, but these experiments were unsuccessful. Then, after having other mechanical assistance, he filed his patent, No. 12,340 of 1848. It was headed variously "Perforating Postage Stamps, Tickets, Labels, &c." and "Archer's Apparatus for Separating Postage Stamps, Tickets, Labels, &c.," he having been granted a provisional patent on Nov. 23, 1848, for his invention of "Improvements in Facilitating the Division of Sheets or Pieces of Paper, Parchment, or other similar Substances." The specification is dated May 23, 1849; the text, other than the formal parts, reads:

"The principal object of this Invention is to enable persons when using postage stamps, tickets, or other small labels to separate one or more from a sheet without the employment of a cutting instrument. This improvement I effect by cutting

Separation. Archer patent, Figure 4. Sectional sideways view exhibiting details of plunger, pins or punches and matrix plate.

or stamping round the margin of every stamp, ticket, or label a consecutive series of holes, whereby the tearing up of the sheets of paper or parchment into pieces of uniform size will be greatly facilitated, while there will be sufficient adherence of the several stamps, tickets, or labels, which are printed on one sheet of paper or parchment, to ensure their retaining the form of a sheet until they are intentionally separated for use.

In the accompanying Drawing I have shewn several views of a stamping press, whereby I am enabled to effect the stamping process with great expedition.

Fig. 1 is a side view; Fig. 2 a front view; and Fig. 3[4] a vertical section taken in the line 1 . . . 2, Fig. 2. *a, a,* is the main framing of the press; *b, b,* are horizontal bracket arms bolted to a cross bar *a**, of the framing *a,* and provided with V-bars, over which a sliding frame *c* traverses. This frame *c* is intended to carry the sheet of paper or other substance intended to be pierced with holes, and for this purpose it is provided at front and back with a set of clips or holders *d, d**, for grasping the edges of the sheet, the jaws of one set of clips *d* being stationary as regards their position on the frame *c, c,* and those of the other *d** being capable of sliding so as to draw the sheet of paper or other material to a suitable tension to be pierced. The construction of these clips is best shewn at Fig. 3. The lower jaw of the moveable set of clips *d** carries the upper jaw, and a continuation of the lower jaw passes through and slides in a bearing attached to the frame. A coiled spring surrounding this continuation of the lower jaw of each clip *d** bears against a nut on the end thereof, and against the piece through which the tail of the jaw slides. The object of this spring is to give the clips a tendency to recede from the clips *d* at the other end of the frame *c,* and thus to keep the sheet of paper or other substance in tension. On the top of the cross bar *a**, a slotted plate *e* is bolted, and over the slot a perforated plate *f* is fixed. These parts are shewn best in the detached sectional view Fig. 4, which represents the punches and the parts in connection therewith on an enlarged scale.

The perforated plate *f* is a matrix to receive the ends of the punches; the mode of supporting and working which I will now describe. *g* is a plate in which a series of pins are set in such order of lines as will allow of their circumscribing each

---

[4]In the drawings accompanying the specification, of which photocopies are available from the Patent Office, what should be "Fig. 3" is incorrectly headed "Fig. 1," and is, in fact, the first figure on the sheet. This is an error of transcription when the drawings were lithographed, and the first and second figures are both headed "Fig. 1" instead of "Fig. 3" and "Fig. 1," respectively. This error does not occur on the original drawings filed in the Public Record Office, London (Chancery Close Roll 1849 — C. 54/13905). The Patent Office photocopies are of the second edition of Archer's specification, printed in 1857, after world-wide interest in stamp perforations had been aroused. I have not seen any copy inscribed "first edition" or its equivalent, and so cannot state whether the error dates from earlier than 1857.

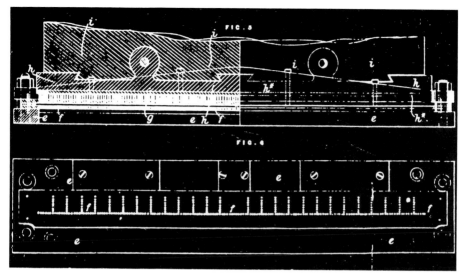

Separation. Archer patent, Figures 5 and 6. Sectional elevation of plunger, pins or punches and matrix plate, and plan of matrix plate showing lay-out of holes to receive the pins for "comb" perforation of British stamps in 1848. Note that this arrangement provided for two complete sheets, each of 240 stamps (twelve across), to be accommodated side by side.

stamp of a row of stamps and punching corresponding holes in the sheet of paper or parchment containing such stamps. The arrangement and fixing of the pins will be better understood on referring to Figs. 5 and 6, which shew the parts in connection therewith in sectional elevation and plan view, on a scale corresponding to Fig. 4. The matrix plate *f*, Fig. 6, shews the mode of arranging the pins when sheets of British postage stamps are to be pierced, but it will be obvious that sheets containing round or oval stamps, or stamps or labels of any size or form, may also be pierced with facility, a difference only in the arrangement of the pins and the perforations of the matrix plate being necessary.

h is a metal plate which carries the plate *g* with its pins, and is attached to and forms part of the plunger *i*. This plunger (see Fig. 2) is provided at its upper part with guides, which work against smooth surfaces of the framing, as is usually employed in such machinery for steadying its movement, and it is jointed to a rod *k*, pendant from a strap piece which embraces an excentric *l*. *h** is a guide embracing the lower end of the plunger, and intended to ensure the proper action of the punch with respect to the matrix plate *f*; *m* is a shaft having its bearings in the upper part of the frame *a*, and carrying at about the middle of its length the excentric *l*. At one end of this shaft, a hand wheel *n* is keyed for working the machinery, and at the other end the shaft carries a disc *o*, which has a straight dovetail slot running across its centre. This slot is intended to receive an adjustable stud pin of a connecting rod *p*, the lower end of which is secured by a pin to two arms *q*, *q**, projecting from loose bosses on the short shaft *r*.

To the inner end of the shaft *r*, a pinion is keyed, which gears into a rack on the side of the frame *c*, and is intended to drive forward that frame together with the sheet of paper or other substance which it carries, so as to bring a different part of the sheet under the action of the punches at each descent of the block *i*. This movement is regulated by the following means: On the shaft *r* a disc wheel

s is mounted, which is provided on its periphery with nicks or indentations to receive a pawle or catch t suspended from the arm q^*; the boss of the arm q has also an arm q^1 which is connected to the lower end of the catch t by a rod u; the upper end of the arm q^* is slotted, so as to allow of a little play the rein of the connecting rod p.

When the rod p is, by the rotation of the disc o, depressed, it will force down the arms q, q^*, and with them the catch t, which being in a notch of the disc will drive round that disc and consequently the shaft r, together with its pinion, which takes into the racks of the frame c; thus the frame c will be moved forward a given distance proportionate to the excentricity of the pin of the connecting rod p in the groove of the disc o, but on the rising of the rod p by the continued rotation of the disc o, it will raise the arm q, and simultaneously the arm q^1 whereby the rod u will be made to lift the catch t out of the notch in the disc s; and as soon as the pin which connects the rod p with the arms q, q^*, has traversed the slot of the arm q^*, the catch (to which latter arm it is directly attached) will be drawn upwards until it drops into the next succeeding notch, when it is ready to act as before. To ensure the quiescence of the arm q^*, when the pin of the rod p has ceased to act upon it, and is traversing the slot in that arm, a spring friction piece attached to the arm q^* is made to embrace a segmental piece attached to the framing a.

It will now be understood that when the hand wheel n is turned, the excentric l will depress the plunger i (which carries the punch), and the paper or other substance beneath will be pierced as required; but immediately before the punch begins to act, the apparatus for bringing forward the paper will have acted, as above described, and thus successive rows of the stamps, labels, or tickets will be pierced at their circumference, as required.

Having now described my Invention, and the machinery which I prefer for carrying the same into effect, I wish it to be understood that I do not confine myself to the use of such machinery, nor to the punching of round holes in the margins of stamps, tickets, or labels, for other machinery might doubtless be devised to effect such purpose, and instead of punched holes, consecutive short slits, formed by straight cutting edges similar to a lancet point, might be adopted to facilitate the after separation of the labels; I therefore wish it to be understood that what I claim under the herein-before in part recited[5] Letters Patent, is the preparation of sheets or pieces of paper, parchment, and other similar substances, which contain stamps, tickets, labels, and other analogous impressions upon them, so that they may be divided with facility when the natural tenacious adherence of the fabric, as a whole, is destroyed (for the above described object) by either of the operations of piercing, cutting or stamping.

It is to be noted that, while Archer's patent was substantially limited to the stroke process, it embraced both of what philatelists refer to as perforation and rouletting. A further point of interest, which seems to have escaped general observation, is that the pins and matrix plates were constructed for perforating at one operation two sheets side by side. In fact, in operation, some half dozen or so thicknesses of paper were placed in the machine. In later models of his machine, Archer replaced the clips d, d^* by a double tympan to hold the sheets.

A much later improvement in the operation of machines acting on the stroke principle was the abandonment of the tympan and the incorporation of a "stripping plate" — that is, an additional plate that moves up and down on

---

[5]The recital appears in the formal parts, which have been omitted here.

but never leaves the pins, and pushes the paper clear of them as they rise and before the paper is moved forward for the next operation. In such cases, the paper is held in position on the moving frame by studs that fit into previously punched holes in the paper. Some of these, and other developments of the stroke perforator, are referred to later in this chapter.

Bemrose

Archer's very early experiments were carried out with a machine that employed piercing rollers,[6] but these experiments were abandoned because the table on which the sheets were laid quickly wore out. It was typical of Archer's impracticability that he abandoned this simple procedure in favor of the much more complicated stroke process that involved comb perforation.

The first application of rotary perforation to postage stamps by machine was patented by William Bemrose the younger and Henry Howe Bemrose, who described themselves as booksellers, printers and stationers, of Derby. Their provisional patent was dated Dec. 11, 1854, and their specification, No. 2607 of 1854, was sealed on Jun. 8, 1855, under the heading of "Improvements in the Mode of and Machinery for Punching and Perforating Paper and other Substances."

The text, other than the formal parts, reads:

Our said Invention relates to the punching or perforating of paper and other substances by means of circular perforators or punches, placed on a cylinder, which is made to rotate at a rate equal to that of the material to be perforated or punched, such material being passed under such perforators or punches by being placed on a counterpart roller or carrier beneath them. Any number of these perforators or punches may be placed upon the cylinder or spindle, and may be adjusted in any convenient manner to suit the materials to be perforated or punched. It is obvious that this arrangement, in addition to being applicable to marking or perforating division lines of paper, &c. to be divided, is also applicable to the production of ornamental patterns or devices upon card and other materials, the main feature of the Invention being the application of the rotating perforators or punches, to perforating, punching, or ornamenting materials, when such materials are carried by apparatus also rotating.

And in order that our said Invention may be more properly understood, we shall now proceed to describe and refer to the several Figures on the Sheet of Drawings hereunto annexed, the same letters of reference referring to corresponding parts throughout the various Figures.

Figure 1 of the Drawings represents a front elevation of our perforating machine; and Figure 2 is a corresponding vertical section of the same, taken through the centre of, and at right angles to, Figure 1. The rest of the Figures are various details which we shall herein-after more fully refer to. The paper or other material to be perforated or ornamented, which is represented by the blue lines, is laid upon the fixed bed or table A, which is supported by brackets cast on the side standards B, B, of the machine, and is fitted with a moveable gauge C, against the edge of which the sheet is placed, and pushed forward until it comes in contact with the punching or perforating rollers D, E, when it is carried forward and perforated.

The lower one E of these rollers serves as a counterpart to the upper roller D.

---

[6]*Report from the Select Committee on Postage Label Stamps* (1852), Page 3, question 11.

653

Fig. 1.

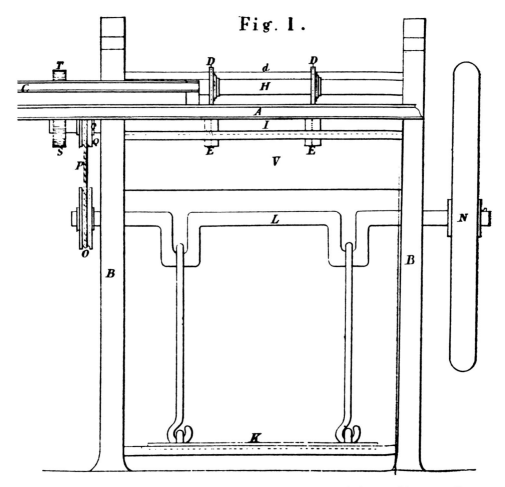

Separation. Bemrose patent, Figure 1. Front view of the machine (treadle-operated). Only two pairs of rollers are shown but, when used for sheets of stamps, the machine had as many pairs as were necessary. The sheet was laid immediately above *A*, with one side resting against the right-hand edge of the guide *C*, which could be set as required.

It is represented in full sized detail side and edge view, at Figures 5 and 6. Any number of pairs of rollers may be used on one machine, according to the number of rows of holes to be perforated at one time; in our Drawings we have only represented two pairs of perforators. The perforating rollers are secured on the shafts *H* & *I* by the set screws *J*, and are actuated or rotated by means of the treadle *K* in connection with the cranked driving shaft *L*, which works in suitable brasses *M* in the side standards of the machine, and carries a fly wheel *N* to regulate the movements of the same.

On the extremity of the crank shaft is keyed a grooved pulley *O*, which, by means of the driving band *P*, gives motion to the second grooved pulley *Q*, fast on the end of the lower spindle, *I*, which carries the lower or counterpart rollers *E, E*. On the end of this shaft is keyed a small spur wheel *S*, gearing with a cor-

Fig. 2.

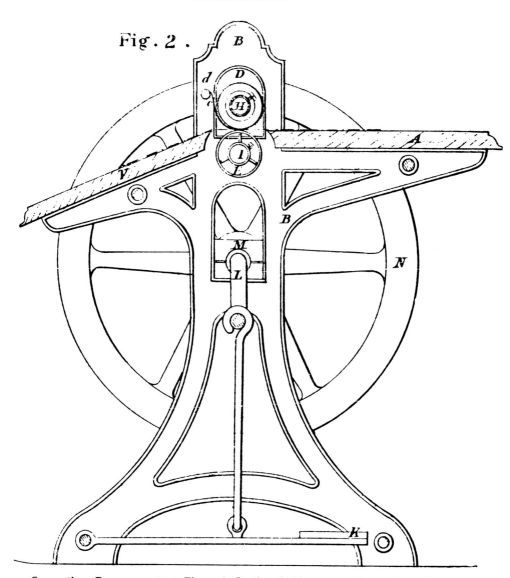

Separation. Bemrose patent, Figure 2. Sectional side view of the machine. The sheet was laid on the table *A* and is represented in the drawing by the interrupted line *A* _____ *V*, in blue on the original drawing.

responding spur wheel *T*, fast on the end of the upper spindle *H*, which carries the perforating rollers *D*. The sheets on being perforated are received on the sloping table *V*, whence they are removed to be placed in boxes or other convenient receptacles. In place of the counterpart and punching rollers, represented in Figures 3, 4, 5, & 6, a counterpart roller of the construction shewn by the detail side and edge views, Figures 7 and 8, may be employed, in conjunction with the knife-edged perforating roller, represented in side and edge view at Figures 9 and 10, and in section at Figure 11.

Fig. 3.

Fig. 4.

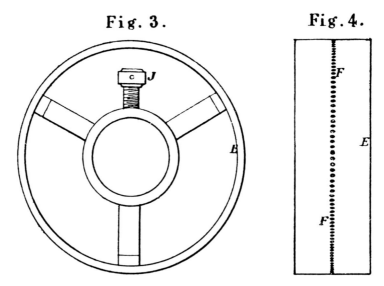

Separation. Bemrose patent, Figures 3 and 4. Perforation. Side and front views of the counterpart roller E containing holes to receive the punches that are set around the periphery of roller D. Note the thinness of roller E; it was thin so that the punched-out pieces of paper might fall through it.

Fig. 5.

Fig. 6.

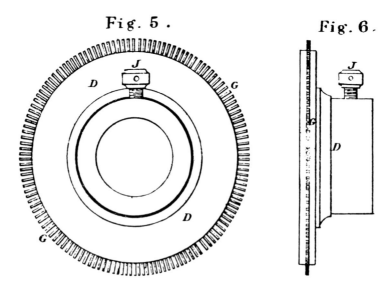

Separation. Bemrose patent, Figures 5 and 6. Perforation. Side and front views of the perforating roller D, bearing around its periphery the punches that fit into the holes on roller E when the rollers rotate on the machine.

Fig. 7.

Fig. 8.

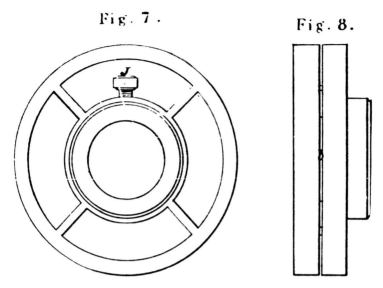

Separation. Bemrose patent, Figures 7 and 8. Rouletting. Side and front views of the roller that acts as a counterpart when the machine is operating with the rouletting roller shown in Figures 9, 10 and 11.

Fig. 9.

Fig. 10.

Fig. 11.

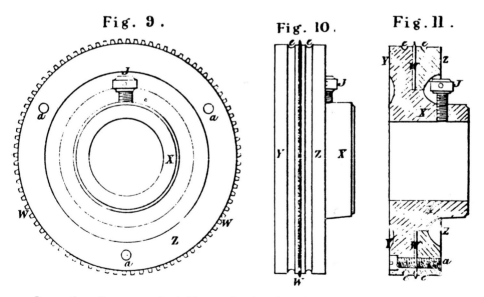

Separation. Bemrose patent, Figures 9, 10 and 11. Rouletting. Side, front and sectional views of the rouletting roller, which comprises three parts, Y and X being one part, W (the blade) another and Z the third.

Fig. 12.

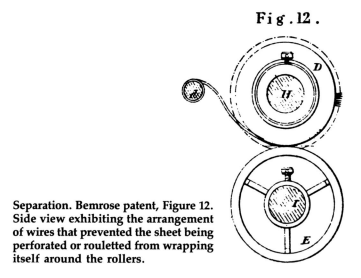

Separation. Bemrose patent, Figure 12. Side view exhibiting the arrangement of wires that prevented the sheet being perforated or rouletted from wrapping itself around the rollers.

This roller does not actually punch out a portion of the material, as is the case with the last-described rollers, but merely perforates it. The perforating portion is composed of a disc of thin metal W, which is serrated or toothed at its periphery, and is fitted on to the boss X of one-half of the roller Y. It is secured in that position by the other half Z of the roller, which is also fitted onto the boss, and is secured thereon by the screws a, a, a, which pass transversely through the roller and through the disc W, as is clearly shewn in the section, Figure 11. The counterpart of this roller has a continuous slit b formed in its periphery, in which slit the teeth of the perforating disc W enter when the two rollers are working together.

In order to ensure the paper leaving the perforators after passing through the rollers, and to prevent its being carried round with them, we employ two curved pieces of wire c, represented more clearly in the detail, Figure 12, which pieces of wire are fitted or soldered at one end to a short tube capable of sliding along the fixed rod d. They are situated on each side of the perforating teeth or punches, and their lower ends are curved slightly and fit into the grooves e, e (Figures 10 & 11), formed in the upper or perforating roller. By this means the paper or other material is taken off the points of the perforators as fast as it passes through the rollers. In place of wires and grooves, a strip of thin brass or other suitable material may be used and applied in connection with the perforator, Figures 5 and 6; but we prefer to use the wires herein-before described and illustrated in Figure 12 of the Drawings. The same principle of punching or perforating apparatus is obviously applicable to the perforating of various devices on paper or other similar materials, for the purpose of ornamenting the same, by using cylinders or rollers with punchers or perforators suitably disposed thereon, in conjunction with corresponding counterpart cylinders or rollers.

Having now described and particularly ascertained the nature of our said Invention, and the manner in which the same is or may be used or carried into effect, we would observe, in conclusion, that we do not confine or restrict ourselves to the precise details or arrangements which we have had occasion to describe or refer to, as many variations may be made therefrom without deviating from the principles or main features of our said Invention; but what we consider to

be novel and original, and therefore claim as the Invention secured to us by the herein-before in part recited[7] Letters Patent, is,—
The system or mode of punching or perforating sheets of paper, cardboard, parchment, or other similar materials by the aid of rotary, punching, or perforating cylinders or rollers, in conjunction with corresponding counterpart cylinders or rollers, for the purpose of facilitating the subsequent division of such sheets, or for ornamenting the same.

It is to be noted that, while the Bemroses's patent was, substantially, limited to the rotary process, it embraced both of what philatelists refer to as perforation and rouletting. Indeed, philatelic ''perforation'' is often referred to as ''punching,'' and ''rouletting'' is often referred to as ''perforating'' in the specification so that the philatelist, to avoid being misled, must read it with close attention to the sense in which the words are used.

Clearly, in order to perforate or roulette a sheet of stamps as specified by the Bemroses, even though the machine was fitted with as many pairs of rollers as could be accommodated on the shafts (H and I), the sheet would have to be passed through the machine twice — once for the vertical rows of separation, and again, after the distances between the pairs of rollers had been appropriately adjusted, for the horizontal rows of separation. Alternatively, the sheet would have to be passed through a combination of two different and appropriately set machines, and be rotated through a right-angle after passing through the first machine. This type of combination perforator has been widely used for stamps, particularly in the United States, where the mechanism is termed ''the 'L' type perforator.''

Improvements in or variations on the Bemrose principle of rotary separation have been made from time to time. For example, in New South Wales and other parts of Australia, stamps were perforated by rotary ''triple cutters,'' which was the term used to designate what is more usually referred to philatelically as a ''comb'' perforator. Further, in the United States, the development of the ''electric eye perforator'' involved the incorporation in the machine of another pair of cylinders with long rows of pins and holes, each row being stamp-depth away from the next row, that effected the horizontal perforations immediately after the vertical perforations were made, thus eliminating the necessity for turning the sheet through a right-angle.

Some of the variations and developments of the rotary perforator are referred to later in this chapter.

'Measurement' and Separations

Before the various separations and variations are discussed in detail, it will be helpful if some consideration is devoted to the classification of separation by means of measurement or gauging.

In the earliest days of collecting, when notice was taken of the fact that increasing numbers of stamps were appearing with separation, attempts were made to classify the separations by reference to the number of teeth or indentations that appeared along the length and width of individual stamps.

---

[7]The recital appears in the formal parts, which have been omitted here.

A typical reference of that period is found, for example, in *The Stamp-Collector's Magazine* for August 1866 (Vol. 4, Page 127): "the French make petty distinctions between . . . the number of holes made by the perforating machine. . . . Their leading journal gravely chronicles the fact, that whereas the number of perforations on the Russian 1, 3 and 5 kopec stamps was formerly 15 by 11, it is now 18 by 13!" French philatelists were, undoubtedly, the leaders in paying ever closer attention to significant differences that could be found between one stamp and another, and in classifying stamps according to those differences, giving rise to what was termed "the French school of philately," in contrast to the so-called "English school," which differentiated only between stamps bearing different designs. The influence of the "French school" spread rapidly among discerning collectors in Europe, England and America, but the "English school" fought a rear guard action for many years, particularly in North America.

In the early attempts at classifying separations according to the number of holes appearing along the length and width of a stamp, the longer dimension — usually the height — was noted first, then the shorter. This gave results as in the instances of the Russian stamps referred to in the quotation from *The Stamp-Collector's Magazine*.[8] Later in the same volume, however (Page 191), E.L. Pemberton, referring to the same stamps, stated: "The first perforated set of Russia has 10 by 14 dents, and during the past month a fresh series has been emitted, 12 by 17. . . ." He was one of the earliest philatelists to note the horizontal measurement first and then the vertical, a practice that has long since become universal.

After a while, it became clear, at least to Dr. J.A. Legrand, that the height and width of individual stamps varied by reason of the method of separation itself. Thus, counting the number of teeth or indentations along those dimensions was not a satisfactory method of classification, because stamps of widely differing sizes and having obviously similar perforations yielded figures that gave no indication of the similarity. For example, U.S. 1861-66 5c. was noted as "16 by 15" and U.S. Newspaper Stamps 1865 5c. was noted as "58 by 32," yet both were perforated by the same machines. Nor, of course, did such figures give any idea whether the teeth on different stamps were more or less close together.

Dr. Legrand, therefore, sought for and applied a system of measurement or gauging based on a standard that had no direct reference to the stamps themselves. He published his findings over his pseudonym, "Dr. Magnus," in a paper entitled "Dentélés et non Dentélés" that appeared in the Belgian magazine, *Le Timbre-Poste*, beginning with the number for October 1866 (Vol. 4, Pages 79 onward) and continuing in successive numbers until April 1867.

Dr. Legrand observed that the height of ordinary stamps varied somewhat around two centimeters, and adopted two centimeters as the conventional

---

[8]That is, Russia 1864 (Jul. 10) 1k. to 5k. perforated 12½, and 1865 1k. to 5k. perforated 14½, 15, respectively. They are listed in *Scott's Standard Postage Stamp Catalogue* as Nos. 5-7 and 12-14, and in *Stanley Gibbons Priced Postage Stamp Catalogue* Part 10 as Nos. 9-11 and 12-14, respectively.

Separation. Perforation. U.S. 1861-66 5c. and U.S. 1865 10c. Newspaper Stamp (face and back, to show perforation). In 1866, the separation on these stamps was noted in the philatelic press as "16 by 15 dents" and "58 by 32 dents," respectively. This was before Dr. J.A. Legrand invented his "odontometre" and determined that both stamps were "perf 12."

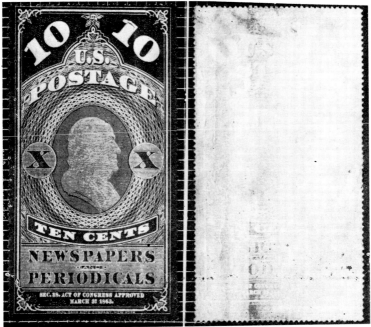

standard length along which to count or gauge the number of teeth or indentations. By counting the number of teeth or indentations occurring within that length, it became possible at once to ascertain what he suggested it was important to establish — that is, whether the teeth were more or less close together — and thus, by reference to a number, to evoke a mental picture of the separation itself. He preferred to count the number of indentations and not the teeth, because the indentations — or, rather, the holes — were themselves the direct product of the machine, but he pointed out that

Separation. "Susse perforation."
Greece 1862-67 5 l. with "Susse" perforation. This perforation, gauging 7,
was the coarsest known to Dr. J.A.
Legrand in 1866 — but he recorded it
only on France 1861 1c. to 80c. The
Greek stamp with this perforation is
not known used; it was, probably, a
trial.

counting either teeth or indentations produced identical results with the same
stamp. He discovered that sometimes it was necessary to measure fractions,
but disregarded any fraction smaller than one-half.

Although Dr. Legrand noted that some stamps had different gauges of perforation vertically and horizontally — for example, France 1862-71 1c. to 80c.
gauged 14 horizontally and only 13½ vertically — he contented himself with
limiting his record to vertical measurements, stating that he did this because
he knew of no stamp (with separation) that measured less than two centimeters vertically, and he, therefore, eliminated a source of possible error
in that he had both a starting point and a finishing point on the stamp within
his two-centimeter scale. He pointed out that, if the only lengths available
on the stamp were less than two centimeters, the proper gauge could be arrived at by counting the indentations occurring within one centimeter and
multiplying the number by two.

As for the gauges themselves, Dr. Legrand found that the coarsest or largest
he knew was 7, and the finest or smallest was 16, and he constructed a
graduated scale, which he called an *odontomètre* (from the Greek), by placing
various stamps on a piece of card, and marking it appropriately from their
separations. This scale, the first perforation gauge, is illustrated earlier in this
work.[9]

Dr. Legrand published a list of the stamps he had used to construct his
odontometer. Reproduced is a translation of that list; the details in italics have
been added:

7 — France with "Susse" perforation, *1861 (1853-60)*.
9 — Prince Edward *Island* 2d., n. *1861 (Jan. 1)*.
9½ — Austria fourth issue, *1863-64*.
10 — Wurtemberg (large teeth), *1862*.
11 — Prince Edward *Island* 9d., *1862*.
11½ — St. Vincent 1d. (variety), *1863-66*.

---

[9]See the illustration in the chapter entitled "Philatelic Trends."

Separation. Perforation. Great Britain 1854-55 1d. "perf 16." This, one of the earliest of perforated stamps, bears the finest gauge of perforation that was known to Dr. J.A. Legrand in 1866.

12   — U.S. current series, *1861-66.*
12½ — Russia *1864 (Jul. 10).*
13   — Belgium *1863, one of the vertical perforations.*
13½ — France *1862-71, vertical perforation.*
14   — Great Britain *1858-64 1d.*
14½ — Ceylon 5d. *1861.*
15   — Russia *1865.*
15½ — Natal 1d. star watermark, *1862.*
16   — Great Britain first perforated stamps, *1854-55 1d. and 2d.*

This list of stamps is confined to, and Dr. Legrand's odontometer was constructed with the use of, stamps from perforated sheets. In his paper, he dealt with rouletted issues, but he did not count the number of indentations produced by roulettes; he confined himself to describing their appearance in terms still in use today. They are referred to later in this chapter.

He observed that after the paper had been punched out by the perforating machine — this he termed *piquage* — or cut by the roulettes — termed *perçage* — the remaining paper formed so many bridges from one stamp to another. In both cases, this gave rise, when the paper was torn, to teeth that were much less prominent in rouletting than in perforation, although the indentations (as distinct from the teeth) in rouletting often resulted from the shapes of the roulettes themselves. He employed *dentelé* as the generic term to designate a stamp from a sheet with separation, incorporating both perforation and rouletting, and without attempting to diagnose the actual method of separation employed. Also, he observed, but took no account of, those cases in which, by imperfect action of the perforating machine, the small circles of paper remained more or less attached to the teeth, so giving rise to what are now termed "rough" and "blind" perforations.

Dr. Legrand appreciated the fact that certain characteristics of separation are useful guides in determining whether a piece of printed paper is a genuine stamp or a forgery. In the years that have passed since his day, students have devoted much time to examining and recording these characteristics and the various methods and peculiarities of separation, thereby not only attempting to cater to the student's insatiable thirst for knowledge, but also for the very practical purpose of expertization.

Machines and instruments that produce separation are not, or are not necessarily, perfectly regular in their construction, nor are the pins or teeth that effect the removal or disturbance of the paper necessarily equidistant, so that along a single line of holes and teeth it is possible in some cases to obtain different gauges or measurements. This fact was not properly appreciated by Dr. Legrand,[10] nor was it universally appreciated for many years after he first published his findings. Thus, enthusiastic collectors without sufficient thought eagerly chronicled new varieties of stamps bearing different perforation when the use of perforation gauges revealed hitherto unrecorded "measurements" on those stamps. Further, while in the majority of cases, a simple count either horizontally or horizontally and vertically sufficed to designate a separation, occasionally the situation was rendered more complex by research that revealed that, during the course of time, one machine produced results that bore little or no resemblance to one another because of wear and repair of the pins and holes. This was the case, for example, with some stamps produced by Perkins, Bacon & Company.

It, therefore, became necessary to establish standards reflecting the sizes of the actual holes, and the appearance of the holes themselves, such as "clean cut" when the circles of paper were completely punched out; "intermediate," when the circles were more or less adhering to the teeth; and "rough" or "blind" when the circles were represented by scarcely any removal of paper but instead by saucer-like depressions in the stamp margins.[11]

The difficulties to which unthinking and indiscriminate recording led, and the approach of the thoughtful student, are illustrated by two extracts from *The London Philatelist* for 1922. The first is from an article by Sir E.D. Bacon (Pages 55, 57): "Since the time when collecting stamps began the chief object that all philatelists have concentrated their efforts upon has been to draw up catalogue lists whereby they can arrange their specimens in the correct chronological sequence in which they were issued for postal use. The means of doing this are by a close observation of any variation in the design; change of colour; the particular kind of paper employed; or by the absence or presence of some special variety of perforation.[12] By a careful study and comparison of specimens under these headings it has been found possible to subdivide specimens that were formerly believed to constitute a single issue into their actual printings and to give a full history of each variety with the exact date

---

[10] For instance, in his listing, he in fact derived 14½ for Ceylon 1861 5d. and 15½ for Natal 1862 1d. from irregularly spaced pins.

[11] For these and other complexities in classifying and gauging the separations of Perkins, Bacon & Company for the British Colonies, see *Grenada* etc. by E.D. Bacon and F.H. Napier (1902), Pages 1 to 75.

[12] Curiously enough, Sir E.D. Bacon omitted mention of two other undoubtedly significant factors in some cases: gum and postal markings.

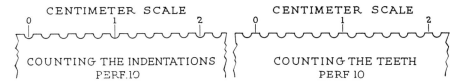

Separation. Ascertaining the gauge with a ruler and by counting the indentations or the teeth.

at which it came into use. . . . Most specialists are so intent on trying to find what they call uncatalogued varieties of the countries they are interested in that they sometimes do not weigh sufficiently the question of whether they are justified or not in the claims they put forward for the inclusion of their so-called discoveries.''

The second extract is from an article by Benjamin Goodfellow (Page 202). Writing about varieties of perforation he stated: ''it is only in so far as they connote, or assist towards the elucidation of, some other factor, which is also of importance, that they are in these days worthy of serious study, or deserve more than a passing reference.''

Conventions in Gauging

In the measurement or gauging and recording of separations, philatelists have adopted certain conventions, and it is convenient here to pause and examine some of those that are in use, especially in the standard catalogues.

First, as has been stated, the universal basis of measurement is a length of two centimeters, and the number of holes, cuts, teeth or indentations occurring within that length is said to be ''the gauge'' or, more loosely, ''the measurement'' of the separation. Thus ''perf 12'' means that, within the length of two centimeters (whether or not the stamp's dimension extends to that distance), twelve indentations or twelve teeth can be counted; if the dimension does not extend to two centimeters, the number occurring within the length of one centimeter is counted and the result is multiplied by two.

This conventional length of two centimeters can be obtained from any source. The philatelist wishing to gauge a perforation need do no more than Dr. Legrand did in the first place — that is, place the edge of the stamp against a ruler marked in centimeters, with the zero line centrally in an indentation, and then count the number of indentations between zero and two centimeters; or, alternatively, place the zero line centrally on a tooth and count the teeth. It is unnecessary to emphasize that, if accuracy is desired, pains must be taken to ensure that the zero line is located and retained at the exact center of the indentation (or the tooth) while the count is being made. For this purpose, a magnifying glass is a useful aid to accuracy. This method of counting is quite satisfactory in the majority of cases, but it has two disadvantages. It is very time-consuming and, for any count involving less than one-half, it is liable to be inaccurate, depending as it does entirely upon judgment of fractions of a millimeter.

Much quicker and more convenient to use in the majority of cases is a per-

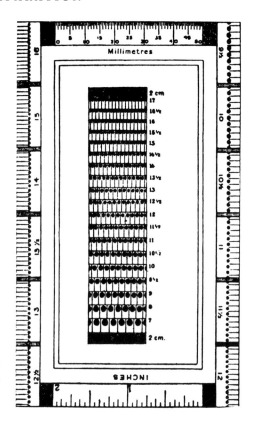

Separation. Perforation
gauge. A typical die-printed
perforation gauge.
(Not to scale.)

foration gauge which, in its usually encountered form, is a more or less
modified but direct descendant of that of Dr. Legrand, referred to earlier.[13]
This type of perforation gauge comprises twenty or so different series of dots
and fine lines, usually in two-centimeter widths, printed on white card or
other substance. The distances between the dots and lines vary among the
series, and each series is marked according to number within the two-
centimeter scale. As a result, a gauge of perforation can be ascertained rapidly
if the edge of the stamp is applied to the various series in turn until one is
found at which a portion of every adjacent dot exactly coincides with every
adjacent indentation (or every adjacent line bisects every adjacent tooth)
within the series — it being quite immaterial whether the edge of the stamp
is equal to or shorter or longer than the series of dots and lines. The appropriate number is the gauge of the perforation.

To gauge the perforation of mounted stamps or those on covers, this type
of perforation gauge is, often, provided with additional series of dots and
lines around the edges. These gauges are reasonably satisfactory in use, but
care must be exercised to avoid errors arising from parallax because of the
thickness of the card or other substance of the perforation gauge itself. Parallax

---

[13]See also the illustration in the chapter entitled "Philatelic Trends."

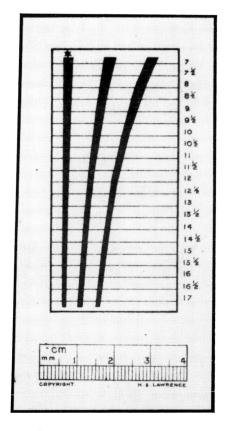

Separation. Perforation gauge. Captain Lawrence's ratio perforation scale. This, one of the earliest perforation gauges to give an infinite number of readings, is simple to use. The stamp is placed so that an indentation is centered on the starred vertical line. The stamp is then moved up and down the scale until indentations are centered on all three lines and the gauge of the perforation is then read at the right. A check is provided in that, if the perforation is accurately gauged, three indentations appear in each space between the vertical lines.

can be practically eliminated by holding the gauge so that its surface and that of the stamp form a right-angle.[14]

These gauges are, usually, limited to differences of one-half, but some are available with differences of one-quarter of a tooth or indentation in two centimeters. However, all of these gauges are, to a certain extent, conventional in that often the series will fit perforations of which the true gauge is a little finer than the one below and a little coarser than the one above in the scale, depending upon whether the bridges are the same size as or smaller or larger than the holes.

In the great majority of cases, this type of perforation gauge is satisfactory when it has been printed from a die that has been accurately engraved. In common with every gauge, it presents difficulties when the perforating pins have been irregularly set in the lines, and the difficulties that arise when the setting of the pins does not accurately conform to measurements made on the one-quarter scale have already been indicated — that is, more than one

---

[14]Because of parallax, this type of gauge printed on transparent plastic is liable to cause error unless the printed side and the stamp are in contact when the gauge is used. The better of such gauges are printed in reverse, so that direct readings may be made through the transparent plastic.

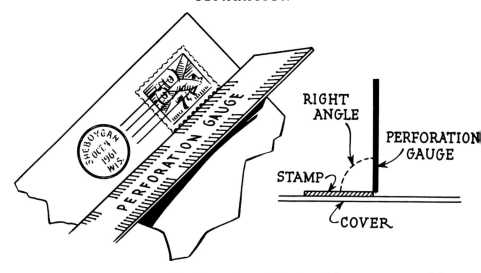

RIGHT
ANGLE

PERFORATION
GAUGE

STAMP

COVER

Separation. Gauging perforations. A method of avoiding errors caused by parallax when using an opaque perforation gauge for a stamp on cover. Hold the gauge so that the surfaces of the cover and gauge form a right-angle.

true gauge of perforation may fit one series of dots or lines, or no series may accurately fit.

When perforating machines are manufactured, the pins are set at distances apart that are dictated by considerations that have nothing to do with the difficulties encountered by the philatelist using the conventional two-centimeter scale. The distances between pins, in different circumstances, can vary almost infinitely — and they have done so since perforation was introduced. Incidentally, the first perforating machines having been manufactured in England, it is quite certain that the inch and not the centimeter was the unit of measurement in manufacture. Also, in all probability, the inch unit was used for the first perforating machines manufactured in America.

For all practical purposes, so far as the issuing authority is concerned, there is no difference between, say, sixteen holes to the inch and sixteen holes within the inch. This difference can be ascertained, when the bridges are equal in width to the holes, by placing the row of perforations against an inch rule in such a position that the zero line is just touching the *left* of the circumference of one perforation hole. If the one-inch mark just touches the *left* of the circumference of the sixteenth perforation hole, there are sixteen pins to the inch; if the one-inch mark touches the *right* of the circumference of the sixteenth perforation hole, there are sixteen pins within the inch.[15] This difference is a difference of interpretation of instructions given to a mechanic, and sometimes accounts for variations in perforation when machines, intended to be identical, have been constructed — and, of course, such differing interpretations can apply where the metric system is used.

---

[15]This subject was first discussed in *The London Philatelist*, Vol. 21, Pages 188, 217 (August, September 1912) in "Notes on Perforation" by Gordon Smith and L.L.R. Hausburg.

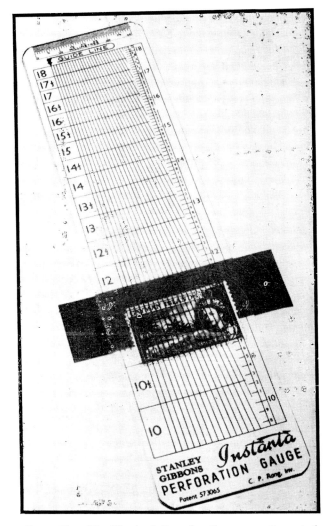

Separation. The "Instanta" perforation gauge. Invented by C.P. Rang after years of experiments, the "Instanta" perforation gauge can be used to give an infinite number of accurate measurements with very fine differences. Printed on the reverse of transparent plastic material, the gauge virtually eliminates errors caused by parallax.

On the type of perforation gauge discussed above, both of these might fit within the same series of dots or lines — 12¾ — yet there is an ascertainable difference between the two. This very difference might indicate the use of different perforating machines, a fact that might, in certain philatelic research, be of importance. It is, therefore, important to be able to gauge the difference and, for the sake of convenience, to be able to do so without laboriously counting and noting whether the perforation hole at the inch mark (or other convenient mark) lies to the left or right of the line or is bisected by it. For this purpose, it is necessary to have a perforation gauge capable of giving unlimitedly fine and accurate readings between each of the points on the gauge. There have been several attempts to solve this philatelic problem. One such attempt was made soon after World War I by Captain N.S. Lawrence, who designed the "ratio perforation scale," based upon a vertical line and two converging curved lines that gave readings from 7 to 17. Reasonably accurate and fairly simple to use, the "ratio perforation scale" did not have a wide circulation, probably because it was marketed by a company[16] that, for other reasons, soon afterward was liquidated.

The most successful of the scales based on converging lines was first marketed about 1944 by Stanley Gibbons Ltd. This is the "Instanta" perforation gauge, invented after years of experiment by C.P. Rang and patented in Great Britain under No. 573065. This gauge, cut in reverse on transparent plastic material so that readings may be made through it, enables every true gauge of perforation between 9.75 and 18.25 to be ascertained, while the main figures, for less exacting use, allow a latitude of one-half a perforation hole each — for example, all measurements between 11.75 and 12.25 are grouped under "12." By its use, accurate readings can be made to within one-fortieth of a perforation per two centimeters. Needless to state, for such fine work, the use of a magnifying glass is most advisable, as is the cross-checking of a reading by gauging not only the indentations but also the teeth.[17]

References have already been made to the fact that the expansion of paper when damp and its subsequent shrinkage when dry are matters that have been sources of difficulty in stamp production since the introduction of perforation, and, to some extent, to philatelists before these characteristics were fully appreciated.[18] However, these problems have very little philatelic significance in regard to the gauging of perforation. The reason is that, almost without exception, perforation is applied to paper that is dry, or substantially so — indeed, it must be dry if perforation is to be entirely satisfactory.[19]

Of course, if a perforated stamp is soaked, the paper expands and, with it, the perforation; consequently, if, while the paper is still wet, the perfora-

---

[16]Fred J. Melville Ltd.

[17]An excellent instance of the results that can be obtained by proper use of the "Instanta" perforation gauge, and the deductions that were drawn from these observations, is to be found in "Early American Perforating Machines — Perforations 1857-1867" by Winthrop S. Boggs in *The Collectors Club Philatelist*, Vol. 33, Pages 61, 145 (March, May 1954). Published as a booklet by the Unitrade Press, Ontario (June 1982).

[18]See, for example, "Shrinkage" in the alphabetical list to the chapter entitled "Paper"; "Wet Printing and Dry Printing" in the chapter entitled "Printing Problems and Varieties"; and "Gumming After or Before Printing" in the chapter entitled "Gum."

[19]Cases are on record in which stamps that occur usually with clean-cut holes are sometimes found with more or less rough perforation because of the absence or insufficiency of humidity control during perforation — perhaps carried out on an exceptionally damp day. Such instances occur, for example, in the case of Great Britain 1858-64 1d., but they are not listed separately in the standard catalogues. Further, other cases are on record in which stamps, perforated on a particular machine with regularly set equidistant pins, yield different readings on different parts of the same row. Such freak occurrences are attributable to dampness present in part of the sheet while perforation was effected.

tion is gauged on a finely graduated perforation gauge, the reading will be at a number appreciably coarser than that yielded by the same stamp when dry. For instance, experiment will reveal that an example of U.S. 1955 (Jan. 15) Pennsylvania Academy of the Fine Arts 3c., which gauges 10.5 x 11.25 when dry, will, after two minutes' soaking, gauge 10.35 x 10.9, and will revert to the original gauge after drying. I know of no instance in which a stamp that is soaked returns to anything but the same gauge or measurement after drying. However, for many years the discussion of the significance of fine differences in gauges of perforation was bedeviled by the mistaken belief that, as a general rule, expansion and contraction of paper during production and subsequent soaking has a residual effect upon the gauge of perforation of the stamp.

Simple and Compound Perforations

No stamp has less than three edges, and the possibility exists that every edge is different so far as separation is concerned. The haphazardness of Dr. Legrand in noting the gauge of only the longer side of the stamp has long since been replaced by a more methodical approach. For the sake of accuracy and record, it is therefore necessary to examine and, perhaps, to gauge each edge independently. Conventionally, the top horizontal edge is noted first, the right-hand edge next, then the lower horizontal edge, and finally the left-hand edge in the case of a rectangular stamp. To avoid unnecessary complications, I shall refer mainly to perforations in the examples quoted.

The simplest expression of a perforation is "perforated" or "perf" followed by a single number. This is one of the most frequent of the conventional types of recording encountered in stamps, and signifies that the perforation gauges the same on all sides of the stamp. Examples chosen at random are U.S. 1959 (Jul. 4) 49-Star Flag 4c., perf 11, and New Hebrides 1953 5c. to 5f., perf 12½.

When the perforation does not gauge the same on all sides of the stamp, it is said to have "compound perforation," but the word "compound" is used in two varying senses in particular circumstances, and they have to be clearly appreciated if confusion is to be avoided. In its primary sense, "compound" is used in regard to what is probably the most frequently encountered type of recording of stamp perforation, two numbers separated by a multiplication sign — for instance, "perf 10½ x 11" as in the case of U.S. 1960 (Aug. 29) World Forestry Congress Issue 4c., and "perf 11 x 12" as in the case of Great Britain 1955 2s.6d. to £1.

The multiplication sign itself is used conventionally in two separate senses, both of them completely different from that of arithmetic. In philately, where two figures only appear, the sign signifies merely that the gauges of perforation on opposite edges of the stamp are equal, the horizontal gauge appearing before, and the vertical gauge appearing after the sign. That is the first conventional use of the multiplication sign and the first sense of "compound." Sometimes in writing, and invariably in speech, the word "by" is used instead of the multiplication sign.

Incidentally, there is, often, a practical reason why such compound per-

Separation. Perforation variations. U.S. 1982 (Jan. 15) Great Americans 13c. "perf 11 x 10½." When the stamp is dry, the perforation gauges 11 x 10.25 on the "Instanta" perforation gauge. After the stamp was soaked for two minutes, and while it was still wet, the perforation gauged 10.9 x 10.19. After drying, it reverted to the original gauge.

foration is adopted in production. Although in practice there is now no manufacturing reason why the pins or punches and the holes in the plates should not be made exactly equidistant from one another, they are often deliberately spaced differently horizontally and vertically. This is done to meet the demands of the authorities supervising the stamp issue and because of the greater strength of paper in one direction than the other. Paper has a greater tearing strength across the grain[20] than with the grain. To prevent the sheets of perforated stamps from disintegrating during handling, the perforation with the grain is made to gauge slightly less than that across the grain. Sometimes a similar objective is attained by making the size of the holes in one direction slightly larger than in the other.

The other sense in which "compound" is used is that the two (if there are only two) gauges given may be found on the stamp but not necessarily on adjoining edges. One gauge may appear on one edge, two edges or three, and the other gauge on the remaining edges or edge. A perforation expressed to be, for example, "perf compound of 12 and 13" means that no fewer than eight permutations are possible, and in setting out these permutations I use the multiplication sign in the second of its conventional meanings:

(1) 12 x 13 x 13 x 13   (2) 12 x 12 x 13 x 13
(3) 12 x 12 x 12 x 13   (4) 12 x 13 x 12 x 13
(5) 13 x 12 x 12 x 12   (6) 13 x 13 x 12 x 12
(7) 13 x 13 x 13 x 12   (8) 13 x 12 x 13 x 12

In this sense, the multiplication sign conventionally has the meaning merely of separating one edge of the rectangular stamp from the other, the first figure referring to the top horizontal gauge, the next figure referring to the gauge on the adjacent right edge, and so on clockwise around the edges of the stamp. Another method of expressing these eight possible permutations, and

---

[20]See "Shrinkage" in the alphabetical list to the chapter entitled "Paper."

Separation. Compound perforation. France 1862-71 40c. "perf 14 x 13½." One of the earliest stamps recorded by Dr. J.A. Legrand as bearing perforations of more than one gauge — "14" horizontally and "13½" vertically.

one that is frequently used when only two gauges are found, is "perf 12 x 13 and compound."

Further, as has been stated, the gauge on all four of the edges may be entirely different, or there may be three different gauges on the four edges. All of these are "compound perforations." Sometimes individual stamps are noted as, for example in the case of Bosnia and Herzegovina 1906-1907 1h. to 5k., "perf 6½ x 6½ x 12½ x 9½," or they are listed in the catalogues as "perf compounds of 6½, 9½ and 12½." The number of possible permutations with such compounds is large indeed, and a particular combination, such as that instanced in the case of Bosnia and Herzegovina, is only one of many possible; the standard catalogue listings indicate this in various ways.[21]

The expression of a perforation by two numbers separated only by a comma is, perhaps, the most confusing and least understood of the conventions. An instance of such a notation is to be found, for example, in Switzerland 1908 (December) Tellboy 2c.[22] "perf 11½, 12." This is no more than a clumsy method of indicating that the perforation gauges neither 11½ nor 12, but should more properly be expressed as "perf 11¾" or such other fraction or

---

[21]As examples, refer, for instance, to the listings of Austria between 1867 and 1899, and Japan between 1872 and 1873.
[22]Scott No. 146, Stanley Gibbons No. 257.

Separation. Compound perforation. Bosnia and Herzegovina 1906-1907 20h. and 30h. "perf compound of 6½, 9½ and 12½." The 20h. gauges 12½ x 12½ x 9½ x 6½; the 30h. gauges 9½ x 12½ x 12½ x 6½.

decimal as more accurate gauging will reveal. Observe that such a notation does *not* usually mean that two distinct stamps exist, one "perf 11½" and another "perf 12." Sometimes a perforation that does not accurately fit any of the series of dots and lines on a perforation gauge is expressed as being "nearly (a gauge)," as in the case, for instance, of New Zealand 1875 (January) Newspaper Stamp ½d. on star watermarked paper,[23] "perf nearly 12." It is said also that the notation "14, 16, 16½" implies that the intermediate gauges do not exist, while "14-16½" means that all intermediate gauges can be found.

Having stated that a notation of a perforation by two figures separated by a comma does not usually mean that two distinct stamps exist, each with one of the gauges, I am constrained also to state that the custom is "honour'd in the breach" as well as in the observance in the United States, and I shall return to it when considering the next conventional expression of a perforation.

The usual, conventional meaning of a perforation expressed by two numbers separated by a dash or by the word "to" is that the holes are irregularly spaced so that the gauge differs along the length of a single line. For example, in the case of Barbados 1861 (½d.) green and (1d.) blue, the perforation is expressed as "clean-cut perf 14 to 16"[24] and bears the meaning of variations between those extremes along the length of a line of perforations. Thus, an individual stamp can be found with a gauge of 14 or 15 or 16, or other measurements between 14 and 16 — and, of course, perhaps one part of one edge of the stamp might gauge 14 and another part of the same edge, say, 15½.[25] However, in the United States, although this convention is often observed, in many instances the word "to" is used as meaning that various different perforations exist between the two numbers, so that individual issues may be found perforated by separate machines having different gauges. For instance, the issues of Fiji between 1878 and 1900 are found with various separate perforations, such as 10, 11 and 12½ and compounds, yet they are listed in the Scott catalogue variously as "perf 10-13½ & compound," "perf 10" and "perf 10-12 & compound."

Line Perforation

Line perforation falls into two main groups. In the first group, only a single line of perforation holes is made in the paper at one operation, and such perforation is, sometimes, termed "single-line perforation." In the second group, several lines of perforation are made in the paper along the same direction at one operation. This, by far the larger of the two groups, is what is usually meant when the term "line perforation" is employed. Indeed, I know of no

---

[23]Stanley Gibbons No. 150; in the Scott catalogue, this perforation is not separately noted, and the perforation of the issue (No. P3) is listed as "12, 12½."

[24]Scott Nos. 13, 14; Stanley Gibbons Nos. 17-19.

[25]Thus, no accurate reading could be obtained over the entire edge by use of one series of dots and lines on a conventional perforation gauge; but a less pronounced difference might not be obvious if the teeth or indentations were counted along the length of two centimeters instead of being gauged.

Separation. "Perforated between stamps." Hohen Rinne (Hungarian Hotel Post) 1906 5h., a block of four from the top left corner of a sheet that was single-line guillotine "perf between stamps," thus saving four strokes of the perforating machine but resulting in the stamp at each corner of the sheet having perforations on only two sides, while the other stamps in the outer rows and columns have perforations on only three sides.

term generally appropriated to this group, although the term "multiple-line perforation" has been used.

Usually, single-line perforation is effected mechanically by a stroke machine, and such a machine is, sometimes, termed a "guillotine" perforator or machine, and sometimes a "single cutter."[26] I know of no instance of sheets of stamps being single-line perforated by a rotary machine.

Reference was made near the beginning of this chapter to the fact that, from the point of view of production, separation may be divided into two broad and exclusive classes — namely "stroke" or "flat bed" and "rotary" — that bear no relation to the effect produced; and to the fact that, from the point of view of philatelic classification, separation may be divided into two broad and exclusive classes — namely, "perforation" and "rouletting" — that bear no relation to the method of production. However, in rare cases, single-line perforation has been carried out by quite exceptional methods that are neither stroke nor rotary.

These cases, really, fall into a class of their own. They are, as has already been stated, neither stroke nor rotary; and also, sometimes, they are neither true perforation nor true roulette. These are cases in which, for want of more appropriate machinery, the stamps have been rendered detachable from the sheet by means of a sewing machine — each gutter on each sheet being passed painstakingly under the rapidly rising and falling needle of that domestically useful appliance.

Such means of separation is termed "sewing machine perforation." Sometimes, however, when the needle has been comparatively thin and sharp, the paper presents the appearance of having been pierced through rather than of having had its substance removed, although when a thick and

---

[26]To distinguish it from a "triple-cutter," which is the term sometimes employed to designate what philatelists almost universally call a "comb" machine.

Separation. "Perforated all around." Holmestrands (Norwegian Local Post of M. Borreston) 1888 (Dec. 1) 10 ö., a block of four from the top left corner of a sheet that was single-line guillotine "perf all around." The stamps at each corner and in the outer rows and columns have perforations on all four sides.

blunt needle, or one with a broken point, has been used, the substance of the paper does appear to have been removed.

Sewing machine perforation can be distinguished, often, by the fact that the lines of holes do not run straight, owing to the absence of adequate guides for the paper in its passage through the machine, or deliberate movement of the paper to negotiate irregular gutters. Sometimes, also, the reverse of the sheet may show numerous small ridges astride the lines of holes, where the pushing mechanism of the machine acted on the paper. Occasionally, the sheet margins provide proof of the use of a sewing machine for perforation. For example, in the case of Tibet 1933, an instance is recorded[27] of a sheet with the perforation in the gutter between the first and second rows of stamps extending into the right-hand sheet margin and turning in a hairpin bend, then continuing unbroken into and along the gutter between the second and third rows. The perforation does not run off the outer edge of the sheet margin at the hairpin bend, and this constitutes adequate proof of the turning of the sheet there, as such a short-radius turn would be virtually impossible with a hand-held rouletting wheel.

Another comparatively modern example of an issue with sewing machine perforation is, for instance, Syria 1921 Killis, no value expressed (1p.),[28] which was issued as a locally prepared provisional because the regular issue was exhausted there owing to the sudden influx of great numbers of refugees from Armenia.

Other issues that can be found with sewing machine perforation include, for example, Bussahir (India) 1895 ¼a. to 1r., Cauca (Colombia) 1903 (1902) 10c. and 20c., and Krefeld (German Local) 1887 (January) 2p.

An outstandingly crude method of line perforation was adopted for the

---

[27]*The Great Wall*, Vol. 4, Page 55 (September 1961).
[28]This stamp is listed in *Scott's Standard Postage Stamp Catalogue* Vol. 4 as Syria No. 91, but is not listed in the Stanley Gibbons catalogue.

early issues of Portuguese India during the 1870s — including, by way of specific example, 1871 10r. The stamps, hand-stamped from a single die, were rendered detachable from contiguous stamps by perforations effected by toothed strips of ivory. As might readily be imagined, the perforation is very irregular, and the gauge varies greatly along the length of a single line.

Single-Line Perforation

The working of a single-line guillotine perforator for stamps is very time-consuming because of the number of separate operations that have to be carried out before a sheet is completely perforated. For example, for a sheet of 100 stamps in ten rows of ten, no fewer than twenty-two separate strokes of the perforator — eleven horizontal and eleven vertical — are necessary if all the stamps are to be perforated around every design.

Sometimes, in an endeavor to reduce the number of operations required, sheets have been perforated only between the stamps. That is, the four stamps at the corners have perforations on only two sides, while the other stamps in the outer rows and columns have perforations on only three sides. This economy reduces to eighteen the number of separate operations necessary on each such sheet. Sheets perforated in this manner are referred to as "perf between stamps," in contrast to sheets with perforations surrounding every design, which are referred to as "perf all around."

Some of the earliest single-line perforations encountered in philately occur on the classic British Colonial issues produced by Perkins, Bacon & Company between 1860 and the end of 1881. The sheets were painstakingly passed through the guillotine perforators by Miss H. Stewart, who was employed by the firm for the exclusive purpose of perforating its stamps (and other productions requiring perforation) from Aug. 17, 1860, onward.

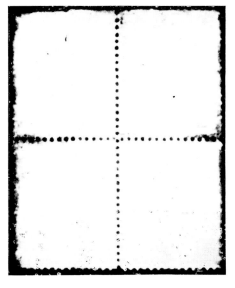

Separation. Single-line guillotine perforation. An example of the clean-cut results produced by the Perkins, Bacon "A" machine during the early stages, before the pins and counterpart holes had begun to wear and yield rough or blind perforations.

No useful purpose would be served in detailing here the differences to be found and the complexities involved in studying the varying perforations produced by that firm's different machines. Such details have long been available in various standard works dealing with the countries concerned. However, I reproduced earlier in this chapter pictures and descriptions of two of the machines, and these illustrate the fundamental principles of the construction and operation of all single-line guillotine perforators worked by hand.

The first of these machines was constructed by James Griffiths, "a machinist, paging machine and press manufacturer" of Clerkenwell, in London. The total cost of the initial machine was £30. The following is a quotation from *Grenada: To Which Is Prefixed An Account Of The Perforations Of The Perkins Bacon Printed Stamps Of The British Colonies:*[29]

The illustration . . . is reproduced from a photograph Messrs. Perkins, Bacon & Co. have kindly allowed us to have taken. . . . [it] obviates the necessity of any very elaborate description of the machine. It was . . . a single-line . . . [machine] in so much that it perforated but one line at a time; . . . the perforation was effected by the descent of a line of pins, of a length suitable to the sheet to be perforated; hence single-line machines of this description are generally termed "guillotine machines."

The machine in question was worked by a hand-wheel, and there was a wooden table attached. On the side of the table on which the sheet of stamps was placed prior to its passage through the machine there was what is called a "guide-plate." This consisted of a flat steel ruler, about an inch in width, under which the sheet was passed on its way towards the line of pins.

The ruler rested on a narrow brass bar fixed parallel to either side of this half of the table; and, attached to each end of the ruler, at right angles, was a steel clamp of about four inches in length with a narrow slit down the middle. These clamps were secured to the brass bars by means of thumb-screws, which fitted into holes drilled in the bars at equal distances apart, and the openings[30] in the clamps allowed the ruler to be moved a certain distance forwards or backwards at any of the holes in the brass bars previous to its being secured in position by the screws.

This ruler had to be properly set, to suit the size of the stamps and the distance between the rows, before the work of perforation commenced, as it acted as a guide to the operator, showing him exactly how far he must push the sheet forward as he perforated it row by row.

The operator, consequently, took no notice of the work done by the line of pins; but, having once set the ruler correctly, he kept his eyes fixed upon it in order to see that the sheet was kept in line and was moved forward the proper distance each time.[31]

The other half of the table, *i.e.,* the part which received the sheet after its passage beneath the pins, had nothing attached to it.

The perforating pins, which were small flat-headed punches, were fixed in the upper part of the machine.

When the wheel was turned the line of pins descended, and worked into a cor-

---

[29]By E.D. Bacon and F.H. Napier (1902), Pages 16ff.

[30]That is, "slits."

[31]In view of the fact that it was *Miss* Stewart who operated this machine, the authors of *Grenada* were less than gallant in referring to the operator as "he."

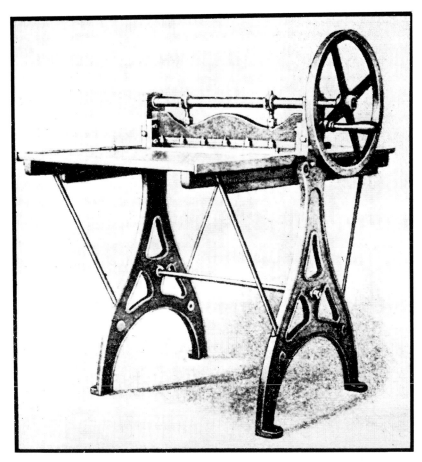

Separation. Single-line perforation. Guillotine machine. The first machine used by Perkins, Bacon & Company (known as the "A" machine), first employed for Trinidad 1860 (August) 1d., 4d. and 6d., yielding clean-cut perf 14 to 16½, the variation occurring because the perforating pins were set at irregular distances apart. The pins were fixed to the bar suspended from the axle across the top of the machine; the bar was moved up and down when the wheel was turned. The pins fitted into holes drilled into the plate on the bed or table of the machine. The operator did not watch the pins at work, but guided the sheets (from the left of the picture, to the right) under a steel ruler, called a "guide plate."

This guide plate was adjusted, before work began, so that the machine could be operated appropriately on the size of stamps to be perforated. When the stamp edges were aligned with the edge of the guide plate, the operator moved the wheel sufficiently to cause the pins to descend and rise again. The operator then moved the sheet until the edges of the next column or row of stamps were aligned with the edge of the guide plate, and again turned the wheel. This was repeated until all the perforations in one direction were applied to the sheet.

This series of operations was performed on sheet after sheet until a whole batch of sheets contained perforations in the one direction. Then the guide plate was adjusted for the different dimension, and the operator applied the perforations in the other direction to every sheet in the batch.

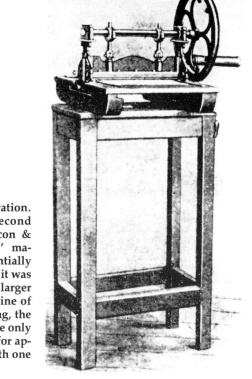

Separation. Single-line perforation. Guillotine machine. The second machine used by Perkins, Bacon & Company (known as the "B" machine). This machine was essentially similar to the "A" machine, but it was smaller, although it produced larger perforation holes. Because the line of holes was only twelve inches long, the "B" machine was suitable for use only with small sheets of stamps, or for applying perforations to sheets with one small dimension.

responding line of holes drilled in a steel plate which was flush with, and formed part of the table.

The flat-headed pins formed, with the drilled holes in the steel plate to which they were nicely fitted, scissor edges that cut or punched out of the interposed sheet minute discs of paper. . . .

. . . the line of pins measured twenty-three inches, so that any sheet of stamps or labels could be perforated up to that length.

It was this machine which . . . is the one they used almost exclusively for perforating colonial stamps from 1860 onwards to 1878. . . . [it is the one referred to in the standard works] as the "A" machine.

The first stamps for which the machine was actually used was the consignment for Trinidad sent off on July 5, 1860. It consisted of 89,000 One Penny, red, 9,000 Four Pence, lilac, and 14,000 Six Pence, green. . . .

All the . . . stamps . . . had perfectly clean cut holes on every side, either when severed or in the sheet, and specimens of them show the nature of the work done by the machine when it was first brought into use.

With regard to the gauge of the machine, of which, as already stated, the line of pins measured twenty-three inches, it may correctly be taken to vary between 14 and 16½ owing to the unequal spacing of the pins, so that in measuring lengths of two centimetres in different parts of the line very different results are obtained, and all gauges between the limits mentioned are to be found in the stamps perforated by it. . . .

Only one sheet was perforated at a time, but as the "guide-plate" required setting differently for the horizontal and vertical rows, Miss Stewart completed the perforation of all the rows in one direction of any batch of stamps she was engaged upon before she turned any of the sheets round to perforate them in the other direction.

During the time this "A" perforating machine was in use for postage stamps — up to September 1879 — the results produced by it varied considerably because of wear and also because of repair and modification. From the clean-cut holes that characterize the earliest productions, the holes deteriorated but improved after the machine received attention. At one period, they were little more than saucer-like depressions in the paper. Then the machine was provided with new pins and bed plate, and the results were entirely different, the holes being smaller and less clean-cut, and the gauge, while still irregular and varying between 14½ and 15½ because of unequal distances between pins, generally measuring 15. Finally the machine was provided with another new set of pins and bed plate, the gauge being 11½.[32]

The next perforating machine acquired by Perkins, Bacon & Company is the one referred to in the standard works as the "B" machine. Again I quote from *Grenada:*[33]

It was purchased May 28, 1862, from a Mr. John Francis, of 21 Essex Street, Islington in London, and . . . is quite a small machine for placing on a table; in fact in size and appearance it is not unlike a small sewing machine. [The table shown in the illustration is the identical one on which the machine was worked by Miss Stewart.] Except for being smaller it works on exactly the same principle as the "A" machine, with a hand-wheel, and also has a "guide-plate," &c.

The line of pins is only twelve inches, and neither the pins nor the plates appear to have been repaired or altered since it was bought. We have been unable to discover for what purpose this machine was originally purchased, but it was certainly not for perforating stamps as the line of pins was far too short to admit most of the sheets of colonial stamps being perforated by it. It is also impossible to say with certainty in what year it was first used for perforating stamps. . . . Miss Stewart . . . says she never used this machine prior to 1866. . . .

There are 175 pins in the line of twelve inches, or 300 mm., which gives a mean gauge of eleven and two-thirds in a space of two centimetres. The pins are, however, extremely irregularly spaced; a few almost touch one another, while others are as much as 1¼ mm. apart, so that the gauge taken at different parts of the line varies from 11 to 12.

As in the case of the "A" machine, when the "B" machine was first used it made perfectly clean-cut holes, but it was not long before the nature of the perforation changed, and we then find very few of the discs of paper entirely removed. . . .

The machine was a good deal used for the stamps of St. Vincent, and it was also employed for the issues of Turks' Islands, and once only for two values of Barbados. . . . In the case of the consignment of Barbados stamps, the machine was used only in conjunction with the "A" machine, as it often was for the stamps

---

[32]This perforation was never used for issued postage stamps, but the machine was employed at the London Philatelic Exhibition in May 1890 to perforate some remainders that were overprinted, in red, "L.P.E. 1890." This accounts for the now only occasionally encountered Mauritius Scott Nos. 7 and 8 and Stanley Gibbons Nos. 39 and 40, thus overprinted and perf 11½. Miss Stewart carried out the perforations at the Exhibition, and the stamps were sold at 6d. each as souvenirs, the proceeds being devoted to Post Office charities.

[33]Pages 34ff.

of St. Vincent, and sometimes for those of Turks' Islands. Whenever so employed we find the horizontal lines of perforation were done by the "B" machine and the vertical lines by the "A" machine. . . .

The reason Miss Stewart gives for using the two machines in conjunction is that the "A" machine, although much the larger, was the easier one to work, and so was mostly used; but some of the values of St. Vincent and the three of Turks' Islands were printed in such narrow sheets, there being only three rows of ten stamps each, that the "guide plate" on the "A" machine was not suitable for them and there was great difficulty in perforating the horizontal lines straight. She found, after trial, she could do the horizontal lines much better by the "B" machine, and from that time she gradually made more and more use of the latter. In working the machine, Miss Stewart tells us, she did not take hold of the handle, but used to move the wheel by catching hold of the rim.

Both the "A" and the "B" machines of Perkins, Bacon & Company were worked by operating a hand-wheel. Other single-line guillotine machines were operated by means of a foot treadle coupled with a wheel to transmit motion to the bar of pins and cause it to rise and fall as required. Most guillotine perforators for postage stamps have been provided with "guide plates," but in some instances they have not.

Multiple-Line Perforation

Multiple-line perforation for postage stamps is effected mechanically by means of rotary machines employing the Bemrose principle referred to earlier in this chapter.

The earliest machine of this type for use with postage stamps in the United States was imported from W. Bemrose & Sons in Derby, England, by Toppan, Carpenter & Company of Philadelphia in 1856 — in Australia, one was imported in 1869 — and such machines have had widespread use.

In these machines, the necessary number of perforating wheels (or "pin wheels") was placed on the upper of two axles. The wheels were spaced the required distances apart, and then secured in position by means of pressure from threaded bolts. The nearness of one set of pins to the next was limited only by the thickness of the pin wheels, and the number of wheels that could be accommodated on the axle was limited only by its length and their aggregate width. Similarly, on the lower of the two axles were secured the counterpart wheels, with the holes that received the ends of the pins and the minute circles of paper that were punched from the sheets during the operation of perforating them.

Each pair of upper and lower wheels had to be carefully and accurately matched, but the pairs of wheels could be moved along the axles so as to produce an infinite number of different spacings. Each machine was, therefore, capable of perforating stamps of widely differing sizes.

It was essential for the satisfactory operating of the machine that not only had the wheels to be set at the correct distances for the width of the stamps, but also the "movable gauge"[34] had to be set at the correct distance to allow

---

[34]The "C" of the specification drawing — see "Bemrose" earlier in this chapter, the specification text, and also Bemrose's Figure 1.

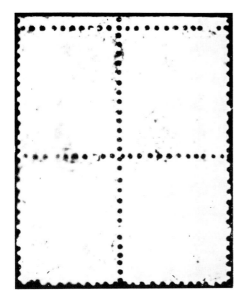

Separation. Single-line guillotine perforation. An example of the clean-cut results produced by the Perkins, Bacon "B" machine during the early stages. Note the irregular spacing between the holes.[35]

for the sheet margins. This movable gauge, when correctly set, ensured that the perforations were made in the stamp gutters.

A picture of a machine in use at the American Bank Note Company during 1861 is to be found accompanying a contemporary article in *Harper's Magazine*.[35]

The picture, part of which is reproduced here, gives a clear idea of the machine in operation. It somewhat resembles an old-fashioned, foot-treadle operated sewing machine; and some of the operating details are described in the article in *Harper's Magazine*, from which the following quotation is taken.

[The machine] consists of a couple of cylinders revolving together. The upper one is studded over with little punches which fit into holes in the lower one. A sheet of stamps — already gummed, dried, and pressed — is passed between these cylinders, and each punch cuts out a piece; the lower cylinder being hollow, these pieces fall into it and do not clog the punches. A hundred stamps are usually printed on a sheet, and 250 of these sheets can be perforated in an hour. . . . The cylinders are made in sections, like a row of wheels, so that the points may be adjusted for stamps of any size.

On being passed through the machine, a sheet was provided with perforations in only one direction at one operation. Before the perforations in the other direction could be applied, the pairs of wheels had to be differently spaced, and the "movable gauge" had to be appropriately reset to allow for the differences between the top or bottom and the side margin of the sheet. This was an operation that occupied some time. Therefore, it was usual to apply one set of perforations to a batch of sheets before altering the setting

---

[35]February 1862. Reprinted in *Ten Decades Ago. 1840-1850* by Winthrop S. Boggs (1949), Pages 56, 73; and also in *Early American Perforating Machines and Perforations 1857-1867* by Winthrop S. Boggs (The Unitrade Press, Toronto, June 1982).

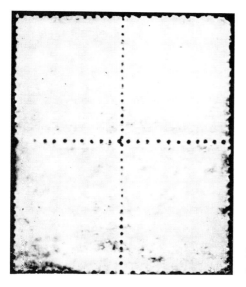

Separation. Single-line guillotine compound perforation. An example of the results produced by a combination of the Perkins, Bacon "A" machine (the vertical perforation) and "B" machine (the horizontal perforation). Some values of St. Vincent and Turks' Islands, printed in sheets of thirty (three across and ten down), were difficult to perforate horizontally on the "A" machine because it was so large, having a line of pins twenty-three inches long. Miss H. Stewart (who carried out all perforations at Perkins, Bacon & Company from 1860 onward) could not align them properly on the "guide plate" of that machine. She therefore used the smaller "B" machine with its twelve-inch line of pins for the horizontal perforations, giving rise to the compound perforation 11 to 12 x 14½ to 15½, of which the picture is an example.

of the wheels and gauge, and then passing each sheet through the machine for a second time to receive the other set of perforations.

The necessity for altering the setting delayed the completion of orders, and busy stamp manufacturers soon realized the advantages to be gained from employing two machines — one machine with the wheels and "movable gauge" set for the vertical, and the other for the horizontal perforations.

In the manufacture of a set of wheels for a machine, it was usual for each pair to be made so as to yield substantially identical results with every other pair. Indeed, unless the pin wheel and its counterpart were very accurately made, the machine would not work, because of the number of pins from each perforating wheel that had to be more or less engaged in its counterpart[36] at any one time when the machine was in operation.[37]

---

[36]It has been demonstrated that in the original Bemrose machine, which gauged "perf 15.25" (producing thirty-nine holes every two inches), the number of pins so engaged was between fourteen and sixteen for every pair of wheels. Therefore, with twenty wheels set for the vertical perforation of the double-pane sheet of U.S. 1857 stamps — only twenty because the interpane gutter was not perforated — parts of not fewer than 280 pins were engaged in the same number of holes in the counterpart wheels at every instant during the perforation process.

[37]It is possible that even greater accuracy than that dictated merely by the number of pins continuously more or less engaged was required in the manufacture of these wheels for the Bemrose machine. A calculation based on measurements taken from photocopies of the patent specification indicates that the counterpart wheel did not necessarily bear the same number of holes as there were pins. The number of holes may have been 154 or 155 as compared with 140 pins. This would indicate that the same pin and hole did not pair as the wheels revolved; and this, in turn, would require great precision in manufacture. However, with sufficient clearance between pin and hole, there may have been the same number of pins and holes. I am indebted to F.M. Johnson for the calculations.

Separation. Multiple-line rotary perforation. From an illustration published in
Harper's Magazine, the machine in use at the American Bank Note Company
in 1861. This machine, constructed on the Bemrose principle, was worked by
foot treadle that caused the rotation of both sets of perforating and counterpart
wheels. The operator has, on the table before her, a sheet of stamps about to
be perforated (in one direction); in the box beyond the perforating wheels are
sheets that have already been perforated. Beyond the operator's left hand and
at the (viewer's) nearest edge of the table at which she is sitting is the "movable
gauge" against which the left-hand (or, as the case might be according to setting, top or bottom) edge of the sheet is placed to ensure that it is fed correctly
into the machine so that the perforations are made in the stamp gutters.

However, when a different pair of wheels was made for that machine, or for a new machine, the new set was not necessarily identical with the old set.[38] Although the differences might be so minute as to be unimportant for most practical production purposes, the exactness of philatelic classification is such that the differences are revealed by careful gauging of the results with a perforation gauge capable of giving unlimitedly fine and accurate readings between each of the points on the gauge.[39]

The use of different sets of wheels for the vertical and horizontal perforations resulted in stamps with perforations that philatelically are designated as "compound." When measurement reveals that a stamp that has been rotary perforated on the Bemrose principle has two even slightly differing gauges of perforation vertically and horizontally, that factor indicates that one machine was used for the vertical perforation and another machine for the horizontal perforation of the sheet.

The indication is not conclusive. It could be controverted by an undoubtedly genuine stamp (or, preferably, several undoubtedly genuine stamps) thus perforated and bearing two differing gauges of perforation in the same direction at each edge. The indication in this event would be that different pairs of pin and counterpart wheels on the same axle had different numbers of pins and holes, each pair of wheels producing a different gauge of perforation. However, this presupposes that, for that particular machine, a solution was found for some not inconsiderable problems of mechanical engineering.

L-Type Perforators

Rotary machines of this nature are, sometimes, termed "one-way" (rotary) perforating machines. The use of two different one-way rotary machines, one for horizontal and the other for vertical perforations, requires that each sheet must be turned through a right-angle after receiving one series of perforations. Frequently, this operation has been carried out by hand — a time-consuming process that necessarily introduces the human element of liability to err.

Perforating units have been assembled to eliminate to a great extent the handling of sheets between the two series of operations. The units comprise an adaptation of the production-line endless band. It is in two sections, one at right-angles to the other. In these units, therefore, instead of the sheet being physically turned through a right-angle, it remains facing in the same direction; but the sheet has imparted to it two different directional movements, one after the other and at right-angles to each other.

The sheet is fed through the first one-way rotary perforator, and is then

---

[38]Quite apart from deliberate variations, there may have been, for instance (as was mentioned earlier in this chapter when "Conventions in Gauging" were discussed), a different interpretation by each of two mechanics of, say, "sixteen pins per inch" — one mechanic producing, in fact, "sixteen pins within the inch," and the other producing "sixteen pins to the inch."

[39]Such as the Instanta perforation gauge.

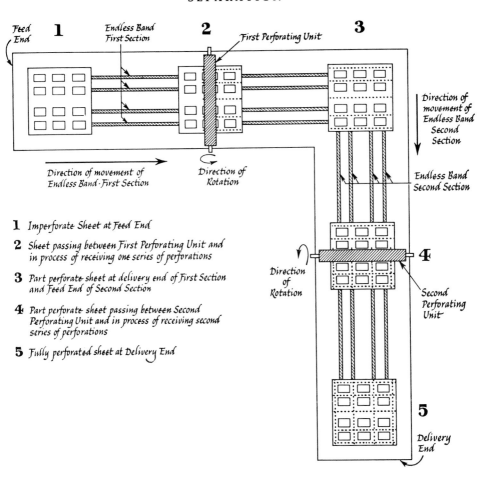

1 Imperforate Sheet at Feed End

2 Sheet passing between First Perforating Unit and in process of receiving one series of perforations

3 Part perforate sheet at delivery end of First Section and Feed End of Second Section

4 Part perforate sheet passing between Second Perforating Unit and in process of receiving second series of perforations

5 Fully perforated sheet at Delivery End

led to the end of the first section of the endless band, where the second section of endless band takes over the sheet and leads it through the second one-way perforator. Because the bands and machines are set at right-angles to one another, and form roughly the shape of the capital letter "L," this sort of perforating assembly is termed the "L-type" perforator.

This type of perforating equipment was in operation at the Bureau of Engraving and Printing at Washington, D.C., and was used, by way of specific example, in the production of U.S. 1957 Flag Issue 4c.

It is characteristic of sheets perforated by these methods using one-way rotary perforating machines that the perforations extend throughout all of the sheet margins.

'Electric Eye' Perforators

Rotary perforators working exclusively on the Bemrose principle are limited in application to sheets. Therefore, when stamps are printed "on the web,"

Separation. Multiple-line rotary perforation. An "L-type" perforator comprising an assembly of two "one-way" perforating machines. In use at the Bureau
of Engraving and Printing at Washington, D.C., for perforating U.S. 1957 Flag
Issue 4c. The sheets were fed, one at a time, beyond the left of the picture, on
to the tapes of the first section of the endless band. They then passed between
the first series of pin and counterpart wheels at the left of the picture, and were
provided with horizontal perforations. The endless band then carried the sheets
toward the operator at the left, where they were transferred to the tapes of the
second section of the endless band. The sheets (still facing in the original direction, but traveling at right-angles to their first stage of travel) passed between
of the second series of pin and counterpart wheels (at the center of the picture),
which imparted all of the vertical perforations. The tapes then carried the fully
perforated sheets to the delivery end, where a finished sheet is being inspected
by the second operator.

or in continuous reels, they have to be cut into sheet form before they can
be perforated.

Partly to overcome the difficulty caused by this break in the flow of production, and partly to provide better control over the registration of perforation, thus reducing waste from spoilage,[40] and for other reasons, the U.S.
Bureau of Engraving and Printing experimented with and developed the so-
called "electric eye" perforator, in which perforation registration is controlled
by photoelectric cells coupled to the machine.

The mechanics of perforation were based primarily on the Bemrose principle, but both vertical and horizontal perforations were provided during a
single passage of the unsevered web, without altering the direction of paper
movement, and without the necessity for turning the paper during the opera-

tion. This was effected by the ingenious yet simple method of substituting, for the second series of pin and counterpart wheels, a single long cylinder bearing around its periphery a series of pins in long rows — each row spaced stamp-depth apart from the next — and a corresponding counterpart cylinder. Thus, the series of pin and counterpart wheels that provides one set of perforations, and the pin cylinder and its counterpart that provide the other set of perforations, rotate in the same direction, and fully perforate a sheet or web at a single passage. Such machines are sometimes termed "two-way" perforating machines.

Experiments were initiated by the Bureau of Engraving and Printing during 1930, and the "experimental" model electric eye perforator was in use for issued stamps, printed from specially engraved plates, in 1933. The first stamp distributed was U.S. 1926 (Dec. 10) Regular 2c., which was sent out to post offices in 1935. Further experiments and development led to the construction of a "pilot" model electric eye perforator — "pilot" because it was to serve as a guide for the production electric eye perforators made by contracting manufacturers.

The "electric eyes" scanned certain marginal markings that at first were hand-engraved on the plates. Later the markings were entered by transfer rollers in the usual way.[41] Over the years, these markings have varied in shape and position, and study of them has led to the creation of a special philatelic terminology. It would be out of place here exhaustively to survey these markings and the different types of plate lay-out. They appear in a standard work.[42] The principal "electric eye" mark philatelic terms include: "dashes" that occur vertically in the center longitudinal gutter separating left and right panes *as printed on the web;* "frame bars" that occur opposite most subjects adjacent to the left or right longitudinal margin *of the printed web* — or, sometimes, in both margins; "margin lines" that appear in the right longitudinal margin *of the printed web,* opposite the lateral gutters separating the panes; and "gutter bars" that occur in the left (and sometimes in the right) longitudinal margin *of the printed web* opposite the lateral gutters separating the panes. Emphasis is laid on "the printed web" because the positions of these marks on post office sheets is determined by the format of the stamp. For example, large vertical-format stamps are rotary printed on the web with the longer dimension across the web, but on the post office sheets the stamps appear upright. Consequently, the post office sheet margins of such stamps, along with the electric eye markings, are at right-angles to their appearance on the printed web.

The "contract" model electric eye perforating machines — five of them — were manufactured by Harris-Seybold of Cleveland, Ohio, in 1941. The

---

[40]Spoilage was reduced from something like thirty-five per cent in 1940 to something like one per cent on the electric eye perforators.

[41]See "Multiplication of the Design Mechanically" in the chapter entitled "Intaglio Printing — I: Line Engraving."

[42]*Electric Eye Terminology,* by the Standardization Committee of The Bureau Issues Association (1948), partly superseded in *The Bureau Specialist* Vol. 33, Pages 70 to 75 (March 1962 and subsequently).

Separation. Electric eye perforator. A "two-way" perforating machine. The "pilot" model, built at the Bureau of Engraving and Printing in Washington, D.C. This machine (made after a series of experiments initiated in 1930 and carried out on an "experimental" model from which stamps were distributed in 1935) was constructed to serve as a guide or "pilot" to manufacturers in the production of "contract" models that were, in fact, produced by Harris-Seybold of Cleveland, Ohio.

In the picture of the "pilot" model, the web or reel of stamps is at the right, by the chair behind the standing operator. Immediately above the reel, and almost obscured by the operator (part of the cable can be seen projecting to the rear), is the first "electric eye" — the photoelectric cell that scans the gutters bearing the "dashes" printed between the left and right panes of stamps as printed on the web. This electric eye controls the longitudinal perforations that are applied by pin and counterpart wheels, obscured by the casing of the machine.

In the picture, to the left of the standing operator's outstretched hand is the second electric eye that scans the margin bearing the "frame bars," and controls the machine's lateral perforations — applied by the cage-like pin cylinder (visible at the top of the machine) and its counterpart cylinder (beneath, hidden by the casing of the machine). The web is severed into full sheets, and they are delivered on to the rack facing the seated operator. She can make adjustments to the registration of each series of perforations by means of the instrument panel beside her.

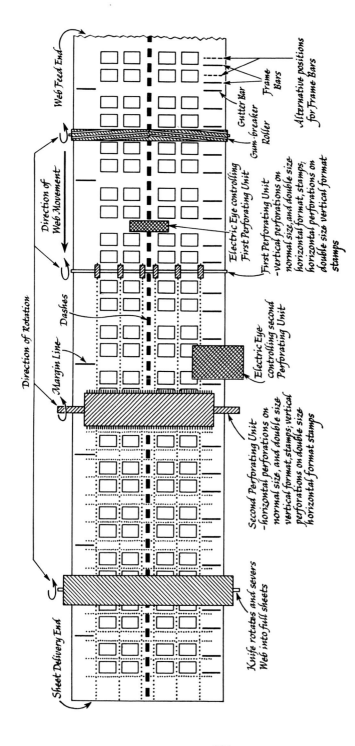

Diagrammatic Representation of
Electric Eye Perforator in Operation

general operation of the machine is reasonably simple to understand, but it is the result of amazingly high-precision mechanical and electrical engineering.

Two gummed and printed rolls of paper — each about eighteen inches wide and 3,000 feet long, with the gummed side outward — are fitted on to axles at the feed end of the machine. These axles are so arranged that they can be cranked into position for the end of the roll to be threaded into the machine. As soon as one roll is exhausted, another is brought into use, and another full roll is fitted on the free axle, with minimum loss of operating time. When the machine is running at speed, a roll is exhausted in well under ten minutes; the web whips through the machine at just under 340 feet per minute!

The end of the roll of paper is led diagonally upward and over a guide roller. Situated immediately above and in the center of this roller is the first "electric eye," a photoelectric cell that controls the centering of the machine's longitudinal perforations — that is, the lines of perforations that are applied throughout the length of the web. It is, strictly speaking, inapt in reference to "electric eye" perforated stamps during production to talk generally about "horizontal" and "vertical" perforations as they appear on post office sheets. The reason is that the stamps are printed on the web according to the dictates of the electric eye perforator. Large, horizontal-format stamps (such as, for example, U.S. 1960 American Woman Issue, 4c.) are printed with the longer dimension across the web from plates of 200 subjects in four panes of fifty each; so also, large vertical-format stamps (such as, for example, U.S. 1960 Fifth World Forestry Congress Issue, 4c.) are printed with the longer dimension across the web from plates of 200 subjects in four panes of fifty each. As a consequence, the *vertical* perforations of the post office sheets of horizontal-format stamps and the *horizontal* perforations of the post office sheets of the vertical-format stamps are *both* longitudinal perforations of the machine. The longitudinal perforations are not applied at the stage of the web's travel under or immediately after the first electric eye, but later; and the electric eye actuates automatic relays. These relays act on the web-carriage of the machine, and shift the web laterally. This lateral control is necessary because, in wet-printed[43] webs, the aggregate width of the impressions on the eighteen-inch web may vary as much as one-quarter inch within the length of a single web, because of uneven shrinkage[44] of paper twice wetted — once before printing and again during gumming. Also, varying humidity will cause paper to expand or contract.

This electric eye itself is focused upon and scans the longitudinal gutter separating the lateral panes as printed on the web and bearing the "dashes."

After passing this electric eye, the web is led between corrugated gum-breaker rollers that have a dual function. The primary purpose of the gum-breaker rollers is to counteract the curling caused by the film of gum on the

(text continues on Page 695)

---

[43]See "Wet Printing and Dry Printing" in the chapter entitled "Printing Problems and Varieties."

[44]See "Shrinkage" in the alphabetical list to the chapter entitled "Paper" and "Gumming After or Before Printing" in the chapter entitled "Gum."

Separation. Electric eye perforator. The "contract" model. Feed end. The end of the printed and gummed reel of stamps is led from below over the roller at the extreme right of the picture, where an "electric eye" — the box-like structure — scans gutter and "dashes" printed between the left and right panes of stamps as printed on the web, and controls the machine's longitudinal perforations, applied later in the web's travel, by a series of pin and counterpart wheels out of view to the left of the picture.

After passing this electric eye, the paper passes under the gum-breaker roller — the first roller in the picture to the left of the electric eye. This roller serves to counteract curling of the gummed paper (and imparts slightly diagonal ridges), and also assists in maintaining the paper at proper tension. The paper then passes under other tensioning and guiding rollers in front of the operator.

In the picture, at the left of her (actual) right hand is another electric eye, and yet another one appears at the extreme left of the picture. These electric eyes control the machine's lateral perforations, the trimming of the right edge of the web, and the web severance into sheets — all these operations being effected later in the web's travel, out of view to the left of the picture.

Note the second reel on the wheel in the foreground. When the reel in use is exhausted, the wheel is turned, and the next web can be fed into the machine — and another reel fitted in place — with very little loss of operating time. The perforator is shown in operation on a reel of 3c. stamps printed for use in books or booklets. The machine's longitudinal perforations are the vertical perforations on the stamps; the lateral perforations are the horizontal perforations on the stamps.

Separation. Electric eye perforator. The "contract" model. Sheet delivery end. The casing at the top of the machine (and on which the operator at the left is resting her left arm) houses the pin and counterpart wheels for the machine's longitudinal perforations, the pin and counterpart cylinders for the machine's lateral perforations, and the web-edge trimming knife. The operator at the left is regarding the operations subsequent to perforation — including web severance into full sheets. The severed full sheets are delivered, stacked, to the operator at the right. She can make adjustments to the registration of each series of perforations by using the control panel attached to the frame of the machine level with her left shoulder.

printed and gummed web. This is effected by fracturing the gum film — and, incidentally, imparting slightly diagonal ridges to the paper.[45] The secondary purpose of the gum-breaker roll is to assist in maintaining the web of paper at proper tension during part of its passage through the machine.

The web next passes under other tensioning and guiding rollers on its way to two other electric eyes. These eyes scan the outer longitudinal margins of the web for "frame bars," "gutter bars" and "margin lines."[46] These photoelectric cells control the centering of the machine's latitudinal perforations — that is, the lines of perforations applied across the web between stamps. These perforations are not applied at that stage of the web's travel, but later; and the electric eyes actuate automatic relays. These relays act on the pin cylinder and its counterpart, adjusting them longitudinally on the web. This longitudinal control is necessary because, atmospheric humidity apart, in wet-printed webs, the aggregate length of the plate impression of normal-size stamps may vary as much as $\frac{3}{32}$ inch within the same web.

The web, traveling at the rate of about 337½ feet per minute, next passes over the web-carriage that has been shifted laterally into position as the result of the first electric eye signal sent out the previous split-second (when the web was beneath the first eye), and encounters the first perforating unit, which applies the machine's longitudinal perforations. For normal-size stamps, this unit consists of twenty-two pairs of pin and counterpart wheels or, as they are sometimes called, "punch rings" and die rings."

Each ring is 9.91 inches in diameter. The punch ring bears 415 punches set in a corresponding number of holes; the die ring has 415 holes. The accuracy with which the rings and punches are made and the holes drilled is quite remarkable. The punches are of needle steel, ground to a diameter of 0.042 inch. The margin of error permissible in diameter is the staggeringly small figure of 0.00001 inch. The rings themselves are made with similar accuracy. Each hole is drilled 0.039 inch in diameter, and is reamed to 0.044 inch. The punches are soldered into place, and the *accumulated* error in the thirty-one-and-a-bit-inch circumference of the ring must not exceed 0.001 inch. Each such longitudinal perforating unit has 9,130 punches. The twenty-two pairs of rings are drilled and assembled as a unit by the manufacturers, who designed special drilling machines for the job, which is carried out in an air-conditioned room in Cleveland.

Still traveling at a rate of more than five feet per second, the web passes between the rapidly revolving punch and die rings, receiving its longitudinal perforations.

The web next encounters the lateral perforating unit. This unit comprises a two-cylinder assembly. Each cylinder is a cage-like structure of bars mounted on rings; the diameter of the cylinder is thirteen inches. For normal-size

---

[45]See "Counteracting Paper Curl" and the illustration in the chapter entitled "Gum." These corrugated gum-breaker rollers were developed with the electric eye perforators. Sometimes, in addition to these rollers, other longitudinal gum-breaker rollers are used. These impart, on normal-size stamps, vertical ridges that are much less pronounced than are the diagonal ridges.

[46]When present.

Separation. Electric eye perforator. The "contract" model. An overall view of the machine from the sheet delivery end. The machine is fed with a printed reel about eighteen inches wide and 3,000 feet long, bearing stamps printed in "full" sheets — that is, for example, for ordinary issues, four panes each of 100 subjects. On the same wet-printed web, the overall printed dimensions may vary up to about one-quarter inch across the eighteen-inch web, and about three thirty-seconds inch in the length of a full sheet. The paper web passes through the machine at the rate of about 337½ feet per minute. The first electric eye causes automatic relays to shift the web carriage into register so that the machine's longitudinal perforations coincide with the stamp gutters. The second electric eye causes automatic relays to adjust the cylinders for the machine's lateral perforations and to register them in the other stamp gutters. Because of these correcting movements the web is in a continual "weaving" motion as it passes through the machine.

The pins (or "punches") and counterparts (or dies") that effect the perforations are the results of extremely high-precision engineering, carried out on specially designed machines. The pin cylinder, thirteen inches in diameter, has up to forty-four bars — according to the shape of the stamps to be perforated. Each bar bears 247 "punches" of needle steel in its eighteen-inch length; the pin measures 0.042 inch in diameter; the distance between centers is 0.07 inch. The pins must be fitted by soldering into each punch bar with a cumulative error of not more than 0.001 inch on the eighteen-inch bar! The hole in the bar to receive the pins measures 0.044 inch after reaming. The pin and counterpart wheels (called "punch rings" and "die rings") each have 415 holes in a circle of 9.91-inch diameter.

The cylinders and rings are assembled as units. For normal-size stamps, a set of units consists of a pin cylinder of forty-four punch bars, a corresponding counterpart cylinder of forty-four die bars, and twenty-two punch rings and twenty-two die rings. This means that, for each such set of units, four less than 40,000 holes have been drilled with hair-splitting precision, and 19,998 punches have been soldered into place on the relevant bars and rings. Each bar unit is guaranteed to perforate a minimum of 4.5 million sheets, and each wheel unit 3.5 million sheets. Some units have perforated as many as 13 million sheets, but the average is 6 million and 5 million sheets, respectively. About 2.5 million perforation holes are punched out every minute, and in five minutes' running time the punched-out circles of paper weigh 22 lbs. 4 oz.

These are sobering thoughts for the collector caviling at the post office for selling a stamp that is perforated off-center by a fraction of a millimeter!

The machine is shown at work on a reel of 3c. stamps for use in books or booklets. The stamps are printed from 360-subject plates, and the machine severs the web into "full" sheets of 360 stamps. These whole sheets are then machine-collated with wax-impregnated separator paper and corresponding top and bottom covers. After collating, the assemblies of full sheet size are cut into six sections, three stamps deep and twenty stamps wide. The sections are glued, examined, counted, stitched, and later cut into individual books or booklets.

stamps, each cylinder has forty-four bars, all made with the same hair-splitting accuracy as the rings. Each bar is eighteen inches long, and has been drilled with 247 holes, the distance between centers being 0.07 inch. Each punch bar has 247 pins that are fitted into it with an accumulated margin of error not greater than 0.001 inch in the eighteen-inch bar. The pins and holes extend just under 17¼ inches of the eighteen inches. The two cylinders are assembled as a unit by the manufacturers, and each such lateral perforating unit has 10,868 pins.

Still traveling at a rate of more than sixty-seven inches per second, the web passes between the rapidly revolving punch and die cylinders, receiving its lateral perforations.

It is characteristic of sheets perforated by the electric eye perforator that one set of perforations (the machine's longitudinal perforations) extends throughout the sheet margins, while the other set of perforations (the machine's lateral perforations) stops short of the sheet edge by one-quarter inch or more.[47]

On its further travel through the machine, the web is severed[48] into "full" sheet form — that is, for normal-size stamps, into sheets bearing four panes, each of 100 subjects. These full sheets are delivered, stacked, at the delivery end of the machine. The sheets are then examined, counted and assembled in bundles of 100. Next a manila board is placed top and bottom. The assembled sheets and boards are stitched together with wire staples to form units. The unit of 100 sheets and two boards is then cut into quarters on a guillotine, and thus the post office sheets come into existence.

Harrison & Sons Ltd., printers of British stamps, experimented with rotary perforation on the web of printed stamps. The objective was to speed production. Previously, production was slowed because the printed web had to be cut into sheets that were then comb stroke-perforated. The experiment was based on a machine colloquially known as "the lawnmower," because of its "cutting" action. The machine, which was termed "the APS machine," had nothing to do with the American Philatelic Society. The acronym, in fact, signified the name of the Swedish firm, Aktiebolaget Produktion Service, but was used also to signify "Alternative Perforating System."

The basis of operation was a revolving cylinder with a surface consisting of short pins or pimples arranged according to the gutters in what were to become the sheets of stamps to be perforated. The printed web was led over the pin-surfaced cylinder. As this was happening, the other side of the paper came into contact with a counter-revolving cylinder consisting of blades that chipped or ground away the paper protruding on the pimples. The paper was thus holed, or perforated, by a revolutionary new method, different from either the Archer stroke principle or the Bemroses's rotary principle.

The experiment was not successful, and Harrison & Sons developed a machine with the capability of intaglio printing in both line engraving and

---

[47]For example, see the illustration of electric eye markings — on perforated stamps — in the chapter entitled "From Design to Printed Sheets."

[48]Compare the "cross-cutter" in the Swiss machine, illustrated in the chapter entitled "Intaglio Printing — I: Line Engraving."

VISCOUNT CUNNINGHAM/HMS WARSPITE

Separation. Perforation. Rotary perforation on the web. Great Britain 1982 (Jun. 16) Maritime Heritage 29p. One stamp in a series of five perforated by a Kampf unit of two cylinders, one with pins that push into holes on the other cylinder and pierce the paper as it passes between them. The series was printed by Harrison & Sons Ltd. on the Jumelle press and bears designs printed in both photogravure and recess engraving. The speed of the paper, printed and perforated on the web, exceeds 490 feet a minute.

photogravure on the web as it passes on its single passage through the various banks of cylinders. The machine is known as the "Jumelle" press. Integral parts of the machine are two Kampf units, which are sets of perforating cylinders that work on a development of the Bemroses's principle. In each case, one cylinder has pins protruding from the surface and the other cylinder has holes into which the pins fit. The web of paper passes between the two cylinders in the set that is being used and is thus perforated. The perforating cylinders operate at a speed that enables 150 meters of printed web a minute to pass through. That is equivalent to something more than eight feet a second. A single instance, chosen at random, of a stamp that was printed on the Jumelle press, perforated by the Kampf units and printed in both photogravure and line-engraved recess is Great Britain 1982 (Jun. 16) Maritime Heritage 29p.

Comb Perforation

Comb perforators, as stated earlier in this chapter, are sometimes termed "triple-cutters," because, in the simplest form of the operation, perforations are supplied to three sides of the stamps in a row or column at a single operation of the machine. The term "comb" was adopted philatelically because the effect on the paper of a single stroke somewhat resembles in appearance a comb with widely spaced teeth. Sometimes, however, when reference is made to the components of this effect, the long row of holes is referred to as "the line," and the short, widely spaced rows at right-angles to the line are referred to as "the legs."

Comb perforation falls into two main groups. In the first group, only a single row of perforations, comprising a line and legs, is made in the paper at one operation, and such perforation is, sometimes, termed "single-comb perforation." In the second group, at one operation, one or more rows or columns of stamps are perforated on all sides, and an additional row or column is provided with perforation between the stamps, so that the last row or column is imperforate throughout one edge. Machines that perforate complete rows or columns are termed "double-comb" if one row or column is completely perforated and the next row or column is provided with legs; "triple-

Separation. Comb perforation. Single-comb perforator. The effect of (part of) one stroke of a single-comb perforator. Termed "comb" because the effect somewhat resembles in appearance a comb with widely spaced teeth, the components of this effect are occasionally referred to as "the line," representing the long row of holes, and "the legs," representing the short rows at right-angles to the line.

At the first stroke, a single-comb perforates three sides of one row or column of stamps. The paper is then moved into position and the next stroke completes the perforation of the first row or column and provides holes (the legs) in the gutters between the stamps of the second row or column. At this stage, if the paper movement has been accurately controlled, the effect resembles exactly one stroke of a double-comb perforator. (The effects produced when the paper movement has not been accurately controlled are illustrated later.)

At the third stroke of the perforator, the perforation of the second row or column is completed and that of the third row or column is partly effected. At that stage, again if the paper movement has been accurately controlled, the effect resembles exactly one stroke of a triple comb. At the fourth stroke, the perforation of the third row or column is completed, and so on.

comb" if two rows or columns are completely perforated and the third provided with legs; "quadruple-comb," and so on. Usually comb perforation is effected mechanically by a stroke machine, although cases are on record, as long ago as 1890, of rotary triple-cutters in use at Adelaide, South Australia, and such machines were used subsequently in Victoria, New South Wales.[49]

A unique variation of double-comb perforation was used experimentally for a short while for New Zealand 1960 (Jul. 11–Sep. 1) to 1964 ½d. to 8d. (except 2½d.). At one operation, one row of stamps was completely perforated on all sides and half-legs were provided to the rows below and above. This exceptional perforation is termed "Chambon" after the name of the firm providing the head.

In fundamental principle of operation, the two main groups of stroke comb perforators are identical. The only substantial difference between them is the distance the paper travels between consecutive descents of the perforating pins. The control and regulation of this paper movement provide clues from

---

[49]The rotary triple-cutter in use at Adelaide was driven by electric power, having been made to the design of the South Australian stamp printer, Cooke, by a man called Nash. These rotary triple-cutters were, undoubtedly, developed locally from a Bemrose machine that had been sent out from England in 1869. I am indebted to J.R.W. Purves for much of this information. Also, for example, Victoria 1901-12 (1910) 1d., Scott No. 218, Stanley Gibbons No. 434, can be found perf 11½ x 12¼ from a rotary comb machine.

Separation. Comb perforation. Double-comb perforator. The effect of (part of) one stroke of a double-comb perforator. A double-comb, at one operation, perforates a single row or column of stamps on all sides and provides perforations (the legs) between the stamps in the next row or column. At this stage, the effect exactly resembles two strokes of a single-comb perforator when the paper movement has been accurately controlled. At the second stroke of a double-comb perforator, the perforation of the second row or column is completed, and that of the third row or column is provided, as are the legs for the fourth row or column. At that stage, if the paper movement has been accurately controlled, the effect exactly resembles that of four strokes of an accurately controlled single-comb perforator, or one stroke of a quadruple-comb perforator. If, with the double-comb perforator, the paper movement has not been accurately controlled, the effect will be that the irregularity will be apparent at every alternate row or column where the legs should accurately meet the line, and some of these effects are illustrated later.

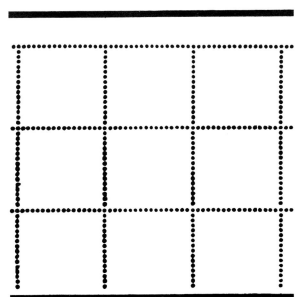

Separation. Comb perforation. Triple-comb perforator. The effect of (part of) one stroke of a triple-comb perforator. A triple-comb at one operation perforates two complete rows or columns of stamps on all sides and provides perforations (the legs) between the stamps in the third row or column.

701

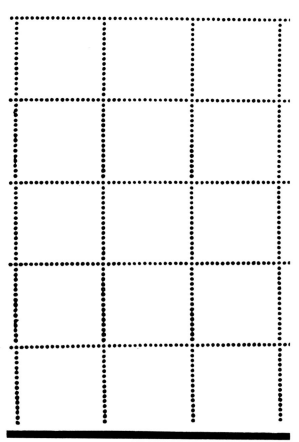

Separation. Comb perforation. Quintuple-comb (or five-comb) perforator. The effect of part of one stroke of a quintuple-comb perforator. A quintuple-comb, at one operation, perforates four complete rows or columns of stamps on all sides and provides perforations (the legs) between the stamps in the fifth row or column.

which the philatelist can usually determine whether the perforating head comprised a ''single-comb,'' ''double-comb'' or so on.

From the earliest days of stamp perforation, the necessity of moving the paper between the descents of the pins has caused difficulty to stamp perforators; the requisite adjustment is a very fine one indeed. Maladjustment of the control, or malfunctioning of it, leads to results that are unsatisfactory to the stamp-issuing authorities and, sometimes, puzzling to the student.

Controlling Paper Movement

Reference was made earlier in this chapter to Henry Archer's specification and, incidentally, to the arrangement of rack, pinion and pawl originally adopted by his engineers for controlling paper movement between descents of the pins. One of Archer's chief difficulties was the shrinkage of paper. He was quite impractical and set about obtaining a machine that was too rigid in operation to cope with the almost infinite variety of dimensions resulting from shrinkage of paper twice wetted before perforation — once before printing, and again when gummed. That he, early on, entirely failed to realize

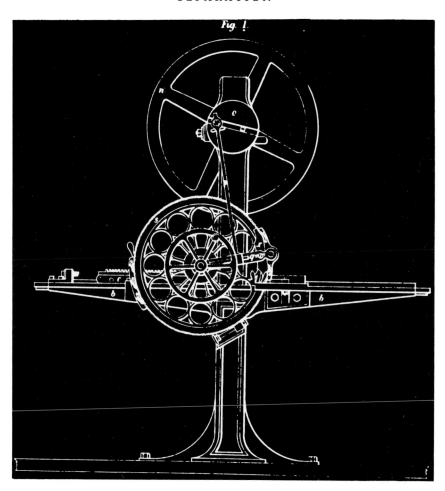

Separation. Variable feed motion. Archer's later experimental model. The (lower) large-toothed wheel, coupled with the rack and pawl, enabled the paper travel between descents of the pins to be varied accurately within narrow limits, and so enabled accurate perforation to be carried out on sheets that, because of irregular shrinkage of paper, were different sizes. Compare this complex arrangement with the crude control on the patent specification model identified as "Archer Patent, Figure 1" pictured earlier in this chapter.

the magnitude of the problem is evident from a perusal of the *Report from the Select Committee on Postage Label Stamps* (1852). He even went to the trouble of taking measurements from the printing plates in an attempt to produce a foolproof pin- and bed-plate arrangement. He succeeded only in alienating the sympathies of Perkins, Bacon & Company.

Archer's specification and patent drawing — Figure 1, properly numbered and illustrated and discussed earlier in this chapter — shows the rudimentary control by means of rack and pawl first adopted to move the sheets forward between descents of the pins. Part of his difficulty was caused by the

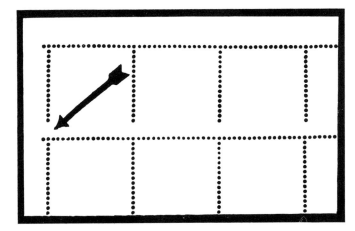

Separation. Single-comb perforator. Paper movement too great for length of legs. The effect that results from two strokes of a single-comb perforator when the paper movement has not been accurately controlled to the length of the legs, resulting in too large a gap.

differing lengths of stamps in the sheet, part by the different widths of the gutters. He operated with a single-comb head and legs of a single length. As he, or his engineers, began to appreciate the situation, experiments were made with a complex arrangement that enabled the distance of paper travel to be varied between consecutive descents of the pins. His pamphlet, *Perforated Postage Label Stamps* (1851), produced during the heat of battle for adequate compensation, contains an illustration of this complex arrangement. That it worked satisfactorily during trials cannot be doubted, for he was

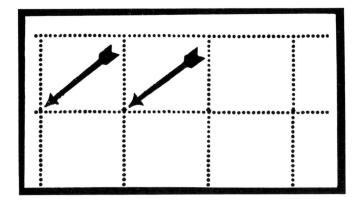

Separation. Single-comb perforator. Paper movement slightly too little for length of legs. The effect that results from two strokes of a single-comb perforator when the paper movement has not been accurately controlled to the length of the legs. The result is a slight encroachment of the holes at the ends of the legs and the corresponding holes in the line, which produces the effect usually associated exclusively with the crossing of line perforations.

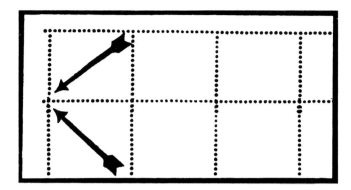

Separation. Single-comb perforator. Paper movement much too little for length of legs. The effect that results from two strokes of a single-comb perforator when the paper movement, owing to maladjustment or interference, has been substantially too little for the length of the legs. This has resulted in "short" stamps in the first row, and encroachment of the upper holes of vertical perforations between the stamps in the second row.

awarded compensation of £4,000, a very considerable sum in those days.[50]

However, when the government took over the Archer patent and had new machines made by David Napier & Sons, the complex arrangement for variable movement was scrapped. Security veiled the scene, but, practically speaking, all that seems to have happened was that racks of different lengths were prepared to cope with sheets of different lengths. On each rack, the teeth were spaced a standard length apart, but that length was different on each rack, and the difference was minute. A rigid and unadjustable forward movement of the paper resulted from the rack and pinion. However, for stamps of grossly different sizes, different pin and base plates were used, and these had perforation legs of different lengths to cope with different stamp dimensions.

When the rack was appropriate to the spaces, the pin and bed plates were appropriate to the stamp dimensions, and the machine was properly adjusted, it produced good work. But, sometimes, maladjustment of the rack and pawl caused the malfunctioning of the machine, and imperfectly perforated stamps resulted. For example, numerous instances have been recorded of "long" and "short" stamps perforated by these machines.[51]

When the pin spacing ("gauge" of perforation) and the paper movement were in sympathy, it mattered not whether the length of the legs was, substantially, equal to the dimension of the stamp, or longer than that dimension. If the legs were the correct length, the subsequent descent of the pins

---

[50]The Prince Consort essay was brought into existence as a result of the difficulties encountered by Henry Archer during the experimental period. See the illustration in the chapter entitled "From Design to Issued Sheets."

[51]"Long" and "short" or "wide" and "narrow" stamps frequently result from line perforation, but they are not unusual. Such variations from the intended norm in comb-perforated stamps are, however, much less frequently encountered.

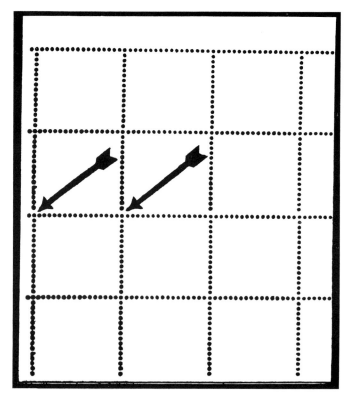

Separation. Double-comb perforator. Slightly maladjusted paper movement, resulting in a slight gap between the legs in the second row and the line between the second and third rows, the bridges between each two holes being wider than the bridges on the rest of each leg. This gap, occurring every two rows, is sufficient to identify the perforator as a double comb.

was made after the paper had moved exactly the correct distance to ensure that the spacing between the hole made by the pin at the end of the leg and the hole made by the appropriate pin in the line representing the other end of the leg was equal to the spacing between the pins comprising the legs themselves. If the legs were longer, some pins coincidentally re-entered holes previously made.

However, when the paper movement and pin spacing were out of sympathy, the effects differed accordingly as the legs were equal to or longer than the stamp dimension. If the legs were the correct length, insufficient paper movement resulted in the two holes encroaching upon, or being too close to, one another — presenting the appearance usually associated exclusively with the crossing of single-line perforation. Too much paper movement resulted in the bridge between the two holes being wider than the bridges on the rest of the leg. If the legs were longer, the relevant holes of each leg, in one extreme of the case, were slightly ovoid, and, in the other extreme of the case, comprised close serrations usually associated with the error or variety "double perforation."

706

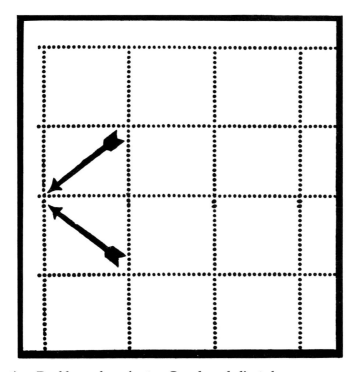

Separation. Double-comb perforator. Grossly maladjusted paper movement. The effect that results from two strokes of the double comb, producing "short" stamps in the second row, and encroachment of the holes of the vertical perforations between stamps in the third row.

The next development in variable feed motion for perforating stamps in England resulted from the joint efforts of S.J. Sworder, the practical mechanician at Somerset House, and Thomas Peacock, who later became Inspector of the Stamping Department. Their device, which is illustrated, was first published on Jun. 26, 1874, in *The Engineer*, from which the following text is adapted:

The accompanying sketch shows a side elevation and a plan of mechanical arrangement applied to the feeding apparatus of one of the stamp-perforating machines in the stamping department at Somerset House, whereby a single rack is made to do the work of a number of racks differently graduated, and a gain of full ten per cent is obtained in the rate of perforation. In drying, after printing and gumming, the sheets of stamps shrink unequally. In the process of perforation, therefore, as the sheets are perforated only one row of holes at a time, although in packs from five to seven sheets thick, it is necessary that they should be sorted out into their various lengths by a graduated gauge. As the perforating machine was originally constructed this difference of length of sheet in the various parcels of stamps was met by the frequent and troublesome change of a number of racks, the length of which corresponded with the various lengths as shown on the gauges. Under the improved arrangement, here shown, a single rack only is used, being made by a simple adjustment for all lengths of sheet. As there is practically no limit to the nicety of this adjustment, a much greater accuracy of

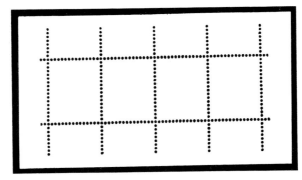

Separation. Chambon perforation. The shape of part of the experimental head provided by Messrs. Chambon and used experimentally by De La Rue & Company for a short time for New Zealand 1960 (Jul. 11 – Sep. 1) to 1964 ½d., 1d., 2d., 3d., 6d. and 8d.

perforation results; and, the rack never being removed from the machine, all the loss of time of the frequent changes is saved. The action of the apparatus is as follows:—

The moving carriage is brought by its weight into its starting position. A parcel of sheets, pinned on a tympan frame, is then placed in a fixed position on the carriage. The machine is started; and, by the action of the pawl upon the rack, the sheets are fed forward one row of stamps at a time till the whole rack is perforated. The pawls are then automatically thrown off, and the frame comes back to its starting place in readiness for a fresh supply of sheets. The rack slides longitudinally on the carriage to the extent of about five-eighths of an inch, bearing at one end against the side of a wedge C, at the other end being guided by a stud upon the carriage working in a slot in the rack. Now it is obvious that when the lever A is in a horizontal position the wedge C, which is in connection with it by means of the block D, which slides in a groove in the side of this lever, receives no motion during the passage of the sheets under the punches, and their perforation intervals correspond exactly with the length of the teeth of the rack. When, however, the lever A is raised out of the horizontal position the wedge (against which the pawl holds the rack) rises at each onward movement of the pawl, and the rack slides slowly forward on the carriage. This has, in result, the effect of shortening slightly each tooth of the rack, and consequently their collective length. The rack resumes its starting position as the carriage is brought back by its weight, retiring against the advance of the wedge as the block D slides down the groove of the lever. It will be readily seen that, by means of this mechanism, as many lengths of rack may be obtained as there are degrees of adjustment of the incline of the lever A. Twelve adjustments are shown in the drawing. Practically the only limit is the eyesight of the sorter. [Illustration Page 710.]

Grover Stroke Comb Perforators

In modern stroke comb-perforating machines, the distance of paper travel between descents of the pins is governed by micrometer adjustments, so that spacing between the strokes can be controlled within very fine limits. Grover & Company Ltd., which has supplied perforating machines to many postage stamp-issuing authorities in Africa, America, Asia, Australia and Europe, has provided me with detailed drawings illustrating these operations; I am in-

Separation. Chambon perforation. Slightly maladjusted paper movement. The back of a strip of three showing the effect that resulted from three strokes (reading downward, part of a stroke, a whole stroke, and part of a stroke) of the Chambon perforating head, used for a short while for New Zealand 1960 (Jul. 11 – Sep. 1) to 1964 ½d., 1d., 2d., 3d., 4d., 6d. and 8d. The first stroke supplied (so far as the picture is concerned) the perforations across the top and the top half of each of the sides of the top stamp; the second stroke supplied (a) the perforations of the lower half of each side of the top stamp, (b) all the perforations of the middle stamp, and (c) the perforations of the top half of the lowest stamp. The third stroke supplied (so far as the picture is concerned) the perforations of the lower half of each side and across the bottom of the lowest stamp. Because paper movement was slightly too little between the first and second strokes, a very narrow tooth resulted on each side of the top stamp, and because paper movement was slightly too much between the second and third strokes, an over-large tooth resulted on each side of the lowest stamp. These varieties, of course, occurred throughout those particular rows, and were caused, almost certainly, by slight buckling and subsequent automatic straightening of the paper during operation of the perforating machine.

debted to them, and also to Harrison & Sons Ltd., which has provided me with many details of that firm's perforating operations.

The Grover sheet-fed machine comprises four main units assembled on a frame: the driving gear and mechanism; the beam and stripping gear that control the perforator unit; the feeding table; and the delivery grippers. In operation, the sheets pass from the feeding table, through the perforator unit to the delivery table, their movement, after the initial feed, being controlled by the delivery grippers.

At the time the sheets are printed, holes are punched in the margins on each side or at the top and bottom of each sheet. These holes are so positioned as to ensure accurate registration of the subsequent operation of perforating, their location sometimes being indicated also by some printed ''per-

Peacock and Sworder

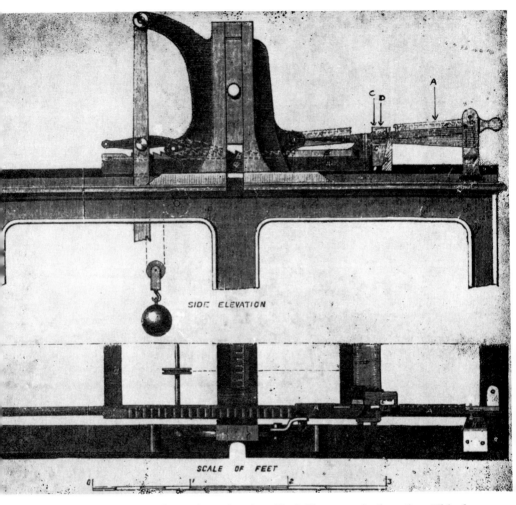

Separation. Single comb perforation. Variable paper feed motion. This drawing, first published in *The Engineer* for Jun. 26, 1874, shows a side elevation and a plan of the device for varying almost infinitely the distance of paper travel between descents of the perforating pins, developed by Thomas Peacock and S.J. Sworder at Somerset House.

foration guide.''[52] Accurate control of the destination of the small discs of punched-out paper is essential, otherwise they may adhere to unprinted sheets and result in the creation of the partial albino ''confetti'' variety.[53]

The printed sheets, usually face-upward, are gathered in batches, usually of seven sheets, on the feeding table. This is a carriage, suitably mounted on ball bearings, with a movement controlled by hand. The movement,

(Register Pin)   (Register Pin)

Separation. Comb perforation. Grover perforator. Feeding table, with the covers removed, showing the two bars, each bearing a register pin on to which the sheets are fitted by means of the holes punched in the sheet margins when the sheets are printed. The handle for moving the feeding table is shown at the right.

termed the initial feed, is from the rear position forward to the perforating unit. The feeding table has two flat bars on which are mounted "boxes" that carry the register pins or studs on to which the sheets are fitted by means of the holes in the sheet margins. The positions of these studs can be varied widely to suit sheets of different sizes up to twenty-five inches wide, and stamps and sheets of different formats.

The direction in which the sheets are to be perforated relative to the printed designs is predetermined; however, there is not an absolute factor for determining this direction. Usually, perforating takes place in the same direction as the printing. Philatelically speaking, therefore, usually the perforation is applied vertically upright. That is, if the top sheet of the batch is viewed face-upward, the upper parts of the designs are nearest to the perforator unit, the line of the comb being nearest the delivery end, with the legs pointing toward the feeding table. Sometimes perforation is applied vertically inverted, and reversed perforation has been carried out — that is, the sheets are placed face-downward on the feeding table.

---

[52]See "Perforation Guide" and "Register Mark" in the alphabetical list to the chapter entitled "From Design to Issued Sheets."

[53]See "Albino" in the alphabetical list to the chapter entitled "Printing Problems and Varieties."

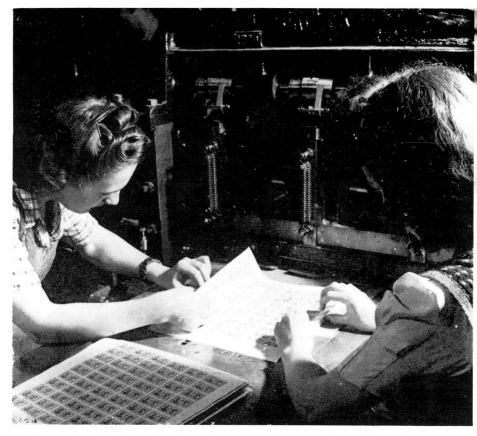

Separation. Comb perforation. Grover perforator. Feeding table. The picture shows two operators fitting a batch of seven sheets on to the register pins to ensure accurate registration of the perforation. The stamps [Southern Rhodesia 1947 (Apr. 1) Royal Visit 1d.] are to be perforated vertically upright. Therefore, the tops of the designs are nearest the perforating head, and the sheets are face-upward. Other sheets, ready to be perforated, are stacked at the left of the picture. The handle for moving the feeding table is partly obscured by the operator at the right of the picture.

For these variations of procedure, which are governed by many factors, including variations in paper stock, gum and humidity, no alteration in the perforator unit is necessary, because the format of the stamps is the same — the same lengths of edges are presented to the line, and the gutter spacing for the legs is the same. If, however, for whatever reason, a decision is taken to perforate sheets of stamps [54] horizontally or sideways (whether from

---

[54]The more usual reasons for what is an apparent horizontal (sideways) perforation is that the arrangement of subjects on the printing base resulted in the sheet formation being printed "sideways." Because perforation is usually effected in the same direction as the printing, such sheets have what is termed "horizontal comb perforation"; this occurs especially when stamps are printed and perforated on the web.

712

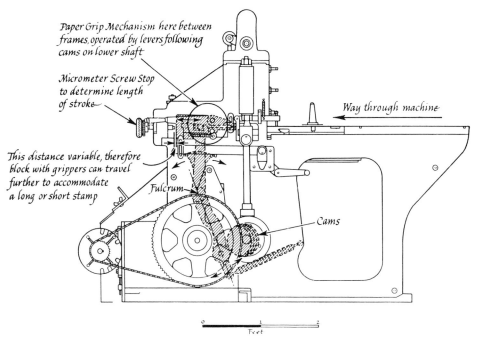

Paper Grip Mechanism here between frames, operated by levers following cams on lower shaft

Micrometer Screw Stop to determine length of stroke

Way through machine

This distance variable, therefore block with grippers can travel further to accommodate a long or short stamp

Fulcrum

Cams

Feet

Separation. Comb perforation. Grover perforator. Side section showing the delivery grippers (paper grip mechanism) that control paper movement between descents of the pins. The actual movement is provided by the levers actuated by the cams, which have four paths enabling various amounts of movement to be imparted. The micrometer screw stop at the left determines the length of the movement, which can be adjusted within very fine limits. The handle for moving the feeding table is at the right.

left-to-right or from right-to-left), then, unless the stamps are square, a different perforator unit or a different arrangement of pins must be adopted. The reason is, of course, that different lengths of edges are presented to the line, and the gutter spacings for the legs are different when the sheets are viewed vertically and horizontally.

In operation, the sheets are fed appropriately on to the register pins by two operators, one on each side of the feeding table. The feeding table is then pushed forward to receive the first stroke of the perforator unit.

At the first stroke, the register pins are knocked out of the holes in the sheet margins, thus releasing the feeding table to be drawn backward and fed again with a new batch of sheets.[55]

At the same time, the sheets have been caught on each side by the delivery

---

[55]No precise figures are available for the speed of operation with postage stamp perforation on these machines. The capacity, with average operators on the Grover perforator, Type 1, feeding seven sheets at a time is claimed to be not less than 2,000 sheets per hour. The time taken to perforate each batch of sheets, however, depends on the size of the stamp, the quality and caliper of the paper, and the size of the sheet.

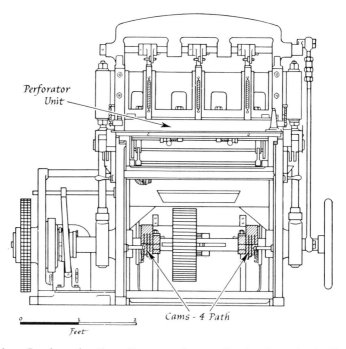

Separation. Comb perforation. Grover perforator. Section from the feeding table end, showing the four-path cams that enable various amounts of movement to be imparted when the levers are actuated.

grippers, which from then on control the movement of the batch of sheets through the perforator unit. Although the next stage in the series of operations is the actual working of the perforator unit, it is convenient here to make brief reference to the operation of the delivery grippers.

The delivery grippers grip the edges of the sheets when the perforation pins are rising. As soon as the pins are clear of the paper, the grippers move the paper forward, bringing it into correct register for the next stroke. While the pins are perforating the paper, the grippers release their grip, move an appropriate distance, grip again and, when the pins are up, again move the sheets forward ready for the next stroke.

The travel of the grippers equals the exact length of movement required from row to row or column to column of stamps. Control, as has been stated, is by micrometer adjustment, while the movement itself is applied by two levers, each actuated by a cam having four paths, to give greater flexibility to the amount of possible movement. Travel is adjustable within very fine limits, from three-quarters inch to two inches, and may be adjusted so that it is greater on one side than on the other, if necessary, to accommodate distortion of the paper owing, for example, to the influence of gum. Further, the Grover perforator incorporates a "slewing gear," as it is termed, that enables the paper to be given a slightly diagonal movement by the grippers during the stroke, thus accommodating sheets that have become bow-shaped by

714

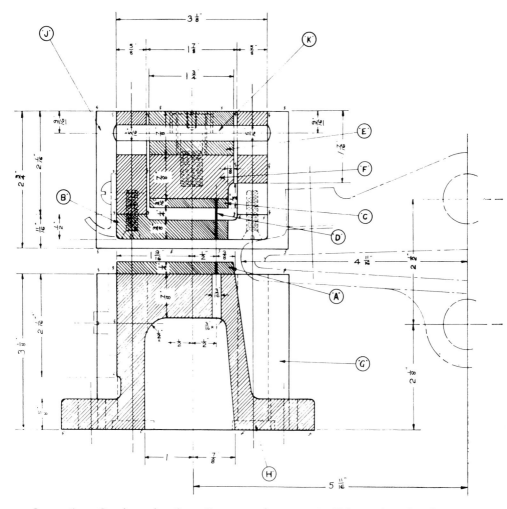

Separation. Comb perforation. Grover perforator unit. Side section showing detail of a perforator unit, together with measurements of the various components. The paper travels between the stripping plate and the die plate, the movement being from left-to-right. Only one pin is shown, representing a pin in the "line"; the "legs" would extend, from the pin shown, toward the left of the drawing.

(A) die plate; (B) stripping plate; (C) pin plate; (D) perforating pins; (E) top pin bar; (F) bottom pin bar; (G) base; (H) guide pins; (J) bridle; (K) cross pin.

distortion. This slewing gear is also controlled by micrometer. The philatelic effects of these adjustments are to produce reasonably centered stamps on sheets that otherwise would contain badly off-center stamps. As the rows or columns of stamps themselves, because of the paper distortion, are out of true on the paper, the effects are obtained by the apparent irregularity of the lines of perforation holes when the sheets are viewed as a whole. These

Separation. Comb perforation. Drilling a die plate for a triple-comb perforator in an air-conditioned room on a special machine at the works of Harrison & Sons at High Wycombe, Buckinghamshire. The tolerances are minute, even by precision engineering standards.

occurrences are rare in the case of stamps produced under conditions of accurate air-conditioning and temperature control.

The perforator unit has as its main components, philatelically considered, the pin plate and pins, and the die plate. But there are also several other components, of which the stripping plate (which "strips," that is, frees the paper from the pins after perforation) sometimes gives rise to the philatelic variety known as "stripped color."[56]

In operation, the pin plate with its pins is set in the upper part of the unit, with the pins pointing downward. They fit through the stripping plate. Up-and-down movement is provided by the main beam, which is actuated by an eccentric and strap on each side of the main shaft of the driving gear. The sheets of paper pass between the stripping plate and the die plate, which is set in the lower part of the unit. The sheets are perforated as the pins descend into the die plate.

---

[56]See "Stripped Color" in the alphabetical list to the chapter entitled "Printing Problems and Varieties."

Separation. Comb perforation. Great Britain 1957 (Sep. 12) 46th Inter-Parliamentary Union Conference 4d. and 1958 (Jul. 18) 6th British Empire and Commonwealth Games 3d. These two stamps exemplify perforation by one and the same perforation head. For the small-size stamps, the pin plate held its full complement of pins. For the double-size stamps, the pins were removed from alternate "legs."

As the pins are withdrawn into the stripping plate (they are never, in operation, withdrawn from it), it pushes the paper clear of the pins, thus freeing the paper for forward movement. The object of the stripping gear is to lock the perforating unit in register with the stamp sheets while the perforating operation is completed. Positive lock of the stamp sheets is obtained by a spring control, which ensures a lock whether seven sheets or fewer are fed in at each operation. The firmness of this lock can be adjusted to ensure a positive hold without causing the gummed sheets to stick together. Usually, too, this adjustment will obviate the ink setting off on to the stripping plate. But sometimes, too firm a pressure, or other conditions, give rise, as has been mentioned, to the variety "stripped color."

The pin plate, die plate and stripping plate contain an identical arrangement of holes, the spacing and distances between the legs depending upon the sizes of the stamps to be perforated. On the die plate and stripping plate, the holes are the same diameter throughout; however, on the upper surface of the pin plate, the holes are countersunk so that appropriately shaped, noncutting ends of the pins fit into the holes and make a flush upper surface. The pins are prevented from slipping out of the top of the pin plate by pin bars, which can be removed to enable the pin arrangement to be altered as required. The pin plate and bars are attached to a "bridle," and the whole assembly is, sometimes, referred to as "the perforating head," or "the perforating box." The die plate is secured to a base, and two guide pins at each end ensure unvarying register between the pin plate, stripping plate and die plate during the up-and-down movements.

The firm Harrison & Sons Ltd. makes all its own pin, die and stripping plates. An important feature of the Harrison method of working is that the drilling is carried out on a special machine in an air-conditioned room. The margin of permissible error is minute even by precision engineering standards. However, it is Harrison's standard practice to make some pins longer

Separation. Comb perforation. A single-comb perforator unit separated to show the pins and die plate. (The stripping plate is not shown.) The pin and die plates have been drilled to accommodate pins for perforating small-size stamps, but the excess pins have been removed, and the head is set for perforating double-size stamps. The two, large, upright guide pins at the extreme right of the picture (and two other such pins at the left, only one of which is visible) fit into corresponding holes in the head of the perforator unit and ensure continuous and unvarying register between the pin plate, stripping plate and die plate during operation of the machine.

than others in the same perforating head, to reduce the pressure needed to pierce the paper.[57]

The actual arrangement of holes drilled, as has been stated, depends upon the particular work to be effected, and this, to a large extent, depends upon the size of the stamps to be perforated. However, because it is a comparatively simple matter to remove the pins from the pin plate, and because it is not necessary to have a pin entering every hole in the stripping plate or die plate during operation, one arrangement of holes can be made to serve in perforating more than one size of stamps. This is frequently done in the case of stamps that are exactly twice the size of others.

What happens is that the pin, die and stripping plates are drilled to accommodate the small-size stamps. When used for them, the pin plate bears its full complement of pins; when, however, the double-size stamps are to be perforated, the perforating head is dismounted, the excess pins are re-

---

[57]The pressure necessary to perforate seven layers of paper and gum, using pins of the same length, is many tons. This was one of the difficulties encountered by Henry Archer during his experiments in 1848 in using steam power to operate his perforator. In *Perforated Postage Label Stamps* (1851), he stated that, when the machine was first tried, the force necessary to pierce the five layers of paper and gum resulted in the permanent bending of one of the supports, a bar of iron six inches in circumference.

Separation. Comb perforation. Great Britain 1958 (Jul. 18) 6th British Empire and Commonwealth Games 6d. Part of unsevered sheets superimposed in register on the separated single-comb pin and die plates (the stripping plate is not shown) showing how double-size stamps are perforated on plates drilled to take a sufficient number of pins to perforate small-size stamps. Note that the sheet gutter is exactly the size to accommodate a small-size stamp, with the pins removed from the "line." Note also that, for the purposes of this illustration, the usual position of the pin and die plates appears to have been inverted; in operation, the pin plate is set in the upper part of the unit, with the legs pointing toward the feed end. The illustration represents a view downward on to the unsevered sheets as they emerge (at the delivery end) after passing through the perforating head, the perforation having been effected vertically upright. (Stamps are usually perforated in the direction of printing.)

moved and the head is reassembled. It is then used, with the same die and stripping plate, in the same manner as if special pin, die and stripping plates had been made. Among the many instances of such occurrences may be mentioned Great Britain 1957 (Sep. 12) 46th Inter-Parliamentary Union Conference 4d. (small-size stamp), and 1958 (Jul. 18) 6th British Empire and Commonwealth Games 3d., 6d. and 1s.3d. (double-size stamps).

The opportunities for the use of a perforating head for stamps of different sizes are, however, comparatively limited, and the general rule is that a different die, pin and stripping plate must be used for every different size of stamp. Also, of course, two different sets of plates will be required if a stamp

Separation. Comb perforation. Reel perforator. An overall view, from the delivery end, of a Grover reel perforator in operation at the works of Harrison & Sons in High Wycombe, Buckinghamshire, England. The web of stamps, printed in sheet formation, can be seen in the feed end of the machine (with a new web on a trolley in the background, ready to be inserted in the perforator after the web in the machine is finished). The beginning of the web is engaged in the perforator unit, and the machine then operates automatically until the web is exhausted. When the web has passed through the perforator unit, it is automatically severed into sheets by a knife in the machine near the operator, and the sheets are delivered to her on the delivery table. On the trolley at the right is a pile of severed sheets in post office sheet form awaiting collection and removal to the checking room. Such machines, without the severing knife, are used for webs printed in continuous (non-sheet) formation for rolls or coils, and sometimes two such webs in register are passed through the machine at one operation.

is to be put through the perforator upright for some sheets and sideways for others — unless the stamp happens to be square, which is a rare occurrence.

Some perforator units, instead of comprising a continuous pin and die plate and other components, consist of two separate sets of components linked by adjusting plates. These linkages are termed "perforating units with lateral adjustments," and they are used in Grover perforators. Before these units were made, sheets that were distorted laterally from being wet-printed or from other causes presented great difficulty for accurate perforation. In the adjustable perforating unit, a screw movement enables a maximum of three-sixteenths-inch adjustment to be made between the left and right halves of the unit, to accommodate lateral distortion. Thus, it is possible to produce what are, philatelically, reasonably well-centered stamps throughout a distorted sheet where badly off-center stamps would have resulted without the use of the lateral adjustment.

To remedy wear in the unit, the pins and die plate may be redressed by grinding. Grover & Company Ltd. states that as many as 600 reams of stamps have been perforated before dressing has been necessary, but that the usual practice is to carry out this repair after perforating each 450 reams of gummed paper. The number of times this operation can be carried out depends on the wear, which again is entirely dependent on the quality and type of paper being perforated. In average circumstances, a unit will usually give months of continuous service.

Stroke comb-perforating machines are used for perforating stamps on the web, or on continuous reels of paper, and for severing the web into sheets. Once the end of the printed web has been fed into the machine, the machine operates automatically. No question, in the usual run, arises of feeding again until the web has been completely perforated and severed. Such machines also are used for the perforation of stamps printed in continuous (non-sheet) formation for use in coils, where sheet severing is unnecessary. Such machines are termed Grover ''reel'' perforators. Sometimes more than one web is fed into the machine at a time; the webs, in register, are then perforated throughout.

Harrow Perforators

Near the outset of this chapter, I summarized and grouped the several different classes of standards evolved philatelically for classifying stamps issued with or without separation; and in the third class, *perforation,* in the first of the five standards, that *based upon the form of application,* the third division is referred to as ''harrow perforation,'' being perforation applied to a whole pane or sheet at one time. The name is derived from the rough similarity in appearance between the pin plate, or the effect, and the farm implement of that name.

When comb perforation was limited to a single comb, the distinction between ''comb'' and ''harrow'' was real and marked. However, with the development of multiple-comb perforators, the difference of effect in the distinction, though still drawn and, in some cases, still real, has increasingly lessened. In some cases today, it is distinction without a difference. Moreover, in some modern instances, it is not usually possible, philatelically, to diagnose the method as ''harrow''; nor, sometimes, can this be ascertained without definite knowledge of the perforating head actually used.

That is not to say that no philatelic advantage derives from the ability to distinguish harrow from comb in many cases. On the contrary. For example, in the case of the first issue of Sweden, the philatelic exercise of ''plating'' — that is, reconstituting the sheet as printed — has been accomplished exclusively by noting the irregularities inherent in the pin and die plates, or rather, the irregularities of the resultant perforations. By the infinitely

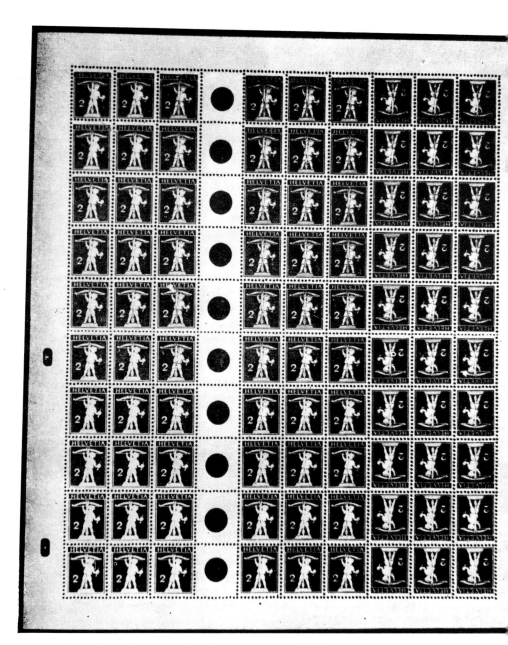

Separation. Harrow perforation. Switzerland 1909 2c. A sheet with no perforations extending into the sheet margins, presenting the classic characteristic of harrow perforation. The sheets were printed in this formation for booklet production, and the large circular holes in the unprinted column were punched out with the objective of preventing fraudulent use of unprinted stamp paper. See also "Gutter Ornaments" and "Pillars" in the alphabetical list to the chapter entitled "From Design to Issued Sheets."

Separation. Harrow perforation. A pin plate with pins set to perforate a pane of 100 subjects in ten rows of ten, but with an extra row of legs that will cause holes to extend across one of the margins of the sheet. This will make certain diagnosis of the method of perforation difficult to accomplish by examination of the sheets alone. In fact, the pin plate can be regarded as a ten-comb perforator, but the sheets are termed harrow-perforated because a whole pane is perforated at one stroke. The picture shows the pin plate being "dressed" — that is, the operating ends of the pins are being ground by a rapidly revolving whetstone so that the edges become sharp and cut clean holes in the paper. The plate is used in the Swiss machine described and illustrated in the chapter entitled "Intaglio Printing — I: Line Engraving."

painstaking process of matching the denticulations and bridges, the sheets have been reconstituted.[58]

Among other early issues that were harrow-perforated were those of Austria 1858 (Nov. 1) 2kr. to 15kr. Indeed, the harrow machine remained in use in Austria until 1898. It was constructed by Aloys Auer in the workshops of the Austrian State Printing Works, and he designed it after studying a sheet of Great Britain 1854-55 1d. that had been perforated on the comb machine made by David Napier & Sons. Whether Auer realized that that sheet was perforated as the result of repeated descents of a comb operating on paper that was moved between descents is not known, but Auer's machine, foot

---

[58]Were it not almost tragic in revealing a lack of appreciation of what can be involved in philatelic study and is, indeed, involved in that particular study, it would be comic to hear, as I have heard, condition faddists caviling that a sheet so reconstituted contained stamps that were — and this was the very phrase used — "badly centered"!

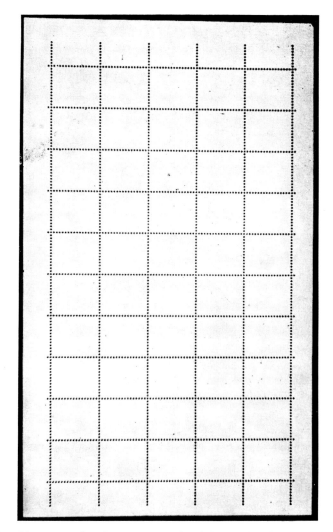

Separation. Harrow perforation. An example of the results of a harrow perforator with extra rows of legs top and bottom. When the sheet is trimmed top and bottom, the extra holes appear to extend throughout the sheet margins, thus rendering diagnosis of the actual method of perforation difficult.

operated, perforated the whole sheet at one operation. The issues of Portugal, beginning with 1867-70 5r. to 240r., were perforated, five to ten sheets at a time, on a harrow machine bought by the Portuguese from Gouweloos Freres of Brussels. It had sixty-one pins in each horizontal row and 120 in each vertical row, gauging perf 12½ — but other harrow machines were in use later.

Instances of comparatively modern issues that, strictly, qualify as being "harrow"-perforated that may be mentioned include those printed in Switzerland on the machine illustrated in the chapter entitled "Intaglio Print-

Separation. Harrow perforation. Luxembourg 1937 (July) Dudelange 2f. souvenir sheet. A comparatively modern miniature example of harrow perforation.

ing — I: Line Engraving.'' That complex machine operates on a reel of paper, in the web, printing the stamps in panes (of fifty or 100 subjects), perforating them at one stroke, and then severing the web into sheets. The perforating unit for the sheets of 100 consists of what is really a ten-comb head — that is to say, at one stroke, ten complete rows of stamps are perforated, and legs protrude from the lowest line. As the panes consist of ten rows of stamps, the protruding legs encroach into the pane margin — and to the edge of the sheet when trimmed. Similarly with panes of fifty subjects with appropriately set pins. As a result, one of the erstwhile invariable characteristics of harrow perforation no longer universally obtains.

That one characteristic used to be, and still is in some cases, a certain test for distinguishing harrow from comb perforation. Examination of a sheet of stamps that was harrow-perforated would reveal no perforations in the margins of the sheets as perforated, with the exception, sometimes, of one or two holes deliberately extending the lines. That is to say, to all intents and purposes, all four sheet margins were imperforate[59] on a sheet that was harrow-perforated.

Some modern perforators that perforate a whole pane at a single stroke have an extra row of legs extending upward from the top line, as well as

---

[59]As contrasted with comb-perforated sheets where, generally speaking, three of the four margins were imperforate; and line perforation, in which the perforations extended throughout all four margins.

one extending downward from the lowest line. Sheets perforated on such a machine and subsequently trimmed reveal perforations extending throughout two opposite margins of the pane, making certain diagnosis of the exact method of perforation difficult indeed. It can be accomplished sometimes if, for example, one hole or more is out of alignment. The fact that the characteristic misalignment occurs only once on the sheet indicates harrow perforation; had the misalignment been on a comb head, the characteristic would have repeated as many times as the comb operated on the sheet.

On a small scale, yet also qualifying for the appellation "harrow-perforated," and much in use in comparatively recent years, are miniature or commemorative sheets — one or a few stamps in an expanse of paper that has been perforated so as to leave the miniature sheet margins imperforate. As instances may be mentioned, say, Luxembourg 1937 (July) Dudelange 2f. and Bermuda 1986 (May 22) Ameripex 86 International Stamp Exhibition, Chicago, $1.50. In such cases, usually, several thicknesses of about ten such unsevered sheets are perforated at a time, and the large sheets are severed to make the miniature sheet.[60]

Irregular and Interrupted Perforations

So far in this chapter, reference has been made to lines, or lines and legs, where the intention has been to provide series of holes of uniform size and, usually, spacing, and lines that are straight — although in practice those desiderata may not always have been attained. For example, in the case of Montenegro 1874, there can be little doubt that the desire of the Austrian State Printing Works, where the perforation was effected, was to produce a pin and bed plate that would result in straight lines of regularly spaced holes. That the resultant lines strayed substantially from rectitude, and that the distances between holes was anything but regular, was a result of low-grade mechanical workmanship.

Irregularities also have occurred temporarily and occasionally in more recent years on perforations produced by Chambon, Grover and Kampf perforators. Originally, needle steel, which is very brittle, was used for perforating pins. In use, sometimes, pins fractured. The result was that damage — more or less damage depending on the particular circumstances — was caused to adjacent stamps.

The number of such fractures caused the adoption of a somewhat more flexible steel, which enabled pins to bend slightly before fracturing. As before, a bent pin would not enter the hole intended to receive it, but would hit the solid metal of the die plate or die cylinder. As a consequence, the paper between would receive a pseudo-perforation hole out of distance and out of register. Of course, the pin would break. However, the effects of the bending and break were less severe than those resulting from fractured needle

---

[60]By no means all such perforated miniature sheets are harrow perforated; and the examination of a number of them will reveal variations in alignment and spacing that can result only from the employment of single-line machines with appropriately set pins.

Separation. Harrow perforation. Bermuda 1986 (May 22)
Ameripex '86 International
Philatelic Exhibition, Chicago, $1.50 miniature sheet. A
modern example of harrow
perforation.

steel. Nevertheless, a sheet or a few sheets would exhibit an irregularity of perforation at the relevant place or places.

After the pin broke, the gutter beside the stamp at the relevant place would have a "blind" perforation hole — that is, no perforation hole where one should have been. The amount of protrusion of the pins and the amount of bending are slight, but the bending can be enough to damage adjacent holes.[61]

There also have been occasions when the spacing between holes has been deliberately irregular, however, and, indeed, when the sizes of the holes have been varied deliberately. I am not, of course, referring here to those instances in which, because of the different tearing strengths of paper with and across the grain, the vertical and horizontal gauges of perforation have been made to differ and result in compound perforation.[62]

The best known instances of deliberately irregular spacing between perforation holes probably occur on the stamps of the Netherlands — for instance, 1924-26 1c.[63] Originally intended for automatic machine coils, the "interrupted" or "syncopated" perforations, as they are termed, were later available in whole sheets.

---

[61]According to an article titled "Abnormal Perforations from Stroke and Rotary Perforators" by Aubrey Walker published in the *(British) Philatelic Bulletin* Vol. 19, Pages 94-96 (March 1982), the protrusion of a pin on the Kampf perforator is about 0.0060 inch from the drum, and it can bend by about 0.0020 to 0.0025 inch at the tip before fracture. A pin on the Grover can bend by 0.0025 to 0.0030 inch before fracture. The distance between perforation holes is only 0.0017 inch and, accordingly, a protruding bent pin can cause damage to existing and adjacent holes. (See illustration Page 728.)

[62]See "Simple and Compound Perforations" earlier in this chapter.

[63]Such varieties are, of course, to be distinguished from the somewhat similar effects that sometimes result from a damaged comb with one or more missing pins, the missing perforation holes being repeated as often as the comb descended onto the sheet.

Many varieties of perforation holes, differing in shape and number, and cuts of various shapes and sizes are to be found on singles and strips of stamps of the United States issued between 1906 and 1927. These are the products of various vending and affixing machine manufacturers, who were supplied with imperforate sheets of stamps that they then cut into strips and perforated or cut as required. These officially countenanced productions include those of the Brinkerhoff Company, the Farwell Company, the Mailometer Company and its predecessor, the Schermack Mailing Machine Company.

Similarly, in other countries, also, stamps obtainable from automatic vending machines, or "penny in the slot machines," exist with unusual separations, actual or apparent. For example, New Zealand 1905-1906 Universal 1d. exists imperforate except for two large holes in the vertical gutters,[64] and also with, additionally, various forms of separation vertically.

While reference is being made to automatic vending machines, it will not be out of place here to mention an occurrence that produces an effect that is puzzling until accounted for. It is that of a freak stamp, centered very high or low (or, as the case may be, sideways) so that portions of two stamps appear with a normal line of perforations through the gutter between the two portions, the top and bottom (or the two extreme edges) of the freak each bearing denticulations of a completely different gauge and shape from those of the normal perforations. This effect is caused by maladjustment or malfunctioning of the vending machine.

Such machines are constructed and regulated to deliver forward a carefully predetermined length of the stamp coil, exactly a stamp length (or width) at a time. To hold the remainder of the coil in position in the machine, and

---

[64]New Zealand Scott No. 108c; Stanley Gibbons Nos. 365-66.

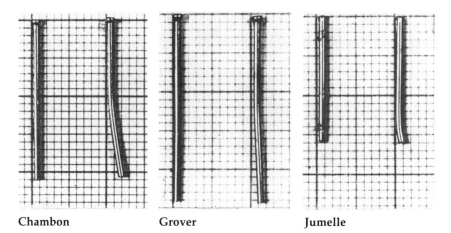

Chambon   Grover   Jumelle

Separation. Perforation. Bent pins. Pictures of pins from Chambon, Grover and Jumelle (or "Kampf") perforating units. The pictures demonstrate the degree of bending that is found in practice. The small grids, in fact, are 1 mm square.

728

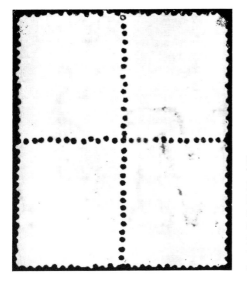

Separation. Irregular perforation. The reverse of a block of four Montenegro 1874-81 perf 12 exhibiting characteristic irregularity of the lines of holes. So outstanding is this irregularity that, philatelically, it led to the coining of a term, "Montenegrin perforation," to indicate any irregular perforation.

to facilitate the tearing of the stamp delivered forward, pins or blades in the machine rise during the forward movement of the stamp, and then descend after it has stopped. While various systems obtain, often these pins or blades — which usually are fewer in number than there are holes of perforation across (or down) the coil strip — are intended to pass through some of these holes. When this happens as it should, the stamp detached from the coil left in the machine bears little or no evidence of the operation of the pins or blades.

However, if the coil has been inserted out of register in the machine, or if, through some faulty action, a greater length of paper than intended is fed forward at one stage, these pins or blades will descend upon and pierce

Separation. Interrupted perforation, or syncopated perforation. Netherlands 1926-30 6c. with interrupted perforation, showing the characteristic missing perforation holes on two sides, the corners only, of a sheet. At first sight, it appears as if the perforating machine was badly adjusted so as to cause too much paper movement between descents of the head. But that was not the case, as can be seen by comparing this picture with that at the top of Page 704. In the case of maladjusted paper movement, no gap occurs between the line and its own leg, but only between the end of one leg and the line of the next stroke of the machine.

through the paper itself. When the part of the coil that has been delivered forward is torn off, the pins or blades cause the appearance of denticulations resulting from rough perforation or a form of rouletting. With repeated use of the machine, these denticulations appear both at the top and bottom (or both sides) of each freak stamp, and they usually continue to appear until the coil is exhausted, unless, indeed, the machine or coil is adjusted. Such freaks are to be found on the stamps of many countries, and must, of course, be distinguished from stamps of which the perforation is merely so badly out of register that portions of two stamps appear within the rectangle of perforated paper. The immediate point of distinction is that, in a case of badly registered perforation, the gutter between the two portions of stamps is imperforate, while in the case of faulty delivery from a vending machine, the gutter is perforated as usual.

Not only has the spacing between holes deliberately been made irregular, but also the size of the holes in the line has occasionally been varied deliberately. The most outstanding instance of such an occurrence is to be found in a perforating head specially made for the Mexican authorities and used for several issues between 1939 and 1946 — for example, Mexico 1939 National Census 2c. — in which alternately one small hole and one large hole appear along every line of perforations.

A type of separation akin to perforation in that the substance of the paper is removed, but in forms other than the circular holes usually associated with perforation, is to be found on some stamps of the United States — for example, U.S. 1912 1c. with "slotted" or "hyphen-hole" perforation, the Schermack Type III vending and affixing machine perforations that already have been mentioned. Somewhat similar, but with smaller apertures, is the hyphen-hole perforation found on U.S. Revenues — for example, Documentary 1898 $1, with the perforation gauging 7.

Akin to these is the lozenge perforation encountered on Bulgaria Postage Due 1884 5s. to 50s., so termed because the paper removed is lozenge- or diamond-shaped.

Other angular separations are to be encountered, for example, in the so-called square holes found on Mexico 1872 6c. to 100c., and Queensland 1862-67 1d. to 1s.

Perforation Characteristics

It is rarely possible with certainty accurately to diagnose the method of perforation — line, comb or harrow — from inspection of a single stamp; and, sometimes, difficulty is presented even when a whole sheet is available for inspection. However, there are certain characteristics and general rules that serve, in the majority of cases, but the exceptions must be borne in mind.

Generally speaking, if a stamp has regular corners, the sheet has been comb- or harrow-perforated; if a stamp has irregular corners, the sheet has been line-perforated. It must, however, be emphasized that those rules are subject to exceptions. Stamps with irregular corners can result from comb-perforated sheets and, more rarely, from harrow-perforated sheets, while stamps with regular corners occasionally occur by chance in line-perforated sheets.

Separation. Vending and affixing machine perforation. U.S. 1923-26 2c. with Schermack Type III perforation.

Separation. Pseudo-separation caused by malfunctioning vending machine. Distinguishable from a stamp with badly registered separation by the horizontal gutter perforation.

Separation. "Penny in the slot" perforation, or vending machine perforation. New Zealand 1905-1906 Universal 1d. with automatic vending machine perforation — two large holes in the vertical gutters.

Separation. Perforation. Large and small holes. Mexico 1939 National Census 2c., a pair from front and back showing the perforation for which the special head incorporating large and small pins was used. Various issues in this or the double-size format were perforated with this head.

Separation. Perforation characteristics. Comb perforation. The "typical" effect presented by a stamp from a comb-perforated sheet. All four corners are regular (Enlargements of the corners are shown.)

Separation. Perforation characteristics. Line perforation. The "typical" effect presented by a stamp from a line-perforated sheet. All four corners are irregular. (Enlargements of the corners are shown.)

There is, as has been stated, in line perforation — even in a two-way per-forator — no mechanical interrelation between the lateral and longitudinal, or horizontal and vertical perforations. As a consequence, where the lines cross one another, pure chance dictates whether the holes coincide, overlap or are regularly spaced. In the vast majority of cases, this chance ensures that the points of intersection are irregular, and results in stamps with ir-regular corners. Occasionally, however, particularly when there is a harmony between the dimensions of the stamp and the gauge of perforation, exact or substantial coincidence of holes results at all four corners of several stamps in the sheet, with the consequence that, when they are detached from it, they have regular corners.

On the other hand, in comb perforation, there is a calculated and micrometrically adjusted mechanical interrelation between the length of paper travel and the length of the legs (or "teeth" of the comb). As a consequence, when the machine has an accurately drilled head with legs the correct dimen-sion for the stamp design and is properly adjusted and functioning correct-ly, all the stamps in the sheet will have perfectly regular corners. Sometimes, however, something falls short of perfection; for example, if the legs are not entirely straight or at right-angles to the line, the last hole in each leg will be opposite two holes instead of one hole of the next line when the head descends again. This will repeat as often as the comb descends on the sheet, and, as a consequence, the stamps when separated will have two irregular corners at the first stroke of the comb, and four afterward. Or, again, the

Separation. Perforation characteristics. Line perforation. A block of four U.S. 1954-60 (Nov. 18, 1955) Theodore Roosevelt 6c. exhibiting "typically" irregular crossing of lines of perforation at all points of intersection that result in the "typically" irregular corners of stamps from line-perforated sheets.

length of the legs may be too great for the dimension of the stamp design, and the machine will be deliberately adjusted so that the paper movement is sufficient to bring the line within the gutter, irrespective of the fact that, thereby, one or more holes of each leg may be infringed by the line, or by it and the top of each leg, resulting in stamps with, perhaps, four irregular corners.[65]

Irregularity of a corner or corners in harrow perforation is very unusual, and occurs only if the holes have not been drilled accurately for the pin and bed plates.

Some general observations may be made about the characteristics imparted to sheets by different perforation methods. What follows does not pretend

---

[65]See also "Controlling Paper Movement" and the accompanying illustrations earlier in this chapter.

Separation. Perforation characteristics. Line perforation. A block of four U.S. 1954-60 (Dec. 12, 1958) from a line-perforated sheet exhibiting chance substantial coincidence of holes at all points where the lines of perforation cross one another. Single stamps from such fortuitous positions have substantially regular corners and are virtually indistinguishable from those detached from comb-perforated sheets.

Separation. Perforation characteristics. Comb perforation. A "typical" effect on the reverse of a block of four from a sheet single-comb perforated from side to side. The paper movement was properly adjusted, and the legs ("teeth" of the comb) were the correct length for the stamp dimension (the width). Note the "perforation characteristic": In the horizontal row of holes, the fourth and fifth holes (counting from the right) are slightly misaligned; this misalignment recurs on the left-hand subject, and, coupled with the fact that the sheet margin is imperforate, provides adequate evidence that perforation was effected by a single-comb head, and also that the sheet was perforated from side to side, in fact from left-to-right in relation to the designs.

to be an exhaustive code of rules, but it should enable the majority of doubts to be resolved.

If all the sheet or pane margins are imperforate, apart from, possibly, encroachment or extension holes at the ends of the lines of perforation, the sheet has been harrow-perforated. However, not all harrow-perforated sheets or panes have imperforate margins, because, occasionally, sheets and panes have been perforated on harrow heads capable of accommodating a greater number of subjects, with the consequence that one, three or even all the sheet or pane margins are perforated.[66]

If one sheet margin is perforated and the other three are imperforate, the sheet has, probably, been comb-perforated. It may, however, have been harrow-perforated, the harrow having an extra set of legs. Also, if one sheet margin is imperforate and the other three are perforated, usually, the sheet will have been comb-perforated. If adjacent sheet margins are imperforate, and the other two margins are perforated, the sheet, almost invariably, will have been comb-perforated. Probably the sheets as perforated were two abreast (and, possibly, two deep) and were trimmed in the inter-sheet gutter (or gutters) subsequent to perforation.

If all the sheet margins are perforated, the sheet has, in all probability, been line-perforated, especially if the holes at the points of intersection of the lines of perforation encroach on one another.

---

[66]See also "Harrow Perforation" and the accompanying illustrations earlier in this chapter.

Separation. Perforation characteristics. Comb perforation. A block of four of Newfoundland 1932-38 2c. from a comb-perforated sheet exhibiting encroachment of holes of legs and the line, resulting in the effect, at the corners of the stamps, usually associated with line perforation. Single stamps from such sheets are virtually indistinguishable from those detached from line-perforated sheets. Note the ''perforation characteristic'': In the vertical line of perforations (counting from the bottom), the bridge between the eighth and ninth holes is broken; this recurs on the left-hand stamp, and, coupled with the fact that the sheet margin is imperforate, provides adequate evidence that the perforation was effected by a single-comb head and also that the sheet was perforated from side to side (right-to-left) in relation to the designs. The encroachment of holes was caused because the legs were slightly too long for the width of the stamps, and the perforating machine was adjusted to reduce the amount of paper movement between descents of the pins so that the line should fall in the vertical gutters.

If two opposite sheet margins are perforated throughout, and in the other two margins the perforations stop short of the edges of the sheet, the probability is that the sheet was perforated in a two-way perforator, the electric eye rotary line perforator.

If one perforation characteristic (for example, a missing or misaligned hole) occurs on opposite sides of a stamp, and a different characteristic occurs on another side, and the characteristics are repeated on every stamp of a column, the sheet was certainly single-comb perforated. If the characteristics repeat on every stamp of a row, the sheet was certainly single-comb perforated from side to side. An exception to this rule exists in the Chambon perforations of New Zealand 1960 (Jul. 11–Sep. 1) to 1964 ½d., 1d., 2d., 3d., 4d., 6d. and 8d. See the illustrations of Chambon perforations earlier in this chapter, Pages 708, 709.

If characteristics repeat every second, third or fourth row or column, the sheet was certainly double-, triple- or quadruple-comb-perforated.

If a perforation characteristic occurs on opposite sides of a stamp, and is repeated throughout a column, and a different perforation characteristic occurs on the adjacent sides of the stamp and is repeated throughout a row (but not in that column), the sheet was certainly line-perforated.

If the gauge of perforation in either direction is not entirely regular, this points to stroke rather than rotary perforation. If the vertical perforation differs in gauge from the horizontal, the indication is in favor of comb- rather than line-perforation; as a corollary, if the vertical and horizontal perforations are exactly the same gauge, that is an indication in favor of line- rather than comb-perforation.

If the width or height of stamps differs frequently — that is, if wide and narrow, or short and long stamps commonly exist — the probability is that single-line perforation was employed.

If all stamps are the same overall size in one dimension, but vary occasionally in the other dimension, the indication is that the sheets were comb-perforated, the legs of the comb having straddled the constant dimension.

Rouletting

Reference was made at the beginning of this chapter to the fact that Henry Archer's earliest experiments were with a machine that employed, not perforating pins to stamp circles of paper from the sheets, but rollers[67] that pierced or cut the paper without removing its substance.[68] I also mentioned that neither Archer nor the Bemroses limited the claims made in their respective patent specifications to perforations as they are philatelically understood.[69] Archer's roulette is known on the stamps of Great Britain, 1841 1d., plates 70 and 71, used about 1848; rouletting that has been attributed to the Bemroses is known on U.S. 1851 3c.

Historically and philatelically considered, therefore, rouletting is older than perforating, although rouletting has had, comparatively, far less use than perforating for postage stamps. Incidentally, and perhaps curiously, in connection with rouletting there is no word in philatelic use to designate the absence of rouletting as contrasted with the absence of perforation. "Imperforate" is an omnibus term, used to indicate the absence of separation; such terms as "unrouletted" and "unpierced" have no general use.

As with perforation, so with rouletting. The effect has been produced by both methods of application: rotary and stroke. However, while hand-applied perforation is, substantially, unknown, hand-applied rouletting has been effected on a number of occasions. Indeed, it is from the rowel wheel of the hand-roulette that the philatelic term "rouletting" is derived, disregarding the fact that the majority of roulettes are produced mechanically and by the

---

[67]Later he experimented with blades set in a fly-press. See *Report From the Select Committee on Postage Label Stamps* (1852) Page 3, question 11.

[68]See "Bemrose" earlier in this chapter.

[69]See "Archer" and "Bemrose" earlier in this chapter.

Separation. Rouletting. Hand-roulette wheel. Typical of all hand-rouletting implements is this converted bookbinder's tool used by Thomas Short, who is said to have been the first to realize that stamps might be divided by a less laborious method than cutting with scissors. The wheel, a flat disc of metal, was filed to make eighty-five teeth, of which three (hidden by the curved shaft) have broken off. The wheel produces a roulette gauging about 7, and is preserved in the offices of W. Pickering & Sons Ltd. at Hinckley, Leicestershire, England.

stroke, not the rotary, process. Unqualified, the term "rouletting" or "rouletted" usually means that the paper has been pierced with straight cuts forming a straight line.

Hand-Rouletting

Because of the inherent simplicity of a little, toothed, tracing wheel on an axle fixed to a small shaft fitting into a handle and capable of being guided easily over the paper, it is not surprising to find that, when imperforate stamps were issued as a matter of course, those little wheels were used by business houses to supply privately what the officially issued stamps lacked — an easy method of separation. Most of the early imperforate issues are found with some form of privately applied roulette.

In England, in Leicestershire, at Hinckley, there is still cherished, in the offices of W. Pickering & Sons Ltd., a converted bookbinder's tool that Thomas Short, founder of the business, used for the purpose of rouletting sheets of the early stamps of Great Britain. Indeed, it has been claimed that he was first to realize that they might be divided by a less laborious method than by cutting with scissors. He, it is claimed, invented the perforator. Because history does not record when, where or how the impractical Henry Archer, the original patentee, hit upon the idea, it is difficult to controvert the claim made for Thomas Short. His wheel, a flat disc of metal, was filed to make eighty-five teeth — three of them have since been broken off — and the rouletting gauges 7.

That implement illustrated is a model of all such rouletting wheels operated by hand; it cut straight slits in the paper because the original disc was flat. In other instances, the discs themselves have been shaped, and have imparted the section of their shape to the paper they pierced. For instance, the edges of the disc used for the several roulettes of the early issues of Finland — for example, Finland 1866 (Jan. 1) 20p. — presented the appearance of pieces of miniature corrugated iron sheets, and impressed cuts of a sharply waved line that has been termed "serpentine"; however, the cutting edge was interrupted minutely by file cuts to prevent the stamps from separating until they were torn apart. Other and differently shaped corrugated discs have been used from time to time: from the gentle undulations of the so-called "Treasury roulette" or "Gladstone roulette" found on Great Britain 1841

737

Separation. Rouletting. Archer roulette, Great Britain 1841 1d. plate 71 with rouletting applied by Henry Archer during his early experiments with separation.

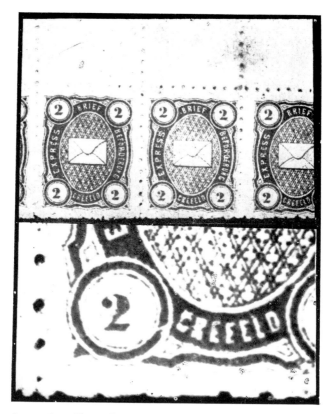

Separation. Pin roulette, sometimes termed pin perforation. Kerfeld (German local) 1886 (December) 2p., part of a strip of five pin-rouletted, and an enlargement showing the effect of a particular application of this type of rouletting, gauging 10.

1d., to the acute oscillations of Helsingfors (Finnish local) 1866-68 10p., and the shallow waves sometimes found on Victoria 1854-58 (Dec. 5, 1857) 6d.

One other type of hand-roulette calls, perhaps, for separate mention. That is a wheel bearing not a disc with a cutting edge, but an arrangement of sharp-pointed pins around its periphery, such as was used, for example, by Perkins, Bacon & Company for Barbados 1860 no value expressed (½d.) and (1d.); Trinidad 1859 (September) no value expressed (1d.) to (1s.), and Krefeld (German local) 1886 (December) 2p. Properly termed "pin rouletting" because the paper is merely disturbed, this form of separation has often been referred to as "pin perforation." Sometimes the effect of this form of rouletting is referred to by the unqualified term "rouletted," which is usually sufficient to distinguish it from perforation, but is liable to cause confusion when considered in general with the more usual use of the unqualified term as designating a straight line of cuts.

Machine-Rouletting

Machine-applied rouletting has been carried out by most of the processes used for perforation: single-line guillotine, harrow, and rotary. An instance of the effects of a guillotine rouletting operation is provided by, for example, Tasmania 1864 1d., 4d. and 6d., rouletted by J. Walch & Sons at Hobart. The machine had two steel knives, used in one line and secured to a bar that rose and fell, and produced a roughly punctured effect, gauging about 8.

An instance of the effects of a harrow-stroke rouletting operation is provided by Queensland 1899 1d., where various lengths of printer's perforative rule were set into a chase and spaced appropriately by printer's furniture representing the stamps. The perforative rule was brass, and its cutting edge presented a zigzag; the rouletting is termed "zigzag roulette."[70] Thirteen 9¼-inch lengths of rule were used for rouletting the horizontal gutters and to extend into the sheet margins. Each of the eleven lines for rouletting the vertical gutters comprised twelve pieces, each 24 mm in length, with, at the end of the line, a further piece just over 10 mm long, which extended into the sheet margin.

Because of the difficulty of obtaining accurate register between the stamp gutters and the rouletting, which was applied by a separate operation after the stamps were printed, the foreman in charge of the rouletting operation gave instructions for the perforative rule to be inked. Because the ink, which was black, was deposited in the gutters, this experiment resulted in better register. The experiment gave rise to the separation variety "rouletted in color," and, in this particular instance, "zigzag rouletted in color." After accurate register was obtained, the use of the ink roller was discontinued. Stamps are to be found with uncolored or colored roulette, or a combination of both.

---

[70]In the United States, the term often used is "serrated roulette."

In South Australia, where harrow-rouletting was carried out on issues from 1858 onward, the notches in the printer's perforative rule were not cut with care, so that the gauge was uneven, and there was no uniformity in the arrangement of the pieces of rule. Sometimes the horizontal gutters were cut by continuous lengths, and the vertical gutters, by short lengths; sometimes the vertical gutters were cut by continuous lengths, other short lengths being used for the horizontal gutters.

Another instance of harrow-rouletting is provided, for example, by Thurn and Taxis, Southern District, 1867 1k. to 9k. In this case, however, instead of the rouletting being applied after the stamps were printed, as in the case of Queensland, it and the printing were effected at the same time. The stamp subjects on the printing base were each surrounded by lengths of printer's perforative rule. This, being slightly more than type high, was inked at the same time as the stamp subjects. When the stamps were printed, the ink on the perforative rule was deposited on, while the rule itself pierced, the paper. As a consequence, of course, all the stamps are well-centered in relation to the rouletting. The stamps are referred to as "rouletted in colored lines"; of course, they also are examples of stamps "rouletted in color."

An instance of the effects of a rotary rouletting machine, hand-operated, is provided, for example, by Victoria 1857-60 Emblems 1d. and 4d., described as rouletted 7-9. The machine, which was used at the stamp window of the post office, was used like the housewife's rolling pin. Indeed, it was called the "rolling-pin rouletter" and, according to the Government Printer,[71] consisted of:

. . . an iron spindle with a wooden handle at each end, similar in shape to the handles of an ordinary rolling-pin, and seven circular steel cutters like spurs arranged between the handles, and separated from each other at equal distances by iron tubular washers. The spindle is 14½ inches long, and the central portion of it, six inches in length, is half-an-inch in diameter, while the remaining 4½ inches at each end, over which the handles are fixed, tapers from three-eights of-an-inch diameter next the central portion to ¼-inch diameter at the ends, forming shoulders with the central portion for the handles to be fixed against. The handles, which are hollow to allow the spindle ends to pass through them, are 4⅛ inches long, and vary in diameter to suit the hand, being about one inch at the thickest part; they have brass caps or ferrules on one end, and iron washers on the other. One of them is firmly fixed to one end of the spindle which passes through it, and is rivetted over the iron washer, while the other is moveable, and can be fixed by a nut which screws on a worm at the other end of the spindle. The circular steel cutters are three-sixteenths of-an-inch by 1¼-inch diameter at the cutting edges, having 44 teeth of one-sixteenth of-an-inch in width, with gaps of one-fiftieth of-an-inch between them (approximate measurement). The iron washers are five-eights of-an-inch diameter by five-eights of-an-inch, and ¾-inch in length respectively, according as they are used for the sides, or top and bottom of the stamps, having to be changed in each case.

In using the rouletter the sheet of stamps was laid upon a block of boxwood, planed perfectly true on the upper surface, and about two inches thick, 6½ inches wide and 12 inches long; the rouletter being rolled firmly over the sheet so that

---

[71]See *Vindin's Philatelic Monthly*, Vol. 5, Page 178 (July 1892).

Separation. Zigzag roulette, often called, in the United States, serrated roulette. Queensland 1899 1d. with zigzag roulette, and an enlargement showing the effect of a particular application of this type of rouletting gauging 13. The stamp has been photographed on a white mount to emphasize the details of separation.

Separation. Rouletted in color. The rouletting was applied at a single separate operation to the whole sheet after the stamps had been printed. To assist in obtaining register for the rouletting, the perforative rule was inked, in black, and deposited ink on the paper as it was pierced, so that the stamp illustrates the term "rouletted in color."

Separation. Double roulette. Before the experimental inking of the perforative rule, rouletting was applied to some sheets, but difficulty was experienced in registering the roulettes in the gutter. This rouletting was uncolored or plain. Afterward, these sheets were rouletted again in color. The picture shows the variety "double roulette." The two roulettes were not coincident with each other. In the stamp pictured, the teeth of the vertical line of the uncolored roulette are to the right, and opposite the indentations of the colored roulette. This has resulted, at the left of the stamp where one of the colored teeth has separated, in the separation also of part of the uncolored roulette and an exaggerated indentation at that place.

the cutters came between the rows of stamps, two rolls each way being required to complete a sheet of 120 stamps.

Rouletting Terms

More than passing reference in connection with perforation was earlier made in this chapter[72] to the series of articles entitled "Dentelés et non Dentelés" written by Dr. J.A. Legrand under his pen name Dr. Magnus and published in Le Timbre-Poste, beginning with the issue for October 1866 (Vol.

---

[72]See "Measurement and Separations" earlier in this chapter.

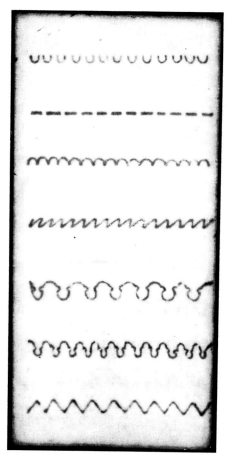

Separation. Rouletting. The original line drawings by Dr. J.A. Legrand, representing the appearances, as he saw them, of various forms of separation, reproduced on Page 81 of *Le Timbre-Poste*, Vol. 4, October 1866. The drawings were un-numbered, but he referred to them as though they were numbered from "1" at the top to "7" at the foot. No. 1 represents perforation (*piquage*); No. 2, (straight) line roulette [*percé en ligne (droite)*]; No. 3, arc roulette (*percé en arc*); No. 4, saw-tooth roulette (*percé en scie*); No. 5, serpentine roulette (*percé en serpentin*), as found on stamps of Finland; No. 6, a variation of the Finnish serpentine, as found on Helsingfors (Finnish local); No. 7, zigzag roulette (in the United States, often termed serrated roulette) (*percé en pointe*), as found on La Guaira 1864 (October).

4, Pages 79 onward) and continuing in successive numbers until April 1867. Those articles are also the fundamental sources of the philatelic classification of rouletting. It is, therefore, necessary to refer in some greater detail to this work.

Seven line drawings were reproduced,[73] under the heading "Sundry Species of Indentations," representing the appearances, as Dr. Legrand saw them, of various forms of separation to which he referred in the articles, and I reproduce those drawings. Although they were, in fact, unnumbered, in his references to them in the text he made it clear that he intended them to be numbered from "1" at the top to "7" at the foot. Number 1 represented perforation. He wrote:[74]

Pierced Stamps. We describe, under this name, stamps of which the separation is effected by a simple disturbance of the material of the paper, without loss of

---

[73]*Le Timbre-Poste*, Vol. 4, Page 81 (October 1866).
[74]*Le Timbre-Poste*, Vol. 4, Pages 88-89 (November 1866). I have added the bracketed material to the text.

Separation. Plain roulette. Thurn and Taxis, Northern District, 1865 ¼s. with plain roulette, and an enlargement showing the effect of a particular application of this type of rouletting gauging 16. The term "plain roulette" or "uncolored roulette" is available when it is necessary to distinguish issues similar except for color or the lack of it in the method of separation.

substance. Several varieties of these stamps may be distinguished:-

On the most frequently encountered, the piercing results in little straight lines, of varying lengths, separated by very small bridges, where the continuity of one stamp with another is preserved. After tearing, one finds straight lines separated by very small protrusions or jagged hollows formed by the remains of these little bridges. Examples are to be found in the Prussian eagles [Prussia, 1861-65] and a certain number of German stamps. There is a great variety in the length of the severing lines, which may vary, from one series to another, from one to three millimeters. I have not yet found it of interest to record the differences. We shall call these stamps *percés en ligne droite* [straight-line roulette] or simply *percés en ligne* [line roulette] [No. 2].

Next to them, we shall place the variety to be found principally on the stamps of Hanover [Hanover, 1864] and Brunswick [Brunswick 1864, 1865]. In the stamp

Separation. Rouletted in colored lines. Thurn and Taxis, Southern District, 1866 (November) 3k., rouletted in colored lines, and an enlargement showing the effect of a particular application of this type of rouletting gauging 16. (The stamp has been photographed on a white mount to exaggerate the details of separation.) The sheets were harrow-rouletted and printed at the same operation, the ink being applied to the printer's perforative rule as well as to the subjects, each of which was surrounded by the rule. As a consequence, the rouletting is in the color of the stamp, and the registration of the stamp design and rouletting does not vary from sheet to sheet.

Separation. Rouletting. *Percé en arc.* Hanover 1864 1g., a block of four *percé en arc,* and enlargements showing the effect of a particular application of this type of rouletting gauging 16. At the left of the block of four is an enlargement of part of the vertical gutter with its rouletting. The effect of this type of rouletting is, especially on single stamps, difficult to distinguish from that of *percé en scie* and, in the United States, both of these types of rouletting often are referred to as serpentine roulette.

gutters one finds a series of very small equal arcs of a circle, of which the extremities touch one another. After separation one finds, on the one side, sunken acute angles separated by convex projections, and, on the other side, acutely pointed projections separated by concave semi-circles. We shall propose calling these stamps *percés en arc* [arc roulette]. It is easy to confuse, after they have been torn apart, stamps divided by this process, with perforated stamps. The cavities of one of these sides recalls the loss of substance of perforation, as the acute projection recalls the tooth; but if one examines the other side of the tearing, the convexities separated by sunken angles, which we have already mentioned, indicate that there is no loss of substance and, hence, no perforation. Resulting as it doubtless does from the arrangement of the piercing machine, it is worthy of remark that on one stamp, most usually two of the sides, one vertical, the other horizontal, present one of these arrangements, the other existing on the other two sides. This does not always occur [No. 3].

A third method of piercing is that which one sees on the majority of the stamps of Bremen [Bremen 1861-64]. It closely compares with the previous one. Instead of little arcs, one finds a succession of teeth comparable with those of a saw[75]

---

[75]Only some saws, rip saws, have such curved teeth, resembling somewhat a wave on the point of turning over before breaking.

Separation. Rouletting. *Percé en scie.* Bremen 1861-64 3s., a strip of three *percé en scie,* and enlargements showing the effect of a particular application of this type of rouletting gauging 16. Across the foot of the picture is an enlargement of part of the gutter with its rouletting between stamps two and three of the strip, with the upper part of the gutter at the left of the picture. The effect of this type of rouletting is, especially on single stamps, difficult to distinguish from that of *percé en arc,* and, in the United States, both of these types of rouletting often are referred to as serpentine roulette.

Separation. Serpentine roulette. Finland 1866 5p. tête-bêche pair, *percé en serpentin,* and an enlargement showing the effect of a particular application of this type of rouletting gauging 7½-8.

having alternately one side oblique and one nearly at right angles, and a blunt tip.[76] As a result, on two stamps thus divided, one finds a complete set of teeth which ought to fit in one with the other, but there is no difference between the sides of the one stamp as in the preceding case except in the direction of the right-angle. On one side, the right-angled edge of the tooth faces downwards, on the other it faces upwards. This is *percé en scie* [saw-tooth roulette] [No. 4].

A fourth method of piercing is to be found in use on the stamps of Finland, of the third and fourth issues (rectangular stamps) [Finland 1860 (Jan. 1), 1866-67]. We shall propose for this species the name *percé en serpentin* [serpentine roulette] [No. 5]. If one examines two stamps still joined, one will notice that the gutter

---

[76]*Une pointe mousse.*

Separation. Serpentine roulette. Helsingfors (Finnish local) 1866-68 10p. *percé en serpentin,* and an enlargement showing the effect of a particular application of this type of rouletting gauging 10½, a variation of the type shown on the tête-bêche pair of Finland 1866 5p.

Separation. Rouletting. *Percé en pointe.*
Enlargement showing the effect of a
particular application, La Guaira 1864
(October), *percé en pointe,* of this type
of rouletting gauging 10. This type of
rouletting is more frequently termed
zigzag rouletting or *percé en zigzags,*
and, in the United States, serrated
roulette.

between is run through by a line having that form. After separation, one finds
on each side of the stamps, rounded teeth, the tip slightly swollen, much longer
than those which result from perforation, and separated by indentations which
are much more marked, because they equal the teeth in length. In bringing
together again the two stamps, one sees them combine like pieces of that children's
game called a jig-saw puzzle, and without loss of substance. The stamp of Helsingfors [Helsingfors (Finnish local) 1866-68 10p.] forms a variation of this method
of piercing [No. 6].

A fifth species, closely allied to the preceding, differs from it by the triangular
form of the teeth. This type is furnished to us by the stamps of the steamship
office of Robert Todd serving for correspondence from St. Thomas to the coast
of Venezuela [La Guaira 1864 (October)]. Here the teeth are sharp, but their sides
are equally oblique, which, apart from their length, distinguishes them from the
saw-teeth of Bremen. It is the layout of the jig-saw puzzle, but rudimentary. We
shall call it, in order to distinguish it from the preceding, *percé en pointe* [zigzag
roulette[77]] [No. 7].

Alongside these methods of separation of stamps, one may place that used for
certain French essays [France, 1853-60], separated with the assistance of a perforation, a true pin perforation [pin roulette]. But this method is not usually used.

Later he wrote:[78]

Since publication of the last number we have encountered a new species of
piercing. It consists of a succession of small lines, about one millimeter long and
two millimeters apart, and parallel to one another, but perpendicular to the gut-

---

[77]In the United States, this is often referred to as "serrated roulette."
[78]*Le Timbre-Poste,* Vol. 4, Page 98 (December 1866).

Separation. *Percé en lignes obliques.* La
Guaira 1864 (October) ½r. *percé en
lignes obliques.* When he first described this form of rouletting on the
stamps of this issue, Dr. Legrand seemed doubtful whether it was different
from *percé en pointe.* He stated (*Le
Timbre-Poste,* Vol. 5, Page 29, April
1867) that "tearing produces inequalities resembling no geometric
figure," and this is amply demonstrated at the left of the stamp pictured,
while the oblique lines are clearly
perceptible at the right. This form of
separation was not very efficient and
the stamps were often cut apart.

ter. This last arrangement, together with the parallelism, of the little lines completely distinguishes this piercing from that of *en ligne droite.* We propose the name
percé en parallel [parallel line roulette]. More often than not one finds a second
row of these small lines in the intermediary spaces; but, while the lines of this
row offer between themselves the same symmetry, they are disposed with the
greatest irregularity in regard to those of the first, touching them sometimes or
extending beyond their sides. After separation, the sides of the stamps present
the most varied jaggedness that it is possible to imagine. We have met it on the
stamps of 5 and 10 silbergroschen and 15 and 30 kreuzer of the office of Thurn
and Taxis [Thurn and Taxis, Northern District, 1859-60 5s. and 10s., and Southern
District, 1859 15k. and 30k.]. The form of piercing places it between No. 2 and
No. 3.

Separation. Combined separation.
Union of South Africa 1942-44 Bantams
3d. with combined separation, perforation and rouletting. Because of the
small size of the subjects, they could
not be perforated completely by the
comb perforating heads available. The
sheets of stamps of this horizontal format were, therefore, first comb-
perforated 14 x 15, and the remaining
imperforate gutters were then rouletted 6½. As a result, single stamps exist perf 14 x 15 x roulette 6½ x perf 15;
roulette 6½ x perf 15; and roulette 6½
x perf 15 x 14 x 15. Other stamps of the
same size but in vertical format exist
perf 15 x roulette 6½ x perf 15 x 14; perf
15 x roulette 6½; and perf 15 x 14 x 15
x roulette 6½.

Later in the series, when dealing with the stamps of individual countries, Dr. Legrand wrote:[79]

The same stamps [La Guaira 1864 (October)] present another, different method of piercing which Mons. Moens has just pointed out to us. It is a series of oblique lines, a little more than one millimeter long, the same distance apart, and parallel to one another, in the stamp gutters. One may call it *percé en lignes obliques* [oblique line roulette]. Tearing produces inequalities resembling no geometric figure. Also, at first we confused it with *percé en pointe*. Examination of two stamps still joined shows the difference. It seems improbable to us that it could be accounted for by *percé en pointe* of which one of the sides of the tooth had not parted, because one would find a trace of it at one point of the circumference of the stamp.

Since Dr. Legrand wrote, various other shapes and results of rouletting have been used or noted philatelically. Consequently, other terms have been added to those he listed. On the whole, however, his terminology has been maintained throughout the years, even though there has been a lack of universal standardization in reference to some of the effects. While he did not find it of interest to record the differences of, or even to note, the gauge of roulette on his odontometer — the original "perforation" gauge — since his time, occasions have demanded that, in order to separate the products of one instrument or machine from others, the gauges be recorded. This has resulted in the frequent, and often unnecessary, recording of the gauge of rouletting. This has been done, as with perforation, on the basis of the number of teeth occurring within the length of two centimeters. Not always are they the teeth resulting from separating the bridges (indeed, this obtains only in line rouletting), but the teeth or projections that result from the shape of the roulette itself.

Combined Separation

On rare occasions only can stamps be found bearing the results of both methods of separation — perforation and rouletting. During the past century, this combination occurred occasionally in Australasia, and instances are to be found in Queensland 1899 1d., the issue that created philatelic history by having a zigzag roulette in color — black, in fact — and that may be encountered with the zigzag roulette uncolored and also perf 12½, 13. Further instances occur in South Australia 1868-70 2d., which may be found rouletted, and perforated, and perf 10 x roulette, and also perf 11½-12½ x roulette.

During this century, combination perforations and roulettes occurred in the World War II issues of the Union of South Africa, when economy measures reduced the size of the stamps and resulted in the so-called "Bantams" issue of 1942-44 ½d. to 1s. The comb perforating heads were incapable of dealing with these miniature stamps, and could not be, or were not, altered. Pairs, or strips of three, of the stamps were perforated around the outside by using the heads, and then the sheets were passed under rouletting wheels, resulting in pairs perf 14 x roulette 6½, or, additionally, in the case of the

---

[79]*Le Timbre-Poste*, Vol. 5, Page 29 (April 1867).

1½d., perf 14 x roulette 13, and strips of three perf 15 x 14 x roulette 6½. Single stamps can be found perf 15 x roulette 6½ x perf 15 x 14; perf 15 x roulette 6½; perf 15 x 14 x 15 x roulette 6½; perf 14 x roulette 13; perf 14 x roulette 6½, and other combinations, depending upon whether the format is vertical or horizontal.

Pseudo-Separation

Reference was made in the chapter entitled "Embossing"[80] to stamps that appear to have a form of separation, but in fact were produced singly, and also to those produced on a coil of paper moved forward by prongs that pierced holes in the strip. Although the individual subjects, or die cut stamps,[81] appear to have a form of rouletting in color, this is in fact merely pseudo-separation, the result of a raised cutting edge on the die. The pierced holes of Peru 1862 (Nov. 18)[82] and some later issues have nothing in intention in common with separation — although, for Peru 1873 (Mar. 1) Llamitas, 2c., the Lecoq machine was modified by replacing the prongs with little blades to produce three cuts on either side of the design (in fact, the top and bottom of the stamp) as the coil passed through, with the intention of facilitating the separation of the stamps from the coil.

Also, reference was made, in the chapter entitled "Relief Printing,"[83] to Jammu and Kashmir (India) 1883-94 4a. and 8a. in black, the design being in color on white, so that the whole surface of the printing plate reproduced in color except where the downs[84] were made in the shape of the design. Each subject was surrounded by uncolored circular dots, simulating perforation. These provide another instance of pseudo-separation.

Perhaps the most amusing story in relation to pseudo-separation is told in connection with Sirmoor, or Sirmur (India) 1892 1p. The first issue, 1879-80 1p., perf 11½, which was locally printed, was sold out and collector demand encouraged the postal authorities to consider reprinting. Alas, the original printing plate no longer could be found, nor could the authorities discover the design, nor even a single example of the issued stamp. They, therefore, copied the reproduction from a stamp dealer's catalogue in which the design was reproduced, reproducing in the process the printed pseudo-separation with which the catalogue design was surrounded. To gild the refined gold and paint the lily, the authorities then provided the official imitation, including its pseudo-separation, with a veritable perforation gauging 11½. Perhaps the not least amusing part of the story lies in the sequel. Collector demand for these official imitations was far less than anticipated — there had, in the meantime, been another issue lithographed by Waterlow & Sons in London, 1885-96 3p. to 2a. — so the authorities put those that were left on hand into

---

[80]See especially the sections entitled "Individual Subjects" and "Strip Production."
[81]See "Die Cut Stamps" in the alphabetical list to the chapter entitled "Embossing."
[82]See the illustration in the chapter entitled "Embossing."
[83]See "Mounted Electros and Stereos" in the chapter entitled "Relief Printing."
[84]See "Down" in the alphabetical list to the chapter entitled "Relief Printing."

Separation. Pseudo-separation. Sirmoor (India) 1892 1p., produced by copying a stamp dealer's catalogue illustration of Sirmoor 1879-80 1p. (shown at the left) and reproducing, as part of the design, the catalogue representation of the perforation used for the earlier issue. In addition to the pseudo-separation, the 1892 issue was veritably perf 11½.

postal use, and they were on sale concurrently available for postage with the issue of 1885-96.

Other, similarly printed pseudo-separations are to be found, for example, on Djibouti 1894-1902 1c. to 50f., and Obock 1893 2f. and 3f., which were, in fact, issued imperforate.

A more modern instance of pseudo-separation is to be found in the simulated perforations, printed in dark blue, on Dominican Republic 1953 Columbus Lighthouse souvenir sheet of ten, which was imperforate.[85]

An apparent form of separation, caused by malfunctioning of automatic vending machines, was mentioned earlier in this chapter.[86]

Varieties of Separating

Near the beginning of this chapter I summarized the several different standards evolved philatelically for classifying stamps issued usually with or without separation. In the fifth class are grouped varieties of separating, varieties not of different methods of separation, but varieties that comprise departures from the intended norm, caused by oversight or mechanical defect, which, in the main, do not readily lend themselves to sub-grouping or sub-classification except under individual headings.

In the case of separating, it is especially difficult to draw a distinction between a variety and an error — if, indeed, an "error of separating" is a proper

---

[85]It is listed in Scott as Dominican Republic No. C86a, and in Stanley Gibbons as No. MS617.

[86]See "Irregular and Interrupted Perforations."

Separation. Pseudo-separation. Obock 1893-94 1c., imperf with pseudo-separation framing the design.

concept.[87] It can be argued that, if a sheet should have been perforated before issue and was not, the omission constituted an error, just as much as, say, the omission to print part of the design constitutes an error. Yet, imperforate stamps result also, and with comparative frequency, from malfunctioning of the machine, rather in the manner that, say, a printing machine might deposit a smear of ink on an otherwise well-printed sheet. It would not, for one moment, be seriously contended that the stamp bearing the smear or part of it constituted an "error." Wherein, then, lies the error of separating in imperforate stamps resulting from such malfunctioning?

Indeed, it might be contended that it is an error of omission that the faultily perforated sheet was issued to the public — but, then, the self-same type of omission allowed the smeared sheet to pass. Similarly with a sheet that has been passed through the separating machine twice because of failure to observe that it already has its complement of separations.

Malfunctioning of, particularly, a comb-perforating machine, which may well produce the imperforate stamps already mentioned, produces also a double perforation. If the first-mentioned double perforation can be regarded as an "error," the second cannot — or cannot with any more justification than can the imperforate stamps resulting from an identical cause, that is, failure to prevent the sheet from being issued to the public.

What, also, is the correct classification — error or variety — of a stamp from a sheet on which the perforation has been begun out of register, the machine stopped or reversed, and the perforation begun again in correct register? Further, how does this case differ essentially, if at all, from those cases in which, after perforation has been applied out of register, the sheet, either strengthened by strips of paper applied to the back or without such strengthening, is perforated again in register?

The answer to the philosophic problem of classification into error and variety appears to be that separating errors are matters of degree, and result from involuntary omission rather than from commission and mechanical malfunctioning.

In most cases, diagnosis of the cause of apparently similar variations from the norm cannot be made from inspection of individual stamps. Inspection of the whole sheet, or sufficient of it to enable the cause to be accurately deduced, is essential before a variety of separating can be classed as an error of separating. Furthermore, in some cases, inspection of such a multiple or whole sheet is not enough, unless it is coupled with facts from which the intended norm can be established.

In other words, as in so many instances that occur throughout the study of stamp production — of which separation forms but a part — it is unsound to take any one practice or variation as standard, and to refer exclusively to it for the purpose of establishing the sequence of events or of drawing purported certain deductions in relation to any particular issue. Each issue must

---

[87]See "Error" and "Variety" in the alphabetical list to the chapter entitled "Printing Problems and Varieties."

Separation. Imperf and part imperf. Newfoundland 1932 (Jan. 1) 2c., an enlargement showing a vertical pair imperforate flanked on both sides by a vertical
pair part imperforate, and a reduced photograph of a block of twenty (ten across,
two down) from which the enlargement was taken. These varieties resulted from
an experiment in registering vertical-comb perforation. The sheet was placed
sideways under the single-comb perforating head, which descended five times;
the sheet was then removed, turned through 180 degrees, and again placed
sideways under the perforating head, which descended four times (or vice versa). The sequence of operations is proved by: the imperforate sheet margins at
left and right of the block of twenty; the perforation characteristic — the joined
holes — that occurs between holes 8 and 9 from the bottom in the right half
of the block, and between holes 8 and 9 from the top in the left half of the block;
and the absence of a line of vertical perforation at both the left and the right
of the center pair. NOTE: From an examination only of the places where the
rows of perforation apparently cross, and because of the encroachment of holes
at those places, the perforation at first glance might be thought to be line; that
it was not line is proved by the imperforate sheet margins.

Separation. Staggered perforation. Vertical-comb perf. New
South Wales 1890 (Dec. 22) 2½d., a pair exhibiting the variety
"staggered perforation," and a photograph of the back of the
pair. This variety can be demonstrated satisfactorily only in
pairs or larger multiples.

be studied by reference to the particular practice obtaining in its particular
production.

It is not my purpose to attempt to classify, much less to refer to and illustrate, all types and varieties of separating. They do not, as has been stated,
readily lend themselves to sub-grouping or sub-classification, because, if for
no other reason, apparently similar effects may result from widely differing
causes. As a basis of broad but not exclusive classification, they might be
considered under six heads: faulty register; blind holes; faulty adjustment
resulting in narrow and wide stamps and gaps between perforation rows;
double separation; freaks; and imperforate or part-perforate and part-
imperforate stamps.

The widely differing causes of such varieties generally are, perhaps,
highlighted by reference to a single group of instances — imperforate or part-
imperforate stamps. Imperforate sheets, and stamps from them, of course,
occur for four main reasons: separation formed no part of the plan of issue;
separation was deliberately, or through force of circumstances, omitted;
separation was omitted by error; and incompletely manufactured sheets were
sold surreptitiously or unofficially.

However, partly imperforate sheets, from which imperforate or part-
imperforate stamps may be severed, result from three main causes: failure,
deliberate or accidental, to pass a sheet through a one-way perforator in more
than one direction; failure, deliberate or accidental, to provide complete
separation on single-line guillotine machines; malfunctioning of a comb-
perforating machine resulting in the presence of one row or more, depending upon the type of comb, of stamps without full or without any perforation. There is, thus, a seventh possible cause of an imperforate stamp. But
the list is by no means exhaustive. Another of several other possible causes
of imperforate stamps (omitting all reference, except here, to part-perforate
and part-imperforate stamps) is revealed by the accompanying illustration
of a block of Newfoundland 1932 (Jan. 1) 2c.

A variety not infrequently encountered on single-comb perforated stamps,
and demonstrable only on pairs or larger multiples, gives the appearance
of a perforation that has been staggered. Usually one of the pair, or one row
or column, will be well-centered, while the other is off-center to a marked

degree. Such staggering occurs, usually, only once in the sheet, and is caused by what is, in fact, sideways movement (in addition to the usual forward movement) of the paper during the interval between one descent of the comb and the next. Sometimes an excess of forward movement causes a wider gap than usual between the legs and the next line, but the two symptoms by no means always co-exist. The variety "staggered perforation" occurs both on stamps perforated upright and on those perforated sideways, and such varieties may be found on the earliest and latest perforated issues. They are found on many issues of New South Wales, including, for instance, 1890 (Dec. 22) 2½d.

Terms Relative to Separation

The alphabetical list that follows contains terms that are in philatelic use in connection with separation. To some extent, it is concerned also with collectible condition in so far as that is affected by separation. The list does not pretend to contain exhaustively all the names and terms that have been associated with perforation and rouletting by specialist-students and collectors of particular countries. To have included these would have extended it, already somewhat enlarged, beyond the bounds of what may be considered to be the fundamentals of philately.

Nevertheless, in a few cases, terms and names of mainly specialist interest have been included. They are related to the issues of the United States and the British Commonwealth, and are fundamental to collectors of and in those countries. Also, no list of terms relative to separation could be considered even to approach comprehensiveness were it not to include three names: Archer, the original patentee of stamp perforation; the Bemroses, patentees of rotary separation; and Dr. J.A. Legrand, the original classifier of separation and the inventor of the perforation gauge.

Further, closely allied in subject matter to separations is the stamp that is, in fact, perforated. So some of the terms relative to the branding of stamps find their way on to the list. Here again, no more than the fundamentals are touched upon, and the collector of perfins will search this list in vain for the more specific terms dear to the hearts of those whose special interests are confined to this collecting field.

While there is reasonable identity of meaning on both sides of the Atlantic Ocean in respect to English terms relative to perforation, this felicitous state does not appear to obtain in respect to terms relative to rouletting. There are cases of sometimes confusing lack of uniformity that occur in terminology in reference to different roulettes. To some of these cases of conflict I have drawn attention under the appropriate headings in the list.

A-Perforation — see "B-Perforation."

APS. An acronym for Aktiebolaget Produktion Service, the firm that provided a new form of perforation. It was designed by the Swedish engineer, Sune Lutteman. The paper was run over a pin cylinder that caused one side of the paper to have raised pimples. At the same time, that side of the paper was acted upon by a counter-rotating cylinder of blades that chipped away the paper's substance until it was holed. The pimples on the pin cylinder were arranged appropriately for the stamps as printed. The action of the machine gave rise to its nickname, "the Lawnmower." The acronym may also mean "alternative perforating system."

Arc Roulette. An English synonym, only rarely employed, for *percé en arc*. See *"Percé en Arc."*

Archer Perforation, Archer Roulette. The perforation or rouletting on stamps of Great Britain 1841 1d., respectively, plates 8, 79, 90, 92-101, 105 and 113, and plates 70 and 71, applied by Henry Archer, the original patentee of perforation for postage stamps, whose specification, No. 12,340 of 1848, dated May 23, 1849, related to a stroke, single-comb perforator. See "Comb Perforation"; "Stroke Perforation." Archer's patent rights were purchased by the British government for £4,000 in June 1853. Sheets were issued in February 1854 perforated on machines constructed by David Napier & Sons. Archer perforation, gauging 16, can be recognized on covers or letters dated before Jan. 28, 1854, and on loose stamps with the check letters of Alphabet I. See "Check Letters" in the alphabetical list to the chapter entitled "Stamp Design." Archer roulettes gauge 12, and were applied during his earlier experiments with separation.

Automatic Machine Perforation. (1) Usually, an apparent perforation, additional to that usual for the issue, caused by malfunctioning of an automatic vending machine. The result is that the machine's pins (for retaining the non-delivered part of the coil, and facilitating the detachment of the delivered stamp or stamps), instead of falling within the perforated holes, fall on to an unintended part of the coil and pierce it; so that, when the delivered part of the coil is detached, it bears portions of two stamps (divided by the usual perforation), of which the extremities bear denticulations caused by the piercing. (2) Occasionally, special, privately applied forms or arrangements of holes in coils for automatic vending or affixing machines. Examples include the two large, widely spaced holes and knife cut or cuts used on some U.S. 1c. to 5c. stamps between 1906 and 1912, comprising Brinkerhoff Type II. Other such U.S. private perforations in a variety of forms include "Farwell" (sometimes called "Chambers"), "International Vending Machine," "Mailometer," "Schermack" and "U.S. Automatic Vending Co." See also "Penny in the Slot Perforation."

B-Perforation. Perforation applied by Perkins, Bacon & Company with a hand-operated single-line stroke machine gauging 11-12. The descriptions "A-Perforation" (applied by a similar type of machine yielding varying results) and "B-Perforation" were adopted by Sir E.D. Bacon and F.H. Napier in the complex classifications that are dealt with in *Grenada: To Which Is Prefixed An Account Of The Perforations Of The Perkins Bacon Printed Stamps Of The British Colonies* (1902). These descriptions have, largely, been superseded by notation of the various gauges and states of perforation.

Bars. (1) Those parts of a two-way perforator that effect the latitudinal perforation, across the web or reel of paper, as distinct from the rings that effect the longitudinal perforations. See "Latitudinal Perforation"; "Rings." Bars are either "punch bars" (or "pin bars") drilled with holes into which one end of flat-ended pins or punches are fixed, or "die bars" (or "counterpart bars") drilled with holes only. The bars are fitted, spaced appropriately, to two synchronized counter-rotating cylinders, the free ends of the flat-ended pins entering and leaving the holes of the die bars as the cylinders rotate. The web passes between the cylinders, and the paper is perforated as it passes between them.

(2) Perforation register marks printed on the web for the purpose of controlling

Separation. Perforation. Bars and rings. A punch bar and die bar, a punch ring and various die rings used in the electric eye perforators. Up to forty-four such pairs of bars are mounted on cylinders that apply the lateral perforations to the web. At the left of the picture is a three-row die ring. When it is in position in the machine, a separate punch ring will be set to engage with each of the three sets of holes. At the right of the picture is a two-row die ring; similarly, two separate punch rings will be set to engage with the rows of holes. In the center (resting on the two- and three-row rings) is a four-row die ring. The rings, suitably mounted, apply the longitudinal perforations to the web. These bars and rings are manufactured to very close tolerances. The bars are eighteen inches long, and are drilled with 247 holes, the distance between centers being 0.07 inch. The overall distance of the holes is just under 17¼ inches; and the accumulated margin of permissible error is not greater than one-thousandth part of an inch in the eighteen-inch bar. The pins or punches, needle steel ground to a diameter of 0.042 inch, are soldered in position in the punch bars and rings. The bars and rings are resting on the reverse of a sheet of normal-size U.S. stamps.

its longitudinal movement as it passes through the two-way electric eye perforator used in the production of U.S. stamps. See "Electric Eye Perforator." Previously the term employed was "gutter bar" or "frame bar," according to its position relative to the stamp design. The term now recommended by the Bureau Issues Association is "bar," without the qualifying adjective. The number of bars on each printing plate equals, roughly, the number of (lateral) rows of stamps across the web printed by the plate at one operation. On the printed sheet, the bars appear parallel to one another, like the rungs of a ladder, and are at right-angles to, and in a different sheet margin from, the dashes. See "Dash." Compare "Margin Line." See also "Electric Eye Terminology."

Bed Plate. That part of a stroke perforating machine in which the holes are bored,

Separation. "Blind perforation (2)." Broken pins. Germany 1946 Civil Government 20p., a block of six from the northwest corner of the sheet, single-comb perf horizontally, exhibiting the variety blind perforation caused by broken pins in the second position in the comb. The broken pins were: in the line between the second and third leg, the fifth and tenth; and in the third leg, the first, fourth and twelfth. Because the head was a single-comb, the blind perforations repeat in the stamp below, and were repeated throughout that column in the sheet. They continued to repeat on every subject in the second column until the pins were replaced. This variety is somewhat similar in appearance to some interrupted perforations (syncopated perforations), but those occur on every subject, unlike the blind perforations, which occur on only the subjects perforated by the comb position affected.

and into which the free ends of the flat-ended pins of the pin plate descend in order to effect the perforation. Used as synonyms for bed plate are "counterpart plate," "die plate," and "matrix plate." Compare "Pin Plate."

Bemrose Perforation. Perforation applied by the rotary line principle patented by William and Henry Howe Bemrose, whose specification No. 2607 of 1854 was dated Jun. 8, 1855. See "Rotary Perforation (1)."

Blind Perforation. (1) Usually, an indentation in, as opposed to a hole punched out of, the paper, and caused by the bed plate holes becoming clogged with paper or, occasionally, by the edges of the flat-ended pins and the holes in the bed plate becoming worn and the stroke of the machine being too short to pierce the paper. In this sense, the term "perforated" is used, despite the absence of the holes, as connoting the intention to perforate. See "Perforated"; "Perforation." Compare "Clean-Cut Perforation." (2) Occasionally, a missing perforation hole resulting from a broken or missing pin.

Blitz Perforation. The name given to the perforations on New Zealand 1936-43 ½d. to 3s. (except 2½d.) gauging 12, 14, and 14 x 15, printed and perforated by

Waterlow & Sons Ltd. in 1940-41 when the works of De La Rue & Company Ltd. was damaged by Nazi "blitzkreig" bombing raids on London.

Box. The container of the head. See "Head."

Branded Stamps — see "Perforated (2)."

Bridge. That part of the paper remaining between one roulette cut or perforation hole and the next, forming a continuous surface, or "bridge," between contiguous stamps or a stamp and pane or sheet margin. When the stamps are separated, the bridge in perforation invariably, and in rouletting sometimes, becomes a tooth or nib. See "Teeth"; see also "Nibbed Perforation."

Brinkerhoff Perforation — see "Automatic Machine Perforation (2)."

Centered — see "Centering."

Centering. The relation of the printed design to the surrounding perforation or rouletting. "Centered" and "well-centered" indicate that the design is surrounded by equal opposite margins. "Off center" indicates that at least one margin is narrower than its opposite margin, and may mean that the design is infringed by the separation. "Centered to left" indicates that the left-hand stamp margin is narrower than the right; "centered low" indicates that the bottom margin is narrower than the top; similarly with "centered to right" and "centered high." These terms, and appropriate combinations of the qualifying adjectives, reflect the degree of accuracy of registration of the separation, and are concerned, primarily, with standards of collectible condition of stamps. See "Registration"; "Staggered Perforation."

Chambers Perforation — see "Automatic Machine Perforation (2)."

Chambon Perforation. The name given to the perforation applied to New Zealand 1960 (Jul. 11 – Sep. 1) to 1964 ½d., 1d., 2d., 3d., 4d., 6d. and 8d. from a specially made head, a unique variation of a double-comb head, whereby, at one operation, one row of stamps was completely perforated on all sides, and half-legs were provided to the paper or stamps above and below that row, the second stroke completing the legs of the row below, completely perforating the next row, and providing half-legs for the row or paper below that. When the paper travel was perfectly adjusted, the Chambon perforations were indistinguishable from results produced by the more usual comb heads perfectly adjusted; slight maladjustment of paper travel did not result in irregular corners, but did result in unusually close or wide spaces between vertically neighboring holes at the center of each side of each stamp in a row, with a compensating difference in the stamps of the next but one row vertically below or above. The perforating head was made by Messrs. Chambon and was used experimentally by De La Rue & Company Ltd. The perforation gauges 14. Perforating machines and heads manufactured by Messrs. Chambon have been widely used in stamp production.

Chicago Perforation. The name given to an unofficial perforation, gauging 12 to 13, found on U.S. 1851 1c. (Type II and Type IV) and 3c. (Type I).

Clean-Cut Perforation. The punched-out paper has been entirely removed, leaving sharply defined edges. Compare "Blind Perforation"; "Intermediate Perforation"; "Rough Perforation."

Colored Roulette — see "Rouletted in Color."

Comb Perforation. The simultaneous punching out of paper from three gutters surrounding a stamp, leaving the fourth gutter (if any) to be perforated at the next stroke. The term "comb" derives from the fancy that a long row of perforation holes and short rows at right-angles to it resemble a comb with widely spaced teeth. See "Legs"; "Line." Comb perforation was first adopted by Henry Archer. See "Archer Perforation." His machine perforated (partly) only one row of stamps at a stroke, and the effect is termed "single-comb perforation." Such machines are termed also "triple cutters," because of their three-sided operation — see "Triangular Comb Perforation." Other machines, termed "multiple-comb perforators," at one stroke perforate all four gutters surrounding each stamp in one or more rows and provide perforations between the stamps of the next row. Such perforation is termed "double-comb perforation" if one complete row and part of the second are perforated; "triple-comb perforation" if two complete rows and part of the third are perforated; "quadruple-" or "four- comb perforation," and so on. See "Multiple-Comb Perforation."

Combination Perforations. Perforations from more than one perforating head on the same sheet of stamps. Such combinations are of comparatively infrequent occurrence except in cases of multiple-line perforation. Combinations of comb and line were used, for instance, in Hungary 1908, 20f., 1k. and 5k., perforated 15 by a comb head. Where the comb did not operate (usually at the foot of the sheet, leaving the bottom margin imperforate), the missing row of perforations was supplied by a single-line machine, gauging 11½, so that the resultant stamps were comb-perforated 15 on three sides and line-perforated 11½ on the other. Similarly, for instance, in Victoria, 1901-10 ½d., the design of the stamp was too small to be completely perforated by the comb head, which accommodated two stamps within the rectangle surrounded by perforations gauging 12 x 12½. The imperforate gutters vertically between alternate stamps in the sheet were provided with perforations from a single-line machine gauging 11, and also another single-line machine gauging 12½, so that the resultant stamps are found with combination perforations, comb 12 x 12½ on three sides, and line 11 or 12½ on the remaining side. Combination perforations of two different comb heads yielding different gauges of perforation on the same sheet are found in New Zealand 1915-16 3d. to 8d. and 1915 (Jul. 30) to 1925 1½d. to 1s., in which one comb, used for the four top rows of stamps, gauges 14 x 13½, and the other comb, used for the six lower rows, gauges 14 x 14½. This combination perforation occurred because irregularity of alignment resulted in the spoilage of too large a proportion of sheets perforated throughout by the head gauging 14 x 13½, which was introduced in 1914; the authorities found that satisfactory results could be obtained by partly perforating the sheets on one head, and then transferring them to the other head for the remainder of the perforating operation. As a consequence, from each sheet, vertical pairs of stamps existed with the different gauges *se tenant.*

Combined Separation. Both rouletting and perforation applied to the same subjects in the sheet. Instances are to be found in Queensland 1899 1d. which exists, for example, zigzag rouletted (serrated roulette) 13 and perforated 12½, 13; South Australia 1868-70 2d. which exists, for example, perf 10 x roulette; and Union of South Africa 1942-44 Bantams ½d., 1d. and 3d., which exist, for example, perf 15 x 14 x 15 x roulette 6½.

Compound Perforation. (1) Perforation of which one gauge is common to the horizontal rows of holes, and another gauge is common to the vertical rows of holes. Such compound perforation is expressed by two figures separated by a multiplication sign, the first figure representing the horizontal gauge in relation to the design; for example, "11 x 10½" on U.S. 1960 (Jul. 19) Pony Express Centennial 4c., and "10½ x 11" on U.S. 1960 (Aug. 28) Employ the Handicapped 4c.

(2) Perforation of which the gauge on one side of the stamp differs from the

Separation. Combination perforation. New Zealand 1915-22 Official 8d., a vertical pair, the upper stamp perf 14 x 13½, the lower stamp perf 14 x 14½, resulting from the use of two different single-comb perforating heads to perforate the sheet. Accurate registration could not be obtained by perforating the sheet throughout with the head gauging 14 x 13½ because of irregularity of alignment. This gave rise to the variety "combination perforation" on these stamps.

Separation. Staggered perforation. Horizontal-comb perf. When it was inserted under the second perforating head, the sheet was not quite in register, so that the pair exhibits also the variety "staggered perforation."

gauge (or gauges) on at least one other side. Such perforation is expressed in various ways according to the circumstances. In the case of an individual stamp, it is usual to state the gauges, beginning with the top line and continuing clockwise around the stamp — for instance, Bosnia and Herzegovina 1906-1907 20h. can be found gauging 9½ x 12½ x 12½ x 6½. In the case of sheets or series of stamps, it is usual to state the gauges together with the word "compound" — for instance, Austria 1890 (Sep. 1) 1k. to 2g. "perf various compounds of 9 to 13½," or "perf 9 to 13½, also compound." Compare "Combination Perforation."

Concurrent Perforations. The perforations of one value or a series simultaneously and normally available from official sources with various gauges of compounds of perforation. In some cases, concurrent perforations indicate philatelically no more than that the manufacturer possessed several perforating machines and used them indiscriminately in producing the stamp or issue. Sometimes, however, one gauge rather than another has been employed on stamps for a particular use, such as in automatic vending machines. Cases in which concurrent perforations occur normally lack the philatelic significance of those for which the periods of issue of the stamps can be determined by different gauges or compounds used during different periods of manufacture because, for instance, of repair to the machine, or because of the introduction of a new one.

Counterpart Bar — see "Bars (1)."

Counterpart Plate — see "Bed Plate."

Counterpart Ring — see "Rings."

Counterpart Wheel — see "Rings."

Separation. Double perforation. Constantinople (Turkish local) Liannos 20p., and an enlargement of part of one edge showing the "classic" effect of close serrations associated with double perforation. It is known that this issue, printed by Perkins, Bacon & Company, was horizontal-comb perf 14 at Somerset House, London. Because the stamp is imperf x double perf, and both edges near the top are imperf for a short distance, it is possible to deduce that the sheet, one of a batch of five or seven, was inserted in the perforator with the foot of the design nearest to the "line," that at some time during passage of the batch of sheets through the perforator the paper movement was interrupted, and that the pins descended to make the first of the two strokes, of which the effect is visible on the stamp illustrated. The result of the first of those strokes was to perforate the "line" through the designs of the row below in the sheet (when viewed upright) approximately level with the "P" of "POSTE." The legs, instead of extending the height of the design, terminated at that "P" on the stamp illustrated. The second of the descents of the pins occurred in almost the same place, because the paper movement mechanism had failed utterly. As a result, the horizontal gutters between the two rows, and the next row above in the sheet (when viewed upright) or the top sheet margin were imperforate. Subsequently, the stamps were cut apart.

Cross Roulette. An English synonym for *percé en croix*. See "Diamond Roulette"; "Lozenge Roulette"; *"Percé en Croix"*; "X-Roulette."

Dash. One of a series of perforation register marks printed on the web for the purpose of controlling its latitudinal movement as it passes through the two-way electric eye perforator used in the production of U.S. stamps. On the printed sheet, the dashes are placed end to end, and simulate a thick line broken by spaces of the same length as the dashes; they are at right-angles to, and in a different sheet margin from, the bars. See "Bars (2)"; compare "Margin Line." See also "Electric Eye Terminology."

Separation. Double perforation. Grenada 1875 (December) 1d., a bottom marginal strip of four exhibiting the variety "double perforation." These stamps, printed by Perkins, Bacon & Company, were perforated at Somerset House on one of the single-comb machines used for the stamps of Great Britain. On one batch of sheets, the horizontal perforation provided by the "line" was well-registered, but the vertical perforation provided by the "legs" was badly registered on at least two (possibly all) rows of the sheet, being too far to the left. The rows affected were subjected to further perforation, so that the "legs" fell in the vertical gutters. This resulted in early double vertical perforation on the strip illustrated, which bears evidence of two separate double descents of the pins — that is, four descents, in all, one double descent on the stamps, the other on the sheet margin. The two "lines" were so closely registered that the holes in the horizontal rows are only slightly ovoid, this being most marked on the outer stamps. Any of these stamps, if the paper outside the inner perforations were detached, would be a "narrow stamp" and, probably, would be condemned as "reperforated"; such a stamp might not measure up to the absolute standards of condition set by some collectors, but would be an example of the effects sometimes resulting from double perforation.

Denticulated, Dentilated. These are terms suggested, but infrequently used philatelically, as descriptive of the edges of a stamp detached from a perforated or rouletted sheet. Despite the illogicality, such a stamp is referred to as "perforated," even though no hole is pierced through it. See "Perforated."

Diamond Roulette. An uneasy translation into English of *percé en losanges,* which was derived from the fancy that the shape of the crosses comprising *percé en croix* resulted in formations resembling heraldic lozenges or diamond shapes. See "Cross Roulette"; "*Percé en Croix.*"

Die Bars — see "Bars (1)."

Die Plate — see "Bed Plate."

Die Ring — see "Rings."

Die Wheel — see "Rings."

Double Comb — see "Comb."

Double Perforation. Perforation twice applied to the same sheet or part of a sheet in error, or to rectify bad registration, or because of malfunctioning of the

Separation. Double perforation. U.S. 1857-60 3c. rotary perforated, a lower-left corner strip of four with attached margin exhibiting the effect of double perforation resulting from inserting the sheet into the perforator out of register, stopping and reversing the movement, and then re-inserting the sheet in proper register. The first set of out-of-register perforations stops abruptly, and the missing or blind holes (occurring in the three pairs of vertical rows of holes at the left) repeat in each row.

perforating machine. The effect of double perforation varies widely according to the perforating head used and the distance between the two sets of holes. The classic effect associated with double perforation on a detached edge consists of the close serrations that result from the second set of perforations having fallen on the bridges left by the first set. When the second set of perforations is more closely in register with the first set, the holes are ovoid. Double rotary perforations result, sometimes, from feeding a sheet out of register into a one-way rotary perforating machine, stopping and reversing it, and then, without any attempt to strengthen the sheet, feeding it into the machine in correct register; such a sheet will exhibit only partially double perforation. See ''Narrow Stamp''; compare ''Mixed Perforations.'' Double perforations are entirely inconstant varieties, and are liable to be encountered on most perforated issues. See ''Error (3).''

Double Roulette. Rouletting twice applied to the same sheet or part of a sheet. Double roulette occurs, usually, through error, or because the first roulette was applied with insufficient force to pierce the paper adequately. An unusual instance of double rouletting, deliberately applied, is found in Queensland 1899 1d., zigzag rouletted (serrated roulette) in black and also plain. In a special sense, ''double roulette'' is applied to Union of South Africa 1942 (August) Bantams 1½d., rouletted 13, in which the rouletting was effected by pairs of discs, each disc producing a line roulette gauging 6½, the intention being that the cuts of the one disc should fall in the bridges left by the other, and the two discs should produce a single line of cuts. In most cases, the object was attained; but in others, two parallel lines of cuts, gauging 6½, appear.

Double Separation — see ''Double Perforation''; ''Double Roulette.''

Electric Eye Markings. Perforation guides used in conjunction with electric eye perforators. See ''Perforation Guide'' in the alphabetical list to the chapter entitled ''From Design to Issued Sheets''; ''Bars (2)''; ''Dash''; ''Margin Line.'' See also ''Electric Eye Terminology.''

Separation. Double perforation and part imperforate varieties. "Double Perforation" and "Imperforate (3)." Great Britain 1941-42 2d., a block of twelve (two across, six down) from the right margin of a post office sheet exhibiting the varieties double perf clearly on the top pair, less obviously on the second, and part imperf on the fourth and fifth pairs. The sheet was perforated by a triple-comb head and, because of malfunctioning of the machine (caused, probably, by the paper bulging increasingly), the stroke that should have perforated the third and fourth rows completely and the fifth row partly fell on the already completely perforated first pair and partly perforated second pair — re-entering, with almost exact coincidence, some of the perforation holes already present — providing only legs on part of the fourth pair. When the pins rose clear of the paper, the bulge straightened, and the paper grippers took over their normal functions so that, on the next stroke, the paper was properly positioned and, indeed, the perforation better registered than the first stroke that first perforated the top of the block. The first stroke to perforate the block perforated also the row above in the sheet; the last stroke to perforate the block perforated also the next two rows below in the sheet.

Electric Eye Perforator. A two-way perforating machine operating on a continuous reel (or "web") of printed stamps, registration being controlled by electric eye markings scanned by photoelectric cells, one of which is coupled to apparatus that adjusts the lateral siting of the web between the rings and so controls the registration of the longitudinal perforations, and another of which is coupled to apparatus that adjusts the siting of the cylinders bearing the bars and so controls the registration of the latitudinal perforations. See "Bars (1)"; "Electric Eye Markings"; "Rings"; "Two-Way Perforator." An experimental model electric eye perforator was used by the Bureau of Engraving and Printing in Washington, D.C., in 1933, the first stamps distributed with electric eye perforations being U.S. 1926 (Dec. 10) Regular 2c., plate 21149, which were sent out to post offices in 1935. Contract model electric eye perforators manufactured by Harris-Seybold came into use in 1941.

Electric Eye Terminology. The nomenclature adopted philatelically to designate the various electric eye markings and the various arrangements of subjects on the printing plates used for printing the reels (or "webs") of stamps perforated by electric eye perforators. See "Electric Eye Markings" and "Electric Eye Per-

Separation. Imperforate. "Error (1)." Great Britain 1854-57 1d., re-engraved die (Die II), a cover bearing a strip of six imperforate. To recognize this as an error of separating, knowledge is necessary that enables stamps of Die I to be distinguished from those of Die II. It is also important to know that all Die II sheets should have been issued perforated — in fact, by a single-comb machine.

forator" above, and "Lay Out" in the alphabetical list to the chapter entitled "Printing Problems and Varieties." The position of the electric eye markings on the post office sheets is determined by the format of the stamp. Large vertical-format stamps and large horizontal-format stamps are printed the same way in relation to the web — that is, with the longer dimension across the web — and the electric eye markings occupy the same position in relation to the web whatever the format. However, in the post office sheets, when viewed with the designs upright, the markings occupy different sheet marginal positions in the two formats. See "Latitudinal Perforation."

Encroachment. (1) Extension into the pane — or sheet — margin of a row of separation, stopping short of the edge of the pane or sheet. Such encroachment comprises, usually, either one hole or two or, occasionally, more holes extra of perforation at the end of each row of holes, and occurs on both comb- and harrow-perforated sheets. Used as synonyms are "extension hole," and the plural.

(2) Overlapping of holes of perforation, particularly of the holes of a line and the end of a leg. See "Legs"; "Line."

Error. In connection with separating, the term "error" is used, strictly, to designate (1) sheets issued wholly imperforate because of inadvertent failure to pass the sheet through the perforating or rouletting machine [Sometimes the term "unperforated" is used to distinguish this error from those cases in which separation either formed no part of the plan of issue, or the absence of separation was deliberate, for which cases the term "imperforate" is used. This class does not, therefore, include sheets that have been issued normally, or sold unofficially or surreptitiously, imperforate. See "Imperforate (1d)."]; to designate (2) sheets issued partly imperforate because of inadvertent failure to provide the missing perforation or rouletting (This class does not, therefore, include sheets that are

766

Separation. Part imperforate. "Error (2)." Southern Rhodesia 1937 (May 12) Coronation 3d., an upper marginal horizontal pair with the (marginal) horizontal line of perforation omitted. The sheets were line-perforated, and the marginal row of perforation was omitted in error.

partly imperforate because of malfunctioning of the machine providing separations.); to designate (3) sheets issued with complete or part double separation applied deliberately but only because of failure to notice the first provision of separation — see "Double Separation" (This class does not, therefore, include sheets that bear complete or part double separation because the second set of separations was deliberately applied to remedy badly registered separation applied earlier — see "Mixed Perforations"; nor does this class include sheets bearing part double separation because of malfunctioning of the machine providing separations.); and to designate (4) sheets issued with perforation resulting from the use of a perforating head with a gauge different from that officially required. Official requirement of the use of a particular gauge or a particular head is a rare

occurrence. Therefore, this class, as an error, is very small. Many cases occur in which different sheets of the same stamp have been perforated in the normal course of events with different heads yielding different gauges of perforation. See "Concurrent Perforation," "Variety (2)." See also "Variety (2)" in the alphabetical list to the chapter entitled "Printing Problems and Varieties."

Extension Hole — see "Encroachment (1)."

Fantail. A stamp with attached sheet margin from a sheet perforated only between stamps. Compare "Wing Margin." See "Imperforate Margin."

Separation. Fantail. Pskov Russian Zemstvo 1896 (June) 1k. and a "fantail" at the foot, being a stamp from the bottom of the sheet that was perforated only between stamps.

Farwell Perforation — see "Automatic Machine Perforation (2)."

Fine Perforation. Small holes, close together and, usually, clean-cut. The term "fine" mainly is used comparatively. Compare "Coarse Perforation."

Flapper — see "Wing Margin."

Flat-Bed Perforation — see "Flat-Bed Separation."

Flat-Bed Rouletting — see "Flat-Bed Separation."

Flat-Bed Separation. Perforation or rouletting applied by a machine operating with a stroke movement as opposed to a rotary movement. See "Rotary Perforation"; "Rotary Rouletting"; "Stroke Perforation"; "Stroke Rouletting."

Frame Bar. The electric eye term formerly recommended for use to designate a perforation register mark that appeared opposite most subjects adjacent to the left or right longitudinal margin of the printed web, or, sometimes, in both those margins. The position of this mark on the post office sheet was determined by the format of the stamp. Large vertical-format stamps being printed in the web with the longer dimension across the web, the frame bar appeared in the post

Separation. Freak or wild perforation. Germany 1922 (May) – 1923 (February) 8m. (Type 1, flat-plate printing), a copy from the southwest corner of the sheet and part of the sheet margin, photographed folded and opened out to show the varieties. The paper was pre-gummed (see "Pre-Gummed Paper" in the alphabetical list to the chapter entitled "Gum"), and, when the sheet was being printed, the southwest corner became folded over forward so that part of the design and some of the marginal markings (see "Marginal Markings" in the alphabetical list to the chapter entitled "From Design to Issued Sheets") were printed on part of the fold and on the gum, while the rest of the design was printed normally. The normal, perforated sheet margin having been removed at some time, the closed and open fold reveal the following varieties: freak or wild perforation in the sheet margin; partial albino (see "Albino" in the alphabetical list to the chapter entitled "Printing Problems and Varieties"); and partially printed on the gum (see "Printed on the Gum" in the alphabetical list to the chapter entitled "Gum").

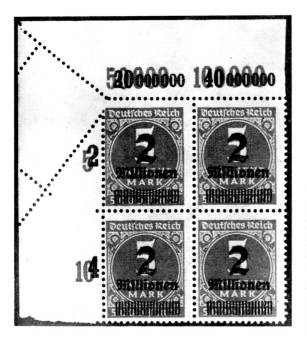

Separation. Freak or wild perforation. Germany 1923 (August–October) 2 mil. on 5 th. m., a block of four from the northwest corner and part of the sheet margin exhibiting the variety "freak" or "wild perforation," caused by a folding over backward of the paper before the sheet was perforated.

office sheet bearing the design upright in the top or bottom margin of the sheet; in large horizontal-format stamps, the frame bars appeared in the side margins of the sheet. See "Bars (2)"; "Longitudinal Perforation."

Freak Separation. Apparently wildly irregular separation usually confined to part of a sheet, with a row or rows of holes or cuts at extravagantly irregular angles, and sometimes passing through parts of some designs, caused by the application of separation to paper while folded or creased and subsequently straightened, or caused by slipping of the paper during passage through the machine, resulting, perhaps, from badly punched stud holes — see "Stud Hole" — or faulty paper grippers. The term "wild separation" is often used as a synonym for freak separation. See also "Registration."

Gauge — see "Perforation Gauge."

Guide — see "Perforation Guide."

Guide Plate. In a guillotine perforator, an adjustable ruler (under which the sheet to be perforated was passed) against the edge of which the rows of stamps were aligned in sequence to ensure that the perforations fell in the gutters. The line of perforations was made one or two stamp rows away from the guide plate, and the alignment did not control the stroke operating in the gutter aligned at the instant of the stroke.

Guillotine. A machine for applying single-line stroke separation. An instance of stamps guillotine-perforated is found in Trinidad 1860 (August) no value expressed (1d.), clean-cut perf 14-16½. An instance of stamps guillotine-rouletted is found in Tasmania 1864 1d. roughly punctured roulette about 8. See "Imperforate (2b)"; "Stroke."

Gutter Bar. The electric eye term formerly recommended for use to designate a perforation register mark that appeared in the left (and sometimes the right) longitudinal margin of the printed web opposite the lateral gutters separating the panes. The position of this mark on the post office sheet was determined by the format of the stamp. Large vertical-format stamps being printed in the web with the longer dimension across the web, the gutter bar appeared in the post office sheet bearing the design upright in the top or bottom margin of the sheet; in large horizontal-format stamps, the gutter bars appeared in the side margin of the sheet. See "Bars (2)"; "Longitudinal Perforation."

Gutter Snipe. A U.S. stamp with attached paper from the central gutter of the sheet as printed, having one row of perforation close to the stamp and another row of holes or teeth at the other edge of the gutter, caused by the sheet having been severed out of register. The severing took place, as is usual, after perforation, and should have occurred in the center of the gutter, leaving the post office sheet with merely a narrow selvedge having an imperforate edge. Compare "Wing Margin." Contrast "Double Perforation."

H-Roulette. A term derived from the shape of each cut found on certain stamps of New Zealand 1859-62 1d., 2d. and 6d., rouletted at Nelson.

Harrow Perforation — see "Harrow Separation."

Harrow Rouletting — see "Harrow Separation."

Harrow Separation. Perforation or rouletting applied to a whole pane or sheet at a single descent of the head. See "Head." An instance of stamps harrow-perforated is to be found, for example, in Sweden 1855 (Jul. 1)–1858 4s., harrow-perforated 14. An instance of stamps harrow-rouletted is to be found, for example, in Luxembourg 1865-72 1c. to 40c., rouletted in color. The erstwhile invariable characteristic of sheets harrow-perforated was that all margins were imperforate (except, possibly, for encroachment holes — see "Encroachment"); but, with the development of multiple-comb perforation, this characteristic no longer universally obtains. See "Multiple-Comb Perforation."

Head. The unit of a stroke machine that effects the perforation, comprising the pin plate, the die plate and, sometimes, the stripping plate. See "Bed Plate"; "Box"; "Pin Plate"; "Stripping Plate."

Horizontal-Comb Perforation. Comb perforation applied to the sheet so that the line appears horizontally and the legs vertically on what is or becomes the post office sheet. See "Comb Perforation"; "Legs"; "Line". Because, in the post office sheet, the stamp designs usually appear upright, horizontal-comb perforation necessarily implies that the sheet is fed vertically through the perforating machine, either head first or foot first. Compare "Vertical-Comb Perforation." In fact, apart from different spacing of legs in the heads and adjustment of the distance of paper travel between descents of the pins, there is no difference in the perforating machine; machines are, usually, capable of applying both horizontal- and vertical-comb perforation. See "Head."

Horizontal Perforation. In relation to the stamp designs viewed upright, perforation in the horizontal gutters, as opposed to "vertical perforation," which lies in the vertical gutters. See also "Latitudinal Perforation."

Hyphen Holes. Small, oblong, rectangular slots resembling hyphens. An instance of stamps hyphen-hole perforated is to be found, for example, in U.S. Revenues Proprietary 1898 2c., hyphen-hole perf 7. Similar, but larger, oblong rectangular slots are to be found on U.S. issues between 1906 and 1923, where two slots appear, one above the other, in the vertical gutters on, for example,

770

Separation. Sheet partly imperforate. "Imperforate (2b)." New Guinea 1937 Coronation 3d. exhibiting the error left-hand vertical row of perforations omitted. The six stamps at the left of the sheet have perforations on only three sides. In this case, the circumstances of production are known, and the failure to perforate fully can be assigned to an error of omission. When circumstances of production are not fully known, single stamps, such as the center four of the six from the left of this sheet, might be considered to be "fantails" from a sheet perforated only between stamps.

Separation. Imperforate and part imperforate variety. "Imperforate (2c) and (3)." Great Britain 1941-42 1d., a block of eighteen (six across, three down) from the top of a post office sheet exhibiting the varieties imperforate on twelve stamps, and part imperforate (or imperf on three sides) on six stamps. This sheet was perforated by a triple-comb head, and because of malfunctioning of the machine, the pins failed to descend for what should have been the first stroke. Nevertheless, the grippers moved the paper forward and, on the second stroke, the next three rows of stamps were perforated. The "line" at the top of the comb is represented by the teeth in the bottom margin of the stamps in the picture.

U.S. 1923-26 2c., the Schermack Type III vending and affixing machine perforations. Such holes are sometimes referred to as "slotted perforation." See "Automatic Machine Perforation (2)."

Imperf. Imperforate.

Imperforate. Not provided with separation. See "Separation." The term "unrouletted" is not used, and references to imperforate stamps embrace stamps without perforation and without rouletting. (1) Imperforate sheets occur because (a) separation formed no part of the plan of issue — for example, Great Britain 1840 1d. and 2d., and U.S. 1847 5c. and 10c. (see "Unperforated"); (b) separation was deliberately, or through force of circumstances, omitted from the sheet — for example, U.S. 1934 National Stamp Exhibition 3c. souvenir sheet, issued deliberately imperforate under the authority of Postmaster General James A. Farley, and Netherlands 1923 5c. and 10c., issued imperforate because of a printers' strike; or Russia (Provisional Government) 1917 1k. to 10r. issued imperforate because of damage to the perforating machines; (c) separation was, by error, omitted from the sheet; and (d) incompletely produced stamps were surreptitiously or unofficially sold — for example, for New Zealand 1936-43 ½d. to 3s., some values are known imperforate from unfinished sheets that had been in the works of De La Rue & Company Ltd., which were bombed during World War II.

(2) Partly imperforate sheets occur (a) because of failure to pass a sheet through

Separation. Imperforate between. U.S. 1857 (Aug. 24) 12c. horizontal pair, imperf between. This variety was caused by bad registration of the sheet in the rotary perforating machine. The printed sheets comprised two panes of 100 (ten x ten) side by side, separated by a pane gutter. The perforating machine was set to perforate only twenty vertical rows of perforation on such sheets;

so that, usually, on the stamps adjoining the pane gutter, the gutter edges of the stamps were imperforate. Registration of the perforation was obtained by laying the edge of the sheet against an adjustable guide; and the printed and perforated sheets were severed later. The operator fed the sheet into the machine out of register to the extent that, instead of the gutter edge being imperforate, one of the interstamp gutters was imperforate, resulting in the ten horizontal pairs being imperforate between.

a one-way perforator in more than one direction, resulting in the absence of all vertical or all horizontal perforations or rouletting (see "Imperforate Between"; "Imperforate Horizontally"; "Imperforate Vertically"); (b) because of deliberate or accidental failure to provide complete separation on single-line guillotine machines — for example, in the Hohe Rinne (Hungarian Hotel Post) 1906 5h., the sheets were perforated only between stamps, resulting in the stamp at each corner of the sheet having perforation on only two sides, while the other stamps from the outer rows and columns have perforations on only three sides [see "Imperforate Margin (1)"]; and New Guinea 1937 Coronation 3d. with the left-hand vertical row of perforation omitted, resulting in the six stamps of the left-hand vertical column of the sheet of thirty having perforations on only three sides [see "Imperforate Margin (2)"]; (c) because of malfunctioning of a comb machine resulting in the presence of one row or more, according to the type of comb, of stamps without full perforations.

(3) Imperforate stamps, or stamps with only part separation, may come from imperforate or partly imperforate sheets. Stamps that exist from both imperforate and line-perforated sheets, or stamps that exist normally line-perforated and imperforate or part perforated by error, are best collected, imperforate or part perforated, in pairs, because line perforation, whether stroke or rotary, inherently has the capacity to produce abnormally "wide" or "long" or (both wide and long in combination) "large" stamps owing to unequal paper movement between strokes, or lateral movement of insufficiently secured pairs of rollers on the shafts of rotary machines — or, possibly, because, say, the vertical perforation was effected on a rotary machine with the wheels set for the wider-spaced horizontal perforation; such stamps can be, and have been, trimmed to give the appearance of being imperforate.

(4) Stamps with only part separation may also result from special manufacturing requirements. For example, some stamps for coils used in automatic vending machines are perforated in only one direction, vertically for sideways-delivery coils or horizontally for end-delivery coils — for instance, U.S. 1954 (Oct. 8) Regular 1c., which exists imperforate horizontally and perforated 10 vertically (such stamps are often referred to as "imperf x perf 10"), and U.S. 1960 (Jun. 17) Regular 1¼c., which exists imperforate vertically and perforated 10 horizontally (such stamps

SEPARATION

are often referred to as "perf 10 x imperf"). See "Imperforate Horizontally"; "Imperforate Vertically." Also, some stamps from some books or booklets are imperforate on two adjacent sides or, sometimes, three sides — for instance, Canada 1954 1c. exists imperforate on two adjacent sides and perforated 12 on the other two sides from booklet panes of five stamps and one label, and Canada 1953 (May 1) 1c. exists imperforate on three sides (top, right and bottom) and perforated 12 at the left from booklet "panes" that were, in fact, strips of three.

Imperforate and Perforated. Imperf x perf. See "Imperforate (4)."

Imperforate and Rouletted. Imperf x roulette. See "Imperforate (2a)."

Imperforate Between. Without separation in the stamp gutter common to two or more stamps. The variety is invariably referred to as "pair (or other multiple) imperforate between," with an indication of whether the pair is vertical or horizontal. The necessity for demonstrating the absence of separation by means of not less than a pair arises from the inherent capacity of single-line separation to produce wide, long and large stamps. See "Imperforate (3)." Imperforate between, almost invariably, is an error resulting from the accidental failure to provide one line of separation by hand operation — for example, Trinidad 1860 (August) no value expressed (1d.) clean-cut perf 14-16½, imperf between horizontal pair, with the vertical row of perforation missing as the result of failure to operate the guillotine when the paper was moved; and Trinidad 1859 6d. pin-rouletted 14, imperf between vertical pair, with the horizontal row of rouletting missing as a result of failure to direct the rouletting wheel along that horizontal row.

Cases are on record, however, in which imperforate between is a variety caused by bad registration — that is, misplacement of sheets in a rotary perforator — for example, U.S. 1857 (Aug. 24) 12c., horizontal pair imperf between. The rotary perforating machines were set to perforate the printed sheets, which comprised two panes of 100 (ten x ten) side by side separated by a pane gutter; only twenty vertical rows of perforation were applied to these sheets, so that, usually, on the stamps adjoining the pane gutter, the gutter edges of the stamps were imperforate, and the printed sheets were severed into post office sheets of 100 after perforation. Registration of the perforation was obtained by laying the edge of the sheet against an adjustable guide. Occasionally the operator fed a sheet into the machine out of register to the extent that, instead of the gutter edges being imperforate, one of the interstamp gutters was imperforate, resulting in horizontal pairs imperforate between. Imperforate between must be distinguished from both imperforate vertically and imperforate horizontally. See "Imperforate (2)"; "Imperforate (4)"; "Imperforate Horizontally"; "Imperforate Vertically."

Imperforate Horizontally. Not provided with horizontal separation. Imperforate horizontally occurs (1) because of error — see "Imperforate (2a)"; and (2) because of intention — see "Imperforate (4)"; "Variety."

Imperforate Margin. (1) The edge without separation of a stamp from an outer row or column of a sheet perforated only between stamps. Contrast "Imperforate Horizontally"; "Imperforate Vertically." The term "straight edge" is often used as a synonym for imperforate margin. A stamp with such a margin is, sometimes, termed a "fantail." Compare "Wing Margin." Such stamps have, frequently, been provided with faked perforations; these, however, can often be detected because the gauge, or the size or shape of the holes, differs from that offically applied, or because of characteristics in the design of the stamp that prove it to have occupied a sheet — or pane — marginal position. See "Re-Perforated."

(2) The edge without separation of a stamp from an outer row or column of a sheet with a row of separation omitted in error. See "Imperforate (2b)." In this

774

case, the stamps from the corner of the sheet will have perforation on three sides, and can, on that account, be distinguished from stamps from the corners of sheets perforated only between stamps, because they are perforated only on two adjoining sides.

Imperforate Vertically. Not provided with vertical separation. Imperforate vertically occurs (1) because of error [see "Error"; "Imperforate (2a)"]; and (2) because of intention [see "Imperforate (4)"; "Variety"].

Instanta. The trade name of a perforation gauge (invented by C.P. Rang, British Patent No. 573065, and marketed by Stanley Gibbons Ltd.) based upon a series of lines converging on a vertical, to give an infinite number of readings, and with a graduated scale between 9.75 and 18.25. See "Perforation Gauge."

Intermediate Perforation. The discs of paper neither have been punched out entirely nor remain attached to the edges of what should be holes. A state of perforation between clean-cut and rough. Only rarely is it necessary to draw the distinction indicated by intermediate perforation. Compare "Clean-Cut Perforation"; "Rough Perforation."

International Vending Machine Perforation — see "Automatic Machine Perforation (2)."

Interrupted Perforation. Perforation with holes missing. The gaps in the rows of holes result from the removal at regular intervals of pins from the pin plate. The gauge of interrupted perforation is regular, apart from the gaps. The term "syncopated perforation" is often used as a synonym for interrupted perforation. This form of separation was originally adopted for coils of stamps used in automatic vending machines to lessen the weakening effect on the paper of perforation, but has been used for stamps sold in sheet form. An instance of interrupted perforation is to be found, for example, on Danzig 1924-39 5p. Such perforation is to be distinguished from the similar effects that sometimes result from a damaged comb on which pins have been broken off. Interrupted perforation occurs on every stamp in the sheet, while the effect of broken pins will be repeated only so often as the comb descended on the sheet, and only in the position or positions affected. See "Blind Perforation (2)."

Irregular Perforation. (1) Perforation of which the gauge varies along the same row — see "Perforation Gauge." Such perforation is, sometimes, referred to as being "roughly [a gauge]," or as two gauges separated by the word "to," or a dash. Instances of such irregular perforation are to be found, for example, in Antigua 1863-67 1d. rough perf 14 to 16; and in New Zealand 1935 (May 1) 2½d. perf 13-14 x 13½, in which each row of horizontal perforations on each stamp is in two gauges, one half gauging 13 and the other half 14. (2) Perforation of which the holes in the rows are in uneven alignment — for example, Montenegro 1874-81 irregular perf 12. The characteristic irregularity of the perforation occurring on those stamps gave rise to the term "Montenegrin perforation" to designate any such irregular perforation.

Kampf. The name of a German-made perforating unit in the Jumelle machine constructed to the requirements of Harrison & Sons Ltd., the British printers, by various manufacturers in several different countries and partly by Harrison & Sons itself. The Jumelle machine, which was put into use in 1972, prints, perforates and severs into sheets stamps printed on the web. The Kampf unit perforates the printed stamps as the web continues on its passage through the Jumelle machine. Two cylinders are involved. One has protruding pins and the other has holes to receive the ends of the pins as the cylinders revolve with the paper passing between them. The pins push through the paper, which is thus perforated.

L-Perforator or L-Type Perforator. An assembly of two one-way rotary perforating machines operating at right-angles to one another and some distance apart, the intervening space being occupied by two endless bands, the assembly being arranged in the shape of the letter "L." The sheet is put on the first endless band and led through the first perforator, which applies all the horizontal (or vertical) perforations. Then, still facing in the same direction, the sheet is carried on to the second endless band and is led through the second perforator, which applies all the vertical (or horizontal) perforations.

Large Stamp. In connection with separation, the term "large stamp" refers not to the design, but to the paper area, and the fact that the spacing between the rows of perforation or rouletting on the sheet or sheets was irregular in both directions, so that some stamps detached from the sheet have substantially larger areas of paper than intended ("large stamps"), while other stamps from the same or different sheets have substantially smaller areas of paper than intended ("small stamps"). Variations in only one direction result in "wide stamps" and "narrow stamps," or "long stamps" and "short stamps." This occurs sometimes in hand-controlled, single-line guillotine perforation in which the spacing depends upon the ability of the operator. It occurs also, sometimes, in rotary perforation when pairs of wheels are either insufficiently secured in position and move sideways on the axles, or when the wheels are spaced for vertical perforation (the height of the stamps being greater than the width) and the machine is used for horizontal perforation, and vice versa. For these reasons, stamps that exist normally perforated and also imperforate or part perforated by error are best collected (imperf or part perf) in pairs. See "Imperforate (3)." Large stamps occasionally occur with comb perforation, but the difference is usually only slight, when, distances between stamps permitting, two differently spaced heads have been used for the same issue. See "Head"; "Short Stamp."

Lateral Perforation — see "Latitudinal Perforation."

Latitudinal Perforation. Perforation across the web applied by the bars in a two-way perforator. See "Bars (1)"; "Two-Way Perforator." Sometimes the term "lateral perforation" is used as a synonym for latitudinal perforation. The longer dimension of large format stamps lies across the web as printed. After perforation, the web is severed into post office sheets, and on them the designs appear upright, whether the vertical or the horizontal dimension is longer. Compare "Longitudinal Perforation." While the web is in the two-way perforator, it is, therefore, inapt to refer to vertical and horizontal perforation without qualification. See "Electric Eye Terminology"; "Horizontal Perforation."

Lawnmower, The — see APS.

Legrand. In connection with separation, Dr. Jacques Amable Legrand is remembered as the philatelist who first distinguished between the effects of perforation and rouletting, who was the originator of the perforation gauge (see "Perforation Gauge") and who originally coined the terms by which the majority of the different forms of rouletting are known. Under his pen name "Dr. Magnus," he published his observations and findings in a paper entitled "Dentelés et non Dentelés" (*Le Timbre-Poste*, Vol. 4, Pages 79ff.; Vol. 5, Pages 4ff., from October 1866 to April 1867).

Separation. Electric eye perforation. "Longitudinal" and "lateral" perforation. U.S. 1960 (Jun. 2) American Woman Issue 4c., and 1960 (Aug. 29) Fifth World Forestry Congress Issue 4c. Both of these stamps were printed (from 200-subject plates bearing four panes of fifty) with the longer stamp dimension across the web of paper. The stamps were perforated by the electric eye perforator on the web, which then was cut into "full" sheets of four panes. Later, these full sheets were quartered to make post office sheets. The post office sheets show the designs upright. The vertical perforations of the stamp at the left, and the horizontal perforations of the stamp below were both applied by the electric eye perforating machine's longitudinal perforating unit. The other two sets of perforations were both applied by the machine's lateral perforating unit. For this reason, the electric eye marginal markings appear at right-angles to one another when post office sheets of these and similar stamps are compared.

Legs. In comb perforation, the short rows of holes usually at right-angles to the line. See "Line (1)." Sometimes the legs are referred to as "the teeth of the comb." See also "Triangular Comb Perforation."

Line. In connection with separation, the term "line" is used in two distinct senses. (1) As a noun, in connection with comb perforation, the line is the long row of holes from which the legs extend, usually at right-angles. See "Legs"; see also "Horizontal Comb Perforation"; "Vertical Comb Perforation."

(2) As an adjective, "line" is employed in conjunction with both "perforation" and "roulette." See "Line Perforation"; "Line Roulette."

Line Perforation. Perforation applied in rows or lines as opposed to comb or harrow perforation. See "Comb Perforation"; "Harrow Separation." There are two main groups of line perforation:

(1) "single-line," where at one operation only one row of holes, applied by a stroke machine, is made in the paper (see "Guillotine"); and (2) "multiple-

Separation. Lozenge perforation. Bulgaria 1884 Postage Due 25s. exhibiting in the vertical gutters true lozenge perforation.

line," where at one operation several rows of holes, applied by rotary action, are made in the paper in the same direction by a one-way perforator, or in both directions by a two-way perforator. See "One-Way Perforator"; "Two-Way Perforator."

Line Roulette. An English synonym for *percé en ligne*, the most widely used form of rouletting employed for stamps. Among U.S. issues with this form of separation may be mentioned the Kansas City roulette, found on U.S. 1912 1c. and 2c., resulting from the use of ordinary tracing wheels on imperforate sheets unsold and unrequired for vending machines, and left on hand in the post office at Kansas City. To make the imperforate stamps salable over the post office counter, they were rouletted with the approval of the Post Office Department; 93,600 of the 1c. and 69,200 of the 2c. stamps were thus rouletted. Other U.S. line-rouletted stamps include U.S. Revenues, Documentary, 1898 1c. See also *"Percé en Ligne"; "Percé en Lignes Colorées."*

Long Stamp. In connection with separation, the term "long stamp" refers not to the design, but to the paper dimension. See "Large Stamp." Occasionally, long stamps have occurred with comb perforation, on sheets perforated with a horizontal comb on which the legs were longer than the height of the design. The distance of paper movement was regulated for the length of the legs, and only after one or more descents of the pins was the paper movement re-adjusted to the required shorter distance. The long stamps resulted from the early stroke or strokes of the machine. Instances of such long stamps are to be found, for example, in India 1869 1a. Similarly, with vertical comb perforation, a "wide stamp" results. Compare "Short Stamp." See "Horizontal-Comb Perforation"; "Vertical-Comb Perforation." Minute differences in the length and width of stamps occur also because of micrometric adjustment of the distance of paper travel during the course of perforating by a comb head.

Longitudinal Perforation. Perforation along the length of the web applied by the rings in a two-way perforator. See "Rings"; "Two-Way Perforator." The

Separation. Perforation. Margin line. U.S. 1926 (Dec. 10) 2c. plate 21149, a marginal block of twenty (two across, ten down) exhibiting, at the upper right, the margin line. The plate number is opposite the eighth horizontal row from the top. From the first distribution, during 1935, of electric eye ("experimental" model) perforated stamps.

shorter dimension of large-format stamps lies along the web as printed; after perforation, the web is severed into post office sheets, and, on them, the designs appear upright whether the horizontal or the vertical dimension is the shorter. Compare "Latitudinal Perforation." While the web is in the two-way perforator, it is, therefore, inapt to refer to vertical and horizontal perforations without qualification. See "Electric Eye Terminology"; "Horizontal Perforation."

Lozenge Perforation — see "Lozenge Roulette."

Lozenge Roulette. An English misnomer for *percé en croix*, perpetrated because of the fancied resemblance of the shapes, resulting from the series of crosses, to those of the heraldic lozenge. The only true lozenge-shaped form of separation encountered in philately is found in Bulgaria Postage Due 1884 5s. to 50s., from the gutters of which the lozenges were cut out and, therefore, constituted "lozenge perforation" as opposed to rouletting. Some stamps referred to in the United States as being lozenge-perforated are merely *percé en croix* — for example, Madeira 1868 20r. to 100r. (Scott Nos. 2c, 3a, 4b and 5a). See "Cross Roulette"; *"Percé en Croix."*

Machine Perforation. Perforation applied by machine, as opposed to so-called "pin perforation" applied by hand and any other means of rouletting. See "Pin Perforation."

Mailometer Perforation — see "Automatic Machine Perforation (2)."

Margin Line. A perforation register mark printed on the web for the purpose of controlling each plate impression by varying the longitudinal position of the web passing through the two-way electric eye perforator used in the production of U.S. stamps. Only one margin line appears on each printing plate, and the margin line is printed on the right-hand outer margin of the web in alignment with the center gutter separating the upper and lower panes as printed. On the post office sheet, the position of the margin line depends upon the format of the stamp. Compare "Bars (2)"; see "Electric Eye Terminology."

Matrix Plate — see "Bed Plate."

Measurement. In connection with separation, the term "measurement" is used loosely as indicating the ascertaining of the gauge of a separation. See "Perforation Gauge."

Misplaced Separation — see "Registration."

Missing Perforation — see "Blind Perforation (2)."

Mixed Perforations. Perforations twice applied to the same sheet, the first set having been applied out of register, the sheet having then been strengthened with paper strips pasted on the underside of the sheet covering the holes, and the second set having been applied in register. When a stamp from a sheet with mixed perforations has been used and removed from the mail it franked, the soaking involved usually removes the strengthening strip of paper, so leaving an apparent double perforation — or, perhaps, a narrow stamp if the gutter has become detached. See "Narrow Stamp." Mixed perforations occur in New Zealand, including, for instance, 1874-75 3d. and 6d., originally rotary perf 10 out of registration, and then perforated 12½ in correct register; and 1901 ½d. mixed perf 14 and 11; in Victoria, for instance, Postage Due 1890 2d. Compare "Double Perforation"; see "Error."

Montenegrin Perforation. See "Irregular Perforation (2)."

Multiple-Comb Perforation. Perforation applied by a head that, at one stroke, perforates all four gutters surrounding each stamp in one or more rows and also provides perforations between the stamps of the next row. See "Comb Perforation"; "Head"; "Legs." Multiple comb heads are drilled to perforate as many as ten complete rows, apart from the extra legs. An instance of stamps perforated by such heads is provided, for example, by Switzerland 1949 3 (c.) to 70 (c.), which were printed in the web in panes of fifty (five across, ten down), and the extra legs extended into pane margins. With the development of multiple comb heads, the distinction between comb and harrow perforation has lost much of its significance. See "Harrow Separation."

Multiple-Line Perforation — see "Line"; "Line Perforation (2)."

Multiplication Sign. In connection with the notation of separation, the multiplication sign ("x") is used conventionally — not in its arithmetical sense of multiplying one figure by another. See "Compound Perforation."

Narrow Stamp — see "Large Stamp"; "Short Stamp." Narrow stamps sometimes result, in vertical-comb perforation, from malfunctioning of the paper grippers, which causes them to slip, and the paper travel to be too short between descents of the pins. Usually this results in all the subsequent vertical perforations being out of register, and a sheet thus perforated would, usually, be rejected if noticed. A "short stamp" similarly occurs in horizontal-comb perforation. Narrow stamps may also result, in horizontal-comb perforation, from double perforation if the sheet is moved sideways and if the stamps are later separated. See "Double Perforation"; "Mixed Perforation."

Nib — see "Bridge."

Nibbed Perforation. A short tooth, or short teeth, resulting from the uneven parting, or cutting apart, of perforated stamps. A stamp exhibiting this effect is referred to, sometimes, as having "one perf short" or "a short perforation."

Oblique Roulette. An English synonym for *percé en lignes obliques*. See *"Percé en Lignes Obliques."*

Odontometer — see "Perforation Gauge (1)."

Official Perforation, Roulette — see "Official Separation."

Official Separation. Separation officially required and applied as part of the plan of issue, as opposed to "unofficial" or "private" perforation or roulette, applied, usually, by business houses to stamps issued imperforate. The first official perforation was applied to Great Britain 1854-57 1d. and 2d. perf 16, first issued in February 1854. The first official perforation in the United States was applied to U.S. 1857-60 1c. to 90c. Among the earliest officially applied roulettes are Finland 1860 (Jan. 1) 5k. and 10k., serpentine roulette 7½ to 8, and Victoria 1854-59 (Dec. 5, 1857) 6d., serpentine roulette 10½. See "Unofficial Perforation"; "Unofficial Roulette."

One-Way Perforator. A rotary perforating machine that applies to the sheet all the perforations in one dimension at one operation. With only one machine in use, it was usual to apply, say, the horizontal perforations to a batch of sheets, then alter the spacing of the wheels and complete the perforation by applying the vertical perforations. Compare "Two-Way Perforator."

Parallel-Line Roulette. An English synonym for *percé en parallel.* See "*Percé en Parallel.*"

Part Imperforate — see "Imperforate Horizontally"; "Imperforate Margin"; "Imperforate Vertically."

Penny-in-the-Slot Perforation. (1) A nickname for the automatic vending machine perforation found on New Zealand 1905-1906 Universal 1d., especially that consisting of two comparatively large holes widely spaced, in the vertical gutters, similar to the two holes in the horizontal gutters on, for example, U.S. 1908-1909 1c. with Brinkerhoff Type II vending machine perforation. (2) Generally, any automatic vending machine special perforation. See "Automatic Machine Perforation (2)."

Percé en Arc. Rouletted with a succession of minute arcs, each approximately a semicircle, and all on the same side of the imaginary line comprising the bases of the arcs, the distance between one semicircle and the next varying between ½ and ¼ mm or less. *Percé en arc* is encountered on Brunswick 1864 ⅓ g. to 3g.; and Hanover 1864 3p. to 3g., gauging 16. The 3g. was reprinted in 1891, and on it the rouletting gauges 13½. The effect, particularly on single stamps, is very similar to *percé en scie.* See also "Serpentine Roulette."

Percé en Croix. Rouletted with a succession of more or less minute diagonal crosses, at distances from one another that vary, often within the length of a single line, and also from line to line, and from one series of roulettes to another. *Percé en croix* is a rare form of rouletting. It is found on Madeira (Portugal) 1868 50r. and 80r. gauge 10, and 100r. in two gauges, 10 and 13½. It is found also on Tasmania 1864-68 1d. and 4d., although this form of rouletting on this issue is not listed in either Scott or Stanley Gibbons, but examples are known to exist. In the Tapling Collection in the British Library, there are seven examples of the locally printed 1d., two bearing pen cancellations dated "5.10.66" and "12.10.66," and two others also pen-canceled, and two examples of the locally printed 4d., one pen-canceled "3.6." All are displayed, as oblique rouletted, in frame 952. See "Cross Roulette."

Percé en Ligne, Percé en Ligne Droite. Rouletted with a succession of short straight cuts, making a straight line intended to be parallel to the frames of the

Separation. *Percé en croix.* Tasmania 1864-68 1d. *percé en croix.* The minute crosses forming the roulette can be most clearly distinguished on and immediately above the top frameline. This form of rouletting was not very efficient or satisfactory in use. In fact, the stamp pictured was separated from the one above by knife or scissors cut.

stamps bordering the gutter along which the rouletting appears. The lengths of the individual cuts varies widely from issue to issue, as do the spacings between the cuts. First used by Henry Archer on Great Britain 1841 1d. plates 70 and 71, gauging 12 (see "Archer Roulette"), *percé en ligne* is the most frequently encountered form of rouletting. Gauges vary between, for example, 4½, found on Danish West Indies 1866 3c.; 6, found on Uruguay 1880 (Nov. 10) 1c.; 18, found on U.S. Confederate States General Issues 1861 (September) 5c.; and 20, found on Palestine 1918 (Mar. 5) 1p. See also "Line Roulette."

Separation. *Percé en ligne.* Palestine 1918 1p., *percé en ligne,* 20, and an enlargement of one corner. One of the finest gauges of *percé en ligne* known in philately.

Separation. *Percé en lignes obliques.* Tasmania 1864-70 1d. *percé en lignes oblique* 14 to 15.

Percé en Lignes Colorées, Percé en Lignes de Couleur. Rouletted with a succession of colored, short, straight cuts making a straight line parallel to the frames of the stamps bordering the gutter along which the rouletting appears. The rouletting is in the same color as the stamps, the perforative rule having surrounded each subject on the printing base and having been inked at the same time as the subjects. At one operation, the stamps were printed and the rouletting effected. *Percé en lignes colorées* is to be found, for example, on Luxembourg 1865-72 1c. to 40c. See also "Rouletted in Color."

Percé en Lignes de Couleur — see "*Percé en Lignes Colorées.*"

Percé en Ligne Droite — see "*Percé en Ligne.*"

Percé en Lignes Obliques. Rouletted with a series of short, straight cuts, each cut being set slanting to the frames of the stamps bordering the gutter in which the rouletting appears or was intended to appear, the cuts in each gutter being parallel to one another and arranged, in the vertical gutters, one above the other and, in the horizontal gutters, side by side so as to make in each gutter a row intended to be parallel to the frames. *Percé en lignes oblique* is to be found, for example, on La Guaira 1864 (October) ½r. and 2r., and Tasmania 1864-70 1d. to 1s., on which two different gauges, 10, 10½ and 14 to 15, are found. (Scott does not differentiate between the gauges — see Tasmania Nos. 39 to 43; however,

Separation. *Percé en parallel.* Tasmania 1864-68 1d. *percé en parallel.* The horizontal parallel cuts are clearly visible in the vertical margins. Such horizontal margins as exist are without any trace of vertical cuts.

Separation. *Percé en pointe.* Danzig 1921 80 (p.), a pair *percé en pointe* and an enlargement showing the effect of a particular application of this type of rouletting gauging 13½. This type of separation is also termed "zigzag roulette" and, in the United States, "serrated roulette."

in Stanley Gibbons, the gauges of the oblique roulette are separately listed: 10, 10½ as Nos. 67 to 71, and 14 to 15, used at Deloraine, as Nos. 72 to 77.)

Percé en Lozenges. An uneasy translation into French of the English "lozenge roulette" — a misnomer for *percé en croix.* See *"Percé en Croix."*

Percé en Parallel. Rouletted with a series of short cuts, each cut being set at right angles to the frames of the stamps bordering the gutter in which the rouletting appears, or was intended to appear, the cuts in each series being parallel to one another and arranged, in the vertical gutters, one above the other, and, in the horizontal gutters, side by side, so as to make in each gutter a row intended to be parallel to the frames. First recorded by Dr. Legrand as being used on the stamps of Thurn and Taxis, Northern District 1859-60 5s. and 10s. and Southern District 1859 15k. and 30k., *percé en parallel* is found also on Tasmania 1864-70 1d. See "Legrand." Neither Scott nor Stanley Gibbons lists this variety of rouletting on this issue, but an example is to be found in the Tapling Collection in the British Library displayed as oblique rouletted.

Separation. *Percé en pointe.* Germany 1923 (August–October) 400T. on 40 (p.), and Germany (Russian Zone), Berlin (Brandenburg) 1945 5p., both *percé en pointe.* This type of separation is also termed "zigzag roulette" and, in the United States, "serrated roulette."

Percé en Pointe. Rouletted with a series of short, straight cuts, the cuts in each series being inclined at angles, in alternate directions, and set slanting to the frames of the stamps bordering the gutter in which the rouletting appears or was intended to appear. When separated from the sheet, the stamp appears framed by triangular projections. With different forms of this type of rouletting, the shape of the triangles varies from acute isosceles to equilateral, and oblique isosceles, and the tips of the projections vary from sharply pointed to blunt. Also, the lengths of the projections and the distances between them and, consequently, the gauges, vary in the different forms of this type of rouletting. Originally adopted by Dr. Legrand as descriptive of the shape of the sharply pointed tips of the triangular projections and to distinguish this verbally from the rounded tips of *percé en serpentin,* the term *percé en pointe* has been, virtually, abandoned in favor of, in the United States, "serrated roulette," and elsewhere, "zigzag roulette" and *"percé en zigzags,"* partly because *percé en pointe* does not clearly conjure up a shape and partly from the confusion caused by the ill-named *percé en pointes.* See "Legrand." *Percé en pointe* is to be found, for example, on Danzig 1921 5 (p.) to 10 (m.), gauge 13½; Germany 1923 (October to November) 10 million m. to 50 milliard m., gauge 13½; La Guaira 1864 (October) ½r. and 2r., gauge 10; and Queensland 1899 1d., gauge 13. See "Serrate Roulette."

Percé en Pointes. A term intended to signify piercing by sharp points — that is, rouletting by means of sharp-ended pins, as opposed to perforation by flat-ended pins. Doubtless because of the confusion which would result from the verbal similarity between the terms *"percé en pointes"* and *"percé en pointe,"* the use of *"percé en pointes"* was avoided by Dr. Legrand who, however, referred to "un vrai piquage a l'épingle" (*Le Timbre-Poste,* Vol. 4, Page 89, November, 1866) in connection with the privately applied pin rouletting found on some examples of France 1853-60 1c. to 80c. See "Legrand." The current French rendering of *percé en pointes* is *"perforé trous d'épingle,"* which neatly sidesteps the difficulty of choosing between *percé* (rouletted) and *piqué* (perforated) and avoids the incorrect implications of the frequently employed English term "pin-perforated" when accuracy demands the use of "pin-rouletted." See "Pin-Rouletted."

Percé en Scie. Rouletted with, occasionally, a minutely waved line more sharply inclined on one side of each crest than on the other, and interrupted at short, irregular intervals, or rouletted with minute arcs, sometimes semicircles, sometimes less, or with more minute curved lines meeting at a sharp angle, all on one side of an imaginary line joining the ends of the bases of the arcs. Theoretically, the edges of a single stamp so separated represent the teeth of a saw, hence the term; but practically, the effect of this form of rouletting is almost indistinguishable from that of *percé en arc.* The terms *percé en scie* and its direct synonym in English, "saw-tooth roulette," are misleading, because the effect bears little resemblance to the sharply pointed projections usually associated with a saw-edge, which is the effect intended to be conveyed by *"percé en pointe"* and "zigzag roulette," or, in the United States, by "serrate roulette." *Percé en scie* has been recorded as existing on Bremen 1861-64 2g. to 5s. and, for example, on France 1853-61 1c. to 80c., and Venezuela 1866-70 ½c. to 2r. See "Saw-Tooth Roulette"; "Serpentine Roulette."

Percé en Serpentin. Rouletted with a continuous, sharply undulating line, minutely interrupted to form bridges. When separated from the sheet, the stamp appears framed by almost straight-sided projections, each rounded at the tip and springing from rounded troughs. The length of the projections varies with different types of this form of rouletting, as does the gauge. Four different lengths of teeth and gauges, three official, one unofficial, are to be found on Finland 1860 (Jan. 1) 5k. and 10k., and 1866-71 5p. to 1m., and others on Helsingfors (Finnish local) 1866-68 10p., and 1871-77 10p. Shallow teeth and less abrupt projections are to be found on Victoria 1854-59 (Dec. 5, 1857) 6p., which is sometimes referred to as having a "wavy line roulette." See also "Serpentine Roulette."

Percé en Zigzag. A French synonym for zigzag roulette, which (with "serrated roulette" in the United States) has virtually superseded *"percé en pointe"* to describe the effect of triangular more or less sharp-pointed projections. See *"Percé en Pointe"*; "Serrate Roulette."

Perf. Perforated or perforation.

Perfin — see "Perforated (2)."

Perforated. (1) Having small circular or other-shaped holes punched out of the paper to assist in rendering a stamp or part of a stamp easily detachable as a unit from contiguous paper or stamps; as distinct from rouletted. See "Rouletted." See also "Blind Perforation"; "Hyphen Holes"; "Lozenge Perforation"; "Square-Hole Perforation." The overwhelming majority of stamps have been thus perforated, while some issues have perforations additional to those in the interstamp gutters — for example, issues of Belgium from 1893 to 1914. For instance, Belgium 1912 1c. was issued complete with a dominical label or tablet bearing instructions not to deliver on Sunday, and with an extra row of perforation between the tablet and the other portion of the design. Other examples include some Italian parcel post stamps, for instance, Italy 1946-54 Parcel Post 20c., a bipartite stamp with a row of perforations between the two parts; and some provisional issues that have been made by dividing each stamp into two by a row of perforations. An instance of a stamp perf about 15 bisected vertically by a row perf 12 is provided by St. Vincent 1880 1d. on 1872-73 one-half of 6d., and an instance of a stamp perf 12½ bisected diagonally by a row perf 12 is provided by Guatemala 1935 (November)–1936 (October) (½c.), being one-half of the 1c. of that issue. See "Perforation Gauge (1)." When a stamp, or part of a stamp, from a perforated sheet is detached from it as a unit, the edges of the stamp or part have teeth and indentations [see "Denticulated"; "Teeth (1)"] but, by common usage, it is referred to as "perforated." This has caused difficulty in distinguishing between such a stamp or part and one, in fact, having holes punched out of its paper [see "Perforated (2)"].

(2) Having small circular holes punched out of the paper as an identifying or security device (see "Perfins" in the alphabetical list to the chapter entitled "Philatelic Trends"). Such stamps are termed variously "branded stamps," "perfins" (*perforated initials*, or *perforated identifications*), "punchies," "punch perforated," "punctured," and "spifs" (*stamps perforated with the initals of firms and societies, or stamps perforated for insurance against frauds*). Such stamps fall, broadly, into two classes:

(a) Those to which the perforation was applied officially or by official request as part of the issue. One of the earliest of such devices was used for Western Australia 1854 1d. official postage stamps, and consisted of a single hole, about 3 mm in diameter. This must be distinguished from, for example, Spanish stamps between 1869 and 1901, including Spain 1899 (Oct. 1) 5c., with a similar circular hole punched out of the paper, signifying that the stamp had been used telegraphically. Other issues and uses include Tunisia, issues to 1901, for instance, 1888-93 1c. perforated with ten or eleven holes to form the letter "T" as signifying postage due; British Guiana 1882 1c. and 2c. perforated "*Specimen*" diagonally as a precaution against fraud on the revenue by forgery (to be distinguished from

Separation. Perforated bisect. "Perforated (1)." Vertical.
St. Vincent 1880 1d. on 1872–73 one-half of 6d.

issues of many countries perforated with the same word, or its equivalent, supplied by issuing authorities as examples of their postage stamps; see "Specimen Stamps" in the alphabetical list to the chapter entitled "Philatelic Trends"); and Argentina 1917 5p., 10p. and 20p. perforated with holes forming part of the word *"Inutilizado,"* signifying that the stamps had been canceled by the perforation (usually in sheets) in payment of postage on bulk mailing of newspapers.

(b) Those to which the perforation was applied privately, but with official permission, as a protection against pilferage. In Great Britain, such perforation was officially authorized in 1868, and one of the earliest users of a private device was T.J. Allman, a London publisher, whose perforation was "T.J.A. 463." In the United States, a postal regulation of May 8, 1908, officially permitted the use of perforated initials, which are found on issues from 1902 onward. Such private perforations are to be found on the stamps of well over 100 countries.

Perforated All Around. Of a sheet: with perforations not only in the interstamp gutters but also close to the outside edges of stamps in the outer rows and columns of the pane or sheet. Of a stamp: having perforations in all margins, as contrasted with a stamp having one margin or more imperforate. See "Perforated between Stamps."

Perforated and Imperforate. Perf x imperf. See "Imperforate (4)."

Perforated between Stamps. Of a sheet: having perforations in only the interstamp gutters so that stamps from the outer rows and columns of the pane or sheet have one or two margins imperforate. See "Imperforate Margin (2)." Contrast "Perforated All Around."

Perforated Bisect — see "Perforated (1)."

Perforating Head — see "Head."

Perforation. The effect of the actual or intended removal from the paper of small circular or other-shaped holes. Compare "Rouletting"; see "Perforated." Per-

Separation. Perforated bisect. "Perforated (1)." Diagonal. Guatemala 1935 (November)–1936 (October) (½c.), a pair, being two copies, se-tenant, of one-half of the 1c. of that issue.

Separation. "Perforation gauge (2)." Singapore (Malaya) 1948 50c. perf 17½ x 18, one of the finest gauges of perforation encountered in philately.

foration by the stroke process for postage stamps was first patented by Henry Archer. See "Archer Perforation." Perforation by the rotary process was first patented by the Bemroses. See "Bemrose Perforation." See also "Perforation Gauge."

Perforation Characteristic. A peculiarity imparted by a particular method of perforation or by a particular perforating head — see also "Perforation Gauge (2)." (1) Characteristics imparted by the method of perforation consist, mainly, in variations in spacing between rows of holes, and in whether the rows extend across the pane or sheet margins. As general rules: (a) if, at each place where the rows of perforation holes cross, two holes encroach on one another, and especially if the sheet margins are all perforated throughout, the perforation was line (see "Line Perforation"); if there is a substantial irregularity of spacing between holes in the rows, the perforation was not rotary (see "Rotary Perforation"); (b) if, where the rows of perforation holes apparently cross, the holes do not encroach on one another, and especially if one, two or three sheet margins are imperforate, the perforation was comb; if there is, at two horizontal or vertical corners of the stamps in a row or column, an appreciably larger gap or shorter distance between holes than obtains elsewhere on the stamps, the perforation almost certainly was comb, and the size of the comb head can be determined by noting at how many rows' or columns' distance the gap or shorter distance occurs (see "Comb Perforation"); (c) if all the sheet or pane margins are imperforate, the perforation was harrow (see "Harrow Separation"). The last rule, while not covering every case of harrow perforation, is absolute; however, the others are all subject to exceptions in particular cases, and the converse of each rule does not apply.

(2) Characteristics imparted by individual perforating heads consist, usually, in slight misalignment of a hole or holes, or variations in the distances between holes within a particular row, and thus enable the student to identify the work done by that head and, usually (because of the pattern of repetition or nonrepetition of the characteristics), to determine the formation of the head.

Perforation Gauge. (1) A scale for ascertaining the number of teeth or bridges and holes or cuts resulting from perforation or rouletting in a standard length of two centimeters. See "Bridge"; "Perforation"; "Rouletting"; "Teeth." The standard length was set and the perforation gauge originally devised by Dr. Jacques Amable Legrand (see "Legrand") and printed in *Le Timbre-Poste* (Vol. 4, Page 84, October 1866). Named by Dr. Legrand the "odontometre," the device consisted of a series of lines of differently spaced dots, with a number at the side of each line; the numbers ranged from 7 to 16, including halves. To use the gauge, the perforation is placed against the lines in turn until one line is found of which

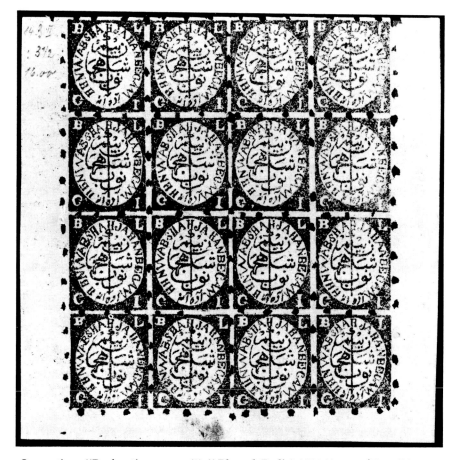

Separation. "Perforation gauge (2)." Bhopal (India) 1891 ½a. perf 3 to 4½, one of the coarsest gauges of perforation encountered in philately.

each dot falls centrally within every different hole of the row of perforation along the length of the line, or of which every different dot is covered by the center of every tooth that appears within the length of the line. The number of holes or teeth of the perforation in the length of two centimeters is the number printed at the side of that line. Perforation gauges substantially similar to that of Dr. Legrand are in use today. As an instrument of precision, however, such a gauge suffers from its inability to provide more finely graduated readings, and other gauges, based upon converging lines, have been developed. See "Instanta."

(2) The number of holes occurring in each length of two centimeters, and resulting from the number of pins in the pin plate or ring and, when present, bar. See "Bars (1)"; "Multiplication Sign"; "Pin Plate"; "Rings." The first stamp-perforating machines were made in England, and the pins were spaced by reference to the inch; in later machines manufactured in Europe, the pins were spaced by reference to the metric system. The first perforating machines had about twenty pins to the inch, providing a perforation gauging 16 in the substantially arbitrarily set standard of two centimeters — see "Perforation Gauge (1)." Since that time, widely varying gauges have been used — for example, 3 to 4½ for Bhopal (India) 1891 ½a., as among the coarsest, to, for example, 17½ x 18, as the finest,

used for many issues of Malaya beginning in 1949, and including, for instance, Malacca 1949 (Mar. 1)–1952 1c. to $5. Usually the intention is that the spacing of the pins should be regular and in alignment along any one row, but the intention has not always been carried out, resulting in irregular perforation. In such cases, the perforation is expressed to gauge two numbers separated by a comma, dash or the word "to," the numbers representing the coarsest and finest gauges along the length of the row of pins. Or it is expressed to gauge "roughly" a number — see "Irregular Perforation." The spacing of the pins is, often, related to the tearing strength of the paper, which is stronger across the grain than with it. See "Grain" in the alphabetical list to the chapter entitled "Paper." This is one explanation of why compound perforation is frequently used — see "Compound Perforation (1)."

Perforation Guide — see "Perforation Guide" in the alphabetical list to the chapter entitled "From Design to Issued Sheets."

Perforation Register Mark — see "Register Mark (3)" in the alphabetical list to the chapter entitled "From Design to Issued Sheets."

Perforation Register Pin — see "Stud."

Perforation Short — see "Nibbed Perforation."

Pin. (1) A flat-ended, solid piece of needle or tempered steel, usually cylindrical, employed as a punch for perforating. Sometimes the term "punch" is used as a synonym for pin. See "Bars (1)"; "Hyphen Holes"; "Lozenge Perforation"; "Pin Plate"; "Rings"; "Square-Hole Perforation."

(2) A needle-pointed piece of, usually, cylindrical steel, one of a series fixed around the periphery of a wooden disc used in applying pin rouletting. See "Pin Roulette."

(3) A sharp, pointed projection, sometimes termed a "register pin," in a frame or tympan upon which sheets for perforating were fixed for registration, the appropriate position being indicated on the sheet by a printed pin mark. See "Perforation Guide" in the alphabetical list to the chapter entitled "From Design to Issued Sheets"; "Registration."

Pin Bars — see "Bars (1)."

Pin Mark — see "Perforation Guide" in the alphabetical list to the chapter entitled "From Design to Issued Sheets."

Pin Perforation. An English translation of *piquage a l'épingle,* and a misnomer for pin rouletting. See "Pin Roulette."

Pin Plate. That part of a stroke comb- or harrow-perforating machine in which are fixed the flat-ended pins. The free ends of the pins descend into holes bored in the bed plate and punch perforation holes in the paper. See "Bed Plate"; "Pin (1)." Sometimes the term "punch plate" is used as a synonym for pin plate.

Pin Ring — see "Rings."

Pin Roulette. Rouletted with a series of, usually, round holes pricked by sharp-pointed pins, as opposed to punched by flat-ended pins. The sizes of holes and distances between holes vary in different instances of use of this form of rouletting, and the edges of different issues are, consequently, more or less ragged. Pin rouletting is to be found, for example, on Barbados 1860 no value expressed (½d.) and (1d.), gauging 14 and 12½; Krefeld (German Local) 1886 (December) 2p., gauging 10¾; New Zealand 1858-59 1d. to 1s., gauging 10; and Venezuela

1868-70 ½c. to 2r. An instance of pin rouletting with square holes is recorded, for example, on Persia 1875 8s. Sometimes this form of rouletting is referred to as "pin perforation," an English translation of *piquage a l'épingle,* to which Dr. Legrand referred in *Le Timbre-Poste* for November 1866. See "Legrand"; "*Percé en Pointes.*" See also "Square Holes."

Pin Wheel — see "Rings."

Plain Roulette. Uncolored rouletting, as contrasted with rouletting in color. See "Rouletted in Color." An instance of the same value existing with both forms of rouletting is provided, for example, by Luxembourg 1865-71 1c. plain (line) roulette, and 1865-72 1c. rouletted in color. Sometimes the term "uncolored roulette" is used as a synonym for plain roulette.

Private Perforation, Roulette — see "Official Separation." See also "Automatic Machine Perforation (2)."

Pseudo-Separation. This term is used to describe cuts or marks that appear to be, or were intended to appear to be, but are not perforation or rouletting. Instances of pseudo-separation are provided, for example, by Jammu and Kashmir (India) 1883-94 4a. and 8a. imperf with uncolored circles like perforation holes in the stamp gutters; Dominican Republic 1953 Columbus Lighthouse souvenir sheet of ten imperf with dark blue circular dots simulating perforation holes; Djibouti 1894-1902 1c. to 50f. imperf with printing in the gutters representing denticulation; Peru 1862 (Nov. 18) 1d. with two holes simulating rouletting widely spaced in the vertical gutters caused by prongs that moved the strips of paper — the stamps were produced in strips — forward in the printing machine; and Czechoslovakia 1918 (October) Scout Stamps 20h. seemingly arc-rouletted in color by the raised cutting edge of each die from which the stamps were produced one at a time.

Punch. In relation to separation: (1) a synonym for pin. See "Pin (1)."
(2) A tool with a circular, hollow sharp end, used in conjunction with a hammer, for cutting comparatively large circles from paper. Such tools were used, for example, in Switzerland between 1910 and 1927 for cutting the circular holes, between 9 mm and 11.5 mm in diameter, out of the interpane gutters of stacks of ten harrow-perforated sheets used for booklet production, including, for instance, Switzerland 1909 (1910) 2c. Contrast "Punch" in the alphabetical lists to the chapters entitled "Printing Problems and Varieties," "Embossing," and "Relief Printing."

Punch Bar — see "Bars (1)."

Punch Perforated. (1) A synonym for a stamp perforated with a device. See "Perforated (2)."
(2) Diagnostically descriptive of interpane gutters with large circular holes. See "Punch (2)."

Punch Plate — see "Pin Plate."

Punch Ring — see "Rings."

Punch Wheel — see "Rings."

Punctured — see "Perforated (2)."

Reel Perforator. A perforating machine adapted for perforating stamps printed on continuous reels or webs of paper, as distinct from perforators that operate

Separation. Bad registration. South Australia 1893-94 2½d. on 4d. green (type of 1890), showing the effect of bad registration of the perforation, which should have fallen in the horizontal gutters. The bar obliterating the value tablet, on a well-registered stamp, appears below the provisional surcharge. Because no perforations appear in the horizontal gutter between what are, in fact, the portions of two stamps, this type of variety can easily be differentiated from the pseudo-separation resulting from malfunctioning of an automatic vending machine. Compare this illustration with that of pseudo-separation that appears earlier in this chapter.

only on sheets of paper. Once the end of the printed web has been fed into the reel perforator, it operates automatically. Such perforators are either stroke-comb (as in the Grover reel perforator) or stroke-harrow (as in the machine used by the Swiss PTT), or else rotary, as in the two-way electric eye perforator used by the U.S. Bureau of Engraving and Printing at Washington, D.C. Reel perforators are to be distinguished from merely rotary perforators. See "Comb Perforation"; "Line (2)"; "Line Perforation (2)"; "Rotary Perforation"; and the illustration of the machine used by the Swiss PTT that accompanies the chapter entitled "Intaglio Printing — I: Line Engraving."

Register Mark. See "Register Mark (3)" in the alphabetical list to the chapter entitled "From Design to Issued Sheets."

Register Pin. (1) A synonym for stud. See "Stud." (2) A synonym for pin. See "Pin (3)."

Registration. In connection with separation, "registration" is used to designate the positioning of the perforation in relation to the design, and is employed in reference to machine-applied separation. The centering of a design within the area of separated paper depends upon registration — see "Centering." Registration has been effected by various devices — for example, by means of thin, sharp pins upon which the sheets were impaled by hand, location being guided by pin marks printed in the sheet margins when the stamps were printed; by holes punched in the sheet margin at the time the stamps were printed, and used for securing the sheet upon studs in the perforator; by an adjustable guide against which sheets were placed by the operator; and by means of electric eye marks. See "Perforation Guide" in the alphabetical list to the chapter entitled "From Design to Issued Sheets"; "Electric Eye Markings"; "Imperforate Between"; "Stud." Misplaced perforation results, usually, from a defect in one or more of the devices for ensuring registration. See also "Freak Separation."

Repaired Perforation — see "Mixed Perforation."

Reperforated. Having had perforation applied (unofficially and, usually, fraudulently) to an imperforate margin, or close to the design in the case of a wing margin. Sometimes, also, having had a missing tooth, or more than one, supplied by paper graft. See "Fantail"; "Imperforate Margin (1)"; "Wing Margin."

Reversed Perforation. Perforation applied to the back instead of, as usual, to the front of the sheet.

Rings. Those parts of a one-way rotary perforator that effect the perforation, and of a two-way perforator that effect the longitudinal perforation along the length of the web or reel of paper, as distinct from the bars that effect the latitudinal perforation. See "Bars (1)." Rings are either "punch rings" (or "pin rings") drilled with holes into which one end of flat-ended pins or punches are fixed, or "die rings" (or "counterpart rings") drilled with holes only. The rings, spaced appropriate distances apart, counter-rotate on axles turned by a treadle or mechanical power, the free ends of the flat-ended pins entering and leaving the holes of the die rings as rotation occurs. The sheet or web passes between the die rings and pin rings, and the paper is perforated as it passes between them. Sometimes the term "wheel" is used as a synonym for ring.

Rosback Perforation. Perforation gauging 12½ applied to 6,641 sheets of U.S. 1919 1c.; so named after the F.P. Rosback Co. of Benton Harbor, Michigan, which furnished the machine used for the perforation.

Rotary Perforation. Perforation applied by passing the paper between two counter-rotating wheels, or sets of wheels, one with flat-ended pins extending from the periphery, and the other bored with holes that free ends of the pins enter and leave; the principle patented by the Bemroses (see "Bemrose Perforation"), who used solely line perforation. See "Line Perforation"; "Rings." Used mainly for line perforation, although rotary perforation was employed in conjunction with triple cutters for, for example, Victoria 1901-12 (February 1910) 1d. See "Comb Perforation." A modification of the rotary perforator resulted in the two-way perforator. See "Two-Way Perforator."

Rotary Rouletting. Rouletting applied by discs or wheels rolled over the paper (or under which the paper is passed) as opposed to blades or perforative rules that descend upon and pierce the paper. Compare "Stroke Rouletting."

Rough Perforation. The paper has not been removed from the edges of some or many of what should be perforation holes. Compare "Clean-Cut Perforation."

Roughly Perforated — see "Irregular Perforation (1)."

Rouletted. Having small straight or other-shaped cuts or holes that have pierced but not removed any part of the substance of the paper, to assist in rendering a stamp or part of a stamp easily detachable as a unit from contiguous paper or stamps; as distinct from perforated. See "Perforated." The implication of the use of the unqualified term "rouletted" is that the form of separation referred to is *percé en ligne* — see "*Percé en Ligne.*"

Rouletted and Imperforate. Roul. x imperf. See "Imperforate." Instances of such stamps are to be found, for example, in Mexico 1915 (Sep. 16) 10c.

Rouletted in Color. This term is used to embrace all forms of rouletting in which, because the perforative rule was inked, ink was deposited on the paper at the time the rouletting was effected. An instance of simultaneous stamp printing and rouletting in color — the color of each stamp — is provided by Thurn and Taxis, Northern District, 1868 ¼s. to 3s., where the separation was rouletting in colored lines. An instance of colored rouletting applied at a subsequent operation — in black — after the stamps were printed, is provided by Queensland 1899 1d., where the separation was zigzag rouletting. Other instances of rouletting in color are provided by Bundi (India) 1914-18 ¼a. to 5r., and Luxembourg 1865-72 1c. to 40c. Sometimes the term "colored roulette" is used as a synonym for rouletted in color. Compare "Plain Roulette." See also *"Percé en Lignes Colorées."*

Rouletted in Colored Lines. An English synonym for *percé en lignes colorées.* See *"Percé en Lignes Colorées."*

Rouletted on Colored Lines. A misnomer for rouletted in colored lines. See *"Percé en Lignes Colorées."*

Rouletting. The effect of the making of small straight or other-shaped cuts or holes that have pierced but not removed any part of the substance of the paper.

Saw-Tooth Roulette. An English synonym for *percé en scie* and its verbal equivalent, although the visual image of a saw-toothed edge would suggest *percé en pointe* — that is, zigzag rouletting — rather than the convexities or concavities of the saw-tooth roulette. Because of the similarity in sense between saw-tooth roulette and serrate roulette, these two terms are, sometimes, used synonymously. See *"Percé en Pointe"*; *"Percé en Scie"*; *"Serrate Roulette."*

Schermack Perforation — see *"Automatic Machine Perforation (2)."*

Separation, Separations. The effect of the use of methods for rendering a stamp or part of a stamp easily detachable as a unit from contiguous paper or stamps; generically embracing the effects of perforation and rouletting. See *"Perforation"*; *"Rouletting"*; *"Sewing Machine Perforation."*

Serpentine Roulette. An English synonym for *percé en serpentin.* In the United States, often "serpentine roulette" is used as a term that embraces the effects of *percé en arc, percé en scie,* and *percé en serpentin* — see, for example, the listings in Scott of Brunswick 1864, 1865 (and Hanover 1864), Bremen 1861-64 and Finland 1860. See *"Percé en Serpentin."*

Serrate Perforation — see *"Serrate Roulette."*

Serrate Roulette, Serrated Roulette. English equivalents (being derived from the Latin "serra," a saw) of *percé en scie,* and, thus, synonyms of saw-tooth roulette, with the same confusing conflict between visual and verbal images. In fact, serrate roulette is often described as a "fine kind of arc rouletting," thus emphasizing the difficulties of distinguishing satisfactorily between the effects of *percé en arc* and *percé en scie.* However, the implicit distinction between "fine" (as serrate roulette) and "coarse" or otherwise (as *percé en arc*) is illusory. Sometimes this form of rouletting is referred to as "serrate perforation." To add to the confusion, the term "serrate roulette" has, in the United States, increasingly attracted the meaning of the visual image of a saw-toothed edge, and is there employed to designate zigzag rouletting. Serrate roulette (or serrated perforation), in the sense of *percé en arc* or *percé en scie,* has been recorded, in various gauges, for example, on New Zealand, 1858-59 1d. to 1s., gauging about 16 to 18; 1862 (August) 1d. to 1s., gauging 14 to 16; Tasmania 1868-69 1d. to 6d., gauging 19; and Victoria 1857 4d., gauging 19. For examples recorded in the sense of zigzag rouletting, see *"Percé en Pointe."*

Sewing Machine Perforation. Separation applied by passing the paper under the needle of a sewing machine. Distances between holes vary considerably; if the needle is flat-ended, the effect resembles rough perforation; if the needle is sharp, the effect resembles pin-rouletting. Instances of sewing machine perforation are to be found, for example, in Colombia (Cartagena issues) 1899-1900 5c.; Persia (Iran) 1906 1c. to 6c.; and U.S. Revenues 1871 Second Issue 25c. and 30c.

Short Perforation — see *"Nibbed Perforation."*

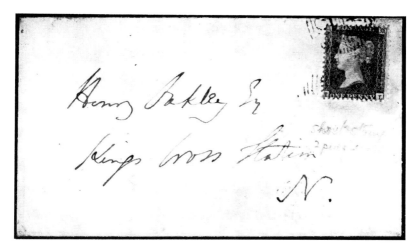

Separation. Short stamp. Great Britain 1854-57 1d. lettered "T-L," on cover exhibiting the variety "short stamp," together with a normal stamp similarly lettered for comparison. The sheets were horizontally comb-perforated and, because of maladjustment of the paper movement in relation to the height of the design and the length of the legs of the comb in the case of the stamps in the row above the short stamp in the sheet — i.e., the "S" row (the sheet having been perforated from the bottom upward) — two holes of each leg were re-entered by the pins during the second descent to ensure that the line of the comb did not pierce holes above the value tablet. Probably on the subsequent stroke the perforation was adequately registered on the stamps in the row above that — i.e., the "R" row.

Short Stamp. In connection with separation, the term "short stamp" refers not to the design, but to the paper dimension. See "Large Stamp." Short stamps have occurred with horizontal comb perforation when, because of maladjustment of the paper movement in relation to the height of the design, one hole or more of each leg has been re-entered at a subsequent descent of the pins and the line has not occupied the gutter as intended but has encroached the stamp design; or, because of adjustment of the paper movement after one descent or more of the pins, the line did in fact occupy the gutter, which, without the adjustment, would not have been occupied. Short stamps from this cause are of comparatively frequent occurrence — for example, on the top and bottom rows of Great Britain 1854-55 1d. and 2d., and 1858-64 1d. — and have been recorded on other stamps perforated at Somerset House to 1878. Similarly, with vertical-comb perforation, a "narrow stamp" results. Compare "Long Stamp." See "Horizontal-Comb Perforation"; "Narrow Stamp"; "Vertical-Comb Perforation."

Sideways Perforation. Comb perforation applied by passing the sheet through the machine with the design not vertical but horizontal to the line. See "Line (1)"; "Vertical-Comb Perforation."

Single-Comb Perforation — see "Comb Perforation."

Single-Cutter. A perforating machine that applies only a single row of holes to the paper at one operation; as opposed to triple-cutter. See "Guillotine"; "Single Line"; "Triple-Cutter."

Single Line. Separation applied so that only a single row of holes or cuts is made in the paper at one operation. See "Guillotine."

Slotted — see "Hyphen Holes."

Small Stamp — see "Large Stamp."

Spifs — see "Perforated (2)."

Square Holes. Small, more or less rectangular and equal-sided holes; the shape of a type of perforation and roulette. For example, an instance of square-hole perforation is provided by Queensland 1862-67 1d. to 1s. perf 12½ square holes x perf 13 round holes; and an instance of square-hole rouletting is provided by Mexico 1872 6c. to 100c. See also "Pin Rouletting."

Staggered Perforation. Comb perforation out of alignment because of sideways as well as forward movement of the paper between descents of the pins, and resulting in well-centered and off-center stamps *se tenant* vertically in the case of horizontal-comb perforation, and horizontally in the case of vertical-comb perforation. Usually the staggering is limited to one position in the sheet. See "Centering"; "Horizontal-Comb Perforation"; "Se Tenant" in the alphabetical list to the chapter entitled "From Design to Issued Sheets"; "Vertical-Comb Perforation."

Straight Edge — see "Imperforate Margin (1)."

Straight-Line Roulette. An English synonym for *percé en ligne droite*. See *"Percé en Ligne."*

Stripping Plate. A plate drilled with holes through which the pins of the pin plate project, which moves up and down on, but is never clear of, the pins, and which, after the pins have perforated the paper, pushes it clear of the pins — that is, "strips" the sheet of paper from the pins. Stripping plates are used mainly in comb-perforating heads. See "Head." See also "Stripped Color" in the alphabetical list to the chapter entitled "Printing Problems and Varieties."

Stroke Perforation. Perforation applied by passing the paper under a pin plate (and, perhaps, a stripping plate) that descends on to a bed plate and punches the holes from the paper during the descent; the principle patented for comb perforation by Henry Archer. See "Archer Perforation"; "Bed Plate"; "Flat-Bed Separation"; "Pin Plate"; "Stripping Plate." Also guillotine and harrow perforation have been applied by the stroke process. See "Guillotine"; "Harrow Separation." See also "Stroke Rouletting."

Stroke Rouletting. Rouletting applied by a blow or straight descent, as opposed to rotary movement. See "Guillotine"; "Harrow Separation"; "Stroke Perforation." Compare "Rotary Rouletting."

Stud. A projection (usually one of two on the feeding table of a comb-perforating machine) by which the sheet is held in position to be pushed for the initial feed under the perforating head; a perforation registering device — see "Registration." The terms "perforation register pin" and "register pin" are used as synonyms for stud. See also "Stud Hole." After the initial feed, the studs are automatically removed and paper grippers take over in moving the paper forward.

Stud Hole. A hole (usually one of two) punched in the margin of a sheet, by which the sheet (usually one of a batch of from five to seven) is positioned on

Separation. Staggered perforation. Vertical-comb perforation. Siam (Thailand) 1908 (Nov. 11) Jubilee 1a., a block of four exhibiting the variety staggered perforation. The sheets were passed sideways, from right-to-left relative to the designs, through the single-comb perforating head. During the interval between one descent of the pins and the next, in addition to normal forward movement of the paper (sideways relative to the designs), there was sideways movement (upward relative to the designs), causing the legs ("teeth") of the comb to encroach on the tops of the stamps at the left of the picture. These two stamps are badly off-center, while the two at the right are centered high and to the right. Compare this illustration with that of Siam (Thailand) 1905 (December) 1a.

Separation. Staggered perforation. Vertical-comb perforation. Siam (Thailand) 1905 (December) 1a., a block of four exhibiting the variety staggered perforation. The sheets were passed sideways, from left-to-right relative to the designs, through the single-comb perforating head. During the interval between one descent of the pins and the next, there was, in addition to forward movement of the paper (sideways movement relative to the designs), sideways movement of the paper (upward relative to the designs). This caused the centering of the horizontally adjacent stamps to vary and to exhibit the variety "staggered perforation." Also, registration of the vertical perforation varies because the forward movement of the paper was, at the same time, slightly excessive. Compare this illustration with that of Siam (Thailand) 1908 (Nov. 11) Jubilee 1a.

the stud, and the perforation is registered. See "Registration"; "Stud." If the stud hole is misplaced or damaged, freak perforation usually results. See "Freak Perforation."

Susse Perforation — see "Unofficial Perforation."

Syncopated Perforation — see "Interrupted Perforation."

Teeth. (1) A synonym for legs. See "Legs." (2) Projections that result from tearing apart perforated or line-rouletted paper; broken bridges. See "Bridge." (3) Projections that result from the shape of the cuts in rouletting, other than line-rouletting. See "H-Roulette"; "*Percé en Arc*"; *Percé en Croix*"; *Percé en Lignes Oblique*"; *Percé en Parallel*"; *Percé en Pointe*"; *Percé en Pointes*"; *Percé en Scie*"; *Percé en Serpentin*"; *Percé en Zigzags*"; "X-Roulette"; "Y-Roulette."

Treadle Perforator. A perforating machine operated by a lever worked by the foot to produce either the up-and-down movement for the stroke machine, or the rotary movement for the rotary machine. Many early line, comb and harrow perforators were worked by treadle — for example, the stroke harrow perforator constructed by Aloys Auer and used for Austrian issues between 1858 and 1898, and the rotary line perforators used by the American Bank Note Company for issues of the United States of 1861 among others.

Triangular-Comb Perforation. Perforation in which the legs are set to the line in such a manner that the rows of holes form triangles, for the purpose of perforating triangular stamps so arranged that the stamps in the row are alternately upright and inverted, and the apex of each triangle is centrally positioned on the base of the triangle in the row above or below. At one stroke, a whole row of stamps is perforated. See "Comb Perforation"; "Legs"; "Line (1)." An instance of triangular-comb perforation is provided, for example, by Austria 1916 (Oct. 1) Express (Special Handling) 2h. printed in sheets of 100 (seven rows of thirteen across, one row of nine and four blank spaces). Such perforation can be termed "horizontal triangular-comb perforation." An instance of triangular-comb perforation in which, at the first stroke, a whole column of upright stamps was perforated, and, at the second stroke, perforations were supplied to the remainder of the next column of (inverted) stamps and the whole of the following column of (upright) stamps, is provided by Malaya (Federation) 1962 (Jul. 21) National Language Month 10c., 20c. and 50c. In sheets of these stamps, the left-hand top and bottom margins are imperforate, but the right-hand margin is perforated by the last stroke of the perforator that completed the perforations for the last column of (inverted) stamps. Such perforations can be termed "vertical triangular-comb perforation."

Triple-Comb Perforator — see "Comb Perforation."

Triple-Cutter — see "Comb Perforation"; compare "Single-Cutter."

Two-Way Perforator. A rotary perforating machine that applies to the printed web all the perforations in both dimensions by means of bars and rings during one passage through the machine; one of the electric eye perforators used by the U.S. Bureau of Engraving and Printing. See "Bars (1)"; "Electric Eye Perforator"; "Rings." Compare "One-Way Perforator."

U.S. Automatic Vending Perforation — see "Automatic Machine Perforation (2)."

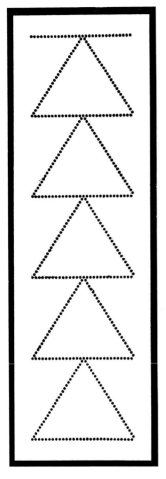

Triangular-comb perforation.

Separation. Wing margin. Great Britain 1865-67 4d. plate 11, stamp lettered "J-F" exhibiting the variety wing margin. These sheets contained the stamps in pane formation and were perforated so that, in the vertical interpane gutters, only one central row of perforations was applied, with the result that each stamp adjacent to the gutter, when detached from the sheet, has perforation teeth close to the design on three sides but at a distance equal to half the interpane gutter on the other side.

Uncolored Roulette — see "Plain Roulette."

Unofficial Perforation. Perforation applied other than by, or at the request of, the issuing authority to stamps issued imperforate. One of the best known instances of unofficial perforation is found on France 1861 1c. to 80c. "Susse" perf 7, a harrow-perforation with large holes, that was applied by Susse Frères, of Paris. As a vendor of stamps, the firm received two per cent discount on face value; it applied the perforation for the convenience of its buyers and to stimulate sales, and sold the stamps without extra charge.

Unofficial Roulette. Rouletting applied other than by, or at the request of, the issuing authority to stamps issued imperforate. Unofficial rouletting is to be found on most imperforate issues; among the earliest known is a line roulette gauging about 7 on Great Britain 1841 1d.

Unofficial Separation — see "Unofficial Perforation"; "Unofficial Roulette"; compare "Official Separation."

Unperforated. Intended to be, but not in fact, provided with perforation; as distinct from "imperforate," which implies that separation formed no part of the original plan of issue. See "Imperforate (1a)." "Unperforated" is rarely used in the defined sense, and, generally, is employed as though it were a synonym for imperforate.

Unrouletted — see "Imperforate."

Unseparated. Se tenant. See "Se Tenant" in the alphabetical list to the chapter entitled "From Design to Issued Sheets."

Variety. In connection with separations, the term "variety" is used in two main, distinct senses. (1) Variety of separation: (a) In relation to separation generally, each particular method, form and gauge used for rendering a stamp or part of a stamp easily detachable as a unit from contiguous paper or stamps is a "variety of separation." (b) In relation to particular stamps, if one stamp has separation applied by one method or form and in one gauge, while another stamp has, or other stamps have, separation applied by a different method, form or gauge (or different methods, forms or gauges), even though both (or all) are normal to the stamps, the stamps are said to be "perforation varieties," or "rouletting varieties," or "separation varieties" of one another, or to exhibit "varieties of perforation," "varieties of rouletting," or "varieties of separation." Compare "Variety of Separating."

(2) Variety of separating: A variation from the intended norm of separation for the stamp or issue caused by oversight, faulty operation or mechanical defect. Varieties of separating owe their existence to the hazards of production that can be encountered in all methods and forms of separation. Such varieties include all errors of separating, but not all such varieties are errors. See "Error." Varieties of separating include blind perforation, stamps off-center, double separation, freaks and wing margins. See "Blind Perforation"; "Centering"; "Double Separation"; "Freak Perforations"; "Staggered Perforation"; "Wing Margins."

Vertical-Comb Perforation. Comb perforations applied to the sheet so that the line appears vertically and the legs horizontally on what is, or becomes, the post office sheet. See "Comb Perforation"; "Legs"; "Line (1)." Because in the post office sheet, the stamp designs usually appear upright, vertical-comb perforation necessarily implies that the sheet is fed horizontally through the perforating machine, from side to side. Compare "Horizontal-Comb Perforation." In fact, apart from differently drilled heads, and adjustment of the distance of paper travel between descents of the pins, there is no difference in the perforating machine; machines are usually capable of applying both vertical- and horizontal-comb perforation. See "Head."

Vertical Perforation — see "Horizontal Perforation."

Wavy-Line Roulette. A term used, occasionally, to designate a shallow-toothed serpentine roulette, to be found on Victoria 1854-57 (Dec. 5, 1857) 6d.

Wheels — see "Rings."

Wide Stamp — see "Large Stamp"; "Long Stamp"; "Narrow Stamp."

Wing Margin. The margin of a stamp from a sheet printed in pane formation and perforated so that, in the vertical interpane gutters, only one central row of perforations was applied, with the result that each stamp adjacent to the gutter, when detached from the sheet, had perforation teeth close to the design on three sides but at a distance equal to half the interpane gutter on the other side; an extended vertical margin with teeth at its extremity and none close to the design. See "Teeth (2)." Contrast "Fantail"; "Gutter Snipe." Sometimes the term "flapper" is used as a synonym for wing margin. Wing margin stamps occur in most of the issues of Great Britain and the British Commonwealth relief-printed by De La Rue & Company Ltd. and perforated at Somerset House, including, for example, British Honduras 1866 (January) 6d. and 1s., printed se tenant; Jamaica 1860 (Nov. 23)–1863 1d. to 1s. After 1878, when the printers took over the perforating, new perforating heads were drilled so that rows of holes were made close to the interpane vertical margins of the stamps, and wing margins no longer occurred. Stamps with wing margins have, frequently, been subject to reperforation. See "Imperforate Margin (1)"; "Reperforated."

x — see "Multiplication Sign."

X-Roulette. A synonym for cross-roulette and, thus, an English synonym for *percé en croix.* See *"Percé en Croix."*

Y-Roulette. A term derived from the shape of each cut found on certain stamps of New Zealand 1859-62 1d. and 1s. rouletted at Nelson.

Zigzag Roulette. An English synonym for *percé en pointe.* See *"Percé en Pointe."*

Index

Gini Horn, librarian of the American Philatelic Research Library, prepared this index to the revised edition. It is based on the index to the original edition compiled by James Negus, F.R.P.S.L.

* Indicates that the item is illustrated or that reference should be made to the caption to an illustration.
† Indicates a footnote to the page cited.

"A" perforating machine, Perkins, Bacon, 677-82*, 684*, 755
"Abnormal Perforations from Stroke & Rotary Perforators" (Walker, 1982), 727†
Acacia gum, 629, 634
Account letter, 138*
Acheson Colloids Ltd., 587, 603
Acid resist, 324, 330, 520, 522, 529, 534
Aciérage (steel facing), 535-36, 558
Added-metal repair, relief printing, 497, 558
Adhesive stamps
  definition, 19
  self, 633
  without gum, 607
Advertisements in booklets, 133
Affixing machines, 136-37, 728, 731*
Afghanistan
  1875 1s., hand-drawn stone, 309-10*, 367
  1880-90 1a., 2a., batonne paper, 51*
  1880 issue, thin paper, 64
  1889-90 1a., batonne paper, dies, 440
  1927 10p. Independence, half-tone block, 184
"After hardening" die proof, 130, 464*
"After striking" die proof, 131, 468†
Air and moisture bubbles in stereotyping, 473-74, 481-82
Air hole flaw, 482*, 558
Airmail collecting, 15, 18
Aktiebolaget Produktion Service, 698, 755
Albino (*see also* Partial albino), 154*-55, 178, 408, 432, 433*
Album, Lallier, 2*
Albumen sensitizing, 306, 334, 522
Aleppo, *see* Syria : Aleppo
ALF, *see* Automatic letter facing

All-over watermarks, 70, 76
Allman, T.J., 787
Alsace-Lorraine, *see* Germany : Alsace-Lorraine
Altered relief, 216
Alternative Perforating System, 698, 755
Alto, 232
Alum, 330-31
Aluminum foil, 56, 583, 601
Aluminum lithographic plates, 329, 358*, 359*
American Bank Note Company
  gum, 620
  multiple-line perforator, 683-86*, 798
  printing before gumming, 613
Amick, George, 633†
Anchor, 558
  mark, 558
Angola, *see* Portuguese Colonies : Angola
Aniline, 582, 597
  color, 582, 599, 605
  scarlet, 599
Anode, electrodeposition, 476, 479*
Antigua
  1863-67 1d., irregular perf., 775
  1921-29 2d., shifted *découpage*, 542*, 563
  1949 1s. U.P.U., printing characteristics, 180
  1969, glazed paper, 59
Antioquia, *see* Colombian States : Antioquia
"Antique" type, 448
AOP, 603
Approaches to Philately (D.B. Armstrong), 92†
APS machine, 698, 755
Arabic gum, *see* Gum arabic
Arc roulette, 742*, 744-45*, 755, 781, 791
Archer, Henry, 117-18, 646, 737

802

Congreve plates, 561
Congreve, Sir William, 561
Consecutive number, 141*, 147
Constant
  flaw, 162
  printing flaws, 162, 368
  variety, 178
Constantinople, *see* Turkey : Locals
Contemporary die proof, 130
Continental Bank Note Company, gum, 620
Continuous
  Jubilee lines, 546
  tone designs, 333*, 335
  watermarks, 74
Control, 138*, 141
  letters, 138*, 141
  number, 138, 141
  private, 141
Cook Islands
  1892 issue, toned paper, 64
  1893-1902 2½d., impacted metal flaws, 470, 566
  1902 (2d.), value omitted, 176, 177*
  1937 1d. Coronation, fancy-type overprint, 445*, 446
Cooke, J.B., 700†
Copper
  die, 438*, 440, 457
  flashed, in electrotyping, 475, 479*
  moulds, relief printing, 467, 487
  plate engraving, 199, 207
  shell, electrotype, 455, 477-80
Copper sulfate electrolyte, 477, 479*
Corbould, Henry, 114
Corn grain, 268*, 269, 282, 294
Corner
  block, 140
  letters, 101*, 102
  ornament, 102
  square, 102
Corrosion flaw, 245, 246*, 518, 518†
Costa Rica
  1953 5c. on 45c. Air, lightface surcharge, 446
Counter, *see* Counterpart, embossing
Counterpart
  bar, 756, 761
  cylinder, 687-702*
  embossing, 389, 394, 393*, 395*, 397, 401-03, 407, 428, 431
  in relief printing, *see* Punch ; Transfer Roll
  plate, 758, 761

ring, 761, 793
  wheel, 682-86*, 688*, 693-97*, 761
Country collections, 20
Courvoisier
  diapositive checking, 293*
  issues with grilled gum, 625*, 629,
  master negative, 256*, 257*
  rotary photogravure printing machine, 289*
Covers
  campaign, 19
  combination, 20
  definition, 20
  first day, 16*-17, 21
Crabtree two-color offset press, 354-5*
Cracked
  electro, 495-96*, 560
  frame, 497-98*, 563
  gum, 632, 634-35, 639*
  plate, 158, 169
Crackly gum, 632, 635*, 639*
Cracks, 158, 169, 465-66*, 487
  gripper, 228
Crawford, Earl of, 12
Crazed gum, 632, 635*, 639*
Crease, gum, 637
Creased
  paper, 53*, 58
  transfer, 320*-21, 361
Cross
  cutter, 238*, 556-57
  line screen, photogravure, 270, 292
  pin, 715*
  roulette, 761, 801
Crust flaw, 537, 561-62, 571, 601
Cuba
  1942 1c. to 13c. Democracy in America, ungummed, 611
Curacao, *see* Netherlands Antilles
Curling, counteracting, 618, 627-29, 640, 692, 693*
Current number, 141
Curved plates, 152-53, 227-28, 239
  in gravure, 253
  in line-engraving, 227-28*, 239
  in relief printing, 513*
Curved stereos, 480
Curving working die, in embossing, 422-24*
Cut, 562
  edge, 472, 514-15*, 562
  transfer, 316-19*, 360, 361
Cutting press, 418-20*, 428
Cyclostyle, 199, 202*

window, production, 427*
Epargne, en (see also relief printing), 200, 435, 458
"Epaulettes" (Belgium, 1849), 104
Errant entry, 31*, 224, 247
Errors
artists', 96-99*
contrasted with varieties, 751-55*
definitions, 21, 178
of color, 31*, 161*, 224, 504* 506
of inscription, 161-2
of paper, 58, 82
of separating, 751-55*, 766-67*, 800
of value, 161-62, 317, 506
of watermark, 82-85*
types of, 161
Essai sur les Filigranes (Dr. Magnus), 73
Essay-Proof Society, 116, 132
Essays *(see also* under Essays in individual countries), 21, 115-18*, 129
Estonia
1923-33 Issues, burelage, 53*, 57
Etching, 200
deep offset, 343*
in making die, 126
in making plates, 232-33
lithographic plates, 329, 358*
lithographic stones, 324, 326
photomechanical, *see* Photomechanical etching
resist, 267, 281-83, 324, 330, 520, 522, 529, 534
to repair line-engraved plate, 226
Ethiopia
1947 70c. Postal Jubilee, fugitive color, 582
Exhibitions, 13
Eden Musée (1889), catalogue, 13*
Vandermaelen Museum, Brussels, Belgium (1852) 12, 14*
Wiener Philatelisten-Club, 13
Expertizing, re-gummed stamps, 615
separations as guide in, 664
Exposure, diapositive, 280
Extended type, 448
Extension hole, 766, 767
External distortion flaw, 471, 491-95*, 564
Extrinsic flaw, 362
Fabrica Nacional del Sello, Madrid, 535
Facsimiles, 5, 6
Face (facing), *see* Facing
Face of type, 449, 564-65
Face (value), 107, 565

Faced plate, 169, 565
Facing *(see also* Surfacing)
in relief printing, 475†, 477†
line-engraved plates, 227, 228, 233
Facsimile, collecting, 5
Fakes, definition, 21
Falkland Islands
1904-12 ½d. to 5s., plates, 232
1964 6d., center transposed, 157*, 158
Fancy type, 445*, 446
Fantail, 771*, 767*, 774
Farley, James A., 772
Farwell Company, 728, 756, 768
Fast color, 601
FCP, 601
Feeding table, 708, 709-13*, 796
Female die, 397, 401, 405-06, 408, 430, 431, 432
Fenton, Adelaide Lucy, 6, 600, 645,
Ferric chloride etching, 281-82
Fiji
1870-71 Times Express, quadrille paper, 52
serifed type, 444
1871, sheet watermark, 71
1874-76 issues, fancy-type overprints, 444
1878-1900 issues, perfs., 674
Times Express rules, 572
Final flaws, 363, 381
Fine
grain, 294
impression, 544*, 569
mesh, 294, 296
perforation, 644, 768
print, 544*
screen, 272, 294, 296
Finger print variety, 322, 323*, 363
Finished designs, 114-15
Finland
1860 issue, serpentine roulette, 746, 781, 786, 794
1866-71 issues, serpentine roulette, 737, 742*, 746-47*, 786
1882-84 20p., *tête-bêche*, 165
1945 1m. to 7m., Sports Fund, invisible gum, 632, 639
1957 30m. Ida Aalberg, color printing, 248
Finland : Locals
Helsingfors 1866-68 10p., roulette, 739, 742*, 746*, 747, 786
1871-77 10p., serpentine roulette, 786

perforated, 645, 786, 791
plate, 790, 791
ring, 695, 696-97*, 791, 793
struck plate, 509-12*, 571
wheel, 791
Punchies, 786
"Punching" (perforation), 659
Punctured, 645, 791
Purves, J.R.W., 700†
PVA, 640

Quad, 571
Quadrille paper, 50*, 52*
Quadruple-comb perforation, 700, 736, 760
Quartz lamp, 604
Quasi-watermarks, 70, 74-76*
Quaternary
flaws (lithography), 363, 367-68
stone, 367, 368
Queensland
1862-67 1d. to 1s., square-hole perf., 730, 796
1879-81 2d., electrotypes, 476-77*
1895-96 ½d., burelage, 57
1899 1d., rouletting, 739, 741*, 749, 760, 764, 785, 793
recess printing, see Intaglio
Quintuple-comb perforation, 702*
Quoins, 490, 559, 571

Randers, see Denmark : Locals
Rang, C.P., 670, 775
Ratio perforation scale, 667*, 670
Rawsthorne, John, 618
Ream, weights of, 41
Recess engraving, 202, 204, 207
Recessed dies, 122*, 123
Recurring flaws, 161-62
Recut, 223*, 249*-50
die, 170-71, 572
Recutting, 223, 226
in relief printing, 498
Redrawing, lithographic, 368-69*
Redrawn die, 170-71, 572
Reducer bleaching agent, 342
Reducing machine die, 412, 416*, 428, 432
Reduction punch, 412, 416*, 432, 434
Reel
perforator, 720-21*, 791-92
rod, 556
Re-engraved die, 158, 170-01, 572
Re-entry, 31*, 221-22, 224, 225, 226, 518†

non-coincident, 221*, 224, 249
Re-facing relief plates, 535-36, 573
Regensburg, see Germany : Regensburg
Register
embossing-printing, 431
mark, 142, 147, 790, 791
marks, lithographic stone, 346
perforation, 752, 754, 773*, 792
pin or stud, 711-12*, 790, 791, 796
Registration
during printing, 171, 182, 241
flaw, 431, 434
mark (printing), 147
point, watermark, 69
Registry marking (in printing), 147
Reglet, 490-92*, 564, 566, 571, 572, 573
flaws, 490-92*, 571, 573
Re-gumming, 615, 641
Reinheimer, Adolph, drawing of Vandermaelen Museum Philatelic Exhibition, 12, 14*
Relief, 571, 574
dies, 122*, 123
engraving, 202, 204
foreign, see Errant entry
stamping, 385, 397-98, 434
transfer, 214, 215*
transfer-roller, 214, 215*
Relief printing, 435-575
added metal, 497, 559
anchor marks, 483-85*, 544, 559
"bite", 183
blank duty dies, 458-61*, 464*, 564, 570
blanket, 540-41*, 559
block, 559
bounce, 559
bump retouching, 497
cameo-stamping from, 398†, 401*, 411
characteristics, 182, 183*, 184, 190*
cliche, 158, 175, 467-68, 559
cold striking, see Punch-struck plate
color separation, 199
combined line and half-tone, 525*, 528-29
compartment line, 514-15*, 544, 560
composite die, 560-61
compound plate, 552, 561
Congreve plates, 561
cracked electro, 495-96*, 560
crust flaw, 537, 561-62, 572, 601
cut, 562
cut edge, 472, 514-15*, 562
cylinder presses, 537-41*, 552-56*